AMERICA

☆ IN THE ☆

TWENTIETH CENTURY

★ Fifth Edition ★

AMERICA ☆ IN THE ☆ TWENTIETH CENTURY

★ Fifth Edition ★

Frank Freidel
University of Washington

Alan Brinkley
Massachusetts Institute of Technology

Alfred A. Knopf  New York

THIS IS A BORZOI BOOK
PUBLISHED BY ALFRED A. KNOPF, INC.

Fifth Edition
987

Library of Congress Cataloging in Publication Data

Freidel, Frank Burt.
  America in the twentieth century.
    Bibliography: p.
  Includes index.
  1. United States—History—20th century. I. Brinkley,
Alan. II. Title.
E741.F7 1982   973.9   81–18597
ISBN 0–394–32780–2   AACR2

Manufactured in the United States of America

Cover design: Jurek Wajdowicz

To the Memory of
William Best Hesseltine
1902-1963

Preface

More than two decades have passed since the first edition of *America in the Twentieth Century* appeared in 1960. Those years have not only produced a history of their own; they have changed the way Americans look at the entire reach of their national past. This fifth edition, therefore, is in many respects an entirely different book from the four editions that have preceded it. We have continued to give careful and thorough attention to the political and diplomatic events of twentieth-century America. But we have added major new coverage of the social, economic, and cultural phenomena that form the context for the public history of the era. In particular, we have introduced new material on the history of women; on the experience of blacks, Hispanics, Native Americans, and other minorities; on the rise of mass culture; and on the changing structure of the American economy. And we have, finally, thoroughly reorganized and rewritten the full text and included new photographs, maps, charts, and bibliographies.

We are deeply grateful to Richard N. Current for his advice and assistance in the preparation of this edition, as well as to the anonymous scholars and teachers who have reviewed the manuscript and offered corrections and suggestions. We wish to acknowledge as well the careful editorial work of the staff at Alfred A. Knopf: David Follmer, the acquiring editor; Irene Pavitt, the project editor; Evelyn Katrak, the copy editor; Lynn Goldberg, the photo editor; and the many others who have contributed to the preparation of this new edition.

Frank Freidel
Seattle, Washington

Alan Brinkley
Cambridge, Massachusetts

October 1981

Contents

Illustrations

Charts

Maps

Designed by Theodore R. Miller

America in the Twentieth Century

★ Fifth Edition ★

One

The New Century and the Old

The American people entered the twentieth century on the heels of an unusually turbulent era. In little more than three decades, the United States had transformed itself from a predominantly rural, agrarian society into a highly industrialized, urbanized one. It had moved from a position of relative unimportance in world affairs to that of a major international power. It had changed from a fragmented, largely provincial society into an increasingly centralized and consolidated one. It had become a modern nation.

It had also become a nation with a sharply divided vision of itself and its future. On the one hand, Americans took pride in their country's remarkable economic growth, in its great technological advances, in its enhanced world power. At the same time, however, they looked with alarm at the wrenching social dislocations that rapid growth and change had created: crowded cities, oppressed minorities, concentrations of power, disparities of wealth, political corruption, general instability. Modernization, they realized, had brought not only progress but chaos and injustice. The American people greeted the new century, therefore, with both optimism and foreboding.

THE PROMISE OF INDUSTRIALIZATION

The reasons for optimism were obvious. America was by 1900 the leading industrial nation on earth, and the potential of its economy seemed to be virtually unlimited. Its natural resources were plentiful. Its labor supply was large and growing. Its technological and administrative capabilities were becoming increasingly sophisticated. The United States was, its people sensed, on the eve of an era of unbounded prosperity.

3

Sources of Growth

America's industrial revolution had been the result of many factors and many years. Industrialization had begun as early as the 1820s, but it was in the decades following the Civil War that manufacturing truly emerged as a major force in the nation's economy. It was then that a great surge of railroad building helped knit the sprawling country together, opening enormous new supplies of raw materials and creating a vast, national market for manufactured goods. Between 1860 and 1900, the nation constructed almost 170,000 miles of railroad lines to create a national total of 200,000 miles—the most comprehensive transportation network on earth.

Those same years saw the opening of new, more fertile farmlands in the West and the introduction of improved agricultural techniques. As a result, fewer farmers could now produce the nation's food, and a rapid flow of men and women from rural areas into the growing industrial cities provided the new factories with a ready source of labor. So did the rising tide of immigration from Europe—more than 12 million new arrivals between 1860 and 1900. By the turn of the century, American industry employed 13 million workers, nearly double the number employed in agriculture and almost five times as many as had worked in industry forty years before.

Equally important was the emergence of institutions capable of using these resources productively. Preeminent among them was the modern corporation. Beginning during and shortly after the Civil War, an increasing number of American entrepreneurs began to discover the potential of the corporation for rapid capital formation. No longer did a merchant or a manufacturer have to rely on his personal wealth to finance new ventures. By forming a corporation, he could raise money through the sale of stock to investors, who then stood to share in the profits of the enterprise when and if they materialized. The great railroad companies were the first successful such organizations. Following in their footsteps, other industries—steel, coal, food, tobacco, soap, merchandising—adopted the corporate structure to expand and consolidate their activities. Protected by government from foreign competition through a complex system of tariffs, unrestrained by environmental concerns, and free from burdensome taxes, the corporate industrialists created an economic system whose productivity and abundance had no precedent in the history of the world. By the turn of the century, American industry was producing $11 billion worth of manufactures a year, more than five times what it had produced forty years before.

That American society had gained much from this economic transformation could hardly be disputed. During the last thirty years of the nineteenth century, per capita output in America increased at an average annual rate of better than 2 percent, more than double that of the years before the Civil War. The real wages of workers also rose steadily: by more than 50 percent between 1860 and 1890, by more than 33 percent in the twenty years that followed. The length of the average workweek was declining, providing workers with increased leisure time. The cost of producing manufactured goods, foodstuffs, and other staples was

BUILDING THE RAILROADS. Workers set new speed records as they lay track across the bare plains in the Dakota and Montana territories in 1887, helping to create the new network of railroads that would assist in the industrialization of late-nineteenth-century America. (*Burlington Northern photo*)

dropping, in response to the increasing efficiency of production. New techniques of retailing—the department store, the mail-order house, and others—made a wide range of goods available to the average consumer. And new techniques of advertising helped create demand for those goods, further fueling the economic growth.

The New Technology

Even more dramatic was the impact of technological advances, which not only made possible much of the industrial progress but reached out to transform the American landscape and alter the daily lives of most citizens. There were scores of significant new inventions and innovations: steel rails, bridges, skyscrapers, elevators, electric lights, electric streetcars, subways, gasoline engines, telephones, and new industrial and agricultural machinery. Their social and economic effects were profound.

Innovations in transportation changed the face of American cities, allowing people to live miles from their places of employment and to travel back and forth on the new forms of public transportation. The inventions of steel beams and of

CHICAGO, 1905.   Automobiles, electric streetcars, and tall buildings illustrate the changing landscape of American cities. (*Chicago Historical Society*)

elevators altered American architecture, permitting the construction of buildings far taller than had once been possible. A nationwide telephone system helped connect distant areas of the country and proved an inestimable boon to business-men attempting to extend the scope of their enterprises across the nation. Indus-trial and agricultural technology made it possible for a single worker to produce far more than he or she had been able to do in the past. Plumbing, electricity, and new household appliances freed many women from much of the drudgery of housework, making possible a significant expansion in the scope of their activities and interest. The changes had been staggering, and few doubted as the new century began that there would be even greater ones in the years to come.

In 1907, Henry Adams, a detached sexagenarian, looked back over his own lifetime, recalled the development of the ocean steamer, the railway, and the telegraph, and reflected upon a future that promised still more change. He wrote in his famous autobiography, *The Education of Henry Adams:*

> He could see that the new American—the child of incalculable coal-power, chemical power, electric power, and radiating energy, as well as new forces yet undetermined—must be a sort of God compared with any former creation of nature. At the rate of progress since 1800, every American who lived into the year 2000 would know how to control unlimited power. He would think in complexities unimaginable to an earlier mind. He would deal with problems altogether beyond the range of earlier society.

To Adams, a natural pessimist, the changes that lay ahead may have seemed vaguely troubling. To other Americans, however, the new century seemed to promise a brave new world of industrial and technological progress.

THE PRICE OF PROGRESS

The rapid transformation of the United States had not, however, come without cost, and Americans in 1900 were acutely aware of the problems that industrializa-tion and urbanization had produced. To many, it seemed that the nation had sacrificed stability for economic progress. To others, it appeared that the country had sacrificed justice. In fact, America had sacrificed much of both.

The Problem of Monopoly

The most troubling problem, many believed, was the rapid concentration of wealth and power in the hands of a few enterprising, even unscrupulous, men. Modern industry encouraged scale, and the small, independent enterprises that had once characterized the American economy were facing a powerful challenge from the emergence of great industrial combinations. A group of new industrial titans—men of a wealth and power unknown to earlier generations—had suc-ceeded in consolidating control of industry after industry in a very few firms, creating either monopolies or oligopolies, and in either case effectively limiting the influence of competition as a force to drive down prices.

Their most celebrated vehicle of control was the trust—a financial arrangement whereby members of an industry would join together in a loose consortium controlled by a central body of trustees, who set prices and production quotas for all. The most powerful member of a trust often controlled its decisions. Thus it was, for example, that John D. Rockefeller had by the end of the nineteenth century won control of virtually the entire American oil industry. In other areas, different methods produced a similar consolidation. When John Pierpont Morgan bought out Andrew Carnegie's giant steel company in 1901 and merged it with others to create the United States Steel Corporation, he not only produced the nation's first billion-dollar enterprise; he created a combination that controlled almost two-thirds of the nation's steel production—a combination able to set prices for steel from which no smaller company dared to deviate.

Companies such as Rockefeller's Standard Oil and Morgan's U.S. Steel were only the most conspicuous examples of a growing trend: small businesses absorbed by larger ones, competition in decline, prices artificially inflated. Indeed, the consolidation of American industry proceeded so rapidly in the last years of the century that many observers feared the death of free competition altogether. By the turn of the century, the number of corporate mergers had soared from dozens annually to thousands. By 1904, there were 318 so-called trusts, with a capitalization of more than $7 billion—combinations that reached not only into such primary industries as oil, steel, copper, and railroads, but into such consumer-oriented fields as tobacco, sugar, and whiskey. As a result, 1 percent of the corporations in America were able to control more than 33 percent of manufacturing.

From the beginning, large segments of the population looked at the proliferation of trusts and other combinations with hostility and mistrust. The popular description of such men as Rockefeller, Carnegie, and Morgan as "robber barons" suggests the attitude of much of the public. So do the reports of numerous conferences, commissions, and study groups, which pointed with alarm to the effects of consolidation upon the marketplace. The United States Industrial Commission reported in 1902:

> In most cases the combination has exerted an appreciable power over prices, and in practically all cases it has increased the margin between raw materials and finished products. Since there is reason to believe that the cost of production over a period of years has lessened, the conclusion is inevitable that the combinations have been able to increase their profits.

Convinced that the trusts were responsible for rising prices, and fearful that the power of the industrial leaders was so extensive as to threaten the nation's individualistic traditions, a startling range of groups had by the end of the century begun to assail monopoly and economic concentration. Laborers, consumers, small manufacturers, farmers, conservative bankers and financiers, advocates of radical change—all joined the attack.

Industrialists and their allies defended themselves by citing the new, purportedly scientific doctrine of Social Darwinism, which argued that the evolution of the economic structure, like the evolution of species, reflected the "survival of the fittest." Others pointed to the successes of such men as Rockefeller and Carnegie as evidence of the opportunities available to the "self-made man," a powerful myth popularized in the novels of Horatio Alger. But the strongest argument on behalf of consolidation was a simpler and more plausible one: efficiency. Small firms simply were not suited for the kind of large-scale manufacturing that the new economy demanded, corporate leaders claimed. Economic concentration enhanced the efficiency and productivity of American industry. Yet even many defenders of the new order were filled with misgivings about the potential for abuse inherent in the great combinations. Few issues engaged so wide a spectrum of American public opinion.

The Unstable Economy

Defenders and opponents of the trusts alike looked with concern at the disturbing pattern of instability in the late-nineteenth-century economy. Although industrial and agricultural production had expanded rapidly, other areas of the economy could not always keep pace. The nation's banks and financial institutions were neither strong enough nor efficient enough to meet the demands for their services adequately. The increasingly important stock market was riddled with corruption. Above all, the market for goods was not growing as rapidly as the supply.

The result was that even in the best of times, manufacturers and other businessmen flirted constantly with bankruptcy and battled one another ruthlessly for control of existing markets. It was the fear of this cutthroat competition that drove many industrialists to join trusts and other combinations. But not even consolidation could remove the underlying problem: too much production, too little demand. Beginning in 1873 and continuing until nearly the end of the century, the economy moved in an erratic cycle of booms and busts, with severe recessions creating economic havoc every five or six years, until finally in 1893 the system seemed on the verge of a total collapse.

Disparities of Wealth

One reason for the economic instability was that the new industries did not pass on enough of their profits to their workers to create an adequate market for the goods they were producing. And this growing disparity in the distribution of wealth was producing not only an imbalance between supply and demand, but a deep popular resentment. The standard of living may have been rising for virtually everyone, but the gap between rich and poor was visibly widening into an enormous chasm.

According to one estimate early in the century, 1 percent of the families in America controlled nearly 88 percent of the nation's assets. A small but conspicuous new class had emerged whose wealth almost defied description, whose fortunes were so vast that great feats of imagination were often required to enable them to be spent. Andrew Carnegie earned $23 million from his steel company in 1900 alone, and that was only part of his income (in an era in which there was as yet no income tax). John D. Rockefeller's personal wealth was estimated at one time to exceed a billion dollars. By the 1890s, highly publicized surveys disclosed that there were more than 4,000 American millionaires; decades earlier there had been only a few hundred.

Some of the wealthy—for example, Carnegie—lived relatively modestly and donated large sums to philanthropic causes. Others, however, lived in a conspicuous luxury that earned the resentment of much of the nation. Like a clan of feudal barons, the Vanderbilts (a family of steamship and railroad magnates) maintained, in addition to many country estates, seven garish mansions on seven blocks of New York City's Fifth Avenue. Other wealthy New Yorkers lavished vast sums on parties. The most notorious, a ball upon which Mrs. Bradley Martin spent $368,-000, created such a furor that she and her husband fled to England to escape the public abuse. A less exceptional dinner, served on gold plates at the old Waldorf-Astoria in 1899, cost $10,000 for forty people, or $250 apiece. For the average workingman, $250 represented six months' wages.

Observing these flagrant displays of wealth were the four-fifths of Americans who lived precariously, and the one-eighth of the population (10 million people) who lived below the poverty line. To those in difficult economic circumstances, the sense of relative deprivation could be as embittering as the poverty itself.

The Ordeal of the Worker

Workers in the mills and factories of the industrial titans were painfully aware of how meager their standard of living remained in comparison with that of their employers. Statistics showed a steady and significant increase in the wages of laborers, but to many workers the reality was much different. The boom-and-bust cycle of the economy left them with little job security, and even those who were spared unemployment often found their wages suddenly and substantially cut in difficult times. In factory towns such as Pullman, Illinois, the home of the railroad car manufacturing company, workers found themselves dependent upon their employers for housing and services; and they were often even more firmly tied by their debts to the company store. In Illinois in 1884, even skilled workers earned an average of less than $2.50 per day, an adequate but hardly luxurious wage at the prices of the day. The average for all workers was $1.51, barely enough for survival.

But American laborers faced a wide array of other hardships as well. There was, first, the painful adjustment to the nature of modern industrial labor: the performance of routine, repetitive tasks, often requiring little skill, on a strict and monotonous schedule. To rural men and women, accustomed to flexible and changing work patterns, the new routine was harsh and disorienting. To skilled craftsmen, whose once-valued tasks were now performed by machines, the new system was impersonal and demeaning. Factory workers were employed, moreover, in plants free from effective government regulation or inspection. The result was workplaces that were often appallingly unsafe or unhealthy. Industrial accidents were frequent and severe. Compensation to the victims, either from their employers or from the government, was rare.

Particular notoriety attached to the plight of women and children working in factories. One-fifth of American women worked in industry, often for wages as low as $6 to $8 a week, a sum below the minimum necessary for survival. The magazine writer O. Henry (William Sidney Porter) was reflecting a widespread indignation when he described in his short stories the strong temptation of these nearly starving workers to succumb to predatory men. Advocates of a minimum wage law for women created a sensation when they brought several women to a hearing in Chicago to testify that low wages and desperate poverty had driven them to prostitution. (It was not, however, sensational enough for the Illinois legislature, which promptly defeated the bill.)

Child labor, which had always existed in the United States, had by 1900 become a national disgrace. At least 1.7 million children under sixteen were employed in factories and fields; 10 percent of all girls between ten and fifteen, and 20 percent of all boys, held jobs. Under the pressure of outraged public opinion, thirty-eight

CHILD LABOR, 1909. These girls working at the spindles of a Carolina textile mill in 1909 were typical of hundreds of thousands of young children employed in the nation's factories. Working long hours for minimal wages, they were far more likely than adults to suffer serious injury or to succumb to disease. (*Lewis Hine. International Museum of Photography, George Eastman House, Rochester, N.Y.*)

state legislatures had passed child labor laws; but these laws were painfully insufficient. Sixty percent of child workers were employed in agriculture, which was
typically exempt from the laws; such children often worked twelve-hour days
picking or hoeing in the fields. The laws were hardly more effective for children
employed in factories; they set a minimum age of twelve years and a maximum
workday of ten hours, but employers often ignored even these minimal standards.
In the cotton mills of the South, children working at the looms all night were kept
awake by having cold water thrown in their faces. In canneries, little girls cut fruits
and vegetables sixteen hours a day. Exhausted children were particularly susceptible to injury while working at dangerous machines, and they were maimed and
even killed in industrial accidents at an alarming rate.

Yet as much as the appalling conditions of many women and children workers
tugged at the national conscience, conditions for men were often worse. As early
as 1877, Massachusetts had required safety devices on machinery and elevators.
Other states passed laws mandating mine inspection. But there was no effective
enforcement of such laws; indeed, personnel for enforcement usually did not exist.
In mills and mines, and on the railroads, the American accident rate was higher
than that of any industrial nation in the world. As late as 1907, an average of
twelve railroad men a week died on the job. In factories, thousands of workers
faced such occupational diseases as lead or phosphorus poisoning, against which
employers had taken few precautions.

An effective union movement among the industrial work force might have
offered solutions to some of these problems; but unions in the late nineteenth
century were for the most part weak and ineffective. Divided by ethnic and racial
animosities, unskilled workers often spent more energy battling one another than
demanding improvements in wages and working conditions. The leading labor
organization, the American Federation of Labor (A.F. of L.), was dominated by
skilled and relatively privileged workers, more concerned with protecting themselves from competition from below than with challenging the power structure
above. Samuel Gompers, the conservative, at times timid leader of the A.F. of L.,
strongly opposed violence and disorder and was reluctant to approve most strikes.
His constituents, unwilling to risk their hard-won gains through militant action
against their employers, usually supported his moderate approach, even though
the position of skilled workers was steadily deteriorating in the face of technological advances that were making their skills obsolete.

On occasion, workers did rebel against the wage cuts, the dangerous working
conditions, and the refusal of employers to recognize unions. Almost always,
however, the strikes ended in frustration. Supported by the courts and by both
federal and local governments, and strengthened by the availability of a large,
cheap supply of immigrant labor to replace any recalcitrant workers, industrialists
were able to withstand even the most militant challenges from labor organizers.
American workers entered the new century, therefore, with their economic position gradually improving, but with a still minimal share of the national wealth and
little power to demand more.

SAMUEL GOMPERS. Gompers's elegant wardrobe was a symbol of the middle-class aspirations of most leaders of the American Federation of Labor early in the century. Despite the declining importance of skilled labor in modern industry, the A.F. of L. stubbornly resisted allying itself with the mass of unskilled workers to produce a united labor movement. (*National Archives*)

Cities and Immigrants

The problems of rapid economic growth were perhaps most obvious to those who looked at the nation's cities. No change had been more dramatic in the last decades of the nineteenth century than the rapid growth in the size of urban areas. In 1860, only 6 million Americans had lived in communities of 2,500 or more people. By 1900, that number had swelled to 30 million—nearly 40 percent of the population. The arrival of rural men and women, who had left their farms in search of factory work, and even more importantly, the arrival of millions of new European immigrants looking for new beginnings, placed strains upon American cities that few were prepared to handle. Because existing dwellings were insufficient, most new residents lived in crowded, hastily built tenements or in shanties, tents, and abandoned stables. In New York, two-thirds of the city's 3.5 million residents lived in tenement houses, most of which had direct light and air in only four of the fourteen rooms on each floor. The rest received what ventilation they could through dank, gloomy airshafts. The demand for water in crowded cities far exceeded the ability of most municipalities to provide it, and primitive methods of sewage disposal made many urban neighborhoods a menace to the health of all who lived in or passed through them.

Inadequate housing and deficient sanitation were only part of the ordeal of the new urban residents. The new wave of immigrants, an increasing number of them uneducated peasants from southern and eastern Europe, faced the problems of assimilation: of learning a new language, adapting to a new culture, and countering the prejudice and hostility they met with from the native population. Immigrants and native rural migrants alike faced the dilemma of supporting themselves in an alien environment, in which they could not grow their own food, jobs were often difficult to find, and social services to help them through times of need barely existed.

Increasingly, they turned to the "machines"—political organizations such as Tammany Hall in New York that provided certain basic services to their constituents in exchange for votes. Controlled by "bosses" who were often themselves first- or second-generation immigrants, the machines gained steadily in political influence by mobilizing the growing numbers of lower-class urban residents behind them. Gradually, they won control of municipal governments in some of the nation's largest cities; and once in power, they horrified the urban middle classes with their casual indulgence in graft and corruption: selling city franchises for exorbitant fees, taking kickbacks for government contracts, diverting public money to their own use. Few city bosses were as expansively corrupt as Tammany's William M. Tweed, whose notorious "ring" once spent $11 million of city funds to build a modest courthouse; but Tweed's exuberant excesses established a pattern that other machine politicians often emulated in the years following his demise in 1872. Even more than the crowding and the poverty of the immigrant neighborhoods, the graft and corruption of the bosses persuaded the middle class, at least, that the new urban society had produced intolerable problems.

The Agrarian Malaise

Urban dwellers and factory workers may have been the most conspicuous victims of the new economic order. But modernization was also imposing costs on those whose lives continued in more traditional patterns. The American farmer, in particular, was faced with a dual problem. In a society in which urban life, urban values, and urban fashions were becoming increasingly dominant, in which the agricultural economy was becoming relatively less important, in which political power was flowing increasingly to the more populous, industrialized regions, it was easy for rural Americans to think of themselves as being somehow left behind, to believe that their own lives were being devalued by their society. The rapid movement of young men and women from the farms to the cities seemed to

ETHNIC NEW YORK. Mulberry Street in New York City, one of many crowded immigrant neighborhoods from which urban machines such as Tammany Hall derived their strength. (*Library of Congress*)

emphasize to those who remained the increasing irrelevance of rural life in American culture.

In addition to these psychological strains, farmers faced a real economic decline. Agriculture, like industry, had experienced a boom in the years after the Civil War, and vast new agricultural lands had been quickly settled and cultivated. By the late 1880s, however, it was becoming clear that the agricultural sector had overexpanded. In some regions, climatic changes turned once-fertile lands into arid prairies, leaving new settlers suddenly unable to produce enough to survive. Even in areas that remained fertile, excess production and dropping prices were producing economic distress. Because of the cyclical nature of their work, farmers had always relied upon loans—borrowing money for planting in the spring, repaying it after the harvest and sale of crops in the fall. As more and more farms began to operate at a loss, farmers found themselves unable to repay their debts and were forced increasingly to assume large mortgages on their land at high rates of interest simply to survive. Unable to control their markets and unable to escape from their growing indebtedness, American farmers were by the 1890s in the midst of a historic crisis.

The Matter of Race

Most black Americans were farmers in the late nineteenth century; and like other farmers, they suffered from the decline in agricultural prices and the general agrarian malaise. As they had throughout their history, however, they faced additional problems of their own. Concentrated in the rural South, blacks were for the most part confined to a system of sharecropping and tenant farming under which they owned no land and supported themselves only on the small proportion of their crops that their landlords allowed them to retain. Constantly in debt, their ability to survive was often in the hands of the local merchant, who served as their only source of needed supplies and with whom they had constantly to negotiate terms for receiving credit. It was a form of servitude only slightly removed from slavery. Emancipation from legal bondage had not freed blacks from economic domination.

By the mid-1890s, moreover, white southerners were moving aggressively to strip blacks of the few social and political privileges won in the aftermath of the Civil War. A system of draconian "Jim-Crow" laws created a legal structure of segregation which ensured that black children would not have access to white schools, that blacks would be restricted to separate (and almost invariably inferior) public facilities, and that few blacks would retain the right to vote. The number of registered black voters in Louisiana, for example, fell from 130,000 in 1896 to 1,300 by 1904. During the same period, blacks and whites ceased eating in the same restaurants, riding in the same railroad cars, using the same public parks, sitting in the same waiting rooms, or attending the same theaters. The Supreme Court sanctioned the new statutes in an 1896 decision, *Plessy* v. *Ferguson*, a ruling that would stand for nearly sixty years.

There were also other, more direct assaults. Capricious lynchings of blacks suspected of crimes reached a peak of 235 in 1892; and although by the beginning of the new century the number had declined, 50 or 60 blacks a year continued to die at the hands of mobs. Local courts and state governments in the South took little action to defend the victims or punish the guilty. Agitation for a federal antilynching law fell on deaf ears in Washington. The new century began with black southerners excluded—economically, politically, and socially—from the life of their region. It is little wonder that a stream of migrants was beginning to establish substantial black communities in such northern cities as New York, Chicago, and Washington, D.C. There, blacks were spared some of the indignities of life in the South but little of the deprivation. "The great majority of the Negroes of New York live in poverty," a social worker noted at the turn of the century. "Negroes pay more and get less for their money than any other tenants."

Invisible Minorities

Few Americans were aware by the end of the century of the plight of other, even more troubled minorities, who also were experiencing the effects of the nation's transformation.

American Indians had by 1890 suffered such complete defeat in their military struggles against white expansion that they had no choice but to accept the meager lands the government set aside for them as reservations. Yet even on the reservations, the Indians were unable to resist encroachments from white society. The most glaring evidence of their plight was the 1890 clash between members of the Sioux tribe and United States soldiers at Wounded Knee, South Dakota, where several hundred Indian men, women, and children were killed. The bloodbath followed the efforts of whites to stop an Indian religious ritual that they considered dangerous and inflammatory.

Three years earlier, Congress had called for an even more drastic change in the nature of Indian society. The Dawes Act of 1887 decreed that residents of reservations would no longer live as traditional tribes but would move instead onto 160-acre farms parceled out of their lands by the government. Few Native Americans knew how to farm; most of the land they received was unsuitable for family farming in any case. Gradually, a substantial portion of their reservations came under the control of land speculators. Further legislation over the next two decades hastened the erosion of tribal authority and further diminished tribal landholdings. It was the willful destruction of a traditional way of life; and the result was to create a troubled, rootless people, drifting through an alien culture and increasingly dependent upon the government for support.

Ever since the annexation of the southwestern lands in the 1840s, a Spanish-speaking minority had lived in poverty and subjugation in American territory. Their plight did not improve during the economic growth of the late nineteenth century. By 1900, the demand for cheap labor in the expanding Southwest was leading to the importation of more than 100,000 workers from Mexico. In raw, western cities, they crowded together in slums as wretched as those in the industrial East. "When the heavy rains come in winter," a social worker visiting a Mexican-American community reported, "imagine those shacks and tents that have no floors! Sick women lie on damp mattresses which are embedded in mud. . . . And the household stays wet till the sun shines again."

THE CRISIS OF THE 1890s

Americans in 1900 were particularly aware of the problems facing their society, for they had just lived through a decade of crisis such as the nation had not experienced since the Civil War. For several years, beginning in 1892, it had seemed that all the accumulated injustices and instabilities of the previous decades were bursting to the surface at once. Many feared that the nation faced revolution or collapse. Virtually everyone was forced to recognize that American society, for all its progress, faced serious maladjustments.

Depression and Unrest

Most devastating was a major economic depression, the worst in American history to that point, which began, like a later depression, with a dramatic stock market panic in May 1893. The next several years were ones of increasing misery. Banks failed; railroad construction ground to a halt; industrial production declined and in some industries virtually ceased; millions of workers lost their jobs. By 1894, some 20 percent of the work force, as many as 3 million people, were unemployed.

The depression seemed to many Americans to emphasize the dangers inherent in an industrial economy controlled by a few large institutions. It also emphasized the unhappy position of American workers. The layoffs, the factory closings, the reduced wages—all helped produce a disturbing upsurge of strikes and labor violence. Even before the depression, there had been unrest. A battle between striking steelworkers and Pinkerton detectives in Homestead, Pennsylvania, in 1892 had left sixteen dead. Two years later the walkouts and conflicts had become a virtual epidemic. When the federal government sent troops into Chicago in 1894 to suppress a strike by Pullman workers, twenty strikers died. A wave of labor radicalism, some of it real, much of it imagined by a frightened middle class, made the labor crisis seem even more alarming.

The Agrarian Revolt

While workers created turmoil in industrial cities and factory towns, American farmers were engaged in an even more powerful revolt of their own. The depression of the 1890s only accentuated a longstanding economic crisis in agriculture, and rural Americans responded by increasing the political agitation in which they had long been engaged. In 1892, agrarian insurgents formally created the People's party (better known as the Populist party), nominated candidates for President and Vice President, and issued a wide-ranging set of demands for major reforms of the nation's political structure, its economy, and its currency. The new party showed impressive strength in the 1892 elections, and it continued to perform well in many areas in 1894. By 1896, the Populists were in decline as an independent force, but the discontent they had unleashed helped pressure the Democratic party to nominate the agrarian spokesman William Jennings Bryan for the presidency. The People's party also subsequently endorsed Bryan. Although far less radical than the orthodox Populists, Bryan was deeply alarming to conservative easterners, who viewed his demand for abandonment of the gold standard and the issuance of currency backed by silver as a threat to the foundations of the American economy. Not even the decisive victory of Republican William McKinley in the presidential election erased the fears of those who believed that the spirit of revolution had now won control of one of the nation's two major parties.

America Overseas

The 1898 war between the United States and the Spanish Empire was not a direct result of the economic and social crisis; but it was, in some respects, a tentative

WILLIAM JENNINGS BRYAN.   Bryan campaigns in 1908 beside a
photograph of himself taken twelve years earlier, when he ran as the
presidential candidate of both the Democratic party and the People's party.
His crusade for the free coinage of silver terrified eastern conservatives in
1896. (*Library of Congress*)

response to the nation's disorder. The depression of the 1890s had emphasized
to many American businessmen the perils of surplus production and the need for
expanded markets for manufactured goods. Unwilling to distribute their profits
in a way that would strengthen the market for their products at home, industrialists had for some years been working to expand American trade overseas. And so
they looked with particular alarm at the savage civil war in nearby Cuba between
natives of the island and Spanish imperial forces.

At first, few businessmen urged American intervention in the conflict, fearing
that a war would place strains on an already troubled domestic economy. Gradually,
however, public sentiment for involvement began to build. Some of it was a result of
agitation by those who feared that American investments in Cuba—more than $50
million—might be endangered by the fighting. Some of it stemmed from an
inflammatory campaign of "yellow journalism" in the newspapers of William
Randolph Hearst, who wasted no opportunity to publicize alleged atrocities committed by the Spaniards against the native rebels. Some of it stemmed from public
outrage after the mysterious blowing up of the United States battleship *Maine* in
Havana harbor. And some of it stemmed from a growing concern among businessmen and government officials that the possessions of the shaky Spanish Empire,
already a target of American trade, might fall into hostile hands.

THE *MAINE*. The wreckage of the U.S. battleship *Maine* rests in the mud in Havana harbor in 1898 after an explosion of undetermined origin. The sinking became the spark that ignited the Spanish-American War. (*Library of Congress*)

The war, once it began in April 1898, was almost ridiculously brief and easy. After three months of successful combat and ardent jingoism, America emerged victorious. It emerged as well with a substantial new empire of its own: Cuba, Guam, Puerto Rico, the Philippines, and (although its acquisition was only indirectly related to the war) Hawaii. Despite the opposition of a small but vocal anti-imperialist movement, President McKinley persuaded Congress to accept the new territories. And although in the following years the nation moved to give some of its overseas possessions political independence in varying degrees, it was careful to ensure that they would remain available as markets for American goods. The war had given the United States exclusive access to markets in the Caribbean; and the annexation of the Philippines gave the nation a strategic position in the Pacific, which ensured that China would remain open to American trade as well.

The Need for Reform

The "splendid little war," as Secretary of State John Hay described it, had helped briefly to divert the nation's attention from its domestic turmoil. And much of the turmoil itself had by the turn of the century started to subside. The economy had begun an impressive recovery. Labor unrest had declined, in part because of the return of prosperity, in part because of ruthless suppression by employers and government, which broke the spirit of all but the most militant workers. The Populist revolt, after the defeat of Bryan in 1896, had quickly faded, and the agricultural economy was beginning slowly but steadily to improve.

Neither the war nor the economic stabilization, however, could erase the memory of the crisis of the mid-1890s. Nor could they obscure the clear evidence that the nation continued to face serious structural problems, that the causes of the crisis had not been removed. And so it was that the American people entered the new century with both high hopes and deep concerns. They were aware that their powerful industrial economy offered them the potential for great growth and progress. Yet they were concerned, too, that the transformation of their society had been too rapid, that the changes had often been heedless and destructive. If America was to profit from its industrial growth, a growing number of Americans were coming to believe, it would first have to make some major adjustments and reforms. It would have to stabilize the disordered new society.

SUGGESTED READINGS

For general accounts of the last decades of the nineteenth century, see Robert H. Wiebe, *The Search for Order* (1967), and Samuel P. Hays, *The Response to Industrialism* (1957). Useful economic studies include Edward C. Kirkland, *Industry Comes of Age* (1961); Thomas C. Cochran, *American Business in the Twentieth Century* (2nd ed., 1972); David F. Noble, *America by Design: Science, Technology, and the Rise of Corporate Capitalism* (1977); and Alfred D. Chandler, *The Visible Hand: The Managerial Revolution in American Business* (1977). For information on changing living standards, see Albert Rees, *Real Wages in Manufacturing, 1890–1914* (1961), and R. H. Bremner, *From the Depths: The Discovery of Poverty in the United States* (1956). On labor, consult David Brody, *Steelworkers in America: The Nonunion Era* (1960); Philip Taft, *The A.F. of L. in the Time of Gompers* (1957); and Melvin Dubofsky, *We Shall Be All: A History of the Industrial Workers of the World* (1969). See also Herbert Gutman, *Work, Culture, and Society in Industrializing America* (1976), and Stephan Thernstrom, *Poverty and Progress* (1964).

Valuable studies of immigration include Oscar Handlin, *The Uprooted* (1951), and John Higham, *Strangers in the Land* (1955). For the agrarian crisis and the Populist revolt, see Lawrence Goodwyn, *Democratic Promise: The Populist Moment in America* (1976), and a shorter, paperback version of the same work, *The Populist Moment* (1978). Important earlier studies include John D. Hicks, *The Populist Revolt* (1931), and the relevant chapters in Richard Hofstadter, *The Age of Reform* (1955). On racial attitudes and practices, see C. Vann Woodward, *The Strange Career of Jim Crow* (1974); August Meier, *Negro Thought in America* (1880–1915); and Nell Painter, *Exodusters* (1978). Dee Brown's *Bury My Heart at Wounded Knee* (1971) is a popular account of the 1890 massacre. More general accounts of the plight of Indians in the late nineteenth century include R. W. Mardock, *Reformers and the American Indian* (1970), and Wilcomb E. Washburn, *The Indian in America* (1975). An overview of the Hispanic experience in America is available in Rodolfo Acuña, *Occupied America* (2nd ed., 1981).

For late-nineteenth-century politics and diplomacy, see especially Morton Keller, *Affairs of State* (1977); C. Vann Woodward, *Origins of the New South* (1951); Morgan Kousser, *The Shaping of Southern Politics* (1974); Richard Jensen, *The Winning of the Midwest* (1971); Ernest May, *Imperial Democracy* (1961); William Appleman Williams, *The Tragedy of American Diplomacy* (1972); and Gerald F. Linderman, *The Mirror of War* (1974).

Two

The Progressive Society

Even before the end of the nineteenth century, a growing number of Americans had begun to embrace a new social outlook, one that expressed the need for imposing order upon the chaos that rapid modernization had created, one that emphasized the necessity of curing industrial society's most glaring injustices. By the early 1900s, the new outlook had acquired a name: progressivism.

Not even the progressives themselves could always agree upon what the word really meant. To some, it suggested simply a broad cultural vision. To others, it meant a cluster of moral and humanitarian goals. To still others, it was a particular set of political reforms (and, later, a particular political party). At times, in fact, it seemed that virtually everyone had become a progressive: middle-class reformers and machine bosses, big businessmen and small entrepreneurs, white segregationists and black activists, industrial workers and farmers, immigrants and immigration restrictionists. More than one historian, looking back upon the era, has suggested that the word *progressive* be dropped from our vocabulary.

Yet if progressivism was a movement of remarkable scope and diversity, it was also one that had a relatively consistent set of central assumptions, assumptions that reflected both the hopefulness and the concern that were the legacy of the late nineteenth century. It was, first of all, an optimistic vision. Progressives believed, as their name implies, in the idea of progress. They believed that society was capable of improvement, even of perfection, that continued growth and advancement were the nation's destiny. There was in progressivism a heady, boisterous enthusiasm, a continuing excitement over possibilities.

But progressives believed, too, that growth and progress could not continue to occur recklessly, as they had in the nineteenth century. Order and stability, they claimed, were essential for social betterment. Not all progressives agreed upon the

23

best way to create order, but most believed that government would play an important role in the process. Only government could effectively counter the corrupt special interests that were responsible for social disarray. Only government could provide the services and the regulation that were necessary for future progress. It was essential, therefore, to rescue the nation's political institutions from the influence of selfish interest groups; and it was vital that government expand its role in the society and in the economy. Not all progressive efforts required the assistance of government, but the broad reordering of society that most progressives believed necessary would be impossible without it.

Beyond these central goals, progressivism flowed outward in two broad streams, embodying two varieties of reform. One rested upon a belief in process, in the importance of the organizations and procedures through which society operated. The other reflected a commitment to humanitarian reform, to the alleviation of social injustice. The two streams were not entirely separate; technocratic and humanitarian reform were often synonymous, and there were many progressive efforts, therefore, that combined both impulses. But the distinction was a real one, and in the end the two approaches met different fates.

THE ORGANIZATIONAL IMPULSE

The first, and ultimately the stronger, progressive impulse was the one toward process and organization. Americans of the time placed much emphasis upon the need for rationalizing their society, for making it operate more efficiently and thus more productively. It was natural, therefore, that they should develop a profound concern for the creation of orderly systems and institutions. To many Americans, the process by which a goal was achieved often seemed as important as the goal itself.

Nothing was so valued among many progressives, therefore, as scientific knowledge and expertise. Nothing so characterized their outlook as the belief that even nonscientific problems were subject to scientific analysis. Society could no longer be left in the hands of untrained amateurs. Enlightened experts and scientifically designed bureaucracies must create the order that America so badly needed.

The New Theorists

Nowhere did this impulse receive clearer expression than in the writings of a new group of scholars and intellectuals. Unlike the Social Darwinists of the nineteenth century, these theorists were no longer content with merely justifying the existing industrial system. They spoke instead of the creation of a new civilization, one in which the expertise of scientists and engineers could be brought to bear upon the problems of the economy and society. Their most influential spokesman was the social scientist Thorstein Veblen. Harshly critical of the industrial tycoons of the late nineteenth century—the "leisure class" as he satirically described them in his first major work, *A Theory of the Leisure Class* (1899)—Veblen proposed instead a new economic system in which power would reside in the hands of highly trained engineers. Only they, he argued, could fully understand the "machine process" by which modern society must be governed. Only they could provide the efficiency and order necessary for the industrial economy. By the end of his life, he was calling for government by a "soviet of technicians," who would impose upon the economy their own instinct for rational process.

Veblen found support, if not for his specific proposals then at least for his broad concerns, from a large group of other intellectuals. William James, a famous psychologist (and brother of the novelist Henry James), laid the groundwork for much progressive thought by publicizing the new theory of "pragmatism." Drawing on the work of such earlier philosophers as Charles S. Peirce, James argued that modern society must rely for guidance less upon old ideals and moral principles than upon the test of scientific inquiry. No idea was valid, he claimed, unless it worked. Even religious beliefs, James insisted, were subject to the test of experience. If faith helped an individual to understand his world, then it was valid for him; if it did not, then it was not.

An expanding network of social scientists brought this same concern for scientific inquiry into areas of thought long dominated by traditional orthodoxies. New economists, such as, Richard T. Ely and Simon Patten, challenged old economic assumptions and argued for a more active and pragmatic use of the discipline. Sociologists like Edward A. Ross and Lester Frank Ward urged the adaptation of scientific methods to the solution of social and political problems. Historians like Frederick Jackson Turner and Charles Beard challenged prevailing assumptions by arguing that economic factors more than spiritual ideals had been the governing force in historical development. The philosopher John Dewey, for many decades one of the most influential of all American intellectuals, proposed a new approach to education that placed less emphasis on the rote learning of traditional knowledge and more on a creative, flexible, democratic approach to schooling, one that enabled students to acquire practical knowledge that would help them deal with the realities of their society. The scientific method, he believed, would be the governing principle of this new, "instrumental" education.

Reshaping the Workplace

The scientific method became the basis as well of a far-reaching effort to restructure the operations of America's factories. Convinced that a modern economy required the modernization of industrial production, a wide range of manufacturers, led by automobile executives, began to turn to the new principles of "scientific management." Their guiding spirit was the engineer Frederick Winslow Taylor. Taylor had achieved early renown with his success in revolutionizing the machine-tool industry with carbon steel cutting edges, which could run efficiently at white-hot speed. He soon discovered, however, that the new technology would be of little use unless machinists could begin to operate their lathes at correspondingly fast speeds. It was the first step in applying to the management of workers the same kind of scientific standards that governed the development of technology. If properly managed, he began to argue, fewer and fewer men could perform simpler tasks at infinitely greater speed, increasing productive efficiency manifold. Those who could not contribute to this efficiency, Taylor argued, should be discarded as readily as obsolete machinery. Thus was born a system of management, widely known as "Taylorism," that rapidly gained a large following among the leaders of industry.

Increasingly, industrialists adopted Taylor's scientific-management studies of workers' motions, often hiring outside "efficiency experts" to view and criticize their operations. Scientists and engineers entered the factories to develop new tools and products that would increase productive efficiency. Industrial laboratories became a commonplace feature of large corporations, in large part because of the phenomenal success of such pioneers as Thomas Alva Edison, whose laboratory at Menlo Park, New Jersey, had produced not only the incandescent lamp, the phonograph, and the motion picture, but scores of devices to improve industrial operations.

Out of the new methods and machines came what many people considered the greatest triumph of the organizational impulse: modern mass production and, above all, the moving assembly line, which Henry Ford introduced in his automobile plants in 1914. This revolutionary technique cut the time for assembling a chassis from twelve and a half hours to one and a half hours. It enabled Ford to raise the wages and lower the hours of his workers while cutting the base price of his Model T from $950 to $290. Other industrialists looked and copied.

By 1914, American manufacturers were producing 76 percent more goods than in 1899; and they were doing so with only 36 percent more workers and 13 percent more establishments. To them, such figures were a triumphant vindication of the values of organization and efficiency. Their workers, however, were often more skeptical. Organized labor reacted strongly against many of the innovations of "Taylorism," protesting the reduction in the number of workers employed in particular industries, expressing resentment at efficiency standards that treated them, they claimed, like machines. Labor leaders won a minor victory in 1915 by persuading Congress to forbid the introduction of efficiency systems into government arsenals and navy yards, but such triumphs were few and far between. Gradually, moreover, many workers began to respond to Taylor's argument that increased efficiency meant higher production and thus a higher living standard for all—not only through lower prices for consumers but through higher wages for employees (as the Ford example showed). By the 1920s, some unions had begun to accept the argument and to acquiesce. Scientific management had won a permanent foothold in American industry.

The Professions

The belief in expertise and organization was particularly influential among the expanding new group of middle-class professionals. The late nineteenth century had seen not only a growth of the industrial work force. It had seen, too, a dramatic expansion in the number of Americans engaged in administrative and professional tasks. Industries needed not only workers but managers, technicians, accountants.

THE ASSEMBLY LINE. Henry Ford's assembly line, first introduced in his automobile plants in 1914, revolutionized American industry. It streamlined production, both by isolating tasks and by establishing a continuous, routinized flow to the assembly process. Although the assembly line increased industrial efficiency, its critics charged that it also contributed to the depersonalization of the workplace. (*Ford Archives*)

Cities required a growing range of commercial, medical, legal, and educational services. The demand for technology required scientists and engineers who, in turn, required institutions and instructors to train them. The industrial state, in short, had produced an enormous new infrastructure of specialized, professional services. And by the turn of the century, those performing these services had come to constitute a distinct social group—a new middle class. Unlike the older middle class, whose status often derived from family background and stature within the community, the new middle class placed a far higher value upon education and accomplishment. Almost 6 million strong by 1910, its members were hard at work creating organizations and standards to secure and stabilize their position in society.

As their vehicle, they created the modern, organized professions. The idea of professionalism had been a frail one in America even as late as 1880. When every patent-medicine salesman could call himself a doctor, when every frustrated politician could proclaim himself a lawyer, when anyone who could read and write could present himself as a teacher, it was clear that a professional label would by itself carry little weight. There were, of course, skilled and responsible doctors, lawyers, teachers, and others; but they had no way of controlling the charlatans and other incompetents who presumed to practice their trades. As the demand for services increased, so did the pressures, from both within and without, for reform.

Among the first to respond was the medical profession. Throughout the 1890s, doctors who considered themselves true professionals—who had had formal training in medicine, who understood the new scientific discoveries that were revolutionizing their methods—began forming local associations and societies. In 1901, finally, they reorganized the American Medical Association into a modern, national, professional society. Between 1900 and 1910, membership increased from 8,400 to over 70,000; by 1920, nearly two-thirds of all American doctors were members. The first major effort of the AMA was to insist on strict, scientific standards for admission to the practice of medicine, with doctors themselves serving as protectors of the standards. State and local governments readily complied, passing new laws that required the licensing of all physicians and restricting licenses to those practitioners approved by the profession.

Accompanying the emphasis upon strict regulation of the profession came a concern for rigorous scientific training and research. By 1900, medical education at a few medical schools—notably Johns Hopkins in Baltimore (founded in 1893)—compared favorably with that in the leading institutions of Europe. Doctors like William H. Welch at Hopkins revolutionized the teaching of medicine by moving students out of the classrooms and into laboratories and clinics. New, rigorous standards forced many inadequate medical schools out of existence, and those that remained were obliged to adopt a strict, scientific approach.

One result of these changes was a rapid increase in American medical research and a series of important new discoveries. In 1900, Walter Reed proved conclusively that a striped mosquito was the transmitter of yellow fever; the following year the army began a widespread program to exterminate the insect. Tropical diseases had been more effective than Spanish bullets in killing American soldiers in the Spanish-American War; during the building of the Panama Canal, army doctors were able virtually to eliminate yellow fever and malaria. A new cure for hookworm had a dramatic impact upon health in the rural South. The medical profession's insistence upon milk inspection (in response to the discoveries of Louis Pasteur) and chlorination of water similarly helped eliminate much disease. In the first twenty years of the new century, the nation's death rate dropped by more than 20 percent, a figure that seemed to justify the strenuous professionalization of American medicine.

There was similar movement in other professions. By 1916, lawyers in all forty-eight states had established professional bar associations; and virtually all of them had succeeded in creating central examining boards, composed of lawyers, to regulate admission to the profession. Increasingly, aspiring lawyers found it necessary to enroll in graduate programs, and the nation's law schools accordingly expanded greatly, both in numbers and in the rigor of their curricula. Teachers made similar efforts to organize and regulate their profession. They established a vast network of teachers' colleges and schools of education and, in 1905, created the National Education Association, which fought, among other things, for government licensing of teachers. Businessmen supported the creation of schools of business administration and created their own national organizations: the National Association of Manufacturers in 1895 and the United States Chamber of Commerce in 1912. Even farmers, long the symbol of the romantic spirit of individualism, responded to the new order by forming, through the National Farm Bureau Federation, a network of agricultural organizations designed to spread scientific farming methods, teach sound marketing techniques, and lobby for the interests of their members.

The behavior of the professions—in creating organizations, in imposing scientific standards upon their members, in stressing technical training and expertise —reflected impulses that were coming to characterize American society as a whole. Modern society was too complex, many people now believed, to be left to individuals or to local institutions. Centralized, scientific management, through efficient organizations staffed by experts, was the key to a successful future. The increasingly bureaucratic society that began to emerge as a result did indeed perform great tasks and solve many difficulties. Only slowly did Americans become aware that it would bring with it serious problems of its own.

THE HUMANITARIAN IMPULSE

While many progressives were emphasizing science and organization as the vehicles for bringing order to America, others were turning to the task of humanitarian social reform. The social reformers were not always distinct from the technocratic progressives; often, they brought to their work the same belief in science and organization. The humanitarian efforts, however, were less directly concerned with stabilizing the position of the middle class than with attacking the problems of the poor—in working, as some put it, for "social justice."

Reformers brought to these efforts one of the strongest elements of progressive thought: its belief in the influence of the environment upon individual development. Social Darwinists such as William Graham Sumner had argued that a person's fortunes reflected his inherent "fitness" for survival; progressive theorists disagreed. Ignorance, poverty, even criminality, they argued, were not the result of inherent moral or genetic failings or of the workings of divine providence. They were, rather, the effects of an unhealthy environment. To elevate the distressed, therefore, required an improvement of the conditions in which they lived.

The Urban Ghetto

The immigrant ghettoes that had expanded so dramatically in the last decades of the nineteenth century were the most logical targets of such efforts. In 1890, Jacob Riis, himself a Danish immigrant, but a determinedly middle-class man, published a shocking exposé of life in the immigrant neighborhoods of New York City, *How the Other Half Lives.* His lurid descriptions of the physical conditions of the ghetto, along with his equally sensational photographs, aroused public sentiment for reform. Riis managed in the following years to lead an effective movement on behalf of slum clearance, a movement that resulted in the destruction of some of the worst slum dwellings in New York but made no provision for the relocation of displaced residents.

Other progressives adopted more sensitive approaches to urban problems. Borrowing ideas from reform movements in Europe, especially England, committed

LIFE IN THE IMMIGRANT GHETTO.   Jacob Riis took this picture of an Italian mother and her baby (apparently in the basement of a New York City tenement) around 1900 to illustrate the appalling conditions of ghetto life. Riis crusaded for many years on behalf of slum clearance; later he joined with his friend Theodore Roosevelt to call for immigration restriction. Critics charged that Riis sensationalized his depiction of immigrant life to arouse popular support for his proposals. (*Jacob A. Riis Collection, Museum of the City of New York*)

men and women established a network of settlement houses in immigrant neighborhoods. Staffed by members of the middle class, these institutions sought to help immigrant families adapt to the language and customs of their new country. Settlement houses offered educational services, staged community events, built libraries, and in general tried to enhance the lives of their neighborhoods without adopting the stance of disapproving moral superiority that had hampered the efforts of earlier philanthropic efforts. Jane Addams's Hull House, founded in Chicago in 1889, became a model for more than 400 similar institutions throughout the nation.

The proliferation of settlement houses helped expose another major change in progressive society: the expanding role of women. Increasingly, middle-class women found themselves not only free from much of the burden of housework —a result both of their own affluence and of technological advances—but aroused to public service by new forms of education. Vassar, founded in 1865, was the first of a growing number of women's colleges that awakened their students to the possibility of a more active social role. It was these educated women who were by the end of the nineteenth century staffing settlement houses, forming clubs to agitate for social reform, and helping to elevate the humanitarian issues of the era to the level of compelling national questions.

The settlement houses also helped to spawn another important institution of reform: the profession of social work. Workers at Hull House, for example, maintained a close relationship with the University of Chicago's pioneering work in the field of sociology; and a growing number of programs for the professional training of social workers began to appear in the nation's leading universities, partly in response to the activities of the settlements. The professional social worker combined a compassion for the poor with a commitment to the values of bureaucratic progressivism: scientific study, efficient organization, reliance upon experts. The new profession produced elaborate surveys and reports, collected statistics, and published scholarly tracts on the need for urban reform. Settlement houses ultimately faded from view; social workers survived.

The Social Gospel

The professional social workers combined their sensitivity to human problems with a belief in organization and expertise. Other urban reformers emphasized instead the social demands of religion. A powerful movement within American Christianity (and, to some extent, within American Judaism), often known as the Social Gospel, had emerged by the early twentieth century as a vigorous force in the effort to redeem the nation's cities. The Salvation Army, which had come to the United States from England, boasted a corps of 3,000 officers and 20,000 privates by 1900, offering both material aid and spiritual service to the urban poor. Ministers of many denominations, priests, and rabbis left traditional parish work to serve in the troubled cities, and their efforts soon became part of the folklore of their time. Edward Sheldon's *In His Steps* (1898), the story of a young minister who abandoned a comfortable post to work among the needy in Chicago, sold more than 15 million copies and established itself as the most successful novel of the era.

Others made similar appeals to religious faith on behalf of social reform. Walter Rauschenbusch, a Protestant theologian from Rochester, New York, published a series of influential discourses on the possibilities for human salvation through Christian reform. To him, the message of Darwinism was not that the individual was engaged in a brutal struggle for survival of the fittest, but that all individuals should work for a humanitarian evolution of the social fabric. "Translate the evolutionary themes into religious faith," he wrote, "and you have the doctrine of the Kingdom of God." American Catholics seized upon the 1893 publication of Pope Leo XIII's encyclical *Rerum Novarum* as justification for their own crusade for social justice. Catholic liberals such as Father John A. Ryan took to heart the Pope's warning that "a small number of very rich men have been able to lay upon the masses of the poor a yoke little better than slavery itself. . . . No practical solution of this question will ever be found without the assistance of religion and the church." For decades, he worked to expand the scope of Catholic social welfare organizations.

The Social Gospel was never the dominant element in the movement for urban reform. Some of the most influential progressives dismissed it as irrelevant moralizing; others viewed it as little more than a useful complement to their own work. But the engagement of religion with reform had a lasting impact, bringing to progressivism a powerful moral component, a belief that society's mission was not simply to cure disorder in the cities but to redeem the lives of even the lowliest residents. Walter Rauschenbusch captured some of both the optimism and the spirituality of the Social Gospel with his proud comment, after a visit to a New York slum known as Hell's Kitchen: "One could hear human virtue cracking and crashing all around."

PROGRESSIVISM AND BLACKS

American blacks may have been the group most conspicuously in need of assistance from progressive reformers in the first years of the new century. They were also the group most consistently ignored by middle-class whites. Trapped in a debilitating economic system in the rural South, forced to live in the least desirable areas of the northern cities to which some were beginning to migrate, burdened in both places by the effects of an unrelenting racial prejudice that was shared by virtually all whites, black Americans had little reason to share the optimism of the rest of the population as they viewed the years ahead. Yet even without the assistance of white reformers, many blacks became imbued with the spirit of progressivism and began important efforts to elevate the position of their race.

Booker T. Washington

The most widely admired black leader at the beginning of the twentieth century was the southern educator Booker T. Washington. Born into slavery, educated at

BOOKER T. WASHINGTON.
Washington was born into slavery and rose from poverty to become the most admired black leader of his era. His efforts on behalf of black vocational education won him the appreciation of many members of his own race; his reluctance to challenge segregation earned him the approval of moderate whites. (*Harvard University Library*)

Hampton Institute in Virginia, the founder and president of the successful Tuskegee Institute in Alabama, Washington was a classic example of the self-made man. Blacks looked upon him as a symbol of their own aspirations. White progressives admired him as an example of the possibilities for black advancement through private, unthreatening efforts. Not until Martin Luther King, Jr., more than fifty years later would a single black leader so clearly establish himself as the leading spokesman for his race.

Washington's message was a cautious one. Blacks could not hope for advancement in American society, he argued, except through their own efforts at self-improvement. They should attend school, learn skills, and establish a solid footing in agriculture and the trades. They should, moreover, refine their speech, improve their dress, and adopt habits of thrift and personal cleanliness. Only thus could they win the respect of the white population, the prerequisite for any larger social gains. In a famous speech in Georgia in 1895, Washington outlined a philosophy of race relations that became widely known as the Atlanta Compromise. "The wisest among my race understand," he said, "that the agitation of questions of social equality is the extremest folly." Blacks should, rather, engage in "severe and constant struggle" for economic gains; for, as he explained, "no race that has anything to contribute to the markets of the world is long in any degree ostracized." It was important for blacks to gain all the rights and privileges of citizenship, he argued, but first they must show that they were "prepared for the exercise of these privileges."

In the context of his time, Washington's message was not as timid and conservative as it would later sound. As the first black leader to acquire a wide audience among members of his race, he offered a powerful challenge to those whites who strove to discourage blacks from acquiring an education or winning any economic gains. He encouraged the strengthening and expansion of black technical schools and agricultural colleges—institutions like Hampton and Tuskegee Institutes. He helped inspire new organizations such as the Urban League, founded in 1910, which attracted the support not only of urban blacks but of some middle-class whites. The League helped blacks obtain improved housing, recreational facilities, and employment. It even attempted to win admission for blacks into labor unions. Booker T. Washington, in short, helped awaken the interest of a new generation in the possibilities for self-advancement.

But Washington's message was comforting to southern whites as well: as an implicit promise that blacks would not challenge the system of segregation then carefully being erected, and as evidence that the burden of racial injustice would be borne not by the oppressor but by the oppressed. And it was for this reason that Washington soon encountered a passionate challenge from the spokesman for another philosophy.

W. E. B. Du Bois

W. E. B. Du Bois, unlike Washington, had never known slavery. Born in Massachusetts and educated at Harvard, he grew to maturity with a far more expansive view than Washington of the goals of his race and the responsibilities of white society to eliminate prejudice and injustice. In *The Souls of Black Folk* (1903), he launched an open attack upon the philosophy of the Atlanta Compromise, accusing Washington of encouraging white efforts to impose segregation and of unnecessarily limiting the aspirations of his race. "Is it possible and probable," he asked,

> that nine millions of men can make effective progress in economic lines if they are deprived of political rights, made a servile caste, and allowed only the most meagre chance for developing their exceptional men? If history and reason give any distinct answer to these questions, it is an emphatic *No.*

Rather than content themselves with education at the trade and agricultural schools Washington advocated, talented blacks should accept nothing less than a full university education. They should aspire to the professions. They should, above all, fight for the immediate restoration of their civil rights, not simply wait for them to be granted as a reward for patient striving.

The NAACP

In 1905, Du Bois and a group of his supporters met in Niagara Falls, Ontario, Canada (no hotel on the American side of the Falls would have them), and launched what became known as the Niagara Movement. Four years later, after

W. E. B. DU BOIS. Du Bois, the first black to receive a Ph.D. from Harvard University, challenged Booker T. Washington's belief in tacit acceptance of racial discrimination. He was a founding member of the NAACP and one of the first historians to devote serious study to the experience of black Americans. In his later years, he became a champion of radical politics. (*Harvard University Library*)

a race riot in Springfield, Illinois, they joined with white progressives sympathetic to their cause to form the National Association for the Advancement of Colored People (NAACP). White men held most of the offices; but Du Bois, its director of publicity and research, was the guiding spirit. In the ensuing years, the new organization led the drive for equal rights, using as its principal weapon lawsuits in the federal courts.

Within less than a decade, the NAACP had begun to win some important victories. In *Guinn* v. *United States* (1915), the Supreme Court supported their position that an Oklahoma law excluding blacks from the ballot was unconstitutional. The statute denied the vote to any citizen whose ancestors had not been enfranchised in 1860—a so-called grandfather clause, typical of many southern states, plainly intended to exclude the descendants of slaves from the polls. In *Buchanan* v. *Worley* (1917), the Court struck down a Louisville, Kentucky, law requiring residential segregation. Disenfranchisement and segregation would survive through other methods for many decades to come, but the NAACP had established a pattern of black resistance that would ultimately bear important fruits. It had also established itself, particularly after Booker T. Washington's death in 1915, as one of the nation's leading black organizations, a position it would maintain for over fifty years.

The NAACP was not a radical, or even an egalitarian, organization. It relied, rather, on the efforts of the most intelligent and educated members of the black race, the "talented tenth" as Du Bois called them. And it stressed not so much the elevation of all blacks from poverty and oppression as the opportunity for exceptional blacks to gain positions of full equality. Ultimately, its members believed, such efforts would redound to the benefit of all blacks. In the meantime, however, the NAACP, like many white progressive organizations, remained largely a force of and for the middle class.

THE NEW ENLIGHTENMENT

Few areas of American life could escape the influence of progressive beliefs. It was a widely shared article of faith that the nation was entering not simply a new century but also a new era. There was broad agreement, too, that future progress required the casting off of incrusted traditions and the reform of outmoded institutions. Such assumptions applied not only to governments, businesses, and cities, but to literature and the arts as well. Writers, poets, painters, sculptors, architects, musicians—all looked upon the early years of the twentieth century as a time of revolutionary change. Some attempted to link their work to the wider efforts for social reform; others concentrated on reshaping the arts themselves. Together, they managed within a very few years to produce a major transformation of American culture.

The Literature of Oppression

It was American literature that felt most directly the impact of the progressive impulse toward reform and revulsion from oppression and human suffering. By the beginning of the twentieth century, a new generation of novelists was abandoning the genteel literary traditions of an earlier age and turning instead to the social dislocations of their time, writing with passion and commitment of the injustices of modern life. Among the most prominent was Theodore Dreiser, one of the first of the new "naturalists," who in 1900 published the startling *Sister Carrie,* the story of a poor young woman caught in and corrupted by the maelstrom of modern urban life. So shocking were the novel's contents to some readers (including, apparently, the publisher's wife, who demanded its suppression) that it was with-drawn from the market for twelve years. Such setbacks did not, however, stop Dreiser from hewing out a series of massive novels in the ensuing decades that exposed the social costs of the American class system and established naturalism as a leading force in American literature.

Many of Dreiser's contemporaries joined him in chronicling the oppression of America's poor. In 1901, Frank Norris, striving for a "big, epic, dramatic thing," published *The Octopus,* an account of a struggle between oppressed wheat ranch-ers and powerful railroad interests in California. Another novel, *The Pit* (1903), the second volume of a trilogy Norris did not live to complete, attacked exploita-tion in the grain markets of Chicago. Upton Sinclair's *The Jungle* (1906) exposed abuses in the American meat-packing industry, and Ellen Glasgow's *The Descen-*

dant (1897) told of the travails of the southern poor white. Other writers would respond to the spirit of the new century in different ways, but the naturalists established a tradition of social commitment in American literature that would persist for many decades.

Art and Social Realism

A similar interest in the grimmer aspects of modern life was beginning to characterize American art. Artists committed to the traditional academic style (the brilliant portraitist John Singer Sargent, for example) continued to flourish; but a new school of younger painters began to vie with them for attention. Influenced by the work of the French Impressionists but shaped too by the tenor of American urban life, members of the so-called Ashcan School joined in revolt against traditional forms and subjects to produce work startling in its naturalism and stark in its portrayal of the social realities of the era. John Sloan, for example, attempted to capture the dreariness of American urban slums; George Bellows caught the vigor and violence of his time in paintings and drawings of prize fights; Edward Hopper chose as his theme the starkness (and occasionally the loneliness) of the modern city. Ultimately, many of these young artists would move beyond the Ashcan revolt to explore the fields of expressionism and abstraction. At the time, however, their work seemed to parallel the efforts of progressive novelists. The prevailing theme of serious art in America, one critic wrote in 1902, "is sadness, heart-searching, misgiving, melancholy—now spiritual, now sensuous—revolt against surrounding circumstance."

The New Music

No area of American culture seemed as resistant to change as music. The most prominent institutions of the age were the great symphony orchestras, particularly the ensembles of Boston, Philadelphia, and New York. And to them, the mission of American musicians was to perform the established classical repertory. The works of Beethoven (whose name was lovingly inscribed above the proscenium arch of Boston's Symphony Hall, opened in 1900) remained the staples of orchestral programs; other nineteenth-century masters—Brahms, Wagner, Tchaikovsky, Schubert—and some eighteenth-century composers—Bach, Mozart, Haydn—followed close behind. Americans paid little attention to twentieth-century music, least of all to the work of their own countrymen. The most popular American composer of the era, Edward McDowell, received some public attention for his pale imitations of European classics. But even the Boston Symphony Orchestra, the acknowledged leader in the performance of new music, devoted only about 6 percent of its repertoire to the work of Americans.

There was, however, a small group of innovative American composers who, although unheard by most of their contemporaries and scorned by much of the musical establishment, nevertheless established a new tradition of musical mod-

THE ARMORY SHOW, 1913. The famous 1913 art exhibition at the
New York City Armory shocked traditionalists by displaying the work of such
European "moderns" as Cézanne and Matisse. The armory show helped
move many young American artists beyond the Ashcan revolt and into new,
nonrepresentational fields. (*Museum of Modern Art*)

ernism in the United States. Openly rebelling against the classical tradition, which
had, they believed, exhausted itself by the end of the nineteenth century, they
began to experiment with new musical techniques—dissonance, atonality,
chromaticism—and to champion the work of such European iconoclasts as Arnold
Schoenberg, Béla Bartók, Paul Hindemith, and Igor Stravinsky. Charles Ives made
enthusiastic use of polytonal harmonies and unconventional rhythms, often paro-
dying traditional American songs. Younger musicians—Walter Piston, for example—were beginning long and productive careers in composition by emulating the
techniques of European musical radicals. Decades later, the often harsh and highly
intellectualized compositions of the modernists would still be unpopular with
much of the public. But music, like art and literature, continued to explore new,
antitraditional forms.

Artists and intellectuals, in the progressive era as in other periods, had limited
influence. Relatively few Americans read the works of serious novelists, saw the
paintings of serious artists, heard the music of serious composers. Popular culture,
although it too underwent important changes (for example, the widespread popularity of jazz music beginning in 1917), was far more likely to continue in traditional, conventional patterns. But if the innovative and iconoclastic artists of the

early twentieth century did not succeed in shaping American life, they did manage to reflect some of its dominant themes: the driving, questing pace of change, the heady belief in the promises and possibilities of the future, the fervent opposition to the incrusted obstacles to progress. Progressivism was above all else a spirit; and it was out of that spirit that the progressive political movement emerged.

SUGGESTED READINGS

Historians have disagreed sharply in their interpretations of progressivism. Among the contending views are Richard Hofstadter, *The Age of Reform* (1955); Robert Wiebe, *The Search for Order* (1967); Gabriel Kolko, *The Triumph of Conservatism* (1963); and James Weinstein, *The Corporate Ideal in the Liberal States, 1900–1918* (1969). Studies of progressive thought include Morton White, *Social Thought in America* (1949); D. W. Marcell, *Progress and Pragmatism: James, Dewey, Beard and the American Idea of Progress* (1974); and Charles Forcey, *The Crossroads of Liberalism: Croly, Weyl, Lippmann* (1961). Sudhir Kakar's *Frederick Taylor* (1970) examines the father of "scientific management." Burton Bledstein's *The Culture of Professionalism* (1976) provides a critical view of the rise of the professional ethic. Donald Fleming's *William H. Welch and the Rise of Modern Medicine* (1954) examines changes in the medical profession. The progressive response to the cities is examined in Allen F. Davis, *Spearheads of Reform: The Social Settlements and the Progressive Movement, 1890–1914* (1968); Roy Lubove, *The Progressives and the Slums: Tenement House Reform in New York City* (1962); Sheila M. Rothman, *Woman's Proper Place* (1978); and Henry May, *Protestant Churches and Industrial America* (1949).

Louis Harlan's *Booker T. Washington* (1973) examines the career of the preeminent black leader of the era, while Elliott Rudwick's *W. E. B. Du Bois* (1969) chronicles the life of his major challenger. George Fredrickson's *The Black Image in the White Mind* (1968) is an overview of white racial attitudes. For a discussion of the arts in the progressive era, see Alfred Kazin, *On Native Grounds* (1942); Van Wyck Brooks, *The Confident Years* (1952); and Kenneth Lynn, *The Dream of Success* (1955).

Three

Progressive Politics

Sooner or later, most progressive goals required the involvement of government. Social workers wanted laws to protect woman and child workers and to improve health and housing in the ghettoes. Professionals advocated legal standards for admission to the practice of medicine, law, and other disciplines. Consumers felt the need for legislation to curb the power of the trusts. And many businessmen urged government regulation of industry to limit the cutthroat tactics of some entrepreneurs. Only government, progressives increasingly agreed, could provide the centralized regulation and control necessary to impose order and justice upon modern society.

But American government at the dawn of the new century was, the progressives believed, peculiarly ill-adapted to perform these ambitious tasks. At every level—federal, state, and local—political institutions were outmoded, inefficient, often corrupt. Powerful special interests had succeeded in subverting government to their own ends; dishonest politicians were using their power for selfish gain. Government was essential to the effective reordering of society, but first it would be necessary to reform government itself. And so progressives launched themselves energetically into the task of transforming American politics.

THE CHALLENGE OF MUNICIPAL REFORM

It was the cities, many progressives believed, that posed the greatest challenges to American society. And it was city government, therefore, that became the first target of those working for political reform. As urban areas staggered under the burden of increased demands for services, as new (and, many believed, dangerous) elements swelled their populations, as existing policies proved increasingly inadequate to the tasks at hand, a powerful movement for reshaping municipal government gained force throughout the nation.

The Muckrakers

Although settlement houses, social workers, and scholars had all attempted to focus public attention upon urban problems and the need for political reforms to combat them, it was a new breed of journalists who were most successful in arousing public outrage at the rampant corruption and incompetence in city government. The muckrakers, as they were called, gave to "exposure" (or what would later be called investigatory) journalism a scale and force unknown in previous decades. And while some attracted widespread attention with their harshly polemical but carefully researched attacks on the great trusts and corporations, others had an even greater impact through their exposure of the evils of "boss rule."

Exposure journalism was not new to the twentieth century. What was new, however, was the availability of mass-circulation magazines and newspapers to print it. Technological innovations had reduced printing costs dramatically in the last decades of the nineteenth century, permitting the rise of inexpensive popular newspapers, such as those of the Hearst chain, and of new magazines intended for a wider audience than the serious journals of the nineteenth century. At the height of the muckraking movement, which first attracted attention in 1902 and peaked in 1906, at least ten major magazines, with a combined circulation of about 3 million, were devoting considerable space to the new exposés. Publishers who had achieved success through the use of inflammatory "yellow journalism" in the 1890s, began to consider muckraking a logical complement to their sensational techniques. Hearst's *New York World* was only one of many newspapers that allotted substantial space to the muckrakers. It was this fusing of sensational revelation with mass circulation that gave the muckrakers their remarkable influence.

The many young journalists who achieved wide renown through muckraking included Ida Tarbell, Ray Stannard Baker, Samuel Hopkins Adams, William Allen White, and Upton Sinclair. The most influential, however, was Lincoln Steffens, a reporter for *McClure's* magazine, who traveled through much of the country in the first years of the century and produced a series of articles on municipal corruption that aroused a major public outcry. His devastating portraits of "machine government" and "boss rule," his exposures of "boodlers" in cities as diverse as St. Louis, Minneapolis, Cleveland, Cincinnati, Chicago, Philadelphia, and New York, his tone of studied moral outrage (as reflected in the title of his series and of the book that emerged from it, *The Shame of the Cities*)—all combined to persuade urban progressives of the need for a militant response.

The Assault on Boss Rule

Steffens and his fellow muckrakers struck a responsive chord among a powerful group of urban middle-class progressives. For several decades after the Civil War, "respectable" citizens of the nation's large cities had avoided participation in municipal government. Viewing politics as a debased and demeaning activity, they shrank from contact with the "vulgar" elements who were coming to dominate public life. By the end of the century, however, a new generation of activists —some of them members of old aristocratic families, others a part of the new middle class—were taking a renewed interest in government. The nineteenth-century middle class had abdicated control of politics to the urban masses; the twentieth-century middle class, appalled by the abuses and failures that had ensued, would win it back.

They faced a formidable array of opponents. In addition to challenging the powerful city bosses and their entrenched political organizations, they were attacking a large group of special interests: saloon owners, brothel keepers, and, perhaps most significantly, those businessmen who had established cozy and lucrative relationships with the urban machines and viewed reform as a threat to their profits. Allied with these interests were many influential newspapers, which ridiculed the reformers as naïve do-gooders or prigs. Finally, there was the great constituency of city working people, mostly of immigrant origin, to whom the machines were a source of needed services. To them, the progressives often seemed to be middle-class prudes, attempting to impose an alien and unappealing life style. Gradually, however, the reformers gained in political strength—in part because of their own growing numbers, in part because of the increasingly conspicuous failures of the existing political leadership. And in the first years of the twentieth century, they began to score some important victories.

One of their first major successes came in Galveston, Texas, where the old city government collapsed in ineffectuality in the wake of a destructive tidal wave in 1900. Capitalizing on public dismay, reformers won approval of a new city charter. The mayor and council were replaced by a commission whose five members would jointly enact ordinances and run the main city departments. In 1907, Des Moines, Iowa, adopted its own version of the commission plan, and other cities soon followed. Another approach to reform was the city-manager plan, by which elected officials hired an outside expert—often a professionally trained business manager or engineer—to take charge of the government. Responsible not to the voters but to the councilors or commissioners who appointed him, the city manager would presumably remain untainted by the corrupting influence of politics. Staunton, Virginia, was one of the first municipalities to hire a city manager, in 1908. Five years later, Dayton, Ohio, attracted wider attention to the device when it adopted the new system after a major flood. By the end of the progressive era, almost 400 cities were operating under commissions, and another 45 employed city managers.

The new systems brought to government many of the same assumptions that progressives had brought to business and the professions: faith in process and organization, reliance upon disinterested experts, and a yearning for order and efficiency. City commissions resembled corporate boards of directors; city managers operated much like modern business executives. Partisan politics, the reformers argued, was irrelevant to the demands of city government; businessmen and engineers were far better equipped than politicians to deal with the complex technological and administrative tasks of the modern metropolis.

Some of the most successful reformers, however, emerged not from the new commission and city-manager systems, but from conventional political structures. Tom Johnson, the celebrated reform mayor of Cleveland, waged a long and difficult war against the powerful streetcar interests in his city, fighting to raise the ridiculously low assessments upon railroad and utilities properties, to lower streetcar fares to three cents, and ultimately to impose municipal ownership upon certain basic utilities. After Johnson's defeat and death, his talented aide Newton D. Baker won election as mayor and helped maintain Cleveland's reputation as the best-governed city in America. Hazen Pingree of Detroit, Samuel "Golden Rule" Jones of Toledo, and other mayors succeeded where advocates of city-manager and commission systems occasionally failed—in creating city governments that were both honest and humane, and in establishing reform as a politically viable force in their communities.

The successes of Johnson, Pingree, and Jones helped illustrate the reasons for the failure of so many other urban reformers. Administrative efficiency may have been appealing to businessmen, professionals, and engineers; but the great mass of urban residents judged their government not merely on the basis of its structure but by the services it provided them. Reformers who attacked the corruption and inefficiency of machines without offering a means to replace their services found little support among the working classes; and they left the door open for skillful machine politicians not only to endure but to strengthen themselves.

Reform by Machine

Political bosses were usually intelligent men, and as such they often recognized that it was necessary to change in order to survive. Determined to maintain their grasp upon city government, some machine leaders allowed themselves to become vehicles of social reform in ways that middle-class progressives usually refused to acknowledge. The best example was New York's Tammany Hall, the nation's oldest and most notorious city machine. Its extraordinarily astute leader, Charles Francis Murphy, began in the early years of the century to fuse the techniques of boss rule with some of the concerns of social reformers. In the process, he ushered his organization into one of the most successful eras in its history.

Murphy did nothing to challenge the fundamental workings of Tammany Hall. The machine continued to mobilize working-class immigrant voters to support its candidates; it continued to offer them favors and services in return; its members continued to use patronage and even graft to strengthen their positions and expand their bank accounts. At the same time, however, Tammany began to take an increased interest in state and national politics, which it had traditionally scorned; and it used its political power on behalf of legislation to improve working conditions, protect child laborers, and eliminate the worst abuses of the industrial economy.

In 1911, a sudden fire swept the factory of the Triangle Shirtwaist Company in New York; 146 workers, most of them women, died. Many of them had been trapped inside the building because management had locked the emergency exits to prevent malingering. It was the worst industrial tragedy in the city's history, and the outrage it produced echoed across the nation. For the next three years, a broad-based state commission studied not only the background of the fire but the general condition of the industrial workplace; and by 1914, it had issued a series of reports calling for major reforms in the conditions of modern labor.

The report itself was a classic progressive document, based on the testimony of experts, replete with statistics and technical data. Yet when its recommendations reached the New York legislature, its most effective supporters were not middle-class progressives but two Tammany Democrats: Senator Robert F. Wagner and Assemblyman Alfred E. Smith. With the support of Murphy and the backing of other Tammany legislators, they steered through a series of pioneering

THE TRIANGLE FIRE, 1911. The charred remains of the interior of the Triangle Shirtwaist factory in New York, where 146 workers, all but 21 of them women, died in a fire in 1911. The tragedy drew national attention to the dangerous conditions of many American workplaces. (*Brown Brothers*)

labor laws that imposed strict regulations on factory owners and established effective mechanisms for enforcement. Tammany Hall, the incarnation of evil in the eyes of many progressives, had itself become an effective agent for reform.

PROGRESSIVISM IN THE STATEHOUSE

Often frustrated in their assault upon boss rule in the cities, many progressives turned to state government as an agent for reform. Crusading district attorneys such as Hiram Johnson in California and Joseph W. Folk in Missouri left their cities to become reform governors. In other states, progressive leaders arrived in the statehouse by other routes. Whatever their background, however, a growing number of reformers agreed that state government must take a leading role in the task of stabilizing American life.

Democratizing the States

State-level progressives generally agreed not only on the importance of reform but on the unfitness of existing state governments to provide it. They looked with particular scorn upon state legislatures, whose ill-paid, relatively inconspicuous members were, they believed, generally incompetent and often corrupt. The progressives found support from muckraking journalists, who subjected state legislatures to the same withering criticism they had directed at urban machines. "The legislature met biennially," William Allen White wrote of Missouri in a 1905 issue of *McClure's*, "and enacted such laws as the corporations paid for, and such others as were necessary to fool the people, and only such laws were enforced as party expediency demanded." If the legislatures were unfit, reformers argued, it would be necessary to circumvent them; only by returning political power directly to the people could the influence of special interests be eliminated.

The result was a wave of reforms in state after state that attempted to "democratize" state government by limiting the authority of elected officials and increasing the influence of the electorate. Two of the most important changes were innovations first proposed by leaders of the populist movement in the 1890s: the initiative and the referendum. The initiative gave reformers the ability to circumvent their legislatures altogether by submitting legislation directly to the voters in general elections. The referendum provided a method by which actions of the legislature could be returned to the electorate for approval. Oregon, in 1902, became the first state to enact such reforms. By 1918, nineteen other states had followed.

Progressives also attempted to improve the quality of elected officials, and for this purpose they created two more "democratic" devices: the direct primary and the recall. The primary election was an attempt to limit the influence of party machines upon the selection of candidates. The recall gave voters the right to remove a public official from office at a special election, which could be called after a sufficient number of citizens had signed a petition. Mississippi adopted the nation's first direct primary in 1902, and by 1915 every state in the nation had instituted primary elections for at least some offices. The recall encountered a more difficult road. No progressive measure so horrified conservatives as this effort to subject officeholders to voter censure before the end of their terms, and they blocked the adoption of the recall more effectively than any other reform. At one point, President William Howard Taft vetoed a bill admitting Arizona to the Union because its proposed constitution authorized the recall of judges. Only when the offensive provision had been removed was Arizona granted statehood (although the state's voters restored the provision shortly thereafter).

Just as progressives had emphasized process and order in their creation of commissions and city managers at the municipal level, so at the state level they were emphasizing the creation of systems as the cornerstone of reform. And just as such systems were not always effective in cities, so they often failed in the states. Initiatives and referendums could just as easily become vehicles for conservative changes as for progressive ones. Primaries could, and often were, dominated by machines, whose ability to mobilize their constituencies far exceeded that of the reformers. The recall proved cumbersome and found only occasional use. Reform efforts proved most effective in states that elevated vigorous and committed politicians to positions of leadership. In New York, Charles Evans Hughes exploited progressive sentiment to create a commission to regulate public utilities. In California, Hiram Johnson used the new reforms to limit the political power of the Southern Pacific Railroad in the state. In New Jersey, Woodrow Wilson, the Princeton University president elected Governor in 1910, used executive leadership to win a substantial array of reforms designed to end New Jersey's widely denounced position as the "mother of trusts." If he did not succeed in making the state a model of progressivism, Wilson did manage to eliminate some of its most glaring political and economic flaws. Like the cities, state governments were finding that men were often more effective than systems in securing reforms. Perhaps the best evidence of this came from the state that virtually all progressives agreed had become the nation's leading center of reform: Wisconsin.

The Laboratory of La Follette

In his later years, Robert M. La Follette served as a national symbol of committed, crusading progressivism. He began his political career in Wisconsin, however, as a fervent defender of free enterprise against its "radical" challengers. First elected to the United States House of Representatives in 1884, he served three terms as a defender of laissez-faire economics, urging discontented farmers and workers to rely on their own, private efforts for advancement.

Like many politicians of his generation, however, La Follette emerged from the 1890s a changed man. Not only had his conservative positions helped lose him his congressional seat in 1890, but his observations of the distress of farmers and workers in his state during the depression had shaken his confidence in the existing orthodoxies. When he returned to Wisconsin politics in 1898, he did so as the enemy of the bosses, the railroads, the trusts, and the financiers—the special interests that were, he argued, corrupting American life. Elected Governor in 1900, he called for a new concept of politics: as the vehicle for enhancing the public interest, rather than an arena in which special interests contended for favors.

In the years that followed, La Follette turned Wisconsin into what reformers across the nation described as a "laboratory of progressivism." He won approval of direct primaries, initiatives, and referendums. He secured the effective regulation of railroads and utilities. He obtained the passage of laws to regulate the workplace and provide compensation for laborers injured on the job. He instituted graduated taxes on inherited fortunes, and he nearly doubled state levies on railroads and other corporate interests.

More than that, however, La Follette brought to progressivism his own fervent, almost evangelical, commitment to reform; and he used his charismatic leadership to widen public awareness of progressive goals and to mobilize the energies of many previously passive groups. Reform was not simply the responsibility of politicians, he argued, but of newspapers, citizens' groups, educational institutions, and business and professional organizations. Progressivism, he suggested, must become a part of the fabric of American life. Ultimately, La Follette would

LA FOLLETTE CAMPAIGNING.   Robert M. La Follette, beloved among progressives as "Battling Bob," helped introduce a series of reforms in his home state that became known as the "Wisconsin Idea" and served as a model for much of the nation. He and his sons dominated the politics of the state for almost forty years. (*State Historical Society of Wisconsin*)

find himself overshadowed by other national progressive leaders. In the early years of the century, however, few men were as effective in publicizing the message of reform. None was as successful in bending state government to that goal.

NATIONAL PROGRESSIVISM

The federal government was somewhat slower to respond to the demands of progressive reformers than were governments at the state and local levels, but it was hardly immune to their influence. From the beginning, many progressives had viewed national politics as the most important vehicle for reform. As the years passed and the limitations of local efforts became clearer, the demand for federal action grew stronger. Most importantly, a series of highly charged issues emerged that required, their proponents believed, national, not state or local, attention. And it was around these issues that some of the most powerful pressures on the federal government emerged.

Order and Exclusion

Some of these reforms seemed to many progressives to be decidedly illiberal, but they nevertheless expressed at least one current of progressive thought. Two such movements were those on behalf of the prohibition of alcoholic beverages and the restriction of immigration.

To some progressives, the elimination of alcohol from American life was a necessary step in the task of restoring order to society. Workers in settlement houses and social agencies (particularly women) abhorred the effects of drinking upon working-class families: scarce wages vanished as workers spent hours in the saloons; drunkenness spawned violence, and occasionally murder, within urban families. Employers, too, regarded alcohol as an impediment to industrial efficiency: workers often missed time on the job because of drunkenness or, worse, came to the factory intoxicated and performed their tasks sloppily and dangerously. Critics of economic privilege denounced the liquor industry as one of the nation's most sinister trusts. And political reformers, who looked upon the saloon (correctly) as one of the central institutions of the machine, saw an attack upon drinking as part of an attack upon the bosses. Out of such sentiments emerged the prohibition movement.

Despite substantial opposition from immigrant and working-class voters, pressure for prohibition grew steadily through the first decades of the new century. The sporadic protests of its opponents could not compete with the disciplined efforts of such organizations as the Woman's Christian Temperance Union and the newer Anti-Saloon League. With the support of rural fundamentalists, who opposed alcohol on moral and religious grounds, progressive advocates of prohibition in 1917 finally steered through Congress a constitutional amendment embodying their demands. Two years later, after ratification by every state in the nation except Connecticut and Rhode Island (bastions of Catholic immigrants) the Eighteenth Amendment became law, to take effect in January 1920. The federal government, many progressives believed, had taken an important step toward eliminating a major source of social instability. Only later did it become clear that prohibition would create far more disorder than it was able to cure.

A similar concern for order fueled the movement demanding the restriction of

PASSAGE TO THE NEW WORLD.   Alfred Stieglitz's famous photograph *The Steerage* conveys the arduous conditions of passage for the millions of European immigrants who traveled to America in the last years of the nineteenth century and the first years of the twentieth. (*Museum of Modern Art*)

immigration, which likewise gained force throughout the progressive era. While virtually all reformers agreed that the burgeoning immigrant population had created social problems, there was wide disagreement on how best to respond. Many progressives, convinced that open immigration was one of the nation's most valued traditions, believed that helping the new residents adapt to American society was the proper approach. Others, however, argued that efforts at assimilation had failed and that the only solution was to limit the flow of new arrivals.

The first decades of the century, therefore, saw a steady growth in pressure on the federal government to close the nation's gates. New scholarly theories, designed to appeal to the progressive respect for expertise, argued that the introduction of immigrants into American society was polluting the nation's racial stock. The spurious "science" of eugenics spread the belief that human inequalities were hereditary and that immigration was contributing to the multiplication of the unfit. Skillful publicists like Madison Grant, whose *The Passing of the Great Race* (1916) established him as the nation's most effective nativist, warned of the dangers of racial "mongrelization" and of the importance of protecting the purity of Anglo-Saxon and other Nordic stock. As on other issues, progressives in Washington established a special commission of "experts," chaired by Senator William P. Dillingham of Vermont, to study the problem of immigration. Supported by elaborate statistics and scholarly testimony, the commission's report argued that the newer immigrant groups—largely southern and eastern Europeans—had proven themselves less assimilable than earlier immigrants. Immigration, the report implied, should be restricted by nationality.

Racial arguments mobilized impressive support behind the restriction movement, but even many who rejected such arguments supported limiting immigration. It was, they believed, creating unmanageable urban problems: overcrowding, unemployment, strained social services, social unrest. The combination of these concerns gradually won for the nativists the support of some of the nation's leading progressives: Theodore Roosevelt, Henry Cabot Lodge, and others. Powerful opponents—employers who saw immigration as a source of cheap labor, reformers who valued the ethnic culture of immigrant communities, immigrants themselves and their political representatives—managed to block the restriction movement for a time. But by the beginning of World War I (which itself effectively blocked immigration for a time), the nativist tide was clearly gaining strength. Progressivism, it was apparent, did not always come in a humane and liberal guise.

Suffrage for Women

A movement that bore more immediate fruits, and one that reflected a larger spirit, was the effort of women to win the right to vote. If the agitations for prohibition and immigration restriction were attempts to remove dangerous influences from American life, the suffrage movement was an attempt, its supporters believed, to inject into society a healthy new force. Giving women the right to vote, suffrage advocates claimed, was not only a matter of abstract principle; it was a practical measure to strengthen the forces of reform.

The movement for woman suffrage had already experienced a long and often frustrating history as the twentieth century began. Women had played an important role in the crusade for the abolition of slavery in the 1840s and 1850s, and they had included suffrage among their political demands after the Civil War. Spurned by political leaders who insisted that this was "the Negro's hour," suffragists continued their efforts through the last decades of the nineteenth century, winning a few victories in some of the new western states but lacking sufficient power to change national policy.

It was the merging of the suffrage movement with other reform efforts in the first years of the new century that transformed it from a small interest group into a major national force. As women became active in settlement houses, social work, and other humanitarian activities, they began to argue that their participation in politics would strengthen demands for social welfare reforms. As many of the same women joined the growing prohibition movement, they linked votes for women with elimination of alcohol. Others argued in more general terms: that women would bring to politics a humane and gentle spirit that would help cleanse the nation of selfishness and corruption. As the reform spirit grew, such arguments attracted the support of an increasing number of progressive men.

Women themselves, however, remained the major force in the movement. Under the spirited leadership of Anna Howard Shaw, a Boston social worker, and Carrie Chapman Catt, a journalist from Iowa, the National American Woman Suffrage Association grew from a membership of about 13,000 in 1893 to over 2 million in 1917. The involvement of such well-known and widely admired women as Jane Addams brought added attention to the cause. The Triangle fire in New York and other such incidents strengthened the arguments of suffragists that woman laborers needed the protection of woman voters. The movement made steady gains in the first decades of the progressive era. By 1919, thirty-nine states had granted women the right to vote in at least some elections; fifteen had allowed them full participation. In 1920, finally, suffragists won ratification of the Twentieth Amendment, which guaranteed political rights to women everywhere. Encouraged by that success, many feminists turned their energies to a new goal: enactment of an equal rights amendment that would prohibit all discrimination on the basis of sex, a battle that would continue for more than sixty years.

The suffrage movement may have gained important strength from its identification with humanitarian reform, but the Social Gospel was not the only impulse behind it. The movement was a coalition of diverse elements; while much of its support was based on a broad and humane social outlook, some of its appeal was to a far narrower view. Some women argued that they needed the vote to counteract the political influence of corrupt and illiterate immigrants who were polluting the electorate. Others claimed that women deserved at least the same political rights as black men. While some feminists tried to fuse the movement with efforts to elevate the status of the immigrant and the black, others supported literacy tests for potential voters and insisted that suffrage would not threaten the system of segregation. The demand for the vote united a wide spectrum of feminine opinion (although by no means all of it), but on other issues women were often no more in agreement than men. Once enfranchised, the new voters did little to support

SUFFRAGETTES. Women played a particularly important role in the promotion of progressive reform. In addition to working for social action to aid the urban poor, they launched a major effort on their own behalf: the fight for their right to vote. (*Culver Pictures*)

the arguments of those suffragists who had claimed that women would operate in politics as a coherent force for reform.

The National Economy

Prohibition, immigration restriction, woman suffrage—these and other issues attracted large but limited constituencies. Of more general concern to progressives of all backgrounds was the state of the nation's economy. From the beginning, it had been animosity toward the great industrial combinations—the trusts—that had formed the core of much progressive sentiment. It was to the task of limiting the power of the giant corporations, therefore, that reformers devoted their greatest energies.

On the need for the assistance of the federal government to accomplish this task, most reformers agreed. On how best to deal with the trusts, however, there emerged a wide range of opinion. Some reformers believed in the importance of careful government regulation. Others argued for steps to destroy the trusts and restore competition. Yet others, moving beyond the strictures of progressivism, argued that the problem lay not in the abuses of the economic system, but in the system itself—that the solution lay in replacing capitalism with socialism.

The Dream of Socialism

At no time in American history, except perhaps briefly in the 1930s, did radical critiques of the capitalist system attract more support than in the period between 1900 and 1914. Although never a force to rival, or even seriously threaten, the two major parties, the Socialist party of America grew during the progressive era into a force of considerable strength. In 1900, it had attracted the support of fewer than 100,000 voters; in 1912, its durable leader and perennial presidential candidate, Eugene V. Debs, received nearly 1 million ballots. Strongest in urban immigrant communities (particularly among Germans and Jews in New York, Chicago, Milwaukee, and elsewhere), it won the loyalties, too, of a substantial number of Protestant farmers in the South and Midwest. Socialists won election to over a thousand state and local offices, and they attracted the admiring attention of some journalists and intellectuals as well as of members of the lower class. Lincoln Steffens, the crusader against municipal corruption, ultimately became a defender of socialism. So for a time did Walter Lippmann, the brilliant young journalist who was to become one of the nation's most important social critics.

Virtually all socialists agreed on the need for basic structural changes in the economy, but they differed widely on how drastic those changes should be. Some endorsed the sweepingly radical goals of European Marxists; others envisioned a more moderate reform that would allow small-scale private enterprise to survive but nationalize the major industries. There was still less agreement on tactics. Militants within the party favored drastic, even violent, action. Most conspicuous was the radical labor union the Industrial Workers of the World (IWW), known to opponents as the "Wobblies." Under the leadership of William ("Big Bill") Haywood, the IWW advocated a single union for all workers and abolition of the "wage slave" system; it rejected political action in favor of strikes and industrial sabotage. Although small in numbers, the "Wobblies" struck terror into the hearts of the middle class with their inflammatory rhetoric and their occasional dynamiting of railroad lines and power stations.

More moderate socialists advocated peaceful change through political struggle, and it was they who dominated the party. They emphasized a gradual education of the public to the need for change, and patient efforts within the system to enact it. But it soon became clear that the years before World War I were not the first stages of an effective socialist movement but the last. By the end of the war,

THE "WOBBLIES" AND THE MILITIA. IWW organizers came to the assistance of striking mill workers in Lowell, Massachusetts, in January 1912. Although the strikers were protesting a wage cut, the "Wobblies" attempted to use the dispute to win new recruits to the union. Their presence served as a pretext for the mayor to call out the militia, shown here confronting the strikers with guns. Before the strike ended, one woman had been killed in a clash with police. (*Library of Congress*)

socialism was virtually dead as a significant political force. Party leaders continued to talk of the need for change, but hardly anyone was listening.

Decentralization and Regulation

A far more influential debate was raging at the same time between those who believed in the essential premises of capitalism but urged reforms to preserve it. The debate centered around two basic approaches: decentralization and regulation.

To many progressives, the greatest threat to the nation's economy was the effect of excessive centralization and consolidation on competition. The trusts had made it impossible for the free market to work as it should; only by restoring the economy to a more human scale could the nation hope for stability and justice. Few such reformers envisioned a return to a society of small, local enterprises; some consolidation, they recognized, was inevitable. They did, however, argue that the federal government should take forceful action to break up the largest combinations, to enforce a balance between the need for bigness and the need for competition. It was a viewpoint often identified with the brilliant lawyer and later Justice of the Supreme Court Louis D. Brandeis, who spoke and wrote widely (most notably in his 1913 book *Other People's Money*) about the "curse of bigness."

To other progressives, competition was an overrated commodity. Far more important was efficiency. And since economic concentration tended to enhance efficiency, the government, they believed, should not discourage it. What government should do, however, was to ensure that "bigness" did not bring with it abuses of power. It should stand constant guard against irresponsibility and corruption in the great corporations. It should distinguish between "good trusts" and "bad trusts," encouraging the good while disciplining the bad. Some progressives—for example, Herbert Croly, whose *The Promise of American Life* (1909) became one of the most influential of all progressive documents—argued that America had entered a new era. Economic consolidation, they foresaw, would remain a permanent feature of society, but continuing oversight by a strong, modernized government would be vital.

The Need for Leadership

Whatever their differences, then, most progressives agreed that the federal government was an essential partner in the work of reform. But first, most of them realized, there must be reform of the government itself. The tired, partisan politics of the nineteenth century were unsuitable to the demands of the twentieth. A government that was to shape a modern economy must itself become a modern institution: employing the services of professionally trained experts, bringing principles of organizational efficiency to bear on its operations, and, above all, shaking off its traditional lassitude and becoming a dynamic agent of change.

Few reformers expected such changes to emanate from Congress, which remained firmly under the control of traditional politicians. "Uncle Joe" Cannon, Speaker of the House through much of the progressive era, still operated under the autocratic powers "Czar" Thomas B. Reed had seized in 1890. A genial man, Cannon nevertheless controlled committee appointments and legislative debates so firmly that progressives could have little impact in the lower chamber. The Senate, similarly, was under the domination of an intelligent and skilled oligarchy of conservatives, exemplified by such men as the tall, austere Nelson Wilmarth Aldrich, a wealthy Rhode Island banker. Progressives could expect little response from that body either.

Reformers did make serious efforts to change the congressional power structure. Republican insurgents combined with Democrats in 1909 in a strong but unsuccessful effort to unseat Speaker Cannon. The following year they did succeed in breaking his iron control of many House functions. Progressives nationwide, in the meantime, were agitating for a constitutional amendment providing for the direct popular election of Senators to replace the traditional method of election by state legislatures. The reform would, they argued, remove the power of party bosses and special interests from the process. The Senate itself managed to block the amendment for more than a decade; but in 1912, in the wake of widespread indignation over revelations of corruption among its members, it acquiesced. The Seventeenth Amendment easily won ratification from the necessary states and became law in 1913.

Such changes, however, were slow and uncertain. Even a reformed Congress, moreover, could not be expected to provide the kind of coherent leadership that the progressive agenda required. If the federal government was to fulfill its mission, if it was to become the principal agent in the reshaping of the nation's economy, it would, most reformers agreed, have to do so largely through the executive branch. It would have to recruit men of exceptional talent and commitment, men able to mold public opinion and mobilize the forces of change. It would require, above all, strong, central leadership from the one office capable of providing it: the presidency.

SUGGESTED READINGS

Important studies of progressive journalism, and in particular muckraking, include Harold S. Wilson, *McClure's Magazine and the Muckrakers* (1970), and C. C. Regier, *The Era of the Muckrakers* (1932). Studies of individual reporters include Justin Kaplan, *Lincoln Steffens* (1974), and Leon Harris, *Upton Sinclair* (1975). Urban political reform movements receive attention in Zane Miller, *Boss Cox's Cincinnati* (1968); John D. Buenker, *Urban Liberalism and Progressive Reform* (1973); J. Joseph Huthmacher, *Senator Robert F. Wagner and the Rise of Urban Liberalism* (1971); and Oscar Handlin, *Al Smith and His America* (1958). For state-level progressive reform, see George E. Mowry, *California Progressives* (1951), a pathbreaking work whose conclusions have been challenged by, among others, David P. Thelen, *The New Citizenship: Origins of Progressivism in Wisconsin* (1972), and Sheldon Hackney, *Popu-*

lism to Progressivism in Alabama (1969). See also Robert S. Maxwell, *La Follette and the Rise of Progressivism in Wisconsin* (1944); Richard M. Abrams, *Conservatism in a Progressive Era: Massachusetts* (1964); Robert F. Wesser, *Charles Evans Hughes: Politics and Reform in New York State, 1905–1910* (1967); and David Thelen, *Robert La Follette and the Insurgent Spirit* (1976).

For discussion of national progressive issues, see J. H. Timberlake, *Prohibition and the Progressive Movement* (1963); Joseph Gusfield, *Symbolic Crusade: Status Politics and the Temperance Movement* (1963); John Higham, *Strangers in the Land* (1955), an indispensable study of American nativism; and Aileen S. Kraditor, *Ideas of the Woman Suffrage Movement* (1965). James Weinstein's *The Decline of Socialism in America* (1967) examines one approach to economic reform. Robert Wiebe, *Businessmen and Reform* (1962); Sidney Fine, *Laissez Faire and the General Welfare State* (1956); and James Weinstein, *The Corporate Ideal in the Liberal State* (1969) examine other progressive economic beliefs.

Four

Theodore Roosevelt and the Progressive Presidency

"Presidents in general are not lovable," Walter Lippmann, who had known many, said near the end of his life. "They've had to do too much to get where they are. But there was one President who was lovable—Teddy Roosevelt—and I loved him."

He was not alone. To a generation of progressive reformers, Theodore Roosevelt was more than an admired public figure; he was an idol, a man before whom, as one supporter noted, "one's normal critical faculties fail." To the American public at large, he became a focus of attention and devotion to a degree unmatched by any President before him and few since. His youth, his vigor, his enthusiasm, what one newspaper called his "opulent efficiency of mind and body" enabled him to dominate not only American politics but, to a considerable extent, world opinion. The King of England called him "the greatest moral force of the age." The German Kaiser openly admired him. A noted French poet once told a visitor, "If I could go to your America, it would be to take *him* by the hand."

Yet Roosevelt was far from the era's most advanced progressive. In many respects, he was decidedly conservative. Born to a family of New York aristocrats and educated at Harvard, Roosevelt had entered politics not so much to crusade for justice as to rescue government from the hands of the "rabble." A strong believer in the essential goodness of American institutions, he scorned those who threatened the existing order. In 1894, during the Pullman strike, he wrote, "I know the Populists and the laboring men well and their faults. . . . I like to see a mob handled by the regulars, or by good State-Guards, not overscrupulous about bloodshed." Even years later, as the hero of reformers, he retained a loathing for anything that smacked of radicalism. When the conservative Republican boss

THEODORE ROOSEVELT. Roosevelt's public presence in the first years of the twentieth century was so powerful that hobbies and sports he enjoyed became national crazes and casual phrases he used, such as "Bully!", became part of everyday language. For generations, the most popular toy in the nation was a stuffed animal named for the President: the Teddy Bear. A biography for youths, *A Boy's Life of Theodore Roosevelt*, remained for decades one of America's most successful books. And Roosevelt's exhortations on behalf of the outdoors and the "strenuous life" left a lasting imprint upon the values of his society. (*Theodore Roosevelt Collection, Harvard University*)

Mark Hanna advised him early in his presidency to "go slow," Roosevelt replied, "I shall go slow." And so, for much of his term of office, he did.

Roosevelt earned his extraordinary popularity less because of the extent of the reforms he championed than because of the vigor and dynamism with which he approached them. "There adheres in the Presidency," he once asserted, "more power than in any other office in any great republic or constitutional monarchy of modern times." He made clear from the beginning that he was not afraid to use that power, operating under the assumption that the President might do whatever was not forbidden by the law or the Constitution; and when questioned in later years about his tactics, he explained simply: "I did not usurp power, but I did greatly broaden the use of executive power." Roosevelt's policies may have been, for the most part, relatively cautious; but his style of leadership made him seem the very model of the committed, crusading, progressive reformer.

THE ACCIDENTAL PRESIDENT

Roosevelt was not intended by his party for the presidency. Republican leaders had nominated him to run for Vice President with William McKinley in 1900 largely to remove him from the governorship of New York, where he was proving troublesome to party bosses. When President McKinley suddenly died in September 1901, the victim of an assassination, Roosevelt was only forty-two years old, the youngest man ever to assume the presidency. Already, however, he had achieved a notoriety that caused party leaders to feel something close to despair. "I told William McKinley that it was a mistake to nominate that wild man at Philadelphia," Senator Mark Hanna was reported to have exclaimed. "I asked him if he realized what would happen if he should die. Now look, that damned cowboy is President of the United States!"

The Rough Rider

Roosevelt's reputation as a wild man was, characteristically, a result less of the substance than of the style of his early political career. As a young member of the New York legislature, he had displayed an energy seldom seen in that lethargic body. As a rancher in the Dakota Badlands (where he retired briefly after the sudden death of his first wife), he had helped capture outlaws. As New York City police commissioner, he had been a flamboyant battler against crime and vice. As commander of a volunteer regiment known as the "Rough Riders," he had led a heroic, if militarily useless, charge up San Juan Hill in Cuba during the Spanish-American War.

Never, however, had Roosevelt openly rebelled against the leaders of his party; and once in the White House, he continued to balance his personal dynamism against the demands of the political establishment, becoming a champion of cautious, moderate change. Reform was, he believed, less a vehicle for remaking American society than for protecting it against more radical challenges. "I cannot say," he once admitted, "that I entered the presidency with any deliberately planned and far reaching scheme of social betterment." His greatest ambition, it seemed, was to be elected President in his own right.

Managing the Trusts

For all his cautiousness, however, Roosevelt did bring certain assumptions to the presidency that markedly differentiated him from his predecessors. Imbued with progressive ideas about the importance of the efficient, modern management of society, he envisioned the federal government not as the agent of any particular interest but as a mediator of the public good. The President would be the central figure in that mediation.

Such attitudes found open expression in Roosevelt's policies toward the great trusts. Like William McKinley, he was not opposed to the principle of economic concentration. Unlike McKinley, however, he acknowledged that consolidation produced abuses of power that could prove harmful to society. From the beginning, therefore, he allied himself with those progressives who urged regulation (but not destruction) of the trusts. "There is a widespread conviction in the minds of the American people," he said in his first presidential message to Congress in December 1901,

> that . . . trusts are in certain of their features and tendencies hurtful to the general welfare. This . . . is based upon sincere conviction that combination and concentration should be, not prohibited, but supervised and within reasonable limits controlled; and in my judgment this conviction is right.

Finley Peter Dunne, the popular humorist, sensed the careful balancing of Roosevelt's conservatism with his zeal for reform and, through his famous character Mr. Dooley, commented: "Th' trusts, says he, are heejoous monsthers built up be th' enlightened intherprise iv th' men that have done so much to advance progress in our beloved country, he says. On wan hand I wud stamp thim undher fut; on th' other hand not so fast."

At the heart of Roosevelt's policy, therefore, was his desire to win for government the power to investigate the activities of corporations and to publicize the results. The pressure of educated public opinion alone, he believed, would eliminate most corporate abuses. Government could legislate solutions for those that remained. The new Department of Commerce and Labor (later to be divided into two separate departments), established in 1903, was to assist in this task through its investigatory arm, the Bureau of Corporations.

Roosevelt was not above an occasional flamboyant gesture on behalf of a more drastic approach to reform. Although not a trustbuster at heart, he engaged in several highly publicized efforts to break up notorious combinations—actions that strengthened his credentials as a progressive without offering any fundamental challenge to the structure of the economy. In 1902, he ordered the Justice Department to invoke the Sherman Antitrust Act against a great new railroad monopoly in the Northwest, the Northern Securities Company, a $400-million enterprise pieced together by J. P. Morgan, E. H. Harriman, and James J. Hill. To Morgan, accustomed to a warm, supportive relationship with Republican administrations, the action was baffling. Hurrying to the White House with two conservative Senators in tow, he told the President, "If we have done anything wrong, send your man to my man and they can fix it up." Roosevelt proceeded with the case nonetheless, and in 1904 the Supreme Court ruled that the Northern Securities Company must be dissolved. At the same time, however, he assured Morgan and others that the suit did not signal a general campaign to dissolve the trusts. Other monopolistic corporations, such as United States Steel, he would challenge only if "they have done something we regard as wrong." Although he filed more than forty additional antitrust suits during the remainder of his presidency, and although he succeeded in dissolving several important combinations, Roosevelt made no serious effort to reverse the prevailing trend toward economic concentration. Regulation, with the government serving as mediator between corporate and public interests, remained his central goal.

Government and Labor

A similar commitment to establishing the government as an impartial regulatory mechanism shaped Roosevelt's policy toward labor. In the past, federal intervention in industrial disputes had almost always meant action on behalf of employers, as in the Pullman strike in 1894. Roosevelt, however, was willing to consider labor's position as well.

He displayed this willingness during a bitter strike in 1902 by members of the United Mine Workers employed in the anthracite coal industry. Miners, under the leadership of John Mitchell, were demanding a 20 percent wage increase, an eight-hour day, and recognition of their union. Management, represented by the truculent George F. Baer, was responding with conspicuous arrogance and contempt. When the strike threatened to drag on long enough to endanger coal supplies for the coming winter, Roosevelt decided to step in—not to assist management but to invite both the operators and the miners to the White House, where he asked them to accept impartial federal arbitration. Mitchell readily agreed. Baer balked.

Furious at the obstinacy of the mine owners (who had already alienated public opinion), Roosevelt threatened drastic action. He would, he told them, order 10,000 federal troops to seize the mines and resume coal production. Under pressure from politicians, the press, and, perhaps most significantly, J. P. Morgan, the operators finally relented. Arbitrators awarded the strikers a 10 percent wage increase and a nine-hour day, but no recognition of the union. It was a meager reward for a long and costly strike, but it was more than the miners might have won without the government's intervention.

Despite such episodes, Roosevelt viewed himself as no more the champion of labor than of management. On several occasions, he ordered federal troops to intervene in strikes on behalf of employers—in Arizona in 1903 and in Colorado in 1904. And although he believed in the right of workers to join a union, he believed, too, in the right of employers to refuse to bargain with it. Just as with trusts, so with labor: Roosevelt's major goal was not structural change but regulative tinkering.

WORKERS EMERGING FROM THE MINES.   Powder men in the Perrin coal mine about 1902. Theodore Roosevelt's intervention in the United Mine Workers' strike of that year averted what might have been a disastrous blow to the nation's economy by forcing the resumption of coal production. It resulted, however, in only minor improvements in the position of mine workers. (*Harvard University Library*)

THE SQUARE DEAL

Even if Roosevelt had wished to move more quickly on economic reforms (and there was little evidence that he did), he would have been reluctant to do so during his first term as President. Much of his energy in those years he was devoting to the business of winning reelection. Above all, he was working to ensure that the conservative Republican Old Guard, which bristled at even the most modest of reforms, would not block his nomination in 1904.

It was a legitimate concern, for men like Nelson Aldrich and Mark Hanna in the Senate and Joseph Cannon in the House were not only influential within the party but suspicious of the new President. Had Roosevelt engaged them in open battle, they might well have destroyed him in 1904. As it was, however, quite the opposite occurred. By skillfully dispensing patronage to conservatives and progressives alike, by reshuffling unstable Republican organizations in the South, by winning the support of northern businessmen while making adroit gestures to reformers, he succeeded in all but neutralizing his opposition within the party and won its presidential nomination with ease. And in the general election, where he faced a pallid conservative Democrat, Alton B. Parker, he stormed to one of the largest victories in the nation's history. Roosevelt captured over 57 percent of the popular vote and lost not one state outside the South. Now, relieved of immediate political concerns, he was free to display the full extent (and the real limits) of his commitment to reform.

Roosevelt and the Railroads

During the 1904 campaign, Roosevelt boasted that he had worked in the anthracite coal strike to provide everyone with a "square deal." In his second term, he became noticeably more aggressive in his efforts to extend the square deal even further. He continued to operate from the political center, offending many of the business interests that had contributed to his campaign and, at the same time, offending many midwestern progressives who subscribed to what he termed "the La Follette type of fool radicalism." But he delighted the great majority of Americans who believed in careful, moderate change.

Among his most important targets was the railroad industry, for nearly half a century one of the most powerful forces in the nation and for much of that time a target of all those who feared unrestrained corporate power. The Interstate Commerce Act of 1887, establishing the Interstate Commerce Commission (ICC), had been an early effort to regulate the industry; but over the years, the courts had virtually nullified its influence. Roosevelt, through a series of intricate maneuvers, pushed a new, more forceful regulatory law through Congress, a law that would give the government considerable power over the setting of railroad rates.

Roosevelt managed to win approval of a particularly strong version of the bill in the House (partly at least because he agreed in return not to push for a tariff reduction). The legislation gave the ICC broad powers to set shipping rates in response to complaints from shippers and to investigate corporate records and supervise accounting methods. In the Senate, however, the Republican Old Guard insisted upon amendments to increase the power of the courts to review ICC rulings (an important change given the prevailing conservatism of the judiciary). During the negotiations between the two bodies that followed, Roosevelt finally agreed to the conservative changes, and in June 1906 the Hepburn Railroad Regulation Act became law.

It was a classic example of the cautiousness with which Roosevelt, even after his 1904 mandate, approached reform. At first, he had seemed to support the position of militant progressives like La Follette, who wanted to give the ICC power to evaluate railroad property as a basis for determining rates. Ultimately, however, he settled for legislation that even many conservatives considered accept-able. La Follette, who believed the President had betrayed him, never forgave Roosevelt—not even after many of the stricter measures he had advocated became law in 1910, with the Mann-Elkins Act, nor when, in 1913, La Follette won approval of legislation authorizing ICC valuation of railroad property.

Extending Regulation

The Hepburn Act was the most conspicuous reform legislation of Roosevelt's second term, but only one of many new regulatory measures. The President won approval of laws providing for compensation by employers to injured workingmen in the District of Columbia and certain other, limited areas. He pressured Con-gress to enact the Pure Food and Drug Act, which, despite weaknesses in its enforcement mechanisms, did restrict the sale of some dangerous or ineffective medicines. When Upton Sinclair's powerful novel *The Jungle* appeared in 1906, featuring nauseating descriptions of the preparation of meats in the nation's stockyards, Roosevelt insisted upon passage of the Meat Inspection Act, which, despite a shaky start, ultimately succeeded in eliminating many diseases once transmitted in impure meat. In every case, what Roosevelt got was far less than what the most fervent progressives wanted. But it was, he argued, a beginning.

Starting in 1907, moreover, he seemed to expand his vision of regulation and began to propose even more stringent measures: an eight-hour day for workers, broader compensation for victims of industrial accidents, inheritance and income taxes (which ultimately required a constitutional amendment in 1913 before they could be instituted), regulation of the stock market, railroad property valuation (the La Follette proposal he had previously abandoned), and others. He was openly and self-consciously moving to the left; and in the process he started openly to criticize conservatives in Congress, who were blocking much of this legislation, and to denounce the judiciary, which was striking down many of the measures that did pass. The result was not only a general stalemate in Roosevelt's reform agenda, but a widening gulf between the President and the conservative wing of his party.

Conservation

Nothing contributed more to the creation of that gulf than Roosevelt's aggressive policies on behalf of conservation. An ardent sportsman and naturalist, he had long been concerned about the unregulated exploitation of America's natural resources and the despoiling of what remained of the nation's wilderness. Using executive powers, he began early in his presidency to restrict private development in millions of acres of undeveloped land still controlled by the government, adding them instead to the hitherto modest system of national forests and parks. When vigorous conservative and western opposition finally resulted in legislation in 1907 to restrict his authority over public lands, Roosevelt and his chief forester, Gifford Pinchot, worked furiously to seize all the forests and many of the waterpower sites still in the public domain, before the bill became law. By the time he left office,

Roosevelt had added about 125 million acres to the national forest system, reserved to the government 4.7 million acres of phosphate beds, and withdrawn 68 million acres of coal lands from the public domain—all the known coal deposits still under government jurisdiction.

Roosevelt was the first President to take an active interest in the new and struggling American conservation movement, and his policies had a lasting effect upon national environmental policies. More than most public figures, he was sympathetic to the concerns of the naturalists—those within the movement committed to protecting the natural beauty of the land and the health of its wildlife from human intrusion. Early in his presidency, Roosevelt even spent four days camping in the Sierras with John Muir, the nation's leading preservationist and the founder of the Sierra Club. In the end, however, Roosevelt's policy tended to favor less the preservationists than another faction within the conservation movement—those who believed in carefully managed development. The leading conservation figure in government, therefore, was not Muir, but Gifford Pinchot. The first professionally trained forester in the United States, Pinchot supported rational and efficient human use of the wilderness. The Sierra Club might argue for the "aesthetic" value of the forests; Pinchot insisted, in contrast, that "the whole question is a practical one." Trained experts in forestry and resource management, such men as Pinchot himself, should, Roosevelt believed, apply to the landscape the same scientific standards that others were applying to the management of cities and industries. The President did side with the preservationists on certain issues, but the more important legacy of his conservation policy was to establish the government's role as manager of the continuing human development of the wilderness.

To much of the Old Guard, the extension of government control over vast new lands smacked of socialism. Even worse, Roosevelt's use of executive powers to achieve that control smacked of dictatorship. Many of these same interests, however, displayed no such scruples in supporting another important aspect of Roosevelt's natural resource policy: public reclamation and irrigation projects. In 1902, the President supported the Newlands Reclamation Act, which provided federal funds for the construction of huge dams, reservoirs, and canals in the West —projects to open new lands for cultivation and provide cheap electric power. By 1915, the government had invested $80 million in twenty-five such projects, the largest of which—a dam on Arizona's Salt River—carried Roosevelt's name. It was the beginning of many years of federal aid for irrigation and power development in the western states, a tradition that survived virtually unchallenged for more than seven decades.

The Panic of 1907

The flurry of reforms Roosevelt was able to enact, and the enormous popularity he attracted as a result, made it easy for members of his administration to believe that finally the government had imposed a strong, effective set of regulations upon the new industrial economy. The chaos of the late nineteenth century, they began

ROOSEVELT AND JOHN MUIR.   Muir escorted the President on a camping trip during Roosevelt's visit to the Yosemite Valley in California in 1906. Conservationists have long believed that Muir's influence was crucial to Roosevelt's later decision to include the valley in the national park system. (*Bettmann Archive*)

to tell themselves, was becoming a thing of the past. In actuality, the Roosevelt record—although impressive when compared with that of his predecessors—had been a relatively modest one, and the economy at large remained essentially uncontrolled. That truth was harshly brought home to Roosevelt and his allies in 1907, when a serious panic and recession revealed how flawed the nation's economic structure remained. The scenario was eerily familiar to those who remembered 1893. Once again, American industrial production had outrun the capacity of either domestic or foreign markets to absorb it. Once again, the banking system and the stock market had displayed pathetic inadequacies. Once again, irresponsible speculation and rampant financial mismanagement had helped to shatter a prosperity that many had come to believe was now permanent. Banks failed; industries cut or ceased production; workers suffered layoffs and wage cuts.

To many conservatives, Roosevelt's "mad" economic policies were the obvious cause of the disaster. The President, naturally and correctly, disagreed; but the panic was clearly unnerving to him, and he acted quickly to reassure business leaders that he would not interfere with their recovery efforts. J. P. Morgan, in a spectacular display of his awesome financial power, helped construct a pool of the assets of several important New York banks to prop up shaky financial institutions. The key to the arrangement, Morgan told the President, was the purchase by U.S. Steel of the shares of the Tennessee Coal and Iron Company currently held by a threatened New York bank. He would, he insisted, need assurances that no antitrust action would ensue. Roosevelt tacitly agreed, and the Morgan plan proceeded. Partly as a result, the panic soon subsided.

For eight years to come, until the outbreak of war in Europe reinvigorated the economy, the nation continued to stumble through a series of modest booms and partial busts, never fully able to stabilize its financial position. The efficient, scientifically managed economy that so many progressives had advocated and that some had come to believe they had achieved was still far from reality.

THE BIG STICK

At the heart of Roosevelt's domestic policies was a continuing concern for imposing order and stability upon the troubled American economy. The same concern dictated his behavior in international affairs. Only by expanding overseas markets for America's industrial products, most progressives believed, could the nation avoid the disastrous economic collapses that had marred the 1890s. And only by acting forcefully to prevent disorder in those regions important to American trade could the markets be secured. For Roosevelt, as for many later Presidents, foreign affairs had an additional attraction. There, he could act without fear of a recalcitrant Congress or conservative courts. There, he could free himself from concerns about public opinion, for most of the public thought like Walter Lippmann, who once wrote: "I cannot remember taking any interest whatsoever in foreign affairs until after the outbreak of the First World War." Overseas, the President could exercise power unfettered and alone.

Sea Power and Civilization

Roosevelt was well suited, both by temperament and by ideology, for an activist foreign policy. A vigorous athlete and once an enthusiastic college boxer, he spoke often of the virtues of the "strenuous life" and viewed physical combat as an ennobling, manly challenge. His fondness for battle was not dampened by his famous charge up San Juan Hill, a crucial event in the development of his political career.

Roosevelt believed, moreover, that an important distinction existed between the "civilized" and "uncivilized" nations of the world. "Civilized" nations, as he defined them, were predominantly white and Anglo-Saxon or Teutonic; "uncivilized" nations were generally nonwhite, Latin, or Slavic. But racism was only partly the basis of the distinction. At least as important was economic development. Thus it was that Japan, a rapidly industrializing society, seemed to Roosevelt to have earned admission to the ranks of the civilized.

There was, of course, another important aspect of this global division. Civilized nations were, by Roosevelt's definition, producers of industrial goods; uncivilized nations were suppliers of raw materials and markets. There was, he believed, an economic relationship between the two parts that was vital to both of them; and it was natural, perhaps, that he should come to believe in the right and duty of the civilized societies to intervene in the affairs of "backward" nations to preserve order and stability. The economic health of the globe might depend on the result.

Accordingly, Roosevelt early became an outspoken champion of the development of American sea power. A friend and admirer of Alfred Thayer Mahan, world-famous champion of the importance of naval force, Roosevelt had believed since his days as Assistant Secretary of the Navy in 1897 that the United States must move rapidly to expand the size and power of its fleet. Only thus, he argued, could the nation play an active and important role in world affairs. To Roosevelt, as to many other early-twentieth-century internationalists, the concept of sea power soon assumed the same central significance that the concept of air power would assume in later decades. By 1906, Roosevelt's support had enabled the American navy to attain a size and strength surpassed only by that of Great Britain (although Germany was fast gaining ground).

Frustrations in Asia

The new strength was not, however, always enough to enable the President to have his way in global developments, as events in the Pacific soon illustrated. The United States had long taken an active interest in the affairs of Asia—both as an imperial power in the Philippines and as a commercial power elsewhere. Roosevelt believed that it was vital to maintain an "open door" for American trade in the Pacific and to prevent any single nation from establishing hegemony there. He looked with alarm, therefore, at the military rivalries involving Japan, Russia, Germany, and France in the region.

He was particularly concerned by Russian efforts to expand southward into Manchuria, a province of China; and when in 1904 the Japanese attacked the Russian fleet at Port Arthur in southern Manchuria, Roosevelt, like most Americans, was inclined to approve. Yet the President was no more eager for Japan to control Manchuria than for Russia to do so. Japanese control might, he believed, "mean a struggle between them and us in the future" over commercial rights in the region. If the fighting between Russia and Japan continued for long, he feared, the Japanese could emerge as the dominant power in the region. In 1905, there-fore, he eagerly agreed to a Japanese request to mediate an end to the conflict. Russia, faring badly in the war—and, as a result, already experiencing a domestic instability that twelve years later would culminate in revolution—had no choice but to agree.

At a peace conference in Portsmouth, New Hampshire, Roosevelt extracted from the embattled Russians a recognition of Japan's territorial gains—control of Korea, South Manchuria, and part of Sakhalin Island, formerly a Russian outpost. Japan, in return, agreed to cease the fighting and expand no further. At the same time, Roosevelt worked to secure American interests by negotiating a secret agreement with the Japanese to ensure that the United States could continue to trade freely in the region.

Roosevelt was pleased with his work at the Portsmouth Conference, particularly when it helped him to win the Nobel Peace Prize in 1906. But his triumph was, in actuality, a hollow one. In the years that followed, relations between the United States and Japan steadily deteriorated, and the careful assurances Roosevelt had won in 1905 proved all but meaningless. Having destroyed the Russian fleet at Port Arthur, Japan now emerged as the preeminent naval power in the Pacific and soon began to exclude American trade from many of the territories it controlled.

It did not help matters that in 1906 the school board of San Francisco voted to segregate Oriental schoolchildren in the city in separate schools; or that a year later, the California legislature attempted to pass legislation limiting the immigra-tion of Japanese laborers into the state. Anti-Oriental riots in California and inflammatory stories in the Hearst papers about the "Yellow Peril" further fanned resentment in Japan.

The President did his best to douse the flames. He quietly persuaded the San Francisco school board to rescind its edict in return for a Japanese agreement to stop the flow of agricultural immigrants into California. Then, lest the Japanese government construe his action as a sign of weakness, he sent sixteen battleships of the new American navy on an unprecedented 45,000-mile voyage around the world that included a call on Japan. Despite fears by some members of Congress that a naval conflict might ensue, the "Great White Fleet," as the flotilla was called, received a warm reception when it arrived in Yokohama. For the moment, Roosevelt's foreign policy—which he once summarized with the African proverb: "Speak softly and carry a big stick"—seemed to have borne important fruit. But the United States had failed to stop Japanese expansion in Asia, and Roosevelt himself had to admit that the situation in the Pacific posed a grave threat to future peace.

Mediation in Europe

At the same time that Roosevelt was attempting to create a balance of power in the Pacific, he was participating in efforts to maintain a balance in Europe. For some years, American relations with Great Britain, which had ranged from chilly

AMERICAN NAVAL POWER ON DISPLAY. The "Great White Fleet" sailed around the world in 1908, demonstrating the new resolve of the United States to behave as an international power. (*U.S. Navy photo*)

to openly hostile through most of the nineteenth century, had been growing increasingly cordial. The friendly settlement of a border dispute between Canada and the American territory of Alaska in 1903, followed by a British agreement to withdraw its naval units from the Caribbean, helped forge an Anglo-American partnership that would grow increasingly important in the years to come. At the moment, however, Roosevelt was chiefly concerned with ensuring that the growth of German power in Europe did not threaten the stability of the Continent or the ability of the British navy to maintain peace in international waters.

When a bitter quarrel arose between Germany and France over control of Morocco in northern Africa, Roosevelt was at first reluctant to involve the United States. "We have other fish to fry," he remarked in 1905. But as the dispute grew more heated, he began to feel compelled to do something "to keep matters on an even keel in Europe." When Kaiser Wilhelm of Germany asked him to help mediate an end to the conflict, Roosevelt persuaded France and Great Britain to send delegates to an international conference in Algeciras, Spain, to establish the status of Morocco. The issue involved more than just Germany and France. The British were deeply concerned by the growth of German naval power and fearful of a permanent disruption of the global power balance in which they played such an important role. They were as committed as the French to limiting German influence in northern Africa, and they supported France's determination to establish a protectorate in Morocco. At the 1906 Algeciras conference, the American delegates sided from the beginning with the British and the French, although they managed to extract some concessions for Germany from the negotiations. The agreement that ensued maintained French control of Morocco and succeeded, Roosevelt believed, in stabilizing the increasingly precarious balance of power in Europe.

The Iron-Fisted Neighbor

Even before the Algeciras conference, Roosevelt had begun to become concerned, some believed almost obsessed, by the possibility of German penetration into Latin America, which the United States had come to consider its exclusive sphere of influence. Unwilling to share trading rights, let alone military control, with any other nation, Roosevelt embarked upon a series of ventures in the Caribbean and South America that established an ominous pattern of American intervention in the region.

Crucial to Roosevelt's thinking was an incident early in his presidency. When the government of Venezuela began in 1902 to renege on debts to European bankers, naval forces of Britain, Italy, and Germany erected a blockade along that country's coast. Roosevelt at first expressed little concern. "If any South American country misbehaves toward any European country," he had written to a friend in Germany, "let the European country spank it." But when that spanking expanded to include a German bombardment of a Venezuelan port and rumors that Germany planned to establish a permanent base in the region, Roosevelt changed his mind. In 1903, he warned the Germans (according to his own later account) that Admiral Dewey and his fleet were standing by in the Caribbean and would act against any German effort to acquire new territory. The German navy finally withdrew.

The incident helped to persuade Roosevelt that European intrusions in Latin America could result not only from aggression but from internal instability or irresponsibility (such as defaulting on debts) in Latin American nations. As a result, he imposed a new interpretation upon the Monroe Doctrine (the 1823 edict proclaiming America's right to prevent any further European colonization of the Western Hemisphere). Roosevelt now claimed that the United States had the right not only to oppose European intervention, but to intervene itself in the domestic affairs of its neighbors if those neighbors proved unable to maintain order on their own. The Roosevelt Corollary, as it soon became known, was not couched in diplomatic niceties. The President stated its premises openly and unapologetically in a 1904 message to Congress:

> Any country whose people conduct themselves well can count upon our hearty friendship. . . . Chronic wrongdoing, or an impotence which results in a general loosening of the ties of civilized society, may in America, as elsewhere, require intervention by some civilized nation, and in the Western hemisphere the adherence of the United States to the Monroe Doctrine may force the United States, however reluctantly, in flagrant cases of such wrongdoing or impotence to the exercise of an international police power.

The immediate motivation for the Roosevelt Corollary, and the first opportunity for putting the doctrine into practice, was a crisis in the Dominican Republic. A revolution had toppled the corrupt and bankrupt government of that nation in 1903, but the new regime proved no better able than the old to make good on the country's $22 million of debts to European nations. Both France and Italy were threatening to intervene to recover their losses, and the new Dominican leaders had turned to the United States for help. Using the rationale he had outlined in his address to Congress, Roosevelt established, in effect, an American receivership, assuming control of Dominican customs and distributing 45 percent of the revenues to Santo Domingo and the rest to foreign creditors. This arrangement lasted, in one form or another, for more than three decades.

Two years later, another opportunity for intervention in the Caribbean arose. In 1902, the United States had granted political independence to Cuba, but only after the new government had agreed to the so-called Platt Amendment to its constitution, giving the United States the right to prevent any foreign power from intruding into the new nation. When, in 1906, a series of domestic uprisings seemed to threaten the internal stability of the island, Roosevelt reasoned that America must intervene to "protect" Cuba from disorder. American troops landed in Cuba, quelled the fighting, and remained there for three years. But American dominance in Cuba survived far longer than that—until the Castro revolution in 1959.

Taking the Panama Canal

The most celebrated accomplishment of Roosevelt's presidency, and the one that illustrated most clearly his own expansive view of the powers of his office and the role of the United States abroad, was the completion of the Panama Canal. Construction of a channel through Central America linking the Atlantic and the Pacific had been a dream of many nations since the mid-nineteenth century, but somehow the canal had never been built. Roosevelt was determined to do better.

The first step was the removal of an old obstacle. In 1850, the United States and Great Britain had agreed to a treaty under which the two nations would construct, operate, and defend any such canal together. The McKinley administration had already begun negotiations to cancel the agreement; Roosevelt completed the process. In 1901, the Hay-Pauncefote Treaty gave the United States the right to undertake the canal project alone.

The next question was where to locate the canal. At first, the Roosevelt administration (and many congressional leaders) favored a route across Nicaragua, which would permit a sea-level canal requiring no locks. A possible alternative was the Isthmus of Panama in Colombia, the site of an earlier, abortive effort by a French company to construct a channel. The Panama route was shorter (although not at sea level), and construction was already about 40 percent complete. When the French company lowered its price for its holdings from $109 million to $40 million, and when it combined this gesture with skillful lobbying efforts in Washington, the President and Congress changed their minds.

Roosevelt quickly dispatched John Hay, his Secretary of State, to negotiate an agreement with Colombian diplomats in Washington that would allow construction to begin without delay. Under heavy American pressure, the Colombian chargé d'affaires, Tomas Herrán, signed an agreement highly unfavorable to his own nation. The United States would gain perpetual rights to a six-mile-wide

ROOSEVELT IN PANAMA. President Roosevelt visited Panama, the nation he had helped to create, during construction of the canal in 1906. He poses here at the controls of an enormous steam shovel being used for excavation at Culebra Cut. (*Library of Congress*)

"canal zone" across Colombia; in return, it would pay Colombia $10 million and an annual rental of $250,000. The treaty produced outrage in the Colombian Senate, whose members angrily pointed out that the defunct French company was to receive four times the amount the government of Colombia was to be paid. The senators refused to ratify the agreement and sent a new representative to the United States with instructions to demand at least $20 million from the Americans plus a share of the payment to the French.

Roosevelt was furious. The Colombians, he charged, were "inefficient bandits" and "blackmailers"; and he began to contemplate ways to circumvent the Bogotá government. He found a ready ally in the person of Philippe Bunau-Varilla, chief engineer of the French canal project and one of the most effective lobbyists in the campaign to persuade the United States to choose the Isthmus of Panama for its own efforts. Bunau-Varilla watched with dismay as the government of Colombia appeared ready to destroy his efforts, and in November 1903 he helped organize and finance a revolution in Panama. There had been many previous revolts, all of them failures. But this one had an important additional asset: the support of the United States. Using an 1846 American-Colombian treaty as justification, Roosevelt landed troops from the U.S.S. *Nashville* in Panama to "maintain order." Their presence prevented Colombian forces from suppressing the rebellion, and three days later the United States recognized Panama as an independent nation. The new Panamanian government, under the influence of Bunau-Varilla, quickly agreed to a new treaty. It would grant the United States a canal zone ten miles wide; the United States would pay it the $10 million fee and the $250,000 annual rental that the Colombian Senate had rejected. Work on the canal proceeded rapidly, despite the enormous cuts and elaborate locks (which alone cost $375 million) that the construction required. It opened in 1914, three years after Roosevelt had proudly boasted to a university audience, "I took the Canal Zone and let Congress debate!" Few at the time would have disagreed.

The Roosevelt Retirement

Theodore Roosevelt loved being President. He had made that plain during his first moments in office, when, torn between his excitement at his new position and his distress at McKinley's death, he had written, "It is a dreadful thing to come into the Presidency in this way; but it would be a far worse thing to be morbid about it." As his years in office produced increasing political and diplomatic successes, as his public popularity continued to rise, more and more observers began to doubt that he would happily stand aside in 1908.

Events, however, dictated otherwise. The Panic of 1907, combined with Roosevelt's growing "radicalism" during his second term, had deeply alienated conservatives in his own party. He would, he realized, have considerable difficulty winning the Republican nomination for a third term. In 1904, moreover, he had made a public promise to step down four years later, a promise that would surely emerge to haunt him if he decided to run again. And so, after nearly eight energetic years in the White House, during which he had transformed the role of the presidency in American government, Theodore Roosevelt, fifty years old, retired from public life—briefly.

SUGGESTED READINGS

An eloquent and popular study of the prepresidential life of Theodore Roosevelt is Edmund Morris, *The Rise of Theodore Roosevelt* (1979). Important full-scale biographies include Henry F. Pringle, *Theodore Roosevelt* (1931), a sharply critical study, and William H. Harbaugh, *Power and Responsibility* (1961), published in paperback under the title *The Life and Times of Theodore Roosevelt.* John Morton Blum's *The Republi-*

can Roosevelt (1954) provides a succinct, interpretive account of TR's career. Other works on Roosevelt's presidency and the national politics of his era include George E. Mowry, *The Era of Theodore Roosevelt* (1958), and G. Wallace Chessman, *Theodore Roosevelt and the Politics of Power* (1969). John A. Garraty's *The Life of George W. Perkins* (1960) chronicles the career of one of Roosevelt's most important political allies. Samuel P. Hays has provided the most penetrating study of progressive conservation policies in *The Gospel of Efficiency: The Progressive Conservation Movement, 1890–1920* (1962).

Howard K. Beale's *Theodore Roosevelt and the Rise of America to World Power* (1956) is the standard work on TR's foreign policy. Other useful studies include Richard Challener, *Admirals, Generals, and American Foreign Policy, 1898–1914* (1973); David H. Burton, *Theodore Roosevelt: Confident Imperialist* (1969); and Julius W. Pratt, *Challenge and Rejection: The United States and World Leadership, 1900– 1921* (1967). On American policy in Asia, see Akira Iriye, *Pacific Estrangement: Japanese and American Expansion, 1897–1911* (1972); Charles E. Neu, *An Uncertain Friendship: Roosevelt and Japan, 1906–1909* (1967); and Charles Vevier, *United States and China* (1955). For American policy in the Caribbean, see Dana G. Munro, *Intervention and Dollar Diplomacy in the Caribbean, 1900–1921* (1964); Dwight C. Miner, *Fight for the Panama Route* (1966); Walter LaFeber, *The Panama Canal* (1978); and David McCullough, *The Path Between the Seas* (1977), a lucid popular history of the building of the canal.

Five

Progressivism Divided

It seemed at first that William Howard Taft, who assumed the presidency in 1909, would be that rare thing among politicians: a leader acceptable to virtually everyone. He had been Theodore Roosevelt's most trusted lieutenant and his hand-picked successor; progressive reformers believed him to be one of their own. He had been one of the first viceroys of the new American empire, serving as governor-general of the Philippines, as Secretary of War, and as special envoy to Japan, and traveling over 100,000 miles between 1900 and 1908; American imperialists trusted him to maintain America's active role in world affairs. He had been a restrained and moderate jurist, a Solicitor General of the United States, and a federal circuit court judge, and he was a man with a punctilious regard for legal process; conservatives expected him to abandon Roosevelt's aggressive use of presidential powers.

It was perhaps unsurprising, then, that in 1908 Taft won election to the presidency with almost ridiculous ease. With the support both of Roosevelt and of much of the Republican Old Guard, he received his party's nomination virtually uncontested. In the general election, he not only inherited most of Roosevelt's enormous constituency; he received, too, the warm support of many business leaders who had come to despise Roosevelt's policies. John D. Rockefeller wired his congratulations after the Republican convention; J. P. Morgan, learning of Taft's nomination, responded, "Good! Good!"; Andrew Carnegie donated $20,-000 to his campaign. Taft's victory in November was a foregone conclusion. Although his popular margin was smaller than Roosevelt's in 1904, it was nevertheless decisive: 51 percent of the votes to 43 percent for the Democratic candidate, William Jennings Bryan, running forlornly for the third time. His electoral margin was a comfortable 321 to 162. Delighted Republican progressives predicted brilliant new achievements. "Roosevelt has cut enough hay," they proclaimed. "Taft is the man to put it into the barn." Republican conservatives rejoiced that they were rid of the "mad messiah." Taft entered office on a wave of good feeling.

It was ironic, therefore, that four years later Taft would leave the White House the most decisively repudiated President of the century, his party deeply, perhaps irrevocably, divided, and the government in the hands of a Democratic administration for the first time in twenty years. It had been his misfortune to bring to the presidency a personality and philosophy of leadership ill-suited to his time, and to preside over an era in which the contending forces of progressivism finally broke into open combat.

THE TROUBLED SUCCESSION

It had been obvious from the start that Taft and Roosevelt were not at all alike, but it was not until Taft took office that the real extent of the differences became clear. Roosevelt had been the most dynamic and charismatic public figure of his age; Taft, by contrast, conveyed a stolid respectability and little more. Roosevelt was an ardent sportsman and athlete; Taft was sedentary and obese—he weighed over 300 pounds and required a special, oversized bathtub to be installed in the White House. Most important, Roosevelt had taken an expansive view of the powers of his office, bringing to the presidency enormous energy and a willingness to act daringly, even recklessly, in performing his duties; Taft, on the other hand, was slow, cautious, even lethargic, insistent that the President must take pains to observe the strict letter of the law. Roosevelt "ought more often to have admitted the legal way of reaching the same ends," Taft once remarked, in the bland, understated tone that characterized his public discourse. Critics were not being entirely fair, perhaps, when they dismissed the new President as "a large, good-natured body, entirely surrounded by people who know exactly what they want." But Taft himself never seemed fully comfortable with the presidency. Shortly after taking office, he wrote a letter to Theodore Roosevelt that revealed how deep were his self-doubts:

> When I am addressed as "Mr. President," I turn to see whether you are not at my elbow.
> . . . I have not the facility for educating the public as you had . . . , and so I fear that a large
> part of the public will feel as if I had fallen away from your ideals; but you know me better
> and will understand that I am still working away on the same old plan.

Yet had Taft been the most dynamic of political figures, he would still have had trouble putting "the same old plan" into operation, for he quickly found himself in the middle of a series of political controversies from which no leader could have emerged unscathed. Having come into office as the darling of progressives and conservatives alike, he soon found that he could not please them both. Increasingly, he found himself, without really intending it, pleasing the conservatives and alienating the progressives.

WILLIAM HOWARD TAFT. Taft suffered from, among other things, a colorless public image that stood in sharp and unfortunate contrast to that of his dynamic predecessor, Theodore Roosevelt. He also suffered public ridicule at times for his enormous weight (at times as high as 350 pounds). Wide publicity attended his installation of a special, oversized bathtub in the White House. (*UPI*)

Congress and the Tariff

The first fiasco occurred in the opening months of the new administration, when Taft called Congress into special session to enact legislation lowering protective tariff rates. Tariff reduction had been a consistent demand of many progressives for nearly a decade. It had reflected less a belief in free trade than a conviction that foreign competition would weaken the power of the great trusts and thus lower domestic prices. Theodore Roosevelt had made several tentative gestures on behalf of tariff reform but had always pulled away from the issue in the end. Taft was determined to do more. "I believe the people are with me," he had written in January 1909, "and before I get through I think I will have downed Cannon and Aldrich too."

But the President was not able to down the Old Guard so easily; often, moreover, he seemed not to be trying to do so. A tariff revision acceptable to most progressives moved relatively easily through the House; but in the Senate, Nelson Aldrich and other conservatives, aided by the relentless efforts of protectionist lobbies, waged a powerful campaign to weaken the bill. For weeks, a spirited battle raged on the Senate floor, conservatives working to amend the bill, progressives (among them La Follette) fighting tirelessly to block them. But the devastating arguments the reformers were able to marshall against the tariff were not enough. They needed help from the White House, and that they never received. Taft agonized, hesitated, made ineffectual efforts to produce a compromise, and ultimately simply withdrew from the controversy. He was, he claimed, reluctant to violate the constitutional doctrine of separation of powers by intervening in legislative matters. Without presidential assistance, the progressive efforts finally failed, with La Follette and his allies embittered by what they considered a betrayal by Taft. On August 5, 1909, the President signed the Payne-Aldrich tariff, passed without the support of the midwestern reformers.

It was not a good bill. Conservatives had made only the slightest concessions to progressives, and tariff rates, when they were not actually raised, were scarcely reduced at all. The act seemed, moreover, conspicuously to favor Nelson Aldrich's New England at the expense of the rest of the nation. Taft, nevertheless, tried to defend the measure as an important progressive victory, "a sincere effort on the part of the Republican party to make a downward revision." On a speaking tour of the Midwest that fall, he increased progressive resentment by standing in the heart of tariff opposition—Winona, Minnesota—and declaring: "On the whole . . . the Payne bill is the best bill that the Republican party ever passed." The rest of his trip, one reporter wrote, was "a polar dash through the world of ice."

The wedge between Taft and the Republican progressives drove deeper as a result of the President's role in efforts to reform the House of Representatives. The almost dictatorial power of Speaker Cannon had been a thorn in the side of progressives for many years; Taft himself harbored a strong dislike for the aging "Uncle Joe." So when reformers began a campaign during the 1909 special session to limit the Speaker's power, Taft at first expressed cautious approval. He soon found, however, that without Cannon's support, his beloved tariff legislation faced almost certain death, and he backed away from the insurgent revolt. Again, congressional progressives watched their reform efforts collapse; again, they blamed Taft for betraying them. The following year, after a fierce debate that raged for nearly thirty hours, progressive Republicans under the leadership of George W. Norris finally succeeded in stripping Cannon of some of his most important powers. Even then, however, they acted without the President's support.

"REVISING THE TARIFF DOWNWARD (?)" J. N. Darling, cartoonist for the progressive *Des Moines Register,* offered this biting commentary on the power of corporate interests in frustrating tariff reform. Indirectly, Darling was commenting on President Taft's ineffectuality in dealing with such interests.

Dollar Diplomacy

Many of those who had admired Theodore Roosevelt's vigorous command of American foreign policy and his strenuous efforts to maintain a world balance of power were similarly dismayed by Taft's performance in international affairs. Although the new President made no decisive break with the policies of his predecessor, and while in some areas he actually extended American involvement abroad, he was in general no readier to exert strong leadership internationally than he was domestically. He worked to advance the nation's economic interests overseas, but he seemed to lack Roosevelt's larger vision of world stability. Worst of all, several of his most important foreign policy initiatives were conspicuous failures.

The thrust of Taft's foreign policy was best symbolized by the man he chose to administer it: Secretary of State Philander C. Knox, a corporation lawyer committed to using his position to promote American business interests overseas. Roosevelt, of course, had promoted American economic interests too; but Knox seemed at times to regard the State Department as little more than an agent of the corporate community. He worked aggressively to extend American investments into underdeveloped regions, motivating critics to label his policies "Dollar Diplomacy."

The Taft-Knox foreign policy faced its severest test, and encountered its greatest failure, in the Far East. Ignoring Roosevelt's tacit 1905 agreement with Japan to limit American involvement in Manchuria, the new administration succumbed to the persuasive powers of Willard Straight, a former diplomat now working as an agent of American bankers, and began to move aggressively to increase America's economic influence in the region. When British, French, and German bankers formed a consortium to finance a vast system of railroads in China, Knox insisted that Americans should also participate; and when in 1911 the Europeans finally agreed to include the United States in their venture, Knox proposed that an international syndicate purchase the South Manchurian Railroad to remove it from Japanese control. Japan responded by signing a treaty of friendship with Russia—a warning to the Europeans—and the entire railroad project quickly collapsed. Having attempted to expand its influence in Asia, America now found the door to Manchuria slammed in its face.

In the Caribbean, the new administration continued Roosevelt's policies of maintaining order and stability in troubled areas without regard for the national integrity of the nations involved; but Taft and Knox went even further. Limiting European influence in the region meant, they believed, not only preventing disorder but establishing a significant American economic presence there—replacing the investments of European nations with investments from the United States. In 1909, Knox tried to arrange for American bankers to establish a financial receivership in Honduras. Later, he persuaded New York bankers to invest in the National Bank of Haiti. But Dollar Diplomacy was not always so peaceful. When a revolution broke out in Nicaragua in 1909, the administration quickly sided with the insurgents (who had been inspired to revolt by an American mining company) and sent United States troops into the country to seize the customs houses. As soon as peace was restored, Knox encouraged American bankers to move into Nicaragua and offer substantial loans to the new government, thus increasing Washington's financial leverage over the country. Within two years, however, the new pro-American government faced a revolt of its own; and Taft, following his policy to its logical extreme, again landed American troops in Nicaragua, this time to protect the existing regime. The troops remained there for more than a decade.

Taft did not entirely abandon Roosevelt's commitment to mediating international conflict. He shared his predecessor's faith in the impartial arbitration of disputes, a cardinal tenet of progressivism, and he sought at times to extend the American role as a world mediator. As in so many other areas where he attempted to emulate Roosevelt, however, he encountered only frustration. The Senate time and again blocked agreements that might force the United States itself to submit to arbitration, and Taft lacked the political strength to advance the scheme on his own.

The Pinchot–Ballinger Affair

With Taft's standing among Republican progressives steadily deteriorating and with the party growing more and more deeply divided, a sensational controversy broke out late in 1909 that helped to destroy for good Taft's popularity with admirers of Theodore Roosevelt. Many progressives had been unhappy when Taft

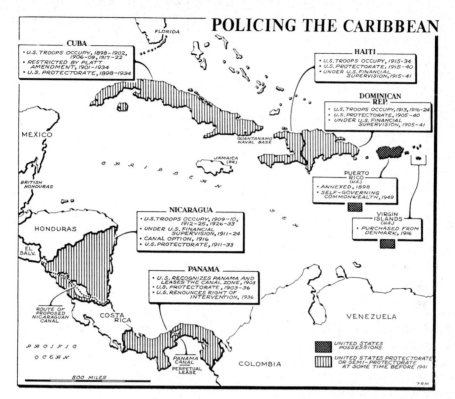

POLICING THE CARIBBEAN

CUBA
- U.S. TROOPS OCCUPY, 1898-1902, 1906-09, 1917-22
- RESTRICTED BY PLATT AMENDMENT, 1901-1934
- U.S. PROTECTORATE, 1898-1934

HAITI
- U.S. TROOPS OCCUPY, 1915-34
- U.S. PROTECTORATE, 1915-40
- UNDER U.S. FINANCIAL SUPERVISION, 1915-41

DOMINICAN REP.
- U.S. TROOPS OCCUPY, 1913, 1916-24
- U.S. PROTECTORATE, 1905-40
- UNDER U.S. FINANCIAL SUPERVISION, 1905-41

PUERTO RICO (U.S.)
- ANNEXED, 1898
- SELF-GOVERNING COMMONWEALTH, 1949

VIRGIN ISLANDS (U.S.)
- PURCHASED FROM DENMARK, 1916

NICARAGUA
- U.S. TROOPS OCCUPY, 1909-10, 1912-25, 1926-33
- UNDER U.S. FINANCIAL SUPERVISION, 1911-24
- CANAL OPTION, 1916
- U.S. PROTECTORATE, 1911-33

PANAMA
- U.S. RECOGNIZES PANAMA AND LEASES THE CANAL ZONE, 1903
- U.S. PROTECTORATE, 1903-36
- U.S. RENOUNCES RIGHT OF INTERVENTION, 1936

MEXICO
BRITISH HONDURAS
HONDURAS
EL SALV.
ROUTE OF PROPOSED NICARAGUAN CANAL
COSTA RICA
PANAMA CANAL PERPETUAL LEASE
COLOMBIA
VENEZUELA
FLORIDA
GUANTANAMO NAVAL BASE
JAMAICA (BR.)
CARIBBEAN SEA
PACIFIC OCEAN

500 MILES

UNITED STATES POSSESSIONS

UNITED STATES PROTECTORATE OR SEMI-PROTECTORATE AT SOME TIME BEFORE 1941

replaced Roosevelt's Secretary of the Interior, James R. Garfield, an aggressive conservationist, with Richard A. Ballinger, a corporate lawyer and a far less fervent environmentalist. Suspicion of Ballinger grew when he attempted to invalidate Roosevelt's actions in removing nearly a million acres of forests and mineral reserves from the public domain. The previous administration had acted illegally, Ballinger insisted; those lands should now be released for private development.

In the midst of this mounting concern, Louis Glavis, an Interior Department investigator, uncovered information that he believed constituted proof that the new secretary had once connived to turn over valuable coal lands in Alaska to a Morgan-Guggenheim syndicate in exchange for personal profits. Glavis took the evidence to Gifford Pinchot, who had remained as head of the Forest Service and had been appalled by Ballinger's retreat from Roosevelt's policies. Pinchot took the charges to the President. Taft listened to Pinchot, heard Ballinger's rebuttal, asked Attorney General George Wickersham to investigate, and finally announced his support for his Interior Secretary. The charges, he insisted, were groundless.

Pinchot, however, was not satisfied. Unhappy that Ballinger remained in office and angry when Taft fired Glavis for his part in the episode, he leaked the story to the press and appealed directly to Congress to investigate the scandal. The President quickly discharged him for insubordination, and the congressional committee appointed to study the controversy, dominated by the Old Guard, exonerated Ballinger. But Taft's victory had come at a high cost. Progressives throughout the country rallied to the support of Pinchot, whom they considered the defender of the public interest against the onslaught of big business. Taft, by contrast, appeared to have capitulated to conservatives and to have repudiated the legacy of Theodore Roosevelt. The controversy aroused as much public passion as any dispute of its time; and when it was over, Taft had alienated the supporters of Theodore Roosevelt as completely as his tariff actions had alienated the followers of La Follette.

Yet Taft had not really repudiated the principles behind Roosevelt's conservation policies in the Pinchot–Ballinger affair. He had, rather, rejected his predecessor's aggressive style of leadership. Although sympathetic to the general aims of the conservationists, he believed that Roosevelt had acted illegally in withdrawing much of the land in Alaska and elsewhere from the public domain. "It is a very dangerous method of upholding reform," he told a protesting progressive Congressman in the midst of the dispute, "to violate the law in so doing, even on the ground of high moral principle, or saving the public."

THE RETURN OF THEODORE ROOSEVELT

During most of Taft's first year in office, Theodore Roosevelt was far from the political fray. He embarked first on a long hunting safari in the jungles of Africa; from there he traveled to Europe for visits to the major heads of state. To the American public, however, Roosevelt remained a formidable presence. Reports of his triumphant European tour dominated the front pages of newspapers across the country. Rumors that he would return to retake control of his party abounded. His arrival in New York in the spring of 1910 was a major public event; and progressives noted that, although he turned down an invitation from Taft to visit the White House, he met at once with Gifford Pinchot (who had already traveled to England to see him several months before).

Roosevelt insisted that he had no plans to return to active politics, but his resolve lasted less than a week. Politicians began flocking immediately to his home at Oyster Bay, Long Island, for endless conferences; Roosevelt himself took an active role in several New York political controversies; and within a month, he announced that he would embark on a national speaking tour before the end of the summer. Furious with Taft, who had, he believed, "completely twisted around the policies I advocated and acted upon," he was becoming convinced that he alone was capable of reuniting the Republican party.

Osawatomie

The real signal of Roosevelt's return to active leadership of the progressives was a speech on September 1, 1910, in Osawatomie, Kansas, where he outlined a set of principles that he labeled the "New Nationalism." The speech made clear how far Roosevelt had moved from the cautious conservatism that had marked the first years of his presidency. Social justice, he argued, could be attained only through

"BACK IN THE OLD PLACE."
Even a continent away, Theodore
Roosevelt continued to dominate the
front pages of American papers. This
cartoon by Nelson Harding of the
Brooklyn Eagle lampoons the former
President's ability to generate publicity
while on safari in Africa shortly after
leaving office. When he returned to
America in 1910, Roosevelt
immediately reestablished himself as a
dominant political figure in the
Republican party.

the vigorous efforts of a strong federal government whose executive acted as the
"steward of the public welfare." Those who thought primarily of property rights
and personal profit "must now give way to the advocate of human welfare, who
rightly maintains that every man holds his property subject to the general right
of the community to regulate its use to whatever degree the public welfare may
require it." Such generalizations were frightening enough by themselves to the
Republican Old Guard, but Roosevelt went beyond them with a list of "radical"
specific proposals: graduated income and inheritance taxes, workers' compensation
for industrial accidents, regulation of the labor of women and children, tariff
revision, and firm regulation of corporations through a more powerful Bureau of
Corporations and ICC. Western progressives were now ready to proclaim him
their next presidential candidate; but among his right-wing opponents, his friend
Henry Cabot Lodge warned him, he was regarded as "little short of a revolution-
ist."

Spreading Insurgency

The congressional elections of 1910 provided further evidence of how far the
progressive revolt had spread through the Republican party and how damaging
it had become. In primary elections, conservative Republicans suffered defeat
after defeat at the hands of progressive insurgents—forty in the House of Representatives alone. Incumbent progressives, moreover, won renomination almost
without exception. In the general election, the Democrats, who were increasingly
offering progressive candidates of their own, won control of the House of Repre-

sentatives for the first time in sixteen years and greatly strengthened their position in the Senate. Progressive insurgency, it seemed, had become a virtual tidal wave. Still, Roosevelt hesitated to move openly to regain the presidency. For months, he claimed that his real purpose was to pressure Taft to return to progressive policies, that he had no wish to break openly with the President. Two events, however, changed his mind.

The first was a 1911 decision by the Taft administration that became, in Roosevelt's eyes, the final, inexcusable indignity. With his strong respect for the letter of the law, Taft had from the beginning been far more active than Roosevelt in enforcing the provisions of the Sherman Antitrust Act, launching dozens of suits against corporate combinations. To Roosevelt, such actions were troubling by themselves, for they reflected what he believed to be a wholly unrealistic attempt to abolish trusts when the proper course was to regulate them. But what truly outraged him was the announcement on October 27, 1911, that the administration was filing an antitrust suit against the United States Steel Corporation, charging, among other things, that the 1907 acquisition of the Tennessee Coal and Iron Company had been illegal. Roosevelt had approved that acquisition in the midst of the 1907 panic, and he was enraged by the clear implication that he had acted improperly. The episode inspired his most strident attacks on the Taft administration to date.

There remained, however, another obstacle to Roosevelt's pursuit of the presidency. Ever since January 1911, Robert La Follette had been working through the newly formed National Progressive Republican League to secure the presidential nomination for himself. Many reformers believed he had established first claim to the leadership of any insurgent revolt, and Roosevelt was at first reluctant to challenge him. But La Follette's candidacy stumbled in February 1912, when, exhausted and plagued by personal worries (including the illness of his daughter), he appeared to suffer a nervous breakdown during a speech in Philadelphia. With almost indecent haste, many of his supporters abandoned him and turned to Roosevelt, who finally announced his candidacy on February 22.

TR Versus Taft

La Follette never forgave Roosevelt for "using" and then "betraying" him, and some diehard loyalists refused to abandon their allegiance to the Wisconsin Senator. But for all practical purposes, the campaign for the Republican nomination had now become a battle between Roosevelt, the champion of the progressives, and Taft, the candidate of the conservatives. In the months that followed, Roosevelt scored overwhelming victories in every presidential preference primary (there were thirteen in all) and arrived at the convention convinced that he had proved himself the choice of the party rank and file. Taft, however, remained the choice of most party leaders, and in the end it was their preference that proved decisive.

The battle for the nomination at the Chicago convention revolved around an unusually large number of contested delegates: 254 in all. Roosevelt needed about

100 of the disputed seats to clinch the nomination. But the Republican National Committee, which ruled on credentials, was controlled by members of the Old Guard; and it awarded all but 19 of the disputed seats to Taft. The President had secured his victory even before the delegates met. Roosevelt and his followers responded bitterly. The decision to seat the Taft delegates, they claimed, was an example of the same corrupt politics that progressives had been fighting for years; once more the people had been thwarted by the special interests. At a rally the night before the convention opened, Roosevelt addressed 5,000 madly cheering supporters and announced that he would not feel bound by the decision of his party if it refused to seat his delegates, that he would continue to fight for a candidacy that had now, it seemed, become a holy cause. "We stand at Armageddon," he told the roaring crowd, "and we battle for the Lord." As good as his word, Roosevelt the next day led his supporters out of the convention, and out of the party. Taft was then quietly nominated on the first ballot.

With financial support from newspaper magnate Frank Munsey and industrialist George W. Perkins, Roosevelt summoned his supporters back to Chicago in August for another convention, this one to launch the new Progressive party and nominate Roosevelt as its presidential candidate. By now, even Roosevelt was aware that the cause was virtually hopeless, particularly when many of the leading insurgents who had supported him during the primaries refused to follow him out of the Republican party. Nevertheless, he approached the battle feeling, as he put it, "fit as a bull moose" (thus giving his new party an enduring nickname). At the meeting in Chicago, he delivered a resounding "Confession of Faith" in which he castigated both of the traditional parties for representing "government of the needy many by professional politicians in the interests of the rich few"; and he produced a platform that embodied a full array of the most advanced progressive reforms.

In later years, many admirers of Roosevelt openly wondered how the former President had allowed himself to become engaged in such a profitless struggle, dividing his own party in order to wage a campaign with virtually no hope of success. Roosevelt himself, however, expressed no such doubts. To him, the Bull Moose crusade was a matter of principle—a protest not only against the political corruption that had, he believed, cost him the Republican nomination, but against the repudiation by Taft and his allies of Roosevelt's own philosophy of government. The New Nationalism promised to restore to the presidency its power to act as mediator of the national interest.

THE RISE OF THE NEW FREEDOM

Yet even while Roosevelt was constructing his New Nationalism as a challenge to conservatives within his own party, a more powerful alternative was emerging from the ranks of the Democrats. The contest, it soon became clear, was not simply one between conservatives and reformers; it was also one between two brands of progressivism expressing two different views of America's future.

Woodrow Wilson

For most of the first decade of the century, the Republican party had often seemed the sole home of progressive reform. In fact, however, progressive sentiment had been gaining strength within the Democratic party as well; and by 1912 it was ready to assert its dominance. At the Democratic convention in Baltimore in June, it appeared at first as though nothing could stop Champ Clark, the conservative Speaker of the House, from securing the presidential nomination. From the beginning, he controlled a majority of the delegates; but on ballot after ballot he failed to assemble the two-thirds necessary to win. For days the battle dragged on inconclusively until finally, on the forty-sixth ballot, Woodrow Wilson, the Governor of New Jersey, emerged as the party's nominee. His victory was in part a result of the last-minute support of Senator Oscar Underwood of Alabama, who had himself been one of the leading contenders for the nomination, and of William Jennings Bryan, who was to become Wilson's Secretary of State. It was also, however, a result of Wilson's position as the only genuinely progressive candidate in the race.

Born in Virginia and raised in Confederate Georgia and Reconstruction South Carolina, Wilson had risen to political prominence by an unusual path. An 1879 graduate of Princeton University, he attended law school and for a time engaged unhappily in practice in Atlanta. He was, however, far more interested in politics and government, and after a few years he enrolled at Johns Hopkins University, where he earned a doctorate in political science. By virtue of his effective teaching and his lucid if unprofound books on the American political system, he rose

THE SPEAKER AND THE NOMINEE.   House Speaker Champ Clark, who had been the early favorite for the 1912 Democratic presidential nomination, visited Woodrow Wilson in Sea Girt, New Jersey, weeks after losing to him at their party's convention. (*Culver Pictures*)

steadily through the academic ranks until in 1902 he was promoted from the faculty to the presidency of Princeton. There, he displayed both the strengths and the weaknesses that would characterize his later political career. A champion of academic reform, he acted firmly and energetically to place Princeton on the road to becoming a great national university. At the same time, however, he displayed during controversies a self-righteous morality that at times made it nearly impossible for him to compromise. Often, he exhibited enormous political skill, revealing a negotiating prowess that left his opponents baffled. On other occasions, however, his personal aloofness, his arrogance, and his stubbornness produced bitter, insoluble stalemates.

It was a series of such stalemates that propelled him out of academia and into politics. Elected Governor of New Jersey in 1910, he brought to his new office the same commitment to reform that he had displayed in the past; and during his two years in the statehouse, he compiled an impressive record of progressive legislation—one that earned him a wide national reputation. At the same time, however, he was gradually alienating conservative party leaders with his intransigence and self-righteousness, and greatly hampering his ability to govern. His nomination for President in 1912 rescued him from what might well have become a political disaster in New Jersey.

The New Freedom

In later years, Wilson's personal characteristics would help polarize the nation. In 1912, however, he sparked controversy by presenting a brand of progressivism that was both forceful and sharply different from Theodore Roosevelt's New Nationalism. His supporters soon began to describe Wilson's program as the "New Freedom"; and although in later years the two phrases began to seem like meaningless slogans, reflecting few important differences, the opposing philosophies—"nationalism" versus "freedom"—were in fact distinct from each other in important ways.

In its narrowest sense, Wilson's New Freedom differed from Roosevelt's New Nationalism in its approach to economic policy, in particular its approach to the trusts. Roosevelt had always believed in accepting economic concentration and using government to regulate and control it. Herbert Croly's *The Promise of American Life,* which appeared in 1909, only clarified and strengthened a view that Roosevelt had long defended. Wilson, by contrast, was a disciple of Louis Brandeis's approach to economic reform. He sided with those who believed that bigness was both unjust and inefficient, that the proper response to monopoly was not to regulate it but to destroy it. The federal government, therefore, should not become the great centralizing force that Roosevelt envisioned. The New Nationalism would create a menacing federal juggernaut that would crush the small entrepreneur and license the financial titans to maintain their dominance. Government should, rather, work to destroy economic privilege and concentration; it should assure small entrepreneurs the chance to prosper and open opportunities for the "man on the make." "This is a second struggle for emancipation," he

ROOSEVELT IN 1912.   Theodore Roosevelt was the most effective
campaigner of his day, and his 1912 presidential effort evoked passionate
enthusiasm from his admirers. It also produced an incident that added
greatly to his reputation for physical courage. As he entered an automobile
in Milwaukee, on October 14, a would-be assassin fired a single bullet into
his chest. It fractured a rib and lodged short of his right lung. Roosevelt
first ordered the crowd not to harm his assailant, then insisted upon
attending a previously scheduled rally, where he spoke to a stunned crowd
for more than an hour. "It takes more than that to kill a Bull Moose," he
told them. (*Theodore Roosevelt Birthplace Association*)

proclaimed in one especially impassioned speech. "If America is not to have free
enterprise, then she can have freedom of no sort whatever."

Wilson seldom explained the New Freedom in terms any more profound than
that, but its implications went far deeper than his economic proposals alone

suggested. For it was, in essence, an alternative vision of what American society should become. To Roosevelt, the essential feature of a modern nation was unity. A centrally organized economy and a forceful federal government were important elements; but there were others. Unity must, he often suggested, extend as well to the nation's values and its social fabric. It was not entirely surprising, therefore, that as time went on, Roosevelt became increasingly antagonistic to immigrant cultures and that he developed a deep, almost unreasonable fear of "foreign" radicalism. In his last years, he was an outspoken champion of the concept of "one hundred percent Americanism" and an advocate of curbs on immigration.

Wilson's progressivism in 1912 suggested a different vision. Progress consisted not of organizing society's energies into a united purpose but of unleashing individual talents and energies. Although no outspoken champion of ethnic traditions, Wilson was more tolerant than Roosevelt of the social diversity that immigration had produced, less fearful of the specter of radicalism, and consistently opposed to efforts to close off immigration. The New Freedom spoke largely in terms of economic reforms that would enhance the position of the little man; but it implied, too, a larger vision of a diverse, pluralistic society. It was an appeal for the preservation of local, state, and regional variations, for the protection not only of the independent merchant but of the independent community. The conflict between "nationalism" and "freedom" that the 1912 campaign offered was, therefore, more than a contest between Roosevelt and Wilson; it was part of a dilemma that American society would continue to face for the remainder of the century.

The Three-Way Contest

Despite the philosophical importance of the issues in 1912, the campaign itself was surprisingly uneventful. Voters seemed generally unaware of the ideological differences between Roosevelt and Wilson, and the election in the end reflected traditional party divisions.

From the beginning, it was a three-candidate election but a two-candidate campaign. William Howard Taft, resigned to defeat, delivered a few desultory, conservative speeches and then lapsed into silence. "There are so many people in the country who don't like me," he sadly explained. Roosevelt campaigned energetically (despite a gunshot wound from a would-be assassin that forced him to the sidelines during the last weeks before the election), and he continued to generate excitement among his Republican followers. He failed, however, to draw any significant numbers of Democratic progressives away from Wilson, who as the campaign wore on was beginning to evoke an enthusiastic national following of his own. The results in November were, therefore, predictable. Roosevelt and Taft split the Republican vote; Wilson held onto the Democratic vote and won. He polled only a plurality of the popular vote: 42 percent, to 27 percent for Roosevelt and a dismal 23 percent for Taft. In the electoral college, however, he produced a landslide: 435 of the 531 votes. Roosevelt had carried only six states, Taft only

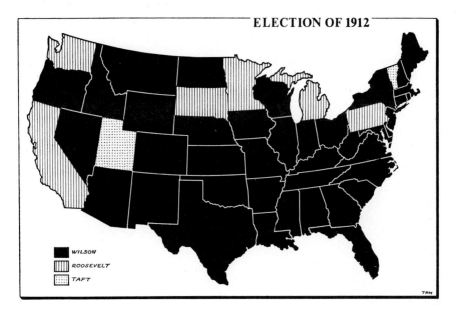

two. It was an impressive mandate for reform. Taft, the only conservative in the race (and even he could make some claim to progressivism), had received less than a quarter of the vote. Nearly 70 percent of the electorate had supported spokesmen for progressive change. Woodrow Wilson entered the presidency with the forces of reform, which had been gathering strength for almost two decades, at the peak of their power.

SUGGESTED READINGS

The standard biography of Taft is Henry F. Pringle's two-volume *The Life and Times of William Howard Taft* (1939), which contrasts its subject favorably with Theodore Roosevelt. Studies of Taft's presidency include Paolo E. Coletta, *The Presidency of Taft* (1973); Norman Wilensky, *Conservatives in the Progressive Era* (1965); and Donald E. Anderson, *William Howard Taft* (1973), which applies a political-science model developed by Richard Neustadt to the Taft administration and finds Taft wanting. The acrimonious Pinchot–Ballinger controversy receives discussion in James L. Penick, *Progressive Politics and Conservation* (1968), and Harold T. Pinkett, *Gifford Pinchot: Private and Public Forester* (1970). For the foreign policy of the Taft years, consult— in addition to the volumes listed at the end of Chapter 4—Walter Scholes and Marie Scholes, *The Foreign Policies of the Taft Administration* (1970). The Republican rift of 1912 is chronicled in George Mowry's *Theodore Roosevelt and the Progressive Movement* (1946).

Six

Progressivism Triumphant

The administration of Woodrow Wilson ended unhappily, both for the President and for the nation. It began, however, in triumph. For nearly five years, until international responsibilities turned his attention elsewhere, Wilson served as the most successful leader of domestic reform of his era. Under his guidance, a remarkable proportion of the progressive agenda was enacted into law. Because of Wilson's political skill, the federal government moved far toward becoming what many reformers had long advocated: a powerful instrument of economic and social control. It was ironic, perhaps, that Wilson, who had campaigned in 1912 in opposition to Theodore Roosevelt's overbearing nationalism, should have become the instrument for completing much of Roosevelt's program. In the flush of the moment, however, few progressives noticed the irony. If Wilson had not become precisely the kind of leader he had promised, he had become exactly the sort of leader for which most reformers had been waiting.

SHAPING THE MODERN STATE

Wilson brought to the White House a conception of the presidency based on long years of scholarly study. His first published book, *Congressional Government* (1898), expressed what remained a lifelong admiration for the British parliamentary system and a belief in its adaptability to American institutions. In his later writings, however, he began to display more interest in the possibilities of presidential leadership. "His is the only voice in national affairs," he wrote of the President only four years before he himself assumed the office. His must therefore be the voice of popular aspirations, the hand that guides public demands into legislative realities.

WOODROW WILSON.   Later generations remembered Wilson for his high idealism and his international vision. To his contemporaries, however, he was at least equally notable for his lack of personal warmth, his frequent unwillingness to compromise, and his tendency to interpret political disagreements as moral conflicts. One of the most successful domestic reformers in American history, he suffered political and personal catastrophe during his relentless fight to win ratification for the Treaty of Versailles. (*National Archives*)

More than William Howard Taft, therefore, more even than Theodore Roosevelt, Wilson concentrated the powers of the executive branch in his own hands. He exerted firm control over his cabinet, and he delegated real authority only to those whose loyalty to him was beyond question. Perhaps the clearest indication of his style of leadership was the identity of the most powerful figure in his administration: Colonel Edward M. House, a man whose only claim to authority was his personal intimacy with the President. Holding no office, attracting little public renown, House nevertheless wielded broad powers on behalf of the President. "He can walk on dead leaves and make no more noise than a tiger," one contemporary noted. That was just what the President wanted. Wilson had little patience with those who attempted to establish an authority within his administration independent of him.

In his dealings with Congress, Wilson viewed himself as the natural leader of the legislative process. It was up to the President to initiate important legislation; it was up to the President to use his powers to guide it to passage. Wilson was not a natural politician, and he often seemed uncomfortable in the presence of those who were. He was, however, unusually adept at using his position as head of his party to pressure and cajole members of Congress into supporting his positions. In his distribution of patronage, he rejected the demands of some reformers that he ignore conservative Democrats and reward progressive ones. Instead, he used his appointive powers to weld together a coalition of conservatives and progressives who would, he believed, support his program. His task was eased, of course, by the existence of Democratic majorities in both houses of Congress and by the realization of many Democrats that the party must enact a progressive program in order to maintain those majorities. But it was Wilson's skillful use of the presidency that provided the most important instrument of reform.

Tariffs and Taxes

Wilson's first triumph as President was the fulfillment of an old Democratic and progressive promise—a substantial lowering of the protective tariff. Roosevelt had avoided the issue; Taft had failed at it. Wilson moved quickly and forcefully to succeed. On the day he took office, he called a special session of Congress. And when it met, he did what no President since Jefferson had done: he appeared before it in person. In a short, graphic message aimed less at the Congressmen than at their constituents, he brought to a blaze the rising public sentiment for genuine tariff reform. With the President's active support, Representative Oscar W. Underwood introduced a bill in the House providing for tariff cuts substantial enough to bring European manufacturers into competition with Americans and thus, progressives hoped, to help break the power of the trusts. Like earlier tariff bills, the Underwood-Simmons tariff, as it became known, passed easily in the House. Unlike earlier bills, however, it survived as well the efforts of conservative Senators to weaken it. Wilson's forceful exercise of party powers mobilized virtually the entire Democratic majority behind it. The law as Wilson finally signed it lowered tariff rates an average of about 8 percent and added many imports to the free list. The economic upheavals of war came too soon to allow the bill to prove the boasts of its supporters that it would lower the cost of living without damaging the health of business. The measure did, however, demonstrate conclusively that the Democrats could unite to enact against great hazards a significant piece of reform legislation.

To make up for the loss of revenue under the new tariff, Representative Cordell Hull of Tennessee drafted an amendment to the bill providing for a graduated income tax, which the recently adopted Sixteenth Amendment to the Constitution now permitted. Hull cautiously set the rates exceedingly low. To his delight, however, progressive Republican and Democratic Senators united to force them substantially higher. This first modern income tax imposed a 1 percent tax upon individuals and corporations earning over $4,000, with rates ranging up to 6 percent on incomes over $500,000. It was the beginning of a fundamental change in the American tax structure, which would slowly shift a proportionately greater share of the cost of government to the wealthy.

Banking Reform

Rather than lose momentum, President Wilson held Congress in session through the sweltering summer to begin work on a major reform of the American banking system. "The great monopoly in this country," he had declared in 1911, "is the money monopoly. So long as that exists, our old variety and freedom and individual energy of development are out of the question." Few progressives would have disagreed. Yet there were apparently conflicting explanations of the nature of the problem, and there were wide differences of opinion about how best to attack it. Wilson attempted to construct a compromise that would reconcile the contending camps.

One of the leading criticisms of the banking system was that it was excessively centralized, that too much control resided in the hands of a few powerful men. Thus it was that the conclusions of a House investigating committee chaired by Arsene Pujo, a Louisiana Democrat, found a ready audience when they were released early in 1913. The committee's figures, widely publicized in Louis Brandeis's *Other People's Money* of the same year, indicated that small banks were depositing their surpluses with larger ones, which were in turn depositing with a few great investment banks on Wall Street. The result was that a small number of men controlled the aggregate savings of millions. They were thus able to dominate the nation's corporations in return for granting them financing, "the lifeblood of business." The Morgan-Rockefeller empire, the Pujo Committee reported, held "in all, 341 directorships in 112 corporations having aggregate resources or capitalization of $22,245,000,000," or more than 10 percent of the entire estimated national wealth. As one railroad president remarked in 1905, "Wherever Morgan sits on a board is the head of the table, even if he has but one share."

The second criticism of the banking system was, paradoxically, that it was excessively decentralized. Because so many banks were small and independent, because they had no larger resources upon which to draw except for the distant and often inaccessible urban clearinghouses, there was a serious weakness in the nation's financial structure at the local level. Independent banks lacked sufficient funds to provide needed credit in agricultural areas, and they were particularly vulnerable to failure in times of economic distress, as the Panic of 1907 had illustrated. There was no way to expand the supply of currency in regions where money was scarce or to shift assets to areas afflicted by financial crisis. Any reorganization of the banking structure, most reformers recognized, must provide some central assistance for the imperiled local institutions.

The two concerns were not, in fact, as incompatible as they seemed. Indeed, the problems fed upon and reinforced each other. The centralization of capital in New York had made it impossible for strong regional banks to emerge, leaving local banks dispersed and without assistance. Nevertheless, reformers disagreed strongly about how to deal with this dual problem, and Wilson faced a formidable task in satisfying all factions. In particular, he faced the problem of reconciling two views of the role of government in a new financial system. Some legislators, of whom Representative Carter Glass of Virginia was one, wanted to decentralize control of the banking system but leave ultimate authority over it with the bankers themselves. Others, whose hatred of the "money trust" was more intense—for example, William Jennings Bryan and fellow agrarians—wanted firm government control. After consultation with Louis Brandeis, Wilson accepted a plan that would place a central supervisory board, overseeing the entire system, in the hands of the government, while maintaining banker control of boards at the regional level. With Bryan mediating and Wilson brandishing every presidential power in his arsenal, the measure passed both houses of Congress and was signed by the President on December 23, 1913. It was the most important piece of domestic legislation of Wilson's administration and one of the most important in several decades.

The Federal Reserve Act created twelve regional banks, each to serve and to be owned and controlled by the individual banks of its district. The Federal Reserve banks would hold a certain percentage of the assets of their member banks in reserve; they would use those reserves to support loans to private banks at an interest (or "discount") rate that the Federal Reserve system would set; they would issue a new type of paper currency—Federal Reserve notes—which would become the nation's basic medium of trade and be backed by the government. Most importantly, perhaps, they would serve as central institutions able to shift funds quickly to troubled areas, to meet increased demands for credit or to protect imperiled banks. Supervising and regulating the entire system was a Federal Reserve Board, whose members were appointed by the President. All national banks were required to join the system; smaller banks were encouraged to do the same. Within a year, nearly half the nation's banking resources were represented in the system; by the late 1920s, the proportion had swelled to 80 percent. Although the American Bankers' Association had strenuously opposed the legislation (fearing government control of their operations), financiers soon found they had little cause for alarm. The Federal Reserve Board, to which Wilson appointed conservative men sympathetic to the bankers' views, looked, one progressive Senator complained, as though the president of the National City Bank had selected its members.

For all its limitations, and there were many, the Federal Reserve Act marked a notable advance in American banking practices, historically among the least stable and efficient in the Western world. The new system provided a more elastic currency, enabling bankers to loan money more easily to farmers and to deal more readily with national financial crises. It contributed to, although it did not approach the completion of, a decentralization of the nation's capital. And it provided the government, through the Federal Reserve Board, with a powerful instrument of economic influence—although it was not until many years later that economists recognized the power that control over the money supply provided. The Great Depression of the 1930s would prove that, despite these changes, the American banking structure remained weak and inadequate; but the Federal Reserve Act was an important first step toward the stabler system that ultimately emerged.

The Problem of the Trusts

The cornerstone of Wilson's campaign for the presidency had been his promise to attack economic concentration, most notably to destroy monopolistic trusts. By the beginning of his second year in office, however, it was becoming clear that his thinking had changed significantly. Increasingly he moved away from his earlier insistence that government dismantle the combinations and toward a commitment to regulating them. On this issue, at least, the New Freedom was giving way to the New Nationalism. Wilson's attitude toward two major pieces of economic legislation symbolized the trend. When in 1914 he began to promote a sweeping plan to deal with the problem of monopoly, two elements emerged at its core. There was a proposal to create a federal agency through which the government would help business police itself—in other words, a regulatory commission of the type Roosevelt had advocated in 1912. There were, in addition, proposals to strengthen the government's power to prosecute and dismantle the trusts—a decentralizing approach more characteristic of Wilson's campaign. The two measures took shape, ultimately, as the Federal Trade Commission Act and the Clayton Antitrust Act.

Wilson fought hard for the Federal Trade Commission Act, which created a regulatory agency of the same name, and he signed it happily when it arrived at the White House. The new commission would, he promised, remove "uncertainty" within the corporate community, allowing businesses to determine in advance whether their actions would be acceptable to the government. It would also have authority to launch prosecutions against "unfair trade practices," which the law did not define, and it would have wide power to investigate corporate behavior. The act, in short, increased the government's regulatory authority significantly. At the same time, Wilson gradually lost interest in the Clayton Antitrust Act and showed a notable lack of vigor in fighting to protect it from conservative assaults. When its opponents in Congress so weakened the bill that progressives complained it lacked enough teeth to masticate milk toast, Wilson did little to strengthen it. When it failed to include any binding guarantees that it would not be used, as earlier antitrust laws had been, as a weapon against unions, Wilson did nothing to change it. Nevertheless, when the emasculated bill finally reached his desk, he lauded it as a major accomplishment. In fact, like the Sherman Antitrust Act before it, this legislation proved to be almost impotent as a weapon against the trusts but a stout club against striking or boycotting unions.

Nor did Wilson act very forcefully within the executive branch to prosecute the trusts. The relative ineffectiveness of the new Federal Trade Commission—to which Wilson appointed men so inept or so sympathetic to the trusts they were supposed to regulate that Brandeis once dismissed them as useless and "stupid" —did nothing to renew his animosity toward monopoly. And the Justice Department remained less than aggressive in its pursuit of illegal combinations. Attorney General James C. McReynolds, who had served in the Roosevelt administration, announced that large corporations doubtful about the legality of their practices could avoid lawsuits if they would straighten their affairs out quietly with the assistance of the government. He managed as a result to win consent decrees from several large combinations, which divested themselves of important acquisitions. But the vigorous legal pursuit of monopoly that Wilson had promised in 1912 never materialized. The future, he had apparently decided, lay with governmental supervision. Economic concentration would survive.

Retreat and Advance

By the fall of 1914, Wilson believed that the program of the New Freedom was essentially complete and that the agitation for reform would now subside. As a result, he himself began a conspicuous retreat from political activism. Citing the doctrine of states' rights, he declined to support the movement for woman suffrage. Accepting the inclinations of the many southerners in his cabinet, he condoned the reimposition of segregation in the agencies of the federal government (a sharp contrast to Theodore Roosevelt, who had ordered the elimination of many such barriers and even taken the unprecedented step of inviting a black man—Booker T. Washington—to the White House). When congressional reformers attempted to enlist his support for new social legislation, he breezily dismissed their proposals as unconstitutional or unnecessary.

The President's complacency could not, however, long survive the congressional elections of 1914. It was disturbing enough that Democrats suffered major losses in the House of Representatives. But it was even more alarming that voters who had in 1912 supported the Progressive party were returning in droves to the Republicans. Wilson would not be able to rely on a divided opposition when he ran for reelection in 1916; he would need more than his 1912 total of 42 percent of the vote, and he would need the support of some of Theodore Roosevelt's former constituency to get it.

By the end of 1915, therefore, Wilson had shed his lethargy and begun to support a second flurry of reforms. In January 1916, he appointed Louis Brandeis to the Supreme Court, making him not only the first Jew but the most advanced progressive to be so named; and he weathered a conservative uproar in the Senate to obtain Brandeis's confirmation. Later, he supported a measure to make it easier for farmers to receive credit and one creating a system of workers' compensation for federal employees. But the real significance of this renewed effort at reform was that Wilson seemed now to have capitulated to the New Nationalism almost entirely; indeed, he had moved beyond it. No longer were there appeals for the restoration of a competitive, decentralized economy. No longer were there warnings about excessive federal power. Instead, Wilson was sponsoring measures that expanded the role of the national government in important ways, giving it new instruments by which it could not only regulate the economy but help shape the economic and social structure itself.

In 1916, for example, Wilson supported the Keating-Owen Act, the first federal law regulating child labor. It was important not only for the problem it addressed but for the means it adopted. The measure prohibited the shipment of goods produced by underage children across state lines, thus giving a new and greatly expanded importance to the constitutional clause assigning Congress the task of regulating interstate commerce. (It would be some years before the Supreme Court would uphold this interpretation of the clause—the Court invalidated the Keating-Owen Act in 1918—but an important precedent for future federal efforts had been established.) The President similarly supported measures that used federal taxing authority as a vehicle for legislating social change. When the Court struck down Keating-Owen, a new bill attempted to achieve the same goal by imposing a heavy tax on the products of child labor. (The Court later struck it down too, but not before yet another important instrument of federal power— the use of the tax codes to induce social change—had been born.) The government's spending authority likewise became an instrument of social control. The Smith-Lever Act, for example, had as early as 1914 offered matching federal grants to states that agreed to support agricultural extension education, a mechanism that would help undermine the autonomy of state governments. Other measures extended the process further: the Smith-Hughes Act of 1917 subsidizing vocational courses in secondary schools; and the Federal Highway Act of 1916, appropriating $75 million to help finance road construction. Functions traditionally performed by states and localities—education, roadbuilding, and others—would now increasingly receive financial support from Washington. The federal government, thereby, would increase its influence over such functions.

Having won a mandate for the New Freedom in 1912, Wilson had by the end of his first term made remarkable strides toward enacting the program of the New Nationalism. He had dramatically expanded the role of the federal government in American society, helping to make it the efficient, centralized regulatory mechanism that Roosevelt and others had long advocated. He had accepted the importance of orderly bureaucratic procedures and enlightened expertise in governing an industrial society, and he had backed away from the vision of a nation liberated from centralized controls. It was not, as one conservative Congressman charged, "the first step away from the old democracy of Thomas Jefferson . . . to the socialism of Karl Marx." But it was an important step toward the creation of the modern state.

It was also virtually the last step in the long progressive campaign for social and economic reform. By the end of 1916, the nation's attention was turning elsewhere; and it would remain for later generations to deal with the problems that remained. They would discover that the progressive accomplishments, significant as they were, did not include any fundamental restructuring of the nation's economy. The corporate community had been forced to abandon some of its most

LOUIS BRANDEIS.
Brandeis was one of the most celebrated legal figures of his age. In the early years of the century, he became the leading spokesman for aggressive government efforts to decentralize economic power, helping to stimulate a debate that would rage for decades. Woodrow Wilson, who deeply admired Brandeis, appointed him to the Supreme Court in 1916, where he became the first Jewish Justice. For the next twenty-five years, he served as one of the Court's most influential members and was a major force for the protection of civil liberties. (*UPI*)

egregious abuses, but its essential power survived. Laborers had received protection from certain afflictions, but they continued to lack effective bargaining power and to receive far less than their proportional share of the national income. Farmers had received a modicum of additional security, but they remained painfully vulnerable to the fluctuations of a market they could not control. Others had fared even less well. Blacks and other minorities had been all but ignored; in many ways, in fact, their position had deteriorated. Urban immigrants had received only scant benefits; they remained, for the most part, isolated from and mistrusted by the bulk of the populace. For a while, it would be possible for many Americans to believe that the fundamental problems of their society had been solved. But the problems would resurface in agonizing form less than a generation later. Future reformers, at least, would be able to face them with a machinery of government that included some effective instruments of change.

DIPLOMACY AND MORALITY

"It would be the irony of fate," Woodrow Wilson remarked shortly before assuming the presidency, "if my administration had to deal chiefly with foreign affairs." It would also, as it turned out, be a tragedy. Wilson faced international challenges of a scope and gravity unmatched by any President before him; and he brought to his treatment of them not only remarkable vision but an often inflexible, even self-righteous morality that would ultimately destroy both him and many of the goals for which he fought. Although the true ordeal of Wilsonian diplomacy did not occur until after World War I, many of the qualities that would help produce it were evident in his foreign policy from his first moments in office.

Wilson was repelled by the crass materialism of Dollar Diplomacy, but he was far from uninterested in America's economic interests abroad. No less than Taft and Roosevelt, he was convinced that the nation's economy required foreign markets in order to survive. The problem, then, was to justify in nobler terms than those used by his predecessors the international actions necessary to secure those markets. Wilson had no difficulty finding the solution, for like many Americans his belief in the nation's economic needs was fused with a conviction that the United States possessed a triumphantly righteous political and economic system. Democracy and capitalism had not only produced a morally admirable society in America; they were essential for creating morally admirable societies abroad. If American intervention overseas was necessary to ensure orderly, constitutional procedures, then there should be no hesitation about resorting to it, even if it meant the use of military force. And if such intervention helped protect and expand the nation's economic interests as well, that should be no reason for shame. The ability of a foreign government to protect American interests within its borders was itself, Wilson believed, a crucial test of its moral legitimacy.

Armed with this powerful rationale (in which he, like many others, sincerely believed), Wilson brought to his conduct of foreign policy many of the same attitudes he brought to the domestic agenda. In particular, he sought new instruments by which the federal government could influence events overseas. The Federal Reserve Board, for example, worked to enhance the competitive position of American bankers attempting to make loans abroad. A new division within the Commerce Department actively assisted businessmen in making overseas investments. New legislation suspended the antitrust laws for businesses engaged in certain international efforts. In the end, however, the most powerful instrument of American foreign policy in the Wilson years was not any of these economic contrivances but the United States military.

Closed Doors

Through much of his administration, Wilson made strenuous but generally unsuccessful efforts to maintain an open door for American trade in China and to resist the expansion of Japanese influence in the Pacific. At the same time, however, the United States was itself working assiduously to close the door to all nations but itself in Latin America. Wilson presided over a foreign policy that not only continued but greatly increased American intervention in the Caribbean and in Latin America, justifying his actions by citing both economic necessity and moral imperative.

The list of American incursions was lengthy and impressive. Having already seized control of the finances of the Dominican Republic in 1905, the United States established a military government there in 1916 when the Dominicans refused to accept a treaty that would have made the country a virtual American protectorate. The military occupation lasted eight years. In Haiti, which shares the island of Hispaniola with the Dominican Republic, Wilson landed the Marines in 1915 to quell a revolution in the course of which a mob had torn an unpopular president limb from limb. American military forces remained in the country until 1934, and American officers drafted the new Haitian constitution adopted in 1918. When Wilson began to fear that the Danish West Indies might be about to fall into the hands of Germany, he bought the colony from Denmark and renamed them the Virgin Islands. Concerned about the possibility of European influence in Nicaragua, he signed a treaty with that country's government ensuring that no other nation would build a canal there and winning for the United States the right to intervene in Nicaragua's internal affairs to protect American interests. In one case after another, the United States was openly disregarding the national integrity of its neighbors, acting instead in response to what Wilson considered a higher mission: the creation of order and, not coincidentally, the protection of American markets and investments. The President had no doubt that the recipients of his attention would become stabler, more democratic nations as a result. In most cases, ultimately, he was wrong.

Mission in Mexico

It was in Mexico that Wilson's missionary view of America's role in the Western Hemisphere received its greatest test and suffered its greatest frustrations. For many years, under the benevolent auspices of dictator Porfirio Díaz, American businessmen had been establishing an enormous presence in Mexico, with investments totaling more than $1 billion. In 1910, however, the corrupt and tyrannical Díaz had been overthrown by Francisco Madero, who excited many of his countrymen by promising democratic reform but alarmed many American businessmen by threatening their investments in his country. With the approval of, among others, the American ambassador in Mexico, Madero was himself deposed early in 1913 by a reactionary general, Victoriano Huerta.

A relieved Taft administration prepared, in its last weeks in office, to recognize the new Huerta regime and welcome back a receptive environment for American investments in Mexico. Before it could do so, however, Huerta murdered Madero, producing horror and outrage around the world. Wilson, therefore, inherited a difficult and unresolved dilemma. But he displayed no hesitation in responding. He would never, he insisted, recognize Huerta's "government of butchers." (In so doing, Wilson added a new weapon to his foreign policy arsenal: never before had the United States withheld diplomatic recognition to signal disapproval of a regime.)

The problem dragged on for years. At first, Wilson hoped that simply by refusing to recognize Huerta he could help topple the regime and bring to power the opposing Constitutionalists, led by Venustiano Carranza. When Huerta established a full military dictatorship in October 1913, however, the President decided on a more forceful approach. First he pressured the British to stop supporting Huerta. Then he offered to send American troops to assist Carranza. Carranza, aware that such an open alliance with the United States would undermine his popular support in Mexico, declined the offer; but he did request and receive from Wilson the right to buy arms in the United States. Still the stalemate continued.

Finally, a minor naval incident provided the President with an excuse for more open intervention. In April 1914, an officer in Huerta's army briefly arrested several American sailors from the U.S.S. *Dolphin* who had gone ashore in Tampico. Although a superior officer immediately released them and apologized to the ship's commander, the American admiral, chafing from inaction, demanded that the Huerta forces fire a twenty-one-gun salute to the American flag as a public display of penance. The Mexicans refused. Wilson seized on the silly incident as a pretext for sending all available American naval forces into Mexican waters; and a few days later, anxious to prevent a German ship from delivering munitions to the Huerta forces, he ordered the navy to seize the Mexican port of Veracruz.

Wilson had envisioned a bloodless action, but he was not to have his way. In a clash with Mexican troops in the city, the Americans killed 126 of the defenders and suffered 19 casualties of their own. With the two nations at the brink of war, Wilson now drew back and began to look for alternative measures to deal with the crisis. His show of force, however, had in the meantime helped strengthen the position of the Carranza faction, which captured Mexico City in August and forced Huerta to flee the country. At last, it seemed, the crisis might find a solution.

It was not to be. Wilson reacted angrily when Carranza refused to accept American guidelines for the creation of a new government, and he briefly considered throwing his support to still another aspirant to leadership: Carranza's erstwhile lieutenant Pancho Villa, who was now leading a rebel army of his own. When Villa's military position deteriorated, however, Wilson abandoned the scheme and finally, in October 1915, granted preliminary recognition to the Carranza government. But by now the President had created yet another crisis. Angry at what he considered an American betrayal, Villa retaliated in January 1916 by taking sixteen Americans from a train in northern Mexico and shooting them. Two months later, he led his soldiers (or bandits, as the United States preferred to call them) across the border into New Mexico, where they murdered nineteen more Americans. His goal, apparently, was to destabilize relations between Wilson and Carranza and provoke a war between them, which might provide him with an opportunity to improve his own declining fortunes. He almost succeeded.

With the permission of the Carranza government, Wilson ordered General John J. Pershing to lead an American expeditionary force across the Mexican

PERSHING IN MEXICO.
General John J. Pershing's expedition into Mexico in 1916 ended in dismal failure. It did not, however, have any appreciable effect on Pershing's later military career; he went on to become the commander of American forces in World War I. But the Mexican fiasco may have served as evidence to Germany of America's lack of preparedness for war, thus encouraging the escalation of submarine warfare against neutral shipping. (*National Archives*)

border in pursuit of Villa. The American troops, during their 300-mile penetration of Mexico, were never able to manage a clash with Villa. They did, however, engage in two ugly skirmishes with Carranza's army, in which forty Mexicans and twelve Americans died. Again, the United States and Mexico stood at the brink of war. By now, however, Wilson's attention was turning to what he considered matters of greater importance in Europe; and he agreed, therefore, to the face-saving expedient of referring the dispute to an international commission, which debated for six months without agreeing upon a solution. In the meantime, Wilson was quietly withdrawing American troops from Mexico; and in March 1917, having spent four years of effort and gained nothing but a lasting Mexican hostility toward the United States, he at last granted formal recognition to the Carranza regime.

THE ROAD TO WAR

The Great War (as it was known to a generation unaware that another, greater war would soon follow) began modestly in August 1914 when Austria invaded the tiny Balkan nation of Serbia. Within weeks, however, it had grown into a widespread conflagration, engaging the armies of all the major nations of Europe and shattering forever the delicate balance of power that had maintained a general peace on the Continent since the early nineteenth century. Americans looked on with horror but also with a conviction that the conflict had little to do with them. They were wrong.

From the beginning, Woodrow Wilson's policy of maintaining American neutrality was based on a false premise. The United States had nothing at stake in this war, he told the nation. In fact, America had a great deal at stake, and as the war dragged on, that stake grew. The nation's economy was critically dependent upon trade with Europe; its shipping had long been dependent upon the maritime stability that the British navy had always provided; and as Europe's own industrial capabilities declined because of the fighting, the American economy roused itself from a recession by taking up the slack. The nation surely was not unaffected by the war. Neither would it long be able to remain uninvolved.

A False Neutrality

Wilson called on his countrymen in 1914 to remain "impartial in thought as well as deed." He himself, however, soon discovered that his own thoughts were far from neutral. Like many Americans of his background, he was a deep admirer of England—its traditions, its culture, its political system; almost instinctively, therefore, he attributed to the cause of the Allies (Britain, France, Italy, Russia) a moral quality that he denied to the Central Powers (Germany and the Austro-Hungarian Empire). More importantly, however, he soon recognized that economic realities made it essential for him to adopt one policy toward England and quite another toward Germany. The neutral rights that he so ardently sought to uphold included, among other things, the right of an impartial nation such as the United States to trade freely with both sides in the conflict. The British, whose control of the seas was their most effective weapon, refused to oblige. They clamped a naval blockade on Germany to prevent munitions and supplies—from neutrals as well as belligerents—from reaching the enemy. Wilson had two choices. He could preserve a genuine American neutrality by denouncing the blockade and imposing an embargo on trade with Great Britain; or he could accept the situation and allow trade with England to continue and trade with Germany to cease. Economic realities, combined with his own inclination to support the British, caused him to choose the latter. The United States could survive an interruption of trade with the Central Powers. It could not, however, easily weather an embargo on trade with the Allies as well, particularly when war orders from Britain and France jumped from $824 million in 1914 to $3.2 billion two years later. The war had produced the greatest economic boom in the nation's history, and no President could afford to destroy it for a matter of abstract principle.

By 1915, therefore, the United States had gradually transformed itself into the arsenal of the Allies. In the process, it had replaced its stance of genuine neutrality with something quite different. Americans would acquiesce quietly, or with feeble protests, in violations of their rights by the British, who periodically seized American ships suspected of carrying supplies destined for Germany. When Germany infringed on neutral rights, however, the response of the United States was harsh and unyielding. The Germans intensified that antagonism by resorting to a new and, in American eyes, barbaric tactic: submarine warfare. Unable to challenge British domination on the ocean's surface, Germany began early in 1915 to use the newly improved submarine to try to stem the flow of supplies to England.

Enemy vessels, the Germans announced, would be sunk on sight, prompting Wilson to declare that he would hold Germany to "strict accountability" for unlawful acts. A test of this pronouncement came only months later, when on May 7, 1915, a German U-boat (short for *Unterseeboot*, undersea boat) sank without warning the British passenger liner *Lusitania*, causing the deaths of 1,198 people, 128 of them Americans. The ship was, it later became clear, carrying not only passengers but munitions; at the time, however, the attack seemed to most Americans to be what Theodore Roosevelt called it: "an act of piracy."

Wilson reacted by initiating an angry exchange of notes with Germany, demanding assurances that such outrages would not reoccur and that the Central Powers would respect the rights of neutral nations, among which, he insisted, was the right of their citizens to travel on the nonmilitary vessels of belligerents. (After one particularly threatening such note, Secretary of State William Jennings Bryan —who argued that equally strenuous protests should be sent to the British in response to their blockade—resigned from office as a matter of principle, one of the few high government officials ever to do so.) The Germans finally agreed to

THE *LUSITANIA.*   The Cunard passenger liner *Lusitania* sailed from New York in the spring of 1915, despite a German warning that "vessels flying the flag of Great Britain, or any of her allies, are liable to destruction." On May 7, a German U-boat torpedoed a large ship off the coast of Ireland; as its bow went high in the air shortly before sinking, the U-boat commander read for the first time the name *Lusitania.* The British and American governments protested loudly against this attack upon an unarmed passenger ship. It later became clear, however, that the *Lusitania* had also been carrying munitions to the English. (*Brown Brothers*)

Wilson's demands, but a pattern of relations had been established that would increasingly bring the two nations into conflict. Early in 1916, American–German relations soured anew when, in response to an announcement that the Allies were now arming merchant ships to sink submarines, Germany proclaimed that it would fire on such vessels without warning. A few weeks later, it did just that, attacking the unarmed French steamer *Sussex* and injuring several American passengers. Again, Wilson demanded that Germany abandon its "unlawful" tactics; again, the German government relented. Lacking sufficient naval power to enforce an effective blockade against Britain, the Germans decided that the marginal advantages of unrestricted submarine warfare did not yet justify the possibility of drawing America into the war.

Preparedness Versus Pacifism

Despite the President's increasing bellicosity in 1916, he was still far from ready to commit the United States to war. One obstacle was American domestic politics. Facing a difficult battle for reelection, Wilson could not ignore the powerful factions that were continuing to insist upon peace. His policies, therefore, represented an effort to satisfy the demands both of those who, like Theodore Roosevelt, insisted that the nation defend its "honor" and economic interests and those who, like Bryan, La Follette, and others, denounced any action that seemed to increase the chance of war. Ranged on one side stood the American military establishment, painfully aware of how unprepared the nation was to fight a major war and adamant that a rapid build-up of its armed forces was essential; American business leaders, insisting that the government act forcefully to ensure that Germany did not interfere with trade with the Allies; and belligerent nationalists, who considered Wilson's policy of neutrality "cowardly" and "dishonorable." On the other side stood German-Americans, who sympathized with their homeland; Irish-Americans, who opposed any assistance to the hated British; large groups of farmers and workers, who saw the war as a battle for commercial and financial supremacy from which they stood to gain little; and a broad, diffuse group who opposed war on moral grounds or who viewed the conflict as antithetical to the progressive precepts around which American society had been shaping itself. The United States, they argued, should remain aloof from the "cesspool" of Europe.

The question of whether America should make military and economic preparations for war provided a preliminary issue over which the two coalitions could battle. Wilson at first sided with the antipreparedness forces, denouncing the idea of an American military build-up as needless and provocative. As tensions between the United States and Germany grew, however, he changed his mind. In the fall of 1915, he endorsed an ambitious proposal by American military leaders for a large and rapid increase in the nation's armed forces to cost more than half a billion dollars; and amid howls of outrage from pacifists in Congress and elsewhere, he worked hard to win approval of it. He even embarked on a national speaking tour early in 1916 to arouse support for the proposal. By midsummer his efforts had in large part succeeded, and rearmament for a possible conflict was well under way.

Still, the peace faction wielded considerable political strength. How much strength became clear to Wilson at the Democratic Convention that met to renominate him in the summer of 1916. The keynote speaker turned his address into a paean of praise for Wilson's efforts to avoid American intervention. He evoked a remarkable response. As he recited a litany of the President's diplomatic accomplishments, the delegates chanted again and again, "What did we do? What did we do?" And the speaker shouted in response, "We didn't go to war! We didn't go to war!" Out of that almost hysterical exchange came one of the most prominent slogans of Wilson's reelection campaign (although one that he himself never used or approved): "He kept us out of war."

In the face of such pressures, therefore, Wilson remained highly cautious. When prowar rhetoric became particularly heated, Wilson spoke defiantly of the nation being "too proud to fight." And when the Republicans chose as their 1916 presidential candidate Charles Evans Hughes, a progressive who attracted the support of the bellicose Theodore Roosevelt, Wilson did nothing to discourage those who argued that Hughes was more likely than he to lead the nation into war. At times, he issued such warnings himself. Wilson's promises of progressivism and peace ultimately combined to give the Democrats, once again a minority party against the reunited Republicans, a narrow victory in November. Wilson won reelection by one of the smallest margins in American history: fewer than 600,000 popular votes and only 23 electoral votes, with the Democrats retaining a precarious control over Congress.

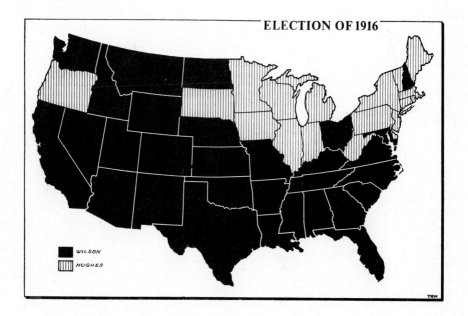

ELECTION OF 1916

WILSON
HUGHES

A War for Democracy

With the election behind him, and with tensions between the United States and Germany unabated, there remained for Woodrow Wilson a final obstacle to involvement in the world war. He required a lofty justification for American intervention, one that would not only unite public opinion but satisfy his own sense of morality. The Germans had gone far toward providing such a justification with their "barbaric" tactics on the seas and their alleged atrocities on land (including, as the American prowar press ardently reported, the use of poison gas and the senseless butchering of women and children). Wilson himself, however, created the most important rationale. The United States, he increasingly insisted, had no material aims of its own in the conflict. It was, rather, committed to using the war as a vehicle for constructing a new world order, one based on the same progressive ideals that had motivated reform in America. The United States, he maintained, could serve as a model and a guide to the Old World in building an international community founded upon democratic principles and governed by impartial commissions that would arbitrate disputes and prevent future conflicts. In a speech before Congress in January 1917, he presented a plan for a postwar order in which the United States would help maintain peace through a permanent league of nations—a peace that would include self-determination and equality for all nations, a "peace among equals," a "peace without victory." For a time, he hoped that he could achieve these goals by providing mediation to end the conflict. As the war dragged on, however, he became convinced that only by playing an active role in ending the fighting would the United States be able to exert its moral authority to shape the peace.

Thus it was that in the first months of 1917, when new provocations once again inflamed German–American relations, Wilson was at last ready to fight. In January, after months of inconclusive warfare in the trenches of France, the military leaders of Germany decided upon one last dramatic gamble to achieve a quick and decisive victory. They would launch a series of major assaults on the enemies' lines in France. At the same time, they would begin unrestricted submarine warfare in an effort to cut off vital supplies from Britain. The Allies would collapse, they hoped, before the United States had time to intervene. Beginning February 1, the German ambassador informed Wilson, U-boats would sink all ships, enemy and neutral alike, in a broad zone around the British Isles. If America chose to continue supplying the Allies, it would have to risk attack.

With that, the President recognized that war was inevitable; the only question remaining was to determine the appropriate time to declare it. Two additional developments helped clear the way. On February 25, the British turned over to him an intercepted telegram from the German foreign minister, Arthur Zimmermann, to the government of Mexico. It proposed that in the event of war between Germany and the United States, the Mexicans should join the struggle against the Americans. In return, they would regain their "lost provinces" to the north when the war was over. Widely publicized in the American press, the Zimmermann telegram inflamed public opinion and helped build up popular sentiment for war.

A second event, in March, provided Wilson with additional comfort. A revolution in Russia toppled the reactionary Czarist regime, which had been tottering ever since the Russo-Japanese War in 1905. A new, republican government took its place. The United States would now be spared the embarrassment of allying itself with a despotic monarchy. The war for a progressive world order could proceed untainted.

On the rainy evening of April 2, two weeks after German submarines had torpedoed three American ships, Wilson appeared before a joint session of Congress and spoke words that brought to an end the years of uncertain waiting:

> It is a fearful thing to lead this great peaceful people into war, into the most terrible and disastrous of all wars, civilization itself seeming to be in the balance. But the right is more precious than peace, and we shall fight for the things which we have always carried nearest our hearts—for democracy, for the right of those who submit to authority to have a voice in their own Governments, for the rights and liberties of small nations, for a universal dominion of right by such a concert of free peoples as shall bring peace and safety to all nations and make the world itself at last free.

The audience in the House chamber roared its approval. In Europe, the Allied nations rejoiced at their deliverance. Even some of Wilson's bitterest enemies, men such as Theodore Roosevelt and Henry Cabot Lodge, offered warm words of praise.

The sentiment for war was not, however, unanimous. For four days, amid cries

THE SINKING OF THE *ILLINOIS*.   The markings of the U.S.S. *Illinois* remain barely visible as the American warship sinks in the North Atlantic on March 18, 1917, victim of a German U-boat attack. The destruction of the *Illinois* was one of a series of crises in the early months of 1917 that culminated in the American declaration of war in April. (*U.S. Navy photo*)

of treason and cowardice, pacifists in Congress carried on their futile struggle. When the declaration of war finally passed on April 6, fifty Representatives and six Senators had voted against it. America was entering a new era, but it was doing so divided and fearful. And Woodrow Wilson, perhaps aware of the ordeal that lay ahead, returned to the White House after his dramatic war address and, according to one account, broke down and wept.

SUGGESTED READINGS

Arthur S. Link, long the nation's preeminent Wilson scholar, is the author of by far the most definitive and intelligent biography, although one that is not yet complete. The five volumes of his *Woodrow Wilson* (1947–1965) follow Wilson's life from birth to the American entrance into World War I. Link is also the author of *Woodrow Wilson and the Progressive Era, 1910–1917* (1954), a general history of the politics of that era, and of *Wilson the Diplomatist* (1957), a series of concise essays on his foreign policies. Other standard studies of Wilson include John Morton Blum, *Woodrow Wilson and the Politics of Morality* (1956), and Alexander George and Juliette George, *Woodrow Wilson and Colonel House* (1956), a psychoanalytic study of the careers of and the relationship between the two intimate friends. John Morton Blum's *Joseph Tumulty and the Wilson Era* (1951) explores the events of the Wilson administration through the career of the President's closest White House associate.

Wilson's foreign policy has spawned a particularly large literature. In addition to the Link essays, see Robert Freeman Smith, *The United States and Revolutionary Nationalism in Mexico, 1916–1932* (1972); David Healy, *Gunboat Diplomacy in the Wilson Era: The U.S. Navy in Haiti, 1915–1916* (1976); and Dana Munro, *Intervention and Dollar Diplomacy in the Caribbean, 1900–1914* (1964). For the story of American entry into World War I, see Ernest R. May, *The World War and American Isolation* (1959), for an excellent account of domestic attitudes. Ross Gregory, *The Origins of American Intervention in the First World War* (1971), and Daniel Smith, *Robert Lansing and American Neutrality* (1958), examine the diplomatic events leading to intervention.

Seven

America
and the World War

By its decision of April 1917, the United States had joined the most savage war in history. For two and a half years the fighting had dragged on, inconclusive, almost inconceivably murderous, engaging not only the armies of the contending nations but their civilian populations as well. It was the first truly "total" war, one that had pitted entire societies against one another and that had by 1917 left Europe decimated and on the brink of utter collapse. By the time of the Armistice, Germany had lost nearly 2 million soldiers in battle, Russia 1.7 million, France 1.4 million, Great Britain 900,000; and although precise figures were impossible to compile, it was clear that the toll of civilian lives, from afflictions directly and indirectly related to the war, was even higher. An entire generation of European youth was being slaughtered; centuries of social, political, and economic traditions were being eroded and destroyed.

For America, the war was the source of a very different experience. As a military struggle, it was brief, decisive, and without great cost; only 112,000 American soldiers died, half of them from disease rather than combat. Economically, it was the source of a great industrial boom, one that helped spark the years of prosperity that would follow. Socially and psychologically, however, the war was a severe, even a traumatic, strain—one that exposed how easily many of the progressive impulses of the preceding decades could be twisted to justify repression and intolerance. America in the war years was not just a nation in search of victory; it was a society in search of unity. And this latter search exposed both the extent and the limits of a generation of reform.

THE LANDSCAPE OF THE GREAT WAR.   The scarred French
countryside suggests the grinding, savage nature of combat in World War I.
American troops fought here in the vast Meuse-Argonne offensive of 1918, one
of the largest and costliest battles of the war. (*U.S. Signal Corps/National Archives*)

OVER THERE

Armies on both sides in Europe were decimated and exhausted by the time of
Woodrow Wilson's declaration of war. The German offensives of early 1917 had
failed to produce an end to the struggle; French and British counteroffensives had
accomplished little beyond adding to the appalling level of casualties. The ghastly
stalemate continued, and only the assistance of the United States appeared to offer
the Allies any hope of victory.

The Naval War

It had been the conflicts at sea that had brought the United States into the war;
and it was upon the naval struggle that American participation had the most
immediate effect. By the spring of 1917, Great Britain was suffering such vast
losses from attacks by German submarines—one of every four ships embarking
from British ports never returned—that its ability to continue ferrying vital
supplies across the Atlantic was coming into serious question. Within weeks of
joining the war, the United States had begun to alter the balance. A fleet of
American destroyers aided the British navy in its assault upon the U-boats; other
American warships escorted merchant vessels across the Atlantic; United States
assistance was crucial in sowing antisubmarine mines in the North Sea. The results
were dramatic. Sinkings of Allied ships had totaled nearly 900,000 tons in the
month of April 1917; by December, the figure had dropped to 350,000; by

October 1918, it had declined to 112,000. The flow of weapons and supplies from the United States to England and France continued; without it, the Allied cause would have been lost.

The Land War

At first, most Americans believed that this naval assistance was all that would be required of them. It soon became clear, however, that a major commitment of American ground forces would be necessary as well. Britain and France by 1917 had few reserves left from which to draw. Russia was in even direr straits; and after the Bolshevik Revolution in November 1917, the new government, led by Nikolai Lenin, negotiated a hasty and costly peace with the Central Powers. Battalions of German troops were now free to fight on the western front. It would be up to American forces to counterbalance them.

In 1917, however, those forces barely existed. The regular army was almost negligible, and little thought had been given to an effective method for expanding it. Theodore Roosevelt, old and ill, swallowed his personal hatred of President Wilson and visited the White House, offering to raise a regiment to fight in Europe. Others, similarly, urged an entirely voluntary recruitment process. The President, however, decided otherwise. Only a national draft, he insisted, could provide the needed men; and despite the protests of those who agreed with House Speaker Champ Clark that "there is precious little difference between a conscript and a convict," he won passage of the Selective Service Act in mid-May. The draft brought nearly 3 million men into the army; another 2 million joined various branches of the armed services voluntarily.

The engagement of these forces in combat was intense but brief. Not until the end of 1917 did the first members of the American Expeditionary Force, or AEF, as it was called, arrive in Europe. Not until the following spring were they there in significant numbers. Eight months later, the war was over. Under the command of General John J. Pershing, whose unhappy experience in Mexico only a year before had not diminished his military reputation, the fresh American troops first joined the existing Allied forces in turning back a series of new German assaults. In May, they assisted the French in repelling a bitter German offensive at Chateau-Thierry, near Paris. Six weeks later, the AEF helped turn away another assault, at Reims, further south. By July 18, the German advance had been halted; and for the first time in what seemed years, the Allies began a successful offensive of their own. On September 26, an enormous American fighting force began to advance against the Germans in the Argonne Forest, part of a grand, 200-mile attack that was to last forty-seven days. Over 1 million American soldiers took part in the assault, using more ammunition than the entire Union army had used in four years of the Civil War; and by the end of October, they had helped push the Germans back to their own border and had cut the enemy's major supply lines to the front.

Faced with an invasion of their own country, German military leaders now began to seek an armistice—an immediate cease-fire that would, they hoped, serve as a prelude to negotiations among the belligerents. Pershing wanted to drive on

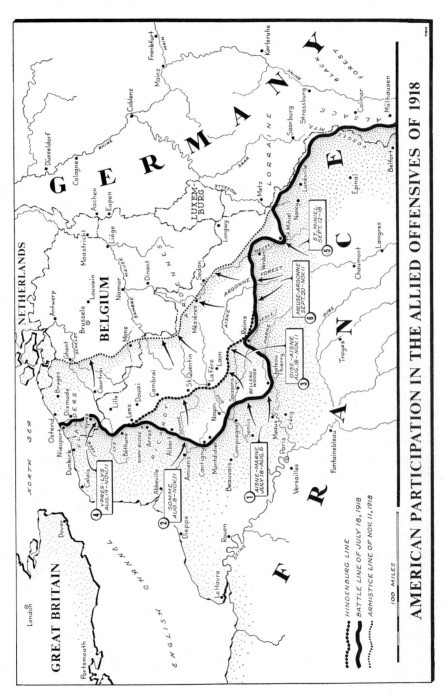

AMERICAN PARTICIPATION IN THE ALLIED OFFENSIVES OF 1918

into Germany itself; but other Allied leaders, after first insisting upon terms so stringent as to make the agreement little different in effect from a surrender, accepted the German proposal. On November 11, 1918, the Great War shuddered to a close. And American troops, having fought in it for only about six months of its four years, boasted proudly that it had been they who had won it. Whether or not the claim was militarily accurate, it was already clear that the United States was the only real victor in the conflict.

ORGANIZING FOR WAR

Back at home, in the meantime, the war was having profound economic and social effects. The conflict had begun to transform the American economy even before the United States joined the struggle. The demand for supplies by the Allies in Europe had created a booming prosperity; the preparedness drive had initiated a movement toward centralized organization. After the declaration of war, both the prosperity and the organization increased; and in the process, the American economy moved far toward becoming the consolidated, centrally directed instrument of which many progressives had long dreamed. At the same time, however, it was becoming clear that such organization could lead to results few progressives had foreseen.

Financing the War

Americans encountered many surprises in 1917. They were surprised when they learned that substantial American ground troops would be necessary in Europe. They were surprised when they discovered that a draft would be necessary to recruit them. And they were surprised above all when they learned how much the war was going to cost them. Many government officials had scoffed at early predictions that the United States would need to spend $10 billion before the fighting ceased; but it soon became clear that even that figure was preposterously low. Before it was over, the federal government had appropriated $32 billion for expenses directly related to the war.

To raise this sum, which by the standards of the time was astoundingly large, the government relied on two devices. First, it launched a major drive to solicit loans from the American people—"Liberty Bonds" they were called. By 1920, the sale of bonds, which was accompanied by a carefully orchestrated appeal to patriotic fervor, had produced $23 billion. At the same time, new taxes were bringing in an additional sum of nearly $10 billion—some of it from levies on the "excess profits" of corporations, much of it from new, steeply graduated income and inheritance taxes that ultimately rose as high as 70 percent in some brackets. There was one conspicuous loophole: many corporations stopped paying heavily taxed dividends to their stockholders and distributed shares of tax-exempt stock instead. Nevertheless, the nation financed the war by spreading the burden widely and reasonably efficiently. It was an experience that persuaded many Americans that major government spending could be accomplished without creating economic chaos.

MARCHING FOR LIBERTY LOANS. The war bond drives of 1917 and 1918 did more than help finance the American military effort. They provided an important vehicle for mobilizing popular enthusiasm for the war. This parade in New Orleans in October 1918 was part of the Fourth Liberty Loan drive, which set out to raise $6 billion shortly before the Armistice. Like earlier bond drives, the loan was oversubscribed. (*National Archives*)

The War Boards

An even greater challenge than raising the necessary funds was the task of organizing the nation's economy to ensure that war needs could be met. It was an undertaking that required an unprecedented degree of centralized regulation and control of American life, an undertaking for which neither the government nor the business sector, despite a generation of progressive reform, was prepared. As a result, much of the early planning fell almost by default into the hands of a small group of engineers and scientists. As early as the summer of 1916, the Civilian Advisory Commission, an offshoot of the new Council of National Defense, began to lay plans and propose techniques for the mobilization of the economy behind the war. Its members, disciples of the engineering gospel of Thorstein Veblen and the "scientific management" principles of Frederick Winslow Taylor, were committed to creating an efficient, rationalized society that reflected their own technocratic values. They urged organizing a series of planning bodies, each to supervise a specific sector of the economy. Thus one agency would control transportation, another agriculture, another manufacturing. Above all, the government would rely on a systematic, scientific use of statistics, modern procedures, and efficient administration. One planner said of William E. Coffin, an engineer influential in the early war efforts, that were he to talk in his sleep, his only words would be "Standardize! Standardize! Standardize!" The administrative structure that slowly emerged reflected many of the technocrats' assumptions, although it seldom worked as smoothly as they had envisioned. It also elevated one impulse of progressivism—efficiency—at the expense of another—the curbing of corporate power.

Shortly after the declaration of war, the Council of National Defense began creating a series of agencies to supervise those areas of the economy deemed vital to the war effort. A Railroad War Board, under the direction of Treasury Secretary William McAdoo, attempted to run the nation's major transportation resource as a single unified system. Using a half-billion-dollar budget for improving equipment and raising wages, McAdoo succeeded in untangling the flow of rail traffic and dramatically increasing the transport of goods to the East, where they could be shipped on to Europe. A new Fuel Administration was charged with allocating the increasingly scarce supplies of coal among the many contending groups seeking to buy it. By raising the price of coal to high levels, it stimulated increased production in what had earlier been only marginally profitable mines. Even so, the fuel shortage continued to intensify, forcing the agency to adopt even more drastic measures. Eastern industries were forced to endure several coal "holidays" early in 1918; some energy consumers were encouraged to forgo using coal altogether and convert to a newer, cheaper, and more plentiful fuel: oil.

Perhaps the most dramatically effective of all the new war agencies was the Food Administration, established under the Lever Act in August 1917 and headed by the brilliant young engineer and business executive Herbert Hoover. Hoover had supervised a spectacularly successful effort earlier in the war to provide food and relief to Belgium, which had been devastated by the German invasion. He brought the same administrative skills to bear on the far greater task of supervising the feeding of the nation, its armies, and its Allies—all of whom were becoming dependent upon the products of American agriculture. At one level, he attempted to increase supplies by encouraging voluntary conservation. Americans should, he announced, plant gardens, observe meatless and wheatless days, substitute plentiful for scarce foods, and cut waste. At the same time, he encouraged increased production of basic foodstuffs such as wheat by arranging for the government to purchase crops at high prices to stimulate farmers to plant as much as possible. Wheat acreage jumped from 45 million in 1917 to 75 million in 1919. Although Hoover avoided rationing and price controls, he worked diligently and effectively to prevent shortages and to keep prices from rising too quickly. Grocers were instructed, for example, to sell no more than two pounds of sugar a month to each customer. To a remarkable degree, these largely voluntary efforts succeeded, partly as a result of Hoover's effective mobilization of public opinion through the use of such slogans as "Food Will Win the War." The nation managed to supply many of the needs of Europe as well as to continue feeding itself; and Hoover emerged from the war as one of the most admired figures in the country.

Government, Industry, and Labor

At the center of the effort to rationalize the economy was the War Industries Board, an agency created in July 1917 to coordinate government purchases of military supplies. It was to become the central mechanism of control over the industrial sector. Casually organized at first, it stumbled badly until March 1918, when Wilson restructured it and placed it under the control of the Wall Street financier Bernard Baruch. From then on, the board wielded powers greater than any governmental agency had ever possessed. Baruch became, in fact, a virtual czar of American industry, using his position not only to coordinate the government's own purchases, but to direct industry itself in many of its most basic decisions. It was Baruch who decided which factories would convert to the production of which war materials; it was he who set prices for the goods that resulted; it was he who imposed standardized production procedures upon industries to increase the efficiency of their operations and to promote interchangeability of parts among their products. When materials were scarce, Baruch decided to whom they should go. When corporations were competing for government contracts, he chose among them. He had become, in some senses, the ultimate expression of the progressive ideals of the New Nationalism. He was providing the centralized regulation of the economy that many reformers had long urged.

There was, however, a crucial difference between Baruch's performance and the progressive ideal. Government regulation, as reformers had envisioned it, was to be disinterested. It was to mediate between the interests of the corporate community and those of the public at large. Baruch, in contrast, viewed himself, openly and explicitly, as the partner of business. Indeed, the relationship between the public and private sectors during the war was so warm and mutually supportive that to many people it began to seem as though the line between the two had all but dissolved. Baruch wielded his powers in constant consultation with the leaders of industry. He ensured that manufacturers coordinating their efforts in accord with his goals would be exempt from antitrust laws. He helped major industries earn enormous profits from their efforts. Steel manufacturers, for example, saw their prices rise 300 percent during a single year of the war. Corporate profits as a whole increased threefold between 1914 and 1919. Rather than working to restrict private power and limit corporate profits, as many progressives had urged, the government was working to enhance the private sector through a mutually beneficial alliance. Business itself, once antagonistic to the idea of any government interference, was beginning to see the advantages of having the state control competition and sanction what were, in essence, collusive arrangements. Having become the partner of private enterprise, the government stood only a few short steps away from becoming its agent.

This growing link between the public and private sectors—the beginning of what would later become known, both in America and in Europe, as corporatism —extended, although in greatly different form, to labor. The National War Labor Board, established in April 1918, served as a kind of supreme court for labor disputes. It pressured industry to grant important concessions to workers: an eight-hour day, the maintenance of minimal living standards, equal pay for women doing equal work, recognition of the right of unions to organize and bargain collectively. In return, it insisted that workers forgo all strikes and that employers not engage in lockouts. Samuel Gompers, president of the American Federation of Labor, sat on the board and supported its decisions; and he watched approvingly as membership in labor unions increased by more than 1.5 million between 1917 and 1919. Yet while labor accomplished more in two years of war than it had been able to do in decades of peacetime, its gains were meager in comparison with those of the corporations. The wage increases workers obtained were almost wiped out by wartime inflation. And many of the organizational gains of the trade unions would not long survive the Armistice.

The Results of Organization

Despite the enthusiasm with which government and business alike adopted their new, cooperative relationship, the material results were often disappointing. The proliferation of government agencies at times created more confusion than order. Bureaucracies occasionally contradicted one another in the directives they issued. Lines of authority were never entirely clear. And excessive regulation sometimes slowed, rather than enhanced, production. The federal government, lacking experience in large-scale planning, was finding that bureaucracies were more difficult to control in reality than they were in theory.

Nor did the planned economy always succeed in its ultimate goal: increasing production for war. There were spectacular accomplishments, of course: Hoover's efficient organization of food supplies, McAdoo's success in untangling the railroads, and others. In some areas, however, progress was so slow that the war was over before many of the supplies ordered for it were ready. The Aircraft Production Board, for example, had promised to deliver 22,000 new planes to the western front by July 1918. By the time the Armistice was signed, it had managed to produce only 1,185 of them. The Emergency Fleet Corporation, created to oversee production of a vast armada of merchant vessels, took more than a year to overcome the effects of its own incompetent management. By the end of the war, American shipbuilding facilities were beginning to produce new ships at a remarkable rate; but most were not completed in time to contribute to the war effort. Had the fighting continued another year, it is likely that the productive machinery the Wilson administration had so painstakingly constructed would have begun to accomplish great feats. As it was, the eighteen months of war were not enough time for the planned economy to learn to function with real efficiency. They were, however, enough to convince many leaders of both government and industry of the economic advantages of a close, cooperative relationship between the public and private sectors.

THE SEARCH FOR SOCIAL UNITY

The idea of unity—not only in the direction of the economy but in the nation's social purpose—had been the dream of many progressives for decades. To them,

THE FIRST WAR FREIGHTER, 1918.   An enthusiastic crowd watches the launching of the first freighter produced for the war at Hog Island, Virginia, in August 1918. The ceremony symbolized both the accomplishments and the limits of the war production effort. Even though the shipbuilding industry had adjusted quickly to meet the demands of war, the first new vessels were being completed only months before the end of the fighting. (*National Archives*)

the war seemed to offer an unmatched opportunity. At last, America was to close ranks behind a great and common cause. In the process, they hoped, society could achieve a lasting sense of mutual purpose. In fact, however, the search for unity that the progressives had so optimistically foreseen became an experience of ugly hysteria and bitter repression. American society remained divided, both in its attitude toward the war and in its larger political and social goals. And the attempt to impose unity on a diverse and contentious people became one of the most painful exercises in the nation's history.

Selling the War

Not long before he launched the United States into the war, Woodrow Wilson reportedly confided to a journalist:

> Once lead this people into war, and they'll forget there ever was such a thing as tolerance. To fight you must be brutal and ruthless, and the spirit of ruthless brutality will enter into the very fibre of our national life, infecting Congress, the courts, the policeman on the beat, the man in the streets.

His words became, in effect, a self-fulfilling prophecy; for it was the government itself that provided much of the impetus behind the "ruthless brutality" that Wilson purportedly feared. Government leaders were painfully aware of how deeply divided public opinion had been up to the moment of America's declaration of war. They knew, too, that many pacifists and isolationists remained opposed to United States participation even after that participation had begun. It was easy to argue, therefore, that a crucial prerequisite for victory was the uniting of public opinion behind the war effort. The government approached that task in several ways.

Most conspicuous was a propaganda campaign far greater than any the government had ever undertaken. It was, indeed, almost entirely without precedent. A Committee on Public Information (CPI), under the direction of journalist George Creel, supervised the distribution of innumerable tons of prowar literature (75 million pieces of printed material in all). War posters plastered the walls of offices, shops, theaters, schools, churches, homes. Newspapers dutifully printed official government accounts of the reasons for the war and the prospects for quick victory. Creel encouraged reporters to exercise "self-censorship" when reporting news about the struggle; and although many people in the press resented the suggestion, the veiled threats that accompanied it persuaded most of them to comply. The CPI employed more than 150,000 people to produce prowar propaganda or to disseminate government doctrine. Over 75,000 volunteers served as Public Information speakers, appearing at almost every conceivable public event to proselytize on behalf of the war.

The CPI attempted at first to distribute only the "facts," believing that the truth would speak for itself. As the war continued, however, their tactics became increasingly crude. Government-promoted films, at first relatively mild in tone, were by 1918 becoming vicious portrayals of the savagery of the Germans, bearing such titles as *The Prussian Cur*. CPI-financed advertisements in magazines appealed to citizens to report to the authorities any evidence among their neighbors of disloyalty, pessimism, or yearning for peace. Creel and his associates were not acting cynically or with deliberate viciousness; but their concern for social unity was producing dark and troubling excesses.

Legal Repression

The inflammatory propaganda of the CPI was perhaps the least damaging aspect of the government's campaign to win public support for the war. The Wilson administration soon began not only to encourage public approval but to suppress opposition. The Espionage Act of 1917 imposed heavy fines and stiff jail terms upon those convicted of spying, sabotage, or obstruction of the war effort. Those crimes were often broadly defined. The law also empowered the Postmaster General to ban from the mails any "seditious" material—an authority he exercised enthusiastically and often capriciously. Far more repressive, however, were two measures of 1918: the Sabotage Act of April 20 and the Sedition Act of May 16. These bills expanded the meaning of the Espionage Act to make illegal any public expression of opposition to the war; in practice, it allowed officials to prosecute those who criticized the President or the government in any way at all.

The most frequent target of the new legislation (and one of the reasons for its enactment in the first place) was the Socialist party and its radical offshoot, the Industrial Workers of the World (IWW). Unlike their counterparts in Europe, American socialists had not dropped their opposition to the war after their country had decided to join it; the impact of this decision upon them was devastating. Many Americans had favored the repression of socialists and radicals even before the war; now, the new government policies made it possible to move against them with full legal sanction. Eugene V. Debs, the humane leader of the party, a pacifist but no friend of Germany, was sentenced to ten years in prison in 1918. Only a presidential pardon ultimately won his release in 1921. The pursuit of other party leaders followed. Big Bill Haywood and members of the IWW were especially energetically prosecuted. Only by fleeing to the Soviet Union did Haywood avoid long imprisonment. In all, more than 1,500 people were arrested in 1918 for the mere act of criticizing their government.

Popular Repression

The federal government did its share to feed the hysteria of the war years, but it was not alone. State governments, local governments, corporations, universities, and above all the actions of private citizens contributed even more to the climate of repression. So obsessed did many Americans become with the need for uniform loyalty that they adopted heavy-handed, often extralegal, and occasionally violent methods to ensure it. Vigilante mobs seemed to spring up spontaneously to "discipline" those who dared challenge the war. Herbert S. Bigelow, a dissident Protestant clergyman in Cincinnati, was pulled from his bed one night by a mob, dragged to a nearby hillside, and whipped "in the name of the women and children of Belgium." Frank Little, an IWW organizer in Montana, was seized by a mob and hanged from a railroad bridge. More corrosive than these scattered episodes of brutality, however, were the actions of a cluster of citizens' groups that mobilized "respectable" members of their communities to root out disloyalty. The American Protective League, probably the largest of such groups, enlisted the services of 250,000 people, who served as "agents"—prying into the activities and thoughts of their neighbors, stopping men on the street and demanding to see their draft cards, opening mail, tapping telephones, and in general attempting to impose upon their communities the unity of opinion of a police state. Attorney General Thomas W. Gregory described them approvingly as a "patriotic organization" engaged in "assisting the heavily overworked Federal authorities in keeping an eye on disloyal individuals and making reports of disloyal utterances." Other vigilante organizations—the National Security League, the Boy Spies of America, the American Defense Society—performed much the same function.

The most frequent victims of such activities were immigrants, who had throughout the early decades of the century been a source of concern to much of American society. Now they became the targets of special abuse. "Loyal" Americans described immigrant communities as spawning grounds for radicalism. Vigilantes devoted special attention to immigrant groups suspected of sympathizing with the enemy. Irish-Americans faced constant accusations because of their historic animosity toward the British and because they had, before 1917, often expressed hopes for a German victory. Jews, who have often been among the first groups to suffer in periods of repression, aroused suspicion because many had expressed opposition to the anti-Semitic policies of the Russian government, until 1917 one of the Allies. Immigrant ghettoes were strictly policed by the "loyalist" citizens' groups. Even settlement workers, many of whom had once championed ethnic diversity, often contributed to their efforts. "We were stirred," one remarked, "to a new sense of responsibility for a more coherent loyalty—a vital Americanism."

The Ordeal of the German-Americans

The greatest target, perhaps the inevitable target, of abuse was the German-American community. Its members had unwittingly contributed to their plight; in the first years of the war in Europe, some had openly advocated American assistance to the Central Powers, and many had opposed United States intervention on behalf of the Allies. But while most German-Americans loyally supported the American war effort once it began, public opinion remained hostile. An almost maniacal campaign to purge society of all things German quickly gathered speed, at times assuming ludicrous forms. Sauerkraut was renamed "liberty cabbage." Hamburger became "liberty sausage." More often, however, the hostility took less innocent forms. Performances of German music were frequently banned; German books were removed from the shelves of libraries; courses in the German language were removed from school curricula. For Americans of German descent, more-over, life became a dangerous ordeal. Germans were routinely fired from jobs in war industries, lest they "sabotage" important tasks. Others were fired from positions entirely unrelated to the war; Karl Muck, the brilliant German-born conductor of the Boston Symphony Orchestra, was forced to resign his position and was interned for the last months of the war. Vigilante groups routinely subjected Germans to harassment and beatings; there was even a lynching—in southern Illinois in 1918. In Minnesota, a pastor was discovered whispering prayers at the bedside of a dying woman who spoke only German; because the minister was speaking in the woman's native tongue, he was tarred and feathered and driven out of town on a rail. Relatively few Americans favored such extremes, but many came to agree with the belief of the eminent psychologist G. Stanley Hall (the man responsible for the first visit of Sigmund Freud to America in 1909) that "there is something fundamentally wrong with the Teutonic soul."

The search for social unity had been a constant theme in the sprawling, hetero-geneous society of the United States for decades. As a part of the progressive movement, it had at times assumed a healthy form. But the war had perverted that quest and turned it to a harsher purpose. It was as if the nation—or at least a powerful segment of its population—had decided at last that diversity was an evil, that unity and conformity were essential to national survival, and that anyone out of step with the dominant culture was a threat to be suppressed or purged. It was not a bright chapter in the life of the nation, and it did not augur well for the years ahead.

PLANNING A NEW WORLD ORDER

It was ironic that in the midst of an unprecedented experience of hysteria and repression at home, the United States should be articulating a vision of a new international order based on lofty democratic principles. Woodrow Wilson had led the nation into war promising a more just and stable peace at its conclusion. Even before the Armistice, therefore, he was beginning preparations to lead the fight for a postwar settlement based on principle, not selfish nationalism.

It was, he realized from the beginning, a difficult task. America had barely joined the war when the new Bolshevik government in Russia began disclosing terms of secret treaties negotiated earlier among the Allies. Britain, France, and imperial Russia had already agreed, according to these reports, on how to divide the colonies of their enemies among them. To Wilson, such treaties ran counter to the idealistic vision for which he was exhorting Americans to fight. It was all the more important, he decided as a result, to build strong international support for his own war aims.

AN "ALIEN" IN CUSTODY. Dr. Ernst Kunwald, former conductor of the Cincinnati Symphony Orchestra, arrested as an enemy alien—one of many American citizens or residents of German ancestry persecuted during World War I as part of the crusade for "loyalty." (*National Archives*)

The Fourteen Points

On January 8, 1918, therefore, Wilson appeared before a joint session of Congress to present the principles for which he claimed the nation was fighting. The war aims fell under fourteen headings, widely known as the Fourteen Points; but their essential elements clustered in three major categories. First, Wilson's proposals contained a series of specific recommendations for adjusting postwar boundaries and for establishing new nations to replace the defunct Austro-Hungarian Empire, all reflecting his belief in the right of every people to self-determination. Second, it contained a set of general principles to govern international conduct in the future: freedom of the seas, open covenants instead of secret treaties, reductions in armaments, free trade, and impartial mediation of colonial claims. Finally, and most important of all to Wilson, there was a proposal for a league of nations that would help to implement these new principles and territorial adjustments, and serve to resolve future controversies. It would be, Wilson announced, "a general association of nations . . . formed under specific covenants for the purpose of affording mutual guarantees of political independence and territorial integrity to great and small states alike." Together, Wilson told the members of Congress, the Fourteen Points would help make the world "fit to live in."

There were serious flaws in Wilson's proposals, a result more of what they omitted than of what they contained. He provided no formula for deciding how to implement the "national self-determination" he promised for subjugated peoples. He made no mention of the new Soviet government in Russia, even though its existence had struck fear in the hearts of all Western governments. He said little about economic rivalries and their effect upon international relations, even though it had been just such economic rivalries that had been in large part responsible for the war. Nevertheless, Wilson's picture of the postwar world was the clearest and most eloquent expression of an international vision that would enchant not only much of his own generation but members of generations to come. It reflected his belief, strongly rooted in the ideas of progressivism, that the world was as capable of just and efficient government as were individual nations; that once the international community accepted certain basic principles of conduct, and once they constructed modern institutions to implement them, the human race could at last live in peace. The rule of law, he promised, would replace the rule of national passions and self-interested diplomacy.

The Fourteen Points came at a low moment in the war—before American troops had arrived in Europe in substantial numbers, at a time when many among the Allies believed the struggle might still be lost. It was greeted, therefore, with special yearning both in America and in Europe. The Allied leaders might have been cool toward the proposals, but there was an enthusiastic popular response among liberals, working people, and others throughout the world. Many Germans, too, welcomed the Wilsonian principles as a promise of a democratic postwar Germany that could assume a position of equality in the community of nations. The Fourteen Points were the most stirring and effective piece of propaganda the war produced.

Wilson was confident, as the war neared its end, that this popular support would enable him to win Allied approval of his peace plan. He seemed at times to expect virtually to dictate a settlement. There were, however, ominous signs, both at home and abroad, that his path might be more difficult than he expected. In Europe, leaders of the Allied powers were marshaling their energies to resist him even before the Armistice was signed. Most of them had resented, since the first days of the war, what they considered his tone of moral superiority. They had reacted unhappily when Wilson refused to make the United States their "ally," but had kept his distance as an "associate" of his European partners. They had been offended by his insistence upon keeping American military forces separate from the Allied armies they were joining. Most of all, however, Britain and France, having suffered incalculable losses in their long years of war, and having stored up an enormous reserve of bitterness toward Germany as a result, were in no mood for a benign and generous peace. They were determined to gain something from the struggle to compensate them for the catastrophe they had suffered.

At the same time, Wilson was encountering signs that he might also face problems at home. In 1918, with the war almost won, Wilson unwisely appealed to the American people to show their support for his peace plans by returning Democrats to Congress in the November elections. A Republican victory, he declared, would be "interpreted on the other side of the water as a repudiation of my leadership." Only days later, the Republicans captured majorities in both houses of Congress. Domestic economic troubles, more than international issues, had been the most important factor in the voting; but because of the President's ill-timed appeal, the results were interpreted both at home and abroad just as he had predicted: as a sign of his own political weakness. The election fiasco contributed as well to another dangerous development: Wilson's alienation of the leaders of the Republican party. They had been furious when he attempted to make the 1918 balloting a referendum on his war aims, especially since many Republicans had been loyally supporting the Fourteen Points. They grew angrier in the ensuing weeks at Wilson's increasing implications that only Democrats were committed to a just peace. And whatever ties may have remained between the President and the Republican party were all but severed when Wilson refused to appoint any leading Republicans to the negotiating team that would represent the United States in Paris, where a treaty was to be drafted. Although such men as Elihu Root and William Howard Taft had supported his war aims, Wilson named only one Republican—a little-known diplomat—to the group.

To the President, who was becoming almost obsessed with his own moral mission, such matters were unimportant. There would be only one member of the American negotiating team with any real authority: Wilson himself. And once he had produced a just and moral treaty, the weight of world and American opinion would compel his enemies to support him. Confident of his ability to create a new world, Woodrow Wilson stepped aboard the steamer *George Washington* and on December 3, 1918, sailed for Europe.

SUGGESTED READINGS

For the military history of the American experience in World War I, see Edward M. Coffman, *The War to End All Wars* (1969); Harvey A. De Weerd, *President Wilson Fights His War* (1968); A. E. Barbeau and Florette Henri, *The Unknown Soldiers: Black American Troops in World War I* (1974); and Russell Weigley, *The American Way of War* (1973). Frank Freidel's *Over There* (1964) is a pictorial history.

David M. Kennedy's *Over Here* (1980) offers the best analysis of the general impact of the war on American society. It should be supplemented with Robert D. Cuff, *The War Industries Board: Business–Government Relations During World War I* (1973), an excellent study of wartime industrial mobilization. George T. Blakey, *Historians on the Homefront* (1970), and J. R. Mock and Cedric Larson, *Words That Won the War* (1939), analyze wartime propaganda and public opinion. H. C. Peterson and Gilbert Fite, *Opponents of War, 1917–1918* (1957), examines dissent and civil liberties; while chapters in John Higham's *Strangers in the Land* (1955) discuss the effects of the war upon immigrant communities.

Eight

The Troubled Peace

It was to have been a "war to end wars," a war "to make the world safe for democracy." It became neither. Instead, World War I led directly to twenty years of international instability that would ultimately generate another great conflict.

It also propelled the United States into a position of almost unquestioned world supremacy. Alone among the great industrial nations, America had survived the fighting with its economy not only unscathed but strengthened. American military power had proved the equal of that of any other nation. While most of Europe began the difficult task of rebuilding after a four-year holocaust, the United States was poised for an era of growth and prosperity. Yet for the first few years following the Armistice, Americans found themselves generally unable to enjoy their triumph. They endured instead a cruel disillusionment, as the idealistic peace settlement for which they thought they had been fighting gradually unraveled and collapsed. They watched the searing personal tragedy of a President they had admired suffering first a political and then a physical and emotional ordeal that left him virtually incapacitated. And they suffered a period of social unrest and violence that helped shatter many of their progressive ideals.

THE LOST PEACE

Woodrow Wilson arrived in Europe in 1919 to a welcome such as few men in history have experienced. To the war-weary people of the Continent, he was nothing less than a savior, the man who would create a new and better world. And when he arrived in Paris on the afternoon of December 13, he saw clear evidence of their adulation in the form of the largest crowd in the history of France. "No one ever heard such cheers," wrote one journalist at the time. "I who heard them

. . . can never forget them in my life. I saw Foch pass, Clemenceau pass, Lloyd George, generals, returning troops, banners, but Wilson heard from his carriage something different, inhuman—or superhuman. Oh, the immovably shining, smiling man!" Said the Premier of France after the jubilant procession, "I do not think there has been anything like it in the history of the world." It was the kind of demonstration that Wilson believed would make it impossible for other world leaders to oppose his peace plans. The negotiations themselves, however, proved far less satisfying.

The Versailles Conference

The meeting at the Palace of Versailles to draft a peace treaty was almost without precedent, and it entailed a sizable risk. International negotiations had traditionally been the province of diplomats; kings, presidents, and prime ministers had generally avoided direct encounters. "Two great princes who wish to establish good personal relations," a fifteenth-century diplomat once wrote, "should never meet each other face to face but ought to communicate through good and wise ambassadors." At Versailles, there were not just two "great princes" meeting face to face, but four: David Lloyd George, the Prime Minister of Great Britain; Georges Clemenceau, the President of France; Vittorio Orlando, the Prime Minister of Italy; and Wilson, who hoped to dominate them all. Some of Wilson's advisers had warned him that if agreement could not be reached at the "summit," there would be nowhere else to go and that it would therefore be better to begin negotiations at a lower level. Wilson, however, was adamant; he alone would represent the United States.

From the beginning, Wilson's commitment to personal diplomacy encountered difficulties. Heads of state in the glare of world publicity were, he soon found, reluctant to modify their nations' demands. The atmosphere of idealism he had sought to create was, therefore, tinged with a spirit of national aggrandizement. There was, moreover, a pervasive sense of unease about the situation in eastern Europe, where starvation seemed imminent and the threat of communism menacing. Russia, whose new Bolshevik government was still fighting "White" counter-revolutionaries, was unrepresented; but the radical threat it seemed to pose to Western governments was never far from the minds of the delegates.

In this tense and often vindictive atmosphere, the Fourteen Points did not fare well. Wilson was unable to win approval of many of the broad principles he had espoused: freedom of the seas, which the British refused even to discuss; free trade; "open covenants openly arrived at" (the Versailles negotiations themselves were often conducted in secret). Despite his support for "impartial mediation" of colonial claims, he was forced to accept a transfer of German colonies in the Pacific to Japan, to whom the British had promised them in exchange for Japanese assistance in the war. His pledge of "national self-determination" for all peoples suffered numerous assaults. Italy, for example, obtained new territory in which 200,000 Austrians lived, and then expressed outrage at not also receiving the port of Fiume, which became part of the new nation of Yugoslavia. Poland received

THE "BIG FOUR" AT VERSAILLES.   Surface amiability disguised
growing tensions among the so-called Big Four, and particularly the growing
resentment of European leaders toward Woodrow Wilson's high moral
posture. From left to right are David Lloyd George of Great Britain,
Vittorio E. Orlando of Italy, Georges Clemenceau of France, and Wilson.
(*National Archives*)

a corridor to the sea which ran through territory that was ethnically German.
Economic and strategic demands were constantly coming into conflict with the
principle of cultural nationalism.

Where the treaty departed most conspicuously from Wilson's ideals was on the
question of reparations. As the conference began, the President was staunchly
opposed to exacting punitive damages from the defeated Central Powers. The
other Allied leaders, however, were intransigent, and slowly Wilson gave way.
Although he resisted the demand of the French government that Germany be
required to pay $200 billion to the Allies, he ultimately bowed to pressure and
accepted the principle of reparations, the specific sum to be set later by a commission. The final figure, established in 1921, was $56 billion, supposedly to pay for
civilian damages and military pensions. Although lower than some earlier demands, it was still far more than the crippled German economy could absorb. The
reparations, combined with other territorial and economic penalties constituted
an effort to keep Germany not only weak but prostrate for the indefinite future.

Never again, the Allied leaders believed, should the Germans be allowed to become powerful enough to threaten the peace of Europe.

Wilson did manage to win some important victories at Versailles. He secured approval of a plan to place many former German colonies in "trusteeships" to be supervised by the League of Nations—the so-called mandate system. He blocked a French proposal to break up western Germany into a group of smaller states, although in return he had to concede to France the disputed territory of Alsace-Lorraine and agree to a demilitarization and Allied occupation of the Rhineland. He oversaw the creation of the new nations of Yugoslavia and Czechoslovakia and the strengthening of Poland. Such accomplishments were of secondary importance to Wilson, however, when compared with his most visible triumph: the creation of a permanent international organization to oversee world affairs and prevent future wars. On January 25, 1919, the Allies voted to accept the "covenant" of the League of Nations; and with that, Wilson believed, the Treaty of Versailles was transformed from a disappointment into a success. Whatever mistakes and inequities had emerged from the peace conference, he was convinced, could be corrected later by the League.

The covenant provided for an assembly of nations that would meet regularly to debate means of resolving disputes and protecting the peace. Authority actually to implement League decisions would rest with a nine-member Executive Council; the United States would be one of five permanent members of the Council, along with Britain, France, Italy, and Japan. The covenant, like the larger treaty of which it was a part, left many questions unanswered, most notably how the League would enforce its decisions. Wilson, however, was confident that once established, the new organization would find suitable answers. The League of Nations, he believed, would become not only the centerpiece of the Treaty of Versailles, but the cornerstone of a new world order. Like other progressives considering other issues, the President was placing his hopes for the future in the process, rather than the substance, of international relations. If rational institutions could be established, then the actual conduct of world affairs would become rationalized as well.

The Battle for Ratification

Wilson was well aware of the political obstacles awaiting him at home. Many Americans, accustomed to their nation's isolation from Europe, questioned the wisdom of this major new commitment to internationalism. Others had serious reservations about the specific features of the treaty and the covenant. On a brief trip to Washington in February 1919, during a recess in the peace conference, the President listened to harsh objections from members of the Senate and others; and although he reacted angrily and haughtily to his critics, he returned to Europe and insisted upon certain modifications in the covenant to satisfy them. The amendments provided that a nation need not accept a mandate (responsibility for overseeing a League territory) against its will, that a member could withdraw from the organization with two years' notice, and that the League would not infringe upon the Monroe Doctrine. Beyond that, however, Wilson refused to go. In particular, he refused to ask for modifications in Article 10, the collective security clause, which had aroused the most opposition in Washington. When Colonel House, his close friend and trusted adviser, told him he must be prepared to compromise further, the President retorted sharply: "I have found that you get nothing in this world that is worth-while without fighting for it."

How bitter that fight would be soon became clear, for there was ample inflexibility and self-righteousness on both sides of the conflict. Wilson presented the treaty to the Senate on July 10, 1919, asking: "Dare we reject it and break the heart of the world?" In the weeks that followed, he consistently refused to consider even the most innocuous compromise. (His deteriorating physical condition—he was suffering from hardening of the arteries and had apparently experienced something close to a stroke in Paris—may have contributed to his intransigence.) The Senate, in the meantime, was raising a host of objections to the treaty. For the fourteen so-called "irreconcilables"—western progressives who included Hiram Johnson, William Borah, and Robert La Follette—the Versailles agreement was totally unacceptable. The United States should never become embroiled in the sordid politics of Europe, they argued; not even the most generous compromise could have won their support for the League. Other opponents, with less fervent convictions, were more concerned with constructing a winning issue for the Republicans in 1920 and with embarrassing a President whom they had not yet forgiven for his political tactics in 1918. Most notable of these was Senator Henry Cabot Lodge of Massachusetts, the powerful chairman of the Foreign Relations Committee. A man of stunning arrogance and a close friend of Theodore Roosevelt (who had died early in 1919, spouting hatred of Wilson to the end), Lodge loathed the President with genuine, unrestrained passion. "I never thought I could hate a man as I hate Wilson," he once admitted. He used every possible tactic, therefore, to obstruct, delay, and ultimately, he hoped, defeat the treaty. Public sentiment clearly favored ratification, so Lodge at first could do little more than play for time. When the document reached his committee, he spent two weeks reading aloud each word of its 300 pages; then he held six weeks of public hearings to air the complaints of every disgruntled minority (Irish-Americans, for example, angry that the settlement made no provision for an independent Ireland). Gradually, Lodge's general opposition to the treaty crystallized into a series of "reservations," amendments to the League covenant limiting American obligations to the organization.

Wilson might still have won approval at this point if he had agreed to some relatively innocuous changes in the language of the treaty. But the President refused to yield. The United States had a moral obligation, he claimed, to respect the terms of the agreement precisely as they stood; in particular, the nation had a moral responsibility to accept the controversial Article 10, which Wilson considered the heart of the covenant. When one Senator warned him that his position was becoming hopeless, that he would have to accept some of the Lodge reservations to have any hope of victory, Wilson retorted: "Never! Never! . . . I'll appeal to the country!"

A COMMENT ON THE RATIFICATION FIGHT. This savage characterization of the partisan opposition to the Treaty of Versailles may not have been fair to all the Senate Republicans opposing ratification. But personal hatred of Woodrow Wilson was a powerful factor in shaping the course of Senator Henry Cabot Lodge, the most important opposition leader. Lodge and Theodore Roosevelt had met frequently during the last months of the former President's life to encourage each other in their deep contempt for Wilson. Lodge reportedly believed that he himself should have been elected President in 1916 and may have resented Wilson even more as a result. (*Library of Congress*)

The Trials of Woodrow Wilson

What followed was a political disaster and a personal tragedy. Against the stern warnings of his physician, Wilson decided to embark on a grueling, cross-country speaking tour to arouse public support for the treaty. For more than three weeks, he traveled by train from city to city, covering more than 8,000 miles, writing his own speeches as he went along, delivering them as often as four times a day, an hour at a time. He received little rest. In the beginning, the crowds were small and the speeches clumsy. As the tour progressed, however, both the size and the enthusiasm of the audiences grew; and Wilson's own eloquence and moral fervor increased. Had it been possible to sway the Senate through public opinion, the tour might have been a success. But it had long ago become plain that the opposition in Washington had little to do with popular sentiment. So the tour was not only an exhausting ordeal for Wilson but a futile one as well.

Finally, the President reached the end of his strength. After speaking at Pueblo, Colorado, on September 25, he collapsed with severe headaches. Canceling the rest of his itinerary, he rushed back to Washington, where, a few days later, he suffered a major stroke. For two weeks, he was close to death; for six weeks more, he was so seriously ill that he could conduct virtually no public business. His wife and his doctor formed an almost impenetrable barrier around him, shielding the President from any official pressures that might impede his recovery, preventing the public from receiving any accurate information about the gravity of his condition. When officials tried to bring important matters to the attention of the President, Mrs. Wilson turned them away. "I am not interested in the President of the United States," she explained. "I am interested in my husband and his health."

Wilson ultimately recovered fully enough to resume a limited official schedule, but he was essentially an invalid for the eighteen remaining months of his presidency. His left side was partially paralyzed; more importantly, his mental and emotional state was precarious and unstable. Like many stroke victims, he found it difficult to control his feelings, often weeping at the slightest provocation. And his condition only intensified what had already been his strong tendency to view public issues in moral terms and to resist any attempts at compromise. When the Senate Foreign Relations Committee finally reported the treaty, recommending nearly fifty amendments and reservations, Wilson refused to consider any of them. When the full Senate voted in November to accept fourteen of the reservations, Wilson gave stern directions to his Democratic allies: they must vote only for a treaty with no changes whatsoever; any other version must be defeated. On November 19, 1919, forty-two Democrats, following the President's instructions, joined with the thirteen Republican "irreconcilables" to reject the amended treaty. When the Senate voted on the original version without any reservations, thirty-eight Senators, all but one a Democrat, voted to approve it; fifty-five voted no.

It did not seem so at the time, but the battle was now for all intents and purposes over; Wilson's long and painful struggle for a new world order was lost. There were sporadic efforts to revive the treaty over the next few months; on March 19, 1920, the day of the final vote, the amended version came as close as 7 votes short of the necessary two-thirds majority. But Wilson's opposition to anything but the precise settlement he had negotiated in Paris remained too formidable an obstacle to surmount. He was, moreover, becoming convinced that the 1920 national election would serve as a "solemn referendum" on the League, that the force of public opinion could still compel ratification of the treaty. He even spoke, somewhat pathetically, of running for reelection himself. By now, however, public interest in the peace process had begun to fade—partly as a reaction against the tragic bitterness of the ratification fight, but more in response to a series of other crises that seemed for a time to threaten the stability of the nation.

POSTWAR INSTABILITY

Even during the Paris Peace Conference, the attention of many Americans was directed less toward international matters than toward events at home. There were increasing economic problems; there was widespread social unrest and violence; there was even a growing fear of revolution. Some of this unease was a legacy of the almost hysterical social atmosphere of the war years; some of it was a response to issues that surfaced after the Armistice. Whatever the reasons, however, America was, in the immediate postwar years, a turbulent and often unhappy place.

The Troubled Economy

Citizens of Washington the day after the Armistice found it impossible to place long-distance telephone calls. The lines were jammed with officials of the war agencies canceling government contracts. The fighting had ended sooner than anyone had anticipated; and without warning, without planning, the nation was launched into the difficult task of economic reconversion.

At first, to the surprise of almost everyone, the wartime boom continued. But it was a troubled and precarious prosperity, based largely on the lingering effects of the war (government deficit spending continued for some months after the Armistice) and on sudden, temporary demands (a booming market for scarce consumer goods at home, a strong European market in the war-ravaged nations). It was accompanied, moreover, by raging inflation, a result in part of the precipitous abandonment of wartime price controls. Through most of 1919 and 1920, prices rose at an average of more than 15 percent a year.

Finally, late in 1920, the economic bubble burst, as many of the temporary forces that had created it disappeared and as inflation began killing the market for consumer goods. Between 1920 and 1921, the Gross National Product (GNP) declined nearly 10 percent; the index of wholesale prices fell from 227.9 to 150.6; 100,000 businesses went bankrupt; 453,000 farmers lost their land; nearly 5 million Americans lost their jobs. Recovery began quickly, and by 1923 it was complete. But the experience of dizzying inflation followed suddenly by a crushing recession was a frightening and disorienting one at the time. It was not a situation likely to produce social stability.

THE BOYS RETURN HOME. American troops, one of them displaying a captured German helmet, return home on board the transport ship *Leviathan* in December 1918. The reintroduction of thousands of veterans into the labor force helped produce the economic instability of the immediate postwar years. (*National Archives*)

Labor Unrest

Perhaps the most visible result of the postwar economic problems was a dramatic increase in labor unrest. American workers had refrained from strikes during the war. But with the fighting over, they were willing to be patient no longer. Many factors combined to produce labor discontent: the raging inflation, which wiped out what had been at best modest gains in wages during the war; concern about job security, heightened by the return to the labor force of hundreds of thousands of veterans; arduous working conditions—such as the perpetuation of the twelve-hour day in the steel industry. Employers aggravated the discontent by using the end of the war (and the end of government controls) as an excuse for taking back some of the benefits they had been forced to concede to workers in 1917 and 1918 —most notably recognition of unions. Mine owners even reneged on promised wage increases. In such a climate, conflict was inevitable.

The year 1919 saw, therefore, an unprecedented wave of strikes—more than 3,600 in all, involving over 4 million workers. Several of the strikes received wide national attention and raised particular alarm. In January, a walkout by shipyard workers in Seattle, Washington, evolved into a general strike that brought the entire city to a virtual standstill. The mayor requested and received the assistance of United States Marines to keep the city running, and eventually the strike failed.

STEEL STRIKE, 1919.   Police arrest a striking steelworker in Pittsburgh during the great strike of 1919. The labor unrest of the postwar years reflected widespread unhappiness about the rampant inflation, which was eating away at the limited wage gains workers had won during the war. It also was a result of the miserable working conditions to which many laborers were subjected. At Carnegie Steel, workers often logged over eighty hours a week—working twelve hours a day, seven days a week. Semiskilled workers earned less than $2,000 per year, unskilled workers less than $1,500 (the generally acknowledged poverty line). One steelworker described in his diary the conditions of labor: "You lift a large sack of coal to your shoulders, run towards the white hot steel in a 100-ton ladle, must get close enough without burning your face off to hurl the sack, using every ounce of strength, into the ladle and run, as flames leap to the roof. Then you rush out to the ladle and madly shovel manganese into it, as hot a job as can be imagined." (*Brown Brothers*)

But the incident was widely cited as evidence of the vulnerability of any community to disruption from labor agitation. In September, there was an even more alarming episode: a strike by the Boston police force, which was demanding recognition of its union. Seattle had remained generally calm; Boston did not. With the police off the job, the city erupted in violence and looting. Efforts by local businessmen, veterans, and college students to patrol the streets proved ineffective; and finally Governor Calvin Coolidge called in the National Guard to restore order. (His public statement at the time that "There is no right to strike against the public safety by anybody, anywhere, any time" attracted national acclaim.) Eventually, Boston officials dismissed the entire police force and hired a new one.

Of all the strikes of 1919, the greatest was the one, also in September, by 350,000 steelworkers in several midwestern cities. They were demanding an eight-hour day and recognition of their union; but Elbert Gary, president of United States Steel, led the industry management in standing firm. The strike was long and bitter, marked by frequent violent conflicts, and climaxed by a riot in Gary, Indiana, in which eighteen strikers were killed. With the assistance of their own armed guards, steel executives managed to keep most plants running with nonunion labor; and by January, the strike had collapsed. Public opinion had turned so decisively against the strikers that the timid A.F. of L. had finally repudiated them. It was a setback from which organized labor would not recover for more than a decade.

The Red Scare

Viewed objectively, the great wave of strikes, most of which ended in failure, was evidence of the weakness of the labor movement and the strength of the corporate establishment. To much of the public, however, the industrial warfare was a frightening omen of social instability. More than that, it was a sign of a dangerous increase in domestic radicalism. The mayor of Seattle claimed that the general strike was an attempt by revolutionaries "to establish a Soviet government." The leaders of the steel industry insisted that "radical agitators" had stirred up trouble among their employees, who were, they claimed, content with things as they were. That such charges were virtually groundless did not diminish their effectiveness.

This was in part because other evidence emerging at the same time likewise seemed to suggest the existence of a radical menace. The Russian Revolution of November 1917 had been disturbing enough by itself—so disturbing to Woodrow Wilson, in fact, that in 1918 he permitted the landing of American troops in the Soviet Union. They were there, he claimed, to help a group of 60,000 Czech soldiers trapped in Russia escape. But the Americans soon became involved, both directly and indirectly, in assisting the White Russians in their fight against the Bolsheviks. Some American troops remained as late as April 1920. Wilson's actions failed to undermine Lenin's communist regime; they did, however, become the source of lasting Russian–American hostility and mistrust. American concerns about the communist threat grew even more intense in 1919 when the

Soviet government announced the formation of the Communist International (or Comintern), whose purpose was to export revolution around the world. No one in the United States seemed to notice that the Russian communists had not yet even secured their own revolution, that they were in no position to begin any overseas adventures.

In America, in the meantime, there was, in addition to the great number of imagined radicals, a modest number of real ones. And when they heard the frightened warnings that a revolution was imminent, they tended to believe them. Some, therefore, engaged in sporadic acts of terrorism to speed the supposed crisis on its way. It was these small bands of radicals, presumably, who were responsible for the series of bombings in the spring of 1919 that produced great national alarm. In April, the Post Office intercepted several dozen parcels addressed to leading businessmen and politicians that were triggered to explode when opened; several reached their destinations, one of them severely injuring the servant of a Georgia public official. Two months later, eight bombs exploded in eight cities within minutes of one another, suggesting a nationwide conspiracy. One of them damaged the façade of Attorney General A. Mitchell Palmer's home in Washington.

In response to these and other provocations, the nation embarked on a crusade against radicalism that resembled in many ways its wartime crusade against disloyalty and dissent. Nearly 30 states enacted new peacetime sedition laws imposing harsh penalties on those who promoted revolution; some 300 people went to jail as a result. Citizens in many communities removed "subversive" books from the shelves of libraries; administrators in some universities dismissed "radical" members from their faculties. A mob of off-duty soldiers in New York City ransacked the offices of a socialist newspaper and beat up its staff. Another mob, in Centralia, Washington, dragged IWW agitator Wesley Everest from jail and castrated him before hanging him from a bridge. Perhaps the greatest contribution to the Red Scare, as it later became known, came from the federal government. Attorney General Palmer, angered by the bombing of his home and ambitious for his party's 1920 presidential nomination, ordered the Justice Department to take steps to quell what he later called the "blaze of revolution . . . sweeping over every American institution of law and order." On New Year's Day, 1920, he orchestrated a series of raids on alleged radical centers throughout the country and arrested more than 6,000 people. Little evidence of wrongdoing seemed necessary; in Hartford, Connecticut, people asking at the police station about friends and relatives who had been arrested were themselves taken into custody. The Palmer Raids had been intended to uncover huge caches of weapons and explosives; they netted a total of three pistols and no dynamite. Nevertheless, many of those arrested spent days and weeks in jail with no formal charges filed against them. Most were ultimately released, but about 500 who were not American citizens were summarily deported. For these egregious violations of civil liberties, A. Mitchell Palmer received a barrage of favorable publicity and enjoyed a period of intense (if brief) national popularity.

The ferocity of the Red Scare soon abated, but its effects lingered well into the

1920s, most notably in the celebrated case of Sacco and Vanzetti. In May of 1920, two Italian immigrants, Nicola Sacco and Bartolomeo Vanzetti, were charged with the murder of a paymaster in Braintree, Massachusetts. The evidence against them was at best questionable; but because both men were confessed anarchists, they faced a widespread public presumption of guilt. The judge in their trial, Webster Thayer, was openly prejudiced; and it was perhaps unsurprising under the circumstances that they were convicted and sentenced to death. Over the next several years, however, interest in the case grew in many quarters—among a group of young journalists, among disenchanted progressives, among many intellectuals, and among an increasing number of others who were impressed with the courage and dignity the two condemned men continued to display. Again and again, supporters of Sacco and Vanzetti filed requests for a new trial or a pardon; repeatedly, judges, the governor, and finally a special review board (whose members included the presidents of Harvard and MIT) denied all appeals. After years of frustrating debate, the struggle ended; on August 23, 1927, Sacco and Vanzetti, still proclaiming their innocence, died in the electric chair. All over the world, crowds demonstrated in protest. In the United States, thousands of men and women expressed anger, shame, and sorrow. It was a cause that a generation of Americans never forgot, an episode that kept the bitter legacy of the Red Scare alive for many years.

Racial Unrest

No group suffered more from the inflamed climate of the postwar years than American blacks. To them more than to most, the war had seemed to offer a major opportunity for social and economic advancement. Over 400,000 blacks served in the army, half of them in Europe; and they expected to earn the gratitude of the nation in return. Several hundred thousand more migrated from the South to northern industrial cities in search of the factory jobs that the war was rapidly generating. Almost overnight, the nation's racial demographics were transformed; suddenly there were enormous black communities crowding into the urban North, which had received only a relatively few Negroes in the past. Just as black soldiers expected their military service to enhance their social status, so black factory workers regarded their move north as an escape from racial prejudice and an opportunity for economic gain.

Even before the war ended, however, the racial climate had begun to sour; and in 1919, it turned savage and murderous. In the South, there was a sudden increase in lynchings—more than seventy blacks, some of them war veterans, died at the hands of white mobs in 1919 alone. In the North, conditions were even worse. Black veterans were cruelly disillusioned when they returned to find a society still unwilling to grant them any significant social or economic gains; black factory workers were facing layoffs as returning white veterans displaced them from their jobs. These economic difficulties contributed to an already tense situation. The Great Migration that had begun in 1915 had thrown thousands of blacks into close proximity with northern whites who were unfamiliar with and generally hostile

SACCO AND VANZETTI.   Nicola Sacco and Bartolomeo Vanzetti, shown here being led handcuffed into court in 1927, were the most celebrated victims of the Red Scare of 1919 and 1920. They were arrested, initially, more because they were professed anarchists than because of any conclusive evidence tying them to the murder with which they were charged. They were finally executed in 1927; the *Boston Herald* explained their demise by asserting: "The momentum of the established order required the execution of Sacco and Vanzetti, and never in your life or mine, has that momentum acquired such tremendous force." (*Brown Brothers*)

to them. As they jostled together on the streets, trolleys, and subways of the overcrowded cities, tensions escalated; and as whites became convinced that black workers, with their lower wage demands, were hurting them economically, the animosity grew further. The result was a rash of disorder and violence. As early as 1917, there had been serious race riots in cities as diverse as Houston, Philadelphia, and East St. Louis (where forty-nine people, thirty-nine of them blacks, were killed). In 1919, things grew far worse. In Chicago, a black teen-ager swimming in Lake Michigan on a hot July day happened to drift toward a white beach. Whites on shore allegedly stoned him unconscious; he sank and drowned. The incident became the match that ignited already severe racial tensions in the city;

and for more than a week, Chicago was virtually at war—black and white mobs roaming through each other's neighborhoods, beating and shooting passersby, destroying homes and properties. In the end, 38 people died—15 whites and 23 blacks—and 537 were injured; over 1,000 people were left homeless. The Chicago riot was the worst but not the only riot during the so-called red summer of 1919; in all, 120 people died in such racial outbreaks in the space of little more than three months.

Blacks responded to the turmoil in various ways. Some were simply bewildered, deeply disillusioned at the shattering of their hopes, frightened by the savagery to which they were now exposed. Others were defiant. The NAACP urged blacks to fight back, to defend themselves and demand government protection. At the same time, a black Jamaican, Marcus Garvey, began to attract a wide American following with an ideology of black nationalism. Black culture was superior to that of white society, he told his supporters; blacks should leave America and return to Africa, where they could create a new society of their own. At the peak of his popularity, Garvey claimed a following of 4 million. In the end, however, blacks had little choice but to acquiesce in the social and economic subjugation being forced upon them. Although they continued to make certain limited gains, and although within their own communities they were sustaining a strong and creative black culture, it would be more than thirty years before they made any substantial progress toward equality.

RACE RIOT, 1919. Whites stone a black man to death during the vicious race riot in Chicago in 1919. The Great Migration of blacks to northern cities, which accelerated during and after the war, produced severe tensions in many urban, industrial areas, as blacks and whites competed for scarce industrial jobs.

The Retreat from Idealism

The economic problems, the labor unrest, the fear of radicalism, the racial tensions—all combined in the years immediately following the war to produce a general sense of disillusionment. By 1920, the American people were tired: tired of idealism, tired of reform, tired of the controversy and instability they believed these impulses had caused. For decades, they had been living in turbulent times: through a series of social crises in the 1890s, through a highly charged era of reform in the first decade and a half of the new century, through an intense and savage war, through a troubled and bitter peace. They yearned now for tranquillity.

How deeply they yearned for it became apparent in the election of 1920. Woodrow Wilson wanted the campaign to be a referendum on the League of Nations; instead, in effect, it became a referendum on the future. The Democratic candidates, Ohio Governor James M. Cox and Assistant Secretary of the Navy Franklin D. Roosevelt, worked hard to keep Wilson's ideals alive. The Republican presidential nominee, however, offered a different vision. He was Warren Gamaliel Harding, an obscure Ohio Senator whose only real asset seemed to be his pliability; party leaders had settled on him late one night in a "smoke-filled room" in a Chicago hotel, confident that he would do their bidding once in office. In the course of his brief and spiritless campaign, Harding offered no soaring ideals, only a vague and comfortable assurance of stability, the promise of a return, as he later phrased it, to "normalcy." He won in a landslide. The Republican ticket received 61 percent of the popular vote and carried every state outside the South. The party made major gains in Congress as well.

Woodrow Wilson, for so long a symbol of many of the nation's highest ideals, stood repudiated. Early in 1921, he retired to a house on S Street in Washington, where for the next three years he lived quietly and inconspicuously. On February 3, 1924, he died.

SUGGESTED READINGS

As an introduction to the vast literature on postwar diplomacy, consult Arthur S. Link, *Wilson the Diplomatist* (1957); N. Gordon Levin, Jr., *Woodrow Wilson and World Politics* (1968); and two works by Thomas A. Bailey, *Woodrow Wilson and the Lost Peace* (1944) and *Woodrow Wilson and the Great Betrayal* (1945). A controversial analysis of the Versailles Conference, emphasizing the influence of anticommunist sentiment upon the negotiations, can be found in Arno Mayer, *Wilson vs. Lenin* (1959) and *Politics and Diplomacy of Peacemaking* (1965). For the battle over ratification, see, in addition to the above, John A. Garraty, *Henry Cabot Lodge* (1953), and Ralph Stone, *The Irreconcilables* (1970). Gene Smith's *When the Cheering Stopped* (1964) is a moving popular account of Wilson's last years. George Kennan, *Decision to Intervene* (1958), and John L. Gaddis, *Russia, the Soviet Union, and the United States* (1978), examine American intervention in the Soviet Union during the Revolution.

Postwar economic turmoil is summarized in Burl Noggle, *Into the Twenties* (1974). Stanley Coben's *A. Mitchell Palmer* (1963), and Robert K. Murray's *The Red Scare* (1955), examine the antiradicalism of the postwar years. Roberta Strauss Feuerlicht, *Justice Crucified* (1977), is one of many studies of the Sacco-Vanzetti case. David Brody, *Labor in Crisis* (1965), examines the steel strike of 1919; while William M. Tuttle, Jr., *Race Riot* (1970), analyzes the Chicago riot of the same year.

Nine

The New Era

To many reformers at the time, the 1920s seemed to mark an end to the nation's long involvement with progressivism. An age of governmental activism and social dynamism was, it appeared, giving way to a decade of stagnant, materialistic conservatism. To other Americans, however, the 1920s represented something very different. Progressivism had not died, they believed. It had triumphed. The nation was at last building the stable, prosperous, organized social order of which progressives had long dreamed. The United States had entered a "New Era" of limitless potential.

There was some truth in both views. Progressivism had always embodied two basic impulses: an idealistic, even humanitarian commitment to correcting social and economic injustices; and a harder, more pragmatic concern with order, efficiency, and process. The 1920s witnessed the debilitation of the former and the strengthening of the latter. The nation did indeed retreat noticeably from the progressive commitment to reform, which had become identified in the postwar years with radicalism and disorder. At the same time, however, America was making great strides toward fulfilling the progressive dream of national unity and consolidation. Far from being a stable, passive era, the 1920s were years of crucial political, economic, and cultural changes. As a result, they were also years of social turbulence and conflict.

REPUBLICAN GOVERNMENT

The federal government in the 1920s gave ample evidence of how progressivism simultaneously increased its influence and narrowed its focus. Beginning in 1921, both the presidency and the Congress rested securely in the hands of the Republi-

147

can party—a party in which the power of reformers had dwindled to almost nothing, a party with little interest in attacking social injustice and even less in attempting to curb corporate power. Yet the government of the New Era was more than the passive, pliant instrument that critics often described. It was in many respects an active and powerful agent of economic change.

Warren G. Harding

Nothing seemed more clearly to illustrate the death of crusading idealism in the 1920s than the characters of the two men who served as President during most of the decade. The progressive era had produced Theodore Roosevelt and Woodrow Wilson. The New Era produced Warren G. Harding and Calvin Coolidge.

Harding was elected to the presidency in 1920 having spent many years in public life doing absolutely nothing of note. He had advanced from the editorship of a newspaper in his hometown of Marion, Ohio, to the state legislature by virtue of his good looks, polished speaking style, and geniality. He had moved from there to the United States Senate as a result of his party regularity. And he had moved from there to the White House as a result of a political agreement among leaders of his party who considered him, as one noted, a "good second-rater."

The new President had few illusions about his own qualifications for office. Awed by his new responsibilities, he made sincere efforts to perform them with distinction. He appointed capable men to the most important cabinet offices; he attempted to stabilize the nation's troubled foreign policy; and he displayed on occasion a vigorous humanity, as when he pardoned socialist Eugene V. Debs in 1921. Even as he attempted to rise to his office, however, he displayed a sense of bafflement about his situation, as if he recognized his own unfitness. "I am a man of limited talents from a small town," he reportedly told friends on one occasion. "I don't seem to grasp that I am President." When complex policy matters reached his desk, he expressed bewilderment and dismay. "I don't know anything about this European stuff," he once said in reply to a reporter's question. On another occasion, he commented on a piece of economic legislation by explaining resignedly, "I can't make a damn thing out of this tax problem." Unsurprisingly, perhaps, Harding soon found himself delegating much of his authority to others: to members of his cabinet, to political cronies, to Congress, to party leaders. In the meantime, the nation's press, overwhelmingly Republican, was portraying him as a wise and effective leader.

It was Harding's personal weaknesses as much as his political naïveté that finally resulted in his demise. He realized the importance of capable subordinates in an administration in which the President himself was reluctant to act. At the same time, however, he lacked the strength to abandon the party hacks who had helped create his political success. One of them, Harry Daugherty, an Ohio party boss, he appointed Attorney General. Another, Albert B. Fall, he made Secretary of the Interior. Members of the so-called Ohio Gang filled important offices throughout the administration. It was widely known within the government that the President's cronies led active, illicit social lives; that they gathered nightly at the famous

THE PRESIDENT AND THE BABE.   Two pleasure-loving heroes of the 1920s:
President Warren G. Harding, whose handsome geniality made him widely beloved
until the exposure of scandals within his administration; and Babe Ruth, the "Sultan
of Swat," whose popularity rested not only on his record-breaking hitting for the New
York Yankees but on his free-spirited life style as well. (*Bettmann Archive*)

"House on K Street" to drink illegal alcohol, play poker, and entertain attractive
women; and that the President himself often joined in all these activities.

What remained for a time generally unknown was that Daugherty, Fall, and
others were engaged in a widespread pattern of fraud and corruption. They sold
government offices and favors, bribed Congressmen and Senators to support
legislation favorable to their interests, and plundered the agencies and departments in which they worked of millions. Jesse Smith in the Justice Department
accepted thousands of dollars from private interests in return for protecting them
from prosecution; when Harding finally dismissed him, he committed suicide.
Charles R. Forbes of the Veterans' Bureau stole nearly $250 million from the
agency; when threatened with exposure, he resigned and fled the country.

The most spectacular scandal involved the rich naval oil reserves at Teapot Dome, Wyoming, and Elk Hills, California. At the urging of Albert Fall, Harding transferred control of those reserves from the Navy Department to the Interior Department. Fall then secretly leased them to two wealthy businessmen—Harry F. Sinclair and Edward L. Doheny—and received in return nearly half a million dollars in "loans" to ease his private financial troubles. Fall was ultimately convicted of bribery and sentenced to a year in prison; Harry Daugherty, his partner in the scheme, barely avoided a similar fate.

For several years, apparently, Harding himself remained generally unaware of the rot infecting his administration. But by the summer of 1923, only months before Senate investigations and press revelations brought the scandals to light, he began to realize how desperate his situation had become. "My God, this is a hell of a job," he confided to one journalist. "I have no trouble with my enemies. . . . But my damned friends, my God-damned friends . . . they're the ones that keep me walking the floor nights!"

Tired and depressed, the President left Washington for a speaking tour in the West and a visit to Alaska. In Seattle late in July, he suffered severe pain, which his doctors diagnosed as food poisoning. A few days later, he seemed to rally and traveled on to San Francisco. There, on August 2, he died. He had suffered two major heart attacks. No one could prove that his illness had been related to his knowledge of the impending scandals, but his obvious desperation had surely contributed to his physical problems. As the revelations of corruption in the administration gradually eroded Harding's public image in the months following his death, Alice Roosevelt Longworth—daughter of a President and wife of the Speaker of the House—expressed the sentiments of many who had known him. "Harding was not a bad man," she said. "He was just a slob."

HARDING IN THE WEST.
President Harding speaks from the rear of his train during his western trip in 1923. Unknown to the public, Harding was already suffering from both physical and political ills that would, within months, lead first to his sudden death in California and then to disclosure of widespread corruption in his administration. (*National Archives*)

Calvin Coolidge

In many ways, Calvin Coolidge, who succeeded to the presidency upon the death of Harding, was utterly different from his predecessor. Where Harding was genial and garrulous, Coolidge was dour and silent. Where Harding adopted a loose, even debauched life style, Coolidge lived soberly and puritanically. And while Harding was, if not personally corrupt, then at least tolerant of corruption in others, Coolidge was honest beyond reproach. The image of stolid respectability that he projected was so unassailable that the Republican party managed to avoid any lasting damage from the Teapot Dome and related scandals. In other ways, however, Harding and Coolidge were similar figures. Both represented no soaring ideals but an unadventurous conservatism. Both took a decidedly passive approach to their office. Both were, essentially, political mediocrities.

Like Harding, Coolidge rose to the presidency on the basis of virtually no substantive accomplishments. During his years in Massachusetts politics, he had won a reputation as a safe, trustworthy figure; and largely as a result of that, he had become governor in 1919. His response to the Boston police strike won him

CALVIN COOLIDGE AT LEISURE.   Coolidge presented a sharp contrast to Harding in his public demeanor. A silent man of simple tastes (shown here on his family's farm in Vermont), he helped ease the impact upon his party of the Teapot Dome and Elk Hills scandals. Like Harding, however, he took few initiatives in public policy. (*Harvard College Library*)

national attention and, in 1920, his party's vice-presidential nomination. Three years later, news of Harding's death reached him in Vermont; and there, by the light of a kerosene lamp on a kitchen table, he took the oath of office from his father, a justice of the peace.

If anything, Coolidge was an even less active President than Harding, partly as a result of his conviction that government should interfere as little as possible in the life of the nation and partly as a result of his own personal lassitude. He took long naps every afternoon. He kept official appointments to a minimum and engaged in almost no conversation with those who did manage to see him. He proposed no significant legislation and took little part in the running of the nation's foreign policy. "He aspired," wrote one of his contemporaries, "to become the least President the country ever had. He attained his desire."

In 1924, he received his party's presidential nomination virtually unopposed. Running against Democrat John W. Davis, a wealthy corporate lawyer who had served in the Wilson administration, he won a comfortable victory: 54 percent of the popular vote and 382 of the 531 electoral votes. Robert La Follette, the candidate of the reincarnated Progressive party, received only 16 percent of the popular vote and carried only his home state of Wisconsin. Coolidge's negative, custodial view of the presidency clearly had the approval of the great majority of the American people. Four years later, it still did. The President could probably have won renomination and reelection easily in 1928. Instead, in characteristically laconic fashion, he walked into a press room one day and handed reporters a slip of paper containing a single sentence: "I do not choose to run." He retired from office a living symbol of the nation's disinterest in idealism and reform.

Government and Business

The story of Harding and Coolidge themselves, however, is only a part—and by no means the most important part—of the story of their administrations. However inert the New Era Presidents may have been, much of the federal government was working effectively and efficiently during the 1920s to adapt public policy to the widely accepted goal of the time: helping business and industry to operate with maximum efficiency and productivity. The close relationship between the private sector and the federal government that had been forged during World War I continued almost without interruption, but with a crucial difference. During the war, government had forged a partnership with business to ensure that the nation's military needs would be met. In the 1920s, government often seemed to become an agent of private industry, working to enhance the ability of business itself to grow and to prosper.

In the executive branch, the most active efforts came from members of the cabinet. Secretary of the Treasury Andrew Mellon, the extraordinarily wealthy steel tycoon who became one of the most influential and respected figures in government, devoted himself to working for substantial cuts in taxes on corporate profits and personal incomes and inheritances. Largely because of his efforts, Congress cut them all by more than half, actions that redounded largely to the

benefit of the wealthy. The result, Mellon claimed, would be to stimulate investment and ensure general prosperity. Others worked to make the government a
positive instrument of economic change. Henry C. Wallace, for example, used his
position as Secretary of Agriculture to promote the wider distribution of knowledge of scientific farming techniques and to encourage the modern, efficient
marketing of agricultural goods.

The most prominent member of the cabinet was Commerce Secretary Herbert
Hoover, a man active in so many areas that he often seemed to be running the
entire federal government single-handedly. Above all, he used his position to
promote a better organized, more efficient national economy. Only thus, he
claimed, could the nation hope to fulfill its most important task: the elimination
of poverty. During his eight years in the Commerce Department, Hoover constantly encouraged voluntary cooperation in the private sector as the best avenue
to stability. But the idea of voluntarism did not require the government to remain
passive; on the contrary, public institutions, Hoover believed, had a duty to play
an active role in creating the new, cooperative order.

A great believer in the value of standardization, he elevated to a position of
importance the National Bureau of Standards, which helped businesses agree on
common production techniques that would permit the interchangeability of parts.
He organized innumerable national conferences, bringing together members of
particular industries and interest groups so that they could share information and
coordinate activities. He placed commercial attachés in American embassies, to
ease the path of corporations attempting to do business overseas. Above all, he
became the champion of the concept of business associationalism, a concept that
envisioned the creation of national organizations of businessmen in particular
industries. Through such trade associations, private entrepreneurs could, Hoover
believed, stabilize their industries and promote efficiency in production and marketing. Hoover strongly resisted those who urged that the government sanction
collusion among manufacturers to fix prices, arguing that competition was essential to a prosperous economy. He did, however, believe that shared information
and limited cooperation would keep that competition from becoming destructive
and thus improve the strength of the economy as a whole.

Hoover not only encouraged associationalism; he played an active role in creating it. For some industries, he drew up the rules and structures for the new
organizations himself; on occasion he even chose their directors. He worked, in
short, to bring the power of managers, experts, and engineers to bear on the
problems of the economy. That kind of expertise could be most effectively employed, he believed, if the economy was organized along national, centralized
lines. It was little wonder that many Americans considered him the nation's most
vigorous and effective progressive.

This combination of open, unembarrassed enthusiasm for the business community and a sober devotion to the principles of centralized and efficient management found reflection in other areas of government in the 1920s. The regulatory
commissions, for example, had in the prewar era made at least token efforts to
restrict the power of private enterprise. In the 1920s, particularly as Harding and

"THE TRAFFIC PROBLEM IN WASHINGTON, D.C." J. N. Darling of the *Des Moines Register* lampoons the wide renown of Commerce Secretary Herbert Hoover, who seemed during much of the 1920s to be running virtually the entire government single-handedly. President Coolidge, shown here directing the traffic, privately resented Hoover's popularity and mistrusted his progressive tendencies.

Coolidge filled them with members of the very businesses they were supposed to regulate, the agencies began to believe that their role was not to regulate industry but to assist it. The Interstate Commerce Commission, for example, openly helped railroad companies to negotiate lucrative contracts with shippers. Meetings to discuss these agreements often took place in the offices of the commissioner himself. The Federal Trade Commission, which Wilson had established to serve as a watchdog over monopolistic business practices, now became a virtual service agency for private industry and its trade associations. Businessmen gathered frequently in the offices of the FTC to discuss ways to cooperate on setting prices and limiting production costs.

The Supreme Court in the 1920s further confirmed the business orientation of the federal government, particularly after the appointment of William Howard Taft as Chief Justice in 1921. The court struck down federal legislation regulating child labor (*Bailey* v. *Drexel Furniture Company,* 1922); it nullified a minimum wage law for women in the District of Columbia (*Adkins* v. *Children's Hospital,* 1923); and it sanctioned the creation of trade associations, ruling in *U.S.* v. *Maple Flooring Association* (1925) that they did not violate antitrust statutes as long as some competition survived within an industry. Five years earlier, in *United States* v. *U.S. Steel,* the Court had applied the same doctrine to the monopolistic United States Steel Corporation; there was no illegal "restraint of trade," it ruled, as long as U.S. Steel continued to face any competition, no matter how slight.

The federal government in the 1920s was, in short, doing two things. First, it was working to emasculate virtually every serious restraint upon the power of business that had been erected during the progressive era. At the same time, it was working actively to encourage an efficient, modern consolidation of American industry by promoting centralized organization and a reliance on scientific expertise. The progressive concern for reform on behalf of social and economic justice had faded; the technocratic values of progressivism survived and flourished.

The pro-business policies of the Republican administrations were not without their critics. There survived in Congress throughout the 1920s a large and influential group of progressive reformers of the old school, whose vision of public power as an antidote to private privilege remained very much alive. They continued to criticize the monopolistic practices of big business, to attack government's alliance with the corporate community, to decry social injustices, and to call for economic reform. Occasionally they were able to mobilize enough support to win congressional approval of progressive legislation, most notably an important scheme to assist farmers in marketing their goods (the McNary-Haugen Act) and an ambitious proposal to use federal funds to develop public power projects on the Tennessee River at Muscle Shoals. But clearly, the progressive reformers were not any longer the dominant force in American political life. When the President vetoed the legislation they had promoted, as he almost always did, they lacked the strength to override him. No longer was there a national consensus on behalf of reform. Instead, in the 1920s, there was an equally overwhelming consensus in favor of the celebration of American business.

[THE MYTH OF ISOLATION] *After Text 1*

Critics of American foreign policy in the New Era often used a single word to describe the cause of their disenchantment: isolationism. Having rejected the Wilsonian vision of a new world order, the nation had, many charged, turned its back on the rest of the globe and taken no active role in international affairs. In fact, quite the opposite was the case. The United States did indeed refuse to participate in most efforts to promote international cooperation and collective security. It did so, however, not because it wanted to isolate itself from world affairs but because it wanted to participate in them on its own terms. There would, Americans believed, be a new world order. But it would be one shaped and dominated by the United States.

Replacing the League

It was clear when the Harding administration took office in 1921 that American membership in the League of Nations was no longer a realistic possibility. As if finally to bury the issue, Secretary of State Charles Evans Hughes promptly secured from Congress legislation declaring the war with Germany at an end and then proceeded to negotiate separate peace treaties with the former Central Powers. Through these treaties, American policymakers believed, the United States would receive all the advantages of the Versailles Treaty with none of the burdensome responsibilities. Hughes was, however, committed to finding something to replace the League as a guarantor of world peace and stability. He embarked, therefore, on a series of efforts to build safeguards against future wars —but safeguards that would not hamper American freedom of action in the world.

The most important of such efforts was the Washington Conference of 1921, an attempt to prevent what was promising to become a costly and destabilizing naval armaments race among America, Britain, and Japan. Hughes startled the delegates by proposing in his opening speech a plan for dramatic reductions in the fleets of all three nations and a ten-year moratorium on the construction of large warships. He envisioned the actual scrapping of nearly 2 million tons of existing ships. As a British observer exclaimed: "Secretary Hughes sank in 35 minutes more ships than all the admirals of the world have sunk in centuries." Even more surprising than the proposal, perhaps, was that the conference ultimately agreed to accept most of its terms. The Five-Power Pact of February 1922 established both the limits for total naval tonnage and a ratio of armaments among the signatories. For every five tons of American and British warships, Japan would maintain three and France and Italy 1.75 each. (Although the treaty seemed to confirm the military inferiority of Japan, in fact it sanctioned Japanese dominance in East Asia. America and Britain had to spread their fleets across the globe; Japan was concerned only with the Pacific.) The Washington Conference also produced two other, related treaties: the Nine-Power Pact, pledging a continuation of the Open-Door Policy in China, and the Four-Power Pact, by which the United States, Britain, France, and Japan promised to respect one anothers' Pacific territories and cooperate to prevent aggression.

Taken as a whole, the Washington Conference did much to advance American international goals. It ensured the United States of at least an equal position in world trade; it eroded the longstanding economic alliance between England and Japan and created instead a stronger financial relationship between Japan and the United States; and it guaranteed that China would remain open to American trade. At the same time, it bound the United States to no cooperative international agreements that might limit its freedom of action; and it promised to reduce the importance of armaments and elevate the influence of an instrument of international power that the United States was far better prepared to wield: economic strength.

The Washington Conference began the New Era effort to protect the peace without accepting active international duties. The Kellogg-Briand Pact of 1928 concluded it. When the French Foreign Minister, Aristide Briand, asked the United States in 1927 to join an alliance against a resurgent Germany, Secretary of State Frank Kellogg (who had replaced Hughes in 1925) proposed instead a multilateral treaty outlawing war as an instrument of national policy. Fourteen nations signed the agreement in Paris on August 27, 1928, amid great solemnity and wide international acclaim. Forty-eight other nations later joined the pact. It contained no instruments of enforcement but rested, as Kellogg put it, on the "moral force" of world opinion. Some critics would later ridicule it as an "international kiss," but to the American people (and many others) at the time, it was a triumph of peaceful diplomacy.

THE PEACETIME NAVY. A repair base in California maintains the American destroyer fleet in 1923. Because of the tonnage limitations imposed by the 1921 Washington Conference, the navy put renewed emphasis on refitting existing ships. It also began construction of medium-sized cruisers, which experts scorned as reflecting the restrictions imposed by the treaty more than the optimal demands of the navy itself. (*Title Insurance and Trust Company, San Diego*)

Stabilizing Europe

The first responsibility of diplomacy, Hughes, Kellogg, and others agreed, was to ensure that American overseas trade faced no obstacles to expansion and that, once established, it would remain free of interference. Preventing a dangerous armaments race and reducing the possibility of war were two steps to that end. So were new financial arrangements that emerged at the same time. Most important to the United States was Europe, upon whose economic health American prosperity in large part depended. Not only were the major industrial powers there suffering from the devastation of war, but they were staggering under a heavy burden of debt. The Allied powers were struggling to repay $11 billion in loans they had contracted with the United States during and shortly after the war, loans that the Republican administrations were unwilling to reduce or forgive. "They hired the money, didn't they?" Calvin Coolidge replied when queried about the debts. At the same time, an even more debilitated Germany was attempting to pay the enormous reparations levied against it by the Allies. With the financial structure of Europe on the brink of collapse as a result, the United States stepped in with a solution.

Charles B. Dawes, an American banker, negotiated an agreement in 1924 among France, Britain, Germany, and the United States under which American banks would provide enormous loans to the Germans, enabling them to meet their reparations payments; in return, Britain and France would agree to reduce the amount of those payments. The Dawes Plan became the centerpiece of a growing American economic presence in Germany. It also became the source of a troubling circular pattern in international finance. America would loan money to Germany, which would use that money to pay reparations to France and England, which would in turn use those funds to repay war debts to the United States. The flow was able to continue only by virtue of the enormous debts Germany was acquiring to American banks and corporations.

Those banks and corporations were doing more than providing loans. They were becoming a daily presence in the economic life of Europe. American automobile manufacturers were opening European factories, capturing a large share of the overseas market. Other industries were establishing in the 1920s subsidiaries worth more than $10 billion throughout the Continent, taking advantage of the devastation of European industry and the inability of domestic corporations to recover. American oil companies worked desperately to establish a stake in the petroleum-rich lands of the Middle East, finally agreeing with Britain and France in 1928 to a division of the region among the corporations of the three nations. Some American investors even pumped money into the Soviet Union, hoping to establish an economic foothold there as well. (That attempt ultimately failed.) Some groups within the American government warned that the reckless expansion of overseas loans and investments, many in enterprises of dubious value, threatened disaster; that the United States was becoming too dependent upon unstable European economies. The high tariff barriers that the Republican Congress erected (through the Fordney-McCumber Act of 1922) created additional problems, such skeptics warned. European nations unable to export their goods to the United States would find it difficult to earn the money necessary to repay their loans. Such warnings fell, for the most part, on deaf ears; and American economic expansion in Europe continued until disaster struck in 1929.

Expanding in Latin America

The federal government felt even fewer reservations about assisting American economic expansion in Latin America. The United States had, after all, long considered that region its exclusive sphere of influence; and its investments there had become large even before World War I. During the 1920s, American military forces maintained a presence in numerous countries in the region, despite Hughes's withdrawal of troops from the Dominican Republic and Nicaragua. But it was the American economic presence that most policymakers considered the key to a stable Latin America. United States investments in the region more than doubled between 1924 and 1929; American corporations built roads and other facilities in many areas, partly, they argued, to weaken the appeal of revolutionary forces in the region, but at least equally to assist their own exploitation of Latin America's rich natural resources. American banks were offering large loans to Latin American governments, just as they were in Europe; and just as in Europe, the Latin Americans were having great difficulty earning the money to repay them in the face of the formidable United States tariff barrier. By the end of the 1920s, resentment of "Yankee imperialism" was already reaching alarming proportions; the economic troubles after 1929 would only accentuate such problems.

THE NATIONAL ECONOMY

Both at home and across the globe, the federal government was actively engaged in promoting the interests of American business. The recipients of this attention did much to justify such efforts, for the American economy in the 1920s had become one of the wonders of the world. After the recession of 1921–1922, the United States began a period of almost uninterrupted prosperity and economic growth. At the same time, the nation continued the process of organization and consolidation that was reshaping the structure of American economic life.

Economic Performance

No one could deny the remarkable, some believed miraculous, feats that the American economy was performing in the 1920s. The nation's manufacturing output rose by more than 60 percent during the decade; the Gross National Product increased at an average of 5 percent a year; output per worker rose by more than 33 percent. Inflation was negligible. Unemployment averaged only slightly more than 2 percent (and dropped as low as 0.8 percent during the boom year of 1929). Per capita income increased from $522 in 1921 to $716 in 1929. A mild recession in 1923 momentarily interrupted the pattern of growth; but when it subsided early in 1924, the economy expanded with even greater vigor than before. It was little wonder, then, that Americans referred to the 1920s as the New Era, that critics of capitalism became more and more difficult to find, that many people could predict, as Herbert Hoover did late in the decade, the impending elimination of poverty.

The economic boom was a result of many things. The most obvious cause, perhaps, was the debilitation of Europe after World War I, leaving the United States for a time the only truly healthy industrial power in the world. The economy benefited as well from benign government policies at home and abroad: protective tariffs, favorable tax schedules, the easing of regulatory and antitrust pressures, aggressive policies to open and protect international markets. Most important, however, was the emergence of new industries or the expansion of older ones within the United States itself. The automobile industry, for example, grew from a relatively modest size in the years before the war to become one of the most important forces in the nation's economy. Americans bought 1.5 million cars in 1921; in 1929 they purchased more than 5 million. Expansion in one industry meant, of course, expansion in others. Auto manufacturers purchased the products of steel, rubber, glass, and tool companies. Auto owners bought gasoline from the oil corporations. Road construction in response to the proliferation of motor vehicles became itself an important industry. The increased mobility that the automobile afforded increased the demand for suburban housing, spawning a boom in the construction industry. Other new industries—electronics, motion pictures, airplanes, home appliances—contributed as well to the economic growth.

Technological advances made possible much of this expansion. The modern assembly line, which Henry Ford had first introduced shortly before the war, was vital not only to the automobile industry but to many others. So were countless other new production techniques, many of them developed during the war. Improved methods of extraction and transportation made greater supplies of more varied raw materials available. Cheap, readily available energy—from newly discovered oil reserves, from the expanded network of electric power, and from the nation's abundant coal fields—further enhanced the ability of industry to produce. Improvements in management techniques also played a role in increasing productivity. More and more industries were subscribing to the "scientific-management" theories of Frederick Winslow Taylor, making deliberate efforts to improve the efficiency of their operations.

The New Organizations

The quest for improved efficiency in industry was only part of a larger trend. American business in the 1920s was making rapid strides toward national organization and consolidation. The process had begun, of course, decades before; but the New Era witnessed an acceleration of such trends. Large national organizations were becoming increasingly important in industry after industry; smaller, more local firms were disappearing. By the end of the decade, 8,000 small mining and manufacturing companies had been swallowed up into larger combinations; 5,000 utilities had disappeared, most of them into great holding companies. Local merchants floundered and vanished as national chain stores cornered more than a quarter of the nation's food, apparel, and general merchandise markets. In some industries, power resided in so few firms that competition had all but vanished. Four rubber companies controlled almost 66 percent of the rubber market; four tobacco companies monopolized more than 90 percent of the tobacco market. U.S. Steel, the nation's largest corporation, controlled its industry almost alone; its dominance was suggested by the widely accepted use of the term "Little Steel" to refer to all of its competitors combined.

The consolidation of the economy was accomplished in various ways. Great corporations, adopting new management structures, expanded to control not only a large proportion of their own industries but many related (and ultimately even unrelated) industries as well. General Motors, which was by 1920 not only the largest automobile manufacturer but the fifth largest American corporation, was a classic example. Beginning early in the century, GM's founder, William C. Durant, had begun acquiring the smaller companies that produced the parts and accessories that went into his automobiles: an axle manufacturer, a spark plug company, and others. In the years immediately following the war, he bought twenty more such concerns in a spectacular surge of expansion. The company was growing not only horizontally—capturing a larger and larger share of the automobile market—but vertically—acquiring more and more of the enterprises that contributed to automobile production and marketing. Durant, however, had little interest in efficient organization, and his giant enterprise floundered during the recession of 1921. It was then that Pierre du Pont, a major GM stockholder, recruited Alfred P. Sloan to take over the company and introduce a modern management structure. Professionally trained as both an engineer and a manager, Sloan began immediately to impose centralized order upon Durant's chaos, creating in the process one of the first truly modern corporations. Sloan first split GM into a series of divisions, each defined scientifically by its function. (Durant had generally allowed the companies he purchased to operate semiautonomously, even if several different companies were engaged in the same activity.) Overseeing Sloan's varied divisions was a central administrative structure, staffed by trained experts and managers and supervising the entire General Motors empire.

By 1925, the new structure was in place, and the corporation was flourishing. GM's share of the market rose from under 19 percent in 1924 to over 43 percent by 1929. The Sloan innovations became models for other major corporations. They also became a vehicle for further economic consolidation. Once corporate leaders ceased operating primarily as manufacturers, directly supervising their factories and marketing, and more as aloof managers, delegating responsibilities and evaluating results, there was little to prevent them from expanding into new areas, even into areas unrelated to the original industry from which their company had emerged. After the 1920s, therefore, corporations would expand not only by integrating the functions within an industry, but by diversifying into new fields.

Other industries proved less susceptible or more resistant to domination by a few great corporations. Nevertheless, even those characterized by the survival of a great number of relatively small companies often experienced a marked consolidation. The vehicles of consolidation were the trade associations—the national organizations promoted by Herbert Hoover to permit central coordination of an industry. Cotton textile manufacturing was a leading example. Hampered by vicious competition among many small producers, the industry in the early 1920s was in marked decline. In 1926, therefore, leading textile producers met with Hoover and agreed upon a new organization: the Cotton Textile Institute (CTI). It was to provide a central apparatus through which individual manufacturers could share information and coordinate activities; it was to fulfill a vision of, as one textile executive put it, "every mill radiating from a central point." Disinterested experts on the CTI staff would distribute information on production and pricing to members. "The day of the individual has passed," said an advertisement in the CTI newspaper attempting to attract new members. "Cooperation has

AT WORK ON THE EMPIRE STATE BUILDING. Symbolic of the exuberant self-confidence of American business in the 1920s was the rapid construction of huge new skyscrapers to house the offices of modern corporations. This construction worker sits astride a beam of the new Empire State Building in New York, completed in 1931, which remained the world's tallest building until the late 1960s. (*International Center for Photography, George Eastman House*)

solved the problem for others. Are you willing to try it?" By 1928, more than two-thirds of all textile manufacturers had joined the Institute (whose first president, a Wall Street lawyer, was selected by Hoover). With assurances from the Justice Department that there would be no antitrust actions, the CTI was, in effect, controlling a large part of the industry: helping its members decide how much to produce and how much to charge. Although never entirely successful in stabilizing the troubled market for textiles, the Institute did convince many manufacturers of the value of expert, centralized direction of their operations. It was a pattern that emerged in many other industries as well.

[THE MARGINAL ECONOMY] *After Test 2*

The remarkable general prosperity and the increasing economic concentration created an image in the 1920s of a nation approaching a solution to all its problems. The reality, however, was quite different. New Era prosperity was real enough, but it was highly maldistributed. More than two-thirds of the population in 1929 lived at no better than what one study described as "minimum comfort level." And half of those were languishing at or below the level of "subsistence and poverty." The affluent middle class, which celebrated the New Era most vocally, had grown and prospered. There were many more, however, who had shared only marginally in the nation's growing wealth. Nor did the pattern of organization and consolidation spread to all sectors of the economy. Large segments of the society remained unable to organize, and they found themselves as a result without sufficient power to protect their economic interests.

Labor's Dilemma

As much as any other group, American labor experienced both the benefits and the deficiencies of the New Era. On the one hand, most workers saw their standard of living rise during the 1920s; many enjoyed greatly improved working conditions and other benefits. At the same time, however, laborers received wage increases that were proportionately far below the increases in corporate profits; and they worked in a climate unremittingly hostile to unionization.

The improvements in wages and working conditions were impossible to ignore. Employers in the 1920s, eager to avoid disruptive labor unrest and forestall the growth of unions, adopted paternalistic techniques that came to be known as "welfare capitalism." Industrialists such as Henry Ford shortened the work week for their employees and instituted paid vacations. Manufacturers such as U.S. Steel spent millions of dollars installing safety devices and improving sanitation in the workplace. Many employers provided medical services for employees; still more built attractive cafeterias and provided new recreational facilities and social diversions. Company welfare workers counseled employees on their family problems, and industrial psychologists attempted to help laborers cope with the strains of monotonous factory tasks. Most important, perhaps, many employers offered their workers substantial raises in pay and other financial benefits. Real wages for laborers increased 26 percent between 1919 and 1929. By 1926, nearly 3 million industrial workers were eligible for pensions upon retirement. In some companies, employees were permitted to buy stock at below market value. When labor grievances surfaced despite these efforts, workers could voice them through the so-called company unions that were emerging in many industries—workers' councils and shop committees, organized by the corporation itself, through which employees could demand improvements in benefits and working conditions.

Yet for all the undoubted benefits that welfare capitalism provided, American workers remained in the 1920s a relatively impoverished and powerless group. Their wages had risen; but the average annual income of a worker remained below $1,500 a year at a time when $1,800 was considered necessary to maintain a minimally decent standard of living. In some industries, such as coal mining and textiles, hours remained long and wages rose scarcely at all. At Elizabethton, Tennessee, mill girls were working fifty-six hours a week for 16 to 18 cents an hour in 1929. Company unions may have been psychologically comforting, but they were for the most part feeble vehicles for demanding benefits. In most companies, the workers' councils were forbidden to deal with questions of wages and hours. Nor could workers do very much to counter the effects of technological unemployment. It may have been true that new mechanical devices, by increasing general productivity, helped in the long run to create more jobs than they eliminated. At the time, however, the new technology posed a real and immediate threat to industrial workers. Total factory employment increased hardly at all during the 1920s, even while manufacturing output was soaring.

Some laborers continued to regard an effective union movement as the best hope for improving their position. But the New Era was a bleak time for labor organization. Part of the blame lay with the workers themselves, many of whom were seduced by the benefits of welfare capitalism and displayed no interest in organizing. Even more of the blame rested with the unions, which failed to adapt to the realities of the modern economy. The conservative American Federation of Labor, the dominant labor organization in the nation, remained wedded to the concept of the craft union, in which workers were organized on the basis of particular skills. Most craft unions, faced with a dwindling demand for their services as new machines made old skills obsolete, devoted their efforts to protecting the privileges of their members. In the meantime, a huge new segment of the work force was emerging: unskilled industrial workers, many of them southern or eastern European immigrants. They received little sympathy or attention from the craft unions and found themselves, as a result, with no organizations to join. The A.F. of L., moreover, remained throughout the 1920s painfully timid about supporting strikes—partly in reaction to the disastrous setbacks it had suffered in 1919. William Green, who became president of the organization in 1924, was committed to peaceful cooperation with employers and strident opposition to communism and socialism.

However much the workers and unions themselves contributed to the weakness of the labor movement, corporate and government policies contributed more. If welfare capitalism was the carrot for inducing workers to accept the status quo, the antiunion policies of most industrialists constituted the stick. Corporate leaders worked hard after the turmoil of 1919 to spread the doctrine that unionism was somehow subversive and un-American, that a crucial element of democratic capitalism was the protection of the open shop (a shop in which no worker could

ON THE JOB IN THE 1920s.   Workers in a Westinghouse Electric plant in south
Philadelphia in the 1920s, where an American flag hangs conspicuously from the
rafters. Employers managed to stem labor protest during the decade with a
combination of increased benefits (which they termed "welfare capitalism") and
heavy-handed suppression of union activities. They christened their commitment to
the open shop the "American Plan," to give it appropriate patriotic credentials. (*UPI*)

be required to join a union). The crusade for the open shop, euphemistically titled
the "American Plan," received the endorsement of the National Association of
Manufacturers in 1920 and became a pretext for a harsh campaign of union
busting across the country. When such tactics proved insufficient to counter union
power, government assistance often made the difference. In 1921, the Supreme
Court declared picketing illegal and upheld the right of lower courts to issue
injunctions against strikers. In 1922, the Justice Department intervened to quell
a strike by 400,000 railroad workers. In 1924, legal agencies refused protection to
members of the United Mine Workers Union when mine owners launched a
violent campaign in western Pennsylvania to drive the union from the coal fields.

The result of all these factors was that union membership suffered a serious
decline in the 1920s. The UMW dwindled from 450,000 members in 1921 to only

150,000 in 1929; and by the end of the decade its members were earning only about half of what they had received at the beginning. Membership in the International Ladies' Garment Workers Union declined during the decade from 120,000 to 45,000. And union membership as a whole fell from more than 5 million in 1920 to about 4.3 million in 1929. Not until the mid-1930s, when a combination of increased labor militancy and active government assistance added strength to the labor movement, would the antiunion syndrome be broken.

The Plight of the Farmer

Despite their other setbacks, many American workers gained at least an increase in income during the 1920s. In contrast, most American farmers of the New Era experienced only decline. Agriculture, like industry, was discovering the advantages of the new technology for increasing production. The number of tractors at work on American farms, for example, quadrupled during the 1920s, helping to open 35 million new acres to cultivation. But while the increases in industrial production were matched by increases in consumer demand, the expansion of agricultural production was not. The bloated European market for American foodstuffs contracted rapidly after the war, when European agriculture began to resume production. At the same time, domestic demand for food rose only slightly and in some cases actually declined; the market for starches, for example, dropped sharply as machines released workers from heavy manual labor. In 1920, moreover, farmers lost the price supports that had stabilized their operations during the war. The result was a disastrous decline in food prices and thus a severe drop in income for farmers. The price of a bushel of wheat, for example, declined from $2.57 in 1920 to less than $1.00 the following year. The prices of other foodstuffs followed. The average income for Americans not engaged in agriculture in 1929 was $870. For farmers, it was $223. In 1920, farm income had been 15 percent of the national total; by 1929, it was 9 percent.

The effects of these changes varied from region to region and from individual to individual. As in other sectors, economic concentration was affecting American agriculture. Those farmers with sufficient resources and energy actually prospered during the 1920s, buying up the land of their struggling neighbors and establishing themselves as virtual agrarian tycoons. With vast landholdings and improved technology, corporate farmers, even those in such troubled areas as the wheat belt, were often able to produce so much that they could profit despite the decline in prices. Their successes, however, only deepened the distress of the smaller farmers unable to adopt their techniques. More than 3 million people left agriculture altogether in the course of the decade. Of those who remained, an alarming number were forced into tenancy—losing ownership of their lands and having to rent instead from banks or other landlords. There were exceptions. Citrus, dairy, and truck farmers continued to flourish even when operating on a modest scale. For the most part, however, the small farmer was suffering severe distress.

In response, farmers began to demand government relief. A few gravitated to such vaguely radical organizations as the Nonpartisan League of North Dakota or its successor, the Farmer-Labor party, which established a foothold as well in Minnesota and other midwestern states. Most farmers, however, adopted a more moderate approach, agitating for a restoration and strengthening of government price supports. Through such organizations as the Farm Bureau Federation, they put increasing pressure upon Congress (where farmers continued to enjoy disproportionately high representation); and while reform sentiment in most other areas made little headway in the 1920s, the movement for agrarian reform rapidly gathered strength.

One price-raising scheme in particular came to dominate agrarian demands: the idea of parity. "Parity" referred to a price for crops determined by a complicated formula. The parity price of agricultural goods was to reflect what farmers called a "fair exchange formula," which was based on the average price of the crop during the decade preceding the war as compared with the general average of all prices during the same period. Its purpose was to ensure that farmers would earn back at least their production costs no matter how the national or world agricultural market might fluctuate. The government would guarantee parity to farmers in two ways: first, by maintaining a high tariff barrier against foreign competition, thus enabling American agriculture to sustain high prices at home; second, by buying up any surplus crops at parity and selling them abroad at whatever the world market would bring. An "equalization fee"—that is, a general tax on all crops—would compensate the government for any loss while spreading the burden evenly among all farmers.

The legislative expression of the demand for parity was the McNary-Haugen Act, named after its two principal sponsors in Congress and introduced repeatedly between 1924 and 1928. In 1924, a bill requiring parity only for grain failed in the House. Two years later, with cotton, tobacco, and rice added to win southern support, the measure passed, only to fall victim to a veto by President Coolidge. In 1928, it won congressional approval again, only to succumb to another presidential veto. Despite the farmers' impressive political strength, as long as agrarian problems did not seem to affect the general prosperity there was little hope for reform.

Coping with Maladjustments

Workers and farmers were perhaps the largest groups suffering from the maladjustments of the New Era economy, but there were many others. Businessmen in a variety of fields failed to share in the prosperity of the decade; "sick" industries —of which railroads, coal mining, textiles, and shipping were examples—fell victim to obsolescence, mismanagement, or overproduction. Blacks, both in the rural South and in the industrial North, suffered not only from the general problems of farmers and workers but from their own historic burdens as well. Black farmers were the first to lose their lands when agricultural prices fell. Black workers were the first to lose their jobs when factories made layoffs, and they were barred from membership in most unions. These displaced black workers joined with similarly displaced whites to form a large, restless underclass; many became virtual nomads, wandering from region to region in search of low-paying temporary or seasonal jobs.

With the gap between the claims of the New Era and the reality of the lives of many of its citizens so large, it was surprising, perhaps, that there was so little resistance to the unquestioned supremacy of business in American life. In part, the passivity of the disadvantaged was a result of cultural pressures. Americans for decades had been taught that individuals were in command of their own destiny, that suffering was the responsibility of the one who suffered. Farmers, skilled workers, and others steeped in these traditional values often tended to blame themselves for their frustrations. In part, moreover, the general calm was a result of the success of the New Era in publicizing itself. The doctrines of efficiency, expertise, and organization that the nation's economic leaders so happily espoused had attractions for those on the margins of the economy as well. Rather than challenging the business ethos, many attempted to borrow it.

Most of all, perhaps, those who did not share in the prosperity of the 1920s failed to protest more forcefully because of a combination of hope and resignation: hope that somehow the wealth they saw around them would eventually filter down to their own level; resignation to the strength of the forces upholding the business culture and reducing most resistance to futility. The smug confidence of the leaders of the 1920s in the virtues of the modern economy is easy to deride from the vantage point of later decades; at the time, however, their complacency stood virtually unchallenged.

SUGGESTED READINGS

Among the best general surveys of politics and society in the 1920s are William Leuchtenburg, *The Perils of Prosperity* (1958); John D. Hicks, *Republican Ascendancy* (1960); Arthur M. Schlesinger, Jr., *The Crisis of the Old Order* (1957); and John Braeman (ed.), *Change and Continuity in Twentieth Century America: The 1920s* (1968). Frederick Lewis Allen's *Only Yesterday* (1931) remains a classic popular account of the decade; while Isabel Leighton (ed.), *The Aspirin Age* (1949), contains a series of entertaining essays on the period.

The Harding presidency is examined in Robert K. Murray, *The Politics of Normalcy* (1973) and *The Harding Era* (1969), and Eugene Trani and David Wilson, *The Presidency of Warren G. Harding* (1977). Burl Noggle, *Teapot Dome* (1962), examines the major scandal of the Harding years. Francis Russell, *The Shadow of Blooming Grove* (1968), and Andrew Sinclair, *The Available Man* (1965), are popular, unadmiring biographies of the twenty-ninth President. A scholarly overview of the Coolidge presidency is available in Donald McCoy, *Calvin Coolidge* (1967); while journalist William Allen White has provided an engaging biography in *A Puritan in Babylon* (1940). The relationships between government and business are explored in James Gilbert, *Designing the Industrial State* (1972); John Hoff Wilson, *Herbert Hoover: Forgotten Progressive* (1975); and David Burner, *Herbert Hoover* (1979). The difficulties of progressive opponents of the administration receive attention in LeRoy Ashby,

Spearless Leader (1972), which focuses upon William Borah; Richard Lowitt, *George W. Norris,* vol. 2 (1971); and David P. Thelen, *Robert M. La Follette and the Insurgent Spirit* (1978).

For the foreign policy of the 1920s, see L. Ethan Ellis, *Republican Foreign Policy, 1921–1933* (1968); Selig Adler, *The Uncertain Giant* (1965); and Merlo J. Pusey, *Charles Evans Hughes,* 2 vols. (1963). Joan Hoff Wilson's *American Business and Foreign Policy, 1920–1933* (1968) and *Ideology and Economics* (1974) discuss corporate influence upon diplomacy and the relationship with the Soviet Union respectively. William Appleman Williams's *The Tragedy of American Diplomacy* (1962) is a revisionist critique of economic influences upon foreign policy. For American policy in the Pacific, see Akira Iriye, *After Imperialism* (1965), and Warren Cohen, *America's Response to China* (1971). Roger Dingman, *Power in the Pacific* (1976), and Thomas Buckley, *The United States and the Washington Conference* (1970), examine the 1921–1922 naval conference; while Robert H. Ferrell, *Peace in Their Time* (1952), studies the Kellogg-Briand Pact. For the United States and Latin America, see Joseph Tulchin, *The Aftermath of War* (1971), and William Kamman, *A Search for Stability* (1968).

On the 1920s economy, see George Soule, *Prosperity Decade* (1947). Alfred Chandler's *Strategy and Structure* (1962) examines the development of several modern corporations (including General Motors); and Louis Galambos's *Competition and Cooperation* (1966) explores the growth of a trade association (the Cotton Textile Institute). A full account of the labor movement in the 1920s is available in Irving Bernstein, *The Lean Years* (1960). See also David Brody, *Steelworkers in America* (1960) and *Workers in Industrial America* (1980), chapter 2. On American agriculture during the decade, consult Gilbert Fite, *George Peek and the Fight for Farm Parity* (1954), and Theodore Saloutos and John D. Hicks, *Twentieth Century Populism* (1951).

Ten

The New Culture
and Its Critics

The decade of the 1920s was notable not only for prosperity, not only for the triumph of the business civilization, and not only for the weakening of social and political reform. It was notable as well for a series of profound cultural changes: changes in the way people lived and thought. Americans of the New Era experienced, first, a marked centralization and nationalization of their culture. They were beginning to live their lives and perceive their world in increasingly similar ways. They were being exposed, second, to a new set of secular values, values that reflected the prosperity and complexity of the modern economy. And they were, finally, experiencing a growing cultural schism, a gulf between those middle-class Americans who welcomed and benefited from the cultural changes, and those less affluent, more provincial Americans who felt threatened and assaulted by them. It was, in short, an era in which the forces of modernism were gaining an ever stronger grip on American life, but one in which those forces were at the same time suffering bitter, determined opposition.

THE NATIONAL CULTURE

Several factors combined in the 1920s to accelerate the trend toward a truly national culture. One such factor was prosperity, and the greatly increased purchasing power it gave to a growing number of Americans. Another was the availability of new consumer products that altered the cultural focus of almost every citizen. Above all, there was a revolution in transportation and communications that eroded local and regional isolation.

The Rise of Consumerism

The United States of the 1920s was for the first time becoming a true consumer society—a society in which not only the affluent, but ordinary men and women bought items not just because of need, but for the sheer pleasure of buying. What they bought, moreover, helped change the way they lived. Middle-class families rushed to purchase such new appliances as electric refrigerators, washing machines, and vacuum cleaners. Men wore wristwatches and smoked cigarettes; women purchased cosmetics and mass-produced fashions. Americans in every part of the country ate commercially processed foods distributed nationally through chain stores and supermarkets.

The clearest illustration of the new consumerism, however, was the frenzied excitement with which Americans greeted the automobile, which was in the 1920s becoming more widely available and affordable than ever before. By the end of the decade, there were more than 30 million cars on American roads—almost as many as there were families. Automobiles had, in the process, become not just a means of transportation, but the first great national consumer obsession. No longer was it possible for automobile manufacturers to do what Henry Ford had once done: offer the public a single model in a single color (black), unchanging from year to year. General Motors now set the pattern for the industry with new models every fall, featuring a wide range of accessories and displaying as much attention to styling and design as to engineering. Automobiles, like other consumer goods, were becoming important to Americans for the status they provided as well as for the functions they served.

No group was more aware of this development (or more responsible for creating it) than a new and growing sector of the economy: the advertising industry. The first advertising and public relations firms (N. W. Ayer and J. Walter Thompson) had appeared well before World War I; but it was in the 1920s, partly as a result of techniques pioneered by wartime propaganda, that advertising truly came of age. Publicists began to see themselves as more than purveyors of information; they no longer considered it their task simply to display a product, describe its features, and tell where it could be bought. They viewed themselves, rather, as agents of the growing American economy; and they advertised products by attempting to invest them with glamor and prestige. Americans were being encouraged to buy consumer goods not just for their practical value but because of the intangible prestige and allure the goods were meant to convey to the purchaser. They were also being encouraged to absorb the values of promotion and salesmanship and to admire those who were effective "boosters" and publicists. One of the most successful books of the 1920s was the work of an advertising executive, Bruce Barton. In *The Man Nobody Knows*, Barton drew a portrait of Jesus Christ, describing him less as a religious prophet than as a "super salesman" who "picked up twelve men from the bottom ranks of business and forged them into an organization that conquered the world." The parables, Barton argued, were "the most powerful advertisements of all time." Perhaps the most telling indication of how clearly Barton's image mirrored popular assumptions was that virtually no one

THE AUTOMOBILE CULTURE.   The expanding importance of the automobile, both to the American economy and to the nation's life style, is suggested by this 1925 photo of the parking lot of a Massachusetts beach. (*Wide World Photos*)

objected to the book as sacrilegious or offensive. Most considered the portrait a flattering one.

Advertising not only increased the appeal of existing wares. It occasionally created a market for utterly useless merchandise or, in one notorious case, for a product that, in effect, did not even exist. By the mid-1920s, largely as a result of the influence of the automobile, the coastal regions of southern Florida were becoming increasingly popular as resort areas and retirement communities. In addition to the real growth in the state, however, there also developed a wild speculative fever, as realtors and advertisers combined to create what became known as the Florida Land Boom. By 1925, there were 2,000 realtors and another 2,500 real estate agents in Miami alone. Aggressive salesmen were selling land all over the state, often to people thousands of miles away who were lured by deceptive advertisements. Much of the property was remote and undeveloped; some of it was worthless swampland. Finally, in 1926, a disastrous hurricane punctured the speculative bubble, and the great land boom collapsed as quickly as it had grown. Real estate prices had continued to climb only because of the success of salesmen and advertisers in creating a demand where none had previously existed.

National Communications

The advertising industry could never have had the impact it did had it not been for the emergence of new vehicles of communication that made it possible to reach large audiences quickly and easily. Nothing was more influential in creating a genuinely national culture than the ability to transmit messages nationally.

Some of the changes occurred within forms of communications that had long existed. Newspapers and magazines were hardly new to the 1920s, but they were undergoing an important transformation. The number of local newspapers, for example, was rapidly shrinking. In Chicago, there were seven morning dailies at the beginning of the decade; by the end there were two. More than 600 papers died between 1914 and 1926, and the average circulation of those that remained rose steadily. Even more significant perhaps was that many of the newspapers that survived were becoming parts of large national chains. By 1927, 55 chains controlled 230 major newspapers. Wire services and syndicates were providing national circulation for columns, features, and comic strips, so that even individually owned newspapers exposed their readers to the same material that people in countless other cities were receiving. There was, as well, a growing number of national, mass-circulation magazines—*Time, Life, Reader's Digest*—aimed at the widest possible audience. In other words, fewer and fewer sources of information were servicing larger and larger groups of people. Increasing numbers of Americans were beginning to share access to the same ideas and experiences.

Even more influential in shaping the popular culture of the 1920s was the popularity of the movies. They too were not new, but they were expanding greatly. Forty million people attended motion pictures in 1922; over 100 million people saw films in 1930, by which time the movies had become a $2-billion industry. Attending the cinema provided Americans with an important, unifying cultural experience. It engaged people in a common activity: going to the movie theater —usually a huge, ornate structure that by itself created excitement. It exposed them to identical experiences: watching the same newsreels, serials, and features. It enabled them to admire the same movie stars and share an interest in the same celebrity gossip. Millions of Americans reveled in news of Clara Bow (the "It" girl), Mary Pickford, Greta Garbo, and Charlie Chaplin. The whole nation mourned when screen idol Rudolph Valentino died in 1926. The addition of sound to motion pictures, beginning with the first "talkie" in 1927, *The Jazz Singer* with Al Jolson, created nationwide excitement. Above all, the movies transmitted to people in every region a common set of values, a shared image of American life. More often than not it was a banal image of conventional middle-class values and stable middle-class life styles. Movie censor Will Hays, the powerful head of the Motion Picture Association who was recruited to improve the industry's image after a series of unsavory scandals in 1921, ensured that all films preached a similar, sanctimonious message. Americans saw little that was jarring or provocative in the products of Hollywood.

The most important communications vehicle of all, however, was the only one that was truly new to the 1920s: radio. The first radio station in America, KDKA in Pittsburgh, began broadcasting on election night in 1920; and the first national radio network, the National Broadcasting Company, took form in 1927. By 1923, there were more than 500 radio stations, covering virtually every area of the country; by 1929, more than 12 million families owned radio sets. Broadcasting became, therefore, the ultimate vehicle for linking the nation together, providing Americans everywhere with instant access to a common source of information and entertainment. It made possible a new social phenomenon: the shared national experience. The entire nation could listen simultaneously to the broadcasting of

THE JAZZ SINGER.   Al Jolson re-created on film a role he had often performed in real life—a vaudeville minstrel singer in blackface—in *The Jazz Singer* (1927), the first feature-length "talkie." The introduction of sound to motion pictures occurred at a moment when the American film industry, long preeminent in the world, was facing stiff competition from abroad, particularly from the Soviet Union. The "talkie revolution" restored Hollywood to the center of international attention. (*The Museum of Modern Art/Film Stills Archive*)

such events as the funeral of President Harding, the flight of Charles Lindbergh, the World Series, the famous Dempsey–Tunney fights.

Fads and Fashions

The combination of the new consumerism, the influence of advertising, and the availability of mass communications media transformed America in the 1920s into a society where national fads and obsessions could emerge suddenly and powerfully. Radio, for example, helped elevate professional sports, and in particular professional baseball, from the level of limited, local activities to the level of a national obsession. Sports heroes such as Babe Ruth, Ty Cobb, Red Grange, and Jack Dempsey vied with politicians and industrialists for the affections of the public. It was now possible for new fads and stunts to achieve national popularity

THE NEW MEDIUM. The changing leisure activities of the 1920s are revealed in this picture of two generations of a middle-class family seated in their parlor. While the parents indulge in traditional evening activities—reading a newspaper or a book— the children suggest the future as they listen through earphones to an early radio set. (*UPI*)

almost overnight. Men and women across the country were bcoming devotees of crossword puzzles, mah jong (a popular game vaguely similar to dominoes), and contract bridge. They shared a pleasure in popular stunts—flagpole sitting, marathon dancing, goldfish swallowing. They shared an interest in national sensations —the birth of the Dionne quintuplets, the sensational Hall-Mills murder trial, the tortuous progress of the Sacco-Vanzetti case. It is not surprising that Frederick Lewis Allen, the brilliant chronicler of the 1920s, referred to the decade as the "Ballyhoo Years."

CHANGING VALUES

Most of the major institutions of the new mass culture—the movie industry, radio, the mass-circulation newspapers and magazines—tried to avoid controversy and to promote traditional values and assumptions. Despite their efforts, however, the American people were in the 1920s being exposed to a wide range of new standards of thought and behavior; and their own values and life styles were often changing as a result. Among members of the prosperous middle class, at least, two sets of values in particular were gaining increasing power. There was, first, the growing influence of secular, material concerns and a corresponding decline in spiritual and idealistic ones. And there was, second, an increasing awareness of the importance of expertise and education in modern society, of the need for specialized, professional training. Together, such changes affected some of the nation's most basic institutions.

Modern Religion

The scientific advances of the late nineteenth and early twentieth centuries had by the 1920s already produced profound changes in American theology. Protestant clergymen in particular had revised religious doctrine to reconcile traditional faith with the theories of Charles Darwin. Ministers in the progressive era had played an important role in promoting social issues; churches had become not only centers of worship but agents of reform. After World War I, the increasing secularism of American society worked even further changes upon both religious faith and religious behavior. Theological modernists, among them Harry Emerson Fosdick and A. C. McGiffert, taught their followers to abandon many of the traditional trappings of religion (literal interpretation of the Bible, belief in the Trinity, attribution of human traits to the deity) and to accept a faith that many believed was only one step removed from agnosticism. One New England clergyman in the 1920s described God as "a sort of oblong blur." Others declined to offer any description at all.

The extremes of religious modernism found acceptance among only a relatively few people. Changes in popular religious assumptions and patterns were, however, widespread. The sociologists Robert and Helen Lynd discovered during a study of community life in Muncie, Indiana, for example, that while most people continued to attend church and express a belief in God, they also were experiencing important changes. Fewer people seemed to believe in hell; many admitted that they "think of Heaven less than they used to." "One infers," the Lynds reported in their famous study *Middletown* (1929), "that doubts and uneasiness among individuals may be greater than a generation ago." Such changes were having an impact upon the outward forms of religious expression as well. Parents were placing less emphasis on religious training of their children than in the past. Families seldom engaged in private prayers any longer, or in any sort of worship outside the church. Religious services during the week were a dying institution; most people thought of Sunday, and Sunday only, as an appropriate time for worship. Yet even Sundays were changing; few middle-class families any longer maintained strict observance of the Sabbath. Churches, forced to compete with secular interests for the attention of their members, often adopted the same competitive salesmanship that was infecting other areas of the society. Ministers began to address businessmen's luncheons and women's clubs; churches increasingly emphasized social and athletic activities; congregations competed with one another over fund raising and over the size and grandeur of new church buildings; sermons increasingly dealt with secular rather than religious matters. Religion, which had for centuries been one of the most powerful forces in American life, was beginning to occupy a secondary place in the daily lives of many members of the middle class.

Women and the Family

Even greater changes were occurring in the structure and behavior of the family. The secularism of the New Era combined with the increasing emphasis on expertise and specialized training to produce a major redefinition of the role of women and the concept of marriage. Technological advances had long ago released many middle-class women from some of the burdens of housework; new, more advanced appliances in the 1920s speeded that liberation even further. Other factors produced additional changes. American society in the first years of the twentieth century had placed a high value on the idea of motherhood, on the belief that a woman's mission was to bear and raise children, on the assumption that women were uniquely and instinctively qualified for parenthood. After World War I, however, an influential group of psychologists—the "behaviorists," led by John B. Watson—began to challenge such assumptions. Maternal affection was not, they claimed, sufficient preparation for child rearing. "No woman," Watson preached, "knows enough to raise a child." Instead, mothers should rely on the advice and assistance of experts and professionals: doctors, nurses, and trained educators in nursery schools and kindergartens. They should avoid "smothering" their children with affection; they should teach them not to expect too much maternal attention.

For many middle-class women, these changes removed what had been an important and consuming activity. They were no longer required to spend endless hours engaged in housework; now they were finding that motherhood occupied far less time as well. Clearly, women needed to discover new activities, a new role to fill the void. For some, that role became entry into a profession. Women in the 1920s were doing far more than those of any previous generation to win for themselves positions in the economic mainstream; in some professions in particular—fashion, publishing, cosmetics, social work, nursing, education—they were making major inroads.

Most women, however, avoided professional activities, discouraged by the historic prejudice against females entering careers, or barred by the powerful obstacles that continued to block women from many supposedly male activities. Instead, they devoted new attention to their roles as wives and companions. A woman's relationship with her husband assumed, therefore, a greatly enhanced importance; and a national cult of "romantic love"—popularized in films, radio serials, and women's magazines—quickly emerged. Women increasingly shared in their husbands' social lives; they devoted attention to cosmetics and seductive clothing in an effort to please their husbands; they tried to prevent children from interfering with the development of marital relationships. Most of all, perhaps, they were encouraged to think of their sexual relationships with their husbands not simply as a means of procreation, as earlier generations had been taught, but as an important and pleasurable experience in its own right, as the culmination of romantic love. Thus it was that the 1920s saw the emergence for the first time of a national birth-control movement, pioneered by Margaret Sanger. Women should, Sanger argued, be free to enjoy the pleasures of sexual activity without relation to the bearing of children.

These changes combined to produce among many women a great sense of liberation. No longer did they feel required to maintain a rigid, Victorian "respectability." They were free to adopt far less inhibited life styles. They could smoke, drink, dance, wear seductive clothes and make-up, and attend lively parties. Married women could share more fully in the lives of their husbands; unmarried women could engage more freely in social and even sexual activity. The popular image of the "flapper"—the modern woman whose liberated life style found expression in dress, hair style, speech, and behavior—became one of the most widely discussed features of the era.

But the changes came, too, at great cost. By placing more and more emphasis upon their relationships with men, women were increasing their vulnerability to frustration and unhappiness when those relationships proved unsatisfactory. It was not surprising, perhaps, that the national divorce rate climbed dramatically in the 1920s; nor that many women who remained married experienced increasing boredom and restlessness.

Education and Youth

The growing secularism of American culture and the emphasis on training and expertise were clearly reflected in the changing role of education, which was beginning to occupy an increasingly important role in the lives of American youths. The changes were evident in numerous ways. First, more people were going to school in the 1920s than ever before. High-school attendance more than doubled during the decade: from 2.2 million to over 5 million. Enrollment in

THE FLAPPER.
Vogue magazine, one of the new mass-circulation women's periodicals of the 1920s, gave wide currency to the image of the "flapper"—the modern, uninhibited woman. (*Condé Nast Publications*)

colleges and universities increased threefold between 1900 and 1930, with much of that increase occurring after World War I. In 1918, there had been 600,000 college students; in 1930, there were 1.2 million, nearly 20 percent of the college-age population. Attendance was increasing as well at trade and vocational schools and in other institutions providing the specialized training that the modern economy demanded. Schools were, in addition, beginning to perform new and more varied functions. Instead of offering simply the traditional disciplines, they were providing training in modern technical skills: engineering, management, economics.

The growing importance of education was contributing as well to the emergence of a separate youth culture. The idea of adolescence as a distinct period in the life of an individual was for the most part new to the twentieth century. It was a result in some measure of the influence of Freudian psychology. But it was a result, too, of society's recognition that a more extended period of training and preparation was necessary before a young person was ready to move into the workplace. Schools and colleges provided adolescents with a setting in which they could develop their own social patterns, their own hobbies, their own interests and activities. An increasing number of students saw school as a place not just for academic training but for organized athletics, extracurricular activities, clubs, fraternities, and sororities; that is, as an institution that allowed them to define themselves less in terms of their families and more in terms of their peer group.

The result, in many cases, was an increasing conformity among high-school and college students, who were subjected to the pressures of their contemporaries to adopt certain social standards and rituals. A college professor at one men's college, for example, complained that the growth of fraternities and other clubs was making students "standardized and uniform, much afraid of being thought unusual or out of step."

Parents expressed alarm at other aspects of the youth culture: the increasing (and increasingly open) freedom of adolescent behavior. Young people in the 1920s were talking differently, dressing differently, and behaving differently from their parents. They often seemed deliberately to flaunt the standards and values of the older generation. Even high-school students were experiencing a liberation from parental control. Those who had access to automobiles could simply drive several miles from home and behave as they wished, free from the gaze of family and neighbors. The automobile made possible other freedoms as well, as a judge in Muncie, Indiana, noted when he described it as a "house of prostitution on wheels."

The Decline of the Self-Made Man

Most of all, however, the increasing importance of education and the changing nature of adolescence underscored one of the most important changes in American society: the gradual disappearance of both the reality and the ideal of the self-made man. The belief that any person could, simply through hard work and innate talent, achieve wealth and renown had always been largely a myth; but it had had enough basis in reality to remain a convincing myth for generations. By the 1920s, however, it was becoming difficult to believe any longer that success was possible without education and training. "The self-made manager in business," wrote *Century Magazine* in 1925, "is nearing the end of his road. He cannot escape the relentless pursuit of the same forces that have eliminated self-made lawyers and doctors and admirals. . . . He is already hiring professionally trained engineers, chemists, accountants, and hygienists. . . . He must himself turn to professional education, or surrender control to those who do."

The "Doom of the Self-Made Man," as *Century* described it, was a difficult development for Americans to accept. It suggested that the individual was no longer entirely in control of his own destiny, that a person's future depended in large part on factors over which he had only limited control. And like many of the other changes of the decade, many Americans greeted this one with marked ambivalence. These mixed feelings were reflected in the identity of three men who

LUCKY LINDY. Charles A. Lindbergh—the greatest hero of the 1920s—is shown here wearing aviation gear in one of the most widely published photographs in the world. Lindbergh's popularity was such that when, in 1928, he endorsed Herbert Hoover for President, the Republicans adopted a campaign song entitled "If He's Good Enough for Lindy, He's Good Enough for Me." (*UPI*)

became the most widely admired heroes of the New Era: Thomas Edison, the inventor of the electric light bulb and many other technological marvels; Henry Ford, the creator of the assembly line and one of the founders of the automobile industry; and Charles Lindbergh, the first aviator to make a solo flight across the Atlantic Ocean. All received the adulation of much of the American public. Lindbergh, in particular, became a national hero the like of which the country had never seen before. And the reasons for their popularity indicated much about how Americans viewed the new epoch in which they were living. On the one hand, all three men represented the triumphs of the modern technological and industrial society. On the other hand, all three had risen to success without the benefit of formal education and largely through their own private efforts. They were, it seemed, genuinely self-made men. Even those Americans who were most happily embracing a new society and a new culture were doing so without entirely diverting their gaze from a simpler past.

THE DISENCHANTED

To a generation of artists and intellectuals coming of age in the 1920s, the new society in which they lived was even more disturbing. They were experiencing a disenchantment with modern America so fundamental that they were often able to view it only with contempt. As a result, they adopted a role sharply different from that of the intellectuals of other eras. Rather than involving themselves with their society's popular culture and attempting to influence and reform the mass of their countrymen, they isolated themselves and embarked on a restless search for personal fulfillment. Gertrude Stein once referred to the young Americans emerging from World War I as a "lost generation." For many writers and intellectuals, at least, it was an apt description.

Sources of Alienation

At the heart of the Lost Generation's critique of modern society was a sense of personal alienation, a belief that contemporary America no longer provided the individual with avenues by which he could achieve personal fulfillment. Modern life, they argued, was cold, impersonal, materialistic, and thus meaningless. The sensitive individual could find no happiness in the mainstream of American society.

This disillusionment had its roots in many things, but in nothing so deeply as the experience of World War I. To those who had fought in France and experienced the horror and savagery of modern warfare—and even to those who had not fought but who nevertheless had been aware of the appalling costs of the struggle—the aftermath of the conflict was shattering. Nothing, it seemed, had been gained. There was no new structure of peace or justice. There was, rather, the same old world back in the hands of the same old men who had always run it. The war had been a fraud; the suffering and the dying had been in vain. Ernest Hemingway, one of the most celebrated (and most commercially successful) of the new breed of writers expressed their contempt for the war in his novel *A Farewell to Arms* (1929). Its hero, an American officer fighting in Europe, decides that there is no justification for his participation in the conflict and deserts the army with a nurse with whom he has fallen in love. Hemingway made it clear that he was to be admired for doing so.

At least equally dispiriting was the character of the nation these young intellectuals found upon their return home at war's end. It was, they believed, a society utterly lacking in vision or idealism, obsessed with materialism, steeped in out-

moded, priggish morality. Worst of all, it was one in which the individual had lost
the ability to control his or her own fate. It was a sleek, new, industrialized and
professionalized world that was organized in a dehumanizing way. Symbolic of it
all was the monotonous, routinized, inhuman quality of modern factory work: men
and women performing the same menial tasks over and over as part of an assembly
line, men and women reduced to the level of cogs in a machine. Sherwood
Anderson satirized the depersonalization of industrial society in his novel *Poor
White* (1920), in which a conveyor belt becomes the master and individual men
its slaves. Charlie Chaplin denounced it some years later in his film *Modern Times*
(1936), in which Chaplin himself, representing the common man, struggles to free
himself from the tyranny of the assembly line by escaping through a maze of gears
and levers.

The Debunkers

One result of this alienation was a series of savage critiques of modern society by
a wide range of writers, the most prominent of whom were often described as the
"debunkers." Most influential was the Baltimore journalist H. L. Mencken, a man
somewhat older than many of the new intellectuals (he was forty years old in
1920), but one who served as a spokesman for the Lost Generation nevertheless.
In the pages of his magazines, first *The Smart Set* and later *The American
Mercury*, he delighted in ridiculing everything Americans held dear: religion,
politics, the arts, even democracy itself. He found it impossible to believe, he
claimed, that "civilized life was possible under a democracy," because it was a
form of government that placed power in the hands of the common people, whom
he ridiculed as the "booboisie." When someone asked Mencken why he continued to live in a society he found so loathsome, he replied: "Why do people go
to the zoo?"

Echoing Mencken's contempt was the novelist Sinclair Lewis, the first American to win a Nobel Prize in literature. In a series of savage novels, he lashed out
at one aspect of modern society after another. In *Main Street* (1920), he satirized
life in a small midwestern town (much like the one in which he himself had grown
up). In *Babbitt* (1922), he ridiculed life in the modern city. *Arrowsmith* (1925)
attacked the medical profession (and by implication professionalism in general);
Elmer Gantry (1927) satirized popular religion. Lewis's message was one of cynicism, despair, and hopelessness. There was nothing redeeming in American life,
he seemed to say, nothing of value. A similar message could be found in the
celebrated collection of essays *Civilization in the United States,* published in 1922
and edited by the young critic Harold Stearns. It included twenty-two articles,
each written by a writer or critic of the new generation, discussing virtually every
aspect of American life: politics, religion, art, journalism, the city, the small town,
literature. All of them, the authors seemed to conclude, were valueless and repel-
lent.

To those who held the values of their society in such contempt, the standard
avenues for advancement held little appeal. Intellectuals of the 1920s turned their

CHAPLIN COMMENTS ON HIS ERA. Charlie Chaplin, the greatest comedy star of 1920s films, depicted in *Modern Times* the bewilderment of the common man in the face of the depersonalized world of the machine. (*Museum of Modern Art*)

backs on the traditional goals of their parents, openly rejecting the "success ethic" that they believed dominated American life. F. Scott Fitzgerald, whose first novel, *This Side of Paradise* (1920), established him as a spokesman for his generation, ridiculed the American obsession with material success in *The Great Gatsby* (1925). The novel's hero, Jay Gatsby, spends his life accumulating wealth and social prestige in order to win the woman he loves. The world to which he has aspired, however, turns out to be one of pretension, fraud, and cruelty, and Gatsby is ultimately destroyed by it. Fitzgerald and his intellectual contemporaries claimed to want nothing to do with conventional American society (although Fitzgerald himself seemed at the same time desperately to crave acceptance by it). They chose, instead, to search elsewhere for fulfillment.

A Refuge in Art

Their quest took them in several different directions, often at the same time. Many Lost Generation intellectuals left America to live in France, making Paris for a time a center of American artistic life. Some adopted hedonistic life styles, indulging in conspicuous debauchery: drinking, drugs, casual sex, wild parties, and a generally flamboyant way of life. (The publicity they received helped set the tone for other, less alienated members of their generation, who began to imitate this uninhibited pursuit of pleasure.) Many intellectuals resorted to an outspoken self-absorption, openly repudiating any responsibility for anyone but themselves. "The great problems of the world . . . do not concern me in the slightest," wrote critic George Jean Nathan. "What concerns me alone is myself and the interests of a few close friends."

For most of these young men and women, however, the only real refuge from the travails of modern society was art—not art for any social purpose, but art for its own sake. Only art, they argued, could allow them full individual expression; only the act of creation could offer them fulfillment. Art was the only escape from dehumanization, the poet e. e. cummings suggested in *The Enormous Room* (1922). What happens to those who do not become artists, a character asks? "I feel nothing happens to them," comes the reply. "I feel negation becomes of them." Some writers and artists attempted to appeal to a broad audience, hoping for commercial as well as critical success. Others, however, rejected the intellectual mainstream far more decisively, producing works of art and literature that were often incomprehensible to anyone other than their creator. The popular artistic school known as Dadaism expressed their outlook. Dadaist art was an entirely personal, individual, at times even random matter. It mattered little if it conveyed no meaning.

The result of this quest for fulfillment through art was not, for the most part, personal satisfaction for the writers and artists involved. They remained throughout the 1920s a restless, usually unhappy generation, searching in vain for contentment. "It is common for young men and women to rebel," Walter Lippmann once wrote of them; "but that they should rebel sadly and without faith in their rebellion . . . that is something of a novelty." They did, however, produce a body of work that made the decade one of the great eras of American art. Most notable were the writers: Hemingway, Fitzgerald, Lewis, as well as others such as Thomas Wolfe, John Dos Passos, Ezra Pound, and Eugene O'Neill—the first great American playwright and the only one ever to win a Nobel Prize. T. S. Eliot, a native of Boston who spent most of his adult life in England, led a generation of poets in breaking with the romanticism of the nineteenth century. His epic work *The Waste Land* (1922) brought to poetry much of the harsh tone of despair that was invading other areas of literature. Yet the writers of the 1920s were notable not only for the effectiveness of their critiques, but for their success in pioneering new literary styles and techniques. Some incorporated Freudian psychology into their work, using literature to explore not only external actions but the workings of the psyche as well. Others produced innovations in form, structure, and dialogue: Ernest Hemingway, with his spare, clean prose; Sinclair Lewis, with his biting satire; John Dos Passos, with his use of the techniques of journalism as well as literature. The literature of the 1920s was escapist; but it was also intensely creative, even revolutionary.

Other Visions

Not all intellectuals of the 1920s, however, expressed such total alienation and despair. Some expressed reservations about their society not by withdrawing from it, but by advocating reform. Older progressive theorists continued to expound the values they had celebrated in the years before the war. Thorstein Veblen, for example, continued to attract a wide audience with his argument that modern society should adopt the "discipline of the machine" and assign control to engineers and technocratic experts. John Dewey remained influential with his appeals for "practical" education and experimentation in social policy. Charles and Mary Beard, perhaps the most influential historians of their day, promoted "progressive" principles. In their book *The Rise of American Civilization* (1927) they stressed economic factors in tracing the development of modern society and suggested the need for social and economic planning. Vernon Parrington, an influential intellectual historian, traced many of the same themes in reviewing American art and literature. In *Main Currents of American Thought* (1927), the epic work he did not live to complete, he explained the evolution of American culture in largely social and economic terms, implying, like the Beards, that positive social programs could have wide-ranging effects. These progressive intellectuals were often harshly critical of the society of the 1920s; yet they were, indirectly, legitimizing some of its most important features. Society was not, they were saying, excessively routinized and disciplined, as members of the Lost Generation were complaining. If anything, it was not disciplined and organized enough.

To another group of intellectuals, the solution to contemporary problems lay neither in escapism nor in progressivism, but in an exploration of their own regional or cultural origins. In New York City, a new generation of black intellectuals created a flourishing Afro-American culture widely described as the "Harlem Renaissance." The Harlem poets, novelists, and artists drew heavily from their African roots in an effort to prove the richness of their own racial heritage (and not incidentally to prove to the white race that the black was worthy of respect). The poet Langston Hughes captured much of the spirit of the movement in a single sentence: "I am a Negro—and beautiful." Other black writers—James Weldon Johnson, Countee Cullen, Claude McKay, Alain Locke—as well as emerging black artists and musicians helped to establish a thriving culture rooted in the historical legacy of their race.

A similar effort was under way among an influential group of southern intellectuals. Known variously as the "Fugitives" and the "Agrarians," these young poets, novelists, and critics sought to counter the depersonalization of industrial society by evoking the strong rural traditions of their own region. In their controversial manifesto *I'll Take My Stand,* a collection of twelve essays by twelve southern intellectuals, they issued a simultaneously radical and conservative appeal for a rejection of the doctrine of "economic progress" and the spiritual debilitation that had accompanied it. The supposedly "backward" South, they argued, could serve as a model for a nation drunk with visions of limitless growth and modernization.

Perhaps the greatest of all American writers of this era avoided such stridency but expressed nevertheless the southerner's strong sense of place and of cultural heritage. William Faulkner, in a remarkable series of novels set in the fictional Mississippi county of Yoknapatawpha—*The Sound and the Fury* (1929), *Absalom, Absalom* (1936), and others—was, like many of his contemporaries, concerned with the problems of the individual seeking fulfillment in the modern world. But unlike others, he painstakingly re-created the bonds of region and community, rather than expressing a detachment from his own society. In the face of the suffocating reality of southern society, Faulkner's most successful characters (usually women and blacks) prove the resilience of the human spirit not by triumphing but by "enduring." Individual destiny, Faulkner—like many other artists of the 1920s—was suggesting, lay in the display of strength and dignity in the face of overpowering obstacles.

A CONFLICT OF CULTURES

The modern, secular culture of the 1920s did not exist alone. It grew up alongside an older, more traditional culture with which it continually and often bitterly competed. One was the society of an affluent, largely urban middle class, committed to a new set of values, adopting a new, increasingly uninhibited life style, linked to a national cultural outlook. The other was a society of less affluent, less urban, far more provincial Americans—men and women who continued to revere traditional values and customs and who feared and resented the modernist threats to their way of life. Beneath the apparent stability of the New Era and its celebrated business civilization, therefore, raged a series of harsh cultural controversies.

Prohibition

When the prohibition of the sale and manufacture of alcohol went into effect in January 1920, it had the support of most members of the middle class and most of those who considered themselves progressives. It was, after all, progressive reformers who had been most responsible for passage of the constitutional amendment requiring Prohibition. Within a year, however, it had become clear that the experiment was not working. What had happened, in essence, was that Americans had simply refused to stop drinking.

The first prohibition commissioner had promised rigorous enforcement of the new law, but the resources available to him were ludicrously insufficient. To keep alcohol out of circulation would have required the constant patrolling of 18,000 miles of coastline and thousands more miles of land borders, across all of which whiskey was being smuggled with reckless abandon. It would have meant guarding the 57 million gallons of industrial alcohol being manufactured every year, much of which was being diverted to human consumption. It would have meant patrolling virtually every community in the country to root out illegal stills, hidden saloons (known as "speakeasies"), and bootleggers. It would have required policing as many as 20 million private homes, where individual citizens were concocting "bathtub gin" and other alcoholic brews.

In the face of such obstacles, enforcement proved impossible, particularly since the government had hired only 1,500 agents at modest salaries to do the job. Before long, it was almost as easy to acquire illegal alcohol in most of the country as it had once been to acquire legal alcohol. One prohibition agent conducted a survey to determine how long it would take him to buy a drink in several major cities. In Atlanta, it took him seventeen minutes from the moment he stepped off the train; in Chicago, twenty-one minutes; in Cleveland, twenty-nine. The fastest purchase was in New Orleans: thirty-five seconds; his cabdriver at the depot

THE "NOBLE EXPERIMENT."   Federal prohibition agents empty bottles of confiscated liquor down a sewer. The head of the Prohibition Bureau once estimated that law-enforcement agencies were catching only about one-twentieth of the alcohol being smuggled into the country, to say nothing of the tremendous quantities that were being produced illegally within the United States. (*Culver Pictures*)

offered him a bottle. The longest was in Washington, D.C., where it took an hour. A local policeman finally showed him where to find a supplier.

More disturbing than the laughable ineffectiveness of the law, however, was the role Prohibition played in stimulating organized crime. An enormous, lucrative industry was now barred to legitimate businessmen; underworld figures quickly and decisively took it over. In Chicago, Al Capone built a vast criminal empire based largely on illegal alcohol. He guarded it against interlopers with an army of up to 1,000 gunmen, whose zealousness contributed to the violent deaths of more than 250 people in the city between 1920 and 1927. Other regions produced gangsters and gang wars of their own. Prohibition, in short, had become not only a national joke but a national scandal. The report of a federal commission appointed in 1929 and chaired by George W. Wickersham provided a devastating indictment of the effects of Prohibition. Most Americans, however, had by then been aware of the problems for years.

Nevertheless, Prohibition survived. The growing strength of repeal forces was more than countered by the increasing militance of defenders of the experiment. Even the Wickersham Commission did not dare recommend outright repeal, for fear of the political outcry such a statement would provoke. The reason was simple. The middle-class progressives who had originally supported Prohibition may have lost interest; but an enormous constituency of provincial, largely rural, overwhelmingly Protestant Americans continued vehemently to defend it. To them, drinking and the general licentiousness with which they associated it were an assault upon their conservative code of morality. More than that, these manifestations represented the encroachments of the new, urban civilization upon their traditional way of life. Drinking symbolized to them the modern city and all its vices. Prohibition had, in short, taken on implications far beyond the issue of drinking itself. It had come to represent the effort of an older America to maintain its dominance in a society that was moving forward in spite of it. As the decade proceeded, opponents of Prohibition (or "wets," as they came to be known) gained steadily in influence. Not until 1933, however, when the Great Depression added weight to their appeals, were they finally able to challenge the "drys" and win repeal of the Eighteenth Amendment.

Nativism and the Klan

Hostility to immigrants was not new to the 1920s. Nor was it restricted to the defenders of the traditional, provincial society. Like Prohibition, agitation for a curb on immigration had begun in the nineteenth century; and like Prohibition, it had gathered strength in the years before the war largely because of the support of middle-class progressives. Theodore Roosevelt toward the end of his life had espoused "100 percent Americanism." Other progressives had echoed his concern that the unbridled flow of immigrants into the country, particularly the flow of uneducated, rural people from southern and eastern Europe, was polluting the nation's racial stock and placing great strains on its social and economic capabilities. Such concerns had not been sufficient in the first years of the century to win passage of curbs on immigration; but when in the years immediately following the war immigration began to become associated with radicalism, popular sentiment on behalf of restriction grew rapidly.

In 1921, therefore, Congress passed an emergency immigration act, establishing a quota system by which annual immigration from any country could not exceed 3 percent of the number of persons of that nationality who had been in the United States in 1910. The new law cut immigration from 800,000 to 300,000 in a single year; but the nativists remained unsatisfied. In 1924, Congress enacted an even harsher law: the National Origins Act, which banned immigration from East Asia entirely (deeply angering Japan) and reduced the quota for Europeans from 3 to 2 percent. The quota would be based, moreover, not on the 1910 census, but on the census of 1890, a year in which there had been far fewer southern and eastern Europeans in the country. What immigration there was, in other words, would heavily favor northwestern Europeans—people of "Nordic" or "Teutonic" stock. The 1924 act cut the yearly flow almost in half, to 164,000. Five years later, a further restriction set a rigid limit of 150,000 immigrants a year. In the years that followed, immigration officials seldom permitted even half that number actually to enter the country.

The legislative expression of nativism reflected largely the doctrines of progressivism, even if a harsh and narrow progressivism. Restricting immigration, its proponents believed, would contribute to the efficient and productive operation of society. There were, however, other expressions of nativism that reflected very different sentiments. To defenders of an older, more provincial America, the growth of large communities of foreign peoples, alien in their speech, their habits, and their values, came to seem a direct threat to their own embattled way of life. This provincial nativism took a number of forms. But the most prominent was the resurgence of the Ku Klux Klan as a major force in American life.

The Klan was originally the product of the first years after the Civil War, when southern opponents of Reconstruction organized to fight what they believed was northern tyranny. That early organization died in the 1870s. But in 1915, shortly after the premiere of the film *The Birth of a Nation,* which celebrated the early Klan, a new group of southerners gathered on Stone Mountain outside Atlanta, Georgia, to establish a modern version of the society. At first, the new Klan, like the old, was largely concerned with intimidating blacks, who were, Klan leader William J. Simmons claimed, becoming dangerously insubordinate. After World War I, however, concern about blacks gradually became secondary to concern about Catholics, Jews, and foreigners. The Klan would devote itself, its leaders proclaimed, to purging American life of impure, alien influences.

It was then that the modern Klan experienced its greatest growth. Membership in the small towns and rural areas of the South soon expanded dramatically; more significantly, the Klan was now spreading northward, establishing a strong foothold particularly in the industrial states of the Midwest. By 1923, there were reportedly 3 million members; by 1924, 4 million. The Indiana Klan, under the leadership of David Stephenson, established effective political control of the state, electing the governor and much of the legislature. In other areas, it was a political force that few dared antagonize. Its success was in part a result of the skillful public relations work of new Klan leaders who began to operate the organization as a lucrative business enterprise. By charging membership fees, selling regalia and other Klan merchandise, and investing the organization with a mystical, fraternal aura, they made themselves and many of their colleagues not only powerful but wealthy. In 1922, a new leader, Hiram Wesley Evans, managed to displace the original hierarchy; but the growth of the Klan continued undiminished.

Members of the Klan adopted a set of secret rituals and used a private language. They wore elaborate white robes, established a hierarchy of "cycklopses," "kleagles," and "wizards," and staged dramatic marches and rallies. In some communities, where Klan leaders came from the most "respectable" segments of society, the society operated much like a fraternal organization, engaging in nothing more dangerous than occasional political pronouncements.

Often, however, the Klan also operated as a brutal, even violent, opponent of

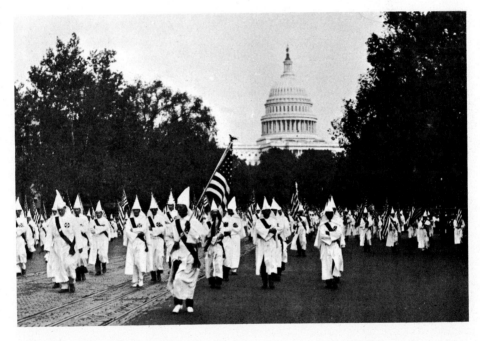

THE KLAN IN THE CAPITAL. Klansmen parade down Washington's Pennsylvania Avenue in 1926, at about the time the organization was beginning to decline in influence. A sordid scandal involving Klan leader David Stephenson, a major figure in Indiana Republican politics, helped speed the movement to its decline. Stephenson was convicted of kidnapping and raping a young woman, then failing to secure medical help when she attempted suicide. The woman, who had been his secretary, ultimately died. (*Culver Pictures*)

"alien" groups and as a defender of traditional, fundamentalist morality. Klansmen systematically terrorized blacks, Jews, Catholics, and foreigners: boycotting their businesses, threatening their families, and attempting to drive them out of their communities. Occasionally, they resorted to violence: public whipping, tarring and feathering, arson, and lynching. But what the Klan most deeply feared, it soon became clear, was not simply "foreign" or racially "impure" groups; it was any group that posed a challenge to their traditional values. Klansmen persecuted not only immigrants and blacks but those white Protestants they considered guilty of irreligion, sexual promiscuity, or drunkenness. The Klan worked to enforce Prohibition; it attempted to institute compulsory Bible readings in schools; it worked to punish divorce. In 1927, Klansmen in Alabama, led by a Baptist minister, staged a public flogging of a divorced woman whose crime was to have married a divorced man. The Ku Klux Klan, in short, was fighting not just to preserve racial homogeneity but to defend a traditional culture against the values and morals of modernity. The organization itself began to decline in influence after 1925, when a series of internal power struggles and several sordid scandals discredited some of its most important leaders. The issues it had raised, however, retained strength among some Americans for many years.

Religious Fundamentalism

The third great cultural controversy of the 1920s revealed even more starkly the growing gulf between the new culture and the old. It was a bitter conflict over questions of religious doctrine and, even more, over the place of religion in contemporary society. By 1921, American Protestantism was already divided into two warring camps. On one side stood the modernists: urban, middle-class people who had attempted to adapt religion to the teachings of modern science and to the realities of their modern, secular society. On the other side stood the fundamentalists: provincial, largely, although not exclusively, rural men and women, fighting to preserve traditional faith and to maintain the centrality of religion in American life. The fundamentalists looked with horror at the new morality of the modern city. (It was they, for example, who formed the core of the defense of Prohibition in the 1920s.) They expressed outrage at the abandonment of traditional beliefs in the face of scientific discoveries, insisting that the Bible was to be interpreted literally. Above all, they opposed the teachings of Charles Darwin, who had openly challenged the biblical story of the creation. Humans had not evolved from lower orders of animals, the fundamentalists insisted. They had been created by God, as described in Genesis.

Fundamentalism in practice assumed several forms. In most places, it involved simply an intensifying commitment to conservative theology. But it included as well a major evangelical movement, particularly in the South and parts of the West. Evangelists, among them the celebrated Billy Sunday, traveled from state to state attracting huge crowds to their revival meetings. In California, Aimée Semple McPherson ministered to many of the new arrivals on the West Coast with a similar diet of fundamentalist evangelicism. Protestant modernists looked upon much of this activity with condescending amusement, but one aspect of fundamentalism they viewed with real alarm. By the mid-1920s, fundamentalists in a number of states were gaining political strength with their demands for legislation to forbid the teaching of evolution in the public schools. To the modernists, such laws were almost unthinkable. Darwinism had to them become indisputable scientific fact; to forbid the teaching of evolution, they believed, would be like forbidding teachers to tell their students that the world was round. Yet they watched with incredulity as one state after another seriously considered the fundamentalist demands. In Kentucky in 1922, an antievolution law failed to pass by a single vote. In Tennessee in March 1925, the legislature actually adopted a measure making it illegal for any public-school teacher "to teach any theory that denies the story of the divine creation of man as taught in the Bible."

The result was one of the most celebrated events of the decade. When the American Civil Liberties Union offered free counsel to any Tennessee educator willing to defy the law and become the defendant in a test case, a twenty-four-year-old biology teacher in the town of Dayton, John T. Scopes, arranged to have himself arrested. And when the ACLU decided to send the famous attorney Clarence Darrow to defend Scopes, the aging William Jennings Bryan announced that he would travel to Dayton to assist the prosecution. Journalists from across the country, among them H. L. Mencken, flocked to Tennessee to cover the trial, which opened in an almost circus atmosphere. Scopes had, of course, clearly violated the law; and a verdict of guilty was a foregone conclusion, especially when the judge refused to permit "expert" testimony by evolution scholars. Scopes was fined $100, and the case was ultimately dismissed in a higher court because of a technicality. Nevertheless, Darrow scored an important victory for the modernists by calling Bryan himself to the stand to testify as an "expert on the Bible." In the course of the cross-examination, Darrow made Bryan's churlish defense of biblical truths appear increasingly foolish and finally tricked him into admitting the possibility that not all religious dogma was subject to only one interpretation. The Scopes trial did not resolve the conflict between fundamentalists and modernists; indeed, four other states soon proceeded to pass antievolution laws of their own. It did, however, expose the anguish of provincial Americans attempting to defend an embattled way of life.

The Ordeal of the Democratic Party

That anguish proved particularly troubling to the Democratic party, which suffered a serious debilitation during the 1920s as a result of tensions between its urban and rural factions. Even more than the Republicans, the Democrats consisted of a diverse coalition of interest groups, linked more by local tradition than common commitment. Among those interest groups were prohibitionists, Klansmen, and fundamentalists on one side, and Catholics, urban workers, and immigrants on the other. In 1924, the tensions between them proved devastating. At the Democratic National Convention in New York that summer, bitter conflict broke out over the platform when the party's urban wing attempted to win approval of planks calling for the repeal of Prohibition and a denunciation of the Klan. Both planks narrowly failed. Far more serious was a deadlock in the balloting for a presidential candidate. Urban Democrats supported Alfred E. Smith, the Irish Catholic Tammanyite who had risen to become a progressive Governor of New York; rural Democrats backed William McAdoo, Woodrow Wilson's Treasury Secretary (and son-in-law), later to become a Senator from California, who had skillfully positioned himself to win the support of southern and western delegates suspicious of Tammany Hall and modern urban life. For 103 ballots, the convention dragged on, until finally both Smith and McAdoo withdrew and the party settled on a compromise: the corporate lawyer John W. Davis. After the humiliating spectacle in New York, Davis was an easy target for Calvin Coolidge and the Republican party in the fall.

In the years that followed, the schism between the two wings of the party continued to plague the Democrats. In 1928, Al Smith finally did manage to secure his party's nomination for President after another acrimonious but less prolonged battle. He was not, however, able to unite his divided party. He became, as a result, the first Democrat since the Civil War to fail to carry the South (he won only six of the eleven states of the former Confederacy). Elsewhere, although he did well in the large cities, he carried no states at all except Massachusetts. Smith's opponent, and the victor in the presidential election, was a man who

AL SMITH. Alfred E. Smith's immigrant origins and progressive policies made him a hero of northern urban residents. But his Catholicism, his harsh New York accent, and his identification with the hated city made him anathema to rural Americans. (*National Archives*)

THE REPUBLICAN NOMINEE. Herbert Hoover won the admiration of the nation during his years as Secretary of Commerce under Harding and Coolidge, and he was the logical Republican candidate for President in 1928. He is shown here beaming at the news that he has just received his party's nomination. (*National Archives*)

perhaps more than any other personified the modern, prosperous, middle-class society of the New Era: Herbert Hoover. The business civilization of the 1920s, with its new institutions, fashions, and values, continued to arouse the animosity of large portions of the population; but the majority of the American people appeared to have accepted and approved it. In 1928, at least, the New Era seemed to be permanently enshrined.

SUGGESTED READINGS

Frederick Lewis Allen's *Only Yesterday* (1931), and Daniel Boorstin's *The Americans: The Democratic Experience* (1973) offer overviews of American culture in the 1920s. Ed Cray, *Chrome Colossus* (1980), and Bernard A. Weisberger, *The Dream Maker* (1979), provide observations on the growing importance of the automobile; while Stuart Ewen, *Captains of Consciousness* (1976), examines the advertising industry. See Larry May, *Screening Out the Past* (1980), and Robert Sklar, *Movie-Made America* (1975), for discussion of the growth of the film industry and its effects on American culture. There is surprisingly little literature on the impact of radio in the 1920s; see, however, Erik Barnouw, *A Tower in Babel*, vol. 1 (1966). Robert Lynd and Helen Lynd, *Middletown* (1929), a sociological portrait of Muncie, Indiana, in the mid-1920s, is invaluable for understanding community life in the decade and particularly useful for examining middle-class religion. Paul Carter, *Another Part of the Twenties* (1977), discusses a range of popular social attitudes. Sheila Rothman, *Woman's Proper Place* (1978), is an important study of the changing roles of women; while Paula Fass, *The Damned and Beautiful* (1977), examines American youth.

Malcolm Cowley's *Exiles Return* (1934) is an eloquent memoir of the Lost Generation. See also Edmund Wilson, *The Twenties* (1975), and Frederick J. Hoffman, *The Twenties* (1949). Nathan Huggins, *Harlem Renaissance* (1971), examines the outstanding black cultural movement of the decade. John Stewart, *The Burden of Time* (1965), is a study of the southern Fugitives and Agrarians. The best critical study of William Faulkner is Cleanth Brooks, *William Faulkner: The Yoknapatawpha Country* (1963).

Norman Clark, *Deliver Us From Evil* (1976), examines the Prohibition movement, tracing it back to its progressive roots. The best study of American nativism is John Higham, *Strangers in the Land* (1963). David Chalmers, *Hooded Americanism* (1965), and Kenneth Jackson, *The Ku Klux Klan in the City* (1965), examine the impact of the Klan. An account of the Scopes trial is available in Ray Ginger, *Six Days or Forever?* (1958); while Norman Furniss, *The Fundamentalist Controversy* (1954), offers a broader view of the fundamentalist movement. The troubled history of the Democratic party in the 1920s can be examined in William Harbaugh, *Lawyer's Lawyer* (1973), a biography of John W. Davis; David Burner, *The Politics of Provincialism* (1967), a particularly useful study; Alan Lichtman, *Prejudice and the Old Politics* (1979), a pathbreaking quantitative study of the 1928 election; and Frank Freidel, *The Ordeal* (1954) and *The Triumph* (1956), volumes covering the 1920s in a biography of Franklin Roosevelt.

Eleven

The Coming of
the Great Depression

Few Americans in the first months of 1929 saw any reason to question the strength and stability of the nation's economy. Most agreed with their new President that the booming prosperity of the years just past would not only continue but increase, and that dramatic social progress would follow in its wake. "We in America today," Herbert Hoover had proclaimed in August 1928, "are nearer to the final triumph over poverty than ever before in the history of any land. The poorhouse is vanishing from among us." Only fifteen months later, however, those words would return to haunt him, as the nation plunged into the severest and most prolonged economic depression in its history. It began with a stock market crash in October 1929, and it continued in one form or another for a full decade, until war finally restored prosperity. The Great Depression not only produced widespread economic misery; it also placed great strains upon the political and social fabric of the nation. And it helped to expose just how much of that fabric Americans were prepared to change, and how much they were determined to preserve.

THE ECONOMIC COLLAPSE

The sudden financial collapse came as an especially severe shock because it followed so closely a period in which the New Era seemed to be performing another series of economic miracles. In particular, the nation was experiencing in 1929 a spectacular boom in the stock market. In February 1928, stock prices began a steady ascent that continued, with only a few, temporary lapses, for a year and a half. By the autumn of that year, the market had become a national obsession, attracting the attention not only of the wealthy but of millions of people of modest

HARD TIMES.   The familiar sight of the unemployed peddling apples in the streets became a symbol to many Americans of the suffering of the Great Depression. Herbert Hoover, however, was less sympathetic. He claimed later that the apple sellers were part of a shrewd marketing strategy adopted by Oregon and Washington state apple growers, who, taking advantage of public sympathy for the unemployed, had "set up a system of selling apples on the street corners in many cities, thus selling their crop and raising their prices. Many persons left their jobs for the more profitable one of selling apples." (*Culver Pictures*)

means, who began pouring their savings into common stocks. The New York Stock Exchange, which through most of the decade had traded an average of only 2 or 3 million shares daily, was routinely experiencing 6-, 7-, or 8-million share days, with the total occasionally rising as high as 12 million. Stockbrokers, who had traditionally serviced only a few, rich patrons, found themselves besieged by new customers eager to share in the quick, easy profits. Some brokerage firms gave added encouragement to the speculative mania by offering absurdly easy credit, requiring purchasers to make down payments of as little as 10 percent of the price of the stock, with the balance to be paid later out of the profits.

A few economists warned that the boom could not continue, that the prices of stocks had ceased to bear any relation to the earning power of the corporations that were issuing them, that the rampant speculation would ultimately produce disaster. But for every voice of caution, there were dozens of voices preaching optimism, particularly as every dip in the market was followed by an even greater and more rapid rise than before. Calvin Coolidge, leaving office in March 1929, expressed the belief that "stocks are cheap at current prices." A Harvard economist said in early October that "stock prices have reached what looks like a permanently high plateau."

The Great Crash

In the autumn of 1929, things began to fall apart. On October 21, the market dipped sharply, alarming those who had become accustomed to an uninterrupted upward progression; but a day later prices began to recover. On October 23, there was an even greater break, sending the index of industrial prices down more than 18 points in a few hours and creating a mood of deep anxiety. The anxiety turned to panic on October 24 ("Black Thursday," as it would later be known), when the market nearly collapsed. In the course of a trading session in which nearly 13 million shares changed hands, in which the ticker tape ran hours behind, and in which major corporations saw the prices of their stocks drop precipitously, it gradually became clear that many traders were simply dumping their shares, trying to salvage whatever they could from their investments and get out of the market.

Black Thursday might have been the final blow to the inflated bull market had it not been for the efforts of a group of powerful bankers, led by J. P. Morgan, Jr., to restore confidence. Meeting quietly in the midst of the panic, the bankers established a $240-million pool and sent Morgan's personal broker, Richard Whitney, onto the floor of the exchange to begin buying large blocks of stock. The effect was dramatic. Other investors took note of this display of support by Morgan and his colleagues and began to make purchases of their own. The market steadied, and for the next several days it showed signs of reviving.

But Morgan's victory was short-lived. On the following Monday, prices once again began to fall; and on October 29, the famous "Black Tuesday," there occurred a panic so devastating that J. P. Morgan could not have stemmed it if he had tried. (He did not.) Sixteen million shares of stock were traded; the industrial index dropped 43 points; stock in many companies became literally worthless, with sellers unable to find buyers at any price. In the weeks that followed, the market continued to decline, with losses in October totaling $16 billion. By mid-November, the price of an average share of stock had fallen 40 percent; the industrial index, which had stood at 380 as recently as August, was

198.7. And in the months and years that followed, things grew steadily worse. Every time analysts began to assure the public that the downward spiral was over, prices would plummet still further. By 1933, stocks that had been worth $87 billion before the crash, and had declined to $55 billion by November 1929, were valued at only $18 billion.

Causes of the Depression

Popular folklore has established the stock market crash as the beginning, and even the cause, of the Great Depression. In fact, it was neither. It was, of course, the most conspicuous sign of the coming of the crisis; and it contributed in several ways to its severity. But the Depression had earlier beginnings and more important causes.

The nation's economy had been showing some signs of distress for months before October 1929, as the two industries most responsible for prosperity began to display evidence of weakness. Construction had passed its peak and was declining rapidly; automobiles were sitting unsold in the showrooms of dealers. Business inventories of all kinds were three times as large as they had been a year before, and other signposts of economic health—freight carloadings, industrial production, wholesale prices—were slipping downward. The extraordinary performance of the stock market kept most Americans from noticing these alarming signs. But the bull market was, in fact, an artificial phenomenon, flourishing at a time when the nation was already slipping into a recession.

The October crash helped increase the nation's economic problems in several ways. The speculative boom of 1929 had to some extent compensated for the decline in consumption by pumping new money into the economy to offset declining sales. After October, that money was no longer available. The market collapse also helped shatter the confidence of Americans in the stability of their economy, discouraging investors and adding to the general sense of distress. But there were other, more important causes of the Great Depression.

Economists and other observers have argued for decades about what was responsible for the crisis; they have agreed only that many factors were involved. There was, first, a serious lack of diversification in the American economy in the 1920s. Prosperity had been excessively dependent on a few basic industries, notably construction and automobiles; when those industries declined, the other sectors of the economy were not large enough or productive enough to take up the slack. More important, there was a fundamental maldistribution of purchasing power in the New Era. As production of goods increased, the proportion of the profits going to farmers, factory workers, and other potential consumers was too small to create a market for the goods they were producing. As long as corporations had continued to expand their capital facilities (their factories, warehouses, heavy equipment, and other investments), the economy had continued to flourish. By the end of the 1920s, however, capital investments had created more plant space than could profitably be used, and factories were pouring out more goods than consumers could purchase. Most Americans would happily have bought more had they been able to afford it. In 1929, only one family in six owned an automobile, only one in five a fixed bathtub. Fewer than 25 percent of all American homes received electric power, and only 10 percent had telephones. But with farm prices and factory wages low, this potential market could not be tapped.

Government policies had contributed as well to the economic dilemma. Taxation had spared the rich and fallen disproportionately on people of modest means, increasing the inequality of incomes. Lax regulation of corporations, banks, and the securities industry had permitted egregious abuses and irresponsible speculation. High tariffs had restricted foreign trade, limiting the ability of American manufacturers to sell their surpluses overseas. Only large American loans had kept the foreign markets alive at all; and those loans were going increasingly into default, expanding the economic crisis even further.

The Depression Economy

Someone asked the British economist John Maynard Keynes in the 1930s whether he was aware of any historical era comparable to the Great Depression. "Yes," Keynes replied. "It was called the Dark Ages, and it lasted 400 years." The Depression did not last 400 years. It did, however, plunge the economy not only of the United States but of most of the Western world into a distress it had not known in the industrial era.

The collapse was so rapid and so devastating that at first it created only bewilderment among those who attempted to explain it. The American Gross National Product plummeted from over $104 billion in 1929 to $76.4 billion in 1932, a 25 percent decline in three years. By 1933, Americans had virtually ceased making investments in productive enterprises. In 1929, they had spent $16.2 billion to promote capital growth; in 1933, they invested only a third of a billion. The consumer price index declined 25 percent between 1929 and 1933, the wholesale price index 32 percent. Farm prices, already depressed in the 1920s, fell even more dramatically. Gross farm income dropped from $12 billion to $5 billion in four years. With economic activity contracting so sharply, it was inevitable that industrial unemployment would greatly increase. By 1932, according to the relatively crude estimates of the time, 25 percent of the American work force was unemployed (some believed the figure was even higher). For the rest of the decade, unemployment averaged nearly 20 percent, never dropping below 15 percent.

It is hard to know whether the suffering was worse in the cities or on the farms. In the industrial Northeast and Midwest, cities were becoming virtually paralyzed by the burden of unemployment. Cleveland, Ohio, for example, had an unemployment rate of 50 percent in 1932; Akron, 60 percent; Toledo, 80 percent. To the men and women suddenly without incomes, the situation was frightening and bewildering. Most had grown up believing that every individual was responsible

BREAD LINE. A bread line stretches across New York City's Times Square in 1932, testimony to the failure of government efforts to meet the escalating demands for relief. (*Wide World Photos*)

for his or her own fate, that unemployment was a sign of personal failure; and even in the face of national distress, many continued to believe it. Unemployed workers walked through the streets day after day looking for jobs that did not exist. When finally they gave up, they often just sat at home, hiding their shame.

An increasing number of families were turning in humiliation to local public relief systems, just to be able to eat. But that system, which had in the 1920s served only a small number of indigents, was totally unequipped to handle the new demands being placed upon it. In many cities, therefore, relief simply collapsed. New York, which offered among the highest relief benefits in the nation, was able to provide families an average of only $2.39 per week. Toledo, Ohio, could offer only a little over 2 cents per person per day. New Orleans in 1931 simply refused to accept any more applicants for relief; St. Louis arbitrarily cut half of its relief recipients from its rolls. Private charities attempted to supplement the public relief efforts, but the problem was far beyond their capabilities as well.

With local efforts rapidly collapsing, state governments began to feel new pressures to expand their own assistance to the unemployed. Most resisted the pressure. Tax revenues were declining, along with everything else, and state leaders balked at placing additional strains on already tight budgets. Many public figures, moreover, feared that any permanent welfare system would undermine the moral fiber of its clients. Thus although several European nations had long maintained programs of unemployment insurance, not a single American state established such a program until Wisconsin did so in January 1932. And while city governments were pleading for state funding of their beleaguered relief agencies, there was little response from the legislatures. Not until September 1931 did the New York State government establish, at the insistence of Governor Franklin D. Roosevelt, the first state relief organization in America: the Temporary Emergency Relief Administration.

As a result of all this, American cities were experiencing scenes that a few years earlier would have seemed almost inconceivable. Bread lines stretched for blocks outside Red Cross and Salvation Army kitchens. Thousands sifted through garbage cans for scraps of food or waited outside restaurant kitchens in hopes of receiving plate scrapings. Men, women, and children suffered, and even died from, malnutrition and starvation. Nearly 2 million young men simply took to the roads, riding freight trains from city to city, living as virtual nomads.

In rural areas conditions were, in many ways, even worse, especially in a large area of the South and Middle West known as the Dust Bowl. Between 1929 and 1932, not only did farm income decline by more than 60 percent; not only did an estimated one-third of all American farmers lose their land through mortgage foreclosures or eviction. Much of the farm belt was suffering as well from a catastrophic natural disaster: one of the worst droughts in the history of the nation. Beginning in 1930, a vast area of the nation—and particularly a group of states stretching north from Texas into the Dakotas—began to experience a steady decline in rainfall and an accompanying increase in heat. The drought continued for a full decade, turning many areas that had once been fertile farm regions into virtual deserts. In Kansas, the soil in some places was devoid of moisture as far as three feet below the surface. In Nebraska, Iowa, and other states, summer temperatures were averaging over 100 degrees. Swarms of grasshoppers were moving from region to region, devouring what meager crops farmers were able to raise, often even devouring fenceposts or clothes hanging out to dry. Great dust storms—"black blizzards," as they were called—swept across the plains, blotting out the sun and suffocating livestock as well as any people unfortunate or foolish enough to stay outside.

It is a measure of how depressed the market for agricultural goods had become that even with these disastrous conditions, American farmers continued through the 1930s to produce far more than American consumers could afford to buy. With the domestic market dwindling and the international market having almost vanished, farmers were able to sell their goods only at prices so low as to make continued operations unprofitable. Thus many farmers, like many urban unem-

THE DUST BOWL. A father and son walk in the face of a relatively mild dust storm in Oklahoma. The heavier storms, or "black blizzards," darkened the sky and forced people to seal themselves indoors for refuge. Even inside the houses, however, the dust often became so thick that occupants had trouble seeing across a room. (*Library of Congress*)

ployed, left their homes and traveled to what they hoped would be better climes. Hundreds of thousands of families, from the Dust Bowl in particular, packed their belongings in rickety cars or trucks and traveled to California, where they found conditions little better than those they had left. Owning no land of their own, they were forced to work as agricultural migrants, traveling from farm to farm picking fruit and other crops at starvation wages.

No nation could survive indefinitely amid such vast economic distress. No people could tolerate for long such widespread and unrelieved suffering. Increasingly, therefore, troubled Americans began to look to their government for a solution to the crisis.

THE DECLINE OF HERBERT HOOVER

Herbert Hoover entered the presidency in March 1929 believing, like most Americans, that the nation faced a bright and prosperous future. He believed, too, that the President could play an important role in stabilizing the economy and ensuring progress. For the first six months of his administration, therefore, he attempted to expand the policies he had advocated during his eight years as Secretary of Commerce and worked to complete what he termed the "American System" of cooperative individualism.

The economic crisis that began before the year was out forced the President to deal with a new set of problems; but for most of the rest of his term, he continued to rely upon the principles that had always governed his public life. He worked hard. He attempted to play an active role in promoting recovery. He rejected arguments that the government should not interfere in the affairs of private enterprise. He was, in short, a more energetic and activist President than any before him. For all his efforts, however, Hoover's continued commitment to the concept of voluntarism, his fiscal conservatism, and his limited view of the role of government doomed his policies to failure; and he left office in 1933 a frustrated and thoroughly discredited man.

Early Programs

Hoover's first response to the Depression was to attempt to restore public confidence in the economy. "The fundamental business of this country, that is, production and distribution of commodities," he said in 1930, "is on a sound and prosperous basis." The Depression, he implied, was a result of panic and confusion. Consequently, he held a series of highly publicized meetings, summoning leaders of business, labor, and agriculture to the White House and urging upon them a program of voluntary cooperation for recovery. He persuaded businessmen not to cut production or lay off workers; he talked labor leaders into forgoing demands for higher wages or better hours. He even tried to convince the public (and perhaps himself as well) that conditions were not as bad as they seemed. When a delegation of businessmen arrived at the White House in June 1930 to discuss further government assistance, Hoover assured them: "Gentlemen, you have come sixty days too late. The Depression is over." For a few brief months, the President's efforts seemed to be having some effect; but by mid-1931, economic conditions had deteriorated so badly that the structure of voluntary cooperation he had erected quickly collapsed. Frightened industrialists soon began cutting production, laying off workers, and slashing wages. Hoover was powerless to stop them.

Hoover also attempted to use government spending as a tool for fighting the Depression. Rejecting the demands of some fiscal conservatives that the government cut back its own programs to ensure a balanced budget, the President proposed to Congress an increase of $423 million—an enormous sum by the standards of the time—in federal public works programs; and he exhorted state

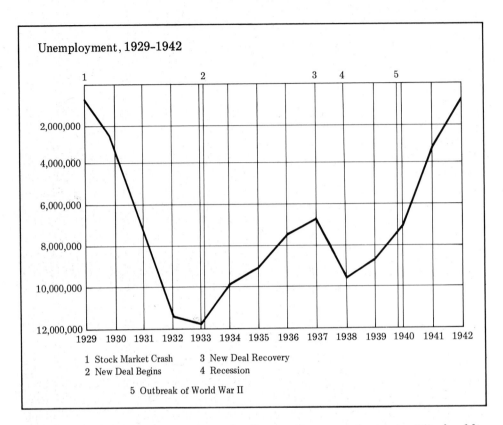

Unemployment, 1929-1942

1   2   3   4   5

2,000,000

4,000,000

6,000,000

8,000,000

10,000,000

12,000,000

1929 1930 1931 1932 1933 1934 1935 1936 1937 1938 1939 1940 1941 1942

1 Stock Market Crash   3 New Deal Recovery
2 New Deal Begins   4 Recession

5 Outbreak of World War II

and local governments to engage in the "energetic yet prudent pursuit" of public construction. Hoover was no more aware of Keynesian ideas of deficit spending than any other public figure of his time, but he did seem to understand the importance of keeping money in circulation during a recession. Nevertheless, Hoover's spending programs were, in the end, no more effective than his efforts at persuasion; for he was not willing to spend enough money, or to spend it for a long enough time, to do any good. He viewed his public works program as a temporary expedient, something to promote a rapid recovery. When economic conditions worsened, he became far less willing to increase government spending, worrying instead about maintaining federal solvency. In 1932, at the depth of the Depression, he proposed a tax increase to help the government avoid a deficit.

Agricultural Marketing

Even before the stock market crash, Hoover had begun to construct a program to assist the troubled agricultural economy. It embodied two major initiatives, which the President proposed to a special session of Congress in April 1929. The Agricultural Marketing Act established for the first time a major government bureaucracy to help farmers maintain prices. A federally sponsored Farm Board of eight members would administer a revolving fund of $500 million, from which it could make loans to national marketing cooperatives or establish "corporations" to buy surpluses and thus raise prices. At the same time, Hoover attempted to protect American farmers from international competition by raising agricultural tariffs. The Hawley-Smoot Act of 1930 contained protective increases on seventy-five farm products and raised rates from the average of 26 percent established by the 1922 Fordney-McCumber Act to a new high of 50 percent.

Neither the Agricultural Marketing Act nor the Hawley-Smoot tariff ultimately helped American farmers in any significant way. The Marketing Act relied on voluntary cooperation among farmers and gave the government no authority to limit production. Hoover's call for a reduction of the wheat crop, for example, resulted in a drop in acreage of only 1 percent in Kansas. The Farm Board, moreover, lacked sufficient funds to deal effectively with the crisis. Prices continued to fall despite its efforts. The Hawley-Smoot Act was an unqualified disaster, as a thousand members of the American Economic Association had warned the President even before he signed it. It provoked foreign governments to enact trade restrictions of their own in reprisal, further diminishing the market for American agricultural goods. And it raised rates not only on farm products but on 925 manufactured goods as well, making industrial products more expensive for farmers.

Reinterpreting the Depression

By the spring of 1931, Herbert Hoover's political position had deteriorated considerably. Democrats had made great gains in the 1930 congressional elections, winning control of the House and making substantial gains in the Senate. Large portions of the public were beginning to hold the President personally to blame for the crisis, and Hoover's name soon became synonymous with economic distress. Miserable shantytowns established on the outskirts of cities were known as "Hoovervilles." Old newspapers were "Hoover blankets," empty pockets were "Hoover flags." Progressive reformers both inside and outside the government urged the President to support more vigorous programs of relief and public spending. Hoover, however, remained adamant in his commitment to voluntarism and local responsibility. When a special commission appointed by the President to study relief recommended a federal program, Hoover ignored the recommendation. Instead, he seized upon a slight improvement in economic conditions early in 1931 as proof that his policies were working.

The international financial panic of the spring of 1931 destroyed the illusion that the economic crisis was coming to an end. At the same time, however, it provided Hoover with a way to reinterpret the Depression and defend his own policies. Throughout much of the 1920s, the European economy had managed to survive the burden of war debts and reparations only by virtue of large loans from American banks. When those loans ceased after 1929, the financial fabric of many European nations began to unravel. In May 1931, the largest bank in Austria collapsed. Over the next several months, panic gripped the financial

HOOVERVILLE, NEW YORK CITY. This shantytown in New York City was typical of the many makeshift villages (or "Hoovervilles") that grew up to house the Depression unemployed. "The signs of collapse were aggressive," wrote one New Yorker. "Dozens of such colonies had sprung up in the city . . . but not nearly enough to accommodate the swelling army of the jobless and dispossessed." (*Culver Pictures*)

institutions of neighboring countries. European governments, desperate for sound assets, withdrew their gold reserves from American banks. European investors, in need of dollars to pay off their loans and protect their solvency, dumped their shares of American stocks onto the market, further depressing prices. More and more European nations were abandoning the gold standard and devaluing their currencies, leaving the United States, which remained tied to gold, at a disadvantage in international trade. American economic conditions quickly declined to new lows, and Herbert Hoover quickly adopted a new approach to the Depression.

It was not the domestic American economy that was to blame for the Depression, he now argued, but the structure of international finance. The proper response to the crisis, therefore, was not to adopt active social and economic programs at home but to work to restore international stability. Hoover's solution was to propose a moratorium—first on the payment of all war debts and reparations, then on the payment of international private debts as well. It was a sound proposal, but it came too late to halt the panic, especially after France balked for several weeks before agreeing to it. Unwilling to act forcefully to deal with the Depression at home, Hoover was finding himself similarly unable to solve the crisis overseas.

New Initiatives

By the time Congress convened in December 1931, conditions had grown so desperate that Hoover finally decided to support an expanded federal role in the economy. Although he still refused to support any system of direct government relief, he accepted the need for public efforts to prevent a collapse of the nation's financial structure. He persuaded Congress to increase funding for federal land banks and to create a system of government home loan banks. Through them, financial institutions holding mortgages on farms, homes, and other properties could receive cash from the government for the mortgages instead of foreclosing on them—thus keeping the banks afloat and, incidentally, preventing many Americans from losing their homes and properties. Hoover also supported the Glass-Steagall Banking Act of 1932, designed to make it easier for American banks to meet the demands of overseas depositors who were withdrawing their gold from the United States. And he encouraged New York financiers to establish a $500-million fund to help troubled banks stay afloat.

The most important piece of legislation of his presidency, however, was a bill passed in January 1932 establishing the Reconstruction Finance Corporation (RFC), a government agency whose purpose was to provide federal loans to troubled banks, railroads, and other businesses. It even made funds available to local governments to support public works projects and assist relief efforts. It was an unprecedented use of federal power; and unlike many earlier Hoover programs, it operated on a large scale. In 1932, the RFC had a budget of $1.5 billion for public works alone.

Nevertheless, the new agency failed to deal directly or forcefully enough with the real problems of the economy to produce any significant recovery. Because the RFC was permitted to lend funds only to those financial institutions with sufficient collateral, much of its money went to large banks and corporations, prompting some critics to dub it a "bread line for big business." The RFC could only provide loans; it could not purchase stock or otherwise provide capital to troubled institutions, even though that was what they most desperately needed. And at Hoover's insistence, it helped finance only those public works projects that promised ultimately to pay for themselves (toll bridges, public housing, and others), thus severely limiting the scope of its efforts. Above all, the RFC did not have enough money to make any real impact on the Depression; and it did not even spend all the money it had. Of the meager $300 million available to support local relief efforts, the RFC lent out only $30 million in 1932. Of the $1.5 billion public works budget, it released only about 20 percent. Even Hoover's most vigorous and expansive program had been crippled by the cautiousness and fiscal conservatism of his administration.

Diplomatic Frustrations

After the relatively placid international climate of the 1920s, the diplomatic challenges facing the Hoover administration must have seemed ominous and bewildering. The world financial crisis was not only creating economic distress; it was producing a heightened nationalism that threatened the international agreements established during the previous decade. Above all, the Depression was toppling many existing political leaders and replacing them with powerful, belligerent governments bent upon expansion as a solution to their economic problems. Hoover was confronted, therefore, with the beginning of a process that would ultimately lead to war; and he was finding himself without sufficient tools to deal with it.

Hoover's policies were most successful in Latin America, where he worked studiously to repair some of the damage created by earlier American actions. He made a ten-week good-will tour through the region before his inauguration. Once in office, he attempted to abstain from intervening in the internal affairs of neighboring nations and moved to withdraw American troops from Nicaragua and Haiti. When economic distress led to the collapse of one Latin American regime after another, Hoover announced a new United States policy: America would grant diplomatic recognition to any de facto government in the region without questioning the means it had used to obtain power. He even repudiated the Roosevelt Corollary to the Monroe Doctrine by refusing to permit American intervention when several Latin American countries defaulted on debt obligations to the United States in October 1931. Hoover had taken a small but significant step toward improving the tenor of relations between the United States and its neighbors.

In Europe, the administration fared less well. When Hoover's debt moratorium failed to produce financial stability, an increasing number of economists and political leaders appealed to the President to cancel all war debts to the United States. Hoover refused, and many European nations promptly went into default, severely damaging an already tense international climate. United States efforts to extend the disarmament agreements of the 1920s met with similar frustration. At a conference in London in January 1930, American negotiators reached agreement with European and Japanese delegates on extending the limits on naval construction established at the Washington Conference of 1921. But France and England, fearful of a resurgent Germany and an expanding Japan, insisted on so many loopholes as to make the treaty virtually meaningless. The increasing irrelevance of Hoover's idealistic commitments became even clearer at the World

Disarmament Conference that opened in Geneva in January 1932. France rejected the idea of disarmament entirely and called for the creation of an international army to counter the growing power of Germany. Hoover continued to urge major reductions in armaments, including an immediate abolition of all "offensive" weapons (tanks, bombers) and a 30 percent reduction in all land and naval forces. The conference ultimately dissolved in failure.

The ineffectiveness of diplomacy in Europe was particularly troubling in view of the character of some of the new governments coming to power on the Continent. Benito Mussolini's Fascist party had been in control of Italy since the early 1920s; by the 1930s, the Mussolini regime was growing increasingly nationalistic and militaristic, and fascist leaders were loudly threatening an active campaign of imperial expansion. Even more ominous was the growing power of the National Socialist (or Nazi) party in Germany. The so-called Weimar Republic, which had emerged as the nation's government at the end of World War I, was by the late 1920s losing virtually all of its popular support, discredited by, among other things, a ruinous inflation. And Adolf Hitler, the stridently nationalistic leader of the Nazis, was rapidly growing in popular favor. Although he lost a 1932 election for Chancellor, Hitler would sweep into power less than a year later. His belief in the racial superiority of the Aryan (German) people; his commitment to providing *Lebensraum* (living space) for his "master race"; his blatant anti-Semitism; and his passionate militarism: all posed a growing threat to European peace.

More immediately alarming to the delegates at the 1932 Geneva Conference was a major crisis in Asia—one that proved to be an early step toward World War II, and one that the United States found itself powerless to resolve. As in the past, it was Japan's international aspirations that were proving troublesome. The Japanese, reeling from an economic depression of their own, had developed an intense concern about the increasing power of the Soviet Union and of Chiang Kai-shek's Nationalist China in Asia. In particular, they were alarmed at Chiang's insistence upon expanding his government's power in Manchuria, which remained officially a part of China, but over which the Japanese had since 1905 maintained effective economic control. When the moderate government of Japan failed to take forceful steps to counter Chiang's ambitions, military leaders staged what was, in effect, a coup in the autumn of 1931—seizing control of foreign policy from the weakened liberals. Only weeks later, they launched a major invasion of northern Manchuria after a small skirmish between Japanese and Chinese troops along the South Manchurian Railway had provided them with a pretext.

The American government had few options. For a while, Secretary of State Henry Stimson continued to hope that Japanese moderates would regain control of the Tokyo government and halt the invasion. The militarists, however, remained in command; and by the beginning of 1932, their conquest of Manchuria was complete. Still, the United States did nothing to halt Japanese aggression. American inaction was the result of a number of factors. First, Hoover feared that a strong United States response would serve to strengthen the militants within the Tokyo regime and perhaps provoke a full-scale war. Second, Hoover and many other Americans had scant sympathy for China, whose increasing nationalism

THE JAPANESE IN MANCHURIA.   Japanese troops enter the ancient walled city of Taonan in western Manchuria after capturing it in 1931. Although Herbert Hoover at first expressed some sympathy for the Japanese during the crisis, Secretary of War Henry Stimson more accurately foresaw the significance of the invasion, warning that it augured a continuing Japanese policy of expansion. "The situation is in the hands of virtually mad dogs," he remarked after militarists had seized power in Tokyo in the fall of 1931. (*UPI*)

struck many policymakers as ominously radical. Japan, many hoped, could serve as a buffer in Asia against the growing power of communism. Third, and most important, Hoover recognized and shared the unwillingness of the vast majority of the American people to become involved in overseas conflicts. He permitted Stimson to issue warnings to Japan and to attempt to use moral suasion to end the crisis. He forbade him, however, to cooperate with the League of Nations in imposing economic sanctions against the Japanese. Stimson's only real tool in dealing with the Manchurian invasion was a refusal to grant diplomatic recognition to the new Japanese territories. Japan was unconcerned and early in 1932 even expanded its aggression further into China, attacking the city of Shanghai and killing thousands of civilians.

The peaceful, idealistic world of which many Americans had dreamed, a world in which self-regulating agreements would maintain the peace without requiring the United States to play any continuing international role, stood exposed in 1931 as an illusion. In the face of economic crisis, the old forces of nationalism and expansionism were emerging resurgent. Yet America seemed unable to adjust. The United States continued to lack either the understanding or the will to deal with international decay.

THE CRISES OF 1932

For the first several years of the Depression, most Americans were either too stunned or too confused to raise any effective protest. By the middle of 1932, however, the crisis had continued so long and had grown so severe that dissident voices began to be heard. With the administration's policies in shambles, with Hoover himself growing increasingly unpopular, and with the economy reaching new lows in almost every sector, it was easy for many Americans to believe that the nation was on the verge of collapse. They responded in many different ways.

Agrarian Unrest

In the Midwest, farmers sensing themselves near economic extinction raised new and louder demands for government assistance. In particular, they called for legislation similar to the McNary-Haugen Act of the 1920s, by which the government would guarantee them a return on their crops at least equal to the cost of production. Lobbyists from the larger farm organizations converged on Washington to pressure members of Congress to act. Some disgruntled farmers staged public protests in the capital. But when neither the President nor the Congress showed any signs of movement, they adopted a more drastic approach. In the summer of 1932, a group of unhappy farm owners gathered in Des Moines, Iowa, to establish a new organization: the Farm Holiday Association. Under the leadership of Milo Reno, the association endorsed the withholding of farm products from the market—in effect a farmers' strike. The strike began in August in western Iowa, spread briefly to a few neighboring areas, and succeeded in blockading several markets; but in the end it dissolved in failure. The scope of the effort was too modest to affect farm prices, and many farmers in the region refused to cooperate in any case. When clashes between strikers and local authorities resulted in several episodes of violence, Reno called off the strike. Nevertheless, the uprising created considerable consternation in state governments in the farm belt and even more in Washington, where the President and much of the Congress were facing a national election.

The Bonus March

A more celebrated protest movement emerged from a less likely quarter: American veterans. In 1924, Congress had approved the payment of a bonus to all those who had served in World War I, the money to be distributed in 1945. By 1932, however, economic distress had mobilized a widespread demand among veterans that the bonus be paid immediately. Hoover would not consider the request, fearing that acquiescence would ruin his hopes for a balanced budget; but the veterans refused to be denied. In June, more than 20,000 veterans, members of the self-proclaimed "Bonus Army," marched into Washington, built crude camps in the city and its environs, and promised to stay until Congress approved legislation to pay the bonus. A few of the veterans departed in July, after Congress had voted down their proposal. Most, however, remained where they were.

Their continued presence in Washington was an irritant and an embarrassment to Herbert Hoover, who had problems enough already and who gradually became defensive and even paranoid about the protestors. Although the veterans had threatened no violence, Hoover increased security at the White House, closed off

THE DEFEAT OF THE BONUS ARMY.   Although General Douglas MacArthur had been instructed only to dislodge Bonus Marchers from abandoned federal buildings in Washington, he pursued the fleeing veterans across the river and burned to the ground the Hooverville they had constructed there for themselves. The general later claimed that the Bonus Marchers had themselves started the fires. (*U.S. Signal Corps*)

surrounding streets, refused to allow pickets in the vicinity, and finally in mid-July ordered police to clear the marchers out of several abandoned federal buildings in which they had been staying. The police arrived; a few marchers threw rocks at them; someone opened fire; and two veterans fell dead. To Hoover, the incident was proof of the dangerous radicalism of the protest; he immediately ordered the United States Army to assist the police in clearing out the buildings.

General Douglas MacArthur, the Army Chief of Staff, chose to carry out the order himself. Dressed in full battle tunic, he led the Third Cavalry (under the command of George S. Patton), two infantry regiments, a machine-gun detachment, and six tanks down Pennsylvania Avenue in pursuit of the motley Bonus Army. The veterans fled in terror as the troops hurled tear gas canisters and flailed at them with their bayonets. MacArthur followed them across the Anacostia River, where he ordered the soldiers to burn their camp to the ground. More than 100 marchers were injured. One baby died. "That was a bad looking mob," MacArthur declared when it was over. "It was animated by the essence of revolution." Not for the last time, Douglas MacArthur had exceeded a President's instructions. Herbert Hoover, however, refused to rebuke him. Instead, he supported the general's decision and endorsed the view that the marchers had been infiltrated by communists and criminals (a view that the Veterans Administration sharply disputed).

The incident served as perhaps the final blow to Hoover's already battered political standing. To much of the public, he now stood confirmed as an aloof and insensitive figure, locked in the White House, uncomprehending of the distress around him. Hoover's own cold and gloomy personality did nothing to change the public image, and some of his embattled public statements at the time made his plight even worse. "Nobody is actually starving," he assured reporters (inaccurately) in 1932. "The hoboes, for example, are better fed than they have ever been." He was not a cruel or uncaring man; but in the midst of the greatest economic crisis in the nation's history, his hard, pragmatic commitment to the old progressive values of order, bureaucracy, and expertise made him a distant and unlovable leader. The Great Engineer, the personification of the optimistic days of the 1920s, had become a symbol of the nation's failure to deal effectively with the Depression.

The Election of 1932

The Farm Holiday Association, the Bonus March, and other movements of popular protest were far from radical, either in their behavior or in their demands. Most of the American people, however, responded to the crisis even more moderately and looked to the 1932 presidential election as their most effective vehicle of protest. No one had any doubts about the outcome. The Republican party dutifully renominated Herbert Hoover for a second term in office; but the lugubrious atmosphere of their convention made it clear that few delegates believed he could carry the November election. The Democrats, in the meantime, gathered jubilantly in Chicago to nominate a candidate who they were certain would be the next President of the United States. Their choice was the Governor of New York, Franklin Delano Roosevelt.

Roosevelt had been a well-known figure in the party for many years already. The son of a wealthy Hudson Valley railroad tycoon and a graduate of Groton, Harvard, and Columbia Law School, Roosevelt had begun his political career in 1910 in the New York State legislature. Because he was handsome, charming, and articulate, and because he was a distant cousin of Theodore Roosevelt (a connection strengthened by his marriage in 1905 to the president's niece, Eleanor), he attracted increasing attention. He served as Assistant Secretary of the Navy under Woodrow Wilson during World War I; and in 1920, he received his party's nomination for Vice President on the ill-fated ticket with James M. Cox. Less than a year later, his public career appeared to come to an end when he was stricken with polio and lost the use of his legs. But Roosevelt worked hard to return to politics; and although he was never again able to walk without the use of crutches and braces, he built up sufficient physical strength to make a courageous appearance at the 1924 Democratic convention to nominate Al Smith. In 1928, when Smith left Albany to run for President, Roosevelt succeeded him as Governor; and in 1930, he easily won reelection.

Roosevelt worked no miracles in New York as the state succumbed to the rigors of the Depression. He did, however, establish enough positive programs of government assistance to provide an effective contrast to Herbert Hoover. At least as important to his political future, however, was his astute effort to win support from both the urban and rural wings of his party. By avoiding such divisive cultural issues as religion and prohibition, and by emphasizing the economic grievances that most Democrats shared, he assembled a coalition within the party that provided him with a majority of the delegates to the convention by the time it assembled. After several ballots of maneuvering, his supporters secured enough additional votes to secure him the necessary two-thirds. And the next day, in a dramatic break with tradition, he flew to Chicago to address the convention in person and accept the nomination.

In the course of his acceptance speech, Roosevelt thrilled the delegates with his ringing promise: "I pledge you, I pledge myself, to a new deal for the American people," giving his program a name that would long endure. Neither then nor in the subsequent campaign, however, did Roosevelt give much indication of what that program would be. In part, of course, it was because there was no need to be specific. Herbert Hoover's unpopularity virtually ensured Roosevelt's election; his only real concern was to avoid offending any voters unnecessarily. In part, however, it was because Roosevelt had no firm or coherent program to describe. Surrounded by advisers holding widely disparate views, the candidate seemed at times to be little more than a genial mediator—listening to everyone, disagreeing with no one. More than one experienced observer agreed with Walter Lippmann that Roosevelt was simply "a pleasant man, who, without any important qualifications for the office, would very much like to be President."

In later years, Lippmann and others readily admitted they had been wrong. Even at the time, however, there was evidence of important differences between Roosevelt and Hoover. Drawing from the ideas of a talented team of university professors (whom the press quickly dubbed the "Brain Trust"), Roosevelt espoused an amalgam of ideas that combined old progressive reform principles with some of the newer ideas of associationalism that had gained currency in the 1920s. Speaking to the Commonwealth Club of San Francisco in September, he emphasized the importance of government in assisting business to develop a stable and well-regulated economic system. The days of unlimited growth and expansion were over, he argued; careful management of the nation's economic resources would be necessary in the future. In addition to these technocratic visions, however, Roosevelt emphasized the right of every citizen to a "comfortable living," and he promised to use public power to ensure that privileged special interests did not frustrate that goal. For all its vagueness, the Commonwealth address and other Roosevelt speeches made clear that he took a more expansive view of the responsibilities of the federal government than his opponent.

There were other important differences as well. Hoover continued to insist that the Depression was international in origin and that any attempt to combat it must be international as well. Roosevelt, in contrast, portrayed the crisis as a domestic (and Republican) problem; and he made it clear that he believed the most important solutions could be found at home. An even more striking difference, however, was in the styles of the two men. Hoover was grim, tired, and deadly serious, traveling the country to warn ominously of the dangers of Roosevelt's "economic radicalism." Republican policies were already winning the battle against the Depression, he somberly insisted. But his speeches were generally so dull, both in delivery and in content (Hoover was the last President to scorn the aid of speech writers), that they evoked little enthusiasm. Roosevelt, on the other hand, was a symbol of energy, enthusiasm, and optimism. His dazzling smile, his floppy broad-brimmed hat, his cigarette holder held at a jaunty angle between his teeth, his skillful oratory, his unfailing wit—all combined to win him a wide personal popularity only vaguely related to the specifics of his programs.

In November, to the surprise of no one, Roosevelt won by a landslide. He received 57.4 percent of the popular vote to Hoover's 39.7. The Socialist party, in this year of despair, garnered only 2.2 percent of the ballots. The communists polled a meager 103,000 votes. In the electoral college, the result was even more overwhelming. Hoover carried Pennsylvania, Connecticut, Vermont, New Hampshire, and Maine. Roosevelt won everything else. And Democrats won majorities in both Houses of Congress. It was a broad and convincing mandate, but it was not yet clear a mandate for what.

The Interregnum

The period between the election and the inauguration (which in the 1930s still lasted more than four months) was traditionally a time of quiet planning and

INAUGURATION DAY, 1933. A grim and silent Herbert Hoover accompanies Franklin Roosevelt to the Capitol on March 4, 1933, where Roosevelt was shortly to take the oath of office as President. After several awkward and unsuccessful attempts to start a conversation with the outgoing President, Roosevelt abandoned the effort and began waving and smiling to the crowd. (*UPI*)

federal inaction. The winter of 1932–1933, however, was a season of growing economic crisis, and traditional patterns seemed to many Americans to be irrelevant. Among those who believed that the President-elect should act forcefully even before taking office was Herbert Hoover, who argued that international economic stability depended upon a clear affirmation by the United States of the sanctity of the gold standard. He argued as well that fear of "radical" economic measures by the new administration was unsettling the domestic financial climate. In a series of brittle exchanges with Roosevelt in the months following the election, Hoover tried to exact from the President-elect a pledge to maintain policies of economic orthodoxy. Roosevelt genially refused.

In February, only a month before the inauguration, a new crisis developed. The American banking system, still among the weakest and least stable in the industrial world, had been in desperate trouble since the middle of 1930. By 1932, it was beginning to collapse. Public confidence in the banks was ebbing; depositors were withdrawing their money in panic; and one bank after another was closing its doors and declaring bankruptcy. The Governor of Michigan, one of the states hardest hit by the panic, declared a "bank holiday" in mid-February, ordering all banks temporarily closed. Other states soon followed, and by the end of the month banking activity was restricted drastically in every state but one. Once again, Hoover wrote to Roosevelt insisting that the problem was a result of "steadily degenerating confidence" in the incoming administration. The only way to restore calm, he insisted, was for Roosevelt to give prompt public assurances that there would be no tinkering with the currency, no heavy borrowing, no unbalancing of the budget. "I realize," he wrote a Republican Senator at the time, "that if these declarations be made by the President-elect, he will have ratified the whole major program of the Republican Administration." Roosevelt realized the same thing and refused to comply.

March 4, 1933, was, therefore, a day not only of economic crisis, but of considerable personal bitterness. The nation waited anxiously as a silent, unsmiling Herbert Hoover, convinced that the United States was headed for disaster, rode glumly down Pennsylvania Avenue with a beaming, buoyant Franklin Roosevelt, who would shortly be sworn in as the thirty-second President of the United States.

SUGGESTED READINGS

Robert Sobel, *The Great Bull Market* (1968), chronicles the Wall Street boom of the 1920s; while John Kenneth Galbraith, *The Great Crash* (1954), examines the bust. Conflicting interpretations of the causes of the Depression are available in Milton Friedman and Anna Schwartz, *The Great Contraction* (1965), a reprint of Chapter 7 of their classic *Monetary History of the United States* (1963), and in Peter Temin, *Did Monetary Forces Cause the Great Depression?* (1976). Friedman and Schwartz's answer to Temin's question is yes; Temin's is no. Overviews of the Depression economy include Broadus Mitchell, *Depression Decade* (1947), and Charles Kindelberger, *The World in Depression* (1973). S. E. Kennedy, *The Banking Crisis of 1933* (1973), examines one of the Depression's low moments. Irving Bernstein, *The Lean Years* (1960), provides a compelling picture of the impact of the Depression upon workers in the first years after the crash, and Arthur M. Schlesinger, Jr., *The Crisis of the Old Order* (1957), offers a picture of the broader impact of the crisis. Valuable oral histories of the impact of the Depression are available in Studs Terkel, *Hard Times* (1970), a series of interviews conducted years after the 1930s. Drawing from interviews conducted in the 1930s are Federal Writers' Project, *These Are Our Lives* (1939); Tom Terrill and Jerrold Hirsch, *Such as Us* (1978); and Ann Banks (ed.), *First-Person America* (1980). Donald Worster, *Dust Bowl* (1979), examines the agricultural crisis in the southern plains.

Important studies of the Hoover presidency include Albert Romasco, *The Poverty of Abundance* (1965); Joan Hoff Wilson, *Herbert Hoover* (1975); David Burner, *Herbert Hoover* (1978); Jordan Schwarz, *The Interregnum of Despair* (1970); and Hoover's own *Memoirs: The Great Depression* (1952). For the foreign policy of the Hoover years, see Robert H. Ferrell, *American Diplomacy in the Great Depression* (1970); Elting Morison, *Turmoil and Tradition* (1960), a biography of Henry Stimson; Alexander DeConde, *Hoover's Latin American Policy* (1951); Raymond O'Connor, *Perilous Equilibrium* (1962), a study of the 1930 London Naval Conference; and Armin Rappaport, *Stimson and Japan* (1963).

John Shover's *Cornbelt Rebellion* (1965) studies the Farm Holiday movement, and Roger Daniels, *The Bonus March* (1971), examines the veterans' efforts in Washington, D.C., in 1932. The emergence of Franklin Roosevelt and the election of 1932 receive extensive treatment in Arthur M. Schlesinger, Jr., *The Crisis of the Old Order* (1957); David Burner, *The Politics of Provincialism* (1967); and Frank Freidel, *The Triumph* (1956). The interregnum of 1932–1933 is examined in Frank Freidel, *Launching the New Deal* (1973); Eliot Rosen, *Hoover, Roosevelt, and the Brains Trust* (1977); and Rexford G. Tugwell, *The Brains Trust* (1968).

Twelve

Constructing the New Deal

Franklin Roosevelt not only served longer as President than any man in American history. He became during his years in office more central to the life of the nation than any Chief Executive before him. And he constructed a series of programs that permanently altered the role and structure of the federal government. Beloved by his admirers, despised by his critics, Roosevelt was a controversial figure in his lifetime. He has remained controversial in the years since his death, not only among historians but among the public at large, who continue to debate his legacy. Was the New Deal, as its defenders have argued, a program of enlightened reform that rescued American government from the special interests and turned it to the service of the people? Was it, as conservative critics have charged, the origin of a cumbersome federal bureaucracy that would ultimately erode the health of the economy and infringe upon personal freedom? Was it, as critics from the left have claimed, an essentially conservative program, designed simply to stabilize the economy and protect American business, and essentially uninterested in the millions of Americans most in need of public assistance?

That Americans have been unable to reach agreement on these and other questions even forty years after the end of the New Deal is an indication not only of the ideological differences in contemporary society, but of the many ideological differences within the Roosevelt administration itself. Pragmatic, experimental, unwedded to any single set of social or economic beliefs, moving in countless directions at the same time, the New Deal defied easy classification or neat description. It did, however, reflect certain basic themes. It was, first, a continuation in many ways of the economic programs of the Hoover years, reflecting, in the beginning at least, the same faith in careful planning and efficient management, and sharing the same commitment to the principles of private enterprise.

221

But it was, in addition, a set of programs that invested far stronger powers in the federal government, powers that gradually took the Roosevelt administration in directions it had neither foreseen nor desired. The New Deal, finally, not only embraced the technocratic values of Hoover's brand of progressivism; it also revived the interest in humanitarian and economic change of an earlier era of reform.

THE RESTORATION OF CONFIDENCE

Before Franklin Roosevelt could begin the work of rebuilding the American economy, he had to stop its decay. In particular, he had to alleviate the panic that was rapidly gripping the nation as he took office in March 1933. He did so remarkably quickly, making use of a new presidential style and a series of rapid legislative actions.

The Roosevelt Style

The new presidential tone of confidence and optimism was evident from the beginning. It was especially clear in Roosevelt's inaugural address, delivered with vigor and eloquence. "This great Nation will endure as it has endured," the new President told a nation eager for reassurance, "will revive and prosper. So, first of all, let me assert my firm belief that the only thing we have to fear is fear itself." In the weeks and months that followed, Roosevelt continued skillfully to craft a warm and comforting public image. His vigorous legislative program during the much-heralded first hundred days of the administration was, of course, his most effective tool. But his rare ability to communicate his dynamism to the public was also important.

Central to Roosevelt's success at establishing himself at the center of the public consciousness was his use of the radio. Presidents before him had used the airwaves infrequently, if at all; Roosevelt used them enthusiastically and often. He was, most observers agreed, a "born radio speaker," one of the first politicians to recognize the crucial difference between addressing a crowd live in an auditorium and addressing families sitting around their radio sets in their living rooms. Among his most celebrated innovations were the "fireside chats"—a series of cozy radio addresses aimed at the average citizen, explaining actions the new administration had undertaken. He delivered his first fireside chat only eight days after his inauguration, and he continued the practice frequently thereafter.

Roosevelt was also a master at handling his relations with the national press. Herbert Hoover, in the last days of his embattled presidency, had become a sour and isolated figure, avoiding reporters as much as possible, snarling when forced to confront them. Roosevelt, in contrast, was remarkably accessible and unfailingly genial. As often as twice a week, he held informal press conferences in the Oval Office, chatting with reporters as if they were close personal friends (as often they were). Thus while the New Deal soon earned the enmity of most newspaper owners, who were overwhelmingly Republican and conservative, the reporters

FRANKLIN AND ELEANOR. Franklin and Eleanor Roosevelt, shown here returning to the White House from the 1941 inaugural, had a tense and at times troubled personal relationship. But theirs was one of the most successful public marriages in history. Mrs. Roosevelt complemented her husband's charm and political skill with her compassion for the poor. She became the most powerful advocate within the government for the rights of blacks and women. She also did extensive traveling on behalf of the President, whose inability to walk restricted his own mobility. (*Tenschert Photo © Ankers Capitol Photographers, Washington, D.C.*)

themselves generally gave the President fair, if not openly supportive treatment. Their respect for Roosevelt, and for the office of President, was such that by unwritten agreement, no news photographer ever photographed the President being lifted into or out of his car or being wheeled in his wheelchair. A substantial portion of the population remained unaware throughout his presidency that Roosevelt was unable to walk.

The First Days

Image alone, however, could not solve the serious economic problems of March 1933; and within twenty-four hours of his inauguration, Roosevelt was moving forcefully to enact legislation that would restore at least momentary stability to the nation. With the banking crisis at a fever pitch and with Congress apparently in a mood to do virtually anything the new President suggested, Roosevelt might well have taken drastic steps, such as nationalizing the banking system. Instead, he worked to restore public confidence in existing financial institutions and to revive business's faith in the economy. On March 6, two days after taking office, he issued a proclamation closing all American banks and stopping all transactions in or exports of gold for four days until Congress could meet in special session. Under other circumstances, the bank "holiday" might have created wide alarm. As it was, however, it produced general relief, providing a momentary hiatus in the disturbing spread of bank failures. Three days later, Roosevelt sent to Congress the Emergency Banking Act, a generally conservative bill (much of it drafted by holdovers from the Hoover administration) designed to protect the solvency of larger banks from the weakness of smaller ones. The measure authorized the Federal Reserve system to issue notes against the assets of the banks, thus increasing financial liquidity; it allowed the Reconstruction Finance Corporation to provide funds to banks by buying their stock; it forbade the hoarding and exporting of gold (thus, in effect, taking the country off the gold standard, a step that would become official on April 19). Perhaps most important to much of the public, the bill provided for Treasury Department inspection of all banks before they would be allowed to reopen. Sound banks would be permitted to resume business; unsafe banks would not and would be forced either to merge with stronger institutions or declare bankruptcy. A confused and frightened Congress passed the bill within four hours of its introduction. The members had not even read it; a rolled-up newspaper had substituted for it in the House because there had not yet been time to print copies.

"I can assure you," Roosevelt told the public on March 12, in his first fireside chat, "that it is safer to keep your money in a reopened bank than under the mattress." And so it was. By his quick and confident action, Roosevelt had averted at least the immediate threat to the banking system and to the capitalist system itself. Three-quarters of the banks in the Federal Reserve system reopened within the next three days, and a billion dollars in hoarded currency and gold flowed back into them within a month. Bank failures all but disappeared in the years that followed.

On the morning after passage of the Emergency Banking Act, Roosevelt sent to Congress another measure—the Economy Act—designed to instill in the public (and especially in the business community) full confidence in the government. The act was designed to balance the federal budget by cutting the salaries of government employees and reducing pensions to veterans by as much as 15 percent. Otherwise, the President warned, the nation faced a $1-billion deficit. The bill revealed clearly what Roosevelt had always maintained: that he was at heart as much a fiscal conservative as his predecessor. And like the banking bill, it passed through Congress almost instantly, although fierce opposition from veterans' organizations produced substantial Democratic opposition in the House. Public pressure soon forced Congress to rescind the pension cuts (over Roosevelt's veto), but the regular expenditures of the federal government remained substantially, if only temporarily, reduced.

So far, except for the gold clause in the banking bill, Roosevelt had done nothing of which Hoover and the Republicans would have disapproved. The effect, however, was the same as if he had done much more. Business confidence began to revive, and the stock market rose 15 percent in a few days. Public hopefulness quickly grew, and Roosevelt's popularity soared. Symbolic of the change in mood, perhaps, was another measure Roosevelt steered to passage during his first days in office: a bill to legalize the manufacture and sale of beer with a 3.2 percent alcohol content (an interim measure pending the repeal of Prohibition, for which a constitutional amendment was already in process). The measure, Roosevelt argued, would stimulate recovery and bring in needed taxes. It also, in urban areas at least, helped lighten the public mood.

THE SEARCH FOR ECONOMIC REFORM

Roosevelt himself was the first to recognize that these initial actions were nothing but stopgaps, that more comprehensive government programs would be necessary before the economy could fully revive. He faced substantial disagreement within his own administration, however, on how best to pursue economic reform. Some members of his celebrated Brain Trust—men such as Raymond Moley and Adolph Berle—advocated a program not far removed from the business associationalism of Herbert Hoover, by which the government would encourage rational planning of the economy by the business community. Others—such as Rexford G. Tugwell—shared this faith in the importance of planning but believed that government itself should be the planner. Still others whose opinions Roosevelt respected—Supreme Court Justice Louis Brandeis, Harvard professor Felix Frankfurter, and others—urged a vigorous program to restore competition in the economy. It was a debate that in many ways mirrored the arguments of twenty years before. Roosevelt responded to it by adopting a series of uneasy compromises that embodied some aspects of each position. At first, however, it was the planners whose arguments proved most influential.

Agricultural Adjustment

The administration's first major reform effort was on behalf of the troubled agricultural economy, and it provided at last active government support for farm prices. More than that, it established an important federal role in the planning of the entire agricultural sector of the economy, a role that it would never relinquish. Farmers had long been renowned for their fierce independence; but for the most part they welcomed the new arrangements, which provided agriculture with preferential treatment from the government.

Roosevelt was faced with two conflicting demands in his effort to satisfy the needs of farmers. The more substantial farm owners—among them the 300,000 members of the Farm Bureau Federation who continued, even in 1933, to pay dues of $10 a year or more—had long advocated a program to limit the planting of crops. The production cuts, they argued, would raise farm prices and allow farmers to make more money at less cost. Other, poorer farmers—members of such organizations as the Farmers' Union and the Farm Holiday Association— argued that they could not afford to cut their already meager production, that they needed instead direct subsidies and forceful inflation of the money supply. Roosevelt attempted to satisfy both groups, but from the beginning it was clear that his primary concern was with the plight of the relatively substantial farmers, who were, he believed, the backbone of the agricultural economy. Within weeks of taking office, he invited members of the various farm organizations to Washington to devise their own plan for agricultural reform. They drafted a sweeping measure that contained scraps and reworkings of many long-cherished schemes but provided most prominently for a system of crop reductions. The reforms were to be administered by the new Agricultural Adjustment Administration (AAA), which began operations in May following Congress's approval of the proposals.

Under the "domestic allotment" system of the AAA, producers of seven basic commodities (wheat, cotton, corn, hogs, rice, tobacco, and dairy products) were to receive benefit payments in return for reducing acreage or otherwise cutting production. A tax on food processing (for example, the milling of wheat) would provide the funds for the new payments; and that tax could then be added to the price of flour and other finished products and passed on to the consumer, who would thus in effect pay the farmer for growing less. Farm prices were to be subsidized up to the point of parity—a level that would provide the same price relationship of farm products to manufactured goods as existed during the period 1909–1914.

Because the 1933 agricultural season was already well under way by the time the AAA began operations, a large-scale destruction of existing crops and livestock was necessary to reduce surpluses. Six million pigs and 220,000 sows about to farrow were slaughtered. Cotton farmers plowed under a quarter of their crop. Wheat crops had been so devastated by bad weather that the AAA did not require any reductions there, but in most areas of the agricultural economy some destruction was necessary. In a society plagued by want, in which many families were suffering from malnutrition and starvation, it was difficult for the government to explain the need for destroying surpluses. The administrators of the AAA might argue that hunger in America was not a result of too little food, but of poor distribution of what food there was. They might point out that 100 million pounds of pork from the slaughtered hogs had been diverted to feed needy families. They might show that cotton farmers, by cutting production only on their poorer lands,

EVICTED SHARECROPPERS ON THE ROAD.   Southern sharecroppers, long among the nation's poorest citizens, benefited little from the reforms of the AAA. The government policy of providing inducements to farmers not to plant caused many landowners to evict the tenants and sharecroppers on their land and collect federal subsidies for leaving the acreage fallow. This 1939 photograph by Arthur Rothstein shows evicted black sharecroppers with their possessions beside a road in Missouri. (*Library of Congress*)

actually ended up growing more cotton in 1933 than they had in 1932. But the image of the government destroying food while poor people starved remained a powerful one and continued to fuel criticism of the Roosevelt administration for years.

The AAA had other tools at its disposal as well. It could, through the Commodity Credit Corporation, lend farmers money on the basis of their existing crops or purchase nonperishable commodities and hold them in storage against future shortages; it could lease land from farmers so as to withdraw it from production; and it could promote new marketing agreements among growers. Smaller farmers, too, received some satisfaction from the new reforms. The act creating the AAA also provided the President with the power to inflate the currency by issuing greenbacks and remonetizing silver (powers he chose not to use). And the new Farm Credit Administration provided farmers with assistance in meeting mortgage payments. Nevertheless, the real thrust of New Deal agricultural policies was toward planning for the farm economy as a whole, not toward protection of individual farmers. As a result, it was the substantial farm owners who benefited most from the new reforms.

The results of the AAA efforts were decidedly mixed. Prices for farm commodities did indeed rise in the years after 1933, and gross farm income increased by half in the first three years of the New Deal. The relative position of farmers in the economy, therefore, improved significantly, even though similarly rising prices for manufactured goods sharply limited their gains. But the AAA did little to help the smaller farmers, most of whom continued to languish at a competitive disadvantage in an increasingly concentrated agricultural economy. At times, even if unintentionally, the agency actually dispossessed them. In the cotton belt, for example, planters who were reducing their acreage fired many field hands and evicted their tenants and sharecroppers.

Industrial Recovery

The dominance within the administration of those who believed in centralized economic planning was even more evident in the New Deal's policy toward industry. The industrial economy in 1933 was, as it had been for nearly three years, suffering from a vicious cycle of deflation. Production and capital investment were falling, causing workers to lose their jobs, reducing consumer demand, driving down prices, and encouraging industry to cut production and employment even further. Only by attacking all these problems simultaneously, New Deal planners believed, could American industry be revived.

Ever since 1931, leaders of the United States Chamber of Commerce had, with others, been urging upon the government an antideflation scheme that would permit trade associations to cooperate in stabilizing prices within their industries. Existing antitrust laws clearly forbade such practices, but businessmen argued that the economic emergency justified a suspension of the restrictions. Herbert Hoover had long been a supporter of the trade association movement, but he had refused to lend his assistance to the scheme. On the contrary, his administration filed suit to force five leading trade associations to dissolve when the Justice Department concluded that they were operating in "restraint of trade"; and the Federal Trade Commission had compelled the trade associations for sixty-two industries to revise their codes to comply with the antitrust laws.

The Roosevelt administration was far more receptive to the idea of cooperation among producers, and even to the demands of some businessmen that the government enforce trade association agreements on pricing and production. But New Dealers insisted on other provisions that would deal with the remaining economic problems as well. Businessmen would have to accept regulation of wages and hours and other concessions to labor to ensure that the incomes of workers would rise along with prices. And lest consumer buying power lag behind and defeat the scheme, the administration added another ingredient: a major program of public works spending designed to pump needed funds into the economy. For three months, the administration worked with businessmen, labor leaders, and others to construct a bill that would embody all these provisions. The result was the National Industrial Recovery Act, which Congress passed in June 1933. Roosevelt, signing the bill, called it "the most important and far-reaching legislation ever enacted by the American Congress." Businessmen hailed it as the beginning of a new era of cooperation between government and industry. Labor leaders praised it as a "magna charta" for trade unions. There was, it seemed, something in the bill for everyone.

At first, moreover, the new program appeared to be working miracles. At its center was a new federal agency, the National Recovery Administration (NRA); and to head it, Roosevelt chose the flamboyant and energetic Hugh S. Johnson, a retired general and successful businessman. Johnson envisioned himself as a kind of evangelist, generating public enthusiasm for New Deal programs. In a sense, it was an appropriate image, for crucial to the success of the NRA was Johnson's ability to persuade the public to accept its provisions. He did so in two ways. First, he called upon every business establishment in the nation to accept a temporary "blanket code," establishing a minimum wage of between 30 and 40 cents an hour, a maximum workweek of 35 to 40 hours, and the abolition of child labor. The result, he claimed, would be to raise consumer purchasing power, increase employment, and eliminate the infamous sweatshop. To generate enthusiasm for the blanket code, Johnson devised a symbol–the famous NRA Blue Eagle–which employers who accepted the provisions could display in their windows. Soon, Blue Eagle flags, posters, and stickers, carrying the NRA slogan "We Do Our Part," were decorating commercial establishments in every part of the country. He composed a pledge, which consumers were to sign as a promise that they would patronize only establishments in compliance with the code. And he mobilized an impressive display of public support: rallies, demonstrations, and parades, including an enormous march down Fifth Avenue in New York in the fall of 1933 that observers claimed was the largest in the city's history.

At the same time, Johnson was busy negotiating another, more specific set of codes with leaders of the nation's major industries—agreements designed to limit the deflationary pressures of "cutthroat competition." These industrial codes set floors below which no company would lower prices or wages in its search for a competitive advantage; and they included agreements on maintaining employment and production. The extraordinary public support Johnson had managed to generate for the blanket code gave him substantial bargaining strength; and in a remarkably short time, he won agreements from almost every major industry in the country. A nation eager for positive action was giving the NRA its fervent support.

From the beginning, however, the New Deal's bold experiment in economic planning was plagued with serious difficulties; and ultimately, under a barrage of public criticism, the entire effort dissolved in failure. The problems were many, some of them a result of the concept of the NRA, some of them a result of its administration. Perhaps the greatest difficulty was in the structure of the industrial codes. In theory, they represented agreement among employers, workers, and consumers, all of whom were represented at the bargaining table. In reality, the power lay with the businessmen themselves, and particularly with the leading figures within each industry. Often, the NRA codes were little more than rewritten versions of existing trade association agreements, strengthened now by the promise of federal enforcement. The result was, first, that most codes favored large

SALUTING THE BLUE EAGLE.　Eight thousand San Francisco schoolchildren assemble on a baseball field in 1933 to form the symbol of the NRA: an eagle clutching a cogwheel (to symbolize industry) and a thunderbolt (to symbolize energy). NRA administrators drew from their memories of the World War I Liberty Loan drives and attempted to establish the Blue Eagle as a symbol of patriotic commitment to recovery. The enthusiasm was widespread at first, but it faded quickly as the economy failed to recover. (*UPI*)

businesses at the expense of smaller ones. Second, they often did more than simply set floors under prices; they actively and artificially raised them—often to levels higher than was necessary to ensure a profit and far higher than market forces would normally have dictated. The NRA had not been intended to promote price fixing, but in practice it did just that. Third, the codes enabled many unhealthy businesses to continue operating when they should have been allowed to fail. And finally, the NRA tended to discourage capital investment, something the country badly needed, by making other investments more profitable.

There were also serious problems in enforcement of the codes, stemming in large part from Hugh Johnson's natural affinity for the business community and his reluctance to employ forceful measures against its members. At first, most manufacturers complied happily with the new agreements, expecting a major industrial revival to result. That revival did not come. Indeed, industrial production actually declined in the months after the establishment of the NRA—from an index of 101 in July 1933 to 71 in November—despite the rise in prices that the codes had helped to create. That failure encouraged an increasing number of firms to begin cutting wages and prices once again or to violate agreements on levels of production. Johnson was not inclined to prosecute them. NRA administrators, moreover, were becoming increasingly mired in efforts to win compliance from small, local firms, spreading their energies so thin that they were unable effectively to police the large enterprises that should have been their first priority.

Another problem was that the attempts to increase consumer purchasing power did not progress as quickly as the efforts to raise prices. Section 7-a of the charter of the NRA gave legal protection to the right of workers to form unions and engage in collective bargaining. But even though union strength increased in the ensuing months, significant wage increases were slow to follow. The public works provisions of the National Industrial Recovery Act were similarly slow to have any impact. The Public Works Administration (PWA) established by the bill to administer the spending programs was placed in the hands of Interior Secretary Harold Ickes, a self-described "curmudgeon" who carefully solicited plans for suitable projects, slowly and punctiliously examined each one to determine its worthiness, and only gradually allowed the $3.3 billion in public works funds to trickle out. Not until 1938 was the PWA budget pumping an appreciable amount of money into the economy.

By the spring of 1934, unsurprisingly, the NRA was besieged by criticism both from within the administration and from without. Businessmen were claiming that the wage requirements of the codes were making it impossible for them to earn adequate profits and were denouncing the provisions requiring them to bargain with unions. Economists were charging that the price fixing encouraged by the codes was undermining efforts to raise purchasing power. Reformers were complaining that the NRA was encouraging economic concentration and monopoly. Critics of all kinds were denouncing Johnson for his cozy relationship with business leaders and his increasingly erratic behavior. A national Recovery Review Board, chaired by the famous criminal lawyer Clarence Darrow, reported in the spring of 1934 that the NRA was excessively dominated by big business and unduly encouraging monopoly; and Hugh Johnson's vituperative response served only to undermine the agency's prestige even further.

Finally, in the fall of 1934, Roosevelt pressured Johnson to resign and established a new board of directors to oversee the NRA. But the agency's effectiveness failed to improve. Then in 1935, the Supreme Court intervened to bring an end to the troubled experiment. The constitutional basis for the NRA had been Congress's power to regulate commerce among the states, a power the administration had interpreted exceptionally broadly. The case before the Court involved alleged code violations by the Schechter brothers, who operated a wholesale poultry business confined to one locality: Brooklyn, New York. The Court ruled unanimously that the Schechters were not engaged in interstate commerce and, further, that Congress had unconstitutionally delegated legislative power to the President to draft the NRA codes. The legislation establishing the agency, therefore, was declared void; and the NRA was forced to cease its operations. Roosevelt expressed outrage at the so-called "sick chicken" decision and denounced the justices for their "horse-and-buggy" interpretation of the interstate commerce clause. In fact, however, the decision proved to be more of a blessing than a catastrophe for the New Deal, providing it with a face-saving way to abolish the decrepit NRA code system. Privately, the President himself expressed relief. "It has been an awful headache," he confided to one colleague.

An Experiment in Regional Planning

In the AAA and even more in the NRA, those New Dealers who favored planning by private interests generally held sway. In other areas, however, those reformers who believed that the government itself should be the chief planning agent in the economy managed to establish dominance. Their most conspicuous success, and one of the most celebrated accomplishments of the New Deal as a whole, was an unprecedented experiment in regional planning: the Tennessee Valley Authority (TVA).

The TVA had its roots in a political controversy that had surfaced repeatedly in the 1920s. Throughout that decade, one of the cherished goals of the progressive reformers remaining in Congress had been public development of the nation's water resources. In particular, they had urged completion of a great dam at Muscle Shoals on the Tennessee River in Alabama, a dam begun during World War I in an effort to increase nitrate production but left unfinished when the hostilities concluded before it could begin operations. The nation's utility companies, predictably opposed to the concept of public power in any form, had fought desperately against completion of the project, spending as much as $35 million annually in lobbying and public relations. The battle had raged on for years. When President Coolidge supported a measure to sell the Muscle Shoals project to Henry Ford for private development, Senator George Norris of Nebraska and other progressives blocked it in Congress. When progressives managed to steer to passage a bill establishing a public power authority in the region, first Coolidge and then Hoover vetoed it. Norris and his allies now argued that the government should not only complete the project but make it the centerpiece of a federal program to develop the resources of the impoverished Tennessee Valley.

By 1933 indignation against the private power interests was burning hot. Monopolistic utility companies had, progressives believed, been gulling investors and overcharging customers for years. The spectacular collapse of the great Insull utility empire in the Midwest in 1932 added credence to their charges. When the public power advocates enlisted the support of Franklin Roosevelt, nothing more stood in their way.

The result was legislation enacted in May 1933 creating the Tennessee Valley Authority, a public corporation whose mandate was "national planning for a complete river watershed." The TVA was intended not only to complete the dam

THE TENNESSEE VALLEY AUTHORITY. Construction of a TVA dam in North Carolina continues under lights at night. (*TVA*)

at Muscle Shoals and build others in the region, and not only to generate and sell electricity from them to the public at reasonable rates. It was to be the agent for a comprehensive redevelopment of the entire region: stopping the disastrous flooding that had plagued the Tennessee Valley for centuries, encouraging the development of local industries, supervising a substantial program of reforestation, and helping farmers to improve productivity. For the most part, it succeeded remarkably well. Although opposition by conservatives within the administration ultimately prevented some of the most ambitious social planning projects proposed by David Lilienthal and other TVA administrators, the project did revitalize the region in countless ways. It improved five existing dams, built twenty new ones, and constructed an extensive (and heavily trafficked) system of inland waterways. The result of all this was virtually to eliminate flooding in the region and to provide electricity to thousands who had never before had it. Indeed, the TVA soon became the greatest producer of electric power in the United States, as well as one of the cheapest suppliers. The price of power in the region dropped from 10 cents a kilowatt hour to 3 cents, once the TVA reached full operation; and throughout the country, largely because of the yardstick provided by the TVA, private power rates soon declined as well. The TVA also produced inexpensive phosphate fertilizers, helped farmers to prevent soil erosion, and generally raised agricultural productivity—and through it the standard of living—for the entire region. The Authority worked no miracles and made many mistakes. The Tennessee Valley remained a generally impoverished region despite its efforts. Blacks, for the most part, were excluded from employment in TVA projects and benefited only marginally from its operations. Nevertheless, no one disputed that the region as a whole was enjoying significant growth and progress as a result of the government's efforts.

Financial Reforms

The primary purpose of New Deal reform, of course, was to promote recovery from the Depression. One approach, embodied in the NRA and AAA, was economic planning to regulate production. Another was to put government money into circulation through the PWA and the many relief agencies the administration established. Still another approach was to manipulate the currency so as to increase the money supply. Roosevelt's willingness to try any number of different experiments led him by the summer of 1933 to endorse that method as well.

According to some economists, the government could raise the prices of commodities almost automatically simply by raising the price of gold, thus inflating the currency. Federal agencies needed only to purchase large quantities of gold and cut the gold content of the dollar (measures already authorized by Congress). Acting on this advice, Roosevelt directed Henry Morgenthau, Jr., head of the Farm Credit Administration (and soon to become Secretary of the Treasury), to make purchases of gold each day along with his purchases of wheat, corn, and oats. A few months later, after Congress had passed the Silver Purchase Act of 1934, the President initiated a similar program for the purchase of silver. The gold- and silver-buying efforts did indeed raise the prices of the precious metals themselves. They did little or nothing, however, to raise prices in the United States; and the silver purchases, in particular, by tripling the price of the metal on the world market, wreaked havoc in nations whose currencies were on the silver standard.

Of more lasting importance than the ill-considered gold- and silver-buying schemes was the administration's early decision to take the dollar off the gold standard. That had been the constant demand of agrarian inflationists since the days of the Populists; until 1933, however, orthodox economists had always forestalled such action by warning that it would lead to financial chaos. Roosevelt was not an inflationist at heart, but he soon came to recognize the gold standard as a major obstacle to the restoration of adequate prices. "I have always favored sound money," he told one critical Congressman, "and do now, but it is 'too darned sound' when it takes so much of farm products to buy a dollar." The Emergency Banking Act of March 1933 had been the first step toward taking the country off the gold standard; on April 18, 1933, the President made the shift official with an executive order (despite the warnings of his budget director, Lew Douglas, who predicted the action would lead to "the end of Western civilization"). A few weeks later, Congress passed legislation confirming his decision. In January 1934, after the failure of the gold-buying experiment, the President finally established a new fixed standard for the dollar, with its gold content set at 59.09 percent of the 1932 amount. The resort to government-managed currency created an important precedent for future federal policies and permanently altered the relationship between the public and private sectors. It did not, however, have any immediate impact upon the depressed American economy.

Through other legislation, the early New Deal advanced even further the shift of financial power from private institutions to the federal government. The Glass-Steagall Act of June 1933 gave the government authority to curb irresponsible speculation by banks. More important, in the public mind at least, it established the Federal Deposit Insurance Corporation, which guaranteed all bank deposits up to $2,500. In other words, even should a bank fail, small depositors would be able to recover their deposits. Roosevelt opposed the FDIC during congressional debate over the bill, but once in operation it proved so successful that he later approved a gradual raising of the limit on guaranteed deposits, which soon reached $15,000.

It was a more difficult task to work out a comprehensive overhaul of the Federal Reserve system so as to remedy the serious financial defects that had appeared during the Depression. Finally, in 1935, Congress passed a major banking act that finally established American finance on a stable footing with constant government supervision. The 1935 act transferred much of the authority once wielded by the regional reserve banks to the Federal Reserve Board in Washington, whose seven members now exercised direct control over interest rates. By lowering the rates, the board could make it easier to borrow money from banks and thus, in most cases, encourage prices to rise.

To protect investors in the once popular and now mistrusted stock market, Congress passed the so-called Truth in Securities Act of 1933, requiring corporations issuing new securities to register them with the Federal Trade Commission and provide full and accurate information about them to the public. In June 1934, Congress went even further and established the Securities and Exchange Commission (SEC) to police the stock market. Among other things, the establishment of the SEC was an indication of how far the financial establishment had fallen in the estimation of the public. In earlier years, J. P. Morgan and other important financiers could have wielded enough influence to stop such government interference in the financial world. Now, Morgan could not even get a respectful hearing on Capitol Hill. The criminal trials of a number of once-respected Wall Street figures for larceny and fraud (including the conviction and imprisonment of Richard Whitney, one-time head of the New York Stock Exchange and the man whose influence had briefly quelled the panic in October 1929) eroded the public stature of the financial community still further.

THE GROWTH OF FEDERAL RELIEF

The most important purpose of the New Deal, Franklin Roosevelt and his colleagues believed, was to reform the economy—to restore stability and enhance productivity so that prosperity would return to the nation. In the meantime, however, millions of Americans were in desperate need of assistance, and the administration quickly recognized the necessity of providing them with relief. It was, they believed, a temporary expedient, to be continued only long enough for the economy to return to health. Gradually, however, it became clear that the government commitment to relief would be far greater and would endure far longer than all but a few New Dealers had envisioned.

Emergency Relief

Like his predecessor, Roosevelt believed that aid to the indigent was primarily a local responsibility and should remain so. But he also recognized that under the circumstances of the Depression, localities were unable to fulfill that responsibility. Among his first acts as President, therefore, was the establishment of the Federal Emergency Relief Administration, which provided cash grants to states (rather than loans, as the Hoover administration had favored) to prop up bankrupt relief agencies. To administer the program, he chose the director of the New York State relief agency, Harry Hopkins, who was ultimately to become the most important member of his administration. Hopkins, unlike Harold Ickes, realized the importance of speed in distributing government funds and disbursed the FERA grants widely and rapidly. Even he, however, shared Roosevelt's basic misgivings about establishing a government dole. "It is probably going to undermine the independence of hundreds of thousands of families," he once lamented. "I look upon this as a great national disaster."

Both Roosevelt and Hopkins felt somewhat more comfortable with another form of government assistance: work relief. Unlike the dole, Hopkins believed, work relief "preserves a man's morale. It saves his skill. It gives him a chance to do something socially useful." Thus when it became clear that the FERA would not be sufficient to pull the country through the winter, the administration established a second program: the Civil Works Administration. Between Novem-

HARRY HOPKINS. Hopkins, the New Deal's "minister of relief," became Roosevelt's most intimate adviser. For some years, he lived in a spare room in the White House. Although in declining health by the 1940s, he traveled extensively during the war on diplomatic missions on behalf of the President. (*National Archives*)

ber and April, it put more than 4 million people to work on temporary projects: some of them of real value, such as the construction of roads, schools, and parks; others little more than make-work, such as raking leaves or supervising playgrounds. The important thing, however, was that the 400,000 CWA projects (with a budget of $1 billion) were pumping money into an economy badly in need of it and were providing assistance to families and individuals with nowhere else to turn.

Like the FERA, the CWA was intended to be a temporary expedient only. Thus as the winter continued, not only congressional critics but Roosevelt himself became increasingly uncomfortable with the program. The FERA, at least, was working through the states and localities. The CWA, even with its work provisions, was too much like a federal dole. By the spring of 1934, therefore, the President began to dismantle the agency, and he ultimately disbanded it altogether. Symbolically, at least, the government was making clear its determination not to become too deeply involved in social welfare. But the New Deal would remain involved despite itself. The President may have abolished the CWA as an administrative entity, but many of its functions continued to be performed by other agencies.

Civilian Conservation

Of all the New Deal relief projects, the one closest to Roosevelt's own heart, and the one he had the least difficulty reconciling with his conservative beliefs, was the Civilian Conservation Corps (CCC). Established in the first weeks of the new administration, the CCC was designed to provide employment to the millions of urban youths who could find no jobs in the cities and who, in many cases, were moving restlessly from one region of the country to another in search of work. At the same time, it was to advance the work of conservation and reforestation—goals Roosevelt had long cherished. The CCC created a series of camps in national parks and forests and in other rural and wilderness settings. There, young men worked in a semimilitary environment on such projects as planting trees, building reservoirs, developing parks, and improving agricultural irrigation. CCC workers planted a "shelterbelt" of trees across the Plains states as an effort to counteract the drought and dust storms afflicting the region. They built towers and other facilities to aid in fighting forest fires. They patrolled public lands and helped refurbish parks and national monuments. As with the CWA, many of the CCC projects were of only marginal value. But the President nevertheless took great pride in the success of the corps in providing jobs to over 500,000 young men, offering them not only incomes but an opportunity to work in a "healthy and wholesome" atmosphere.

Mortgage and Credit Relief

Mortgage relief was a pressing need of millions of farm owners and homeowners. Roosevelt had provided some assistance to farmers in danger of losing their land, through the AAA and particularly through the Farm Credit Administration,

FDR AND THE CCC.   President Roosevelt joins workers at a Civilian
Conservation Corps camp in Virginia for lunch in August 1933. Of all the New Deal
relief programs, the CCC was Roosevelt's personal favorite. Seated with him are,
from left to right, Louis Howe, the President's longtime political adviser; Interior
Secretary Harold Ickes; CCC director Robert Fechner; Agriculture Secretary Henry
A. Wallace; and Rexford G. Tugwell, one of the original members of the Roosevelt
Brain Trust. (*Franklin D. Roosevelt Library Collection*)

which within two years refinanced one-fifth of all farm mortgages in the United
States. The Frazier-Lemke Farm Bankruptcy Act of 1933 went even further,
enabling some farmers to regain their land even after the foreclosure of mortgages.
Despite such efforts, however, small farmers continued to lose their property in
many regions; by 1934, 25 percent of all American farmers had lost their land.
    Homeowners were similarly troubled, and in June 1933 the administration
established the Home Owners' Loan Corporation, which in a three-year period

loaned out more than $3 billion to refinance the mortgages of more than a million householders. Altogether, it carried about one-sixth of the nation's urban mortgage burden. A year later, Congress established the Federal Housing Administration to insure mortgages for new construction and home repairs—a measure that combined an effort to provide relief with a program to stimulate lasting recovery of the construction industry.

The Reconstruction Finance Corporation continued, under the New Deal, to provide loans to troubled businesses. Democrats in Congress, unhappy with the RFC's tendency during the Hoover administration to make most of its loans to large banks and corporations, broadened the agency's authority so as to allow it to lend funds to smaller enterprises. The effort was only partially successful. Some small businesses did benefit from the reforms; but under the conservative management of Jesse Jones, the RFC continued to make loans only to those enterprises it believed likely to repay them. In the eyes of the agency, that meant, for the most part, large organizations.

The Irony of New Deal Relief

The relief efforts of the first hundred days, and even of the first two years, of the New Deal were based on several basic premises. Relief was, Franklin Roosevelt believed, an emergency function of government—as the name of his first relief agency suggested. It was, therefore, to be temporary. Relief was, almost all members of the administration believed, primarily the responsibility of state and local government. Federal assistance, therefore, should be channeled through localities. And relief was, the President and his allies were convinced, a danger to the moral fiber of the nation, threatening to undermine the traditional values of work and self-reliance. Government programs, therefore, should avoid becoming doles, and should emphasize useful work instead.

Even in the early days of the New Deal, however, each of these assumptions was being severely tested; and each of these restraints was being significantly eroded. New Dealers would continue in the years ahead to attempt to limit and qualify the federal government's commitment to relief. But despite their efforts, a national policy of social welfare was beginning to emerge as a permanent element of the modern state.

SUGGESTED READINGS

The best overview of the New Deal is William E. Leuchtenburg, *Franklin D. Roosevelt and the New Deal* (1963). A more thorough account of the first years of the Roosevelt administration, and one more favorable to FDR, is Arthur M. Schlesinger, Jr., *The Coming of the New Deal* (1959). Paul Conkin, *The New Deal* (1967), is a brief revisionist view that is more skeptical of the New Deal's achievements. Another general study of the early Roosevelt years is James McGregor Burns, *Roosevelt: The Lion and the Fox* (1956). The most comprehensive study of Roosevelt himself is Frank Freidel's multivolume biography, *Franklin D. Roosevelt,* 4 vols. (1952–1973), the fourth volume of which follows Roosevelt through his first hundred days in the White House. Joseph P. Lash, *Eleanor and Franklin* (1971), studies the most celebrated of all first ladies and sheds valuable light upon her relationship with her husband.

The first months of the New Deal receive intensive scrutiny in Frank Freidel, *Launching the New Deal* (1973); Raymond Moley and Eliot Rosen, *The First New Deal* (1966); and Herbert Feis, *Characters in Crisis* (1966). An invaluable study of New Deal economic policy is Ellis Hawley, *The New Deal and the Problem of Monopoly* (1966). Bernard Bellush, *The Failure of the NRA* (1975), examines the cornerstone of the early New Deal economic program, and Sidney Fine, *The Automobile Under the Blue Eagle* (1963), examines the impact of the NRA on one industry. Robert F. Himmelberg, *The Origins of the National Recovery Administration* (1976), is another valuable work.

New Deal agricultural policy receives attention in Van L. Perkins, *Crisis in Agriculture* (1969), and Richard S. Kirkendall, *Social Scientists and Farm Politics in the Age of Roosevelt* (1966). David Conrad, *The Forgotten Farmers* (1965), examines those who did not share in the benefits of the AAA. Thomas K. McCraw, *TVA and the Power Fight* (1970), is a valuable study of the most conspicuous social project of the New Deal. Michael Parrish, *Securities Regulation and the New Deal* (1970), and Ralph F. De Bedts, *The New Deal's SEC* (1964), analyze the most prominent of the administration's financial reforms. Searle Charles, *Minister of Relief* (1963), examines the origins of welfare policies through the career of Harry Hopkins. John Salmond, *The Civilian Conservation Corps* (1967), studies the most popular of the relief agencies. James T. Patterson, *America's Struggle Against Poverty, 1900–1980* (1981), is a new and sweeping examination of the growth of social welfare policies, with extensive examination of the New Deal. Paul Mertz, *The New Deal and Southern Rural Poverty* (1978), examines some of the limits of relief.

Thirteen

The New Deal in
Transition and Decline

For nearly two years, Franklin Roosevelt succeeded, if not in ending the Depression, then at least in maintaining a remarkable popularity. Despite the decidedly mixed results of his programs for economic reform, despite the obvious limitations of his new relief agencies, much of the American public came to view the President as the personification of concerned and committed government. He had quelled the panic and despair of 1932. And he had, through the warmth of his personality, projected a promise of better times to come. Although majority parties as a rule lose strength in Congress in off-year elections, Roosevelt's popularity was such that the Democrats actually increased their majorities in both Houses in 1934.

By the spring of 1935, however, the Roosevelt presidency had become deeply troubled. The Depression continued—softened perhaps by New Deal efforts, but generally unabated. Ten million people, 20 percent of the work force, remained unemployed. Farm prices continued to languish far below their 1929 levels. National income was still 40 percent lower than six years earlier. At the same time, the administration seemed to have run out of ideas for dealing with the crisis. The cornerstone of its efforts to create a rational, planned economy—the NRA—had failed to perform as hoped and had, in any case, been invalidated by a conservative Supreme Court. Spending on public works and relief had failed to stimulate recovery. Nothing new had yet emerged to take their place. "Once more," wrote Walter Lippmann at the time, "we have come to a period of discouragement after a few months of buoyant hope."

It was perhaps unsurprising that in the midst of these frustrations the New Deal should find itself subjected to fierce public criticism. But the opposition in 1935 was particularly disturbing to Franklin Roosevelt because it came not just from

241

his traditional opponents—the Republican minority in Congress—but from a whole host of new and unconventional groups. From the right and, even more disturbingly, from the left were emerging powerful, organized movements challenging not only the New Deal but, it seemed for a time, the political system itself.

This dual challenge—the challenge of continuing economic hardship and of growing political danger—was not lost on Franklin Roosevelt. Far from succumbing to despair, he embarked on a major effort to reinvigorate the New Deal with a new program of legislation. And he launched a forceful campaign designed to preempt his critics on the left and isolate his critics on the right. The result was, first, a series of important new reforms and, second, a striking political success for the President in 1936. Still, however, there was no end to the Depression. In the years following Roosevelt's triumphant reelection, in fact, the New Deal faced even greater frustrations than before and fell victim to even more damaging confusion.

THE NEW DEAL BESIEGED

There had been opposition to the New Deal from the beginning: from those who believed Roosevelt was doing too much too quickly, from those who believed he was moving too cautiously and too slowly, and from some who believed he was doing both. At first the administration's critics had difficulty finding any substantial public support for their positions. But by the time two years had passed and the economy had not revived, attacks on the New Deal were generating a substantial response.

Assault from the Right

Roosevelt had for a time worked hard to conciliate the right and, above all, the American business community. He had displayed his fiscal conservatism in the Economy Act of 1933. He had allowed corporate leaders themselves to help design and operate the NRA. He had, he believed, made every reasonable effort to woo big business into the New Deal coalition. By the end of 1934, however, that effort had clearly failed; and Roosevelt had become the target of an unprecedented enmity from American conservatives. They denounced his "reckless spending," his reliance on "economic crackpots," his "socialist" reforms, and perhaps above all, his support for organized labor. The President was, his conservative critics insisted, provoking "class hatred," turning worker against employer, the poor against the rich. He was undermining the work ethic with his fanciful relief programs. He had, in short, become an enemy of the traditional values and institutions of American life. So intense was the conservative animosity that some Roosevelt critics could not even bear to say the President's name. They referred to him simply and bitterly as "that man in the White House."

Some of this opposition came from existing organizations, such as the Chamber of Commerce and the National Association of Manufacturers. In August 1934, however, conservatives created a new society, the American Liberty League,

"A TRAITOR TO HIS CLASS." *New Yorker* cartoonist Peter Arno satirized the deep animosity of many wealthy Americans toward Franklin Roosevelt in this 1936 cartoon. Some conservatives so detested the President that they refused to speak his name, referring to him only as "that man." Others denounced Roosevelt, himself a member of a wealthy aristocratic family, as a "traitor to his class."

"Come along. We're going to the Trans-Lux to hiss Roosevelt."

designed specifically to arouse public opposition to the New Deal. Members of the du Pont family and executives in their great chemical corporation (including John J. Raskob, one-time chairman of the Democratic National Committee) took the lead in establishing the league. Al Smith, both personally and politically embittered toward his former protégé in the White House, served as an officer. The new organization campaigned vigorously against Roosevelt's "dictatorial" policies, accusing him of flouting the Constitution, destroying free enterprise, undermining states' rights, and eroding the strength of the "American Plan" for labor–management relations (in other words, the open shop). The league claimed to be open to membership from Americans of all regions, parties, and backgrounds. In fact, it attracted primarily northern industrialists, most of them Republicans. At its peak, league membership numbered only about 125,000; but the wealth of its constituency provided the organization with a large budget with which it could make itself heard.

The real impact of the Liberty League and other conservative opponents, however, was neither to undermine the President's political strength nor to force him to moderate his positions. It was, rather, to convince Roosevelt that his efforts to conciliate the business community had failed, that conservatives had adopted a selfish, reckless, and unprincipled political stance, and that it was up to the government now to launch a frontal attack upon them—to reform the corporate community for its own good. As late as October 1934, the President had issued such public statements as his message to the American Bankers' Association that "The time is ripe for an alliance of all forces intent upon the business of recovery. In such an alliance will be found business and banking, agriculture and industry, and labor and capital. What an all-American team that would be!" By 1936, he harbored no such illusions. The forces of "organized money," he said near the end of his campaign for reelection, "are unanimous in their hate for me—and I welcome their hatred."

Challenge from the Left

To the lonely denizens of the far left, who had endured public revilement, official repression, and general political feebleness since the beginning of World War I, the Great Depression seemed at first to offer an opportunity for major gains. The Socialist party, now under the leadership of Norman Thomas, cited the economic crisis as evidence of the failure of capitalism and sought vigorously to win public support for its own political program. In particular, it attempted to mobilize support among those groups suffering most severely from the free market economy. The Southern Tenant Farmers Union, for example, was supported by the party and organized in large part by a young Socialist, H. L. Mitchell, a close associate of Norman Thomas. It attempted to create a biracial coalition of share-croppers, tenant farmers, and others that aimed, through political efforts and work actions, to force fundamental reforms in the agrarian economy of the South. Despite some impressive accomplishments, however, the new union made little real progress and after a few years began to dissolve. Similarly, the Socialist party as a whole made no lasting gains as a result of the Depression. On the contrary, by 1936, membership in the party had fallen below 20,000; and Norman Thomas, the Socialist presidential candidate, was able to attract fewer than 200,000 votes —only about 20 percent of his total four years earlier.

The American Communist party was substantially more successful in using the Depression to increase its influence. It attracted some significant support from within the expanding labor movement and exercised actual control over several important unions. It won the backing of an increasing number of prominent intellectuals, and it gained a large following on college campuses. Only a relatively few American communists were fervent, committed revolutionaries, but those activists were occasionally successful in provoking violent confrontations between citizens and authorities. Although official membership in the party (or Popular Front, as it called itself) never rose much above 50,000, its influence spread far wider than that.

Nevertheless, communism in America never gained anything approaching an important foothold even in the worst years of the Great Depression. The vast majority of the population remained unremittingly hostile to the party. And the communists themselves suffered from severe internal divisions and wavering loyalties. Some members protested when, starting in 1935, the party ceased its strident denunciations of Franklin Roosevelt as a "tool of Wall Street" and began instead to call for a broad coalition of liberals and radicals to fight the spread of world fascism. Others were even further disillusioned when in 1936 the party actually endorsed the President for reelection (albeit without enthusiasm). But the real damage to the Popular Front came not from its failure to satisfy its more radical members but from its success in convincing its moderates of the importance of opposing fascism. An increasing number of communists after 1936 drifted out of the party and back to the support of Franklin Roosevelt. And a massive defection occurred in 1939, when the Stalinist regime in the Soviet Union signed a friend-ship pact with Nazi Germany. The communist hierarchy in America endorsed Stalin's decision and, once the war had begun in Europe, denounced all American aid to the antifascist forces. Membership in the party declined drastically as a result. More important, however, public sympathy for the communists dwindled to almost nothing; not even the American alliance with the Soviet Union after 1941 was able to revive it.

The Dissident Specter

Far more menacing to the New Deal than either the far right or the far left was a growing array of dissident political movements that defied easy ideological classification. Some were marginal, "crackpot" organizations with little popular following—exemplified by William Dudley Pelley's Silver Shirts in North Caro-lina and California and Art J. Smith's Khaki Shirts in New York State, both modeled openly on the Nazi and Fascist parties in Germany and Italy. Others were groups that established substantial public support within particular states or regions. Upton Sinclair's vaguely socialist plan to End Poverty in California (the so-called EPIC movement) almost won him the governorship of that state in 1934. The reinvigorated Progressive party did capture political control of Wisconsin. Robert La Follette, Jr., son of the great progressive of earlier years, won re-election to the Senate as a Progressive in 1934, and his younger brother Phil won the governorship. Floyd Olson, leader of the new Farmer-Labor party in Minnesota, was elected Governor on a platform that some believed was essentially socialist. Dissidents of all sorts were winning election to the Senate and the House.

There were, however, only three insurgent movements that succeeded in mobil-izing genuinely national public support. And by 1935, they had attracted such wide followings that members of the administration had come to consider them the greatest threat to the President's political future. Worst of all, there were signs that the movements were beginning to overlap, that they might ultimately form an alliance and pit a powerful third-party candidate against Roosevelt in 1936. It was with great alarm, therefore, that supporters of the New Deal watched the ascent of Dr. Francis E. Townsend, Father Charles E. Coughlin, and Senator Huey P. Long.

Francis Townsend, an obscure and aging physician in Long Beach, California, began to rise to political prominence in 1933 when he became incensed at the miserable poverty he saw afflicting the many elderly citizens of his city and his state. In response, he began to publicize his own program for both aiding the aged and curing the Depression: the Old Age Revolving Pension Plan. Under the Townsend Plan, as it was more widely known, all Americans over the age of sixty would receive a monthly government pension of $200, providing they retired from their current employment (thus freeing jobs for younger, unemployed Americans) and spent the money in full each month (which would pump needed funds into the economy). With the help of an able (if unscrupulous) publicist, Robert Clements, Townsend managed to win a wide public hearing for his plan; and within less than two years, he had created a nationwide organization with more than a million official members and many more sympathizers. Townsendites in Congress proposed legislation embodying the main provisions of the doctor's program; and although the administration succeeded in convincing the House to defeat it, it was clear that the legislators had recognized the political strength of the movement. Almost half of all Congressmen conspicuously abstained from the vote on the measure. Townsend's strength declined considerably after his congressional defeat, particularly when public disclosures of fraud among his staff rocked the organization. But the movement remained alive for many years, reminding the nation of the compelling needs of the nation's elderly, and helping to build public pressure for first the creation and later the expansion of the Social Security System.

For Father Charles Coughlin, fame arrived along a different and somewhat slower path, but it came in even greater measure. A Catholic priest in the small suburban parish of Royal Oak, Michigan (outside Detroit), Coughlin began in the late 1920s to air his Sunday sermons over a local radio station. His natural broadcasting abilities won him a devoted and growing following; he soon began to recruit other midwestern stations, and finally in 1931 the CBS network, to carry his weekly discourses. At first purely moral and theological, Coughlin's sermons became in the early 1930s increasingly political in tone. By 1932, they were almost totally devoted to economic issues. Reflecting the impulses of the Catholic social welfare movement (which drew heavily from papal encyclicals issued by Pope Leo XIII in 1893 and by Pope Pius XI in 1931), he dwelt in large part on the oppression of the worker and the responsibilities of the community to protect the economic rights of all its citizens. Drawing from the populist and other earlier reform movements, he proposed a series of monetary reforms—remonetization of silver, issuing of greenbacks, and nationalization of the banking system—that would, he claimed, restore both prosperity and economic justice.

By 1933, Coughlin was attracting a weekly radio audience of over 40 million people across the nation. He was receiving hundreds of thousands of letters (many of them containing cash donations) from supporters every month. And he was drawing huge and idolatrous crowds when he traveled to distant cities for rallies and public appearances. To many Americans—but particularly to lower-middle- and working-class urban dwellers, many but not all of them Catholics—he had become a figure of rare hope and promise. In 1932 and during the first two years of the New Deal, Coughlin was a loyal, even slavish supporter of Franklin Roosevelt, telling his radio audiences that the choice they faced was "Roosevelt or ruin,"

FATHER COUGHLIN.
During one particularly impassioned 1936 speech, Father Charles E. Coughlin ripped off his coat and clerical collar and denounced President Roosevelt as a "liar" and "betrayer." It was one of the few occasions on which he drew a rebuke from his usually supportive bishop, and he later apologized. After Coughlin supported an unsuccessful third-party campaign against Roosevelt in 1936, his popularity quickly faded. By 1938, he was resorting to anti-Semitism in a desperate effort to restore his public influence. (*Culver Pictures*)

assuring them that "the New Deal is Christ's deal." But when the President failed either to adopt Coughlin's economic programs or to allow the priest sufficient access to the White House, the relationship quickly soured. By the spring of 1935, although the break was not yet complete, Coughlin had become openly critical of the administration. He had established a political organization, the National Union for Social Justice, that many people believed was the first step toward the formation of a third party. And he was displaying what appeared to be remarkable influence in Congress. He had, in short, become a formidable and, in the eyes of the President, dangerous force.

He was not, however, as alarming as the leader of the third major dissident movement: Senator Huey P. Long of Louisiana. Long had risen to power in his home state through his strident attacks upon the banks, oil companies, and utilities, and upon the conservative political oligarchy allied with them that had for decades dominated the Louisiana government. Elected Governor in 1928, he launched an assault on his opposition so thorough and forceful that they were soon left with virtually no political power whatsoever. Long dominated the legislature, the courts, and the executive departments; and he brooked no interference. When opponents accused him of violating the Louisiana constitution, he brazenly replied, "I'm the Constitution here now." Many claimed that he had, in effect, become a dictator. If so, he was a dictator who maintained the overwhelming support of the Louisiana electorate, in part because of his flamboyant personality and in part because of his solid record of accomplishment: building roads, schools, and hospitals; revising the tax codes; distributing free textbooks; lowering utility rates; and more. Barred by law from succeeding himself as Governor, he ran in 1930 for a seat in the United States Senate, won easily, and left the state government in the hands of loyal, docile allies.

Once in Washington, Long, like Coughlin, soon became harshly critical of Herbert Hoover's ineffectual policies for dealing with the Depression. And, also like Coughlin, he supported Franklin Roosevelt for President in 1932. Far more rapidly than the priest, however, Long broke with the New Deal—a break that was all but complete within six months of the inauguration. As an alternative, he advocated a drastic program of wealth redistribution, a program he ultimately named the Share-Our-Wealth Plan. According to Long, the government could

THE KINGFISH. Few public speakers could stir up a crowd as effectively as Huey Long of Louisiana, who was known to many as the Kingfish (a nickname borrowed from the popular radio show "Amos 'n Andy"). It was Long's effective use of the radio, however, that contributed most directly to his spreading national appeal in the early 1930s. (*George Eastman House, Rochester, New York*)

end the Depression easily and quickly simply by confiscating through taxation the surplus riches of the wealthiest men and women in America, whose fortunes were, he claimed, so bloated that not enough wealth remained to satisfy the needs of the great mass of citizens. By limiting incomes to $1 million annually and by limiting capital accumulation and inheritances to $5 million, the government would soon acquire enough assets to guarantee every family a minimum "homestead" of $5,000 and an annual wage of $2,500.

Long made little effort to disguise his interest in running for President. In 1934, he established his own national organization: the Share-Our-Wealth Society, which soon attracted a large following—not only in Long's native South but in New York, Pennsylvania, parts of the Midwest, and above all California. There were no accurate figures to indicate the movement's precise size, but even Long's critics admitted it might have as many as 4 million members. A poll by the Democratic National Committee in the spring of 1935 disclosed that Long might attract more than 10 percent of the electorate running as a third-party candidate, enough to tip a close election to the Republicans.

Observers in the 1930s hotly debated the significance of these dissident movements. Some believed they represented the rise of fascism in America; others claimed they were dangerously close to socialism or communism. In fact, they were neither. They represented, rather, two competing popular sentiments: the urgent desire of many Americans for government assistance in this time of need, and their equally strong desire to protect their ability to control their own lives. Long, Coughlin, Townsend, and others spoke harshly of the "plutocrats," "international bankers," and other remote financial powers who were, they claimed, not only impoverishing the nation but exercising tyrannical power over individuals and communities. They spoke equally harshly, however, of the dangers of excessive government bureaucracy, attacking the New Deal for establishing a menacing, "dictatorial" state. They envisioned a society in which government would, through a series of simple economic reforms, guarantee prosperity to every American without exercising intrusive control over private and community activities.

However much their critics may have disagreed about the merits of these programs, they agreed on one thing: the specter of dissident politics was in 1935 becoming a genuine threat to the established political parties. An increasing number of advisers were warning the President that he would have to do something dramatic to counter their strength.

THE SECOND NEW DEAL

An array of pressures, therefore, was acting in 1935 to move Franklin Roosevelt toward a new set of initiatives. There was the continuing economic hardship. There was the growing political opposition. And there was a flurry of Supreme Court decisions that, like the Schechter ruling, were invalidating many of the early New Deal efforts to deal with the crisis. The result was a group of new programs often described as the Second New Deal. In part, the 1935 proposals were simply an attempt to steal the thunder of the administration's critics. But they represented, too, if not a new direction at least a change in emphasis in New Deal policy. During 1933 and 1934, the President had tended to favor economic planning as the best way to restore prosperity. Now he began to seem more concerned with enhancing the ability of the impoverished to lead decent lives and exercise economic and political power. "We have not weeded out the over-privileged," he told Congress in January 1935, "and we have not effectively lifted up the underprivileged." In the months that followed, he initiated a number of programs designed to do both.

An Assault on Big Business

Perhaps the most conspicuous change in New Deal policy in 1935 was its new attitude toward big business. No longer was the President attempting to conciliate financiers and industrialists. Instead, symbolically at least, he was attacking their power. In March, for example, he proposed to Congress an act to prohibit the increasing concentration of power in the great utilities holding companies, which had earned the hatred of much of the public by their flagrant abuses during the 1920s. In 1935, thirteen such companies controlled three-quarters of the nation's electric power; and Roosevelt spoke harshly of the injustices inherent in their monopolistic position. The companies fought desperately against the "death-sentence" bill, one of them spending $700,000 to lobby against the measure. In the end, neither side emerged entirely victorious. Congress did indeed pass the Holding Company Act of 1935; but the bill contained amendments favored by the companies that sharply limited its effects.

Equally alarming to affluent Americans was a series of tax reforms proposed by the President in 1935, a program conservatives quickly labeled a "soak-the-rich" scheme. Clearly designed to undercut the appeal of Huey Long's Share-Our-Wealth Plan, the Roosevelt proposals called for establishing the highest and most progressive peacetime tax rates in history. Rates in the highest brackets reached 75 percent on income, 70 percent on inheritances, and 15 percent on corporate incomes. In fact, the taxes sounded far more burdensome than they were (as Huey Long quickly pointed out). Nevertheless, the measure approved by Congress shifted a sizable portion of the tax load onto the wealthy.

Labor and Agriculture

The Supreme Court decision in 1935 to invalidate the NRA solved some problems for the administration, but it also created others. The now defunct act had contained, among other things, an important clause guaranteeing to workers the right to organize and bargain collectively. Supporters of labor, both in the administration and in Congress, advocated quick action to restore that protection. With the President himself somewhat slow to respond, the initiative fell to a group of progressives in Congress led by Senator Robert F. Wagner of New York, who in 1935 introduced the National Labor Relations Act. The new bill, quickly dubbed the Wagner Act, provided workers with far more federal protection than Section

7-a of the NRA had offered. It specifically outlawed a group of "unfair practices" by which employers had been fighting unionization. And it created a National Labor Relations Board (NLRB) to police employers, with power to compel them to recognize and bargain with legitimate unions. The President was not happy with the Wagner Act as it moved through Congress. But he recognized the importance of labor to his own political future, and when the measure reached his desk he signed it.

The Supreme Court soon created additional problems for the New Deal, this time in the realm of agricultural policy. In January 1936, the Court struck down those provisions of the Agricultural Adjustment Act authorizing the government to regulate farm production or to tax farmers to induce them to grow less. The administration, however, remained convinced of the importance of the crop reduction program, and within weeks it won congressional approval of a new bill (the Soil Conservation and Domestic Allotment Act) that met the Court's objections while continuing the essential functions of the AAA. Now, instead of reducing production to eliminate surpluses, which the Court had claimed was an unwarranted interference with the market, the government would pay farmers to reduce production so as allegedly to "conserve soil," prevent erosion, and accomplish other secondary goals. The new law also attempted to correct one of the most glaring injustices of the original AAA: its failure to make any provision for sharecroppers and tenant farmers. Now, landlords were required to share the payments they received for cutting back production with those who worked their land. The new requirement had, however, little impact on the problem. By 1937, when the average plantation operator was grossing $8,328, of which $833 came from the soil conservation program, the average tenant family was earning only $385, of which $27 came from the government.

The administration embarked on other efforts to assist farmers as well. The Resettlement Administration, established in 1935, and its successor the Farm Security Administration, created in 1937, attempted through short- and long-term loans to help farmers cultivating submarginal soil to relocate on better lands. The programs ultimately succeeded, however, in moving only a few thousand farmers. Of more importance was the Rural Electrification Administration, created in 1935, which worked to make electric power available to farmers through utilities cooperatives. Since its activities also stimulated private utilities to extend services into the countryside (something they had previously avoided as unprofitable), it aided farmers both directly and indirectly. Power lines had reached only 4 percent of all American farms in 1925. By 1940, they reached 25 percent.

New Directions in Relief

From the first moments of the New Deal, important members of the administration, most notably Secretary of Labor Frances Perkins, had been lobbying patiently for a system of federally sponsored social insurance for the elderly and the unemployed. The popularity of the Townsend movement added strength to their cause, and in 1935, finally, Roosevelt gave his support to what became the Social

Security Act. It provided for several different kinds of relief. For the elderly, there were two types of assistance. Those who were presently destitute could receive up to $15 a month in federal assistance (depending upon what matching sums the states might provide). More important for the future, every working American could qualify for a pension upon retirement. There were severe limits upon the program. Pension payments would not begin until 1942 and even then would provide only $10 to $85 a month to recipients. And wide categories of workers (including domestic servants and agricultural laborers, many of whom were black) were excluded from the program. But it was a first step in what would become the nation's most important social program for its elderly. In addition, the Social Security Act expanded the government's activities on behalf of the unemployed and dispossessed. It provided for a system of unemployment insurance, for federal assistance to dependent mothers and children, and for aid to the blind and crippled.

The Social Security Act exposed many of the reservations New Dealers still harbored about federal relief as well as the extent to which those reservations were eroding. Because the administration still believed that relief should be a local function, social security assistance to the unemployed, the handicapped, and families with dependent children was to be administered by the states. Nevertheless, much of the funding for such programs would come from the federal government; and it would be Washington that would supervise the state agencies, imposing strict standards upon them for disbursing the funds. Because New Dealers continued to oppose the concept of the "dole," social security was established as a system of social "insurance," by which every citizen would in effect pay for his or her own benefits through a separate social security tax. In practice, of course, social security bore little relation to a traditional insurance program. Many workers who, because of their wealth, would never require or qualify for benefits were nevertheless contributing to pensions for people of less affluence. The system performed a redistributive function, not an actuarial one. It was the most important of all New Deal steps toward the modern system of federal welfare.

Social security was designed primarily to fulfill long-range goals. Of more immediate concern were the millions of Americans who remained unemployed and who had not yet found relief through existing government programs. To meet their needs (and not incidentally to replace such early New Deal programs of direct relief as the FERA, with which the President had always felt uncomfortable) the administration established in 1935 the Works Progress Administration (WPA). Like the Civil Works Administration and other earlier efforts, the WPA established a system of work relief for the unemployed. It far surpassed all earlier agencies, however, both in the size of its budget ($5 billion) and in the energy and imagination of its operations. Under the direction of Harry Hopkins, who had by now emerged as the New Deal's "minister of relief," the WPA employed an average of 2.1 million workers at any given moment between 1935 and 1941. As with the CWA, many WPA projects were of little value; and even worthwhile undertakings generally proceeded far less efficiently and profitably than comparable tasks performed by private enterprise. Nevertheless, the agency was responsible ultimately for the erection or renovation of 110,000 public buildings (schools, post offices, office buildings), for the construction of almost 600 airports, more than 500,000 miles of roads, and over 100,000 bridges, and for other projects of genuine social value. More important, however, the WPA provided incomes to those it employed and helped stimulate the economy in general by increasing the flow of money into it.

The WPA also displayed remarkable flexibility and imagination in offering assistance to those whose occupations did not fit into any traditional category of relief. The Federal Writers Project of the WPA, for example, offered unemployed writers support not only to pursue their own creative endeavors but to work on projects initiated by the agency itself. Workers in the project composed a series of state guide books of remarkable quality. They conducted interviews with sharecroppers, factory workers, former slaves, and others, providing an invaluable documentary resource for future historians. The Federal Art Project, similarly, provided aid to painters, sculptors, and others to continue their careers; and it sponsored a series of murals and other artworks for public buildings and monuments. The Federal Music Project and the Federal Theater Project oversaw the production of concerts and of plays, skits, and even a controversial review of public affairs known as the "Living Newspaper," thus creating work for unemployed musicians, actors, directors, and others. Unlike other New Deal programs, the WPA established few lasting precedents. Most of its projects were dismantled as soon as prosperity returned; and the government did not again provide work relief in quite the same form. During the 1930s, however, no other agency of the New Deal reached as widely across the nation to expose the possibilities of federal assistance to the indigent.

Other relief agencies emerged alongside the WPA. The National Youth Administration provided assistance to those between the ages of sixteen and twenty-five, largely in the form of scholarship assistance to high-school and college students. The Emergency Housing Division of the Public Works Administration (the agency that had been established in 1933 along with the NRA, but whose benefits were slow to be felt) began federal sponsorship of public housing. It cleared some of the nation's most notorious slums and built instead some fifty new housing developments, containing nearly 22,000 units—most of them priced too high for those who had been displaced by slum clearance. Not until 1937, when Congress approved Senator Wagner's bill creating the United States Housing Authority, did the government begin to provide a substantial amount of housing for the truly poor.

During the Second New Deal, just as during the first, Franklin Roosevelt and his associates attempted to keep the federal commitment to relief limited and temporary. Once again, however, they discovered that the nation's needs required a far larger response than they had originally envisioned. And future generations would discover that many programs established as temporary expedients ultimately became, in one form or another, permanent parts of the federal government.

The 1936 "Referendum"

The presidential election of 1936 was, it was clear from the start, to be a national referendum on Franklin Roosevelt and the New Deal. And while in 1935, there had been reason to question the President's political prospects, by the middle of 1936 there could be little doubt that he would win a second term. The flurry of legislation of the so-called Second New Deal had more than repaired whatever damage the events of the preceding year had done to his popularity. And his opponents on both the left and the right had by the time of the election declined almost to the point of insignificance.

The conservative opposition to Roosevelt had always been intense but never large. In 1936, it was not even strong enough to win control of the Republican party. Ignoring the anguished pleas of Herbert Hoover and others who detested all aspects of the New Deal, the party nominated the moderate Governor of Kansas, Alf M. Landon, a former Bull Mooser who had never abandoned his progressive commitments. The Republican platform promised, in effect, to continue the programs of the New Deal—but constitutionally, and without running a deficit.

As for the dissidents, their strength seemed to evaporate as quickly as it had emerged. One reason was the violent death of their most effective leader, Huey Long, who was assassinated in a corridor of the Louisiana state capitol in September 1935 by a young Baton Rouge doctor. (No one ever had a chance to discover the motives of the assailant; he was gunned down on the spot by Long's bodyguards.) Another reason was the ill-fated alliance among several of the remaining dissident leaders in 1936. Father Coughlin, Dr. Townsend, and Gerald L. K. Smith (a sycophantic henchman of Huey Long trying unsuccessfully to establish himself as Long's political heir) joined forces that summer to establish a third party—the Union party. But the incessant squabbling among them, combined with the colorlessness of their presidential candidate—a mediocre North Dakota Congressman, William Lemke—made the new party a ridiculous spectacle. It polled only 890,000 votes. The most important reason for the dissidents' collapse, however, was their failure ever to turn their supporters fully against Franklin Roosevelt, who had skillfully undercut the appeal of his dissident critics by espousing many of their ideas.

The campaign was a lopsided contest. Roosevelt drew huge crowds and evoked widespread enthusiasm with his impassioned attacks upon the "economic royalists" and his pledge to help the "one third of the nation" who remained, he claimed, "ill-housed, ill-clad, and ill-fed." Landon's pallid rhetoric and moderate platform could not effectively compete. The result was the greatest landslide in American history, Roosevelt polling just under 61 percent of the vote to Landon's 36 percent. The Republican candidate was able to carry no states except Maine and Vermont. In addition to ensuring Roosevelt of a second term, the election displayed the fundamental party realignment that the New Deal had managed to effect. The Democrats now controlled a broad coalition of western and southern farmers, the urban working classes, the poor and unemployed, and the black communities of the northern cities, as well as traditional progressives and committed new liberals—a coalition that constituted a substantial majority of the electorate. It would be many years before the Republican party could again muster anything approaching a majority coalition of its own.

THE NEW DEAL IN DISARRAY

Roosevelt emerged from the 1936 election at the zenith of his popularity and power, it appeared. Within months, however, the New Deal began to encounter serious new difficulties—both as a result of continuing opposition and as a result of the President's own political errors. His administration would never fully recover. Throughout Roosevelt's second term, recovery from the Depression remained elusive; and the New Deal, stumbling from one policy to another, appeared unable to regain the initiative it once had held.

The Court Fight

If the 1936 election had been a mandate for anything, Franklin Roosevelt believed, it was a mandate to do something about the Supreme Court. No program of reform, he had become convinced, could long survive the ravages of the obstructionist justices, who had already struck down the NRA and the AAA and who threatened to invalidate even more legislation. Foes of such New Deal measures as the National Labor Relations Act, the Social Security Act, and the Holding Companies Act were openly flouting the new laws, confident that the Supreme Court would soon disallow them. Through its narrow interpretation of the federal power over interstate commerce and taxation, and through its broad

ALF LANDON. Landon, the progressive Republican Governor of Kansas, began briefly to believe the magazine polls and other predictions that showed him leading Franklin Roosevelt in the 1936 presidential campaign. Then, according to his own account, he rode a train into Chicago one day and saw a picture of the President in almost every window of the working-class neighborhoods he passed. At that moment, he realized the battle was lost. (*National Archives*)

interpretation of freedom of contract, the Court seemed to have created an economic no man's land within which neither the federal nor the state governments could act.

Some critics of the Court were urging a constitutional amendment to provide the federal government with more extensive powers. The President, however, believed that the Constitution already provided adequate authority to the state, that the problem was the Supreme Court's antiquated interpretation of the document. Even more troubling was that the four or five justices most firmly opposed to New Deal measures showed no signs of weakening or retiring, so there was little immediate promise of change. Roosevelt's solution, therefore, was to propose adding to the Supreme Court additional new justices—justices he would appoint and whose liberal views would presumably counterbalance the conservatism of the existing justices.

It was a bold measure, but it was neither a radical nor an illegal one. The Constitution called for no specific number of Supreme Court justices, and Congress had from time to time changed the size of the Court in the past. Nevertheless, the plan aroused a great public furor, largely because Roosevelt displayed what was, for him at least, an astounding political ineptitude in proposing and promoting it. Had he given an honest explanation of the measure, explaining that it was necessary to stop Court obstructionism, he might well have rallied enough support to win passage of the plan. Instead, he dissembled. Without informing congressional leaders in advance, he sent a surprise message to Capitol Hill in February 1937 proposing a general overhaul of the federal court system and including among many provisions one to add up to six new justices to the Supreme Court. The courts were "overworked," he claimed, and needed additional manpower and younger blood to enable them to cope with their increasing burdens. The explanation fooled almost no one.

Conservatives throughout the country expressed outrage at the "court-packing plan," warning that such constitutional shortcuts were the common route by which dictators seized power. And while in the past few Americans had been disposed to heed such warnings, now, as a result of Roosevelt's heavy-handed tactics, much of the public seemed to agree. In Congress, the controversy cut across party lines. Progressive Republicans such as Robert La Follette, Jr., supported the President, arguing that the Court had already been "packed" for years "in the cause of Reaction and Laissez-Faire." But conservative Democrats, especially from the South, opposed the plan. They had supported the New Deal during its first years largely because of party loyalty and public pressure. Now, convinced that much of the electorate had turned against the administration, they broke loose. Still, the President had considerable political clout at his disposal; and he might well have forced Congress to approve at least a compromise measure had not the Supreme Court itself intervened in the controversy.

Virtually all the justices—including Louis Brandeis, who was at once the oldest member of the Court and the one most disposed to support the President—were outraged at Roosevelt's implication that they were too old to handle their caseload. Chief Justice Charles Evans Hughes even wrote a public letter insisting that they

were not falling behind in their work. The Court's most effective weapon against
the President's plan, however, was a more subtle one: they simply eliminated the
need for it. Even before the court-packing fight began, the ideological balance of
the Court had been a precarious one. Four conservative justices could be relied
upon to oppose the New Deal on almost all occasions; three were generally
inclined to support it. The remaining two tended to waver, with Chief Justice
Hughes often siding with the progressives and Associate Justice Owen J. Roberts
more often voting with the conservatives. Were Hughes and Roberts both to side
with the liberals, there would be a 5 to 4 majority in support of the New Deal
without the appointment of additional justices. And that was precisely what
happened. On March 29, 1937, Roberts, Hughes, and the three progressive
justices voted together to uphold a state minimum wage law—in the case of *West
Coast Hotel* v. *Parrish*—thus reversing a 5 to 4 decision of the previous year
invalidating a similar law. Two weeks later, again by a 5 to 4 margin, the Court
upheld the Wagner Act; and in May, it validated the Social Security Act. The
necessity for Roosevelt's judicial reform bill had vanished. The Supreme Court
had prudently moderated its position in order to avert what it considered a
disastrous precedent. "You may have saved the country," Hughes jubilantly told
Owen Roberts after the first decision favorable to the New Deal in March.

On one level, the affair was a significant victory for Franklin Roosevelt. No

ONE VIEW OF THE COURT FIGHT.   "Nine Old Men," a cartoon endorsing
the President's argument that the members of the Supreme Court were living in the
"horse-and-buggy" days, appeared in the Communist magazine *New Masses* in 1937.
Unfortunately for Roosevelt, there was little similar support from mainstream political
groups for his plan to expand the membership of the Court. (*Brown Brothers*)

longer would the Court serve as an obstruction to New Deal reforms, particularly after a group of older justices began retiring in the following months, to be replaced by Roosevelt appointees. On another level, however, the court-packing episode was a serious defeat for the President, and one that did lasting damage to his administration. By generating public suspicion of his motives, he had reinvigorated the conservative opposition, which only months before had been in disarray. By giving members of his own party an excuse to oppose him, he had helped destroy his congressional coalition. From 1937 on, southern Democrats and other conservatives voted against his measures with alarming consistency; never again would the President enjoy the freedom of legislative action he had had during his first years in office. Roosevelt was not even able to spare himself the embarrassment of having his plan publicly voted down. Although the need for it had vanished by the spring of 1937, Roosevelt, because he had been less than frank about his real reasons for submitting it, had no plausible excuse now to withdraw it. Gleefully, his congressional opponents inflicted upon him a searing personal defeat.

A year later, the President's political situation deteriorated further. Determined to regain the initiative in his legislative battles, Roosevelt launched an ill-considered effort to "purge" Congress of some of its most conservative members. In Democratic primaries that spring, he openly campaigned against members of his own party who had opposed his programs. The effort was a humiliating failure. Not only was Roosevelt unable to unseat any of the five Democratic Senators against whom he campaigned, but his "purge" efforts drove an even deeper wedge between the administration and its conservative opponents, ensuring that Roosevelt would suffer more legislative frustrations in the future.

Retrenchment and Recession

Hard on the heels of the court-packing fiasco came another economic crisis: a severe recession that began in the fall of 1937, continued for more than nine months, and plunged the nation into its worst suffering since 1932. It was a bitter pill for a society that was just beginning to believe that true recovery was under way; and it was a particularly bitter pill for Franklin Roosevelt, whose policies had helped to create the new collapse.

The origins of the 1937–1938 recession lay in the impressive economic progress that had preceded it. By the summer of 1937, it no longer seemed fanciful to believe that prosperity was about to return. The national income, which had dropped from $82 billion in 1929 to $40 billion in 1932, had risen to nearly $72 billion. Other economic indices showed similar improvements. To the President, therefore, the time seemed ripe for a drastic retrenchment in government spending, for allowing the business community, as Roosevelt put it, to stand once again on its own two feet. Not incidentally, it also seemed to be a good time to balance the federal budget, whose mounting deficits had never ceased to trouble the President. And there were even arguments that the real danger now was no longer depression but inflation.

As a result, the administration moved on several fronts to cut back its recovery programs. Roosevelt persuaded the Federal Reserve Board to tighten credit by raising interest rates. More important, he drastically reduced government spending by slashing the budget for one relief program after another. Between January and August 1937, for example, he cut the WPA in half, sending 1.5 million relief workers on unpaid "vacations." It was a clear expression of Roosevelt's continuing belief in orthodox, "sound money" economics; and the result was disaster. The fragile boom quickly collapsed; and the private sector, left to its own devices, proved unable to revive it. The index of industrial production dropped from 117 in August 1937 to 76 in May 1938. Four million additional workers lost their jobs. Farm prices plummeted (although less as a result of administration policies than because an easing of the drought produced a huge surplus).

In retrospect, it is easy to discern the reasons for the collapse. The "boom" of 1937 had never been a stable or self-sustaining one even at its height. Production had increased, to be sure; but 7.5 million people had remained unemployed and 4.5 million families had still been on relief. And there had been no significant increase in capital investment or other private sector expansion, the real signs of economic health. Instead, what recovery there had been was almost entirely a result of government spending: of the billions spent on relief programs, of the increasing momentum of public works projects, of the loans to farmers, and of the payment in 1936 of the veterans' bonus (the result of a bill passed over the President's veto). When the administration began to remove these sources of economic stimulation in 1937, the recession quickly followed.

The new crisis forced yet another reevaluation of policies by the President and his advisers and produced yet another shift of emphasis within the New Deal. The advocates of government spending as an antidote to the Depression had always had to struggle for the President's favor against those who believed in more conservative fiscal policies. Now, it seemed, they stood vindicated; and the notion of using government deficits to stimulate the economy—an idea associated with the great British economist John Maynard Keynes—had established its first, timid foothold in American public policy. In October 1937, the President asked Congress for an emergency appropriation of $5 billion for public works and relief programs, and government funds soon began pouring into the economy once again. By June 1938, the worst of the recession was over, and another tentative recovery seemed to be under way.

At the same time, another group of theorists began to win Franklin Roosevelt's ear: those who feared economic concentration and wanted the government to move forcefully to restore competition. They had been present in New Deal circles from the beginning, but until now their position had been a weak one. By 1937, however, the President was sufficiently disillusioned with the American business community (a disillusionment only strengthened by the 1937 recession, which he tried to blame on "selfish interests") that he was willing to experiment with their approach. In April 1938, Roosevelt sent a stinging message to Congress, vehemently denouncing what he called an unjustifiable concentration of economic power. Less than 5 percent of all corporations owned 87 percent of the nation's assets in 1935, he claimed, producing as a result a serious maldistribution of income. The upper 1.5 percent of the population had a share of the national income as great as the 47 percent at the bottom—all of whom earned less than $1,000 per year per family. The remedy, therefore, was to embark on a thorough examination of concentration with an eye to major reforms in the antitrust laws. In response, Congress established the Temporary National Economic Committee (TNEC), chaired by Senator Joseph O'Mahoney of Wyoming and including representatives of both Houses of Congress and of several executive agencies. At about the same time, Roosevelt appointed a new head of the antitrust division of the Justice Department: Thurman Arnold, a Yale Law School professor who soon proved to be the most vigorous trustbuster to serve in that office in the nation's history. Making new and sophisticated use of the Sherman and Clayton acts, he launched more than 200 investigations over the next two years and filed 92 test cases.

Despite all this, however, the administration's commitment to restoring competition was never a wholehearted one; and the results of its antitrust efforts were ultimately of little lasting importance. The TNEC investigation ran on for nearly three years and produced volumes of testimony, but in the end it made no important recommendations for action. Its real impact was, rather, to delay action on the question of concentration, which was perhaps what the President had in mind in the first place. It was, Raymond Moley once wrote, "the final expression of Roosevelt's personal indecision about what policy his administration ought to follow." Nor did Thurman Arnold's vigorous tenure in the Justice Department result in any major changes in the nation's economic structure. By the time many of his cases were beginning to reach trial, World War II had begun, persuading the President that the time for antitrust activity was over. Arnold was quietly eased out of office, and the New Deal's brief experiment in trustbusting sputtered to a close.

By the end of 1938, therefore, the New Deal had essentially come to an end. Not only did congressional opposition now make it difficult for the President to enact any major new programs; he had, it seemed, no new programs to propose. More important, perhaps, the threat of world crisis hung heavy in the political atmosphere, and Roosevelt was growing more concerned with persuading a reluctant nation to prepare for war than with pursuing any new avenues of reform.

SUGGESTED READINGS

A sweeping account of dissident opposition to the New Deal and of the administration's response is Arthur M. Schlesinger, Jr., *The Politics of Upheaval* (1960). George Wolfskill, *Revolt of the Conservatives* (1962), examines the challenge from the Liberty League. Irving Howe and Lewis Coser, *The American Communist Party* (1957), and David Shannon, *The Socialist Party of America* (1955), chronicle the challenges to the New Deal from the left; Donald Grubbs, *Cry From the Cotton* (1971), is an important study of the Southern Tenant Farmers Union. Opposition to the New Deal from less radical groups is examined in Donald McCoy, *Angry Voices* (1958); the political efforts of disaffected intellectuals receive attention in R. Alan Lawson, *The Failure of Independent Liberalism* (1971). Alan Brinkley, *Voices of Protest: Huey Long, Father Coughlin, and the Great Depression* (1982), chronicles the leading dissident movement, and David H. Bennett, *Demagogues in the Depression* (1969), chronicles their decline. Individual studies of the most prominent insurgents include Abraham Holzman, *The Townsend Movement* (1963); Charles J. Tull, *Father Coughlin and the New Deal* (1965); and T. Harry Williams, *Huey Long* (1969), a highly praised definitive biography. Robert Penn Warren, *All the King's Men* (1946), one of the greatest political novels in American literature, is the story of a southern leader reminiscent of Huey Long.

Most of the general accounts of the New Deal cited after Chapter 12 contain extensive treatment of the 1935 reforms. In addition, see J. Joseph Huthmacher, *Senator Robert Wagner and the Rise of Urban Liberalism* (1968), especially for labor and housing legislation; W. D. Rowley, *M. L. Wilson and the Campaign for Domestic Allotment* (1970), and Sidney Baldwin, *Poverty and Politics: The Farm Security Administration* (1968), for changes in agricultural policy; Roy Lubove, *The Struggle for Social Security* (1968), for the major welfare innovation of the later New Deal; and Paul Conkin, *Tomorrow a New World* (1971), for the government's experimental community program. The WPA has spawned a large literature of its own, much of it focusing upon the innovative art and literature programs. See, especially, Jane deHart Matthews, *The Federal Theater* (1967); Jerre Mangione, *The Dream and the Deal* (1972), on the Federal Writers Project; and William F. McDonald, *Federal Relief Administration and the Arts* (1968). For the 1936 election (and the general issue of electoral realignments in the 1930s), see Samuel Lubell, *The Future of American Politics* (1952), and John Allswang, *The New Deal in American Politics* (1978). An anthology examining the ideological currents in the Roosevelt administration is Howard Zinn, *New Deal Thought* (1966).

The troubled years after 1936 have received less attention from historians, but several important works are available. On the rise of conservative opposition, see James T. Patterson, *Congressional Conservatism and the New Deal* (1967); Frank Freidel, *FDR and the South* (1965); and George Wolfskill and John Hudson, *All But the People* (1969). On the court-packing fight, consult Leonard Baker, *Back to Back* (1967), and William Leuchtenburg, "The Origins of Franklin D. Roosevelt's 'Court-Packing' Plan," in Philip B. Kurland (ed.), *The Supreme Court Review* (1966). Richard Polenberg, *Reorganizing Roosevelt's Government* (1966), and Barry Karl, *Executive Reorganization and Reform in the New Deal* (1963), examine the bureaucratic reform efforts of the second term. James T. Patterson, *The New Deal and the States* (1969), explores the relationship between federal and local governments; and Charles Trout, *Boston: The Great Depression and the New Deal* (1977), examines that relationship in a single city.

Fourteen

The American People in Hard Times

In 1935, the sociologists Robert Lynd and Helen Merrell Lynd published their second major study of society and culture in the city of Muncie, Indiana, which they called Middletown. Ten years earlier, they had described the community in the midst of prosperity. Now, they depicted its struggle to deal with the Great Depression. "The city had been shaken for nearly six years," they wrote,

> by a catastrophe involving not only people's values but, in the case of many, their very existence. . . . the great knife of the depression had cut down impartially through the entire population, cleaving open the lives and hopes of rich as well as poor. The experience had been more nearly universal than any prolonged recent emotional experience in the city's history; it had approached in its elemental shock the primary experiences of birth and death.

What the Lynds were trying to determine by returning to Muncie was what aspects of life in the community had changed as a result of this profound crisis, and what aspects had survived in traditional form. It was a question that many Americans in many places asked throughout the 1930s; and it is a question that historians have continued to ask in the years since. And as with all such questions, there is no clear answer. The Depression was striking for the transformations it wrought in American society; but it was at least equally striking for the important continuities in the nation's institutions and values. That, at least, was the conclusion of the Lynds, who wrote at the completion of their study that "basically the texture of Middletown's culture has not changed. . . . Middletown is overwhelmingly living by the values by which it lived in 1925."

THE CHALLENGE TO SOCIAL PATTERNS

All Americans, but middle-class Americans above all, had by 1929 spent several decades developing a new set of values suitable for their modern, industrial society. The Great Depression put those values to a severe test.

The Survival of the Success Ethic

No assumption would seem to have been more vulnerable to assault during the Depression than that the individual was in control of his or her own fate, that anyone displaying sufficient talent and industry could become a success. And in many ways, the economic crisis did erode that belief, just as the increasingly specialized economy of the 1920s had undermined it earlier. Americans became during the 1930s more accustomed to looking to their government for assistance; they learned to blame corporate moguls, international bankers, economic royalists, and others for their distress; they rejected once and for all the old doctrine of laissez faire and espoused instead the idea that the individual had responsibilities to society and vice versa. But while the Depression may have eroded the success ethic, it did not destroy it. On the contrary, Americans at all levels continued enthusiastically to embrace the ideals of work and individual advancement.

Some of the evidence for this conclusion comes from the reactions of those most traumatized by the Depression: responsible, conscientious working people of all levels who suddenly, bewilderingly found themselves without employment. Some expressed anger, striking out at the economic system that had produced the crisis. More, however, blamed themselves, if not openly, at least subconsciously. There were the hundreds of thousands of unemployed men who dutifully left home every morning as if on their way to work, even though there were no jobs to go to. There were the indigent who spent every day looking for employment, refusing to accept that there was none to be had. And there were the many jobless who hid themselves from public view, unable to face their friends or even their families because of their feelings of humiliation. Stories of unemployed men simply sitting in their living rooms, staring at nothing, day after day, were frequent. So strong was the ideology of individual achievement that many Americans turned their anger upon themselves rather than question their traditional assumptions.

At the same time, millions responded eagerly to reassurances that they could, through their own efforts, restore themselves to prosperity and success. Dale Carnegie's *How to Win Friends and Influence People* (1936), a self-help manual preaching individual initiative, was one of the best-selling books of the decade. Harry Emerson Fosdick, a Protestant theologian who similarly preached the virtues of positive thinking and individual initiative, attracted large audiences with his radio addresses. Although many of the great financial moguls fell into wide disrepute after 1929, the public continued to revere such "self-made men" as Thomas Edison and even, to some extent, Henry Ford. The animosity toward big business in general, moreover, proved remarkably short-lived. By 1938, according to one study, the corporate image had regained much of the luster it had lost in the first years of the Depression.

Women and the Family

In some respects, the 1930s were years of important changes in the position of women in American society. Just as the 1920s had brought many women for the first time into business and the professions, so the 1930s brought an unprecedented number of women into government. The change was most evident within the New Deal, where Franklin Roosevelt not only appointed the first female member of the cabinet in the nation's history—Secretary of Labor Frances Perkins—but more than a hundred other women to positions throughout the federal bureaucracy. He was responding in part to pressure from his wife, Eleanor Roosevelt. A committed advocate of women's rights, she herself, through courageous work on behalf of humanitarian causes, served as an example to countless other members of her sex of the possibilities for public service. Mary Dewson, head of the Women's Division of the Democratic National Committee, was also influential in securing federal appointments for women, as well as in increasing their role within the Democratic party. Several women received appointments to the federal judiciary. And one, Hattie Caraway of Arkansas, became the first woman ever elected to a full term in the United States Senate (running to succeed her husband, who had died in office).

Symbolically important as these political gains may have been, they had little impact on the vast majority of American women, who continued to perform traditional roles as wives and mothers. Indeed the Depression in many ways reinforced popular assumptions that the woman's place was in the home. With jobs scarce and applicants many, an increasing number of men and women alike began to advocate that what positions there were should go to unemployed men. Some, including Frances Perkins, went so far as to argue that women who had jobs should leave them so that men could take their places. Those who continued to work generally earned less than men performing comparable jobs, even on some government projects. Women in the 1930s were, perhaps, less likely to marry young (the average marriage age rose during the decade) or to bear children (the birth rate declined considerably); but neither American men nor even most American women themselves were ready to abandon their traditional views about the proper role of women.

New Views of Ethnicity

One longstanding American attitude, at least, changed considerably during the 1930s: nativism. Hostility to immigrants and their alien cultures had been a powerful force since the nineteenth century, and it had reached special intensity in the early 1920s. It did not disappear during the Great Depression, but it did abate. In part, the lessening of hostility was because of the almost complete absence of new immigrants. The restriction laws of the 1920s had stemmed the flow, and the Depression reduced it even further. Earlier generations of immigrants, at the same time, were becoming more fully assimilated; and the conspicuously alien cultures in which they had lived were becoming increasingly Americanized. There were, moreover, a number of representatives of previously unpopular immigrant groups whose public prominence in the 1930s helped win wider acceptance for their fellow ethnics. Popular heroes in entertainment (where many Jews were becoming prominent), sports (where such idols as Joe DiMaggio were emerging), and even politics (where such men as Mayor Fiorello La Guardia of New York were bringing respectability to the idea of ethnics in public office) had a substantial impact.

At the same time, American intellectuals were abandoning the supposedly scientific doctrines of the 1920s, which had suggested that ethnic differences were inherited and immutable, and that certain cultures, therefore, were superior to others. Instead, a series of new theories, based on scientific observation rather than idle speculation, was changing the academic approach to ethnicity. Anthropologists such as Franz Boas and Ruth Benedict, for example, were arguing for what came to be known as "cultural relativism." Cultural differences were not inherited, they claimed, but learned through the influence of environment. Moreover, no one culture was intrinsically superior to any other; each should be considered on its own terms. Such beliefs did not, of course, win universal or even wide public acceptance. They did, however, help to reinforce the general decline in nativist sentiment. Ethnic prejudice would continue in America, but for the most part in less strident and less vicious form than in the past.

The Survival of Racism

The same could not be said, however, for racism. The Depression was a time of important changes in the lives and outlooks of American blacks, and a time of some improvements in their position in society. But it was not a time in which racism and the discrimination based on it declined in any significant way.

For the first time in American history, supporters of racial equality had, during the Great Depression, an ally in the White House. It was not the President, however, but Eleanor Roosevelt. Throughout the 1930s she exerted continuing pressure upon her husband and upon others in the federal government to ease discrimination against blacks. She was also responsible for what was, symbolically at least, one of the most important events of the decade for American blacks. When the black opera singer Marian Anderson was refused permission in the spring of 1939 to give a concert in the auditorium of the Daughters of the American Revolution (Washington's only concert hall), Eleanor Roosevelt secured government permission for her to sing on the steps of the Lincoln Memorial. Her Easter Sunday concert attracted 75,000 people and became, in effect, one of the first modern civil-rights demonstrations.

The President, although basically sympathetic to the plight of blacks, believed that other problems were far more pressing and was unwilling to risk losing the support of southern Democrats by becoming too much identified with race.

MARIAN ANDERSON IN WASHINGTON, 1939.
Black contralto Marian Anderson's concert on the steps of the Lincoln Memorial in 1939 became a symbol of emerging black aspirations. Banned from singing in the auditorium of the Daughters of the American Revolution, she received permission to perform at the Lincoln Memorial through the intervention of Eleanor Roosevelt. The First Lady resigned her own membership in the DAR to protest the barring of Anderson. (*UPI*)

Typical of his equivocal attitude was his harsh denunciation of lynching combined with his refusal to support legislation making lynching a federal crime. Still, Roosevelt, unlike his Democratic predecessor Woodrow Wilson, did not move to increase government discrimination against blacks; and in many ways, he gave active support to combating racism within the federal government. He appointed a number of blacks to important (if second-level) positions in his administration, creating in the process a network of officeholders that became known as the "Black Cabinet." Roosevelt appointees such as Robert Weaver, William Hastie, and Mary McLeod Bethune consulted with one another frequently and served as an active lobby for the interests of their race.

Perhaps more important, blacks benefited in significant, if limited ways from New Deal relief programs (in large part because Eleanor Roosevelt, a close friend of relief administrator Harry Hopkins, and Harold Ickes worked hard to ensure that the programs did not exclude blacks). By 1935, according to some estimates, nearly 30 percent of all blacks were receiving some form of government assistance. Blacks, who constituted in the 1930s only 10 percent of the population, filled 18 percent of the positions within the WPA. The Farm Security Administration, in addition to directing national attention to the desperate plight of tenants and sharecroppers in the South, black and white, relocated 1,400 black families in FSA "homesteads"—that is, about a quarter of the total number of families so moved. Other New Deal programs, however, discriminated against blacks: the CCC, which established separate black camps; the NRA, whose codes often indirectly permitted blacks to be paid less than whites; and the AAA, whose policies led to the eviction of thousands of black farmers from their lands. But on the whole, the Roosevelt administration offered important, indeed essential, assistance to blacks to an extent unmatched by any of its predecessors.

The result was, among other things, a historic change in black electoral behavior. Blacks had traditionally allied themselves with the Republican party, the party that had aided them after the Civil War and that had continued to oppose the ruling white oligarchy in the South. But the Republican party had done little to aid blacks in recent years; and the emergence of Franklin Roosevelt changed black voting behavior almost overnight. In 1928, the vast majority of black voters had voted Republican; by 1936, more than 90 percent of them were voting for Franklin Roosevelt. That pattern would continue in the future. "Turn Lincoln's picture to the wall," a black leader in the South said at the time. "That debt has been paid in full."

The Depression was a time, too, of important changes in the role and behavior of the leading black organizations. The NAACP, for example, began to work diligently to win a favored position for blacks within the emerging labor movement, supporting the formation of the Congress of Industrial Organizations and helping to erode racial barriers within labor unions. Walter White, secretary of the NAACP, once even made a personal appearance at an auto plant to implore blacks not to work as strikebreakers. Partly as a result of such efforts, more than half a million blacks were able to join the labor movement. In the Steelworkers Union, for example, blacks constituted about 20 percent of the membership.

At the same time, many black leaders were beginning to question their traditional belief that patient lobbying in Congress and through the courts would ultimately produce racial equality. The economic distress of American blacks, combined with adverse judicial decisions and the continuing disinterest of Congress and state legislatures in their problems, caused many to contemplate more direct forms of protest. W. E. B. Du Bois and others, losing faith in their belief that education would provide an effective avenue for racial advancement, were even beginning to question the desirability of integration as a goal for blacks, arguing instead for a form of "black nationalism." Such arguments attracted only a relatively small following; but they helped produce a growing impatience among American blacks.

It is not difficult to understand why black Americans were growing impatient in the 1930s. Despite the benefits they received from the New Deal, blacks continued to languish in almost universal poverty and continued to be the victims of brutal racial discrimination. However much whites were suffering from the Great Depression, blacks were suffering worse. They were victimized, first, by the general pattern by which blacks were the "last hired and first fired"—a pattern that resulted in blacks losing their jobs far more quickly than whites when hard times arrived. Because a disproportionate number of black farmers were tenants and sharecroppers in the South, they suffered disproportionately from the crisis in southern agriculture. Two-thirds of black cotton farmers in the 1930s made no money at all from their crops and survived only by hunting, scavenging, begging, or moving to the cities. And in the cities, both North and South, things were little better. In the past, urban blacks had had access at least to certain menial jobs unattractive to whites—such jobs as street cleaning, garbage collection, and domestic service; now even those jobs were in high demand, and most of them were going to whites. In Atlanta in 1930, an organization called the Black Shirts (consisting largely of unemployed whites) adopted the slogan "No Jobs for Niggers Until Every White Man Has a Job." In New York, department stores, insurance companies, banks, and other institutions simply refused to hire blacks for any position, no matter how modest. Moreover, local relief agencies often provided far more meager benefits to blacks than to whites.

And in addition to the continuing pattern of segregation and economic discrimination, blacks continued to suffer from random violence at the hands of whites and continued to lack effective means of legal redress. In some areas of the country, in fact, the legal system itself became an instrument of oppression. One of the most celebrated racial episodes of the 1930s was the trial and conviction of nine black youths falsely accused of raping two white women on a freight train passing through Alabama. The Scottsboro case, as it was called, attracted wide attention to the racism within the southern judicial system. Even when the

AT WORK IN THE COTTON FIELDS.   Black farm workers picking cotton in the South, in a photograph by Ben Shahn. The New Deal made several symbolic gestures on behalf of blacks during the 1930s, but there were few substantive improvements in the lot of the poorest members of the race. (*Library of Congress*)

authorities received almost incontrovertible proof that the "Scottsboro boys" were innocent, the nine youths remained imprisoned; several of them were not released for years. Few could doubt that similar examples of racism were occurring elsewhere, outside the glare of publicity. In 1936, Franklin Roosevelt spoke at Howard University and declared: "Among American citizens, there should be no forgotten man and no forgotten race." Blacks may not have been forgotten in the 1930s, but another generation would pass before white society would begin to respond in meaningful ways to black demands for social and economic equality.

The Plight of Hispanics and Indians

Most Americans were at least aware of the position of blacks in their society. Two other minorities, one relatively new and one older than the nation itself, received virtually no attention at all from the white majority during the Depression. For Hispanics and for American Indians, the 1930s were years of continuing hardship and, in some cases, increasing discrimination.

America's Hispanic population had been growing steadily since early in the century, largely in California and in the Southwest through massive immigration from Mexico (which was specifically excluded from the restriction laws of the 1920s). Mexican-Americans in the Southwest filled many of the same menial jobs that blacks had traditionally occupied in other regions. Others began to farm on small, marginal tracts. Still more became agricultural migrants, traveling from region to region harvesting fruit, lettuce, and other crops. Even during the prosperous 1920s, it had been a precarious existence. The Depression made things significantly worse. In some parts of the Southwest, and particularly in Texas, public and official pressure combined to force thousands of Mexican immigrants out of the country. In California, local police occasionally raided the *barrios* (Hispanic neighborhoods), rounding up Mexican-Americans and forcing them to return to Mexico. More than half a million Hispanics left the country in response to such pressures.

For those who remained, there were both economic hardships and increasing social discrimination. A few New Deal programs offered assistance to Mexican-Americans; in Texas, the head of the state branch of the National Youth Administration, Lyndon Baines Johnson, worked to ensure that some of the agency's benefits were distributed to Hispanics. More often, however, local administrators excluded Mexicans from the relief rolls or offered them benefits far lower than those available to whites. Mexican-Americans often had no access to schools, and many hospitals refused them admission. Unlike American blacks, who had in response to discrimination established certain educational and social facilities of their own, Hispanics had nowhere to turn. Even those of them who possessed American citizenship found themselves treated like unwelcome foreigners. There were, occasionally, signs of organized resistance by Mexican-Americans themselves, most notably in California, where they attempted to form a union of migrant farm workers. But harsh repression by local growers and the public authorities allied with them prevented such organizations from making significant progress. Like black farm workers, many Hispanic migrants began as a result to settle in western cities, where they lived in a poverty comparable to urban blacks in the South and Northeast.

For the most tragically exploited of all American minorities—Indians—the 1930s were years of several important changes. The Indian Reorganization Act of 1934 reversed the longstanding government policy of encouraging the assimilation of Native Americans into the mainstream of the nation's culture, a policy that had generally served as an excuse for robbing Indians of their tribal lands and reducing them to indigence. The act returned significant authority to the tribes to govern themselves, provided government funds to support education and cultural activities, and perhaps most important, restored the right of tribes to own land as collective entities. Previously, the government had required all Indian land to be owned by individuals. Other New Deal policies also assisted Indians. The Soil Conservation Service, for example, helped the Navajos improve their range lands and offered needed employment to many Indians on soil conservation and erosion prevention projects.

Nevertheless, American Indians remained through the 1930s what they had been for many years: an impoverished and isolated minority. Even with the redistribution of lands under the 1934 act, Indians continued to possess, for the most part, only territory that whites did not want—much of it arid, some of it desert. They continued to lack real authority to govern their own economic and social relationships, even inside their reservations. And they continued to lose property to white encroachment. Most of all, they continued to live in desperate poverty. In 1934, the average income of an American Indian was $48 a year.

THE RISE OF ORGANIZED LABOR

The Depression produced few lasting changes in the lives of some groups of Americans, but upon workers its impact was profound. After many decades of relative powerlessness in dealing with owners and employers, American labor during the 1930s took a giant stride toward establishing itself as a powerful interest group, capable of challenging the power of industrialists and of winning important new benefits.

The New Militancy

During the 1920s, workers had for the most part displayed little militancy in challenging employers or demanding recognition of their unions. They faced the opposition of a powerful and highly popular business establishment, with the support of the government behind it. They were, in large measure, coopted by the system of "welfare capitalism," which provided them with increased wages and benefits in return for their general passivity. And they were saddled with conservative labor organizations, generally unwilling to risk modest gains already won.

In the 1930s, however, all these inhibiting factors quickly vanished. Businessmen and industrialists lost (if only temporarily) the high public standing they had enjoyed in the New Era; and on matters of labor policy at least, they lost the support of the government. Through Section 7-a of the National Industrial Recovery Act of 1933, and more importantly through the Wagner Act of 1935, labor won legal guarantees of their right to organize and bargain collectively, as well as enforcement mechanisms to protect those rights. At the same time, the "welfare capitalism" of the 1920s vanished almost overnight. With the economy in sharp decline, employers quickly rescinded most of the gains they had offered labor in the preceding years. Those workers who kept their jobs often did so only by accepting reduced wages and fewer benefits. Finally, as the decade progressed, new labor organizations emerged to challenge the established, conservative unions. The result was, among other things, an important change in the outlook of many workers: a growing resentment of conditions as they were, and an increasing commitment to the idea of organizing to rectify them.

Industrial Unionism

Even though the American Federation of Labor, under the leadership now of William Green, increased its activities in response to the Depression, it proved painfully inadequate for the task at hand. The A.F. of L. remained committed to the idea of the craft union: the idea of organizing workers on the basis of their skills. As a result, the Federation offered little hope to unskilled laborers, even though it was the unskilled who now constituted the bulk of the industrial work force. It was not only as a result of corporate resistance that union membership had declined by more than 2 million during the 1920s; it was also because the A.F. of L. had made no provision for a vast number of workers.

During the 1930s, therefore, another concept of labor organization emerged to challenge the traditional craft union ideal: the concept of industrial unionism. Advocates of this approach argued that all the workers in a particular industry should be organized in a single union, regardless of what functions the workers performed. All auto workers should be in a single automobile union; all steel workers should be in a single steel union; skilled workers within the mass-production industries should abandon their commitment to exclusivity in their organizations and join with unskilled laborers to produce effective bargaining units. Workers divided into many small unions would, many labor leaders were beginning to claim, lack the strength to deal successfully with the great corporations. United into a single great union, however, they would wield considerable power.

Leaders of the A.F. of L. for the most part opposed the new concept. But industrial unionism found a number of important spokesmen, most prominent among them John L. Lewis. Lewis was the talented, flamboyant, and eloquent leader of the United Mine Workers—the oldest major union in the country organized along industrial rather than craft lines. He was also a charismatic public figure, whose personal magnetism alone helped win thousands of recruits to his cause. Like Franklin Roosevelt, he was to become one of the best-known and most controversial figures of his era.

At first, Lewis and his allies attempted to work within the A.F. of L. In 1934, they won a charter from the Federation empowering them to begin organizing the mass-production industries; but they were sharply warned against encroaching upon existing unions within those industries. That proved an almost impossible restriction to observe, and friction between the new industrial organizations and the older craft unions grew rapidly as a result. At the 1935 A.F. of L. convention, Lewis became embroiled in a series of angry confrontations (and one celebrated fistfight) with craft union leaders before finally walking out. A few weeks later, he created the Committee on Industrial Organization—a body officially within the A.F. of L. but unsanctioned by its leadership. After a series of bitter jurisdictional conflicts, the A.F. of L. finally expelled the new committee from its ranks, and along with it all the industrial unions it represented. In response, Lewis simply renamed the committee the Congress of Industrial Organizations (CIO), established it in 1936 as an organization directly rivaling the A.F. of L., and became its first president. The schism clearly weakened the labor movement as a whole in many ways. But by freeing the advocates of industrial unionism from the restrictive rules of the Federation, it gave important impetus to the creation of powerful new organizations.

JOHN L. LEWIS. Lewis rose from the presidency of the struggling United Mine Workers union to become the founder of the CIO and the father of modern mass-production unionism. His combative nature and his oratorical brilliance often obscured an essentially middle-class outlook. By the mid-1940s, he was supporting Republican political candidates, purging his organization of "disloyal" members, and encouraging the crusade against communist "subversion" in America. (*National Archives*)

Organizing Battles

Those new organizations had begun struggling for recognition even before the schism of 1936. Major battles were under way, in particular, in the automobile and steel industries. Out of a myriad of competing auto unions, the United Auto Workers (UAW) was, during the early and mid-1930s, gradually emerging preeminent. But through 1936, although it was steadily gaining recruits, it was making little progress in winning recognition from the corporations. There was good reason. In 1934, at about the time the organizing drive began, almost half of the workers in the industry were earning less than $1,000 a year. Determined to protect this low wage scale, the auto companies fought vigorously and often viciously against the union—General Motors alone spending nearly $1 million between 1934 and 1936 on private detectives.

In December 1936, however, workers introduced a new and dramatically effective technique for challenging corporate opposition: the sit-down strike. Employees in several GM plants in Detroit simply sat down inside the plants, refusing either to work or to leave, thus preventing the company from making use of strikebreakers. The tactic quickly spread to other locations, so that by February 1937 strikers had occupied seventeen General Motors plants. The strikers ignored court orders to vacate the buildings, and they successfully resisted sporadic efforts by local police to remove them. When Michigan Governor Frank Murphy, a liberal Democrat, refused to call out the National Guard to clear out the strikers, the company had little choice but to relent. General Motors became in February 1937 the first major manufacturer to recognize the UAW; other automobile companies soon did the same. (The sit-down strike proved effective in rubber and other industries as well; but it survived only briefly as a labor technique. It was clearly illegal, and it aroused widespread public outrage and alarm; so labor leaders ultimately abandoned it.)

In the steel industry, the battle for unionization was less easily won. In 1936, the CIO had voted a $500,000 fund to support the Steel Workers' Organizing Committee (later United Steelworkers of America) in a major campaign. Over the next few months, the onslaught began, with the SWOC quickly recruiting tens of thousands of workers and staging a series of prolonged and often bitter strikes. In March 1937, to the amazement of almost everyone, United States Steel, the giant of the industry, relented. Rather than continue a costly strike at a time when it sensed itself on the verge of recovery from the Depression, the company signed a contract with the SWOC, the new organization's first important victory.

The lesser companies (known as "Little Steel") were, however, far less ready to surrender. And three of them, under the leadership of Tom Girdler of Republic Steel, resisted furiously. More than 70,000 steelworkers in twenty-seven plants were on strike in the spring of 1937; but "Little Steel" had mobilized a powerful antistrike force to combat them: 7,000 police; a budget of $4 million; and a large corps of strikebreakers, some of them living in the factories and supplied with food by parachute. On Memorial Day 1937, a group of striking workers from Republic Steel gathered with their families for a picnic and demonstration in South Chicago; and when they attempted to march peacefully (and legally) toward the steel plant, police opened fire on them. Ten demonstrators were killed; another ninety were wounded. Despite a public outcry against the "Memorial Day Massacre," the harsh tactics of "Little Steel" ultimately proved successful. The 1937 strike failed.

But the victory of "Little Steel" was the exception rather than the rule; it was, in fact, one of the last gasps of the kind of brutal, naked strikebreaking that had proved so effective in the past. In the course of 1937, one of the most turbulent years in the history of American labor, there were 4,720 strikes—over 80 percent of them settled favorably to the unions. By the end of the year, more than 8 million workers were members of unions (as compared with 3 million in 1932).

THE MEMORIAL DAY MASSACRE, 1937.   Wielding guns and billy clubs, police attack strikers and their families as they march toward the Republic Steel plant in South Chicago on Memorial Day 1937. Some Hollywood executives attempted to suppress newsreel footage of the "massacre," in which ten strikers died; but the grisly film (of which this photograph is a part) was ultimately released. (*Wide World Photos*)

By 1941, that number had expanded to 10 million and included the workers of "Little Steel," which had finally relented. Workers were somewhat slower to win major new wage increases and benefits than they were to achieve union recognition. But the organizing battles of the 1930s had established the labor movement as a powerful force in the American economy.

THE CULTURE OF DEPRESSION

Prosperity had helped to shape the outlook of American intellectuals and the thrust of popular culture in the 1920s. Economic hardship did the same in the 1930s. During the Great Depression, American intellectuals tended to turn away from the self-absorption and detachment of the New Era and involve themselves with social and political causes. Popular culture, in the meantime, was following an opposite path: turning away from contemporary issues and offering an escape from social difficulties.

The Discovery of Poverty

Just as many progressives had become alarmed when, early in the twentieth century, they "discovered" the existence of widespread poverty in the cities, so many Americans were shocked during the 1930s at their discovery of debilitating rural poverty. The plight of the farmer—and particularly of the southern tenant farmer and sharecropper—became one of the leading themes of Depression intellectual life.

Perhaps most effective in conveying the dimensions of rural poverty was a group of documentary photographers, many of them employed by the Farm Security Administration in the late 1930s, who traveled through the South recording the nature of agricultural life. Men such as Roy Stryker, Walker Evans, Arthur Rothstein, and Ben Shahn and, perhaps more importantly, women such as Margaret Bourke-White and Dorothea Lange produced memorable studies of farm families and their surroundings, studies designed to show the savage impact of a hostile environment upon its victims. Through their work, not only did the problems of poverty receive wider public attention but the art of photography earned new stature.

Writers, similarly, turned away from the personal concerns of the 1920s and, in many cases, devoted themselves to searing exposés of social injustice. Erskine Caldwell exposed many of the same injustices that the FSA photographers had studied, in *Tobacco Road* (1932)—a novel about life in the rural South, which later became a long-running play. James Agee produced one of the most powerful portraits of the lives of sharecroppers, in *Let Us Now Praise Famous Men* (1941) —a careful, nonjudgmental description of the lives of three southern families, illustrated with photographs by Walker Evans. Other writers and artists turned their gaze upon social injustice in other settings. Richard Wright, a major black novelist, exposed the plight of residents of the urban ghetto, in *Native Son* (1940). James T. Farrell, in *Studs Lonigan* (1936), depicted the savage world of urban,

SHARECROPPERS. Photographer Walker Evans and novelist James Agee spent a month in the summer of 1936 living with three families of southern white sharecroppers (one of which is pictured here). The result of their trip was *Let Us Now Praise Famous Men* (1941), one of the literary landmarks of the Great Depression. (*Library of Congress*)

lower-class white youths. The impact of social realism could be seen, as well, in painting—in the work of many of the artists employed by the Federal Art Project and in the paintings of such rural realists as Thomas Hart Benton and Grant Wood.

The Political Impulse

An even larger group of artists and intellectuals moved beyond social realism, combining an effort to expose social problems with a commitment to political solutions. Some argued along specifically Marxist lines; others urged far more moderate solutions. Most, however, agreed on certain things: that the plight of the common people was the most important subject for concern, and that some organized, collective response was essential to correct society's injustices.

It was a group of influential writers who most clearly embodied this impulse. Some were successful novelists of the 1920s who now turned to new themes. Ernest Hemingway, in *To Have and Have Not* (1937), displayed for the first time a concern with social issues by portraying a bitter labor struggle and advocating a collective solution; in *For Whom the Bell Tolls* (1940), he used the Spanish Civil War as a setting through which to illustrate the importance of solidarity in the face of oppression. Other, newer writers were discussing similar themes. John Steinbeck's *The Grapes of Wrath* (1939) portrayed the trials of a migrant family in California, concluding with an open call for collective social action against injustice. John Dos Passos's *U.S.A.* trilogy (1930–1937) attacked modern capitalism in a style that combined the use of literary techniques with the tools of journalism. Playwright Clifford Odets provided a particularly explicit demonstration of the appeal of political radicalism in *Waiting for Lefty* (1935). Critics and historians such as Granville Hicks and V. F. Calverton (both avowed Marxists) denounced the hollow values that capitalism had imposed upon American culture.

Escapist Culture

A few writers and artists—most notably Hemingway and Steinbeck—managed to combine social realism and political commitment with popular success. For the most part, however, the cultural products of the 1930s that attracted wide popular audiences were more effective in diverting attention away from the Depression than in illuminating its problems.

The two most powerful instruments of popular culture in the 1930s—radio and the movies—were particularly careful to provide mostly light and diverting entertainment. The radio industry, still fearful of the possibility of nationalization (as was occurring in other countries just establishing broadcasting systems), made every effort to avoid political or social controversy. Although many stations carried inflammatory programs, among them Father Coughlin's sermons, the staple of broadcasting was escapism: comedies like "Amos 'n Andy"; adventures of the "Superman" or "Dick Tracy" type; and other programs of pure entertainment. Hollywood continued to exercise tight control over its products through its resident censor Will Hays, who, in response to growing pressure from the Catholic church's Legion of Decency, founded in 1934, redoubled his efforts to ensure that movies carried only banal, conventional messages. There were occasional pictures —for example, the film version of *The Grapes of Wrath*—that projected a muted political message. Far more frequent, however, were such movies as the "screwball" comedies of Frank Capra, in which evidence of economic hardship was only occasionally visible.

Popular literature, similarly, offered Americans an escape from the Depression rather than an investigation of it. Two of the best-selling novels of the decade, for example, were romantic sagas set in bygone eras: Margaret Mitchell's *Gone with the Wind* (1936), which became the source of one of the most celebrated films of all time; and Hervey Allen's *Anthony Adverse* (1933). Leading magazines, and particularly such popular new photographic journals as *Life*, did offer occasional glimpses of the ravages of the Depression. But for the most part, they concentrated on fashions, stunts, and eye-catching scenery. Even the newsreels distributed to movie theaters across the country tended to give more attention to beauty contests and ship launchings than to the Depression itself. The American people had not only prevented the Great Depression from destroying their traditional values and institutions; they had, apparently, decided to try as best they could to keep from even being reminded of it.

SUGGESTED READINGS

Many of the secondary works and oral histories cited after Chapter 11 for descriptions of the economic impact of the Depression are also useful for the question of changing values. In addition, see Robert Lynd and Helen Merrell Lynd, *Middletown in Transition* (1935), which examines the impact of the Depression upon Muncie, Indiana, and Frederick Lewis Allen, *Since Yesterday* (1940), a contemporary view of social mores. On the issue of women during the Depression, see Joseph Lash, *Eleanor and Franklin* (1971); Susan Ware, *Beyond Suffrage* (1981); and William Chafe, *The American Woman* (1972). For changing views of ethnicity, consult Richard Krickus, *Pursuing the American Dream* (1976), and Gilman Ostrander, *American Civilization in the First Machine Age* (1970). The most comprehensive study of the experience of blacks during the Depression is Harvard Sitkoff, *A New Deal for Blacks* (1978). Also useful are Raymond Wolters, *Negroes and the Great Depression* (1970); Nancy Weiss, *The National Urban League* (1974); and Ralph Bunche, *The Political Status of the Negro in the Age of FDR* (1973), a reissue of a study originally published during World War II. John Dollard, *Caste and Class in a Southern Town*, 3rd ed. (1957), is a classic study, originally published in 1937, of racial relationships in a southern community. Dan T. Carter, *Scottsboro* (1969), is a compelling account of one of the most celebrated racial issues of the decade. The Hispanic experience during the Depression is considered in the appropriate chapters of Rodolfo Acuña, *Occupied America,* 2nd ed. (1981). Carey McWilliams, *Factories in the Field* (1939), studies the plight of migrant farm workers in California. Donald L. Parman, *The Navajos and the New Deal* (1976), considers the Native American response to the Roosevelt Indian policy.

The most thorough account of the labor movement during the Depression is Irving Bernstein, *Turbulent Years* (1970). See also Melvyn Dubofsky and Warren Van Tine, *John L. Lewis* (1977); David Brody, *Workers in Industrial America* (1980); Jerold Auerbach, *Labor and Liberty* (1966); Bert Cochran, *Labor and Communism* (1977); and Peter Friedlander, *The Emergence of a UAW Local* (1975).

William Stott, *Documentary Expression and Thirties America* (1973), offers a powerful examination of Depression photography and other forms of documentary expression. Richard Pells, *Radical Visions and American Dreams* (1973), is the most thorough study of artistic responses to the Depression. Robert Sklar, *Movie-Made America* (1975), and Andrew Bergman, *We're in the Money* (1971), explore the films of the era. Daniel Aaron, *Writers on the Left* (1961), is an important study of the interaction between literature and politics.

Fifteen

America and the World Crisis

When Franklin Roosevelt assumed leadership of the United States in March 1933, he acquired as well a position of enormous influence in a world already grown frighteningly dangerous. Only eighteen months earlier, Japan had invaded and occupied Manchuria. And only weeks before Roosevelt's inauguration, Adolf Hitler had become Chancellor of Germany on a promise of rapid rearmament and belligerent nationalism. The international agreements of the preceding fifteen years were clearly in disarray, and few governments seemed willing to look beyond their internal economic troubles to deal with the emerging threats to peace. Least of all was the United States prepared to play an active role in maintaining international stability. Having turned away from global commitments in the 1920s, Americans were even less inclined to look beyond their own borders during the Great Depression. Like many other nations suffering economic hardship, the United States was turning within itself.

But the realities of world affairs were not to allow Americans to remain isolated for very long, as Franklin Roosevelt realized earlier than most of his countrymen. The 1930s, therefore, were years not only of growing world tensions but of continuing battles within the United States between those who wished to isolate America from controversies abroad and those who believed that the nation should not and could not remain uninvolved with the world. Only the advent of war finally resolved that dispute.

DEPRESSION DIPLOMACY

From Herbert Hoover, Franklin Roosevelt inherited a foreign policy less concerned with issues of war and peace than with matters of economic policy. And although the New Deal rejected many of the initiatives that the Republicans had begun, it continued for several years to base its foreign policy on the nation's immediate economic needs.

Currency, Debts, and Trade

Perhaps Roosevelt's sharpest break with the policies of his predecessor was on the question of American economic relations with Europe. Hoover had argued that only by resolving the question of war debts and reinforcing the gold standard could the American economy hope to recover. He had, therefore, agreed to participate in the World Economic Conference, to be held in London in June 1933, to attempt to resolve these issues; and in the last months of his presidency, he had tried unsuccessfully to wrest from Roosevelt assurances that the new administration would accept his own commitment to the gold standard.

By the time the conference assembled, however, Roosevelt had already become convinced that the gold value of the dollar had to be allowed to fall in order for American goods to be able to compete in world markets. The American negotiating team, led by Secretary of State Cordell Hull, arrived in London carrying the President's vague promise to cooperate with the European powers to "establish order in place of the present chaos." But on July 3, Roosevelt sent Hull a famous "bombshell" message repudiating the orthodox views of the other delegates and rejecting any agreement on currency stabilization. The conference quickly dissolved without reaching agreement; and not until 1936 did the administration finally agree to new negotiations to stabilize Western currencies.

At the same time, Roosevelt was moving to abandon the commitments of the Hoover administration to settle the issue of war debts through international agreement. In effect, he simply let the issue die. Not only did he decline to negotiate a solution at the London Conference, but in April 1934 he signed a bill, introduced by Senator Hiram Johnson, to forbid American banks from making loans to any nation in default on its debts. The result was to stop the old, circular system by which debt payments continued only by virtue of increasing American loans; within months, moreover, war-debt payments from every nation except Finland stopped for good.

If the new administration had no interest in international currency stabilization or settlement of war debts, it did have an active interest in improving America's position in world trade. Secretary of State Hull, in particular, was a fervent advocate of lowering tariff barriers to permit increased reciprocal trade with other nations; and by January 1934, Roosevelt was ready to listen to him. As a result, he supported the Reciprocal Trade Agreement Act of 1934, authorizing the administration to negotiate treaties lowering tariffs by as much as 50 percent in return for reciprocal reductions by other nations. (The bill also permitted the administration to raise rates up to 50 percent in retaliation against other nations that erected tariff barriers.) The immediate effect of the reciprocal trade agreements negotiated as a result of the act was not impressive. Most agreements in the 1930s were carefully drafted to admit only products not competitive with

CORDELL HULL. Hull was a Democratic Senator from Tennessee when Franklin Roosevelt chose him to serve as Secretary of State in 1933. Although political pressures occasionally caused the President to waver in his public commitment to internationalism, Hull remained a constant advocate of reliance upon international law and liberal trade policies to promote peace. (*Karsh, Ottawa*)

American industry and agriculture; and although by 1939 Hull had succeeded in negotiating new treaties with twenty-one countries (increasing American exports to them by nearly 40 percent), imports into the United States continued to lag. Other nations, as a result, were not obtaining the American currency needed to buy American products; and foreign debts to the United States increased considerably during the period.

The Soviet Union and Latin America

American hopes of increasing its foreign trade produced particular efforts by the administration to improve its diplomatic posture in two areas: the Soviet Union and Latin America. The United States and Russia had viewed each other with mistrust and even hostility since the Bolshevik Revolution of 1917, and the American government still had not officially recognized the Soviet regime by 1933. But powerful voices within the United States were urging a change in policy —less because the revulsion with which most Americans viewed communism had diminished to any great extent than because the Soviet Union appeared to be a possible source of important trade. The Russians, too, were eager for a new relationship. For them, however, the motivation was neither ideological nor economic but military. They were hoping for American cooperation in containing the power of Japan on Russia's southeastern flank. In November 1933, therefore,

Soviet Foreign Minister Maxim Litvinov reached an agreement with the President in Washington. The Soviets would cease their propaganda efforts in the United States and protect American citizens in Russia; in return, the United States would recognize the communist regime.

Despite this promising beginning, however, relations with the Soviet Union soon soured once again. American trade failed to establish a foothold in Russia, disappointing hopes in the United States; and the American government did little to reassure the Soviets that it was interested in stopping Japanese expansion in Asia, dousing expectations in Russia. Soviet propaganda abroad continued, and American hostility toward communism survived unabated. By the end of 1934, the Soviet Union and the United States were once again viewing each other with considerable mistrust. And Stalin, having abandoned whatever hopes he might once have held of cooperation with America, was beginning to consider making agreements of his own with the fascist governments of Japan and Germany.

Somewhat more successful were American efforts to enhance both diplomatic and economic relations with Latin America through what became known as the "Good Neighbor Policy." Latin America was one of the most important targets of the new policy of trade reciprocity, and the United States succeeded during the 1930s in increasing both exports to and imports from the other nations of the Western Hemisphere by over 100 percent. Closely tied to these new economic relationships was a new American attitude toward intervention in Latin America. The Hoover administration had unofficially abandoned the earlier American practice of using military force to compel Latin American governments to repay debts, respect foreign investments, or otherwise behave "responsibly." The Roosevelt administration went even further. At the Inter-American Conference in Montevideo in December 1933, Secretary of State Hull signed a formal convention declaring: "No state has the right to intervene in the internal or external affairs of another." Roosevelt respected that pledge throughout his years in office, refusing to use force against Latin American governments even in the face of strong domestic pressure to do so. Mexico provided the most severe test of the new policy. What many people regarded as a radical Mexican government was outraging American Catholics in the 1930s by seizing lands from and otherwise displaying hostility toward the Catholic clergy within its own country. In 1938, it evoked outrage from American businessmen as well by expropriating all foreign oil holdings in Mexico, offering the United States petroleum companies far less in recompense than the companies believed they deserved. The Roosevelt administration did attempt to persuade the Mexicans to negotiate a fairer price for the oil lands; but it refused otherwise to intervene.

The Good Neighbor Policy did not mean, however, that the United States had abandoned its influence in Latin America. On the contrary, it had simply replaced one form of leverage with another. Instead of military force, Americans could now use economic influence, as the case of Cuba illustrated. A revolution in that nation in 1933 brought to power a new military dictatorship under Fulgencio Batista, who installed a government that American policymakers considered dangerously radical, even communistic. Roosevelt dealt with the problem not by sending in the Marines but by offering Batista an attractive trade package for Cuban sugar. Batista, well aware of the crucial economic importance of Cuba's exports to the United States, quickly agreed to appoint more conservative officials to the government in return. As a result, the President finally consented in 1934 to the official repeal of the Platt Amendment, which had given America the right to intervene in Cuba's internal affairs. The new reliance upon economic rather than military pressure in Latin America eased tensions between the United States and its neighbors considerably, eliminating the most abrasive and conspicuous irritants in the relationship. It did little, however, to stem the growing American domination of the Latin American economy, a domination that would create serious difficulties in later years.

THE RISE OF ISOLATIONISM

The first years of the Roosevelt administration marked more than the death of Hoover's hopes for international economic agreements. They marked, too, the end of any hopes for world peace through treaties and disarmament. Ever since the retreat from Wilsonian idealism after World War I, the United States had attempted to influence world affairs through example and encouragement, but without tying itself to any binding relationships with other nations. Roosevelt attempted to continue that policy and even, on several occasions, to expand upon it. But a combination of domestic opposition and international decay frustrated his hopes.

The Failure of Disarmament

That the international arrangements of the 1920s were no longer suitable for the world of the 1930s became obvious in the first months of the Roosevelt presidency, when the new administration attempted to stimulate movement toward world disarmament. An arms control conference in Geneva had been meeting, without result, since 1932; and in May 1933, Roosevelt attempted to spur it to action by submitting a new American proposal. In exchange for a substantial reduction in armaments, the United States would agree to cooperate with other nations in limited ways to deter future aggression. Specifically, America would respect any embargo imposed against an aggressor, rather than try to assert its neutral rights to trade freely with every nation, as it had tried to do during the early years of World War I. Several European leaders, including Hitler, responded warmly to the proposal; but France continued to resist all efforts to reduce armaments, effectively stalling negotiations.

At the same time, the arms control negotiations were reeling under even more severe blows from other sources. Adolf Hitler withdrew Germany from the talks (and from the League of Nations) in October 1933. Italy abandoned the talks at about the same time, although it retained its membership in the League until 1935. The Geneva Conference, it was now clear, was a failure. Two years later, Japan withdrew from the London Naval Conference, which was attempting to draw up an agreement to continue the limitations on naval armaments negotiated at the Washington Conference of 1921. The movement for world disarmament had collapsed.

Isolationism Triumphant

The breakdown of the fragile international balance of the 1920s presented the United States with a choice. With the world situation clearly deteriorating, Americans could choose between more active efforts to repair it or more energetic attempts to isolate themselves from it. Almost without hesitating, they chose the latter. Support for isolationism emerged from many quarters. Old Wilsonian internationalists had grown disillusioned with the League of Nations and its inability to stop Japanese aggression in Asia; internationalism, they were beginning to argue, had failed. Other Americans were listening to the argument that powerful business interests—Wall Street, munitions makers, and others—had tricked the United States into participating in World War I. An investigation by a Senate committee chaired by Senator Gerald Nye of Colorado revealed exorbitant profiteering and blatant tax evasion by many corporations during the war, and it suggested that bankers had pressured Wilson to intervene so as to protect their loans abroad. Such findings further discredited the forces of internationalism in the eyes of the public, and pressure grew steadily behind efforts to ensure that the same factors did not again drag America into war.

Roosevelt himself shared some of the suspicions of the isolationists and claimed to be impressed by the findings of the Nye investigation. Nevertheless, he continued to hope for at least a modest American role in maintaining world peace. In 1935, he proposed to the Senate a treaty to make the United States a member of the World Court—a treaty that would have expanded America's symbolic commitment to internationalism without increasing its actual responsibilities in any important way. Nevertheless, isolationist opposition (spurred by a passionate broadcast by Father Coughlin on the eve of the Senate vote) resulted in the defeat of the treaty. It was a devastating political blow to the President, and he would not soon again attempt to challenge the isolationist tide.

That tide was growing stronger with every passing month. Through the summer of 1935, it became increasingly clear to the world that Mussolini's Italy was preparing to invade Ethiopia in an effort to expand its colonial holdings in Africa. Fearing that a general European war would ensue, American legislators began to design legislative safeguards to prevent the United States from being dragged into the conflict. The result was the Neutrality Act of 1935.

The 1935 bill, and the Neutrality Acts of 1936 and 1937 that followed, were designed to prevent a recurrence of the events that many Americans now believed had pressured the United States into World War I. The 1935 law established a mandatory arms embargo against both victim and aggressor in any military conflict and empowered the President to warn American citizens that they might travel on the ships of warring nations only at their own risk. Thus, isolationists believed, the "protection of neutral rights" could not again become an excuse for American intervention in war. The 1936 Neutrality Act renewed these provisions. And in

HITLER AT NUREMBERG. The rising power of Nazi Germany provided an ominous backdrop to American foreign policy during the 1930s. Here Hitler passes before troops and ardent followers during one of the Nazi party's enormous, highly disciplined rallies at Nuremberg. (*Photoworld*)

1937, with world conditions growing even more precarious, Congress passed a yet more stringent measure. In addition to maintaining the arms embargo requirement, the new Neutrality Act established the so-called cash-and-carry policy, by which belligerents could purchase nonmilitary goods from the United States only by paying cash and shipping their purchases themselves. Critics ridiculed the measures as laws "to keep the United States out of World War I." But the isolationists were undeterred.

The American stance of militant neutrality was reinforced in October 1935 when Mussolini finally launched his long-awaited attack on Ethiopia. If anyone still believed that a system of collective security could prevent such aggression, the abject failure of the League of Nations to respond effectively to the invasion dispelled their illusions. Mussolini easily defeated the Ethiopians; and when the League protested, he simply resigned from the organization and formed an alliance (or "axis") with Hitler's Germany. American public-opinion polls taken shortly after the Ethiopian conflict illustrated what the crisis had done to reinforce isolationist sentiment. When a November survey asked respondents: "If one foreign nation insists upon attacking another, should the United States join with other nations to compel it to stop?" 28 percent said yes, 67 percent said no.

Isolationist sentiment showed its strength once again in 1936 and 1937 in response to a civil war in Spain. The Falangists of General Francisco Franco, a group much like the Italian Fascists, revolted in July 1936 against the existing government, a moderate constitutional monarchy. Hitler and Mussolini supported Franco, both vocally and with weapons and supplies. The United States joined with Britain and France in an agreement to offer no assistance to either side. Since all three nations were more sympathetic to the Loyalists than to the Falangists, the result of the agreement was to deny what otherwise might have been crucial aid to the anti-Franco forces. Only the Soviet Union actively assisted the Loyalists, a policy that did little to improve the chances of the hopelessly outmatched Spanish government but did much to improve Russia's image in the eyes of some American internationalists. Despite the anguished pleas of those who believed the United States should intervene to stop the fascist challenge in Spain, Roosevelt remained firm in his support of neutrality. "We are not isolationists," he said publicly a month after the Spanish Civil War had begun, "except in so far as we seek to isolate ourselves completely from war."

THE EXPANDING CRISIS

His public statements notwithstanding, Franklin Roosevelt was viewing the events of 1935 and 1936 with growing alarm. Should a major international conflict break out, he believed, America would not be able to remain uninvolved no matter what the isolationists might do. And as the chances for such a conflict appeared to grow, he began to consider ways to increase the American role in world affairs. Slowly, cautiously, Roosevelt attempted to challenge the grip of the isolationists upon the nation's foreign policy. For a time, however, it seemed to be a virtually hopeless cause; and the United States finally proved powerless to prevent the outbreak of war.

The Threat from Japan

While isolationists were busy protecting the United States from the decaying situation in Europe, an equally disturbing scenario was unfolding in Asia, where the growth of Japanese power was becoming a direct threat to international stability. Japan's aggressive designs against China had been clear since the invasion of Manchuria in 1931. In the summer of 1937, Tokyo launched an even more devastating assault, attacking China's five northern provinces with massive military force. This action presented the United States with a major dilemma. Japanese control of China and the Pacific threatened American trade and investments there; it imperiled American access to rubber and other vital materials; and it challenged world peace far more directly than either the Ethiopian invasion or the Spanish Civil War had done. The United States could not, Roosevelt believed, allow the Japanese aggression to go unremarked or unpunished.

In October 1937, therefore, the President set out to arouse public support for a policy of containment in the Pacific. In a speech in Chicago, he warned forcefully of the dangers that Japanese aggression posed to world peace and declared: "The peace-loving nations must make a concerted effort in opposition to those violations of treaties and those ignorings of humane instincts which today are creating a state of international anarchy, international instability from which there is no escape through mere isolation or neutrality." Aggressors, he proclaimed, should be "quarantined" by the international community to prevent the contagion of war from spreading.

The President was deliberately vague about what such a "quarantine" would mean; and there is evidence that he was contemplating nothing more drastic than a break in diplomatic relations with Japan, that he was not considering economic or military sanctions. Nevertheless, public response to the speech was disturbingly hostile, particularly after much of the press, including the Hearst papers, the *Chicago Tribune,* and others, began warning hysterically of the "hurricane of war fright" that the President had produced. As a result, Roosevelt drew back. Although his strong words had encouraged the British government to call a conference in Brussels to discuss the crisis in Asia, the United States now refused to make any commitments to collective action; and the conference produced no agreement.

Only months later, another episode gave renewed evidence of how formidable the obstacles to Roosevelt's efforts remained. On December 12, 1937, Japanese aviators bombed and sank the United States gunboat *Panay* as it sailed the Yangtze River in China. The attack was almost undoubtedly deliberate. It occurred in broad daylight, with clear visibility; and a large American flag had been painted conspicuously on the *Panay's* deck. Even so, the American public seized eagerly upon Japanese protestations that the bombing had been an accident and pressured the administration to accept Japan's apologies and overlook the attack.

Strengthening Hemispheric Defenses

One area in which the President did enjoy some freedom of action was in dealing with the rest of the Western Hemisphere. Indeed, there were no more devout exponents of the Monroe Doctrine than the American isolationists; and they were willing to allow the President to act forcefully to defend the hemisphere from external incursions. In December 1936, therefore, Roosevelt began an effort to construct in Latin America a series of mutual security agreements that he hoped later to extend to other regions of the world as well. Traveling to Buenos Aires, he reached agreement with other national leaders on an expansion of the language

TOJO AND THE EMPEROR.   Premier Hideki Tojo bows respectfully to Emperor Hirohito. Although the Japanese people revered the Emperor as divine, it was military leaders who exercised the real power in the late 1930s as the nation moved closer to war with the United States. (*U.S. Office of War Information/National Archives*)

of the Monroe Doctrine; henceforth, if any outside power threatened the American republics, not only would the United States oppose the aggressors, but all the nations of the hemisphere would consult on providing protection for the endangered country. It was an understanding clearly aimed at the threat of Axis expansion into South America, a matter of growing concern to Roosevelt as he watched German influence increase in various Latin American countries. In 1938, the American nations strengthened the pact at a meeting in Lima, Peru; and the same year, Roosevelt issued a declaration of solidarity with Canada, thus extending the hemispheric agreement to the north.

The Failure of Munich

Despite such successes close to home, Roosevelt was unable to find any politically acceptable way to increase American influence in Europe. It was not yet clear, moreover, that he believed the United States should become involved there in any case, even though the forces of war were rapidly gathering momentum. In 1936, Hitler had moved the now powerful German army into the Rhineland, rearming an area that France had, in effect, controlled since World War I. In March 1938,

German forces marched into Austria; and Hitler proclaimed a union (or *Anschluss*) between Austria, his native land, and Germany, his adopted one. Neither in America nor in Europe was there much more than a murmur of opposition.

The Austrian invasion, however, soon created another crisis; for Hitler had by now occupied territory surrounding three sides of western Czechoslovakia, a region he dreamed of annexing to provide Germany with the *Lebensraum* (living space) he believed it needed. In September 1938, he demanded that Czechoslovakia cede to him the Sudetenland, a region on the Austro-German border in which many ethnic Germans lived. Czechoslovakia, which possessed substantial military power of its own, was prepared to fight rather than submit. But it realized it could not hope for success without assistance from other European nations. That assistance it did not receive. Most Western nations, including the United States, were appalled at the prospect of another war and were willing to pay almost any price to settle the crisis peacefully. Finally, on September 29, Hitler met with the leaders of France and Great Britain at Munich in an effort to resolve the crisis. The French and British agreed to accept the German demands in Czechoslovakia in return for Hitler's promise to expand no farther. "This is the last territorial claim I have to make in Europe," the Führer solemnly declared. And Prime Minister Neville Chamberlain returned to England to a hero's welcome, assuring his people that the agreement ensured "peace in our time." Among those who had cabled him encouragement at Munich was Franklin Roosevelt.

The Munich accords were the most prominent elements of a policy that came to be known as "appeasement" and came to be identified (not altogether fairly) almost exclusively with Chamberlain. Whoever was to blame, however, it became clear almost immediately that the policy was a failure. In March 1939, Hitler occupied the remaining areas of Czechoslovakia, violating the Munich agreement unashamedly. And in April, he began issuing threats against Poland. At that point, both Britain and France decided to stand firm. They quickly gave assurances to the Polish government that they would come to its assistance in case of an invasion; and they even flirted, too late, with the Stalinist regime in Russia, attempting to draw it into a mutual defense agreement. Stalin, however, had already decided that he could expect no protection from the West; he had, after all, not even been invited to attend the Munich Conference. Accordingly, he signed a nonaggression pact with Hitler in August 1939, freeing the Germans for the moment from the danger of a two-front war. For a few months, Hitler continued to try to frighten the Poles into submitting to German rule. When that failed, he staged an incident on the border to allow him to claim that Germany had been attacked; and on September 1, 1939, he launched a full-scale invasion of Poland. Britain and France, true to their pledges, declared war on Germany two days later. World War II had begun.

NEUTRALITY TESTED

"This nation will remain a neutral nation," the President declared shortly after the hostilities began in Europe, "but I cannot ask that every American remain neutral in thought as well." It was a statement that stood in stark and deliberate contrast to Woodrow Wilson's 1914 plea that the nation remain neutral in both deed and thought; and it was clear from the start that among those whose opinions were decidedly unneutral in 1939 was the President himself. There was never any question that both he and the majority of the American people favored Britain, France, and the other Allied nations in the contest. The question was how much the United States was prepared to do to assist them.

First Steps

At the very least, Roosevelt believed, the United States should make armaments available to the Allied armies to help them counteract the remarkably productive German munitions industry. As a result, he called Congress into special session in September and asked for a revision of the Neutrality Acts. The original measures had forbade the sale of American weapons to any nation engaged in war; Roosevelt wanted the arms embargo lifted. Powerful isolationist opposition forced him to accept a weaker revision than he would have liked; as passed by Congress, the 1939 measure maintained the prohibition on American ships entering war zones. It did, however, permit belligerents to purchase arms on the same "cash-and-carry" basis that the earlier Neutrality Acts had established for the sale of nonmilitary materials.

For a time, it was possible to believe that little more would be necessary. After the German armies had quickly subdued Poland, the war in Europe settled into a long, quiet lull that lasted through the winter and spring—a "phony war," as it was beginning to be termed. The only real fighting during this period occurred not between the Allies and the Axis, but between Russia and its neighbors. Taking advantage of the situation in the West, the Soviet Union overran first the small Baltic republics of Latvia, Estonia, and Lithuania, and then, in late November, Finland. Americans were, for the most part, outraged; but neither Congress nor the President was willing to do more than impose a "moral embargo" on the shipment of armaments to Russia. By March 1940, the Soviet advance was complete. The American sanctions had had no effect.

Whatever illusions Americans had harbored about the war in western Europe were shattered in the spring of 1940 when Germany launched an invasion to the west—first attacking Denmark and Norway, sweeping next across the Netherlands and Belgium, and driving finally deep into the heart of France. Allied efforts proved futile against the Nazi "blitzkrieg," and Americans watched in horror as one stronghold after another fell into German hands. On June 10, Mussolini brought Italy into the war, invading France from the south as Hitler was attacking from the north, and prompting Roosevelt to declare angrily: "The hand that held the dagger has struck it into the back of its neighbor." On June 22, finally, France fell to the German onslaught. Nazi troops marched into Paris; a new collaborationist regime began to assemble in Vichy; and in all Europe, only the shattered remnants of the British army, which had been miraculously rescued from the beaches of Dunkirk, remained to oppose the Axis forces.

Roosevelt had already begun to expand both aid to the Allies and, more importantly, preparations for a possible Nazi invasion of the United States. On May 16, he asked Congress for an additional billion dollars for defense (much of it for the construction of an enormous new fleet of warplanes) and received it quickly. With France tottering a few weeks later, he proclaimed that the United States would "extend to the opponents of force the material resources of this nation." But words, of course, were not enough, as the new British Prime Minister, Winston Churchill, quickly reminded him. On May 15, Churchill sent Roosevelt the first of many long lists of requests for ships, armaments, and other assistance without which, he insisted, England could not long survive. Many Americans believed that the British plight was already hopeless, that any aid to the English was a wasted effort. Even some who thought that America would have to enter the war itself argued that the United States should save its weapons for its own needs, not waste them on the hopelessly overmatched British. The President, however, disagreed and made the bold and dangerous decision to "scrape the bottom of the barrel" to make war materials available to Winston Churchill. He even circumvented the "cash-and-carry" provisions of the Neutrality Act by trading fifty American destroyers (most of them left over from World War I) to England in return for the right to build American bases on British territory in the Western Hemisphere; and he returned to the factories a number of new airplanes purchased by the American government so that the British could buy them instead. The President's behavior was becoming, as Churchill himself later wrote, "decidedly unneutral." (It was also becoming, if not openly illegal, of at least dubious legality, as Roosevelt used the powers of his office to evade the clearly expressed will of Congress.)

Roosevelt was able to take such steps in part because of a major shift in American public opinion. Before the invasion of France, most Americans had believed that a German victory in the war would not be a threat to the United States. (Only 43 percent of those surveyed in a March 1940 poll expressed concern about German power.) In July, with France defeated and Britain threatened, opinion had changed dramatically. More than 66 percent of those polled now claimed to believe that Germany posed a direct threat to the United States. And while only 35 percent had favored aid to the British in May, 60 percent favored it in September. Congress was aware of the change and was becoming willing, therefore, to permit expanded American assistance to the Allies. It was even willing to consider the need for internal preparations for war, approving in September the Burke-Wadsworth Act inaugurating the first peacetime military conscription in American history.

The Survival of Isolationism

But while the forces of isolation may have softened their position, they were far from dead. On the contrary, there began in the summer of 1940 a spirited and often vicious debate between those who advocated expanded American involvement in the war (who were often termed, not entirely accurately, "interventionists") and those who continued to insist upon neutrality. The celebrated journalist

William Allen White served as chairman of a new Committee to Defend America, whose members lobbied actively for increased American assistance to the Allies; some of them went so far as to urge an immediate declaration of war (a position that as yet had little public support) and in April created an organization of their own, the Fight for Freedom Committee. Opposing them was a powerful new lobby entitled the America First Committee. The brainchild of a Yale student, R. Douglas Stuart, Jr., the committee attracted some of America's most prominent leaders. Its chairman was General Robert E. Wood, until recently the president of Sears Roebuck; and its membership included Charles Lindbergh, General Hugh Johnson, Senator Gerald Nye, and Senator Burton Wheeler. It won the editorial support of the Hearst chain and other influential newspapers; and it had at least the indirect support of a large proportion of the Republican party. (It also, inevitably, attracted a small fringe of Nazi sympathizers and anti-Semites.) The debate between the two sides was loud and bitter. Through the summer and fall of 1940, moreover, it was complicated by a presidential campaign.

The Third-Term Campaign

Much of the political drama of 1940 revolved around the question of Franklin Roosevelt's intentions. Would he break with tradition and run for an unprecedented third term? The President himself was deliberately coy and never publicly revealed his own wishes. But by refusing to withdraw from the contest, he made it impossible for any rival Democrats to establish a foothold within the party. And when, just before the Democratic Convention in July, he let it be known that he would accept a "draft" from his party, the issue was settled. The Democrats quickly renominated him and even swallowed his choice for Vice President: Agriculture Secretary Henry A. Wallace, a man too liberal for the taste of many party leaders.

The Republicans, again, faced a far more difficult task. As they began to gather for their convention in Philadelphia in June, they received a heavy blow from two of their own most distinguished members. Henry L. Stimson, the elder statesman who had served in the cabinets of William Howard Taft and Herbert Hoover, accepted an appointment as Roosevelt's Secretary of War. Even more embarrassing, Frank Knox, the 1936 Republican vice-presidential candidate, agreed to become the new Secretary of the Navy. The chagrined Republican delegates angrily read both men out of the party; but the episode underscored their dilemma. With Roosevelt effectively straddling the center of the defense debate, favoring neither the extreme isolationists nor the extreme interventionists, the Republicans had few viable alternatives. Their solution was to compete with the President on his own ground. Succumbing to the carefully orchestrated pressure of a remarkable grass-roots movement, they nominated for President a politically inexperienced businessman, Wendell Willkie. Both the candidate and the party platform took positions little different from Roosevelt's: they would keep the country out of war but would extend generous assistance to the Allies.

Willkie was left, therefore, with the unenviable task of defeating Roosevelt by outmatching him in personal magnetism and by trying to arouse public fears of the dangers of an unprecedented third term. An appealing figure and a vigorous campaigner, he managed to evoke more public enthusiasm than any Republican candidate since Theodore Roosevelt. He attracted, too, the support of a number of disenchanted New Dealers, including Raymond Moley, Hugh Johnson, and even John L. Lewis (who threatened to resign as president of the CIO if Roosevelt was reelected, and ultimately did). In the end, however, Willkie was no match for Franklin Roosevelt.

The President tried to give the appearance of not campaigning at all, explaining that he had to devote his full energies to mobilizing the nation's defenses. In the process, however, he managed to make frequent visits to defense plants, army bases, and shipyards across the nation, traveling through major cities at almost every stop. More important, he managed to undercut the only effective issue Willkie was able to muster. The Republican candidate began to argue that if Roosevelt's promise to stay out of war was no better than his promise to balance the budget, then American soldiers were "already almost on the transports." Roosevelt responded in a speech in Boston with his most ringing promise to date: "I have said this before, but I shall say it again and again and again: Your boys are not going to be sent into any foreign wars." (Privately, he had made the mental reservation that if the United States were attacked, the war would no longer be "foreign.")

Although Willkie scrupulously refrained from attacking the President for assisting the Allies, he received the votes of most of those who disapproved of Roosevelt's aid policies. It was not enough. Although the election was closer than either the 1932 or 1936 contest, Roosevelt nevertheless won decisively. He received 55 percent of the popular vote to Willkie's 45 percent; and he won 449 electoral votes to Willkie's 82. (Within weeks, Willkie had openly enlisted in the effort to increase American assistance to the Allies and was serving as an intermediary between Roosevelt and Churchill. In the years that followed, until his death in 1944, he worked tirelessly on behalf of progressive internationalism.)

NEUTRALITY ABANDONED

With the election behind him and with the situation in Europe deteriorating, Roosevelt began in the last months of 1940 to make subtle but profound changes in the American role in the war. To the public, he claimed that he was simply continuing the now established policy of providing aid to the embattled Allies. In fact, that aid was taking new and far more decisive forms—so new and so decisive that by the fall of 1941 the United States was participating in the war in all but name.

Lend-Lease

In December 1940, Great Britain was virtually bankrupt. No longer could the British meet the "cash-and-carry" requirements imposed by the Neutrality Acts;

WENDELL WILLKIE.   The campaign of Wendell Willkie in 1940 was unlike that of any Republican presidential candidate in recent memory. Willkie, shown here riding through Elwood, Indiana, exuded an energy and a folksy charm that stood in marked contrast to the glum sobriety of such candidates as Herbert Hoover and Calvin Coolidge. The popular excitement he created led some observers to believe he had a real chance to defeat Franklin Roosevelt's bid for an unprecedented third term; but while Willkie did better than Alf Landon in 1936, he nevertheless lost decisively. (*UPI*)

yet England's needs, Churchill insisted, were greater than ever. The President, therefore, began to consider ways to provide continued assistance without arousing intense isolationist opposition. He might have asked for the repeal of neutrality legislation forbidding war loans, but he rejected that idea for fear of reawakening old negative feelings about the unpaid debts of World War I. Instead, he suggested a method that would "eliminate the dollar sign" from all arms transactions while still, he hoped, pacifying those who opposed blatant American intervention in the war. The new system was labeled "lend-lease." It would allow the President not only to sell but to lend or lease armaments to any nation deemed "vital to the defense of the United States." In other words, America could funnel weapons to England on the basis of no more than Britain's promise to return them when the war was over. The system would allow the United States to serve, Roosevelt declared, as an "arsenal of democracy." Isolationists attacked the measure bitterly, arguing (correctly) that it was simply a device to tie the United States more closely to the Allies. But public opinion was on the side of the President, and Congress enacted the bill (House Resolution 1776) by wide margins. It empowered the President to spend $7 billion to provide supplies to the Allies, a sum as large as all the controversial loans of World War I combined.

Engagement in the Atlantic

With lend-lease formally established, Roosevelt soon faced another serious problem: ensuring that the American supplies would actually reach Great Britain. Shipping lanes in the Atlantic had become more and more dangerous as German submarines roved the waters destroying as much as a half-million tons of shipping each month. British vessels, of course, were the major victims; and the Royal Navy was losing ships far more rapidly than it could replace them and was finding it increasingly difficult to convoy materials across the Atlantic from America. Secretary of War Stimson argued that the United States should itself convoy vessels to England; but Roosevelt continued to fear isolationist opposition and relied instead upon the concept of "hemispheric defense." By July 1941, arguing that the western Atlantic was a neutral zone and the responsibility of the American nations, he was patrolling the ocean as far east as Iceland, escorting convoys of merchant ships and radioing information to British vessels about the location of Nazi submarines.

At first, Germany did little to challenge these obviously hostile American actions. By September 1941, however, the situation had changed. Nazi forces had invaded the Soviet Union in June of that year, driving quickly and forcefully deep into Russian territory. When the Soviets did not surrender, as many had predicted, Roosevelt persuaded Congress to extend lend-lease privileges to them. Now, American industry was providing the lifeblood to Hitler's foes on two fronts, and the American navy was playing a more active role than ever in protecting the flow of goods to Europe. German submarines had already attacked and sunk an American ship, the *Robin Moor,* off the coast of Brazil in May. While the Nazis had responded to American protests by proclaiming that "Germany will continue to sink every ship with contraband for Britain whatever its name," for several months there were no further incidents. In September, however, Nazi submarines began a far more concerted campaign against American vessels. Early that month, a German U-boat fired on the American destroyer *Greer* (which was radioing the

U-boat's position to the British at the time). Roosevelt responded by ordering American ships to fire on German submarines "on sight." In October, Nazi submarines actually hit two destroyers and sank one of them, the *Reuben James,* killing many American sailors in the process. An enraged Congress now voted approval of a measure allowing the United States to arm its merchant vessels and to sail all the way into belligerent ports. The United States had, in effect, launched a naval war against Germany, as the Chief of Naval Operations privately admitted. Hitler "has every excuse in the world to declare war on us now," he wrote in his diary at the time.

Among those excuses was a series of meetings, some private and one public, that tied the United States and Great Britain ever more closely together. In April 1941, senior military officers of the two nations had met in secret and agreed upon a joint strategy to be followed were the United States to enter the war. In August, Roosevelt met publicly with Winston Churchill aboard a British vessel anchored off the coast of Newfoundland. The President made no military commitments, but he did join with Churchill in releasing a document that became known as the Atlantic Charter, in which the two nations set out "certain common principles" on which to base "a better future for the world." It was, in only vaguely disguised form, a statement of war aims, among which was a commitment to establishing a "wider and permanent system of general security" when the hostilities ceased. More significantly, perhaps, the document called openly for "the final destruction of the Nazi tyranny," a provocative commitment for a nation officially not at war.

By the fall of 1941, therefore, it seemed only a matter of time before the United States became an official belligerent. Roosevelt remained convinced that he could ask for a declaration of war only in the event of an actual enemy attack. As late as November, polls disclosed that only 20 percent of the people favored entering the war. But an attack seemed certain to come, if not in the Atlantic, then in the Pacific.

The Road to Pearl Harbor

The Japanese had not sat idle during the crisis in Europe. With Great Britain preoccupied with Germany, and with Soviet attention diverted to the west, Japan sensed an unparalleled opportunity to extend its empire in the Pacific. In the summer of 1939, the increasingly militant Tokyo government began to threaten the colonial possessions of England and the Netherlands in Southeast Asia. And in September 1940, Japan signed the Tripartite Pact, a defensive alliance with Germany and Italy that extended the Axis into Asia. The United States was determined to resist.

Roosevelt had already displayed his animosity toward the Japanese by harshly denouncing their continuing assault upon China and by terminating the long-standing American commercial treaty with the Tokyo government. Beginning in January 1940, as a result of the latter action, the United States was free to stop shipments to Japan of American oil, scrap iron, and other vital war materials. In the fall, finally, Roosevelt did just that: embargoing aviation fuel, iron, steel, and other raw materials with military potential. Still, the Japanese drive continued. In July 1941, Imperial troops moved into Indochina and seized the capital of Vietnam. The United States, having broken Japanese codes, knew that their next target was the Dutch East Indies; and when Tokyo failed to respond to Roosevelt's stern warnings, the President froze all Japanese assets in the United States, severely limiting Japan's ability to purchase needed American supplies.

Tokyo now faced a choice. It would either have to repair relations with the United States to restore the flow of supplies, or it would have to find those supplies elsewhere, most obviously by seizing British and Dutch possessions in the Pacific. At first, the Tokyo government seemed willing to compromise. The Japanese Prime Minister, Prince Konoye, had begun negotiations with the United States even before the freezing of his country's assets; and in August he increased the pace by requesting a personal meeting with President Roosevelt. On the advice of Secretary Hull, who feared that Konoye lacked sufficient power within his own government to be able to enforce any agreement, Roosevelt replied that he would meet with the Prime Minister only if Japan would give guarantees in advance that it would respect the territorial integrity of China. Konoye could give no such assurances, and the negotiations collapsed.

The breakdown of diplomacy in the fall of 1941 raised serious questions about the wisdom of Hull's and Roosevelt's tactics. By taking an adamant moral position on China, the administration was playing into the hands of Japanese extremists, who cited American intransigence as justification for their own hard-line position. In October, the militants in Tokyo forced Konoye out of office and replaced him with the leader of the war party, General Hideki Tojo. There seemed little alternative now to war. Yet the United States was still far from prepared for a major world conflict. Even had further negotiations failed to produce an acceptable settlement, the Roosevelt administration might at least have delayed the war long enough to permit an expansion of American military strength.

The Tojo government maintained for several weeks a pretense of wanting to continue negotiations. On November 20, 1941, Tokyo proposed a "modus vivendi" highly favorable to itself and sent its diplomats in Washington to the State Department to discuss it. But the effort was merely a charade. Tokyo had already decided that it would not yield on the question of China; and Washington had made it clear that it would accept nothing less than a reversal of that policy. Hull rejected the Japanese overtures out of hand; and on November 27, he told Secretary of War Stimson, "I have washed my hands of the Japanese situation, and it is now in the hands of you and Knox, the Army and Navy." He was not merely speculating. American intelligence had already decoded Japanese messages that made clear that war was imminent, that after November 29 an attack would be only a matter of days.

What Washington did not know was where the attack would take place. Most officials were convinced that the Japanese would move first not against American territory but against British or Dutch possessions to the south. American intelli-

PEARL HARBOR.   December 7, 1941—"a date which will live in infamy"
—propelled an unprepared United States into the most savage war in history.
Not the least of America's problems was the destruction of much of its
Pacific fleet as a result of the Japanese air raid on Pearl Harbor. Here, the
magazine of the U.S.S. *Shaw* explodes during the attack. (*Official U.S. Navy
photo*)

gence took note of a Japanese naval task force that began sailing east from the
Kuriles toward Hawaii on November 25; and a routine warning was sent to the
United States naval facility at Pearl Harbor. Officials were paying far more attention, however, to a large Japanese convoy moving southward through the China
Sea. A combination of confusion and miscalculation caused the government to
overlook clear indications that Japan intended a direct attack upon American
forces.

At 7:55 A.M. on Sunday, December 7, 1941, a wave of Japanese bombers attacked the United States naval base at Pearl Harbor. A second wave came an hour later. Because the military commanders in Hawaii had taken no precautions against such an attack, allowing ships to remain bunched up defenselessly in the harbor, the results of the air raid were catastrophic. Within two hours, the United States lost 8 battleships, 3 cruisers, 4 other vessels, 188 airplanes, and several vital shore installations. More than 2,000 men died, and another thousand were injured. The Japanese suffered only light losses.

America was suddenly rendered almost impotent in the Pacific; and the nation remained unprepared for war in almost every other respect as well. Nevertheless, the raid on Pearl Harbor did overnight what more than two years of effort by Franklin Roosevelt had been unable to do: it unified the American people in a fervent commitment to war. On December 8, the President traveled to Capitol Hill, where he grimly addressed a joint session of Congress: "Yesterday, December 7, 1941—a date which will live in infamy—the United States of America was suddenly and deliberately attacked by the naval and air forces of the Empire of Japan." Within four hours, the Senate unanimously and the House 388 to 1 approved a declaration of war against Japan. Three days later, Germany and Italy, Japan's European allies, declared war on the United States; and on the same day, December 11, Congress reciprocated without a dissenting vote. For the second time in less than twenty-five years, the United States had joined in an awesome international conflagration.

SUGGESTED READINGS

The best and most thorough account of the foreign policy of the Roosevelt administration is Robert Dallek, *Franklin D. Roosevelt and American Foreign Policy, 1932–1945* (1979). New Deal international economic policy is examined in Lloyd Gardner, *Economic Aspects of New Deal Diplomacy* (1964). Frank Freidel, *Launching the New Deal* (1973), examines the London Economic Conference. Beatrice Farnsworth, *William C. Bullitt and the Soviet Union* (1967); Edward E. Bennett, *Recognition of Russia* (1970); Bryce Wood, *The Making of the Good Neighbor Policy* (1961); and David Green, *The Containment of Latin America* (1971), examine two areas that received special diplomatic attention during the first years of the New Deal.

Overviews of the origins of American involvement in World War II include Selig Adler, *The Uncertain Giant* (1966), and Robert Divine, *The Reluctant Belligerent* (1965). William Langer and S. Everett Gleason, *The Challenge to Isolation* (1952) and *The Undeclared War* (1953), are thorough, standard accounts. The rise of isolationist sentiment is chronicled in Selig Adler, *The Isolationist Impulse* (1957), and Manfred Jonas, *Isolationism in America* (1966). Wayne S. Cole, *Charles A. Lindbergh and the Battle Against American Intervention in World War II* (1974), is a valuable specialized study. See also John K. Nelson, *The Peace Prophets* (1967), and Wayne S. Cole,

Senator Gerald P. Nye and American Foreign Relations (1962). The 1940 campaign receives attention in Bernard F. Donahoe, *Private Plans and Public Dangers* (1965).

The final steps toward war are chronicled in James Leutze, *Bargaining for Supremacy* (1977), a valuable study of Anglo-American cooperation; Joseph Lash, *Roosevelt and Churchill* (1976); Warren Kimball, *The Most Unsordid Act* (1970), a study of lend-lease; Herbert Feis, *The Road to Pearl Harbor* (1950); and James MacGregor Burns, *Roosevelt: The Soldier of Freedom* (1970). Roberta Wohlstetter, *Pearl Harbor: Warning and Decision* (1962), is an invaluable study of the 1941 fiasco.

Sixteen

Total War and the Modern Nation

"War is no longer simply a battle between armed forces in the field," an American government report of 1939 concluded. "It is a struggle in which each side strives to bring to bear against the enemy the coordinated power of every individual and of every material resource at its command. The conflict extends from the soldier in the front line to the citizen in the remotest hamlet in the rear."

In many respects, the United States moved quickly and effectively to become the united, "coordinated" society that a "total war" demanded. The nation performed prodigious feats of productivity in arming itself and its allies for the struggle against the Axis. It accepted with striking equanimity the privations and sacrifices that the war imposed. It avoided, for the most part, the bitter social divisiveness that had made World War I a dark chapter in the history of American civil liberties. In other respects, however, World War II not only failed to eliminate, but actually accentuated the deep divisions that remained in American society. Political battles raged furiously throughout the conflict. Racial and ethnic tensions often boiled to the surface. And those who had spent the years of the Great Depression working for social and economic reform had to watch helplessly as conservatives took advantage of the war to halt and even dismantle their efforts.

Both in the unity it imposed and in the divisions it accentuated, World War II reached out to affect the lives of virtually all Americans. And while some of the changes it wrought proved ultimately to be temporary aberrations, others were lasting and fundamental. Americans emerged from the war having experienced permanent transformations in some of their most basic assumptions and institutions: in the role of government, in the structure of the economy, and in the expectations of the populace regarding their own society and the world.

OUTPRODUCING THE AXIS

Well before Pearl Harbor, Franklin Roosevelt had begun to mobilize both the armed forces and the nation's productive facilities for war. By December 1941, however, the United States was still not fully prepared to fight. Preparedness efforts had met consistent opposition from isolationists within Congress and without, forcing the President to moderate his efforts. The administration's first agency to coordinate military procurement, the War Resources Board, aroused particularly strong opposition, in part because of the unfortunate use of the word *war*, rather than *defense*, in its name. The President disbanded the agency only months after establishing it.

In June 1940, the fall of France spurred the administration to new organizational efforts. The President first reestablished a body that had been created in 1939 and then disbanded: the Advisory Commission of the Council of National Defense; and in January 1941, after further bureaucratic problems, he replaced it with the Office of Production Management, under former General Motors executive William Knudsen. Three months later, he created the Office of Price Administration and Civilian Supply, under Leon Henderson, to supervise the civilian economy. Still, because of the bureaucratic reshuffling and conflicting lines of authority of the prewar agencies, the nation continued to lack a coherent administrative structure to supervise the economic demands of war. And since so much of the military output of American factories had been shipped to England, the nation's armed forces continued to lack the weapons and equipment they needed.

Nevertheless, America entered World War II far better prepared than it had entered World War I. In the second half of 1940, the government had awarded $10.5 billion in defense contracts, spurring an enormous boom in the construction of aircraft factories, shipyards, and other defense plants. Even if insufficient materials had been stockpiled for American forces, the capacity to produce those materials quickly had expanded greatly. The United States was by the end of 1941 producing more combat munitions than any nation in the world—almost as much as Germany and Japan combined. Airplane production had risen to a rate of almost 25,000 a year. Shipyards were gearing up for a surge of construction that would ultimately exceed even the most optimistic predictions. More than 2 million men had already been inducted into the armed forces (through a draft instituted in the fall of 1940), and new training camps were under construction to permit the induction of many more. Serious problems and shortages remained, but the groundwork had been laid for the rapid and successful mobilization that was to come.

Mobilizing Production

The attack on Pearl Harbor and the declarations of war that followed suddenly placed intolerable strains upon the already struggling defense bureaucracy. Without efficient central direction, the agencies responded to the emergency by sud-

MUSHROOMING WAR PLANTS. Two pictures taken in the same spot in 1941 (top) and 1942 indicate the speed of construction of the Morgantown, West Virginia, ordnance plant. (*DuPont*)

denly ordering tremendous quantities—indeed far too much—of everything. No procurement officer wanted the war to be lost because he had failed to request enough for his unit. The result was an impossible burden upon American industry —which was already far behind in existing war orders and struggling for access to scarce materials—and a bureaucratic crisis in Washington.

Roosevelt responded in January 1942 by disbanding the Office of Production Management and creating a new "super agency": the War Production Board. It was to be under the direction of Donald Nelson, formerly an executive in Sears Roebuck; and it was to have greatly expanded powers over the economy—although it was always significantly weaker than the War Industries Board had been during World War I. The task of the WPB was an arduous one. It was required, first, to evaluate all procurement requests from military and other sources and decide which were justified and which were not. It was to distribute contracts for government purchases among the many competing manufacturers. And perhaps most difficult, it was to mediate between the military and civilian sectors of the economy, determining how to allot limited materials between the two. In this atmosphere of contending interests, bureaucratic warfare and personality clashes were inevitable.

Donald Nelson, a dedicated, personable, and competent administrator, nevertheless proved unable to withstand the assaults upon his authority. The WPB charter required him to distribute contracts equitably among large and small manufacturers alike; but in the end, most orders went to the larger, more influential corporations. Nelson was also charged with exercising strict civilian control over purchases and materials allotments; as the war progressed, however, the military came to exert increasing authority over such matters. And it was Nelson's responsibility to create a well-balanced production plan for the entire economy; but conflicting interest groups hampered him continually in that task. By late 1942, the war bureaucracy was once again in crisis. Although Roosevelt allowed the WPB to survive and Nelson to remain as its director, he diminished its powers considerably by persuading Associate Justice James F. Byrnes to resign from the Supreme Court and become a sort of assistant president in charge of war production. Byrnes headed first the Office of Economic Stabilization and then, after 1943, the Office of War Mobilization, which finally provided the relatively efficient war administration the President had long been seeking.

Despite all these problems, the WPB in 1942 did manage gradually to impose a measure of order upon the confusion. The first step was a major reduction in the construction of war plants. Nelson and others believed that the remarkable construction boom of 1940 and 1941 had provided the nation with enough plant capacity already, that resources and manpower would be better spent utilizing existing facilities. So despite occasional opposition from regions deprived of new factories and facilities (as when the Higgins shipyards in New Orleans were abandoned), by the middle of 1942 the amount of new construction being started had declined sharply; in another six months, the larger part of the war plants and military facilities had been built.

There remained the problem of coordinating war production, which continued as late as the summer of 1942 to suffer from crippling bottlenecks. The vital shipbuilding program, for example, had to be cut back because of scarcities of such raw materials as steel plate and glass and of such components as valves, turbines, and engines. The WPB eventually broke most of these bottlenecks by establishing effective authority—through the Controlled Materials Plan—over the allocation of raw materials to each manufacturer.

The shortage of rubber became so critical in 1942 that it required special attention. After the WPB failed to solve the problem, Roosevelt appointed a committee under Bernard Baruch to make a special report. This recommended sharp restrictions upon the use of motor vehicles, to be accomplished through gasoline rationing and a national speed limit of thirty-five miles per hour, as well as immediate construction of enormous synthetic rubber plants. Roosevelt ordered the restrictions and appointed a rubber director in the WPB—William M. Jeffers, president of the Union Pacific Railroad—to construct the plants. By the end of 1943 the synthetic rubber industry was producing one-third again as much rubber as the country had normally used before the war.

An indispensable adjunct of the war agencies was the Senate War Investigating Committee, headed by Harry S Truman, a previously little known Senator from Missouri. The Senators consciously patterned it after the Committee on the Conduct of the War of the Civil War period but avoided the pitfalls of their predecessors by ruling out questions of military policy. Instead, they ferreted out incompetence and corruption in the war-production and military-construction programs: outrageous expense in building army camps, improper inspection of airplane engines, a quixotic scheme to build an Arctic pipeline, and the like. The Truman Committee uncovered and stopped hundreds of millions of dollars of waste. In the wartime expenditure of $400 billion there was remarkably little corruption.

The Output

By the beginning of 1944, American war production had proved so successful that factories were more than fulfilling the nation's military needs. Their output was twice that of all the Axis countries combined; and there were even charges that military production was becoming excessive, that a resumption of civilian production should now be encouraged. (The military staunchly and successfully opposed such demands.)

The success of the war mobilization was graphic evidence of the enormous productive capacity of the American economy, a capacity untested during the previous decade of depression. Having begun with virtually no facilities for producing military goods, the United States was by the end of the war the greatest manufacturer of armaments in the world. Its factories had constructed almost 300,000 airplanes, 76,000 ships, 86,000 tanks, and 2.6 million machine guns. It had almost doubled its total plant capacity in the space of six years. It had created new industries—for example, magnesium—and multiplied the size of existing ones many times. Aluminum productive capacity nearly trebled; machine tool production rose sevenfold; the output of electricity increased by nearly 50 percent; production of iron and steel was soon greater than that of the entire rest of the world only a few years earlier.

Among the most remarkable accomplishments of the war years was the rapid expansion of the nation's transportation facilities to meet the demands of the war. Under the direction of the Office of Defense Transportation, created in December 1941, railroads began carrying double the traffic of 1939 with only 10 percent more locomotives and 20 percent more freight cars. When German submarines began attacking coastal tankers in 1942, the government supervised construction of the Big Inch pipeline to carry oil from Texas all the way to Pennsylvania.

Transporting troops and supplies overseas required one of the most spectacular construction programs of all. The Germans had sunk more than 12 million tons of shipping by 1942. To replace it, the United States Maritime Commission had to abandon its program of building fast, efficient ships requiring scarce turbines, valves, and electrical equipment. As early as July 1940, Admiral Emory S. Land, head of the commission, and William Knudsen recommended to Roosevelt mass production of a freighter that, while slow (with a sailing speed of only eleven knots), would be simple to construct and would not require scarce components. By using the existing designs for an old-fashioned British tramp steamer with a reciprocating engine and steam winches, they saved six months in starting production. This "ugly duckling" was the Liberty ship. After a slow beginning, builders substituted welding for riveting and applied prefabrication and subassembly techniques in constructing it. In 1941, construction of a Liberty ship required an average of 355 days; by the end of 1942, the time had been cut to 56 days, and one of Henry J. Kaiser's companies completed one in 14 days. During 1942 alone, 8 million tons of shipping were built; by 1945, the United States had over 36 million tons of ships afloat.

Science and the War

The United States had generally neglected scientific research in the period between the two wars. Germany, in the meantime, had made rapid strides. It was now the task of American science to close the gap. At the urging of Vannevar Bush, a noted scientist, Roosevelt agreed in 1940 to create a committee for scientific research. A year later, he expanded it into the Office of Scientific Research and Development, under the direction of Bush, which mobilized scientists quickly and effectively and helped produce some of the most important products of the war.

The Naval Research Laboratory in Washington had discovered the principle of radar in the 1920s by bouncing a radio beam off a ship on the Potomac River. The British had improved the system and had made effective use of it during the air blitz of 1940–1941. Now, Allied scientists developed radar even further, enabling it not only to detect enemy ships and aircraft but to help direct shells against them. American rocket research, similarly, produced weapons that enormously increased the fire power of airplanes, ships, and tanks (although the Allies never matched the Germans, who by the end of the war were blasting London with enormous V-1 and V-2 rockets).

The most important scientific undertaking of the war years, however, was one conducted in almost total secrecy: the development of the atomic bomb. Reports had reached the United States in 1939, through the Italian physicist Enrico Fermi and the German mathematician Albert Einstein (now living in exile in America), that Nazi scientists had achieved atomic fission in uranium. Next, they warned, might come a bomb more powerful than any weapon ever devised. What had long been theoretically possible now seemed on the verge of accomplishment; and the United States immediately began a race in the dark to develop the weapon before the Germans did.

In December 1942, American physicists produced a controlled chain reaction in an atomic pile at the University of Chicago, solving the first great problem in producing an atomic weapon. There remained the enormous technical problems of achieving the release of this power in a bomb. Over the next three years, the government secretly poured nearly $2 billion into the so-called Manhattan Project —a massive scientific effort conducted at hidden laboratories in Oak Ridge, Tennessee, Los Alamos, New Mexico, and other sites. Hundreds of scientists worked for months on end, many of them not fully aware of what they were working on, to complete two complementary projects. One was the production of fissionable plutonium, the fuel for an atomic explosion; the other, under the supervision of J. Robert Oppenheimer, was the construction of a bomb that could employ the fuel. Frantic to complete the weapon before the Germans and worried that the device might not work when completed, the scientists pushed ahead far faster than anyone had predicted. Even so, the war in Europe had ended by the time they were ready to test the first bomb. (Only later did they discover that the Germans had never come close to constructing a usable atomic device.)

On July 16, 1945, the Manhattan Project scientists stood on a hill near Los Alamos, New Mexico, watching a tower several miles away on which was suspended the fruits of their labor. And just before dawn, they witnessed the first atomic explosion in history: a blinding flash of light brighter than any ever seen on earth, and a huge, billowing mushroom cloud. Some were exhilarated by their success. Others, among them J. Robert Oppenheimer, were already severely troubled by the implications of what they had done. Standing on the New Mexico desert watching the terrible explosion, Oppenheimer thought grimly of the words from Hindu scripture: "Now I am become death, the destroyer of worlds." His concern would trouble countless scientists for many decades to come.

THE WARTIME ECONOMY

The industrial boom created by the war not only produced a remarkable amount of munitions for the American military. It also ended at last the Great Depression. By the middle of 1941, the economic problems of the 1930s—unemployment, deflation, industrial sluggishness—had been replaced with new problems—labor shortages, inflation, and a scarcity of consumer goods. Prosperity had returned; but because of the war, it was a prosperity with unusual characteristics.

Economic Expansion

The most important agent of the new prosperity was federal spending, which within months was pumping far more money into the economy than all the New Deal relief agencies combined. In 1939, the federal budget had been $9 billion; by 1945, it had risen to $100 billion. And the Gross National Product had soared as a result: from $91 billion in 1939 to $166 billion in 1945. The index of industrial production had doubled. Seventeen million new jobs had been created. Perhaps most striking was the increase in personal income, which in some cities soared almost astronomically. In New York, the average family income in 1938 had been $2,760; by 1942, it had risen to $4,044. In Boston, the increase was from $2,455 to $3,618; in Washington, D.C., from $2,227 to $5,316.

Not everyone shared in the new prosperity. Government economists reported in 1943 that 10 million families still received less than the $1,675 per year requisite for a minimum standard of living. Most Americans, however, were relatively more affluent than they had been. The living standard of working people advanced rapidly. This was due less to wage increases than to payment of time and a half for overtime beyond 40 hours. The average workweek lengthened from 40.6 hours in 1941 to 45.2 in 1944. As living costs rose (on a 1935–1939 base of 100) from 100.4 in 1940 to 128.4 in 1945, gross weekly wages went up far more rapidly, from $25.20 to $43.39.

There were, of course, limits upon what the recipients of these expanded incomes could do with their money. Many consumer goods—automobiles, radios, and appliances, even many types of food and clothing—were in short supply. On the whole, however, the American economy proved remarkably successful in meeting the demands of both the military and the civilian sectors simultaneously. While the variety of goods and services available to consumers diminished during the war, the quantity actually increased.

The End of Unemployment

The most persistent and debilitating feature of the Great Depression had been continuing, substantial unemployment—a condition that many people had begun to assume was a permanent feature of American life. The war ended that problem almost overnight and replaced it with another one: a serious labor shortage. After grappling for years with the problem of millions of jobless, the nation found itself hard pressed for sufficient people to swell the fighting forces, man the war plants, till the fields, and keep the domestic economy functioning. There were periodic demands for national service legislation or a labor draft, but unions were so vehemently opposed that no such measure ever passed the Senate. The relatively weak War Manpower Commission tried to coerce workers into remaining at defense jobs at the risk of being drafted, but the war came to an end without any tight allocation of manpower comparable to that of materials. The armed forces had first call upon men through the Selective Service System, which had been in operation since the fall of 1940. Altogether, draft boards registered 31 million men. Including volunteers, over 15 million men and women served in the armed forces during the war. Nevertheless, the working force jumped from 46.5 million to over 53 million as the 7 million unemployed and many previously considered unemployable—the very young and the elderly—and several million women found jobs. The number of civilian employees of the federal government trebled.

Labor: Growth and Restraint

Both the size and the power of labor unions grew rapidly during the war, but their unpopularity among middle- and upper-class Americans increased correspondingly. Unions faced, therefore, not only unparalleled opportunities to enhance the economic positions of their members but serious restraints upon their ability to act freely in the economy.

Union membership rose with the rise in the working force, from about 10.5 million workers in 1941 to over 13 million in 1945. Keeping these workers satisfied was no easy matter. The administration was determined to prevent strikes and to restrain the formidable pressure of the labor unions from forcing wages, and thus all prices, upward. President Roosevelt followed the procedure of World War I by establishing a National Defense Mediation Board in March 1941, made up of representatives of management, labor, and the public. In November 1941 it broke down when the CIO members resigned over the refusal of the board to recommend a union shop (that is, one in which all new workers hired must join the union) in coal mines. In January 1942, Roosevelt replaced it with the National War Labor Board, similarly constituted but much stronger. This board could set wages, hours, and working conditions, and through the war powers of the President it could enforce these in a final extremity by government seizure and operation of plants.

On the union-shop question, which was creating much hostility between management and labor, the board arrived at a compromise, the "maintenance-of-membership" clause. Nonmembers hired into a war plant did not have to join a union, but members had to remain in it, and the union continued as the bargaining agent for the duration of the contract. Pressure for wage increases, which might contribute to inflation, was a more serious question. The board hit upon a solution in ruling upon the Little Steel cases in July 1942. Taking January 1, 1941, as the base date when workers had received a standard wage, it recognized a 15 percent rise in the cost-of-living index since then. Consequently, it felt that a proportionate increase for steelworkers would be equitable. The Little Steel formula, except for those receiving substandard wages (for example, some textile workers), served thereafter as a wage ceiling.

Despite the no-strike pledges of the major unions, there were nearly 15,000 work stoppages during the war, involving the loss of more than 36 million man-days. These stoppages involved only one-ninth of 1 percent of the working time (though they indirectly caused more damage than this). When Lewis's United Mine Workers defied the government by striking against the Little Steel formula

WOMEN WAR WORKERS. One result of the sudden demand for labor was the introduction of many women into the workplace for the first time, many of them in occupations traditionally considered the exclusive preserve of men. These women are working as riveters in a factory producing airplanes for the army—an occupation that inspired a popular song, "Rosie the Riveter," during the war. Women also played important roles in the armed services in the WACS and WAVEs. Some of the wartime advances proved only temporary, however, as men quickly replaced women in many jobs shortly after the end of the war. (*Library of Congress*)

in May 1943, Congress reacted by passing a month later, over Roosevelt's veto, the Smith-Connally Act (War Labor Disputes Act). This act required unions to wait thirty days before striking and empowered the President to seize a struck war plant. In practice, the law did little to limit the power of unions. It simply gave them an additional weapon: the power to threaten a strike, which now carried with it the possibility of government control of the company. But if the federal government remained cautious in curbing union power, public animosity continued to rise. Many states passed laws to discipline the unions; and by the end of the war, pressure was growing for federal action to limit their influence.

Stabilizing the Boom

Union power was not the only factor that threatened to create economic instability. There were other challenges as well, all of which required increasing government activity. By the middle of the war, Washington was exercising a power over the American economy far greater than anything the New Deal had ever attempted or envisioned.

At the beginning of the war, with a two-year supply of surplus wheat, cotton, and corn in storage, there seemed no danger of food shortages in the United States. But within six months after Pearl Harbor, scarcities of many kinds began to develop. The United States felt the increased demand of the armed forces and its allies and the reduction of supplies due to the loss of fibers and oils from Southeast Asia. By 1942, meat production was half again that of the Depression years, but American consumers with their increased buying power were eager to buy even more. Consumer income in 1943 was 65 percent above Depression levels, and much of it was in the pockets of people who had not eaten adequately for years.

A food administrator did exist, Chester Davis, but he resigned in protest when his views (and those of the American Farm Bureau Federation) did not prevail; his successor was Marvin Jones. Neither man had the dictatorial powers to procure the scarce supplies and manpower that the dominant farm bloc in Congress would have liked to bestow upon agricultural producers. Rather, farmers had to depend upon whatever the WPB would allocate to them and upon a generous draft-exemption program they obtained from Congress. They also received legislation raising the ceiling on commodity prices to 110 percent of parity. Since this came into conflict with the anti-inflation efforts of the administration, a dogged struggle developed between the President and the congressional farm bloc over farm prices. Neither side won entirely.

Pressures from business, farmers, and labor, combined with the scarcity of consumer goods and the burgeoning of buying power, created an almost irresistible trend toward inflation. During the prewar period, the Office of Price Administration (OPA), under a vigorous New Dealer, Leon Henderson, lacked real coercive power and failed to halt inflation. Between the invasion of Poland and the attack on Pearl Harbor, prices of twenty-eight basic commodities rose by nearly 25 percent. Immediately thereafter, pressures became so acute that prices went up 2 percent per month. Congress hastily passed a bill authorizing only selective price fixing and setting ceilings with a preferential trap door for agriculture.

In April 1942, the OPA issued a General Maximum Price Regulation that froze prices of consumer goods, and of rents in defense areas only, at their March 1942 level. But the rise of uncontrolled farm prices toward 110 percent of parity forced an upward revision of food prices. This gave ammunition to the labor unions' barrage against fixed wages. In October 1942, Congress, grudgingly responding to the President's demand, passed the Anti-Inflation Act. Under its authority, Roosevelt immediately froze agricultural prices, wages, salaries, and rents throughout the country.

In July 1943, Roosevelt appointed a former advertising executive with remarkable administrative talents, Chester Bowles, to head the OPA. With a small enforcement staff, Bowles braved general unpopularity to hold the increase in living costs during the next two years to 1.4 percent. Altogether, the price level went up less than 29 percent from 1939 to the end of the war, compared with 63 percent between 1914 and the Armistice.

Consumers nonetheless suffered numerous irritations and discomforts. The OPA, through unpaid local volunteers manning 5,600 price and rationing boards, administered the rationing of canned goods, coffee, sugar, meat, butter and other fats, shoes, tires, gasoline, and fuel oil. The OPA could not, however, control deterioration of quality. Black-marketing and overcharging grew in proportions far beyond OPA policing capacity; and in 1943 Congress slashed the funds of the enforcement division.

One of the most important inflationary controls was the sale of war bonds and stamps to channel off some of the excess purchasing power, which for the single year 1945 mounted to nearly $60 billion. Throughout most of the war, personal incomes were at least one-third greater than the value of available civilian goods and services. The Treasury Department, through eight war bond drives and its payroll deduction plans, but with few of the lurid or coercive touches of World War I, sold $40 billion worth of series "E" bonds to small investors and $60 billion more to individuals and corporate entities other than banks.

Had this been the total of government loans, the effect would have been to quell

A RATION COUPON. The Office of Price Administration supervised an elaborate system of rationing in addition to its wage and price controls. The rationing of gasoline was intended less to preserve fuel oil, which was plentiful through most of the war, than to cut down on driving so as to conserve rubber, which became desperately scarce after Japanese forces overran the Pacific countries from which the United States had imported its largest supply. Although a new, domestic synthetic rubber industry grew up remarkably quickly, gasoline rationing continued until after the end of the war. (*Courtesy of G. Litton*) inflation, but the Treasury had to borrow $87.5 billion more from Federal Reserve and commercial banks. Since in effect the banks created new credits that the government then spent, the result was to inflate bank credits and money in circulation by over $100 billion.

Taxes did much more to drain off surplus purchasing power. The government raised 41 percent of its war costs through taxation, compared with 33 percent during World War I. The Revenue Act of 1942, which Roosevelt hailed as "the greatest tax bill in American history," levied a 94 percent tax on the highest incomes; the President had suggested that no one should net more than $25,000 per year during the war. Also, for the first time, the income tax fell upon those in lower-income brackets. To simplify payment for these new millions, Congress enacted a withholding system of payroll deductions in 1943. Corporation taxes reached a maximum of 40 percent on the largest incomes. In addition, excess profits were subject to a 90 percent tax, reclaiming for the government a large part of the return from war contracts. However, these taxes could be rebated to companies to aid them in reconversion (changing back to peacetime production), a provision of future significance. In effect, the government taxed away a large part of the profits of corporations, then returned it later when it was needed. Heavy excise taxes on transportation, communication, luxuries, and amusements completed the levies.

Between 1941 and 1945, the government raised $138 billion through taxation —nearly $100 billion of it from income and excess profits taxes. Those in the top 5 percent of the income scale suffered a serious relative economic loss, as their share of disposable income dropped from 26 percent in 1940 to 16 percent in 1944. Few persons or corporations were able to make fortunes out of the war, and a considerable amount of economic leveling—upward more than downward—did take place. Despite the heavy taxation, by the end of the war consumers possessed an estimated $129 billion in liquid savings.

From 1941 to 1945, the federal government spent twice as much as the total appropriations from the creation of the government to 1941, and ten times as much as the cost of World War I—a total of $321 billion. The national debt rose from $49 billion in 1941 to $259 billion in 1945, yet the black warnings of national bankruptcy that had punctuated the New Deal years all but disappeared.

POLITICS AND SOCIETY

The greatest effects of the war upon American politics and society were generally indirect ones: the restoration of prosperity and full employment, the redistribution of wealth through greatly increased progressive taxation, and the forcing of women into the workplace to compensate for men inducted into the armed forces. But the war had other effects upon the American people that were both direct and deliberate, as various groups used the conflict to justify active efforts to shape society according to their desires.

Selling the War

Perhaps the most serious such effort was by the government itself, which found itself faced with the task of rallying an entire society behind a war being fought thousands of miles from American shores. After the early fear of a Japanese invasion of California or a German invasion of the East Coast subsided, the government realized that it would need to find new methods for making the public feel involved with the conflict. At the same time, the administration felt the need to prevent the publication or broadcast of information that might damage the war effort. The result was a pair of agencies designed to control the flow of public information.

The first to be established was the Office of Censorship, under the direction of former Associate Press executive Byron Price. From Pearl Harbor on, Price attempted to tread the narrow line between concealing information that might be damaging to the war effort (evidence of troop movements, for example) and suppressing information that simply exposed incompetence or corruption. He faced constant charges of attempting to "manage" the news, and on occasion the charges were justified. On the whole, however, the nation's press remained remarkably free to criticize the administration and reveal the truth about the progress of the war. The real censorship came not from the government but from the press itself. War correspondents came to think of themselves almost as members of the military and tended not to disclose discouraging or embarrassing information. Publishers and editors, fearful of public outrage, similarly suppressed material that might sound pessimistic or denigrating.

The second agency controlling the flow of information was established in June 1942: the Office of War Information (OWI), under the direction of a well-known radio commentator, Elmer Davis. Both at home and overseas, the OWI was, in fact, the official propaganda ministry of the United States, proselytizing on behalf of the war. The domestic branch of the agency attempted to persuade Americans that they were fighting not only for a just but for a prosperous future. Official publications, films, and radio broadcasts stressed not only the "four freedoms" (freedom of speech and worship, freedom from want and fear) that the President had enunciated in 1941 but a glittering vision of postwar society. Americans were encouraged to look ahead to an era in which every man would sit behind the wheel of a new, chromium-trimmed automobile and every woman would stand enthroned in a gleaming kitchen filled with modern appliances. Only the successful completion of the war, the government implied, stood in the way of this shining future. With the encouragement of the OWI, private businesses filled the magazines, newspapers, and airwaves with advertisements to arouse public enthusiasm for the war and for the bounties victory would bring. Private enterprise spent more than a billion dollars on such promotion in the first years of the war.

But the OWI also engaged in other types of propaganda that aroused greater controversy. Workers in the OWI's domestic branch often fought bitterly among themselves about what the agency should be promoting. At one point, there was a mass resignation of pamphlet writers because conservatives within the agency managed to block publication of several tracts: one opposing inflation, one on blacks and the war, and one intended to be a "tax primer." Republicans in Congress expressed misgivings about what they considered partisan propaganda emanating from the agency. They cited, for example, a cartoon biography of Franklin Roosevelt (prepared for overseas distribution) and warned that Davis might be preparing to use the agency to promote the President's reelection. In 1943, Congress cut funds for the domestic branch so drastically that it had to stop producing propaganda. But other war agencies expanded their output proportionately, continuing to flood the public with arguments explaining the need for rationing, the importance of economizing, and the value of hard work.

A particularly important propaganda tool was the war bond drives. Although the drives served a legitimate economic purpose—raising money for the war and dampening inflation—they served an important social goal as well. They gave the ordinary citizen, who might have had trouble identifying with a war in which he or she was not directly involved, a way to play a part in the struggle. The government reaped only a modest financial reward from its efforts to induce citizens of modest means to invest small sums in low-denomination bonds or "war stamps." It did, however, reap the benefit of increased public involvement with the war.

Overseas, the OWI projected an idealistic view of American war aims and of the nation's aspirations for a peaceful postwar world. Through Voice of America broadcasts, begun in 1941, and through other programs employing 8,400 people by 1945, the agency made Roosevelt himself an international symbol of these ideals. By the end of the war, the President was more of a hero overseas than he was at home. To the world at large, the OWI presented an image of a nation fighting only for ideals. To Americans at home, that image vied with an equally alluring promise of future prosperity. Still, Americans did emerge from World War II far more committed to the idea of international efforts to preserve the peace than they had from World War I.

The Retreat from Reform

Late in 1943, Franklin Roosevelt publicly suggested that "Dr. New Deal," as he called it, had served its purpose and should now give way to "Dr. Win-the-War." The statement reflected the President's own genuine shift in concern: that victory was now more important than reform. But it reflected, too, the political reality that had emerged during the first two years of war. Liberals in government were finding themselves increasingly unable to enact new programs. They were even finding it difficult to protect existing ones from conservative assault.

Many liberals had expected the war to be an opportunity for progressive national planning, for finally reforming the economy along the lines they had long advocated. They were sorely disappointed. The managers of the wartime economy were not reformers but corporate businessmen. William Knudsen and Donald Nelson had both been recruited from major corporations. Other administrators of wartime economic controls came largely from businesses or from conservative

Wall Street law firms. Washington was flooded with so-called dollar-a-year men
—administrators wealthy enough to work in the war agencies for no salary—and
it was they who supervised many of the programs in which reformers had once
placed such great hopes.

Unsurprisingly, perhaps, economic agencies dominated by men from the corporate world tended to favor that world when distributing contracts. An overwhelming proportion of the orders for armaments and other government purchases went
to large corporations, rather than to the many smaller firms vying for a share of
the bounty. There were sporadic efforts to reverse the trend. In 1942, the Murray-
Patman Act created a Smaller War Plants Corporation within the WPB, whose
purpose was to spread government business more widely. In the end, however, it
had little effect. For two years, it suffered from weak and half-hearted administration. Then, beginning in 1944, it came under the control of Maury Maverick, a
dynamic New Deal Congressman from Texas. Maverick tried hard to force the
letting of contracts to smaller plants and, as attention began to turn to reconversion, to win favored treatment for small businesses in the return to civilian
production. Opposition from conservatives in the war agencies and even more
from the military, which had little faith in the ability of small companies to
perform needed tasks, frustrated his goals. He managed to win the support of
Donald Nelson; but in the end both Maverick and Nelson were forced to resign.

Much the same thing happened to efforts within the government to curb the
growth of the great corporations through antitrust efforts. In the last years before
the war, the head of the antitrust division of the Justice Department, Thurman
Arnold, had launched a major campaign against economic concentration. During
the war, he received continuing support from reformers in Congress and from
many of the findings of the Truman Committee. Nevertheless, Arnold found
himself by the end of 1942 with virtually no power to pursue antitrust activity.
His support from within the administration had all but vanished. Increasingly it
became clear that the corporations he was investigating were ones with which the
government was doing war business and whose cooperation the military considered essential (du Pont, Standard Oil, and others). Secretary of War Stimson
began calling him a "self-seeking fanatic" whose efforts were frightening business
and "making a very great deterrent effect upon our munitions production." Finally, in 1943, the President removed Arnold from office. And although shortly
before the end of the war he appointed another activist to head the antitrust
division, it was clear that any hope for a major government assault upon economic
concentration remained dim.

The greatest assault upon liberal reform, however, came not from within the
administration but from Congress. The war provided conservatives there with the
excuse for which they had been waiting to dismantle many of the achievements
of the New Deal, which they had always mistrusted. By the end of 1943, Congress
had eliminated the Civilian Conservation Corps, the National Youth Administration, and the Works Progress Administration. With budget deficits mounting
because of war costs, liberals made no headway in their efforts to increase social
security benefits and otherwise extend social welfare programs. Congress cut back

substantially upon the one agency committed to helping perhaps the most distressed sector of the economy: poor farmers. The Farm Security Administration was soon virtually impotent.

Even had Roosevelt had the inclination to resist this conservative trend, his awareness of political realities would have been enough to stop him from trying very hard. In the congressional elections of 1942, Republicans gained 47 seats in the House and 10 in the Senate. Within both parties, it was clear, the trend was to the right. Increasingly, the President quietly accepted the defeat or erosion of New Deal measures in order to win support for his war policies and peace plans. He also accepted the changes, however, because he realized that his chances for reelection in 1944 depended upon his ability to identify himself less with domestic issues than with world peace.

The Fourth Term

Republicans approached the 1944 election determined to exploit what they believed was a smoldering national resentment of wartime regimentation and privation and a general unhappiness with the pattern of Democratic reform. They also hoped to play upon concerns about the deteriorating health of the President; and they nominated as their candidate the young and vigorous Governor of New York, Thomas E. Dewey. Roosevelt faced no opposition for the Democratic nomination for President; but because he was so visibly in poor health, there was great pressure upon him to abandon Vice President Henry Wallace, an advanced New Dealer and hero of the CIO, and replace him with a more moderate figure, acceptable to conservative party bosses and southern Democrats. Roosevelt reluctantly succumbed to the pressure. He refused to select the candidate most favored by party conservatives, James M. Byrnes of South Carolina, who had been a central figure in the administration for two years. But he did finally replace Wallace on the ticket with Senator Harry S Truman of Missouri, whose work as chairman of the Senate War Investigating Committee had won him national attention.

Republican and Democratic leaders agreed in advance that the conduct of the war and the plans for the peace would not be an issue in the campaign. The two parties adopted almost identical planks on those issues in their platforms. Instead, the campaign revolved around domestic economic issues and, indirectly, the President's health. Public doubts about his capacity to campaign seemed to provide a shot of adrenalin to Roosevelt. At the end of September, he addressed a raucously appreciative audience of members of the Teamsters Union and was at his sardonic best. He followed this triumph with strenuous campaign appearances in Chicago and with a day-long drive in an open car through New York City in a soaking rain.

Roosevelt's apparent capacity to serve four more years, his international leadership, and his promise to workers to revive the New Deal after the war combined to ensure him a substantial victory. He captured 53.5 percent of the popular vote to Dewey's 46 percent; and he won 432 electoral votes to Dewey's 99. Democrats lost 1 seat in the Senate, gained 20 in the House, and maintained control of both.

THOMAS E. DEWEY. The 1944 Republican candidate appears uncharacteristically relaxed and informal inspecting a tank during his unsuccessful campaign for the presidency. In general, Dewey conveyed a rather frosty public image, prompting Alice Roosevelt Longworth to remark of him once that he looked like "the man on the wedding cake." (*National Archives*)

Blacks and the War

It was not only labor unions, mounting deficits, and economic regimentation that aroused conservative ire during the war. It was a growing fear that American blacks would use the conflict to challenge the system of segregation. The fears were well justified, for black leaders approached World War II with a newly militant outlook.

During World War I, many American blacks had eagerly seized the chance to serve in the armed forces, believing that their patriotic efforts would win them an enhanced position in postwar society. They had been cruelly disappointed. As World War II approached, blacks were again determined to use the conflict to improve the position of their race—this time, however, not by currying favor but by making demands. In the summer of 1941, with preparedness efforts at their height, A. Philip Randolph, president of the Brotherhood of Sleeping Car Porters, a black union, began to insist that the government require those companies receiving defense contracts to integrate their work forces. To mobilize support for the demand, Randolph planned a massive march on Washington, which threatened to bring more than 100,000 protesting blacks into the capital. Roosevelt, fearful of both the possibility of violence and the certainty of political embarrassment, finally persuaded Randolph to cancel the march in return for a promise to establish a Fair Employment Practices Commission. Its purpose was to investigate discrimination against blacks in war industries; and although its enforcement powers, and thus its effectiveness, were limited, it did mark an important step toward a government commitment to racial equality.

The economic realities of the war years greatly increased the migration of blacks from the rural areas of the South into the industrial cities, where there were suddenly factory jobs available in war plants. Five million farmers, many of them black, moved within the South during the war, and another 1.6 million left the region entirely. In the South, the migration produced white resentment and suspicion, including the false rumor among white homeowners that blacks were engaged in a conspiracy to deprive the region of domestic servants. Whites pointed to the purported existence of "Eleanor Clubs," named after Eleanor Roosevelt, a champion of racial justice. The alleged purpose of the clubs (which in fact did not even exist) was to "get a white woman in every kitchen in 1943." In the North, the migration produced much more severe tensions. In Detroit in 1943, a violent race riot erupted when black families began moving into a new housing project near a Polish neighborhood. Thirty-four people died in the rioting, twenty-five of them blacks.

Despite such tensions, the leading black organizations redoubled their efforts during the war to challenge the system of segregation. The Congress of Racial Equality (CORE), organized in 1942 by Randolph, mobilized mass popular resistance to discrimination in a way that the older, more conservative organizations had never done. Randolph, Bayard Rustin, James Farmer, and other, younger black leaders helped organize sit-ins and demonstrations in theaters and restaurants. In 1944, they won a much-publicized victory by forcing a Washington, D.C., restaurant to agree to serve blacks. In other areas, their victories were few. Nevertheless, the war years aroused a defiant public spirit among many blacks that would survive into the 1950s and help produce the civil-rights movement.

Racial agitation was most pronounced in civilian institutions, but the winds of change were blowing within the military as well. At first, the armed forces main-

WELDERS. This Ben Shahn poster was rejected by the Office of War Information, perhaps because of its racial message. It was, however, widely used by the CIO political action committee in its effort to elevate the position of workers during the war. (*Museum of Modern Art*)

tained their traditional practice of limiting blacks to the most menial assignments, keeping them in segregated training camps and units, and barring them entirely from the Marine Corps and the army air force. Gradually, however, military leaders were forced to make adjustments—in part because of public and political pressures, but largely because they recognized that these forms of segregation were wasting manpower. By the end of the war, the number of black servicemen had increased sevenfold, to 700,000; training camps were being integrated, blacks were being allowed to serve on ships with white sailors, and more black units were being sent into combat. But tensions remained. In some of the integrated army bases —Fort Dix, New Jersey, for example—riots occasionally broke out when blacks protested having to serve in segregated divisions. Substantial discrimination survived in all the services until well after the war. But within the military, as within the society at large, the traditional pattern of race relations was slowly but substantially eroding. Not the least of the reasons was the obvious disparity between America's racial practices and the ideals of freedom and brotherhood it was attempting to project to the world. "It must be remembered," Walter White, a black journalist, wrote during the war, "that our failures of omission and commission are being watched by other colored peoples, who constitute a majority of the peoples of the earth."

The Internment of the Japanese-Americans

World War I had produced in America a virtual orgy of hatred, vindictiveness, and hysteria, as well as widespread and flagrant violations of civil liberties. World War II did not. A few papers, among them Father Coughlin's *Social Justice*, were barred from the mails as seditious; but there was no general censorship of dissident publications. A few Nazi agents and American fascists were jailed; but there was no major assault upon those suspected of sympathizing with the Axis. Indeed, the most ambitious effort to punish domestic fascists, a sedition trial of twenty-eight people, ended in a mistrial, and the defendants went free. Unlike World War I, socialists and communists (who generally supported the war effort) were left unpunished and unpersecuted.

Nor was there much of the ethnic or cultural animosity that had characterized World War I. Americans continued to eat sauerkraut without calling it "liberty cabbage." They continued to listen to German and Italian music. They displayed little hostility toward German- and Italian-Americans. Instead, they seemed to share the view of government propaganda that the enemy was less the German and Italian people than the vicious political systems to which they had been subjected.

But there was a glaring exception to the general rule of tolerance: the treatment of the small, politically powerless group of Japanese-Americans. From the beginning, Americans adopted a different attitude toward the Japanese enemy than they did toward their European foes. They attributed to the Japanese people certain racial and cultural characteristics that made it easier to hold them in contempt. Popular portrayals of the "Japs," as they were routinely labeled, stressed unattractive racial characteristics: a leering grin; narrow, slitted eyes; sallow, yellow skin. The Japanese, both government and private propaganda encouraged Americans to believe, were a devious, malign, and cruel people. They had, after all, launched an infamous attack upon Pearl Harbor without warning. (The Japanese were carefully distinguished in all this from America's allies, the Chinese, who were generally portrayed as calm, wise, and tolerant.)

It should not have been surprising, therefore, that this racial animosity soon extended to Americans of Japanese descent. There were not many Japanese-Americans in the United States—only about 127,000 (not counting those in Hawaii), most of them concentrated in a few areas in California. And because they generally kept to themselves and preserved traditional Japanese cultural patterns, it was easy for their neighbors to imagine that they were engaged in conspiracies on behalf of their ancestral homeland. Wild stories circulated about sabotage at Pearl Harbor and plots to aid a Japanese landing on the coast of California—all later shown to be entirely without foundation. Public pressure to remove the threat grew steadily. Wrote one newspaper columnist in California at the time: "Herd 'em up, pack 'em off . . . let 'em be pinched, hurt, hungry, and dead up against it. I hate the Japanese." Said an army general on the West Coast: "A Jap's a Jap. . . . It makes no difference whether he is an American citizen or not."

Finally, in February 1942, the President authorized the army to "intern" the Japanese-Americans. More than 100,000 people, two-thirds of them American citizens, were rounded up, told to dispose of their property however they could (which often meant simply abandoning it), and taken to what the government euphemistically termed "relocation centers" in the "interior." In fact, they were facilities little different from prisons, many of them located in the desert. Conditions in the internment camps were not, for the most part, inhumane. Neither, however, were they especially comfortable. More important, a large group of loyal, hard-working American citizens were forced to spend up to three years in grim, debilitating isolation, barred from lucrative employment, provided with only minimal medical care, and deprived of decent schools for their children. The Supreme Court upheld the evacuation in a 1944 decision; and although most of the Japanese-Americans were released later that year (after the reelection of the President), they were unable to win any compensation for their losses. In time of war, no price seemed too great to pay to win security from the Axis. Infringements upon personal freedoms and civil liberties were, apparently, part of the bill.

Yet the experience of the Japanese-Americans was notable not only because it represented an indefensible violation of civil rights. It was notable too because it stood in such sharp contrast to the experience of the majority of Americans during the war. In the midst of the greatest military conflict in the history of the world, the American people were, to a remarkable extent, able to live as they had always lived—indeed, in many cases to live much better than before. They enjoyed a remarkable level of personal freedom for a people engaged in a "total war." They suffered strikingly few material privations. The ability of the American economy and of American society to absorb the strains of World War II without serious suffering or distortion was a clear augury of the remarkable era of growth and abundance that would follow.

EN ROUTE TO THE CAMPS. Japanese-Americans prepare to load
their belongings for the trip to government internment camps in 1942.
American fear and resentment of the Nisei was in part a result of genuine
concern (however unjustified) about sabotage and espionage. But it was also
a result of cultural and racial animosity and, perhaps, jealousy of the striking
economic success of the Japanese community in California. (*National
Archives*)

SUGGESTED READINGS

General studies of the effects of the war upon American society include John Morton
Blum, *V Was for Victory* (1976), and Richard Polenberg, *War and Society* (1972). For
the story of the war production effort specifically, see Donald Nelson, *Arsenal of
Democracy* (1946), the WPB director's personal memoirs; Bruce Catton, *War Lords
of Washington* (1946); and Eliot Janeway, *Struggle for Survival* (1951). Joel Seidman,
American Labor From Defense to Reconversion (1953), examines the experience of
workers. Leslie R. Groves, *Now It Can Be Told* (1962), is an account of the development of the atomic bomb by the general who commanded the Manhattan Project;
Oscar E. Anderson, Jr., *The New World* (1962), is another valuable study of the

subject. Chester Bowles, *Promises to Keep* (1971), and Lester V. Chandler, *Inflation in the United States, 1940–1948* (1951), are studies of price controls. Alan Winkler, *The Politics of Propaganda* (1978), and Philip Knightley, *The First Casualty* (1975), examine the effects of war upon the press and vice versa.

James MacGregor Burns, *Roosevelt: The Soldier of Freedom* (1970), includes information about domestic politics and the 1944 election. Ellsworth Barnard, *Wendell Willkie* (1966), sheds light on the activities of the Republicans during the war. For wartime civil-rights activities, see Louis Ruchames, *Race, Jobs, and Politics* (1953), a study of the establishment of the FEPC; Neil Wynn, *The Afro-American and the Second World War* (1975); and Herbert Garfinkel, *When Negroes March* (1959). Richard M. Dalfiume, *Desegregation of the U.S. Armed Forces* (1969), examines the racial situation within the military; and August Meier and Elliott Rudwick, *CORE* (1973), studies the emergence of an important civil-rights organization. Roger Daniels, *Concentration Camps, USA* (1971); Audrie Girdner and Anne Loftis, *The Great Betrayal* (1969); and Bill Hosokawa, *Nisei* (1969), study the internment of Japanese-Americans.

Seventeen

Fighting a Global War

Whatever political disagreements and social tensions the war may have produced among the American people, there was from the beginning a remarkable unity of opinion about the conflict itself, "a unity," as one member of Congress proclaimed shortly after Pearl Harbor, "never before witnessed in this country." A few die-hard isolationists might continue to claim that the President had provoked the Japanese into attacking Hawaii so as to "trick" the nation into entering the war. The vast majority, however, accepted not only the justice of the American cause, but the necessity of the United States assuming an irrevocable position of leadership among the world's nations.

That unity and confidence were severely tested in the first, troubled months of 1942. For despite the impressive display of patriotism and the dramatic flurry of activity, the war was going very badly. Britain appeared ready to collapse. The Soviet Union was staggering before the German onslaught. One after another, Allied strongholds in the Pacific were falling to the forces of Japan. American power was capable of turning the tide, most people believed. But no one could be sure whether that power could be mobilized and dispatched in time.

Slowly, however, the full might of American factories and American armies made their presence felt in both the European and Pacific theaters. By 1944, it had become clear that the momentum had shifted, that Allied forces were gradually but steadily breaking down the Axis resistance and heading toward final victory.

324

ON THE DEFENSIVE

It was not only in the production of armaments and the recruitment of troops that America was unprepared for war in December 1941. It was in the planning and organization of the military effort itself. The first months of 1942, therefore, witnessed a series of important decisions about basic policy and strategy.

Organizing the Military

Neither the army nor the navy was particularly well prepared for combat in December 1941, as the fiasco at Pearl Harbor seemed clearly to illustrate. The navy possessed only 300 ships, many of them in need of repair. The army, even after two years of rapid expansion, had enlisted only slightly more than a million men. The army air force, in practice but not in name a virtually independent branch of the service, had only about 200,000 officers and men and only a few thousand aircraft. These were impressive totals in comparison with peacetime levels, but they were only a small proportion of what would be needed for the task ahead. By the end of the war, the army would consist of more than 10 million men; the navy would possess 1,167 ships (all but a few of them built after 1941) and over 3 million sailors; and the army air force would have expanded to over 2 million men.

These vast increases in personnel and equipment forced rapid changes in planning and organization. General George C. Marshall, Chief of Staff of the army, reorganized the army high command in March 1942. That same month, Admiral Ernest J. King, a clear-headed hard driver, became Chief of Naval Operations. Together with General H. H. Arnold of the army air force, these men met with a personal representative of the President, Admiral William D. Leahy, to constitute the Joint Chiefs of Staff. They functioned as the overall command and represented the United States in combined planning with the British or occasional negotiations with the Russians.

Over the Joint Chiefs of Staff was the commander in chief, President Roosevelt, who bore ultimate responsibility for the conduct of the war. Personally, and through such assistants as Harry Hopkins and various cabinet members, he coordinated the war planning of the Joint Chiefs with war production and manpower and with foreign policy. The war plans division of the Army General Staff had pointed out that civilians should decide the "what" of national policies and the professional soldiers the "how." Roosevelt, who had always zealously guarded civilian control even in the Navy Department and the War Department, followed this course throughout the war. He depended heavily upon the advice of the Joint Chiefs of Staff and, once major policy had been decided, seldom interfered with their strategy.

Charting Policy

The President and his policymakers had reached their first major strategic decision more than a year before Pearl Harbor. If the United States were to become embroiled in a war on two fronts, the nation's first goal would be the defeat of Germany, whose superior military force, war production, and weapons development made it the more dangerous foe. The United States confirmed this priority in its initial wartime conferences with the British at the end of December 1941.

That decision did not mean ignoring the Pacific. The war against Japan, unlike the war in Europe, was to be an almost exclusively American operation; and the President was not willing to neglect the effort altogether. As early as August 1941, when the American military build-up was well under way, there was an assumption that there would be fighting on two fronts simultaneously. The President confirmed that assumption after Pearl Harbor by ordering General Douglas MacArthur to lead the American struggle in the Pacific. Nevertheless, there remained for several years a crucial difference between the nation's European and Pacific strategies. The war against Germany was to be offensive. That against Japan was, in the beginning at least, to be primarily defensive.

It was difficult to hold to this policy as the Japanese tide in the Pacific swelled far beyond the bounds that even the most pessimistic planners had anticipated. For Roosevelt, furious over the Japanese treachery at Pearl Harbor, and for the navy, primarily responsible for the Pacific war, it was a particularly hard decision to maintain. General MacArthur, the panic-stricken public on the Pacific coast, and most Americans elsewhere were clamoring for prompt and stern action against the Japanese. But despite these pressures, the administration continued to make the European theater its first priority.

During these first chaotic months of shocking reverses, the armed forces allotted their men and supplies piecemeal to try to meet each new Axis threat. Top strategists, however, emphatically warned that such dissipation of effort might lead to defeat. No one was more insistent than Dwight D. Eisenhower, who had been brought to Washington after Pearl Harbor as a Far Eastern expert and who by the spring of 1942 was head of the operations planning division under General Marshall. In emphatic memoranda Eisenhower hammered away at the need to build up men and supplies in Europe for the invasion of North Africa that Roosevelt and Churchill had decided upon in their December 1941 meeting. Because of his vigor and his important role in developing an invasion plan, Eisenhower became the logical man to send to Britain (in June 1942) as commanding general in the European theater.

The Bleak Months

While the United States was building and equipping its fighting forces, it had to depend upon the Russians and the British to hold off the Germans as best they could. During the discouraging first six months of American participation, the American forces had to stand perilously on the defensive in both the Atlantic and the Pacific. There even seemed to be danger of a breakthrough in Egypt and the Caucasus that might enable the Germans and the Japanese to join forces in the Middle East or India.

Ten hours after the strike at Pearl Harbor, Japanese airplanes hit the American airfields at Manila, destroying half the bombers and two-thirds of the fighter planes. That same day, the Japanese sank two British ships off Malaya, the only Allied warships remaining in the Far East. Three days later Guam fell; then, in the weeks that followed, Wake Island and Hong Kong. The great British fortress of Singapore in Malaya surrendered in February 1942, the Dutch East Indies in March, and Burma in April. In the Philippines on May 6 the exhausted Filipino and American troops, having made brave withdrawals to the Bataan peninsula and the island of Corregidor in Manila Bay, ran down the last American flag in the Far East.

Only one weak outpost, Port Moresby in southern New Guinea, stood as a bulwark against the invasion of Australia. It too seemed likely to fall; but the containment of the Japanese finally began there through the efforts, on land, of Australian and American troops and, on the sea, of American aircraft carriers. In the Battle of the Coral Sea on May 6–7, 1942, the American navy turned back Japanese invasion forces threatening Port Moresby. Under General MacArthur,

MIDWAY, 1942. Japanese airplanes attack the U.S. carrier *Yorktown* during the Battle of Midway, June 1942. Midway was a turning point in the Pacific war, halting Japanese expansion and setting the stage for the American counteroffensives of the following years. (*Official U.S. Navy photo*)

who had escaped from the Philippines, American and Australian army troops began clearing the Japanese from New Guinea.

After the Battle of the Coral Sea, the navy, having intercepted Japanese messages, knew Japan's next move and rushed every available plane and vessel into the central Pacific. Near Midway Island, June 3–6, 1942, these forces inflicted heavy damage on a Japanese invasion fleet and headed off a drive to capture the island and neutralize Hawaii. The United States had achieved its goal of containment in the Pacific, and as men and supplies could be spared from the operations against the Nazis, it could assume the offensive against Japan.

In the Atlantic during the early months of 1942, the Nazis tried by means of submarines to confine the Americans to the Western Hemisphere. By mid-January the Germans had moved so many submarines to the Atlantic coast, where at night they torpedoed tankers silhouetted against the lights of cities, that they created a critical oil shortage. Against convoys bound for Europe they made attacks with devastating success. In the first eleven months they sank over 8 million tons of shipping—1.2 million tons more than the Allies had meanwhile built—and threatened to delay indefinitely the large-scale shipment of supplies and men to Europe. Gradually, the United States countered by developing effective antisubmarine vessels, air patrols, detecting devices, and weapons.

The submarines made it difficult to send assistance to the British and Russians in the summer of 1942, when they needed it most. The German Afrika Korps raced to El Alamein, only seventy-five miles from Alexandria, Egypt, threatening the Suez Canal and the Middle East. At the same time, German armies in Russia were plunging toward the Caucasus. In May the Russian Foreign Minister, Vyacheslav Molotov, visited Washington to demand an immediate second front that would divert at least forty German divisions from Russia; the alternative might be Russian collapse. Roosevelt promised to do everything possible to divert the Germans by invading France. But Churchill arrived the next month, when the Germans were threatening Egypt, and he strongly urged an invasion of North Africa instead.

TURNING THE TIDE: EUROPE

There was controversy both at the time and in years after about the wisdom of launching the first Anglo-American offensive in Africa rather than on the European continent. Some critics claimed that Churchill was trying to protect British colonial interests in Africa (and perhaps also to vindicate the ill-fated strategy he had pursued during World War I of attacking Europe from its "soft underbelly" on the Mediterranean). Other, more cynical observers argued that the western Allies were deliberately denying aid to the Soviet Union, refusing to do anything to divert German forces from the eastern front (a charge for which no evidence exists). Still others claimed that the Allies were simply making a mistake, moving cautiously in a peripheral area of the war when they should have been moving forcefully against the main theater.

In fact, Roosevelt agreed to attack North Africa first largely because he did not believe the Allies were yet capable of launching a successful invasion of the Continent. The overwhelming losses of experienced Canadian troops during an unsuccessful raid on Dieppe, France, in August 1942 seemed to confirm the wisdom of making the first American landing on a relatively unprotected German flank. Only later would the Allies finally decide they were prepared for a direct assault upon the Axis forces in Europe.

The Mediterranean Offensive

Through advance negotiations with officials of the Vichy government of defeated France, the Americans hoped to make a bloodless landing in French North Africa. At the end of October 1942, the British opened a counteroffensive at El Alamein that sent the Afrika Korps reeling back. On November 8, Anglo-American forces landed at Oran, Algiers, and Casablanca, Morocco, with some bungling but gratifyingly few losses. They met determined Vichy French resistance only at Casablanca.

Admiral Jean Darlan, earlier one of the most notorious collaborators with the Nazis, signed an armistice with the Allies on November 12. He ordered a cease-fire and promised the aid of 50,000 French colonial troops. Outraged American liberals protested against making a deal with the Vichyites instead of with the French resistance forces under General Charles de Gaulle. The critics quieted somewhat a few weeks later when Darlan was assassinated.

The Germans tried to counter the invasion by ferrying troops from Sicily into Tunisia at the rate of a thousand a day. Early in 1943 the Afrika Korps, which had retreated westward across Tripoli, joined them and threw the full weight of its armor against the green American troops. The Americans lost heavily; but with the aid of the British, they held on to their bases and gained in experience. Allied air power and the British navy so seriously harassed the Axis supply line from Sicily that Germany decided not to make a major stand in Tunisia. From March into May the British army in the east and the armies in the west under Eisenhower gradually closed a vise on the German and Italian troops. On May 12, 1943, the last Axis troops in North Africa surrendered. The Mediterranean had been re-opened, and the Americans had learned lessons that would be useful in the invasion of France.

That invasion, despite the continued clamoring of the Russians, was not to take place immediately. The fighting in Tunisia had tied up too large a part of the Allied combat resources for too long. Nazi submarines were still taking too heavy a toll of the Allies' inadequate shipping. Some of the ships and production had to be diverted to the antisubmarine war and others to the prosecution of the Pacific campaigns. In addition, the planners in London had come to recognize that an enormous build-up was necessary for a successful cross-Channel invasion. Fortunately for the Allies, the tide turned for the Russians also during the winter of 1942–1943, when they successfully held the Germans at Stalingrad in the Ukraine, eliminating an army of 250,000 men.

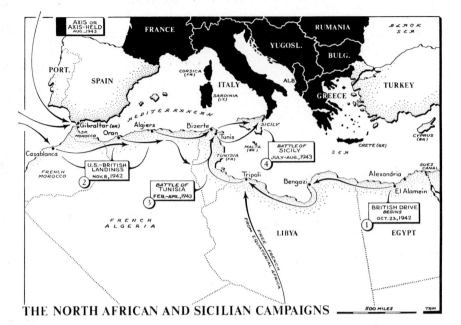

THE NORTH AFRICAN AND SICILIAN CAMPAIGNS ——— 500 MILES

The Invasion of Italy

As early as mid-January 1943, Roosevelt and Churchill and their staffs, while conferring at Casablanca, were looking ahead to their next move after the African invasion. This was to be an invasion of Sicily. General Marshall feared it might delay the invasion of France, but Churchill argued persuasively that the operation in Sicily might knock Italy out of the war and lead the Germans to tie up many divisions in defense of Italy and the Balkans.

On the night of July 9, 1943, American and British armies landed in the extreme southeast of Sicily, where defenses were comparatively light. The Americans made grievous errors, the worst being to shoot down twenty-three planeloads of their own paratroops. Nevertheless, within thirty-eight days, the Allies had conquered the island and were looking toward the Italian mainland. Mussolini now fell from power, to be replaced by the pro-Allied Marshal Pietro Badoglio. At once Badoglio opened complicated negotiations to switch Italy to the side of the Allies. As the negotiations continued, the Nazis moved eight strong divisions into northern Italy, concentrated other troops near Rome, and turned the country into an occupied defense bastion.

A limited but long and punishing campaign opened on the Italian peninsula on September 3, 1943. It started amid great optimism, for that same day the Italian government signed an armistice agreement, and the Allies quickly seized bases and airfields in southern Italy. But the Nazi defenders fought so fiercely from hillside fortifications that by early 1944 they had stopped the slow and deliberately moving Allies at Monte Cassino. When the Allies tried to break behind the line

THE ITALIAN CAMPAIGN

by landing at Anzio, south of Rome, they were almost thrown back into the sea. With relatively few divisions the Nazis were tying down the Allies while concentrating their main effort upon Russia. Finally, in May 1944, the Allies captured Monte Cassino, pressed on from the Anzio beachhead, and on June 4 captured Rome, just before the cross-Channel invasion of France began.

The Liberation of France

In the fall of 1943, Germany was already reeling under incessant blows from the growing Allied air power. Great Britain had begun its mass bombing of German industrial centers in the late spring of 1942 with a thousand-plane night raid on Cologne. In August, the Americans made their first experimental daytime raids on the Continent. Bombing almost around the clock began on a gigantic scale in February 1944. One of the objects of these bombing raids was to draw German fighter planes into battle. By the end of the war, the Americans were flying over 7,000 bombers and 6,000 fighters in Europe, had dropped nearly a million and a half tons of bombs, and had lost nearly 10,000 bombers. British figures were similar. Especially in the last year of the war, the bombing drastically cut German production and impeded transportation. As early as the winter of 1944, it had so seriously demoralized the German people that 77 percent of them already regarded the war as lost.

The bombing attacks, first upon the aviation industry, then upon transportation, did much to clear the way for the invasion in the late spring. By May 1944, the *Luftwaffe* was incapable of beating off the Allied air cover for an invasion. As D-Day (the code name for the date of the Allied landing) approached, the invasion was postponed from the beginning of May until early June, despite the likelihood of worsening weather, in order to obtain an additional month's production of special landing craft. A sudden storm delayed the operation for a day; but on the morning of June 6, 1944, the invasion came—not at the narrowest part of the English Channel, where the Nazis expected it, but along sixty miles of the Cotentin peninsula on the Normandy coast. While airplanes and battleships offshore ceaselessly bombarded the Nazi defenses, 4,000 vessels, stretching as far as the eye could see, brought in troops and supplies.

D-DAY, 1944. A Coast Guard combat photographer took this panoramic shot of the great Allied armada landing on the beaches of Normandy, June 6, 1944. While landing barges ferry troops from the larger ships to the shore, barrage balloons protect the invaders from low-flying enemy aircraft. Long lines of trucks pour off the barges to carry soldiers inland. (*Official U.S. Coast Guard photo*)

Within two weeks after the initial landings, the Allies had put ashore a million men and the equipment for them. They had also captured Cherbourg, only to find that the Germans had blocked its harbor so skillfully that it could not be used until August.

Well into July, the Allies fought mile by mile through the Normandy hedge-rows. The breakthrough came on July 25, 1944, when General Omar Bradley's First Army, using its tanks as cavalry had been used in earlier wars, smashed the German lines in an enormous sweep southward, then eastward. The invasion on the Mediterranean coast, beginning on August 15, quickly seized new ports (until then seriously blocked) and opened new supply lines for the Allies. On August 25 French forces rode into a Paris jammed with cheering throngs. By mid-September the Allied armies had driven the Germans from almost all of France and Belgium, including the port of Antwerp, and had come to a halt against a firm line of German defenses.

Cold weather, rain, and floods aided the Germans briefly. In December they struck with desperate fury along fifty miles of front in the Ardennes Forest, driving fifty-five miles toward Antwerp before they were stopped (in the Battle of the Bulge) at Bastogne. It was the last major battle of the war.

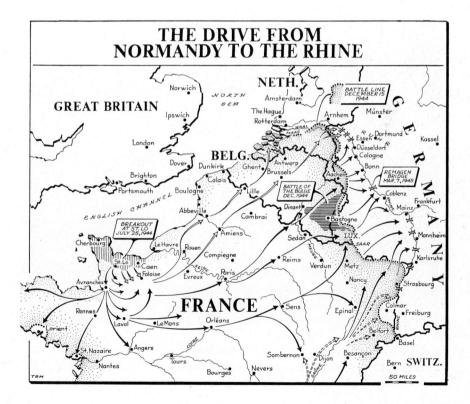

THE DRIVE FROM NORMANDY TO THE RHINE

The Push to Victory

While the Allies were fighting their way through France to the Westwall (German defense line) as well as up the Italian peninsula, the Russians had been sweeping westward into central Europe and the Balkans. The Soviet armies advanced more rapidly than had been expected and, in late January 1945, launched an offensive of over 150 divisions toward the Oder River, far inside Germany.

After liquidating the German thrust into the Ardennes, which had almost exhausted the Nazi fighting capacity, the Allied armies pushed on to the Rhine. The Americans captured Cologne on the west bank on March 6, 1945, and the next day, through remarkable luck, captured a bridge across the Rhine at Remagen. Troops poured across it. By the end of March the last great drives were under way as the British commander, Bernard Law Montgomery, with a million troops pushed across the north while Bradley's army, sweeping through central Germany, completed the encirclement and trapping of 300,000 German soldiers in the Ruhr. Russian troops were about to mount a spring offensive only thirty-five miles from Berlin.

There were fears that the Nazis were preparing for a last stand in an Alpine redoubt centering on Berchtesgaden on the Austrian border. In fact, however, the German western front had been demolished. The only real questions were where

AIR POWER.   A spectacular explosion follows an American air attack on a German ammunition truck. Air support helped speed the Allied push across Europe after the successful Normandy invasion. (*Official U.S. Air Force photo*)

the Americans would drive next and where they would join the Russians. The Americans, capable of moving much farther eastward than had been anticipated, could have beaten the Russians to Berlin and Prague. This would have cost American lives but would have reaped political gain in Europe. General Eisenhower decided, instead, to send American troops to capture the Alpine redoubt and then halt along the Elbe River in central Germany to meet the Russians.

On May 8, 1945, the remaining German forces surrendered unconditionally, and V-E Day arrived amid tremendous celebrations in western Europe and the United States. The rejoicing was tempered only by the knowledge of the continuing war against Japan.

THE WAR IN THE PACIFIC

For nearly a year, the United States, having abandoned most of its possessions in the western Pacific to the Japanese onslaught, engaged in what was essentially a holding action in the Asian war. By late summer 1942, however, American naval forces were beginning offensive operations in the Pacific in an effort to improve their strategic position for later, more direct assaults against the Japanese. Little by little, the war expanded, until the Japanese Empire found itself directly and relentlessly besieged.

The Expanding Offensive

The offensive strategy against the Japanese involved amphibious warfare of a type that the Marine Corps had been developing since the early 1920s. In the Pacific, these new tactics came to be so perfected that troops were able to cross and seize vigorously defended beaches and thus immobilize advanced Japanese strong points when the United States could not by-pass them. At this point the American strategy was, whenever feasible, "Hit 'em where they ain't."

The southern Solomon Islands to the east of New Guinea were being developed as a Japanese base for air raids against American communications with Australia. In August 1942 the navy and the Marines opened an offensive against three of these islands, Gavutu, Tulagi, and Guadalcanal. Around and on Guadalcanal a struggle of unprecedented ferocity developed, as the American and Japanese navies battled for control in a series of large-scale engagements. By the time the struggle was over, the United States and its allies had lost heavily in cruisers, carriers, and destroyers but had sunk forty-seven Japanese vessels. The Japanese navy had lost its offensive strength and thereafter concentrated upon defensive operations.

During the months when the great naval battles had been going against the United States, the Americans had gained control of the air and thus were able to sustain the Marines, and subsequently the army, in their precarious jungle onslaught. By February 1943, Guadalcanal had been won. Through the year, the island hopping continued all around the enormous Japanese-held perimeter: in the South Pacific through the northern Solomons to New Georgia, and in November to Bougainville; in the central Pacific, also in November, the Marine landing on

Makin and the bloody assault on Tarawa in the Gilberts; in the northern Pacific, the inexpert reconquest of Kiska and Attu in the Aleutians.

Victories in the Marshall Islands in February 1944 cracked the Japanese outer perimeter, and before the month was out the navy had plunged far within it to wreck the bastion at Truk and raid Saipan in the Mariana Islands. American submarines were increasingly harassing Japanese shipping, and thus hampering that country's economy. In 1943 the Americans had sunk 284 ships; in 1944 they sank 492—necessitating by summer a cut of nearly a quarter in skimpy Japanese food rations and creating a crucial gasoline shortage. The inner empire of Japan was coming under relentless siege.

Meanwhile, in 1942, the Japanese forced General Joseph H. Stilwell out of Burma and brought their troops as far west as the mountains bordering on India. China was so isolated that the United States could send in meager supplies only through an aerial ferry over the "hump" of the Himalayas. On the return trip, the planes brought Chinese troops for Stilwell to train and arm. Through 1943, Stilwell with Chinese, Indian, and a few American troops fought back through northern Burma, constructing a road and parallel pipeline across the rugged mountains into Yunnan province, China. The Ledo Road—also known as the Stilwell Road—was not open until the fall of 1944, but meanwhile the Air Transport Command managed to fly in sufficient supplies to enable the Fourteenth Air Force (before Pearl Harbor, the "Flying Tigers") to harass the Japanese. The command undertook a still larger task when B-29 bombers struck the Yawata steel mills in Japan from Chinese bases (June 1944). The Japanese retaliated in the next few months by overrunning the bases from which the bombers operated and clearing the coastal area so that they could bring supplies northward from Southeast Asia by rail or road. They drove so far into the interior that they threatened the Chinese terminus of the Ledo Road, and perhaps even the center of government at Chungking.

The great Japanese offensive precipitated a long-simmering crisis in Chinese–American affairs, centering upon the relations between General Stilwell and Chiang Kai-shek. Stilwell was indignant because Chiang was using many of his troops to maintain an armed frontier against the Chinese communists and would not deploy them against the Japanese. What was more, Chiang was clamoring for even more American aid for his battle against the communists. Had the United States provided what he needed, the campaigns against Germany and directly against Japan would probably have been slowed down or postponed.

During 1944, Japan came under heavy blockade from the sea and bombardment from the air. American submarines firing torpedoes and laying mines continued to make heavy inroads on the dwindling Japanese merchant marine.

In mid-June, an enormous American armada struck the heavily fortified Mariana Islands, quickly but expensively capturing Tinian, Guam, and Saipan, 1,350 miles from Tokyo. These were among the bloodiest operations of the war. In September, the Americans landed on the western Carolines. The way was being prepared for the return to the Philippines. For weeks in advance, navy craft swept the central Pacific, and airplanes ranged over the Philippines and Formosa. Fi-

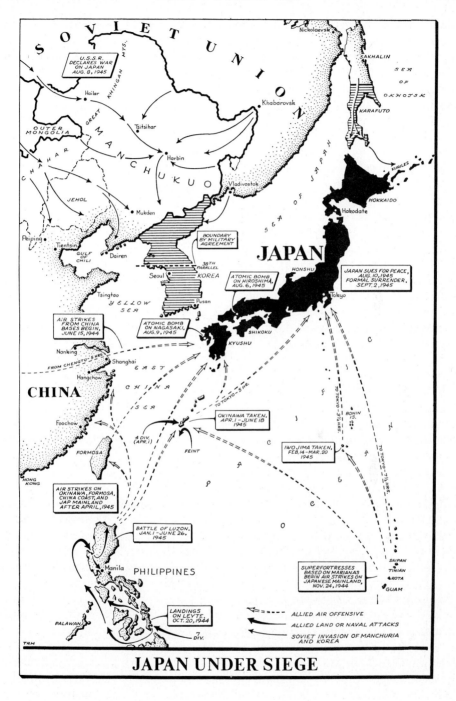

JAPAN UNDER SIEGE

nally, on October 20, General MacArthur's troops landed on Leyte Island in the Philippines. The Japanese, threatened with being fatally cut off from their new empire in Southeast Asia, threw their remaining fleets against the invaders in three major encounters—together comprising the decisive Battle of Leyte Gulf, the largest naval engagement in history—and lost almost all their remaining sea power.

The Final Victory

With remarkable speed but grievous losses, the American forces cut still deeper into the Japanese Empire during the early months of 1945. While fighting continued in the Philippines, the Marines landed in February on the tiny volcanic island of Iwo Jima, only 750 miles from Tokyo. The Americans needed Iwo Jima to provide fighter cover for Japan-bound bombers and a landing place for crippled ones. The Japanese defended the island so grimly that the Marines suffered over 20,000 casualties. It was the bloodiest battle in the history of the Marine Corps.

The battle for Okinawa, an island sixty-five miles long, beginning on April 1, 1945, was even bloodier. This island lies 370 miles south of Japan, and its conquest clearly would be a prelude to an invasion of the main islands. On land and from the air, the Japanese fought with a desperate fury. Week after week they sent Kamikaze suicide planes against the American and British ships, sacrificing 3,500 of them but inflicting great damage. Ashore at night, Japanese troops launched equally desperate attacks on the American lines. The United States and its allies suffered nearly 50,000 casualties on land and at sea before the battle came to an end in late June 1945. The Japanese lost 110,000 killed and 7,800 taken prisoner.

The same kind of bitter fighting seemed to await the Americans when they invaded Japan. But there were signs early in 1945 that such an invasion might not be necessary. The Japanese by now had almost no ships or airplanes with which to fight; and when American forces challenged them, there was little resistance. In July 1945, for example, American warships stood off the shore of Japan and shelled industrial targets (many already in ruins from aerial bombings) with impunity. Moderate Japanese leaders, who had long since decided that the war was lost, were in the meantime increasing their power within the government. After the invasion of Okinawa, Emperor Hirohito appointed a new Premier and gave him instructions to sue for peace. Although the new leader could not persuade military leaders to give up the fight, he did try, along with the Emperor himself, to obtain mediation through the Soviet Union.

The Russians showed little interest in playing the role of arbitrator, perhaps because they had already decided to enter the Pacific war themselves as soon as the fighting in Europe concluded. In any case, other developments intervened to make their participation, either as peacemaker or as warrior, superfluous. At a meeting of Allied leaders in Potsdam, Germany, in mid-July 1945, President Harry S Truman (who had succeeded to the office upon the death of Franklin Roosevelt three months earlier) received word that the first test of an atomic weapon had been successful. In response, he issued an ultimatum to the Japanese (signed jointly by the British) demanding that they surrender immediately or face utter devastation. The deadline was August 3. The Japanese Premier wished to accept the Allied demand, but by the time the deadline arrived he had not yet been able to persuade the military leaders to surrender. With that, Truman ordered the air force to drop an atomic bomb on one of four previously selected Japanese cities.

Controversy has raged for decades over whether Truman's decision was justified and what his motives were for agreeing to use the weapon. Some people have argued that the atomic attack was unnecessary, that had the United States waited only a few more weeks the Japanese would have surrendered without it. Others, including many of the scientists involved in the Manhattan Project, have argued that whatever Japanese intentions, the United States, as a matter of moral conviction, should not have used the terrible new weapon. One horrified physicist wrote the President shortly before the attack: "This thing must not be permitted to exist on this earth. We must not be the most hated and feared people in the world." The nation's leaders, however, showed little concern about such matters. Truman, through no fault of his own, had not even been aware of the bomb's existence until a few weeks before he was called upon to decide whether to use it. And knowing so little about it, he could hardly have been expected to recognize the full implications of its power. He was, apparently, making what he believed to be a simple military decision. A weapon was available that would end the war quickly; he could see no reason not to use it.

Still more controversy has existed over whether there were other motives at work in Truman's decision as well. With the Soviet Union poised to enter the war in the Pacific, did the United States want to end the conflict quickly to forestall an expanded communist presence in Asia? Did Truman use the bomb as a weapon to intimidate Stalin, with whom he was engaged in difficult negotiations, so the Soviet leader would accept American demands? Little direct evidence is available to support either of these accusations, but historians continue to disagree on the issue.

Whatever the reasons, the decision was made. On August 6, 1945, an American B-29, the *Enola Gay,* dropped an atomic weapon on the Japanese industrial city of Hiroshima. With a single bomb, the United States succeeded in destroying most of the hitherto undamaged city. Thousands of civilians died—80,000 according to American estimates, 200,000 according to the Japanese. Many more survived to suffer the painful and crippling effects of radioactive fallout and to pass those effects on to their children in the form of serious birth defects.

Even after the horror of Hiroshima, the Japanese army refused to accept defeat. On August 9, Russia declared war on Japan. And on that same day, another American plane dropped another atomic weapon—this time on the city of Nagasaki—inflicting horrible damage upon yet another unfortunate community. Finally, the Japanese relented. Some military leaders still resisted surrender; but after personal intervention by the Emperor, the government announced on August 14 that it was ready to give up. On September 2, 1945, on board the American battleship *Missouri,* anchored in Tokyo Bay, the articles of surrender were signed.

World War II had come to an end, and the United States had emerged

NAGASAKI.   An enormous mushroom cloud rises over the Japanese city of Nagasaki, August 9, 1945—the second city in a week to be devastated by an American atomic bomb. (*Official U.S. Air Force Photo*)

HIROSHIMA, OCTOBER 1945. The ruins of Hiroshima illustrate the awesome destructiveness of the atomic bomb. In addition to the visible carnage, however, was an unseen effect. Thousands of residents of Hiroshima and Nagasaki who survived the blast developed deadly forms of cancer—particularly leukemia—in the years that followed as a consequence of their exposure to radiation from the blast. The building shown here was left standing, unrepaired, when the city was rebuilt so that it could serve as a reminder of the effects of atomic war. (*National Archives*)

victorious. But it was a victory in which few could take lasting comfort. Fourteen million men under arms had died in the struggle. Perhaps as many more civilians had perished. The United States had suffered only light casualties in comparison with some other nations, but the totals were frightful nevertheless: 322,000 dead, another 800,000 injured. And in spite of having paid so high a price for peace, the world continued to face an uncertain future. The menace of nuclear warfare, which the United States had introduced to the globe, hung like a dark cloud on the horizon. And already the world's two strongest nations—the United States and the Soviet Union—were developing suspicions of and antagonisms toward each other that would threaten the peace for decades to come.

SUGGESTED READINGS

James MacGregor Burns, *Roosevelt: The Soldier of Freedom* (1970), recounts the military struggle through the experiences of the President. Albert R. Buchanan, *The*

United States and World War II, 2 vols. (1962), is an extensive survey of the military experience. See also Samuel Eliot Morison, *Strategy and Compromise* (1958), an analysis of strategic decision making, and *History of United States Naval Operations in World War II*, 14 vols. (1947–1960). A summary of this massive work is *The Two Ocean War* (1963). Winston S. Churchill, *The Second World War*, 6 vols. (1948–1953), is an invaluable account, although not written from an American perspective. Chester Wilmot, *The Struggle for Europe* (1952), and Charles B. McDonald, *The Mighty Endeavor* (1969), examine the American effort in Europe. See also Stephen Ambrose, *The Supreme Commander* (1970), an examination of Eisenhower's wartime command; Michael Howard, *The Mediterranean Strategy in World War II* (1968); and Dwight D. Eisenhower, *Crusade in Europe* (1948). Cornelius Ryan, *The Last Battle* (1966), and John Toland, *The Last Hundred Days* (1966), recount the end of the war in Europe. For the war in the Pacific, see E. J. Kind and W. M. Whitehill, *Fleet Admiral King* (1952); Barbara Tuchman, *Stilwell and the American Experience in China* (1971); John Toland, *The Rising Sun* (1970); and William Manchester, *American Caesar* (1979), a biography of Douglas MacArthur. On the use of the atomic bomb in Japan, see Martin Sherwin, *A World Destroyed* (1975); Gar Alperovitz, *Atomic Diplomacy* (1965); Gregg Herken, *The Winning Weapon* (1980); and W. S. Schoenberger, *Decision of Destiny* (1969). Robert Donovan, *Conflict and Crisis* (1977), an account of the first years of Truman's presidency, examines the new President's decision to use the nuclear weapon.

Eighteen

The Coming of the Cold War

Henry Luce, the flamboyant publisher of *Life*, expressed the expectations of many Americans in his book *The American Century* (1941) when he described the role the United States would play in the postwar world:

> America as the dynamic center of ever-widening spheres of enterprise, America as the training center of the skillful servants of mankind, America as the Good Samaritan, really believing again that it is more blessed to give than to receive—out of these elements surely can be fashioned a vision of the 20th Century to which we can and will devote ourselves in joy and gladness and vigor and enthusiasm.

The world was, in short, about to enter an "American Century."

It was a heady vision—one that by 1945 had seized the imagination of much of the country. It was a vision of a peaceful world, united by bonds of mutual cooperation. But it was also a vision of a world molded in the American image, a world in which the United States would reign unchallenged as the preeminent military, economic, and moral force.

In some respects, the postwar years confirmed Luce's buoyant prediction. The United States did indeed emerge from World War II the world's strongest and most influential power. But the larger hope—the hope for an era of peaceful cooperation in a united international community, the expectation of unchallenged American power—was not to be realized. Within two years following the end of the war (some would argue even before the hostilities concluded), the United States found itself locked in a long, grim, and dangerous struggle for international preeminence with the Soviet Union. The world had moved from the horrors of

343

"total war" to the tensions of another type of conflict: what Walter Lippmann, and later most others, termed the "Cold War."

EARLY ORIGINS

No issue in twentieth-century American history has aroused more debate than the question of the origins of the Cold War. Two questions, in particular, have provoked controversy: When did it begin? Who was to blame? Some have argued that the Cold War could have been avoided as late as 1947 or 1948, others that it was virtually inevitable long before World War II concluded. Some have claimed that Soviet duplicity and expansionism created the international tensions, others that American provocations and imperial ambitions were at least equally to blame. On virtually every aspect of the history of the Cold War, disagreement remains rampant.

But if historians have reached no general accord on these questions, they have gradually arrived at something approaching a consensus on some of the outlines of the debate. Most would agree that the origins of the Cold War can be understood only by looking at both the historic background of Soviet–American relations and the specific events of 1945 through 1948. And most would also agree that wherever the preponderance of blame may lie, both the United States and the Soviet Union contributed greatly to the atmosphere of hostility and suspicion that quickly clouded the peace.

A Legacy of Mistrust

The wartime alliance between the United States and the Soviet Union was an aberration from the normal tenor of Soviet–American relations. Ever since the Bolshevik Revolution of 1917, in some respects since before that, the two nations had viewed each other with deep mutual mistrust. The necessities of war obscured those suspicions briefly, but the legacy of them remained strong.

The reasons for American hostility toward the Soviet Union were both obvious and many. There was, of course, the fundamental American animosity toward communism, which had strong roots in the nation's past and had been a powerful force in society since well before the Russian Revolution. But there were more specific reasons as well. Americans never forgot the separate peace that the Soviet government had negotiated with Germany in 1917, leaving the West to fight the Central Powers alone. They had chafed at the strident attacks emanating from Moscow on the American capitalist system, attacks that proved particularly grating during the 1930s, when that system was under duress. They had long been concerned about the Soviet regime's open avowal of the need for world revolution, as symbolized by the creation of the Communist International. They had felt a deep and understandable revulsion at the bloody Stalinist purges of the 1930s. And they had been deeply embittered in 1939 when Stalin and Hitler agreed to the short-lived Nazi–Soviet Pact.

But Soviet hostility toward the United States had deep roots as well. Russian leaders were well aware of the American opposition to their revolution in 1917, and they never forgot that the United States had sent troops into the Soviet Union at the end of World War I to work, the Russians believed, to overthrow their new government. They resented their exclusion from the international community throughout the 1920s and 1930s; Russia had been invited to participate in neither the Versailles Conference in 1919 nor the Munich Conference in 1938. The Stalin regime continued to resent the long delay by the United States in recognizing the Soviet government; the two nations did not exchange ambassadors until 1933, sixteen years after the Revolution, nine years after Great Britain had recognized the Moscow government. And just as most Americans viewed communism with foreboding and contempt, so did most Russian communists harbor deep suspicions and a genuine distaste for industrial capitalism. There was, in short, a powerful legacy of mistrust on both sides.

In some respects, the wartime experience helped to abate that mistrust. Both the United States and the Soviet Union tended to focus during the war less on the traditional image of a dangerous potential foe and more on the image of a brave and dauntless ally. Americans expressed open admiration for the courage of Soviet forces in withstanding the Nazi onslaught and began to depict Stalin less as the bloody ogre of the purges than as the wise and persistent "Uncle Joe." The Soviet government, similarly, praised both the American fighting forces and the wisdom and courage of Franklin Roosevelt. In other respects, however, the war deepened the gulf between the two nations. Americans did not forget the Soviet invasion of Finland and the Baltic states late in 1939 once the war with Germany had begun in the west. Nor were they unaware, as the war continued, of Soviet brutality—not only toward the fascist enemies but toward supposedly friendly forces: for example, the Polish resistance fighters. Stalin had even greater cause to resent the American approach to the war. Despite repeated assurances from Roosevelt that the United States and Britain would soon open a second front on the European continent, thus drawing German strength away from the assault upon Russia, the Allied invasion did not finally occur until June 1944, more than two years after Stalin had first demanded it. In the meantime, the Russians had suffered appalling casualties—some estimates put them as high as 20 million; and it was easy for Stalin to believe that the West had deliberately delayed the invasion in order to weaken the Soviet Union. So although in most respects the wartime alliance worked well, with both sides making serious efforts to play down their differences, an undercurrent of tension and hostility remained.

Two Visions of the World

At least as important as these deep-seated suspicions was a fundamental difference in the ways the great powers envisioned the postwar world—a difference that was not at first immediately obvious, but one that ultimately shattered any hope for international amity. The first vision was that of the United States, one perhaps best expressed by the title of a famous book by Wendell Willkie, *One World* (1943), and first openly outlined in the Atlantic Charter, drafted by Roosevelt and Churchill in 1941. It was a vision of a world in which nations abandoned their traditional belief in military alliances and spheres of influence. Instead, the world would govern itself through democratic processes, with an international organization serving as the arbiter of disputes and the protector of the peace. No nation would control any other. Every people would have the right "to choose the form of government under which they will live."

The other vision was that of the Soviet Union and to some extent, it gradually became clear, of Great Britain. Both Stalin and Churchill had agreed to sign the Atlantic Charter espousing the "One World" principles. But neither man truly shared them. Britain always had been uneasy about the implications of the self-determination ideal for its own empire, which remained at the close of World War II the largest in the history of the world. The Soviet Union was determined to create a secure sphere for itself in eastern Europe as protection against future aggression from the West. Both Churchill and Stalin, therefore, tended to envision a postwar structure in which the great powers would control areas of strategic interest to them, in which something vaguely similar to the traditional European balance of power would reemerge.

This difference of opinion was particularly serious because the internationalist vision of Roosevelt had, by the end of the war, become a fervent commitment among many Americans. It was a vision composed equally of expansive idealism and national self-interest. Roosevelt had never forgotten the excitement with which he had greeted the principles of Wilsonian idealism during World War I, and he saw his mission in the 1940s as one of bringing lasting peace and genuine democracy to the world. But it was clear, too, that the "One World" vision would enhance the position of the United States in particular. As the world's greatest industrial power, and as one of the few nations unravaged by the war, America stood to gain more than any other country from opening the entire world to unfettered trade. The United States would have a global market for its exports, and it would have unrestricted access to vital raw materials. Determined to avoid another economic catastrophe like that of the 1930s, Roosevelt saw the creation of the postwar order as a way to ensure continuing American prosperity.

Thus when Britain and the Soviet Union began to balk at some of the provisions the United States was advocating, the debate seemed to become more than a simple difference of opinion. It became an ideological struggle for the future of the world. And on that rock the hope for a genuine peace would ultimately founder. Roosevelt was by the end of the war able to win at least the partial consent of Winston Churchill to his principles; but although he believed at times that Stalin would similarly relent, he never managed to steer the Soviets from their determination to control eastern Europe, from their vision of a postwar order in which each of the great powers would dominate its own sphere. Gradually, the irreconcilable differences between these two positions would turn the peacemaking process into a form of warfare.

THE WARTIME ACCORDS

Almost from the moment of Pearl Harbor, the Roosevelt administration devoted nearly as much attention to planning the peace as it did to winning the war. Indeed, the President himself realized that the conduct of the war—the relationships among the Allies in coordinating their efforts—would go far toward determining the shape of the postwar world. Strategic and diplomatic decisions were, therefore, linked from the beginning. And as the war drew to a close and the Allied powers began seriously to negotiate their future relationship, such decisions became virtually inseparable.

Casablanca and Teheran

Throughout 1942, Roosevelt had engaged in inconclusive discussions with the Soviet Union, and particularly with Foreign Minister Vyacheslav Molotov, about how best to implement the principles of the Atlantic Charter, to which all the Allies had in theory subscribed. Until 1943, however, neither nation was ready for any specific commitments. In the meantime, serious strains in the alliance were beginning to appear as a result of Stalin's irritation at delays in opening the second front and his resentment of the Anglo-American decision to invade North Africa before Europe.

It was in this deteriorating atmosphere that the President called for a meeting of the "Big Three"—Roosevelt, Churchill, and Stalin—in Casablanca, Morocco, in January 1943. Stalin declined the invitation, but Churchill and Roosevelt met nevertheless. Because the two leaders agreed that they could not accept Stalin's most important demand—the opening of a second front—they reached another decision designed to reassure the Soviet Union. The Allies, Roosevelt announced, would accept nothing less than the unconditional surrender of the Axis powers. In later years, many people would argue that the unconditional surrender doctrine actually lengthened the war—that it inspired the Germans to last-ditch resistance, that it left the United States with no choice but to use atomic weapons against Japan. At the time, however, the announcement was a signal to Stalin that the Americans and British would not negotiate a separate peace with Hitler and leave the Soviets to fight on alone.

After Secretary of State Cordell Hull had visited Moscow in October 1943 for discussions with his British and Soviet counterparts, optimism rose in Washington about the possibilities for a workable postwar accord. Stalin had seemed to agree to Hull's proposal that the great powers would maintain their alliance after the war as the core of an international system of peaceful cooperation. In that hopeful atmosphere, Roosevelt and Churchill traveled to Teheran, Iran, the following month for their first meeting with Stalin. By now, however, Roosevelt's most effective bargaining tool—Stalin's need for American assistance in his struggle against Germany—had been removed. The German advance against Russia had been halted; Soviet forces were now launching their own westward offensive. New tensions had emerged in the alliance, moreover, as a result of the refusal by the British and Americans to allow any Soviet participation in the creation of a new Italian government following the fall of Mussolini. To Stalin, at least, the "One World" doctrine was already appearing to embody a double standard: America and Britain expected to have a voice in the future of eastern Europe, but the Soviet Union was to have no voice in the future of the West.

Nevertheless, the Teheran Conference seemed in most respects to have been a success. Roosevelt and Stalin established a cordial relationship, one that the President hoped would eventually produce the same personal intimacy he enjoyed with Churchill. Stalin agreed to an American request that the Soviet Union enter the war in the Pacific soon after the end of hostilities in Europe. Roosevelt, in turn, promised that an Anglo-American second front would be established within six months. More important to Roosevelt, all three leaders agreed in principle to a postwar international organization and to efforts to prevent a resurgence of German expansionism.

On other matters, however, the origins of future disagreements could already be discerned. Most important was the question of the future of Poland. Roosevelt and Churchill were willing to agree to a movement of the Soviet border westward, thus allowing Stalin to annex some historically Polish territory. But on the nature

TEHERAN, 1943. Stalin, Roosevelt, and Churchill—the "Big Three" of World War II—pose for photographers during their first meeting, in Teheran, Iran. Roosevelt worked hard to establish what he believed was a warm personal relationship with the Soviet leader—one that he hoped would enable him to work out remaining differences between the Soviet Union and the West after the end of the war. (*National Archives*)

of the postwar government in that portion of Poland that would remain independent, there were sharp differences. Roosevelt and Churchill supported the claims of the Polish government-in-exile that had been functioning in London since 1940; Stalin wished to install another, procommunist exiled government that had spent the war in the Soviet Union. The three leaders avoided a bitter conclusion to the Teheran Conference only by leaving the issue unresolved. There had, however, been little evidence to support hopes that an amicable settlement of the Polish question would be possible.

Yalta

For more than a year, during which the Soviet Union began finally to destroy German resistance and the British and Americans launched their successful invasion of France, the Grand Alliance among the United States, Britain, and the Soviet Union alternated between high tension and warm amicability. In the fall of 1944, Churchill flew by himself to Moscow for a meeting with Stalin to resolve issues arising from a civil war in Greece. In return for a Soviet agreement to cease assisting Greek communists, who were challenging the British-supported monarchical government, Churchill consented to a proposal whereby control of eastern Europe would be divided between Britain and the Soviet Union. "This memorable meeting," Churchill wrote Stalin after its close, "has shown that there are no matters that cannot be adjusted between us when we meet together in frank and intimate discussion." To Roosevelt, however, the Moscow agreement was evidence of how little the Atlantic Charter principles seemed to mean to his two most important allies. The "One World" vision was in serious jeopardy.

It was in an atmosphere of some gloom, therefore, that Roosevelt and Churchill joined Stalin for a great peace conference in the Soviet city of Yalta in February 1945. The American President sensed resistance to his internationalist dreams. The British Prime Minister was already becoming disillusioned about Stalin's willingness to make concessions and compromises, warning even before the conference met that "I think the end of this war may well prove to be more disappointing than was the last." Stalin, whose armies were now only miles from Berlin and who was well aware of how much the United States still wanted his assistance in the Pacific, was confident and determined.

On a number of issues, the Big Three reached amicable and mutually satisfactory agreements. In return for Stalin's promise to enter the war against Japan, Roosevelt agreed that the Soviet Union should receive the Kurile Islands north of Japan, should regain southern Sakhalin Island and Port Arthur, both of which Russia had lost in the 1904 Russo-Japanese War, and could exercise some influence (along with the government of China) in Manchuria.

The negotiators agreed as well on a plan for a new international organization: the United Nations. Tentative plans for the UN had been hammered out the previous summer at a conference in Washington, D.C., at the Dumbarton Oaks estate. At Yalta, the leaders ratified the Dumbarton plan to create a General Assembly, in which every member would be represented, and a Security Council, on which would sit permanent representatives of the five major powers (the United States, Britain, France, the Soviet Union, and China) along with tempo-rary delegates from several other nations. They accepted, too, the provision giving each of the major powers a veto over all Security Council decisions. In addition, Roosevelt acceded at Yalta to Stalin's demand that the Soviet Union be allowed three votes in the General Assembly (to offset the many votes of the British Commonwealth, he claimed). These agreements became the basis for the drafting of the United Nations charter at a conference of fifty nations beginning April 25, 1945, in San Francisco. The United States Senate ratified the charter in July by a vote of 80 to 2 (a striking contrast to the slow and painful defeat it had administered to the charter of the League of Nations twenty-five years before).

On other issues, however, the Yalta Conference produced no real agreement, either leaving fundamental differences unresolved or papering them over with weak and unstable compromises. As in Teheran, the most important stumbling block remained Poland. The conferees reaffirmed the Teheran decision to adjust the border between Poland and Russia; but Churchill and Roosevelt dissented sharply from Stalin's determination to shift the western border of Poland into German territory. More troubling still, fundamental disagreement remained about the postwar Polish government, with each side continuing to insist upon the rights of its own government-in-exile. Stalin, whose armies had by now occupied Poland, had already installed a government composed of the procommunist "Lubin" Poles, to the chagrin of the British and Americans. He had, moreover, inflamed the issue greatly six months earlier during the Soviet military drive into Poland. With Russian armies only fifty miles from Warsaw, members of the Polish underground in that city (most of them anti-Soviet) had risen in revolt against their Nazi occupiers. At that point the Russian advance had slowed—deliberately, many Westerners believed—while Nazi forces systematically slaughtered the re-sisting Poles.

At Yalta, Roosevelt and Churchill protested strongly against Stalin's unilateral establishment of a new Polish government, insisting that the pro-Western "Lon-don" Poles must be allowed a place in the Warsaw regime. Roosevelt envisioned a complete restructuring of the Soviet-controlled government, based on free, democratic elections—which both he and Stalin recognized the pro-Western forces would win. Stalin agreed only to a vague compromise by which an un-specified number of pro-Western Poles would be granted a place in the govern-ment. Although he reluctantly consented to hold "free and unfettered elections" in Poland, he made no firm commitment to a date for them. They never took place. Neither on the Polish border question nor on the structure of the new government, therefore, was there anything like a real agreement.

Nor was there agreement about one of the touchiest issues facing the three leaders: the future of Germany. All three leaders were determined to ensure that Germany could not soon again become a major military power, but there were wide differences in their views of how to accomplish that goal. Stalin wanted to impose $20 billion in reparations upon the Germans, of which Russia would receive half. Churchill protested, arguing that the result would be that Britain and

America would have to feed the German people. Roosevelt finally accepted the $20 billion figure as a "basis for discussion" but left final settlement to a future reparations commission. To Stalin, whose hopes for the reconstruction of Russia rested in part upon tribute from Germany, it was an unsatisfactory compromise.

Roosevelt was uncertain at first about how he wished to resolve the German question. In 1944, he and Churchill had met in Quebec and agreed upon what became known as the Morgenthau Plan—a plan for the pastoralization of Germany. But by accepting the principle of reparations at Yalta, he was clearly abandoning the idea of destroying German industry; without it, the Germans would have no means by which to pay. Instead, he seemed to be hoping for a reconstructed and reunited Germany, one that would be permitted to develop a prosperous, modern economy, but one that would remain under the careful supervision of the Allies. Stalin, by contrast, wanted a permanent dismemberment of Germany, a proposal the British and Americans firmly rejected. The final agreement was, like the Polish agreement, a vague and unstable one. The United States, Great Britain, France, and the Soviet Union would each control their own "zones of occupation" in Germany, zones determined by the position of troops at the time when the war would end. (Berlin, the German capital, was already well inside the Soviet zone, but because of its symbolic importance it would itself be divided into four sectors, one for each nation to occupy.) At an unspecified future date, the nation would be reunited; but no specific agreement was reached upon how the reunification would occur.

As for the rest of Europe, the conference produced a murky accord on the establishment of interim governments "broadly representative of all democratic elements." They would be replaced ultimately by permanent governments "responsible to the will of the people" and created through free elections. Once again, no specific provisions or timetables accompanied the agreements.

The Yalta Accords, in other words, were less a settlement of postwar issues than a general set of loose principles that side-stepped the most divisive issues. Roosevelt, Churchill, and Stalin returned home from the conference each apparently convinced that he had signed an important agreement. But the Soviet interpretation of the accords differed so sharply from the Anglo-American interpretation that the illusion endured only briefly. Stalin continued to believe that Soviet control of eastern Europe was essential and considered the Yalta Accords little more than a set of small concessions to Western punctiliousness. Roosevelt, in contrast, thought that the agreements represented a mutual acceptance of the idea of an "open" Europe, under the direct control of no single nation. In the weeks following the Yalta Conference, therefore, he watched with horror as the Soviet Union moved systematically to establish procommunist governments in one eastern European nation after another and as Stalin refused to make the changes in Poland that the President believed he had promised.

Still, Roosevelt refused to abandon hope. His personal relationship with Stalin was such, he believed, that a settlement of these issues remained possible. Continuing to work to secure his vision of the future, he left Washington early in the

YALTA.   Winston Churchill was appalled at Roosevelt's sickly appearance during the Yalta Conference. Here, the Big Three meet for the last time. Months later, Roosevelt would be dead, Churchill out of office, and the fragile Yalta Accords well on their way to dissolution. (*National Archives*)

spring for a vacation at his private retreat in Warm Springs, Georgia. There, on April 12, 1945, he suffered a sudden, massive stroke and died.

THE COLLAPSE OF THE PEACE

Harry S Truman, who succeeded Roosevelt in the presidency, inherited an international predicament that would have taxed the most experienced and patient statesman. He did not, however, inherit Roosevelt's familiarity with the world situation. (He had served in the administration only a few weeks and had received few substantive briefings on foreign policy.) Nor did he share Roosevelt's belief in the tractability of the Soviet Union. Roosevelt had insisted until the end that the Russians could be bargained with, that Stalin was, essentially, a reasonable man with whom an ultimate accord could be reached. Truman, in contrast, sided with those in the government (and there were many) who considered the Soviet Union fundamentally untrustworthy and viewed Stalin himself with deep suspicion and basic dislike.

There was also a significant contrast between the personalities of the two men. Roosevelt had always been a wily, even devious public figure, using his surface geniality to disguise his intentions. He had, as a result, been an unusually effective negotiator. Truman, on the other hand, was a sharp, direct, and impatient leader, a man who said what he thought and seldom wavered from decisions once he had made them. They were qualities that would win him the admiration of many of his contemporaries and of an even larger proportion of later generations of Americans. They were not, however, qualities well suited to patient negotiation.

But while Truman's impulsiveness may have contributed to the rapid deterioration of Soviet–American relations in 1945 and 1946, it alone did not cause them. The fundamental difference between the Russian and American views of the postwar world finally stood revealed in those years for what they were: an all but insuperable obstacle to peace.

The Failure of Potsdam

Truman had been in office only a few days before he decided upon his approach to the Soviet Union. He would "get tough." Stalin had made what the new President interpreted as solemn agreements with the United States at Yalta. The United States, therefore, would insist that he honor them. Dismissing the advice of Secretary of War Stimson that the Polish question was a lost cause and not worth a world crisis, Truman met on April 23 with Soviet Foreign Minister Molotov and sharply chastised him for violations of the Yalta Accords. "I have never been talked to like that in my life," a shocked Molotov reportedly replied. "Carry out your agreements and you won't get talked to like that," said the President.

In fact, however, Truman had only limited leverage by which to compel the Soviet Union to carry out what he considered to be its agreements. Russian forces already occupied Poland and much of the rest of eastern Europe. Germany was already divided among the conquering nations. The United States was still engaged in a war in the Pacific and was neither able nor willing to engage in a second conflict in Europe. Despite Truman's professed belief that the United States should be able to get "85 percent" of what it wanted, he was ultimately forced to settle for much less.

He conceded first on Poland. When Stalin made a few minor concessions to the pro-Western exiles, Truman recognized the Warsaw government, hoping that noncommunist forces might gradually expand their influence there. Other questions remained, and to settle them Truman met in July with Churchill (who was replaced in the midst of the negotiations by Clement Attlee, who had ousted him as Prime Minister) and Stalin at Potsdam, near Berlin, in Russian-occupied Germany. The British and Americans hoped to use the Potsdam Conference to resolve the question of Germany, and in one sense they succeeded. But the resolution was not, ultimately, to the liking of the Western leaders. Truman reluctantly accepted the adjustments of the Polish–German border that Stalin had long demanded; he refused, however, to permit the Russians to claim any reparations from the American and British zones of western Germany. The result, in effect, was to confirm that Germany would remain divided, with the western zones united into one nation, friendly to the United States, and the Russian zone surviving as another nation, with a pro-Soviet, communist government. Stalin had failed to receive the reparations he wanted, and he had been unable to secure other forms of financial assistance from the West (a failure symbolized by the abrupt termination by the Truman administration in May of all lend-lease assistance). He would, therefore, use eastern Germany to help rebuild the shattered Russian economy. Soon, the Soviet Union was siphoning between $1.5 and $3 billion a year out of its zone of occupation.

The Atlantic Charter principles of an open world had, in effect, been abandoned. And although the Truman administration continued during the ensuing months to try to change the realities of eastern Europe, the world was rapidly being divided into two great, opposing spheres of influence. Not even the atomic bomb, which the United States for the moment controlled exclusively, and which Truman hoped would strengthen his negotiating position, proved sufficient to alter the chain of events.

A Dilemma in Asia

Throughout the frustrating course of its negotiations over the future of Europe, the United States was facing an equally troubling dilemma in Asia. Central to American hopes for an open, peaceful world "policed" by the great powers was a strong, independent China. But even before the war had ended, the American government was aware that those hopes faced a major, perhaps insurmountable obstacle: the Chinese government of Chiang Kai-shek. Chiang was generally friendly to the United States, but he had few other virtues. His government was hopelessly corrupt and incompetent. His popular legitimacy was feeble. And Chiang himself lived in a world of surreal isolation, unable or unwilling to face the problems that were threatening to engulf him. Ever since 1927, the Nationalist government he headed had been engaged in a prolonged and bitter rivalry with the Communist armies of Mao Tse-tung. So successful had the communist challenge grown, with Mao in control of one-fourth of the population by 1945, that through most of World War II, Chiang refused to release his troops to participate in the war against Japan, reserving them instead for his impending battle with Mao. Partly as a result of a bitter dispute between Chiang and General Joseph Stilwell, commander of American forces in China, Roosevelt had decided in 1944 that the Chinese government was hopelessly weak. He had not even invited Chiang to participate in the Teheran and Yalta conferences. By 1945, however, the United States was faced with a bitter choice.

Truman had managed at Potsdam to win Stalin's agreement that Chiang would be recognized as the legitimate ruler of China; but Chiang himself was rapidly losing his grip on his country. Some Americans urged the government to try to find a third faction to support as an alternative to either Chiang or Mao. A few argued that America should try to reach some accommodation with Mao. Truman, however, decided reluctantly that he had no choice but to continue supporting Chiang, despite the weakness of his position. American forces in the last months of the war diverted attention from the Japanese long enough to assist Chiang against the Communists in Manchuria. For the next several years, as the long struggle between the Nationalists and the Communists erupted into a full-scale civil war, the United States continued to pump money and weapons to

Chiang. By late 1947, however, it was clear to the President that the cause was lost. Although he did not abandon China entirely or immediately, it became clear that the United States was not prepared to intervene to save the Nationalist regime.

Instead, the American government was beginning to consider an alternative to China as the strong, pro-Western force in Asia: a revived Japan. During the first years of American occupation of Japan after the war, the United States commander, Douglas MacArthur, provided a firm and restrictive administration of the island. A series of purges removed what remained of the warlord government of the Japanese Empire. Americans insisted, too, upon dismantling the nation's munitions industry. But after two years of occupation, American policy toward Japan shifted. The United States would now encourage a revitalized Japanese economy. It lifted all limitations upon industrial development and encouraged rapid economic growth. As in Europe, the vision of an open, united Asia had been replaced with an acceptance of the necessity of developing a strong, pro-American sphere of influence.

The Containment Doctrine

By the end of 1945, the Grand Alliance was in shambles, and with it any realistic hope of a postwar world constructed along the lines Americans had urged. Although few policymakers were willing to admit openly that the United States must abandon its "One World" ideals, a new American policy was slowly emerging to replace them. Rather than attempt to create a unified, "open" world, the West would work to "contain" the threat of further Soviet expansion. The United States would be the leading force in that effort.

The new doctrine received one test before it was even fully formulated. When Stalin refused in March 1946 to follow the British and American lead in pulling his occupation forces out of Iran, the Truman administration issued a strong and threatening ultimatum. Stalin relented and withdrew. But new crises were emerging—in Turkey, where Stalin was exerting heavy pressure to win some control over the vital straits to the Mediterranean, and in Greece, where once again communist forces were threatening the pro-Western government and where the British had announced they could no longer provide assistance. Faced with these challenges, the President finally decided to enunciate a firm new policy.

It was not an easy task. American opinion was sharply divided over the Soviet Union, many citizens refusing to believe in the reality of a Russian threat to world peace, others refusing to abandon the ideal of "One World." Winston Churchill attempted to shift the nation's attitudes when, in March 1946, in a speech in Fulton, Missouri, he warned Americans that "an iron curtain has descended across the Continent. . . . I do not believe that Soviet Russia desires war. What they desire is the fruits of war and the indefinite expansion of their power and doctrines." Still, strong public support for a policy of confrontation remained elusive.

The crises in Turkey and Greece, therefore, provided Truman with an important opportunity to dramatize the necessity of American firmness. He had for some time been convinced that the Soviet Union, like Nazi Germany before it, was an aggressor nation bent on world conquest. He had accepted the arguments of the influential American diplomat George F. Kennan, who warned that the United States faced "a political force committed fanatically to the belief that with the U.S. there can be no permanent *modus vivendi,*" and that the only answer was "a long-term, patient but firm and vigilant containment of Russian expansive tendencies." On March 12, 1947, Truman appeared before Congress and used Kennan's warnings as the basis of what became known as the Truman Doctrine. "I believe," he argued, "that it must be the policy of the United States to support free peoples who are resisting attempted subjugation by armed minorities or by outside pressures." In the same speech he requested $400 million—part of it to bolster the armed forces of Greece and Turkey, another part to provide economic assistance to Greece. Congress quickly approved the measure.

The American commitment ultimately eased Soviet pressure upon Turkey and helped the Greek government to defeat the communist insurgents. More important, it established a fundamental new doctrine that would become the basis of American foreign policy for more than two decades. Communism, Truman

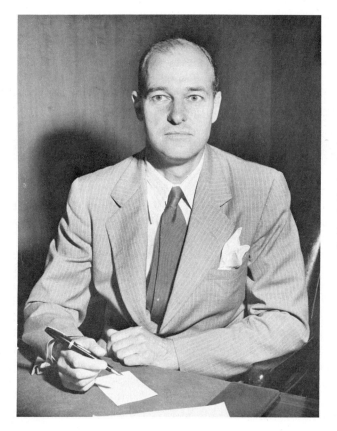

GEORGE F. KENNAN. In later years, Kennan would become one of the most eloquent critics of American foreign policy, denouncing the war in Vietnam and many of the assumptions that lay behind it. In the 1940s, however, he was perhaps the single most influential figure in constructing the theoretical groundwork for the "containment" doctrine. (*UPI*)

claimed, was an ideological threat; it was indivisible; its expansion anywhere was a threat to democracy because, as Secretary of State Dean Acheson had argued, the fall of one nation to communism would have a "domino effect" upon surrounding nations. It was, therefore, the policy of the United States to assist pro-Western forces in any struggle against communism anywhere in the world, whether that struggle directly involved the Soviet Union or not. The Truman Doctrine marked the final American abandonment of the "One World" vision of a generation of idealists. But it replaced it with another, equally unrealistic vision—a vision of two worlds, one enslaved and one free, in which every rivalry and every conflict could be defined as a struggle between the United States and the Soviet Union. In the years to come, the ideology of the Truman Doctrine would often blind Americans to local or regional particularities, with the result that the United States would on more than one occasion interpret an internal revolution as an expression of Soviet expansionism.

The Marshall Plan

The Truman Doctrine was only one half—the military half—of the new containment doctrine. The second, and more effective, part of the new American policy was a proposal to aid in the economic reconstruction of western Europe. There were a number of motives for the assistance. One was a simple, humanitarian concern for the European peoples, whose economies lay in ruins and whose future appeared bleak. Another was practical necessity: until Europe could support itself economically, it would remain a drain upon the United States, which was endeavoring in the meantime to feed it. But there was powerful self-interest at work as well. Without a strong European market for American goods, most policymakers believed, the United States economy would be unable to sustain the prosperity it had achieved during the war. And above all, unless something could be done to strengthen the perilous position of the pro-American governments in western Europe, they might well fall to communism, which was growing increasingly powerful as a result of the economic misery.

In June 1947, therefore, Secretary of State George C. Marshall spoke before a commencement gathering at Harvard University and announced a plan to provide economic assistance to all European nations (including the Soviet Union) that would join in drafting a program for recovery. Although Russia and its eastern satellites quickly rejected the plan, claiming (with some justification) that it represented an American attempt to reshape Europe in its own image, sixteen western European nations eagerly participated. There was substantial opposition at first to Truman's request for an enormous appropriation to fund the effort; but congressional opponents lost power quickly, embarrassed by the unwelcome support of the American Communist party and shocked by a sudden seizure of power by communists in Czechoslovakia, which had hitherto remained at least nominally free of Soviet control. In April 1948, the President signed a bill establishing the Economic Cooperation Administration and providing an initial budget of $4 billion. Over the next three years, the Marshall Plan, as it soon became known, channeled over $12 billion of American aid into Europe, sparking what many viewed as a miraculous economic revival. By the end of 1950, European industrial production had risen 64 percent, communist strength in the member nations was declining, and the opportunities for American trade had been fully revived.

THE COLD WAR ENTRENCHED

With the Soviet determination to maintain control over eastern Europe now clear, and with American commitment to resist communist expansion firmly asserted, the outlines of international relations for the postwar years were well defined. There ensued, however, a period of increasing tensions during which the position of each side became more firmly entrenched. The result, finally, was a system of alliances that gave full, institutional shape to the Cold War.

Mobilization at Home

That the United States had fully accepted a continuing commitment to the containment policy became clear in 1947 and 1948 through a series of measures designed to maintain American military power at near wartime levels. Although the government had moved rapidly in 1945 to release almost 7 million men from

GEORGE C. MARSHALL. Marshall's distinguished military career culminated in his service as Army Chief of Staff throughout World War II. Many believed, however, that his greatest accomplishments came during his years as diplomat and statesman—first as ambassador to China from 1945 to 1947; then as Secretary of State from 1947 to 1949, during which time he presided over the formulation of the containment doctrine and the creation of the European recovery plan, which came to bear his name. He closed his public career by serving as Secretary of Defense in 1950 and 1951. (*UPI*)

the armed forces in the space of a few months, it was not long before the President began to demand a renewal of universal military training through a continuing draft. Congress finally restored the Selective Service System in 1948. The United States had announced shortly after the surrender of Japan that it was prepared to accept an international agreement banning nuclear weapons (through a proposal known as the Baruch Plan). The Soviet Union, arguing that since only America had developed a bomb, America alone should abandon it, resisted any system of international inspection and controls. In response, the United States simply redoubled its own efforts in atomic research, elevating nuclear warfare to a central place in its military arsenal. The Atomic Energy Commission, established in 1946, became the supervisory body charged with overseeing all nuclear research, civilian and military alike.

Perhaps the clearest indication of America's continuing concern with military power, however, came through the National Security Act of 1947. It created a new Department of Defense, whose secretary would combine the traditional functions of the Secretary of War and the Secretary of the Navy and would preside over all branches of the armed services. The National Security Council (NSC), operating out of the White House and including the President, members of his cabinet, and others, would preside over foreign and military policy. The Central Intelligence Agency (CIA) would be responsible for collecting information through both open and covert methods and, as the Cold War continued, for engaging secretly in active political and military operations on behalf of American goals.

This reorganization of the nation's defense establishment did not immediately operate as smoothly as its advocates had hoped. Strong interservice rivalries continued, and the first Secretary of Defense, James V. Forrestal, soon became so exhausted and frustrated by the problems of unification that in 1949 he resigned in a state of deep mental confusion. Just weeks later, he committed suicide. Despite the problems, however, the National Security Act effected important changes in the nation's ability to conduct a cold war. It transferred to the President expanded powers over all defense activities, centralizing in the White House control that had once been widely dispersed. It enabled the administration to take warlike actions without an open declaration of war; and it created vehicles by which the government could act politically and militarily overseas behind a veil of secrecy.

The Road to NATO

At about the same time, the United States was moving to strengthen the military capabilities of western Europe. Convinced that only a reconstructed Germany could serve as the necessary bulwark against communist expansion, Truman abandoned earlier policies designed to restrain German power and forged an agreement with England and France to merge the three western zones of occupation into a new West German republic (which would include the American, British, and French sectors of Berlin, even though that city lay well within the Soviet zone).

Stalin interpreted the move (correctly) as a direct challenge to his hopes for a subdued Germany and a docile Europe. At almost the same moment, he was facing a challenge from inside what he considered his own sphere. The government of Yugoslavia, under the leadership of Marshall Josip Broz Tito, broke openly with the Soviet Union and declared the nation an unaligned communist state. The United States offered Tito assistance.

Stalin's response came quickly. On June 24, 1948, taking advantage of the lack of a written guarantee of Western transit through eastern Germany, he imposed a tight blockade around the western sectors of Berlin. If Germany was to be officially divided, he was implying, then the country's Western government would have to abandon its outpost in the heart of the Soviet-controlled eastern zone. The United States was being given a choice between dropping its plan for a united West Germany or surrendering Berlin. Truman refused to do either. Although he was unwilling to risk war by responding militarily to the blockade, he ordered a massive airlift to supply the city with food, fuel, and supplies. The airlift continued for more than ten months, transporting nearly 2.5 million tons of material, keeping alive a city of 2 million people, and transforming West Berlin into a symbol of the West's resolve to resist communist expansion. Finally, late in the spring of 1949, Stalin lifted the now ineffective blockade. And in October, the division of Germany into two nations—the Federal Republic in the west and the Democratic Republic in the east—became official.

The crisis in Berlin accelerated the consolidation of what was already in effect an alliance of the United States and the countries of western Europe. On April 4, 1949, twelve nations signed an agreement establishing the North Atlantic Treaty Organization (NATO) and declaring that an armed attack against one member would be considered an attack against all. The NATO countries would, moreover, create a joint military force in Europe to defend against what many believed was the threat of a Soviet invasion. The American Senate quickly ratified this first peacetime alliance between the United States and Europe since the eighteenth century. The NATO alliance did more than create a powerful military force in western Europe. It greatly increased American influence there as well. The United States quickly became the most important supplier of the NATO military forces; and an American officer, General Dwight D. Eisenhower, assumed the powerful position of Supreme Commander of Allied forces in Europe.

The Enduring Crisis

The Berlin blockade, the offer of aid to Yugoslavia, the creation of NATO—all had in most respects been expressions of American confidence. Truman had believed, along with most other policymakers, that the United States was easily the more powerful of the two great rivals, that the Soviet Union would not dare provoke war because of the certainty of defeat. For a time, it had seemed that the battle against communism was being won.

But a series of events in 1949 began seriously to erode that confidence and launched the Cold War into a new and more enduring phase. An announcement

THE BERLIN AIRLIFT.   Stalin instituted the blockade of West Berlin in an attempt to force the United States and its allies to abandon the city, which lay completely surrounded by communist East Germany. But the blockade had the opposite effect. The Berlin airlift of 1948 and 1949 made the city a worldwide symbol of resistance to communism. General Lucius D. Clay, military governor of the American zone during the airlift, wrote of scenes such as the one depicted here: "It was inspiring and somewhat heart-rending to witness the spontaneous visits of the women and children of Berlin to Tempelhof airport to show their appreciation . . . bringing with them some precious last possessions as a token of gratitude to the members of the air crews." (*UPI*)

in September that the Soviet Union had successfully exploded its first atomic weapon, years before most Americans had considered it possible, came as a severe shock to the nation. So did the collapse of Chiang Kai-shek's Nationalist government in China, which occurred with startling speed in the last months of 1949. Chiang fled with his political allies and the remnants of his army to the offshore island of Formosa (Taiwan), and the entire Chinese mainland came under the control of a communist government that many Americans believed to be a mere extension of the Soviet Union. The United States, powerless to stop the Communists without a major military commitment that virtually no one wanted, had no choice but to watch the collapse of its ill-chosen ally. Few policymakers shared the belief of the so-called China Lobby that the United States should now commit itself to the rearming of Chiang Kai-shek. But neither would the administration recognize the new Communist regime, particularly after the Maoist government began expropriating American property, expelling American businessmen, and strengthening its ties to the Soviet Union. The Chinese mainland would remain almost entirely closed to the West for a full generation. The United States, in the meantime, would devote increased attention to the revitalization of Japan as a buffer against Asian communism, ending the American occupation of the island, finally, in 1952.

With the containment policy in apparent disarray, and with political opposition mounting at home, Truman called for a thorough review of American foreign policy. The result was an important National Security Council report, commonly known as NSC-68, which outlined a significant shift in the American position. The April 1950 document argued that the United States could no longer rely on other nations to take the initiative in resisting communism. It must itself establish firm and active leadership of the noncommunist world. Among other things, the report called for a major expansion of American military power, with a defense budget almost four times the previously projected figure. It also reinforced what was already a strong sense of mission in the formation of American foreign policy. Upon the United States, the report maintained, lay the sole responsibility of defending freedom in the world. America had, its citizens were beginning to believe, embarked upon a moral crusade. That conviction would help to produce three decades of international tragedy and frustration.

SUGGESTED READINGS

A good introduction to the vast literature on the Cold War is Walter LaFeber, *America, Russia, and the Cold War*, 3rd ed. (1976), which carries the story to 1975. Wartime relations between the United States and the Soviet Union are analyzed in John L. Snell, *Illusion and Necessity* (1967); Gaddis Smith, *American Diplomacy During the Second World War* (1965); Herbert Feis, *Churchill, Roosevelt, and Stalin* (1957); and William McNeill, *America, Britain and Russia* (1953). On the wartime accords, see Diane Clemens, *Yalta* (1970); Herbert Feis, *Between War and Peace: The Potsdam Conference* (1960); Athan G. Theoharis, *The Yalta Myths* (1970); and W. L. Neumann, *After Victory* (1969). Broader studies of the origins of the Cold War include John L. Gaddis, *The United States and the Origins of the Cold War* (1972); George C. Herring, Jr., *Aid to Russia* (1973); Daniel Yergin, *Shattered Peace* (1977); Thomas Paterson, *Soviet-American Confrontation* (1974); Gregg Herken, *The Winning Weapon* (1980); and Martin Sherwin, *A World Destroyed* (1975).

The foreign policies of the Truman administration receive particular attention in Robert Donovan, *Conflict and Crisis* (1977); Lloyd Gardner, *Architects of Illusion* (1970); and Richard Freeland, *The Truman Doctrine and the Origins of McCarthyism* (1971). George F. Kennan, *American Diplomacy: 1900–1950 (1952)* and *Memoirs,*

1925–1950 (1967), are invaluable works by one of the architects of the containment doctrine; Dean Acheson's *Present at the Creation* (1970) is another useful memoir. Joyce Kolko and Gabriel Kolko, *The Limits of Power* (1970), is a highly critical study. Hadley Arkes, *Bureaucracy, the Marshall Plan and National Interest* (1973), examines the European recovery plan.

Akira Iriye, *The Cold War in Asia* (1974), is a valuable overview. John K. Fairbank, *The United States and China*, 3rd ed. (1971), and Edwin O. Reischauer, *The United States and Japan*, 3rd ed. (1965), are both standard works, with chapters on the postwar years. Michael Schaller, *The U.S. Crusade in China* (1979), and Kenneth F. Shewmaker, *Americans and the Chinese Communists* (1971), provide background to the events of 1949. Godfrey Hodgson, *America in Our Time* (1976), is a valuable survey of the development of Cold War ideology. Harry S Truman, *Memoirs*, 2 vols. (1955–1956), is an important document of the time. Ronald Radosh, *Prophets on the Right* (1975), explores some of the domestic pressures upon foreign policy.

Nineteen

Postwar America

Like any nation emerging victorious from a long and difficult war, the United States in 1945 viewed its future with high and fervent hopes. America had become, its citizens believed, the most powerful nation on earth. The postwar world, therefore, would reflect its goals. The American economy had revived from the doldrums of the Depression. After four years of wartime privation, therefore, much of the public was ready to enjoy a bountiful, stable peace.

But the immediate postwar years did much to discourage the American people. The expectation of a peaceful world based on American principles died quickly in the face of the emerging Cold War. And the hopes for prosperity and stability at home suffered a series of shocks before the economy finally began to perform successfully. Harry Truman, the "accidental President," presided over this difficult transition. And the years of his presidency, therefore, were deeply troubled.

POSTWAR ADJUSTMENTS

The increasing dangers overseas were only a part of the frustrations facing the United States after the war. The nation also encountered serious difficulties in adapting its complex economy to the new demands of peace; and the instability that resulted contributed to the creation of a heated political climate.

The Problems of Reconversion

The bombs that destroyed Hiroshima and Nagasaki not only ended the war months earlier than almost anyone had predicted; they propelled the nation precipitously into a process of reconversion. The lack of planning was soon compounded by a growing popular impatience, as civilians clamored to buy the consumer goods denied them during the preceding four years and as returning veterans began to demand jobs, housing, and services. Under intense public pressure, the Truman administration attempted to hasten the "return to normal," despite dire warnings by some planners and economists. The result was a period of severe economic problems.

They were not, however, the problems that most Americans had feared. There had been many predictions that peace would bring a return of Depression unemployment, as war production ceased and returning soldiers flooded the labor market. But there was no general economic collapse in 1946—for several reasons. Government spending dropped sharply and abruptly to be sure; $35 billion of war contracts were canceled at a stroke within weeks of the Japanese surrender. But increased consumer demand soon compensated. Consumer goods had been generally unavailable during the war, so many workers had saved a substantial portion of their wages and were now ready to spend them. A $6-billion tax cut pumped additional money into general circulation. The Servicemen's Readjustment Act of 1944, better known as the GI Bill of Rights, provided substantial economic and educational assistance to veterans, increasing spending even further.

But while the sudden flood of consumer demand ensured that there would be no new depression, it also created rampant, debilitating inflation. For more than two years inflation continued, with prices rising at rates of 14 or 15 percent. In the summer of 1946, the President vetoed an extension of the authority of the wartime Office of Price Administration because Congress had weakened the agency's authority. In so doing, he permitted government price controls, which were already having difficulty holding down price increases, to be removed altogether. A month later, he relented and signed a bill little different from the one he had rejected. But in the meantime inflation had soared briefly to 25 percent.

Compounding the economic difficulties was a sharp rise in labor unrest. Unions had accepted government-imposed restraint on their demands during the war, but now they were willing to wait no longer, particularly as inflation cut into the existing wage scales with painful force. By the end of 1945, there had already been major strikes in the automobile, electrical, and steel industries. Government intervention had helped settle the strikes relatively quickly, but the agreements fueled inflation even further. In the steel strike, for example, the government had approved a settlement granting workers a raise of 18.5 cents an hour and the industry a price increase of $5 a ton.

In April 1946, a fresh crisis emerged when John L. Lewis led the United Mine Workers out on strike, shutting down the coal fields for forty days. The economic impact was devastating. Freight and shipping activity declined by 75 percent; the steel industry made plans to shut down operations; fears grew that without vital coal supplies, the entire nation might virtually grind to a halt. Truman finally forced coal production to resume by ordering government seizure of the mines, but at the cost of conceding to the union most of its demands, which he had earlier denounced as inflationary. Almost simultaneously, the nation's railroads suffered a total shutdown—the first in the nation's history—as two major unions walked out on strike. By threatening to use the army to run the trains, Truman pressured the workers back to work after only a few days. Once again, however, the nation had stared economic chaos in the face.

The strikes and the shutdowns provided only occasional disruptions. More constant reminders of the problems of reconversion were the severe shortages in a wide range of consumer goods. During the war, there had been an excuse for such shortages. Now, many Americans believed, consumer goods should have been plentiful. That they were not seemed to be evidence of mismanagement and disarray. Supplies of appliances, automobiles, nylon, sugar, meat, and many other goods could not approach keeping up with the demand. Far more Americans were attempting to buy or rent housing than there was housing available. The sense of things simply "not working" was impossible to avoid.

Things got better, of course. By the middle of 1947, most of the shortages had disappeared; inflation was slowly beginning to abate; labor unrest had subsided. But the memory of those first months survived to become, like the continuing frustrations in international affairs, a reminder of the gap between the nation's high hopes for the postwar world and the more troubled realities.

The Fair Deal and the Eightieth Congress

On September 6, 1945, only four days after the formal Japanese surrender, Truman submitted to Congress a twenty-one point domestic program outlining what he later termed the "Fair Deal." It called for the expansion of social security benefits, the raising of the legal minimum wage from 40 to 65 cents an hour, a program to ensure full employment, a permanent Fair Employment Practices Act, public housing and slum clearance, long-range environmental and public works

"WEATHER CLEAR, TRACK FAST." A cartoon by D. R. Fitzpatrick for the *St. Louis Post-Dispatch* expresses the widespread national concern about soaring postwar inflation. President Truman's vacillating economic policies and his mishandling of the repeal of wage and price controls helped exaggerate what would have been a serious problem in any case. The inflation contributed to the dramatic Republican victory in the 1946 congressional elections.

planning, and government promotion of scientific research. Weeks later he added other proposals: federal aid to education, government health insurance, prepaid medical care, funding for the St. Lawrence Seaway, and nationalization of atomic energy. The President was, it was clear, declaring an end to the wartime moratorium on reform and creating an impressive new liberal agenda. The announcement of the Fair Deal, he later wrote, "symbolizes for me my assumption of the office of President in my own right."

Truman's proposals greatly heartened Democratic liberals, who had continued to wonder whether the new President would prove a satisfactory successor to Franklin Roosevelt. But the Fair Deal made little progress in Congress. Truman won approval of several defense-related proposals, including creation of the Atomic Energy Commission and unification of the armed forces. And he managed to push through a modest "full-employment bill," although in a form greatly different from what he had proposed. Congress refused to pledge federal deficit spending in times of recession, as the President had urged. Instead, in the Maximum Employment Act of February 1946, it authorized the creation of a three-man Council of Economic Advisers, whose purpose was to engage in economic planning for the general welfare and to help government use its fiscal and monetary powers to stimulate employment. The act was another important step toward the integration of Keynesian theories into American economic policy, a step that ultimately greatly increased the power of the federal government (and of the President). At the time, however, it seemed like a very limited achievement.

These successes were the exception rather than the rule. For the most part, Truman's Fair Deal programs fell victim to the same general public and congressional conservatism that had crippled the last years of the New Deal and had increased during the war. The economic problems and labor unrest of 1946 only intensified congressional resistance to further spending and reform. And what little hope there had been for legislative progress died in November 1946, when the Republican party—making use of the simple but devastating slogan "Had Enough?"—won control of both houses of Congress.

The election results reflected in large part the increasing unpopularity of Truman himself, who had, much of the public was now concluding, simply failed to "measure up." Farmers were returning in droves to the Republican party. Workers, enraged at the President's "antiunion" stance in the coal and railroad strikes, similarly voted against the Democrats in unprecedented numbers. Some New Deal reformers had abandoned the President when Secretary of the Interior Harold Ickes, one of Roosevelt's original cabinet appointees and a symbol of traditional Democratic liberalism, resigned to protest the appointment of a wealthy oilman as Undersecretary of the Navy. Others had departed when Truman fired Secretary of Commerce Henry Wallace because of disagreements over foreign policy. Still more were simply frustrated by the President's apparent inability to control the squabbling and confusion within his own administration and at his continued reliance on political cronies from Missouri.

With the new Congress in place, the retreat from reform rapidly became a stampede. The President bowed to what he claimed was the popular mandate to lift most remaining wage and price controls, and Congress moved further to deregulate the economy. Inflation rapidly increased. When a public outcry arose over the soaring prices for meat, Senator Robert Taft, perhaps the most influential Republican conservative in Congress, advised consumers to "Eat less," and added, "We have got to break with the corrupting idea that we can legislate prosperity, legislate equality, legislate opportunity." True to the spirit of Taft's words, the Republican Congress quickly applied what one Congressman described as a "meat-axe to government frills." It refused to appropriate funds to aid education, increase social security, or support reclamation and power projects in the West. It defeated a proposal to raise the minimum wage. It passed tax measures that cut rates dramatically for high-income families and only moderately for those with lower incomes. Only vetoes by the President finally forced a more equitable bill.

The most notable action of the Eightieth Congress was an open assault upon one of the cornerstones of Depression reform: the Wagner Act of 1935. Conservatives had always resented the enormous powers the legislation granted unions; and in the light of the labor difficulties following the war, such resentments intensified sharply. The result was the Labor-Management Relations Act of 1947, better known as the Taft-Hartley Act, which loosened several of the earlier restrictions upon employers and added some important new prohibitions against the unions. The act made illegal the so-called closed shop (a workplace in which no one could be hired without first being a member of a union). And although it continued to permit the creation of so-called union shops (in which workers must join a union after being hired), it permitted states to pass "right-to-work" laws prohibiting even that. This provision, the controversial Section 14B, remained a target of the labor movement for decades. The act also empowered the President to call for a "cooling-off" period before a strike by issuing an injunction against any work stoppage that endangered national safety or health. These and other provisions delighted conservatives, who viewed union power as one of the nation's greatest social evils. But they outraged workers and union leaders, who denounced the measure as a "slave labor bill" and called on the President to veto it. Truman needed little persuading. He had opposed the Taft-Hartley Act from the beginning and, on June 20, 1947, returned it to Congress with a stinging veto message. Both houses easily overruled him the same day.

The Taft-Hartley Act did not destroy the labor movement, as many union leaders had predicted. But it did seriously damage the position of weaker unions in relatively lightly organized industries such as chemicals and textiles; and it made far more difficult the organizing of workers who had never been union members at all, especially in the South. Powerful unions remained powerful, for the most part; but unorganized or loosely organized workers now faced serious obstacles. Equally important in the short run, the passage of Taft-Hartley served as a symbol of the repudiation of New Deal reform by the Republican party and its Congress, a warning that government innovations that many had come to take for granted were now in jeopardy. "Victories fought and won years ago were suddenly in doubt," a columnist for the *New Republic* wrote at the time. "Everything was debatable again."

LABOR'S PLEA, 1947. Truman did, but it did not help. Congress overrode his veto with ease, and in 1947 the Taft-Hartley Act became law despite the anguished protests of workers, including members of the International Ladies' Garment Workers' Union, who are shown here meeting in New York's Madison Square Garden to demonstrate their opposition. (*ILGWU*)

The Election of 1948

Truman and his advisers were convinced that the American public was not ready to abandon the achievements of the New Deal, that the 1946 election had not been a mandate for a surrender to conservatism. As they planned strategy for the 1948 campaign, therefore, they placed their hopes in an appeal to enduring Democratic liberalism. Throughout 1948, Truman proposed one reform measure after another (including, on February 2, the first major civil-rights bill of the century). Congress, of course, ignored or defeated them all; but the President was effectively building a campaign issue for the fall.

There remained, however, the serious problem of Truman's personal unpopularity—the assumption among a vast segment of the electorate that he lacked stature, that his administration was weak and inept. Many of the qualities that made him such an admired figure in later years—his outspokenness, his impatience, his "common-man" demeanor—seemed at the time to be evidence of his unfitness to fill the shoes of Franklin Roosevelt. Liberals within his own party were actively looking for an alternative candidate. Conservatives were regarding the President with disgust.

All of these tensions came to a head at the Democratic Convention that summer. Two factions abandoned the party altogether. Southern conservatives,

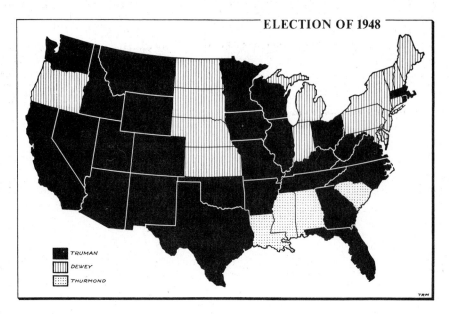

ELECTION OF 1948

TRUMAN
DEWEY
THURMOND

angered by Truman's proposed civil-rights bill and outraged by the approval at the convention of a civil-rights plank to the platform (engineered by Hubert Humphrey, the mayor of Minneapolis), walked out and formed the States' Rights (or "Dixiecrat") party, with Governor Strom Thurmond of South Carolina as its nominee. At the same time, the party's left wing formed a new Progressive party, with Henry A. Wallace as its candidate. The Wallace supporters objected to what they considered the slow and ineffective domestic policies of the Truman administration; but they resented even more the President's confrontational foreign policy with the Soviet Union.

In addition, many Democrats unwilling to leave the party attempted to dump the President in 1948. The Americans for Democratic Action (ADA), a coalition of liberals formed shortly after the war, attempted to entice Dwight D. Eisenhower, the popular war hero, to contest the nomination, certain that he could win the November election while Truman could not. Only after Eisenhower had refused did the party bow to the inevitable and, in near despair, give the nomination to Truman. The Republicans, in the meantime, had once again nominated Governor Thomas E. Dewey of New York, whose substantial reelection victory in 1946 had made him one of the nation's leading political figures. Austere, dignified, and competent, he seemed to offer an unbeatable alternative to the President. That his views on most issues were only marginally different from Truman's appeared further to strengthen his chances of victory.

Nothing, it seemed, could save the President from certain defeat. His party was seriously splintered. Polls showed him trailing so far behind Dewey that late in September public opinion analysts stopped taking surveys. Dewey was conducting a quiet, statesmanlike campaign, behaving much as if he were already President.

Only Truman, it seemed, believed he could win. He had provided a foretaste of what was to come in his speech accepting the Democratic nomination, a blistering attack on the Republican party. As the campaign gathered momentum, he became increasingly aggressive, turning his fire not on Dewey but on the "do-nothing, good-for-nothing" Republican Congress, which was, he told the voters, responsible for fueling inflation and abandoning the workers and the common people. To dramatize his point, he called Congress into special session in July to give it a chance, he said, to enact the liberal measures the Republicans had recently written into their platform. Congress met for two weeks and, predictably, did almost nothing. Truman was delighted.

Before the campaign was over, the President had traveled nearly 32,000 miles and made 356 speeches, delivering blunt, extemporaneous attacks. He had told Alben Barkley, his running mate, "I'm going to fight hard. I'm going to give them hell." He did. He also called for repeal of the Taft-Hartley Act, increased price supports for farmers, and strong civil-rights protection for blacks (he was the first President to campaign in Harlem). He sought, in short, to re-create much of Franklin Roosevelt's New Deal coalition. And to the surprise of virtually everyone, he succeeded. When the returns came in, the nation was stunned to learn that Harry Truman had won a narrow but decisive victory: 49.5 percent of the popular vote to Dewey's 45 percent (with the two splinter parties dividing the small remainder between them), and an electoral margin of 303 to 189. Democrats, in the meantime, had regained both Houses of Congress by substantial margins. It was the most dramatic upset in the history of presidential elections.

How had it happened? In part, it was because Truman's political problems had never been as serious as most observers believed. The desertion of the Wallace wing of the party, for example, proved to be an ephemeral threat. In an atmosphere of growing anticommunist fervor, Wallace's refusal to repudiate the support of a number of American communists seriously undermined his public stature. Even many liberal Democrats, including the ADA, harshly denounced him as a "Soviet dupe." And when the President himself began attacking the Progressives as communist sympathizers, he strengthened his position with many voters who had suspected the Democrats of being "soft" on communism. The Dixiecrat revolt, in the meantime, cost Truman some support in the South and cost him the electoral votes of four southern states. It helped him, however, among northern blacks, who were becoming an important political force in many industrial states.

More important, however, was Truman's ability to arouse public admiration for his feisty, combative campaign style. And most important of all was his success in turning national discontent to his own advantage. He could not argue that the country was entirely healthy and untroubled. But the record of the Eightieth Congress made it possible for him to argue that the problems were the responsibility not of the Democrats but of the Republicans. Democratic liberalism might be in decline, but the election results made clear that—despite, or perhaps because of, the efforts of the Republican Congress to bury it—it was not yet dead.

TRUMAN WINS. The *Chicago Tribune,* a champion of Republican conservatism, indulged in some wishful thinking on election night 1948 and issued a premature prediction in its first edition. The error provided a jubilant Harry Truman with an opportunity to pose for one of the most famous of all American political photographs. (*United Press photo*)

COLD WAR REFORM AND LIMITED WAR

Truman interpreted the 1948 election as a mandate for the revival of liberal reform. But while he enjoyed a few legislative successes in the ensuing months, most of his domestic programs quickly fell victim to his own and the nation's increasing preoccupation with the Cold War. At the same time that the President was urging an array of ambitious new social reforms, he was expanding the Marshall Plan, constructing the NATO alliance, and adjusting to the collapse of Chiang Kai-shek's government in China and the emergence of a communist regime to replace it. In competition with such concerns, the Fair Deal generally suffered. And it faded almost entirely from view when, beginning in 1950, the United States found itself embroiled in a difficult and frustrating war in Korea.

The Fair Deal and the Eighty-first Congress

Despite the Democratic victory in 1948, it often seemed that the Eighty-first Congress was no more hospitable to reform than its Republican predecessor. Truman failed once again to win approval of such major new reforms as aid to education and national health insurance. Nevertheless, his administration managed in the first two years of its second term to consolidate and extend a number of already established New Deal reforms that before the election had seemed to be in jeopardy.

On three issues, in particular, Truman won important victories. Congress raised the legal minimum wage from 40 cents to 75 cents an hour. It approved an expansion of the Social Security System, increasing benefits by 75 percent and extending them to 10 million additional people. And it strengthened the federal commitment to public housing. The National Housing Act of 1949 provided for the construction of 810,000 units of low-income housing over six years, to be accompanied by long-term rent subsidies.

While many of the other initiatives Truman had sponsored before 1948 gradually faded from view, the President continued to press strenuously on what was perhaps the most controversial domestic issue of all: civil rights. His commitment was a result of several factors: sincere personal conviction, a recognition of the growing importance of black voters to the Democratic party, and a desire to remove a glaring social injustice at a time when the Soviet Union was attempting to exploit the issue in its propaganda war with the United States.

The President had little luck persuading Congress to accept the civil-rights legislation he proposed in 1949, legislation that would have made lynching a federal crime, provided federal protection of black voting rights, abolished the poll tax, and established a Fair Employment Practices Commission to limit discrimination in hiring. Although a majority of the Senate appeared ready to support at least some aspects of this package, a vigorous filibuster by southern Democrats (who also controlled crucial committees) managed to block the legislation. Nevertheless, Truman proceeded on his own to battle several forms of racial discrimination. He appointed a federal Civil Rights Commission in 1948, whose report became the first important government call for the total elimination of segregation. Truman publicly approved its recommendations, although he was as yet unable to implement them. He ordered an end to discrimination in the hiring of government employees. He worked to dismantle segregation within the armed forces. And he allowed the Justice Department to become actively involved in court battles against discriminatory statutes. The Supreme Court, in the meantime, signaled its own increasing awareness of the issue by ruling, in *Shelley* v. *Kraemer* (1948), that the courts could not be used to enforce private "covenants" meant to restrict blacks from residential neighborhoods. The Truman record, and the judicial decisions that accompanied it, made only minor dents in the structure of segregation. They did, however, signal the beginning of a commitment by liberal Democrats—and by the federal government as a whole—finally to confront the problem of race.

War in Korea

Truman's domestic policies had had a difficult time from the beginning competing against the nation's obsession with the Soviet threat in Europe. In 1950, a new and more dangerous element of the Cold War emerged and all but killed hopes for further Fair Deal reform. On June 24, 1950, the armies of communist North Korea swept across their southern border and began a major invasion of the pro-Western half of the Korean peninsula to the south. Suddenly, the United States found itself embroiled in a new kind of conflict. The nation was neither fully at war nor fully at peace. It had, rather, discovered the peculiar demands of "limited war."

Korea had long been a source of international controversy. A peninsula of great strategic importance in Asia, it offered easy access to the Soviet Union, Japan, and China. At the end of World War II, therefore, neither the United States nor the Soviet Union—both of which had sent troops into Korea against the Japanese—was willing to leave. As a result, the nation had been divided, supposedly temporarily, along the thirty-eighth parallel. The Russians departed in 1949, leaving behind a communist government in the north with a strong, Soviet-equipped army. The Americans left only months later, handing control of the south to the pro-Western government of Syngman Rhee, a ruthless and only nominally democratic leader and an ardent nationalist. He possessed a far less imposing army than his northern counterparts, and he used it primarily to strengthen his own position against internal political opposition.

STALEMATE IN KOREA.   American fighter pilots trudge off to combat beneath a whimsical sign that expressed the exasperation of many soldiers in Korea. The first "limited war" quickly degenerated into an apparently endless stalemate; and soldiers responded to it with a level of cynicism that far exceeded the ordinary wisecracking of GIs in combat. (*U.S. Air Force photo*)

The situation proved a strong temptation to the Soviet leadership. The communist government of the north, recognizing its military superiority, was eager to invade the south to reunite the nation. The Russians would not, Stalin believed, have to play any direct role themselves. The unification of Korea under a sympathetic communist regime, moreover, would be an important strategic gain to the Soviets, who were looking with concern at American efforts to make Japan an American stronghold in Asia. With much to gain and little, he believed, to lose, Stalin gave his approval to the invasion.

The Truman administration was quick to respond. On June 27 the President ordered American air and naval forces to assist the South Korean army against the invaders; and on the same day he appealed to the United Nations to intervene. Because the Soviet Union was boycotting the Security Council at the time (to protest the council's refusal to recognize the new communist government of China), American delegates were able to win UN agreement to a resolution calling for international assistance to the embattled Rhee government. On June 30, the United States ordered its own ground forces into Korea, and Truman appointed General Douglas MacArthur to command the UN operations there. (Several other nations offered minor assistance to the effort, but the "UN" armies were, in fact, overwhelmingly American.)

The intervention in Korea was the first expression of the newly militant American foreign policy outlined in NSC-68. Very quickly, the administration decided that the war would not simply be an effort at containment, but also at "liberation." After a surprise American invasion at Inchon in September had routed the North Korean forces from the south and sent them fleeing back across the thirty-eighth parallel, Truman gave MacArthur permission to pursue the communists into their own territory. His aim, as an American-sponsored UN resolution proclaimed in October, was to create "a unified, independent and democratic Korea." (Paralleling this decision came new American initiatives in other areas: efforts to strengthen the Chiang regime in Taiwan for a possible future assault upon the Chinese mainland; and assistance to the French, who were attempting to rout communist forces from Vietnam and Laos.)

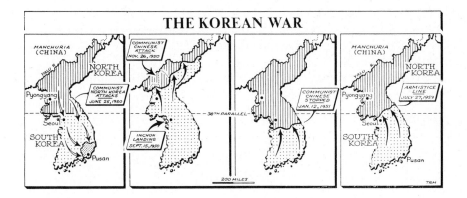

THE KOREAN WAR

From Invasion to Stalemate

For several weeks, MacArthur's invasion of North Korea proceeded smoothly. On October 19, the capital, Pyongyang, fell to the UN forces. At the same time, parachutists managed to trap and immobilize much of the rest of the North Korean army. Victory seemed near. Slowly, however, the United States was becoming aware of the growing presence of forces from communist China; and by November 4, it was clear that eight Chinese divisions had entered the war. Suddenly, the UN offensive stalled and then collapsed. Through December 1950, American forces fought a bitter, losing battle against far more numerous Chinese divisions, retreating at almost every juncture. Within weeks, communist forces had pushed the Americans back below the thirty-eighth parallel once again and had recaptured the South Korean capital of Seoul. By March, the rout had ceased, and the UN armies had managed to regain much of the territory it had so recently lost, taking back Seoul and pushing the communists north of the thirty-eighth parallel for the second time. But with that, the war degenerated into a protracted, brutal stalemate.

It was then that the nation began, for the first time, to experience the true dilemmas of "limited war." Truman had been determined from the beginning to avoid embroiling the nation in a direct conflict with China, a conflict that would, he believed, lead to a world conflagration. As early as December 1950, he had begun seeking a negotiated solution to the struggle; and he continued through the next two years to insist that there would be no wider war. He faced, however, a formidable opponent in General MacArthur, a soldier of the old school who could not accept the idea of any limits upon a military endeavor. The United States was fighting the Chinese, he argued. It should, therefore, attack China itself, if not through an actual invasion, then at least by bombing communist forces massing north of the Chinese border. In March 1951 he gave a public indication of his unhappiness with the administration's policy, sending to House Republican leader Joseph W. Martin a message that concluded: "There is no substitute for victory." His position quickly won wide popular support from a nation frustrated by the long, inconclusive war.

For nine months, Truman had chafed at MacArthur's continuing resistance to his decisions about the conduct of the war. More than once, he had warned him to keep his objections to himself. The release of the Martin letter, therefore, struck the President as intolerable insubordination. On April 11, 1951, he relieved MacArthur of his command.

The result was a virtual firestorm of public outrage. Sixty-nine percent of the American people supported MacArthur in the controversy, a Gallup Poll reported. When the general returned to the United States in 1951, the first time he had set foot in the country since 1935, he was greeted with hysterical enthusiasm. His televised farewell appearance before a joint session of Congress attracted an audience of millions. Public criticism abated somewhat when a number of prominent military figures, including General Omar Bradley, publicly supported the

MACARTHUR COMES HOME. "Old soldiers never die; they just fade away," General MacArthur said at the close of his emotional speech to a joint session of Congress. Many Republicans hoped to nominate him as the party's candidate for President in 1952 (a hope MacArthur himself did nothing to discourage), but in the end it was the moderate forces that prevailed. Dwight D. Eisenhower was a far less controversial and equally revered military hero. MacArthur did indeed "fade away" in the ensuing years. Never again did he play a major role in American public life. (*U.S. Army photo*)

President's decision. But the controversy had cast in sharp relief the dilemmas of limited war.

The dispute between Truman and MacArthur represented not only a conflict over civilian versus military control of the armed forces. It represented, too, sharp disagreement within both the civilian government and the military over America's strategic objectives. Truman and many military leaders believed that the first priority of the United States was Europe, that the nation must limit its Asian commitments to maintain sufficient strength to resist communist expansion in the West. MacArthur and his supporters, in contrast, viewed Asia as the region of greatest importance to the American future and were impatient, therefore, with the limits placed upon American actions there. It was a debate that would continue to rage within the government for many years.

In the meantime, the Korean stalemate continued for what seemed interminable months. In July 1951, negotiations began between the opposing forces at Panmunjom, near the thirty-eighth parallel; but they produced no swift resolution.

Instead, the talks—and the war—dragged on until 1953, placing increasing strains on the American people.

Limited Mobilization

Just as the war in Korea produced only a limited American military commitment abroad, so it created only a limited economic mobilization at home. Although the Truman administration drew heavily upon the experiences of World War II in meeting the demands for armaments and supplies, never was it necessary to create the enormous bureaucracy and pervasive controls that had been required a decade earlier. Nevertheless, the Korean War did place pressure upon the government to control the economy in several important ways. First, Truman attempted to halt a new wave of inflation by setting up the Office of Defense Mobilization to hold down prices and discourage high union wage demands. Then, confronted with the failure of these cautious regulatory efforts, the President took more drastic action. When railroad workers walked off the job in 1951, Truman ordered the government to seize control of the railroads. But the dramatic gesture had little impact; workers ultimately got most of what they had demanded before the railroads were returned to their owners. In 1952, a nationwide steel strike threatened to interrupt vital war production; and again, Truman moved to seize the steel mills, citing his powers as Commander in Chief. This time, however, the courts intervened. In a 6 to 3 decision, the Supreme Court ruled that the President had exceeded his authority, and Truman was forced to relent. A lengthy and costly strike ensued. Clearly, there were special problems in mobilizing the nation's economy for war without mobilizing American society behind a total war effort.

There were, however, important positive results of the military commitment in Korea, most notably the significant boost it gave to national prosperity. Just at the point when some economists believed the postwar consumer demand was about to decline, a new surge of funds was being pumped into the economy by the federal government, which increased military expenditures more than fourfold, to $60 billion in 1953. Unemployment declined. Industry embarked on a new wave of capital expansion. The groundwork was being laid for the remarkable boom years of the 1950s.

But the war had other, less healthy effects upon American life. Coming at a time of rising insecurity about the position of the United States in the world, it intensified anxiety about communism. As the long stalemate continued, producing 140,000 American casualties (and more than 1 million South Korean dead and wounded), frustration increasingly turned to anger. The United States, which had recently won the greatest war in history, seemed unable to conclude what many Americans considered a minor border skirmish in an unimportant country. Many began to believe that something must be deeply wrong—not only in Korea but within the United States as well. Such fears became one of many factors contributing to the rise of the second major campaign of the century against domestic communism.

THE CRUSADE AGAINST SUBVERSION

There has never been a single, satisfactory explanation of why, in the years following World War II, the American people developed a growing fear of internal communist subversion that by the early 1950s had reached the point of near hysteria. Anticommunism was an old and fundamental element of American political thought; and there had, it was true, been red scares before—most notably in the years following World War I. Never, however, had the fear of subversion become as pervasive or lasted for so long as in the years from 1947 through 1953 —years marked by one of the most corrosive assaults upon civil liberties and general tolerance in the nation's history. Only by looking at the convergence of many factors at once is it possible to understand the era of the "great fear."

One factor was obvious. Communism was not an imagined enemy in the 1950s; it had tangible shape, in the person of Joseph Stalin and the Soviet Union, and it had become a dark and menacing threat to America's hopes for the world. The continuing setbacks overseas, the frustrations in Korea, the "loss" of China, the shocking realization that Russia had developed an atomic bomb—all created a sense of unease and a need to find someone to blame. The idea of a communist conspiracy within American borders was a natural outlet. But there were other factors as well, rooted in domestic political rivalries, that took a gnawing uneasiness and whipped it into a public frenzy.

HUAC and Alger Hiss

Much of the anticommunist furor emerged out of the search by the Republican party for an issue with which to attack the Democrats, and out of the efforts of the Democrats to take that issue away. Beginning in 1947, the House Un-American Activities Committee (HUAC), now under the control of Republicans, launched a series of widely publicized and highly inflammatory investigations to prove that, under Democratic rule, the nation had allowed communist subversion to reach alarming levels. The committee turned first to the movie industry, arguing that communists had so infiltrated Hollywood that American films were being tainted with Soviet propaganda. A parade of writers and producers was summoned to testify; and when some of them refused to answer questions about their political beliefs, they were sent to jail for contempt. Others were barred from employment in the industry when Hollywood, attempting to protect its public image, adopted a blacklist consisting of those of "suspicious loyalty."

Far more frightening, however, was HUAC's investigation into charges of disloyalty leveled against a former high-ranking member of the State Department: Alger Hiss. Whittaker Chambers, a self-avowed former communist agent, told the committee in 1948 that Hiss had passed classified documents to him in 1937 and 1938. When Hiss sued him for slander, Chambers produced microfilms of the documents (called the "pumpkin papers," because Chambers had kept them hidden in a pumpkin in his garden). Hiss could not be tried for espionage because the statute of limitations had expired. But because of the committee's efforts (and particularly because of the relentless pursuit of the case by Richard M. Nixon, a freshman Republican Congressman from California), Hiss was charged with lying to the HUAC inquisitors. After a sensational trial, in which a number of leading Democratic liberals—including Adlai Stevenson, Felix Frankfurter, and Dean Acheson—testified as character witnesses for Hiss, the jury was unable to reach a verdict. A second trial produced a conviction for perjury, and Hiss served several years in prison, still proclaiming his innocence. The Hiss case not only discredited a talented young diplomat; it cast suspicion upon an entire generation of liberal Democrats and made it possible for the public to believe that communists had actually infiltrated the government.

The Federal Loyalty Program

The Truman administration, in the meantime, was making its own contribution to increasing the popular fear. Partly to protect itself against Republican attacks, partly to encourage support for the President's foreign policy initiatives, the executive branch in 1947 initiated a widely publicized program to review the "loyalty" of federal employees. A series of "loyalty boards" undertook a sweeping investigation of the government; and in August 1950, the President authorized the dismissal in sensitive departments of even those deemed no more than "bad security risks." The faintest suspicion of disloyalty could cause a federal employee to lose his or her job. By 1951, more than 2,000 government employees had resigned and 212 had been dismissed.

In addition to the Employee Loyalty Program itself being abused, the program served as a signal throughout the executive branch to launch a major assault upon subversion. The Attorney General established a list of dissident organizations and, in 1948, obtained indictments of eleven American communists for "conspiring to teach the violent overthrow of the government." The Federal Bureau of Investigation (FBI), whose director, J. Edgar Hoover, had been obsessed with the issue of communism for years, launched major crusades to investigate and harass alleged radicals. Federal information and education programs began to become tainted with strident anticommunist propaganda.

By now, the anticommunist frenzy was growing so intense that even a Democratic Congress was becoming obsessed with it. In 1950, over the objections of the Department of Defense, the Department of Justice, and the CIA, it enacted the McCarran Internal Security Act. The bill did not outlaw the Communist party. It did, however, require all communist organizations to register with the government and to publish their records. Americans were liable for prosecution on grounds as vague as "fomenting revolution." Communists were barred from working in defense plants and denied passports. Members of overseas "subversive organizations" were denied visas to enter the country. Truman vetoed the bill. Congress easily overrode his veto.

Of particular importance in fanning public fears were the efforts of the FBI and the Justice Department to prove a communist conspiracy to steal America's atomic secrets for the Soviet Union. The early explosion of a Russian nuclear

NIXON AND THE HISS PAPERS. Congressman Richard Nixon of California, whose ardent pursuit of the Alger Hiss investigation helped make him a national figure, examines the so-called pumpkin papers—a microfilm of secret State Department documents that Hiss had allegedly copied and conveyed to the Soviet Union years before. By tracing the documents to a typewriter once owned by Hiss, government prosecutors attempted to prove that the former diplomat had indeed been involved in espionage. Despite staunch support from, among others, Secretary of State Dean Acheson, Hiss was convicted of perjury. He would spend more than thirty years attempting to prove his innocence. (*Wide World Photos*)

weapon made such charges credible. And the testimony in 1950 of Klaus Fuchs, a young British scientist, that he had delivered to the Russians full details of the manufacture of the bomb gave the charges substance. Through an arcane series of connections, the case ultimately settled on an obscure New York couple, Julius and Ethel Rosenberg, whom the government claimed had been the masterminds of the conspiracy. The Rosenbergs had allegedly received the information from Ethel's brother, a machinist who had worked on the Manhattan Project, and passed it on to the Soviet Union. Several witnesses corroborated the story; although the Rosenbergs vehemently denied any guilt, they were found guilty and, on April 5, 1951, sentenced to death. A rising chorus of public protests and a long string of appeals failed to save them. On June 19, 1953, they died in the electric chair.

All these factors—the HUAC investigations, the Hiss trial, the loyalty investigations, the McCarran Act, the Rosenberg case, and more—combined, by the early 1950s, to create a paranoia about communist subversion that seemed to grip the entire country. State and local governments launched loyalty programs of their own, dismissing thousands of employees. Local courts began handing down extraordinarily harsh sentences to defendants convicted of anything resembling subversion. Schools and universities rooted out teachers suspected of teaching "un-American" ideas. Unions found themselves under continuing assault for suspected (and occasionally real) communist leanings. And a pervasive fear settled on the country—not only fear of communist infiltration but the fear of being suspected of communism. Critics of American society became wary of voicing sharp objections lest they be accused of disloyalty. Official and public pressure combined to encourage conformity and discourage serious dissent. It was a climate that made possible the rise of an extraordinary public figure, whose behavior at any other time would have been dismissed as preposterous.

McCarthyism

Joseph McCarthy was an undistinguished, first-term, Republican Senator from Wisconsin when, in February 1950, he suddenly burst into national prominence. In the midst of a speech in Wheeling, West Virginia, he raised a sheet of paper into the air and claimed to "hold in my hand" a list of 205 known communists currently working in the American State Department. No person of comparable stature had ever made so bold a charge against the federal government; and in the weeks to come, as McCarthy repeated and expanded upon such accusations, he emerged as the nation's preeminent leader of the crusade against communism.

He had seized upon anticommunism not out of any real concern but because he needed an issue with which to run for reelection in 1952. And he continued to exploit the issue for the next four years because, to his surprise, it won him fame and notoriety beyond his wildest dreams. His rise was meteoric. Within weeks of his charges against the State Department, he had launched a series of investigations of subversion, investigations that probed virtually every area of the government. His unprincipled assistants, Roy Cohn and David Schine, sauntered arrogantly through federal offices and American embassies overseas looking for evidence of communist influence. One hapless government official after another found himself summoned before McCarthy's special subcommittee, where the Senator belligerently and often cruelly badgered witnesses and destroyed public careers.

In the course of this extraordinary crusade, not once did McCarthy produce conclusive evidence against a federal employee of communist ties. But the public seemed not to care. A growing constituency adored him for his coarse, "fearless" assaults upon a government establishment that many considered arrogant, effete, even effeminate. They admired his efforts to expose the "traitors" who had, he claimed, riddled the Truman administration. They even tolerated his attacks upon public figures who earlier would have been considered unassailable, men such as General George C. Marshall and Governor Adlai Stevenson. Republicans, in particular, rallied to his claims that the Democrats had been responsible for "twenty years of treason," that only a change of parties could rid the country of subversion. McCarthy, in short, provided his followers with an issue into which they could channel a wide range of resentments: fear of communism, animosity toward the country's "eastern establishment," and frustrated partisan ambitions.

For several years, McCarthy terrorized American public life, intimidating all but a very few from speaking out in opposition to him. In 1952, when some Democratic Senators dared to denounce him, McCarthy openly campaigned against their reelection, and several went down to defeat. Journalists and intellectuals, with some notable exceptions, drew back from challenging him for fear of being themselves discredited by his attack. Even the highly popular Dwight D. Eisenhower, running for President in 1952, did not dare to oppose him. Outraged at McCarthy's attacks upon General Marshall, Eisenhower briefly considered issuing a public protest. In the end, however, he remained silent.

McCarthy was, during his brief years of prominence, undoubtedly the most important figure in the nation's obsession with communist subversion—a figure so important that the term "McCarthyism" came to symbolize the entire troubled era. But the Senator from Wisconsin was less the cause than the result of the harsh political climate of the time. And when, beginning in 1953, the paranoia began to subside, McCarthy himself was one of the first political figures to suffer.

The Republican Revival

Public frustration over the stalemate in Korea and popular fears of internal subversion combined to make 1952 an inhospitable year for the Democratic party. Truman, whose own popularity had diminished almost to the vanishing point, wisely withdrew from that year's presidential contest, creating the first open battle for the nomination since 1932. Senator Estes Kefauver of Tennessee launched a spirited campaign, performing well in the primaries. But party leaders ultimately settled on Governor Adlai E. Stevenson of Illinois, whose early reluctance to run seemed only to enhance his attractiveness.

Stevenson's dignity, wit, and eloquence quickly made him a beloved figure to many liberals and intellectuals, who developed a devotion to him that they had never offered Harry Truman. But those same qualities seemed only to fuel Republican charges that Stevenson lacked the strength or the will to combat communism sufficiently. Joseph McCarthy described him as "soft" and took delight in deliberately confusing him with Alger Hiss.

Stevenson's greatest problem, however, was the candidate the Republicans chose to oppose him. Rejecting the efforts of conservatives to nominate either

THE DEMOCRATIC TICKET, 1952. Adlai E. Stevenson stands with his running mate, Senator John Sparkman of Alabama, before the 1952 Democratic National Convention. Although Stevenson lost badly to Dwight D. Eisenhower in both the 1952 and 1956 presidential elections, he remained the hero of American liberals until his death in 1964. Critics scoffed at him as an "egghead," reflecting the wide misconception that Stevenson was an intellectual. But the candidate's wit, urbanity, and unaffected intelligence set him apart from the normal run of political figures. (*National Archives*)

Robert Taft or Douglas MacArthur, the Republicans turned to a man who had had so little previous identification with the party that liberal Democrats had tried to draft him four years earlier. Their choice was General Dwight D. Eisenhower, military hero, former commander of NATO, now president of Columbia University in New York. Despite a vigorous struggle by the Taft forces, Eisenhower won nomination on the first ballot. He chose as his running mate the young California Senator who had won national prominence through his crusade against Alger Hiss: Richard M. Nixon.

Eisenhower and Nixon proved to be a powerful combination in the autumn campaign. While Eisenhower attracted support by virtue of his geniality and his statesmanlike pledges to settle the Korean conflict (at one point dramatically promising to "go to Korea" himself), Nixon effectively exploited the issue of domestic anticommunism. After surviving early accusations of financial improprieties (which he effectively neutralized in a famous television speech), Nixon went

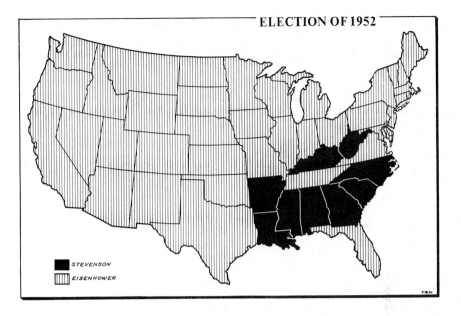

ELECTION OF 1952

STEVENSON

EISENHOWER

on to launch harsh attacks on Democratic "cowardice," "appeasement," and "treason." He spoke derisively of "Adlai the appeaser" and ridiculed Secretary of State Dean Acheson for running a "cowardly college of communist containment." And he missed no opportunity to publicize Stevenson's early support for Alger Hiss as opposed to Nixon's role in exposing Hiss's misdeeds. Eisenhower and Nixon both made effective use of allegations of corruption in the Truman administration and pledged repeatedly to "clean up the mess in Washington."

The response at the polls was overwhelming. Eisenhower won both a popular and an electoral landslide: 55 percent of the popular vote to Stevenson's 44 percent, 442 electoral votes to Stevenson's 89. Republicans gained marginal control of both Houses of Congress; but it was clear that their presidential candidate was far more popular than the party as a whole. Nevertheless, the election of 1952 ended twenty uninterrupted years of Democratic control of the federal government. And while it might not have seemed so at the time, it also helped signal the end of the turbulent postwar era and the beginning of a period marked by a search for cohesion and stability.

SUGGESTED READINGS

On the policies and problems of the Truman administration, see Alonzo Hamby, *Beyond the New Deal* (1973); Robert Donovan, *Conflict and Crisis* (1977); Barton Bernstein (ed.), *Politics and Policies of the Truman Administration* (1970); and Bert Cochran, *Truman and the Crisis Presidency* (1973). Eric Goldman, *The Crucial Decade—And After* (1960), is a breezy account of the era. William Berman, *The Politics of Civil Rights in the Truman Administration* (1970), and Donald McCoy and Richard Ruetten, *Quest and Response* (1973), examine the record on race. R. Alton Lee, *Truman and Taft-Hartley* (1967), explores one of the President's most prominent disputes; and James T. Patterson, *Mr. Republican* (1972), a biography of Senator Robert Taft, examines the career of one of his leading conservative opponents. Maeva Marcus, *Truman and the Steel Seizure* (1977), is a study of one of the administration's flamboyant but unsuccessful attempts to quell instability. On the dramatic election of 1948, see Irwin Ross, *The Loneliest Campaign* (1968); Norman Markowitz, *The Rise and Fall of the People's Century* (1973), a study of the campaign of Henry Wallace; and Allen Yarnell, *Democrats and Progressives* (1974).

For the Korean War, consult Allen Whiting, *China Crosses the Yalu* (1960); Robert Leckie, *Conflict* (1962); John Spanier, *The Truman-MacArthur Controversy* (1959); and Glenn Paige, *The Korean Decision* (1968). A survey of the anticommunist frenzy of the era is David Caute, *The Great Fear* (1978). On the Hiss case, see Allen Weinstein, *Perjury* (1978), which argues that Hiss was guilty. Robert and Michael Meeropol, the children of Julius and Ethel Rosenberg, argue the innocence of their parents in *We Are Your Sons* (1975). Richard Freeland, *The Truman Doctrine and the Origins of McCarthyism* (1971); Athan Theoharis, *Seeds of Repression* (1971); and Alan Harper, *The Politics of Loyalty* (1969), discuss the impact of Truman administration policies upon the anticommunist frenzy. On McCarthy, see Richard Rovere, *Senator Joe McCarthy* (1959); Richard Fried, *Men Against McCarthy* (1976); Robert Griffith, *The Politics of Fear* (1970); and Michael Rogin, *The Intellectuals and McCarthy* (1967). Victor Navasky, *Naming Names* (1980), discusses the sensitive issue of informers during the Red Scare. Joseph Starobin, *American Communism in Crisis* (1972), discusses the plight of the embattled party.

Twenty

The Affluent Society

In later decades, Americans tended to look back on the 1950s and early 1960s as something of a golden age: an era of boundless prosperity, of social stability, of national optimism and confidence. To some extent, that image was simply a result of the nostalgia with which most generations view earlier, apparently happier times. But to a remarkable degree, it was also the image that Americans of the 1950s held of their own society. Seldom before had the United States experienced an era of such pride and self-satisfaction.

Two fundamental realities shaped the mood of the decade. There was, first, a booming national prosperity, which seemed to promise a solution to all the nation's economic and social problems. And there was, second, the continuing struggle against communism, a struggle that created an undercurrent of anxiety but that also encouraged Americans to look even more approvingly at their own society. The combination produced what many observers at the time and many historians later described as a broad consensus—a wide agreement on the basic goals and values of national life. But this apparent consensus often blinded Americans to the serious social tensions that continued to plague their society—tensions that would ultimately help to produce a great cultural crisis in the 1960s.

PROSPERITY AND ITS LIMITS

Perhaps the most striking feature of American life in the 1950s and early 1960s, and one that virtually no observer could ignore, was prosperity—a booming, almost miraculous economic growth that made even the heady 1920s seem pale by comparison. It was, moreover, a prosperity far better balanced and far more widely distributed than that of thirty years earlier. It was not, however, as universal as Americans liked to believe.

Economic Growth

By 1949, despite the continuing problems of postwar reconversion, what some called the "miracle" of American economic expansion had begun. It would continue with only minor interruptions for almost twenty years. The Gross National Product, the most basic indicator of economic growth, alone provides ample evidence of the prosperity of the era. Between 1945 and 1960, the American GNP grew by 250 percent, from $200 billion to $500 billion. That growth appears even more remarkable in view of public expectations in 1945 that the GNP would soon decline, once the extraordinary demands of war production subsided. Unemployment, which during the Depression had averaged between 15 and 25 percent, remained throughout the 1950s and early 1960s at about 5 percent or lower. Inflation, in the meantime, hovered at about 3 percent a year or less.

There was no single cause. Government spending, which had ended the Depression in the 1940s, continued to stimulate growth. There was increasing public funding of schools, housing, veterans' benefits, welfare, and interstate highways (for which the government spent over $100 billion beginning in 1956)—all helping to sustain prosperity. Above all, there was military spending, which continued at almost wartime levels. The Korean War, in particular, helped to spark the economic boom. During the first half of the 1950s, when military spending was at its peak, the annual growth rate was 4.7 percent. For the second half of the decade, with the Korean War concluded and spending on armaments in decline, the rate of growth was only 2.25 percent.

Technological progress also contributed to the boom. Because of advances in production techniques and mechanical efficiency, worker productivity increased more than 35 percent in the first decade after the war, a rate far higher than that of any previous era. The development of electronic computers, which first became commercially available in the mid-1950s, helped improve the performance of many American corporations. And technological research and development itself became an important new sector of the economy, expanding the demand for scientists, engineers, and other highly trained experts.

The national birth rate reversed a long pattern of decline, sparking the so-called postwar baby boom, which peaked in 1957. The nation's population rose almost 20 percent in the decade, from 150 million in 1950 to 179 million in 1960. This growth mirrored a worldwide demographic explosion that would ultimately place great strains upon the resources of the planet. In the United States of the 1950s, however, the baby boom meant increased consumer demand and expanding economic growth.

The rapid expansion of suburbs—whose population grew 47 percent in the 1950s, more than twice as fast as the population of the nation as a whole—helped stimulate growth in several important sectors of the economy. The automobile industry experienced the greatest boom in its history, as the number of privately owned cars more than doubled in a decade. The demand for new homes helped sustain a vigorous housing industry. The construction of roads, which was both a cause and a result of the growth of suburbs, stimulated the economy even further.

Economic Consolidation

The prosperity of the 1920s had been accompanied by a rapid increase in economic centralization and concentration. The prosperity of the 1950s brought with it a similar consolidation. There were more than 4,000 corporate mergers in the course of the 1950s; and more than ever, a few large corporations were controlling an enormous proportion of the nation's economic activity. This was particularly true in industries benefiting from government defense spending. As during World War II, the federal government tended to award military contracts to large corporations. In 1959, for example, half of all defense contracts went to only twenty firms. But the pattern repeated itself in almost all areas of the economy, as an increasing number of corporations moved from being single-industry firms to becoming diversified conglomerates. By the end of the decade, half of the net

FREEWAYS. The rapid construction of interstate highways in the 1950s and 1960s changed the face of the American landscape. It also altered the fabric of American life, both by providing a stimulus to the booming economy and by encouraging the rapid exodus of middle-class families from city to suburb. The Los Angeles freeway system, pictured here, is perhaps the ultimate expression of the nation's fascination with and dependence on the automobile. (*UPI*)

corporate income in the nation was going to only slightly more than 500 firms, or one-tenth of 1 percent of the total number of corporations.

Unlike the 1920s, this increase in corporate consolidation was accompanied by a growth in the power of labor organizations. Corporations enjoying such remarkable growth were reluctant to allow strikes to interfere with their operations; and since the most important unions were now so large and entrenched that they could not easily be suppressed or intimidated, business leaders made important concessions to them. As early as 1948, Walter Reuther, president of the United Automobile Workers, obtained from General Motors a contract that included a built-in "escalator clause"—an automatic cost-of-living increase pegged to the consumer price index. The provision set a crucial precedent—not only for the rest of the automobile industry but for the economy at large. In 1955, Reuther received a guarantee from Ford Motor Company of continuing wages to auto workers even during layoffs (although not the guaranteed annual wage he had demanded). A few months later, steelworkers in several corporations did receive guarantees of an annual salary. By the mid-1950s, factory wages in all industries had risen substantially, to a healthy average of $80 per week.

Not all laborers shared in such gains. The labor movement enjoyed great success in winning new benefits for workers already organized in strong unions. For the majority of laborers who were as yet unorganized, there were fewer advances. Total union membership remained relatively stable at about 16 million throughout the 1950s; and while this was in part a result of a shift in the work force from blue-collar to white-collar jobs, it was at least as much a result of new obstacles to organization. The Taft-Hartley Act and the state right-to-work laws that it spawned made increasingly difficult the creation of new unions that would be powerful enough to demand recognition from employers.

The economic successes of the entrenched unions in the 1950s helped pave the way for the reunification of the labor movement. In December 1955, the American Federation of Labor and the Congress of Industrial Organizations ended their twenty-year rivalry and merged to create a giant new federation, the AFL-CIO, under the leadership of George Meany. But the climate of the era produced other, less welcome changes in the nature of the labor movement. An increasing number of unions, no longer required to engage in the militant crusades against corporate resistance that had dominated the 1930s, were themselves becoming wealthy, powerful bureaucracies. Most continued to operate responsibly and effectively; but some of the most important unions began to face accusations of corruption and indifference.

The powerful Teamsters Union became in 1957 the focal point of a congressional investigation, which charged president David Beck with the misappropriation of over $320,000 in union funds. Beck ultimately stepped down from his office to be replaced by Jimmy Hoffa, who was widely believed to have close ties to underworld crime. Government investigators pursued Hoffa for nearly a decade before finally winning a conviction against him in 1964. After his release from prison in 1971 (on a pardon from President Richard Nixon), he attempted to regain his position in the union. But before he could succeed, he disappeared and

JIMMY HOFFA.
The controversial Teamster president waves to delegates at the annual convention of the Teamsters Union in Miami Beach, July 1961. The convention reelected him the same day, but only three years later a federal jury would convict him of jury tampering. Although "getting" Hoffa became almost an obsession of Attorney General Robert Kennedy, the "labor racketeering" that Hoffa came to symbolize spread far beyond his office and his union. (*UPI*)

was generally presumed to have been murdered. The United Mine Workers, the union that had spearheaded the industrial movement in the 1930s, similarly became tainted by suspicions of corruption and by violence. John L. Lewis's last years as head of the union were plagued with scandals and dissent within the organization. His successor, Tony Boyle, was ultimately convicted of complicity in the 1969 murder of Joseph Yablonski, the leader of a dissident faction within the union. Even more troubling, perhaps, was the growing belief among many union members that the leaders of these and other labor organizations had lost touch with the rank and file. They often appeared to have grown more involved with the internal bureaucratic and political struggles of the union organization itself than with the welfare of the members. Like other Americans railing against other bureaucracies, laborers could discern no easy solution to the problem.

Economic Dislocations

Americans in the 1950s liked to believe that their growing prosperity was reaching virtually every area of the society. It was not. Important groups continued to struggle on the fringes of the economic boom, unable to share in the abundance. Between 1948 and 1956, while national income increased 50 percent, farm prices dropped 33 percent, a victim of enormous surpluses in basic staples. In 1948, farmers had received 8.9 percent of the national income; in 1956, they received only 4.1 percent. In part, this decline reflected the steadily shrinking farm population; in 1956 alone, one out of every eleven rural residents moved into or was absorbed by a city. But it also reflected the deteriorating economic condition of those farmers who remained. They experienced not only a decline in their own income but a steady increase in the prices they paid for consumer goods.

The federal government, in the meantime, was exhibiting some uncertainty about its own role in the agricultural economy. There was great pressure within the Eisenhower administration to reduce the enormous government losses that had resulted from rigid price supports and to end the artificiality in production and distribution that some economists argued had resulted. But the flexible price supports that the government adopted in 1954 came under increasing attack from farmers, who argued that the supports could only "flex" downward. Finally, in 1956, the administration bowed to the demands of farmers and accepted a program of increased subsidies for land left fallow. But neither the new programs nor the billions of dollars the government pumped into the agricultural economy by its purchases of surpluses succeeded in arresting the decline.

Farmers, at least, were able to attract some public attention to their plight. Other, poorer groups languished in virtual obscurity. As middle-class Americans left the cities for the suburbs, it became increasingly easy to ignore the existence of severe poverty in the heart of the major industrial metropolises. Black ghettoes were expanding rapidly in the 1950s, as black farmers joined the general exodus from country to city and as the black population in general expanded rapidly. Continuing racial discrimination helped doom these communities to unmitigated, even increasing, poverty. In New York City and elsewhere, growing Puerto Rican and other Hispanic communities were earning less than what the government considered the minimum necessary for "adequate" living. Urban ghettoes were becoming so isolated from the economic mainstream that their residents were finding it almost impossible to obtain employment. Thus the "inner cities" were becoming virtual prisons for poor people, who had neither the resources to move to areas where jobs were more plentiful nor the political power to force development of their own communities. A similar predicament faced residents of several particularly destitute rural regions—most notably the Appalachian areas of the southern and border states, which were experiencing an almost total economic collapse. Lacking adequate schools, health care, and services, the residents of Appalachia, like the residents of the urban ghettoes, were almost entirely shut off from the mainstream of American economic life. Not until the 1960s, when such exposés as Michael Harrington's *The Other America* (1962) began drawing attention to the continuing existence of poverty in the nation, did the middle class begin to recognize the seriousness of the problem.

THE CULTURE OF AFFLUENCE

The process of cultural consolidation, like the process of economic consolidation, gathered increasing momentum in the 1950s. Middle-class Americans, at least, found themselves living in a society growing more alike from one region to the next and one community to the next. Several important economic and social trends in particular encouraged this homogenization of American culture: consumerism, the growth of the suburbs, the expanding role of the media, and the increasing influence of science and technology. At the same time, however, the nation began to hear a rising chorus of protest from those who found the new culture unsatisfying or dehumanizing.

Consumers and Suburbs

At the center of middle-class culture was a rampant, at times almost obsessive, consumerism. It was a result of many things: the spread of affluence, the increasing variety and availability of products, and the adeptness of advertisers in creating a demand for those products. It was also a result of the growth of consumer credit, which increased by 800 percent between 1945 and 1957. Easily available credit cards, revolving charge accounts, and easy-payment plans made immediate gratification of consumer yearnings not only desirable but possible. Affluent Americans in the 1950s and 1960s showed renewed interest in such longtime consumer crazes

LEVITTOWN, PENNSYLVANIA, 1949. Levittown was one of the first of the sprawling, mass-produced suburbs that would become a feature of the American landscape in the 1950s. Although more affluent developments often attempted to preserve trees and to vary the architecture of their houses, the more modest middle-class suburbs, of which this is an example, made few such efforts. (*UPI*)

as the automobile, as Detroit responded to the boom with ever-flashier styling and accessories. And they responded eagerly to the development of such new products as dishwashers, garbage disposals, televisions, and "hi-fis" and stereos. Because so large a proportion of such goods were produced by a few large corporations, Americans in all areas of the country were making use of identical products. And competition among neighbors to purchase the most recent consumer craze helped further to fuel a growing middle-class conformity.

Suburbs, similarly, helped create an American life style that differed little from one region to another. Since suburban housing developments were usually new and constructed all at once, they tended to be far more similar to one another than older neighborhoods, which had grown up more slowly. The general (and deliberate) isolation of suburbs from congested urban areas made regional variations even fewer. And within the suburbs themselves, homes were often almost indistinguishable from one another. Among the popular symbols of American society in the 1950s were the Levittowns—huge, mass-produced suburban towns, created by developer Arthur Levitt, where street after street was lined with identical single-family houses. Builders across the country followed Levitt's lead and adopted standardized building methods. Separated from urban institutions and surrounded by uniformity, residents of suburbia developed an increasingly homogenized life style. And because there was so little that was distinctive about most suburban communities, there was also little to discourage families from moving elsewhere as economic opportunities appeared. The conformity of suburban life was accompanied, therefore, by an increasing rootlessness among members of the middle class, who often developed no permanent ties to any one region but identified instead with the larger, national culture.

The Media

The postwar era witnessed as well the birth of the most important agent of cultural homogenization of all: television. Television did not even exist as a commercial medium until after World War II. In 1946, there had been only 17,000 sets in the entire country. By 1953, two-thirds of all American homes had televisions. Seven million sets were produced in that year alone. By 1957, there were 40 million television sets in use, almost as many as there were families. More people had television sets, according to one report, than had refrigerators.

The impact of television upon American life was rapid, pervasive, and profound. Television news had by the end of the 1950s replaced newspapers, magazines, and radios as the nation's most important vehicle of information. A small group of anchormen, producers, and reporters, almost all based on the East Coast, exercised virtually total control of how the vast majority of Americans viewed public events. Television advertising exposed the entire nation to new fashions and products. Television entertainment programming, almost all of it controlled by three national networks, created a common image of American life—an image that was predominantly white, middle-class, and suburban. Even those unable to share in

ED AND RALPH. One of the most popular television comedies of the 1950s—*The Honeymooners,* starring Jackie Gleason and Art Carney—was also one of the least typical. Its working-class characters (a bus driver, a sewer worker, and their wives) contrasted sharply with the suburban, middle-class families of most television series. (*UPI*)

the affluence of the era could, through television, acquire a vivid picture of how the rest of their society lived.

The Allure of Science

In 1961, *Time* magazine chose as its "man of the year" not a specific person but the "American Scientist." It was an indication of the widespread fascination with which Americans in the age of atomic weapons viewed science and technology. Major medical advances—for example, Jonas Salk's discovery of a vaccine to prevent polio—seemed to confirm the important role that scientific research would play in promoting progress. So did such technological innovations as the jet airplane, the computer, synthetics, and new types of commercially prepared foods. Nothing, however, better illustrated the nation's veneration of scientific expertise than the popular enthusiasm for the American space program.

The program began, in large part, because of the Cold War. When the Soviet Union announced in 1957 that it had launched a satellite—*Sputnik*—into outer space, the United States reacted with shock and alarm. Strenuous efforts began to improve scientific education in the schools, to develop more research laborato-

REACHING THE MOON. Edwin "Buzz" Aldrin stands on the lunar surface in July 1969, as he and *Apollo XI* commander, Neil Armstrong, become the first men ever to reach the moon. Reflected in his visor are Armstrong, who is taking the photograph, and the lunar module *Eagle,* in which the astronauts landed and in which they would later rejoin the mother ship, *Columbia,* for the return to earth. Although the moon landing created wide excitement, it represented in fact the tail end of America's fascination with the space program. It was in the late 1950s and early 1960s that the romance of space had captured the nation's imagination most completely. Moon landings after 1969 attracted a decreasing level of public interest; and by the late 1970s, the space program was in rapid decline. Enthusiasm seemed to revive early in 1981 with the successful flight of the first reusable "space shuttle," but NASA remained plagued by limited funding. (*NASA*)

ries, and, above all, to speed the development of America's own exploration of outer space. The centerpiece of that exploration was the manned space program, established in 1958 with the selection of the first American space pilots. In the years that followed, these seven "astronauts" became the nation's most widely revered heroes. The entire country watched on May 5, 1961, as Alan Shepard became the first American launched into space (several months after a Soviet "cosmonaut," Yuri Gagarin, had made a similar flight). John Glenn, who on February 2, 1962, became the first American to orbit the globe (again, only after Gagarin had already done so), was soon an even more celebrated national idol. Yet Americans marveling at space exploration were reacting less to the individual men involved than to the enormous scientific effort that lay behind their exploits.

Ultimately, the nation would tire of the space program, which never managed to convince the public that it offered any practical benefits. But interest remained high as late as the summer of 1969, when Neil Armstrong and Edwin Aldrin became the first men to walk on the surface of the moon. Not long after that, the enthusiasm began to subside, and the government began to cut the funding for future missions. The broader faith in science and technology, however, proved more enduring.

Organized Society and Its Detractors

Even more than in the 1920s, Americans in the 1950s and 1960s were aware of the increasing importance of organizations and bureaucracies in their lives. White-collar workers, who in the 1950s came to outnumber blue-collar laborers for the first time, found employment predominantly in corporate settings with rigid hierarchical structures. Industrial workers confronted ponderous bureaucracies in their own unions. Consumers discovered the frustrations of bureaucracy in dealing with the large, national companies from whom they bought goods and services. It was becoming increasingly clear to all Americans that the key to a successful future lay in acquiring the specialized training and skills necessary for work in large organizations, where every worker performed a particular, well-defined function.

As in earlier eras, Americans reacted to these developments with ambivalence, often hostility. The debilitating impact of bureaucratic life upon the individual was slowly becoming one of the central themes of popular and scholarly analyses of national life. William H. Whyte, Jr., produced one of the most widely discussed books of the decade: *The Organization Man* (1956), which attempted to describe the special mentality of the worker in a large, bureaucratic setting. Self-reliance, Whyte claimed, was losing place to the ability to "get along" and "work as a team" as the most valuable trait in modern character. Sociologist David Riesman made similar observations in *The Lonely Crowd* (1950), in which he argued that the traditional "inner-directed" man, who judged himself on the basis of his own values and the esteem of his family, was giving way to a new "other-directed" man, more concerned with winning the approval of the larger organization or community. Others echoed this concern that society was creating crushing pressures on its members to conform. Even those who lived and worked outside bureaucratic settings, such critics argued, were subjected to the homogenizing pressures of a "mass culture," dominated by television and designed to appeal to the "lowest common denominator."

To many Americans, such concerns were the source of a general personal uneasiness, a sense of restlessness or unfulfillment. For no group was this problem more acute than for middle-class American women. Never was the social pressure upon women to avoid careers and serve instead as housewives and mothers stronger than it was in the 1950s. Yet never did that role offer fewer opportunities for fulfillment. For those wives sequestered in isolated suburbs, in particular, there were often intolerable pressures of loneliness, boredom, and frustration. Betty Friedan began to call attention to this "problem that has no name," in *The Feminine Mystique* (1963), which helped signal the beginning of the feminist movement of the 1960s and 1970s.

The most decisive critics of the culture of the affluent society, however, were a number of young poets and writers generally known as the "beats" (or, by derisive critics, as "beatniks"). To them, the conventional society of the American middle class was an object of contempt, a world to be avoided and despised. They wrote harsh critiques of the sterility and conformity of American life, the mean-inglessness of American politics, and the banality of popular culture. Allen Ginsberg, one of the most celebrated of the beats, attracted wide acclaim with his dark, bitter poem *Howl* (1955), decrying the "Robot apartments! invincible suburbs! skeleton treasuries! blind capitals! demonic industries!" of modern life. Jack Kerouac, a talented novelist whose severe alcoholism and early death sharply limited his creative output, nevertheless produced what may have been the leading document of the Beat Generation: *On the Road* (1957), an account of a cross-country automobile trip that depicted the rootless, iconoclastic life style of Kerouac and his friends.

Other, gentler writers nevertheless used their work to express misgivings about the enormity and impersonality of modern society. Saul Bellow produced a series of novels—*The Adventures of Augie March* (1953), *Seize the Day* (1956), *Herzog* (1964), and others—that chronicled the difficulties of modern, urban Jews in finding fulfillment in the dehumanizing environment in which they were forced to live. J. D. Salinger, one of the most popular writers of the era, wrote, in *The Catcher in the Rye* (1951), of the crushing impact of modern life on vulnerable, sensitive individuals. The novel described the dilemma of prep-school student Holden Caulfield, unable to find any area of society—school, family, friends, city —in which he could feel secure or committed. Salinger's series of short stories and novelettes about the Glass family likewise described the assaults of contemporary society upon people of intelligence and sensitivity. In the 1950s and early 1960s, such warnings remained relatively muted, as in the writings of Bellow and Salinger, or had only a limited impact upon the culture at large, as with the work of Ginsberg and Kerouac. By the late 1960s, however, these concerns were becoming crucial to the creation of a widespread and influential "counterculture."

THE SUBWAY (1950). American realist George Tooker used his paintings to convey the same sense of frightened alienation from modern society that many writers of the 1950s expressed in their novels. This dreamlike painting suggests the monotonous and threatening character of the urban environment. (*Collection of the Whitney Museum of American Art, Juliana Force Purchase*)

THE POLITICAL CLIMATE

Among the many phenomena that made the "age of affluence" an extraordinary period in American life was the confident, exhilarating, at times even arrogant tone of the nation's political climate. Americans continued to differ sharply on any number of political issues; but most did so within a framework of agreement about the essential righteousness of American values and about the strength and stability of the American political and economic system. That outlook sustained the relatively calm and unadventurous political climate of the Eisenhower years; it supported the optimistic surge of liberal reform during the Kennedy and Johnson administrations; and it collapsed, finally, in the face of a series of national traumas in the late 1960s. While it survived, however, it exercised a powerful, pervasive influence upon the nation's life at home and upon its role in the world.

The New Economics

Basic to this sense of national confidence was the exciting (and to some surprising) discovery of the power of the American economic system. During the Depression, some had questioned the viability of capitalism. In the 1950s, such doubts all but disappeared. Two features in particular made the postwar economy a source of national pride and confidence.

First was the belief that Keynesian economics made it possible for government to regulate and stabilize the economy without intruding directly into the private sector. Keynes had argued as early as the 1920s that by varying the flow of government spending and managing the supply of currency, the state could stimulate the economy to cure recession and dampen growth to prevent inflation. The experience of the last years of the Depression and the first years of the war had seemed to confirm this argument. And by the mid-1950s, Keynesian theory was rapidly becoming a fundamental article of faith—not only among professional economists but among much of the public at large. The most popular economics textbook of the 1950s and 1960s, Paul Samuelson's *Economics,* imbued genera- tions of college students with Keynesian dogma. Armed with these fiscal and monetary tools, economists now believed, it was possible for the government to maintain a permanent prosperity. The dispiriting boom-and-bust cycle that many had long believed to be a permanent feature of industrial capitalism could now be banished forever. Never again would it be necessary for the nation to experience another Depression.

If any doubters remained, they found ample evidence to dispel their misgivings during the brief recessions the economy experienced during the era. When the economy slackened in late 1953, Secretary of the Treasury George M. Humphrey and the Federal Reserve Board worked to ease credit and make money more readily available. The economy quickly recovered, helping to confirm the value of Keynesian tactics. A far more serious recession began late in 1957 and continued for more than a year. This time, the Eisenhower administration ignored the Keynesians and adopted such deflationary tactics as cutting the budget. The slow, halting nature of the recovery, in contrast with the rapid revival in 1954, seemed further to support the Keynesian philosophy. The new economics finally won full acceptance in 1963, when John Kennedy proposed a tax cut to stimulate economic growth. Although it took Kennedy's death and the political skills of Lyndon Johnson finally to win passage of the measure in 1964, the result was all that the Keynesians had predicted: an increase in private demand, which stimulated eco- nomic growth and reduced unemployment.

In addition to the belief in the possibility of permanent economic stability was the equally exhilarating belief in permanent economic growth. As the economy continued to expand far beyond what any observer had predicted was possible only a few years before, more and more Americans assumed that such growth was now without bounds—that there were few effective limits upon the abundance availa- ble to the nation. This was not only a comforting thought in itself; it also provided a new outlook on social and economic problems. In the 1930s, many Americans had argued that the elimination of poverty and injustice would require a redistribu- tion of wealth—a limitation on the fortunes of the rich and a distribution of this wealth to the poor. By the mid-1950s, reformers concerned about economic deprivation were arguing that the solution lay in increased production. The afflu- ent would not have to sacrifice in order to eliminate poverty. The nation would simply have to produce more abundance, thus raising the quality of life of even the poorest citizens to a level of comfort and decency. Few people claimed that all the nation's social problems had been solved. But many were beginning to argue that the new economics made solutions to such problems possible, and that such solutions would not require wrenching social conflict.

The National Purpose

Some of this confidence in the capabilities of the American economy was well justified by the realities of the 1950s and 1960s. But much of it, as subsequent years would prove, was not. That Americans not only believed in but exaggerated the strength of their economic system was in part a result of their continuing preoccupation with the struggle against communism. The more virtues that could be attributed to the American way of life, the more forceful would be the argument that democratic capitalism was stronger and more just than Marxism.

The combination of faith in the economy and fear of communism produced what may have been the most striking feature of American political life in the 1950s: the virtual disappearance of a serious political left. The far left had never been a powerful force in American society, even in eras of deep distress such as the 1930s. But it had always been audible. Not even the booming prosperity of the 1920s had quelled the voices of those who openly challenged the capitalist system. In the 1950s, however, the few serious critics of the American political and economic structure who remained were all but silenced—either intimidated by the crashing din of the anticommunist crusade or denied access to media by which to make themselves heard.

The labor movement had always been one area in which the left had maintained a secure and influential base. The CIO, in particular, had since the 1930s been the home of a number of outspoken leftists, including some avowed socialists and communists. There had been among some labor organizations a sense that the purpose of a union was not simply to win higher wages for workers, but to promote structural change in the economic system. By the early 1950s, however, the leaders of both the A.F. of L. and the CIO had become convinced that the labor movement, like the rest of the country, had to rid itself of communism. Leftists within the unions either abandoned their beliefs or found themselves repudiated or expelled. Phillip Murray, president of the CIO, announced that his organization had "no use for any damn communists." Walter Reuther, who became president of the United Auto Workers in 1948, engaged in a strenuous campaign against the left in his union. By the time of the AFL-CIO merger in 1957, the labor movement had effectively purged itself of all serious critics of capitalism. The labor left stood almost entirely isolated, almost completely without influence.

The failure of Henry Wallace's Progressive party in 1948 also played a role in this process. The left wing of the Democratic party had always included people with fundamental reservations about the American system—not socialists or communists, perhaps, but men and women who believed in major structural changes in capitalism and in United States foreign policy. It was this group, disillusioned with the domestic timidity and the international belligerence of the Truman administration, that had rallied to the cause of Henry Wallace. But in doing so, they had identified themselves in the public eye with communism and all but entirely isolated themselves from the political mainstream. Taking their place as the left wing of the Democratic party was a far more moderate group of liberals, members of the Americans for Democratic Action.

The only important critics of American society remaining on the left, in other words, were people with no real criticisms to make. Such liberal intellectuals as Arthur M. Schlesinger, Jr., Daniel Bell, Richard Hofstadter, Louis Hartz, and others might point to particular social problems that required remedying. But they argued just as strenuously on behalf of the essential justice and equity of the American political system. Their harshest criticisms were directed toward those "extremists" who threatened to destroy what Arthur Schlesinger once termed the "vital center." Americans were not interested in ideologies, wrote Louis Hartz in *The Liberal Tradition in America* (1955), one of the most influential books of the decade. They had throughout their history shared a belief in the basic values of their society, and they differed only on the practical measures necessary to achieve the broader goals. The United States had never suffered from the class conflict that had plagued European nations, argued historians such as Richard Hofstadter. Populism and similar reform movements, he claimed in *The Age of Reform* (1954), far from being authentic class rivalries, had represented the aberrant behavior of groups who had not yet learned how to operate effectively within the political mainstream.

As the 1950s progressed, liberals who believed so strongly in the strength and justice of their society began to grow increasingly impatient with failures to address those social problems that remained. By the end of the Eisenhower administration, they were complaining loudly about the "drift" in public policy, the lack of a sense of "national purpose." America had the capacity to solve its problems, they believed. And it had a duty to do so—not only for its own sake but to prove to the world that a democratic, capitalist society was preferable to a communist one. In the early 1960s, this liberal faith became the motive force behind a bold new surge of domestic reform.

In the meantime, however, this same liberal faith helped to support the nation's continuing commitment to fighting the spread of communism throughout the world. Because the American way of life was so clearly superior to communism, it was both the right and the duty of the nation to ensure that all peoples had the opportunity to share the fruits of democracy and capitalism. And because the United States was so powerful and resourceful, there was no reason to believe that the nation was not capable of working its will wherever it wished. Along with the surge of domestic reform, therefore, there emerged in the early 1960s an increasing willingness to expand the American commitment to anticommunist struggles. By the end of that decade, the nation would discover that neither solving domestic problems nor opposing communist expansion was as easy or as simple as had been thought.

HERBLOCK ON IKE. Liberal criticism of the Eisenhower administration's "drift" receives expression in this 1957 cartoon by Herblock of the *Washington Post.* While social turmoil builds beneath him, the President hovers complacently above the fray.

The Survival of the Right

Liberals and moderates of both parties spoke frequently in the 1950s and early 1960s of what historian Eric Goldman once described as "the arrival of a broad consensus in the thinking of Americans about the public issues of the day." To some extent, they were correct. Certainly the American left had been effectively emasculated; and the majority of the population seemed by the end of the decade to have accepted both the basic assumptions of the Cold War and the broad ideology of liberal reform. But such observers erred in another assumption: that they had effectively eliminated the right as an important force in American life. What Goldman and others liked to dismiss as "a few shrill voices" was, in fact, a powerful and enduring element in the nation's politics.

The extreme right, to be sure, was able to muster only a small constituency. Such organizations as the John Birch Society, which was militantly anticommunist, and the Ku Klux Klan, which waged a continuing battle to preserve "white supremacy," wielded influence that could not be ignored. Neither of them, however, was a major national force. But the sentiments upon which they thrived— the belief that the United States was insufficiently assertive in its fight against world communism and domestic radicalism, the fear that government reforms would threaten the survival of local customs and institutions—survived among a broad spectrum of the public. Reformers liked to believe that opposition to racial integration, for example, was restricted to a few bigots or to a particular, backward region. They would later discover that conservative attitudes on these and many other issues were far more deeply rooted and far more widespread than they had suspected.

SUGGESTED READINGS

Broad studies of the society of the 1950s include William Leuchtenburg, *A Troubled Feast* (1979); Carl Degler, *Affluence and Anxiety* (1968); John Brooks, *The Great Leap* (1966); and Godfrey Hodgson, *America in Our Time* (1976). On the economy, consult John K. Galbraith, *The Affluent Society* (1958) and *The New Industrial State* (1967); C. Wright Mills, *The Power Elite* (1956); Harold G. Vatter, *The U.S. Economy in the 1950s* (1963); and Robert Heilbroner, *The Limits of American Capitalism* (1965). Joel Seidman, *American Labor From Defense to Reconversion* (1953), and John Hutchinson, *The Imperfect Union* (1970), examine changes in the labor movement. A sociological examination of suburban society can be found in Herbert Gans, *The Levittowners* (1967). The rise of mass media receives attention in Edward J. Epstein, *News From Nowhere* (1973), and David Halberstam, *The Powers That Be* (1979). Tom Wolfe, *The Right Stuff* (1979), is an engaging and perceptive discussion of the origins of the space program. More conventional studies include R. L. Rosholt, *An Administrative History of NASA* (1966), and Walter Sullivan (ed.), *America's Race for the Moon* (1962).

Among the many books examining the effects of modern, organized society upon the individual, several are of particular value. See David Riesman, *The Lonely Crowd* (1950); William Whyte, *The Organization Man* (1956); and C. Wright Mills, *White Collar* (1956). On the beats, see Bruce Cook, *The Beat Generation* (1971), and John Tytell, *Naked Angels* (1976). For Jack Kerouac, see Ann Charters, *Kerouac* (1973), and Dennis McNally, *Desolate Angel* (1979). Good examples of the political and intellectual climate of the era include Arthur M. Schlesinger, Jr., *The Vital Center* (1949); Daniel Bell, *The End of Ideology* (1960); and Richard Hofstadter, *The Age of Reform* (1954). Mary Sperling McAuliffe, *Crisis on the Left* (1978), is a good account of the split among liberals and the origins of the "consensus." Daniel Bell (ed.), *The Radical Right* (1963), is a collection of hostile studies of the survival of extreme conservatism.

Twenty-One

Eisenhower and the "Middle of the Road"

It was appropriate, perhaps, that Dwight D. Eisenhower, a man who had risen to prominence as a great military leader, should preside over an era in which the American people were preoccupied with international tensions. And it was fitting, too, that this essentially conservative man, who enjoyed the company of wealthy businessmen, should serve as President in a period when Americans wanted nothing so much as a lasting stabilization of their newly prosperous economy. It should not have been surprising, therefore, that Eisenhower, the least experienced politician to serve in the White House in the twentieth century, was nevertheless the most politically successful President of the postwar era. At home, he pursued essentially moderate policies, avoiding most new initiatives but accepting the work of earlier reformers. Abroad, he continued and even intensified American commitments to oppose communism but brought to some of those commitments a measure of restraint that his successors could not always match.

THE POLITICS OF PROSPERITY

Eisenhower did little during his eight years in office to challenge the prevailing desire for moderation and security. Instead, he adopted policies designed to allow Americans to preserve their economic gains and to avoid adventuring toward new governmental programs or dogmas. In a nation moderate in its views, Eisenhower clung firmly to the "middle of the road" in his conduct of domestic affairs.

A Business Government

The first Republican administration in twenty years staffed itself with men drawn from the same quarter as those who had staffed Republican administrations in the 1920s: the business community. To his cabinet the President appointed a leading corporation lawyer (Secretary of State John Foster Dulles), the president of General Motors (Defense Secretary Charles E. Wilson), the head of a major financial firm (Treasury Secretary George Humphrey), a New England manufacturer, two automobile distributors, a farm marketing executive, and other wealthy corporate figures. Only Secretary of Labor Martin P. Durkin, president of the plumbers' union, stood apart. "Eight millionaires and a plumber," the *New Republic* caustically remarked. Within eight months, Durkin resigned, to be replaced by yet another businessman. Members of the new administration were not apologetic about their backgrounds. Charles Wilson assured Senators considering his confirmation that he foresaw no conflict of interest because he was certain that "what was good for our country was good for General Motors, and vice versa."

The inclination of the Eisenhower government to limit federal activities and encourage private enterprise received clear illustration in its policies toward government power development. The President, who referred to the Tennessee Valley Authority in 1953 as an example of "creeping socialism" and once talked wistfully of selling "the whole thing," supported the private rather than public development of natural resources. When the TVA proposed building a new steam plant on the banks of the Mississippi, the administration circumvented the agency and awarded the contract instead to the private Dixon-Yates syndicate. The decision provoked two years of controversy, which abated only when the President canceled the contract and allowed the city of Memphis, Tennessee, to build the plant. The President similarly canceled plans for a large federal dam in Hell's Canyon on the Snake River in Idaho and authorized a private power company to build three smaller dams on the site instead. To decentralize resource development even further, he turned over to the states the control of offshore oil-drilling leases along the Gulf of Mexico and the Pacific Coast.

Eisenhower moved in other areas as well to limit government involvement in the economy. In addition to lowering supports for farm prices (see pp. 391–392), he removed the last limited wage and price controls maintained by the Truman administration. He opposed the creation of new social service programs such as national health insurance (although he did support a bill to underwrite private insurance programs, a bill that never passed). He strove constantly to reduce federal expenditures (even during the recession of 1958) and balance the budget. He ended 1960, his last full year in office, with a $1 billion surplus.

The Survival of Social Welfare

Eisenhower's philosophy of "dynamic conservatism," as he saw it, may not have been hospitable to new social programs. But it did permit the survival, and even on occasion the expansion, of some existing ones. The President resisted pressure

THE VICTORS, 1952. President-elect Dwight D. Eisenhower and Vice President-elect Richard M. Nixon acknowledge the cheers of supporters on election night 1952. Between them stand their wives, Pat Nixon and Mamie Eisenhower. Eisenhower paid little attention to Nixon during their years in office together, but the Vice President nevertheless managed to convey the impression of performing an important role in the administration. (*UPI*)

from the right wing of his party to dismantle the welfare policies of the New Deal that had survived the conservative assaults of the war years and after. During his term, a Republican Congress agreed to extend the Social Security System to an additional 10 million new people and unemployment compensation to an additional 4 million people. The minimum hourly wage increased from 75 cents to $1. And the administration did support one positive new government program of great importance: interstate highway construction. The Federal Highway Act of 1956 authorized $25 billion for a ten-year building effort—one that would ultimately expand far beyond that figure.

That Eisenhower did not launch a stronger assault on existing social programs and that he actually supported some liberal reforms was partly a result of his own inclinations. It was also a result of political realities. During his first two years in office, although Congress was nominally under Republican control, a coalition of Democrats and liberal Republicans limited the freedom of conservatives to act. And from 1954 to the end of Eisenhower's years in office (indeed until 1980), both Houses of Congress remained securely in Democratic hands.

Not even Eisenhower's personal popularity was sufficient to bring his party back to power in Congress. In 1956, Eisenhower ran for a second term, even though he had suffered a serious heart attack the previous year. With Adlai Stevenson opposing him once again, he won by another, even greater landslide, receiving nearly 57 percent of the popular vote and 442 electoral votes to Stevenson's 89. Still, Democrats retained control of both Houses of Congress. And in 1958, they increased that control by substantial margins. The nation had endorsed Eisenhower's inclination to moderate the reforming zeal of earlier years, to "hold the line." They were not, however, ready to accept the belief of others in his party that the nation should adopt an even more militantly conservative policy.

The Decline of McCarthyism

The Eisenhower administration did little in its first years in office to discourage the anticommunist furor that had gripped the nation. Indeed, it helped to sustain it. The President actually intensified the already much-abused hunt for subversives in the government, which Truman had begun several years earlier. More than 2,220 federal employees resigned or were dismissed as a result of security investigations. Among them were most of the leading Asian experts in the State Department, who were harried from office because they had shown inadequate enthusiasm for the now exiled regime of Chiang Kai-shek. Their absence was later to prove costly, as the government expanded its commitments in Asia without sufficient knowledge of the political realities within the region.

Among the most celebrated episodes of the first year of the new administration was the case of J. Robert Oppenheimer, director of the Manhattan Project during the war and one of the nation's most distinguished and admired physicists. Although Oppenheimer was now out of government service, he continued as a consultant to the Atomic Energy Commission. But he had angered some officials by his public opposition to development of the new, more powerful, hydrogen bomb. In 1953, the FBI distributed a dossier within the administration detailing Oppenheimer's prewar association with various left-wing groups. And the President responded by ordering a "blank wall" to be placed between Oppenheimer and government secrets. A federal investigation, requested by Oppenheimer himself and conducted in an inflamed and confused atmosphere, confirmed the decision to deny him a security clearance. The episode deeply embittered much of the scientific community and caused a major public outcry.

The strong opposition to the persecution of Oppenheimer was one indication that the anticommunist hysteria of the early 1950s was beginning to abate. A more important signal of the change was the political demise of Senator Joseph

THE ARMY VS. McCARTHY.   Senator Joseph McCarthy of Wisconsin illustrates
his claim of communist infiltration of the country by using an elaborate map during
the 1954 Army–McCarthy hearings, which were televised nationwide. To McCarthy's
left, conspicuously unimpressed with the presentation, is counsel for the army Joseph
Welch. In the course of the hearings, Welch's patient, understated responses to
McCarthy's strident accusations helped undermine public respect for the Senator,
who under the glare of television cameras appeared crude and cruel. (*UPI*)

McCarthy. McCarthy continued during the first year of the Eisenhower administration to operate with almost total impunity. The President, who privately
loathed him, nevertheless refused to speak out in public. "I will not get into the
gutter with that guy," he reportedly explained. But McCarthy finally overreached
himself in January 1954 when he began launching oblique attacks against the
President and a direct assault upon Secretary of the Army Robert Stevens and the
armed services in general. In the face of these outrageous charges, Congress
decided it had no choice but to stage a series of special meetings, the Army–
McCarthy hearings as they became known. They were among the first such
hearings to be nationally televised, and the result was devastating to McCarthy.
Day after day, the public watched McCarthy in action—bullying witnesses, hurl-
ing groundless (and often cruel) accusations, evading issues, and offering churlish
objections at every point. He began to appear less a hero than a villain, and
ultimately less that than a mere buffoon. In December 1954, the Senate voted

67 to 22 to condemn him for "conduct unbecoming a senator." And three years later, with little public support left, he died—a victim of complications arising from serious alcoholism.

The Supreme Court, in the meantime, was also beginning to restrict the official harassment of suspected "subversives." Many people had expected the Court to become more conservative once the new President began to appoint new members. In fact, quite the opposite occurred. In 1953, Eisenhower nominated the former Republican Governor of California, Earl Warren, to be the new Chief Justice. And to the surprise of many, including Eisenhower, Warren became the moving force behind the most strenuous judicial effort to protect and expand civil liberties in the nation's history. In 1957, the Warren Court limited the FBI's latitude in using secret evidence against an opponent. More important, that same year it struck down the Smith Act, ruling that urging the overthrow of the government was not a crime unless it involved direct incitement of illegal actions. The following year the Court forbade the State Department to deny passports to members of the Communist party. There had, it seemed, been a reversal of roles. In the 1930s, the Court had been a conservative impediment to a liberal executive branch. In the 1950s, the justices were moving more boldly than the administration on behalf of civil rights and civil liberties.

THE RISE OF THE CIVIL-RIGHTS MOVEMENT

The Eisenhower years may have represented a national mood of cautious moderation in many areas. On one issue, however, they were a time in which a major social revolution finally commenced. After decades of skirmishes, there began in the 1950s an open battle against racial segregation and discrimination, a battle that would prove to be one of the longest and most difficult of the century. It occurred on several fronts. From the Supreme Court came a series of rulings that began to destroy the legal edifice of segregation. From blacks themselves came concerted, forceful, and increasingly direct challenges to local institutions of discrimination.

The Brown Decision

In 1954, years of patient legal efforts by the NAACP and other black reformers finally bore fruit when, on May 17, the Supreme Court announced its decision in the case of *Brown* v. *Board of Education of Topeka*. In considering the legal segregation of a Kansas public-school system, the Court finally rejected the doctrine of the 1896 *Plessy* v. *Ferguson* decision, which had established that states could provide blacks with separate facilities as long as the facilities were equal to those of whites. Explaining the unanimous opinion of his colleagues, Chief Justice Warren declared: "We conclude that in the field of public education the doctrine of 'separate but equal' has no place. Separate educational facilities are inherently unequal." Communities must work to desegregate their schools, the Court ordered, "with all deliberate speed."

It was not to be so easy. In some communities, compliance came relatively quickly and painlessly, as in Washington, D.C. Far more often, however, strong local resistance produced long delays. Some school districts attempted to circumvent the ruling with purely token efforts to integrate. Others simply ignored the ruling altogether. By the fall of 1957, only 684 of 3,000 eligible school districts in the South had even begun to desegregate their schools. In those that had complied, white resistance often produced angry mob actions and other violence. An increasing number of white parents simply withdrew their children from the public schools and enrolled them in all-white "segregation academies," many of them poorly staffed and equipped. The *Brown* decision, far from ending segregation, launched a prolonged battle between federal authority and state and local governments. In the years to come, federal courts would have to play an ever-increasing role in public education to ensure compliance with the desegregation rulings. And the executive branch, whose responsibility it was to enforce the decisions of the courts, found itself frequently pitted against local authorities attempting to defy the law.

The first of such confrontations occurred in September 1957 in Little Rock, Arkansas. The courts had ordered the desegregation of that city's Central High School. Governor Orval Faubus, a rabid and ambitious segregationist, ordered the National Guard to intervene to stop it. Faubus finally called off the Guard in response to the orders of a federal judge; but an angry mob quickly took its place in blocking integration of the school. Faced with this open defiance of federal authority (and with real danger to the safety of the black students involved), Eisenhower finally responded by sending federal troops to Little Rock to restore order and ensure that the court orders would be obeyed. Central High School admitted its first black students; but controversy continued to plague the Little Rock school system for several years.

The Expanding Movement

The legal assault on school segregation was only one part of the war against racial discrimination in the 1950s. The *Brown* decision seemed also to spark a growing number of popular challenges to segregation by blacks in one community after another. The first and most celebrated occurred in Montgomery, Alabama. There, in December 1955, a black woman, Rosa Parks, was arrested when she refused to give up her seat on a city bus to a white passenger. The incident produced outrage in the city's black community, which organized an almost total black boycott of the bus system to demand an end to segregated seating. Six months later, a federal court ordered the bus company to change its policy.

The real accomplishment of the Montgomery boycott, however, was less in changing the seating policies of the bus system than in establishing a new form of racial protest and in elevating to prominence a new figure in the movement for civil rights. The leader of the boycott was a local Baptist pastor, Martin Luther King, Jr., son of a prominent Atlanta minister and the possessor of a charismatic leadership ability that even he had not suspected. King won national attention

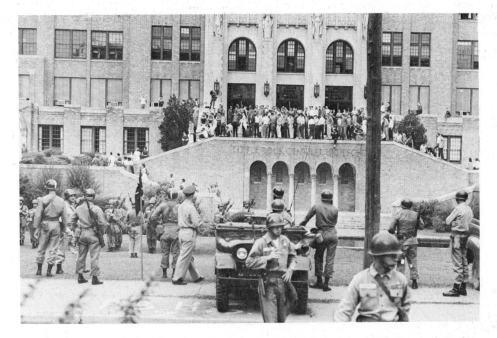

CRISIS IN LITTLE ROCK. Federal troops maintain order outside Central High School in Little Rock, Arkansas, in 1957. President Eisenhower reluctantly ordered the troops into the city after angry white citizens backed up by Governor Orval Faubus had threatened to prevent the court-ordered integration of the school. The incident was one of the first direct confrontations between federal and local authorities over the volatile issue of racial integration. It would not be the last. (*UPI*)

with his doctrine of "nonviolence"—that is, of passive resistance even in the face of direct assaults by white segregationists. Drawing from the teachings of Mahatma Gandhi, the legendary Indian nationalist leader, whose life King had studied while a student in Boston, he urged blacks to engage in peaceful demonstrations; to allow themselves to be arrested, even beaten, if necessary; and to respond to hate with love. King's unparalleled oratorical talents ensured that his message would be widely heard. And for the next thirteen years, he would serve as the most influential and widely admired black leader of the century.

Pressure from the courts, from northern liberals, and from blacks themselves also speeded the pace of racial change in other areas. As early as 1947, one important color line had been breached when the Brooklyn Dodgers signed Jackie Robinson as the first black to play in the major leagues. By the mid-1950s, blacks had established themselves as a major force in almost all professional sports. Within the government, President Eisenhower completed the integration of the armed forces, attempted to desegregate the federal work force, and in 1957 signed a civil-rights act providing federal protection for blacks who wished to register to vote. It was a weak bill, with few mechanisms for enforcement; but it was a signal that the executive and legislative branches were beginning to join the judiciary in the federal commitment to the "Second Reconstruction."

A BALANCE OF TERROR

An undercurrent of anxiety tinged the domestic events of the Eisenhower years, for Americans were well aware throughout the 1950s of how dangerous was the world in which they lived. Above all, they were aware of the horrors of a possible nuclear war, as both the United States and the Soviet Union began to make atomic weapons more and more central to their foreign policies. Yet the nuclear threat had another effect as well. With the costs of war now so enormous, both of the superpowers began to edge away from direct confrontations. And increasingly, the attention of the United States began to turn to the rapidly escalating change and instability in the nations of the Third World.

Dulles and Massive Retaliation

Eisenhower's Secretary of State, and indisputably the dominant figure in the nation's foreign policy in the 1950s, was John Foster Dulles, an aristocratic corporate lawyer with a stern moral revulsion toward communism. As a deeply religious man, Dulles detested the atheistic dogmas of Marxism. As a man closely tied to the nation's financial establishment, he feared the communist challenge to world free enterprise. He entered office denouncing the containment policies of the Truman years as excessively passive, arguing that the United States should pursue instead an active program of "liberation," which would lead to a "roll-back" of communist expansion. Once in power, however, he had to defer to the far more moderate views of the President himself. And Dulles began, instead, to develop a new set of doctrines that reflected the impact of nuclear weapons upon the world.

The most prominent of those doctrines was the policy of "massive retaliation," which Dulles announced early in 1954. The United States would, he explained, respond to communist threats to its allies not by using conventional forces in local conflicts (a policy that had led to such frustration in Korea) but by relying on "the deterrent of massive retaliatory power . . . a great capacity to retaliate instantly, by means and at times of our own choosing." He left no doubt that the retaliation he was envisioning was a nuclear one. The new doctrine reflected in part Dulles's inclination for tense confrontations, an approach he once defined as "brinksmanship"—pushing the Soviet Union to the brink of war in order to exact concessions. But the real force behind the massive retaliation policy was an economic one. With pressure growing both in and out of government for a reduction in American military expenditures, an increasing reliance on atomic weapons seemed, as some advocates put it, to promise "more bang for a buck." Many argued further that smaller, so-called tactical nuclear weapons could replace conventional forces even in limited wars.

DULLES AND EISENHOWER.   Secretary of State Dulles, shown here reporting to the President and the nation over television in 1955, brought to American foreign policy a deep moral antipathy toward communism. His belief in confrontation, or what he at times called "brinksmanship," struck many as a dangerous posture in a nuclear age. But in fact, perhaps because of Eisenhower's moderating influence, the United States found itself engaged in few direct confrontations with the communists during the Republican administration. It was in the early 1960s that the most frightening encounters occurred. (*Department of State*)

The "new look" in American defense policy seemed at first to please almost everyone. It maintained the national commitment (and, its advocates argued, the national ability) to counter communist expansion throughout the world. Yet it did so at greatly reduced cost, satisfying those who were demanding new efforts to balance the budget.

At the same time, Dulles intensified the efforts of Truman and Acheson to "integrate" the entire noncommunist world into a system of mutual defense pacts. During his years in office, he logged almost 500,000 miles in foreign travels to cement new alliances that were modeled on NATO but were, without exception, far weaker than the European pact. By the end of the decade, the United States had become a party to almost a dozen such treaties in all areas of the world. In Southeast Asia, there was the SEATO alliance, which included Thailand and the Philippines but few other Asian nations. In the Middle East, there was the Baghdad Pact, soon renamed the CENTO alliance, which tied the United States to Turkey, Pakistan, Iraq, and Iran. Other, smaller agreements pledged American aid to additional areas as well. Despite Dulles's criticisms of it, the containment policy was clearly alive and well.

Dilemmas in Asia

What had been the most troubling foreign policy concern of the Truman years
—the war in Korea—plagued the Eisenhower administration only briefly. The
new President did indeed "go to Korea" as he had promised in his campaign—
visiting briefly in the months between the election and his inauguration. But peace
came as a result of other things, primarily a softening of both the American and
communist positions. On July 27, 1953, negotiators at Panmunjom finally signed
an agreement ending the hostilities. Each antagonist was to withdraw its troops
a mile and a half from the existing battle line, which ran roughly along the
thirty-eighth parallel, the prewar border between North and South Korea. A
conference in Geneva was to consider means by which to reunite the nation
peacefully, although in fact the 1954 meeting produced no agreement and left the
cease-fire line as the permanent border between the two countries.

In the meantime, however, American attention was being drawn to problems
in other parts of Asia. There was, first, the continuing pressure on the administration from the so-called China Lobby, or "Asia-Firsters," who insisted on active
American efforts to restore Chiang Kai-shek to the Chinese mainland. Such
demands were wholly unrealistic. Chiang had nothing approaching sufficient
military strength to launch an effective invasion. Even had he been able to muster
the forces, he would have found virtually no popular following within China itself.
Nevertheless, the administration continued to supply him with weapons and other
assistance, particularly after the communist regime on the mainland began to
threaten to attack the tiny offshore islands of Quemoy and Matsu, from which
Chiang had launched occasional air attacks on communist installations. The
President even implied that the United States would intervene directly if necessary to defend the islands. Out of the Quemoy-Matsu controversy emerged a
strong new treaty between the United States and Taiwan and a congressional
resolution giving the President nearly unlimited powers to aid Chiang.

Almost simultaneously, the United States was becoming drawn into a long,
bitter struggle in Southeast Asia. Ever since the end of World War II, France
had been attempting to restore its authority over its one-time colony, Vietnam,
which it had had to abandon to the Japanese during World War II. Opposing
the French, however, were the powerful nationalist forces of Ho Chi Minh, which
were determined to win independence for their nation. Ho had appealed on
several occasions to the United States for support in the first years after the war
but had received no reply. By 1954, he was accepting substantial aid from communist China and the Soviet Union. America, in the meantime, had been paying
more than 70 percent of French war costs since 1950. A crisis emerged in early
1954 when 12,000 French troops became surrounded in a disastrous siege at the
city of Dienbienphu, which they were incapable of defending. Only American
intervention, it was clear, could prevent the total collapse of the French military
effort.

Eisenhower spoke out strongly about the importance of preserving a "free"

Vietnam, using the analogy once employed by Acheson of a row of dominoes. If Vietnam fell, he implied, the rest of Asia would soon follow. Yet despite the urgings of Secretary of State Dulles, Vice President Nixon, and others, Eisenhower refused to agree to direct American military intervention in Vietnam, claiming that neither the Congress nor America's other allies would support such action. In fact, Eisenhower seemed to sense how difficult and costly such intervention would be.

Without American aid, the French defense of Dienbienphu finally collapsed on May 7, 1954; and France quickly agreed to a settlement of the conflict at a conference in Geneva that summer. The Geneva Accords of July 1954, to which the United States was not a party, established a temporary division of Vietnam along the seventeenth parallel. The north would be governed by Ho Chi Minh, the south by a pro-Western regime. Democratic elections would serve as the basis for uniting the nation in 1956. The agreement marked the effective end of the French commitment to Vietnam, but it became the basis for an expanded American presence. Realizing that Ho Chi Minh would win any election in Vietnam, Eisenhower and Dulles decided almost immediately that they could not accept the agreement. Instead, they helped establish a pro-American government in the south, headed by Ngo Dinh Diem, a wealthy, corrupt member of his country's Roman Catholic minority. Diem, it was clear from the start, would not permit elections. He felt secure in his refusal because the United States had promised to provide him with ample military assistance against any attack from the north.

Crises in the Middle East

However effective nuclear weapons may have been as a deterrent against direct Soviet aggression, they were—as the events in Asia suggested—less useful in enabling the United States to control local uprisings in the Third World. Yet it was just such uprisings, American policymakers were coming to believe, that now constituted the greatest danger of communist expansion. The dilemma of the 1950s, therefore, became how best to respond to insurgency in remoter, less-developed regions. (Few policymakers pondered seriously the question of *whether* the United States should always attempt to counter that insurgency; nor did America make much of an effort to distinguish between purely indigenous local uprisings and those engineered by the Soviet Union. The assumptions of the containment policy—that communism was unacceptable anywhere outside its existing borders—not only survived virtually unchallenged but blinded the United States to the distinctions among different forms of radicalism.) Such problems arose in many parts of the globe, but nowhere more acutely than in the Middle East. The region was a volatile and important one for two reasons: Israel and oil.

The establishment of a Jewish state in Palestine had been the dream of Zionists in many parts of the world for more than half a century. The plight of the hundreds of thousands of homeless Jews uprooted by World War II, and the international outrage that followed revelations of the Nazi holocaust, gave new strength to Zionist demands in the late 1940s. Palestine had been a British protectorate since the end of World War I; and in deference to local Arab opposition, the British after 1945 had attempted to limit Jewish immigration there. But despite such efforts, Jews came to Palestine in such enormous numbers that they could not be ignored. Finally, Britain brought the problem to the United Nations, which responded by recommending a partition of Palestine into a Jewish and an Arab state. On May 14, 1948, the British mandate ended, and Jews proclaimed the existence of the nation of Israel. President Truman recognized the new government the following day, thus effectively blocking a UN proposal to keep the area under a temporary trusteeship. But the creation of Israel was only the beginning of the battle for a Jewish homeland. Palestinian Arabs, unwilling to accept being displaced in what they considered their own country, fought determinedly against the new state in 1948—the first of many Arab–Israeli wars. And the United States found itself with a new ally whose survival would require years of extensive American aid.

The interest of the United States in preventing the Islamic areas of the Middle East from becoming communist went far beyond the abstract imperatives of the containment doctrine. The region contained the richest oil reserves in the world, reserves in which American companies had already invested heavily. Thus the United States reacted with alarm as it watched Mohammed Mossadegh, the nationalist Prime Minister of Iran, become increasingly resistant to the presence of Western corporations in his nation. In 1951, he ordered the seizure of Iran's oil wells from the British companies that had been developing them. During the next two years, American observers grew convinced that Mossadegh was becoming friendly with the Soviet Union. In 1953, as a result, the American Central Intelligence Agency joined forces with conservative Iranian military leaders to engineer a coup that drove Mossadegh from office. To replace him, the United States favored elevating the young Shah of Iran, Mohammed Riza Pahlavi, from his position as a token constitutional monarch to that of a virtual absolute ruler. In return, the Shah allowed American companies to share in the development of Iranian oil reserves; and he remained closely tied to the United States for the next twenty-five years, even as his regime was becoming increasingly despotic and unpopular.

American policy was less effective in dealing with the nationalist government of Egypt, under the leadership of General Gamal Abdel Nasser. Nasser pressured the British in 1954 to remove their remaining troops from his country, an effort the United States accepted and even assisted. But Dulles and other policymakers were less willing to tolerate Nasser's flirtations with the Soviet Union, which took the form of increasing Soviet shipments of armaments in return for Egyptian cotton. To punish Nasser for his transgressions, Dulles suddenly withdrew American offers of assistance in building the great Aswan Dam across the Nile. A week later, Nasser retaliated by seizing from the British control of the Suez Canal, saying that he would use the income from it to build the dam himself.

During the tedious negotiations that followed, Britain, France, and Israel all began to grow impatient with the pace of American efforts to effect a settlement. Control of the Suez Canal was of vital strategic importance; and Nasser's growing military strength made further delay costly. Thus, on October 29, 1956, Israeli forces struck a preemptive blow against Egypt; and the British and French followed the next day by landing troops to drive the Egyptians from the canal. Dulles and Eisenhower reacted with horror, fearing that the Suez crisis would drive the Arab states toward the Soviet Union and precipitate a new world war. By refusing to support the invasion, and by joining in a United Nations denunciation of it, the United States helped pressure the French and British to withdraw. Egypt and Israel agreed to a cease-fire, and another precarious truce was in place. In the following years, just as Dulles had feared, the government of Egypt turned increasingly to the Soviet Union for assistance, accepting Russian financing of the Aswan Dam and making the Soviets an important force in the Middle East.

In Washington, the President responded in 1957 by enunciating the so-called Eisenhower Doctrine, by which the United States would offer economic and military aid "to secure and protect the territorial independence" of Middle Eastern nations "against overt armed aggression from any nation controlled by international communism." In practice, that meant more than simply opposing Soviet aggression. It meant working to prevent the spread of pan-Arab nationalism: Nasser's efforts to unite all the Arab states into a single nation, in which he would be the dominant force. Egypt and Syria merged to form the United Arab Republic in February 1958, causing modest concern in Washington. But that concern soon turned to alarm as pan-Arab forces began to challenge the pro-Western governments of Lebanon, Jordan, and Iraq. The United States could do little about Iraq, which fell under the control of a pro-Nasser military government in July (although only temporarily). But in Lebanon and Jordan, the situation was different. At the request of the embattled Beirut government, Eisenhower ordered 5,000 American Marines to land on the beaches of Lebanon in mid-July; British troops entered Jordan at about the same time. The effect of the interventions was negligible. The governments of both countries managed to stabilize their positions on their own, and within months both the American and the British forces withdrew.

Throughout the troubled course of American intervention in the Middle East, the Soviet Union was never more than an indirect presence. It provided aid to countries that would accept it. It attempted to increase its influence, just as the United States was doing. It did not, however, make any overt efforts to supplant existing governments. The real concern of the United States in the Middle East was one Americans did not fully understand. It was not communism but nationalism. American policymakers were becoming convinced that they must oppose not only Soviet aggression but internal challenges to the authority of pro-American governments, even if those challenges reflected nationalist far more than communist aspirations. The Third World was no longer the passive, compliant area it had once seemed. And America's difficulty in reconciling the emergence of nationalism there with its own desire for influence was placing increasing strains upon the nation's foreign policy.

Latin America and "Yankee Imperialism"

Such difficulties were particularly apparent in an area important to, but generally neglected by, American foreign policy: Latin America. American economic interests in the region were vast; in some countries, United States corporations were the dominant force in the economy. Yet in most Latin American nations, the American interests were supporting conservative, despotic governments whose members enriched themselves and permitted little wealth to filter down to the mass of the desperately poor and rapidly expanding populations. The United States government, in the meantime, had all but abandoned even the limited initiatives of Roosevelt's Good Neighbor Policy, sending most of its foreign aid to Europe and Asia rather than to Latin America.

Animosity toward the United States, therefore, grew steadily during the 1950s, as an increasing number of Latin Americans began to regard the influence of United States business in their countries as an insidious form of imperialism. Some nationalists in the region had once believed that the United States would support popular efforts to overthrow undemocratic governments. But in 1954, the Eisenhower administration suggested otherwise when it helped topple a new, leftist government in Guatemala that Secretary Dulles believed was potentially communist. Four years later, the depths of anti-American sentiment became clear when Vice President Richard Nixon visited the region, to be greeted in city after city by angry, hostile, occasionally dangerous mobs.

Americans were shocked by the outburst of animosity, and the administration began hasty, belated efforts to improve relations with its neighbors. But the legacy of more than fifty years of casual exploitation of Latin America was too strong to prevent the rise of other nationalist movements hostile to the United States. No nation in the region had been more closely tied to America than Cuba. Its leader, Fulgencio Batista, had ruled as a military dictator since 1952, when with American assistance, he had toppled a more moderate government. Cuba's economy had become a virtual fiefdom of American corporations, which controlled almost all the island's natural resources and had cornered over half of the vital sugar crop. Beginning in 1957, a popular movement of resistance to the Batista regime began to gather power under the leadership of Fidel Castro. By late 1958, the Batista forces were in almost total disarray. And on January 1, 1959, with Batista now in exile in Spain (having taken millions of dollars in government funds along with him), Castro marched into Havana and established a new government.

Despite its long support of the Batista government, the United States had always been vaguely embarrassed by its ties to that corrupt regime. At first, therefore, Americans reacted warmly to Castro, particularly since there was little evidence that he was tied to any communist elements. But as Castro began implementing drastic policies of land reform and expropriation of foreign-owned businesses and resources, Cuban–American relations rapidly deteriorated. The new government was outraging American businessmen by its assaults upon their interests. It was, moreover, causing increasing concern to Eisenhower and Dulles by its growing interest in communist ideas and tactics. When Castro began

NIXON IN SOUTH AMERICA, 1958. Hostile anti-American mobs greet Vice President Richard Nixon during his 1958 tour of South America. Above, students at San Marcos University in Lima, Peru, taunt the Vice President. Some of them threw stones, one of which grazed Nixon's neck. On another occasion, Nixon and his wife found themselves trapped inside their car, completely surrounded by angry demonstrators. The episodes shocked the American public and reminded officials of the extent to which relations with Latin America had deteriorated. (*UPI*)

accepting assistance from the Soviet Union in 1960, the United States cut back the "quota" by which Cuba could export sugar to America at a favored price. Early in 1961, as one of its last acts, the Eisenhower administration severed diplomatic relations with Castro. It had already begun secretly training Cuban expatriates for an invasion of the island to topple the new regime. Totally isolated by the United States, Castro soon cemented a close and lasting alliance with the Soviet Union.

Europe and the Soviet Union

The problems of the Third World would soon become the central focus of American foreign policy. Through most of the 1950s, however, the United States remained chiefly concerned with its direct relationship with the Soviet Union and with the possibility of communist expansion in Europe. The "massive retaliation" doctrine was the first American effort to deter such expansion. The rearming of West Germany was another. Beginning in 1954, the West German government began, within the strict guidelines imposed by the United States, Britain, and France, to develop its first armed forces since the end of World War II. In 1957, the first German forces joined NATO, making the nation a full military ally of the United States.

In the meantime, however, many Americans continued to hope that the United States and the Soviet Union would be able to negotiate solutions to some of their remaining problems. Such hopes were buoyed when, after the death of Stalin in 1953, signs began to emerge of a new Russian attitude of conciliation. The Soviet Union extended a peace overture to the rebellious Tito government in Yugoslavia; it returned a military base to Finland; it signed a peace treaty with Japan; and, above all, it agreed to terminate its long military occupation of Austria, making that nation a neutral state. Pressure for negotiation intensified when, between 1953 and 1954, both the United States and the Soviet Union successfully tested the new hydrogen bomb, a nuclear device of vastly greater power than those developed during the war. These factors seemed briefly to bear fruit in 1955, when Eisenhower and other NATO leaders met with the Soviet Premier, Nicolai Bulganin, at a cordial summit conference in Geneva. But when a subsequent conference of foreign ministers met to try to resolve specific issues, the "spirit of Geneva" quickly dissolved, as neither side could agree to the terms of the other.

The failure of conciliation brought renewed vigor to the Cold War, not only helping to produce tensions between the superpowers in the Third World but spurring a vastly increased Soviet–American arms race. Both nations engaged in extensive nuclear testing in the atmosphere, causing alarm among many scientists and environmentalists. Both nations redoubled efforts to develop effective intercontinental ballistic missiles, which could deliver atomic warheads directly from one continent to another. The apparent Russian lead in such development caused wide alarm in the United States. The American military, in the meantime, developed a new breed of atomic-powered submarines, capable of launching missiles from anywhere in the world.

The arms race not only increased tensions between the United States and Russia; it increased tensions within each nation as well. In America, public concern about nuclear war was becoming an obsessive national nightmare, a preoccupation never far from popular thought. Movies, television programs, books, popular songs: all expressed the pervasive fear. Government studies began to appear outlining the hideous casualties that a nuclear war would inflict upon the nation. Schools, local governments, and individual families built a huge network of bomb shelters for protection against atomic blasts and radioactive fallout. Fear of communism, therefore, combined with fear of atomic war to create a widespread national unease.

Khrushchev and Berlin

In this tense and fearful atmosphere, new Soviet provocations in Berlin in 1958 created a particularly troubling crisis. The linking of West Germany first to NATO and then to the new European Common Market, establishing that nation as a full partner of the West, made the continuing existence of an anticommunist West Berlin a particularly galling irritation to the Soviets. In November 1958, therefore, Nikita Khrushchev, who succeeded Bulganin as Soviet Premier and Communist party chief in 1958, renewed the demands of his predecessors that the NATO powers abandon the city, threatening vaguely to cut its ties to the West if they did not. The United States and its allies refused, and America and Russia were locked in another tense confrontation.

Khrushchev declined to force the issue when it became apparent that the West was unwilling to budge. Instead, he suggested that he and Eisenhower engage in personal discussions, both by visiting each other's countries and by conferring at a summit meeting in Paris in 1960. The United States eagerly agreed. Khrushchev's 1959 visit to America produced a cool but cordial response; and plans proceeded for the summit conference and for Eisenhower's visit to Moscow shortly thereafter. Only days before the scheduled beginning of the Paris meeting, however, the Soviet Union announced that it had shot down an American U-2, a high-altitude spy plane, over Russian territory. Its pilot, Gary Powers, was in captivity. The Eisenhower administration responded clumsily, at first denying the allegations and then, when confronted with incontrovertible proof, awkwardly admitting the circumstances of Powers's mission and attempting to explain them. Khrushchev lashed back in anger, breaking up the Paris summit almost before it could begin and withdrawing his invitation to Eisenhower to visit the Soviet Union. But the U-2 incident was really only a pretext. By the spring of 1960, both Khrushchev and Eisenhower were aware that no agreement was possible on the Berlin issue; and Khrushchev, therefore, was eager for an excuse to avoid what he believed would be fruitless negotiations.

Eisenhower's Farewell

The events of 1960 provided a somber backdrop for the end of the Eisenhower administration. After eight years in office, Eisenhower had failed to eliminate the tensions between the United States and the Soviet Union. He had failed to end the costly and dangerous armaments race. And he had presided over a transformation of the Cold War from a relatively limited confrontation with the Soviet Union in Europe to a global effort to resist communist subversion in the Third World as well.

Yet Eisenhower had brought to these matters his own sense of the limits of American power. He had refused to commit American troops to anticommunist crusades except in carefully limited and generally low-risk situations, such as Guatemala and Lebanon. He had resisted pressures from the British, from the French, and from hardliners in his own government to place American force behind efforts to maintain colonial power in Vietnam and in the Suez. He had placed a certain measure of restraint on those who urged the creation of an enormous American military establishment, warning in his farewell address in January 1961 of the "unwarranted influence" of a vast "military-industrial complex." His caution, both in domestic and in international affairs, stood in marked contrast to the attitudes of his successors, who argued that the United States must act far more boldly and aggressively on behalf of its goals at home and abroad.

SUGGESTED READINGS

General studies of the Eisenhower administration include Charles C. Alexander, *Holding the Line* (1975); Herbert S. Parmet, *Eisenhower and the American Crusade* (1972); Peter Lyon, *Eisenhower: Portrait of a Hero* (1974); and Eisenhower's own memoirs, *The White House Years*, 2 vols. (1963–1965). Other memoirs by important figures in the administration include Emmet John Hughes, *The Ordeal of Power* (1963); Sherman Adams, *Firsthand Report* (1961); and Richard Nixon, *Six Crises* (1962). The foreign policy of the Eisenhower years is discussed in Robert Divine, *Eisenhower and the Cold War* (1981). On Dulles, see Townsend Hoopes, *The Devil and John Foster Dulles* (1973), a generally critical study; and Louis Gerson, *John Foster Dulles* (1967), a more favorable view. On the early stages of American involvement in Vietnam, see Chester Cooper, *Lost Crusade* (1970); Frances Fitzgerald, *Fire in the Lake* (1972); John T. McAlister, Jr., *Vietnam: The Origins of Revolution* (1969); and George Herring, *America's Longest War* (1979). Chester Cooper, *The Lion's Last Roar* (1978), and Hugh Thomas, *Suez* (1967), examine the major Middle Eastern crisis of the era. Mira Wilkins, *The Maturing of Multinational Enterprise* (1974), examines a major source of change in American foreign policy. Kermit Roosevelt, *Counter-coup* (1980), is a first-hand account by the CIA operative who organized the 1954 coup in Iran; and Burton Kaufman, *The Oil Cartel Case* (1978), provides additional insights into United States involvement in Iranian affairs. Robert A. Divine, *Foreign Policy and U.S. Presidential Elections*, 2 vols. (1974), and *Blowing in the Wind: The Nuclear Test Ban Debate, 1954–1960* (1978), are also valuable.

Philip Stern, *The Oppenheimer Case* (1969), examines one of the outstanding internal security controversies of the era. Michael Straight, *Trial by Television* (1954), discusses the decline of McCarthy, as do many of the books on McCarthy cited after Chapter 19. On the Warren Court, see Paul Murphy, *The Constitution in Crisis Times* (1972); Alexander Bickel, *Politics and the Warren Court* (1965) and *The Supreme Court and the Idea of Progress* (1970); Philip Kurland, *Politics, the Constitution, and the Warren Court* (1970); and John Weaver, *Earl Warren* (1967). A thorough and rewarding study of the *Brown* decision is Richard Kluger, *Simple Justice* (1975). On the emergence of the civil-rights movement, see Anthony Lewis, *Portrait of a Decade* (1964); Martin Luther King, Jr., *Stride Toward Freedom* (1958), a personal account of the Montgomery bus boycott; and William Chafe, *Civilities and Civil Rights* (1980), a fine study of the origins of the movement in Greensboro, North Carolina.

Twenty-Two

Kennedy, Johnson, and the Triumph of Liberalism

The calm, reassuring presence of Eisenhower seemed perfectly to match the political mood of the 1950s—a mood that combined a desire for domestic stability with a concern for international security. By the end of the decade, however, an increasing number of Americans were beginning to clamor for a more active and assertive approach to public policy. The nation had, many liberals complained, been allowed to "drift." It was time for an energetic assault on both domestic and world problems. Such sentiments helped produce two Presidents whose activism transformed the nature of their office. And those same sentiments helped launch the nation into extraordinary new commitments both at home and abroad.

THE ACTIVIST PRESIDENCY

The presidency had always been an important institution in American life, and it had grown steadily more important through the twentieth century. The existence of atomic weapons, under the personal control of the President, added a new dimension to the powers of the office in the 1950s. And by 1960, more and more Americans were looking to the presidency as the source of all initiatives, almost as the embodiment of nationhood. Clinton Rossiter, a noted political scientist, once referred to the President as "a kind of magnificent lion, who can roam freely and do great deeds so long as he does not try to break loose from his broad reservation." Richard Neustadt, whose book *Presidential Power* (1960) expressed liberal expectations of the office as effectively as any single work, argued that the President's task is to overcome the limits of his office so as to be able to exercise forceful, positive power.

Such exhortations found a receptive audience in the two men who served in the White House from 1961 until 1969: John F. Kennedy and Lyndon B. Johnson. Although from very different backgrounds and of very different temperaments, they shared a commitment to active leadership. Their administrations expanded the role of the presidency in ways that would produce great triumphs for the liberal philosophy to which they both subscribed, but that would ultimately help as well to produce a major national crisis.

John F. Kennedy and the 1960 Election

The campaign of 1960 produced two young candidates who claimed to offer the nation active leadership. The Republican nomination went almost uncontested to

JFK AND LBJ.   John Kennedy and Lyndon Johnson review their inaugural parade in January 1961. The two men differed so strikingly in background and personality that it remained a source of wonderment to friends of them both that they had agreed to serve together on the same ticket—particularly since Johnson by doing so was sacrificing a powerful position as Senate Majority Leader. Robert Kennedy, the President's brother and a man whose own relationship with Johnson was always difficult, later claimed that John Kennedy had offered the nomination to Johnson only because he was certain Johnson would refuse it. Whether or not the story is true, Johnson always resented what he believed to be the condescending treatment he had received from the Kennedy circle. (*John F. Kennedy Library*)

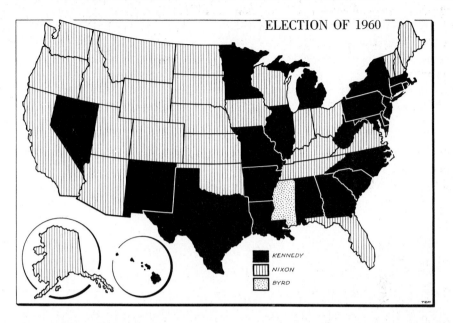

ELECTION OF 1960

KENNEDY
NIXON
BYRD

Vice President Richard Nixon, who for the occasion abandoned the strident anticommunism that had characterized his earlier career and adopted a centrist position in favor of moderate reform. Although he openly associated himself with the Republican record, he attempted to project an image of greater vigor and dynamism than Eisenhower.

The Democrats, in the meantime, emerged from a spirited primary campaign united, somewhat uneasily, behind John F. Kennedy, an attractive and articulate Senator from Massachusetts who had narrowly missed being the party's vice-presidential candidate in 1956. The son of an enormously wealthy, influential businessman who had been a controversial American ambassador to England under Franklin Roosevelt, Kennedy had led a privileged but energetic life. After graduation from Harvard in 1940, he served in the navy in the Pacific, where he was decorated for heroism after saving the lives of some members of the crew of his PT boat. He won election to Congress in 1946, moved on to the Senate in 1952, and in 1956 received a Pulitzer Prize for his book *Profiles in Courage*, a series of portraits of American politicians whose sense of commitment he admired. After winning reelection to the Senate in 1958 by a record margin, he began almost immediately to run for President. And after defeating first a liberal challenge by Senator Hubert Humphrey of Minnesota, and then a more conservative one by Senate Majority Leader Lyndon Johnson of Texas, he emerged as his party's nominee, premising his campaign, he said, "on the single assumption that the American people are uneasy at the present drift in our national course." He was, wrote *New Republic* columnist TRB, "a young man offering positive leadership and presidential power to the uttermost."

He was also a Catholic, a political liability that had almost cost him the nomination and that continued to dog him throughout the campaign. Kennedy compensated for that with his remarkably appealing public image—one that seemed perfectly suited for television—and with an unusually sophisticated and capable campaign. The crucial moment, perhaps, came when he met Vice President Nixon in a series of televised debates. Cool, poised, and relaxed, Kennedy stood in marked contrast to the haggard and somewhat nervous Nixon, who was, during the first debate at least, recovering from an illness. The favorable response Kennedy received from the debates helped propel him to victory.

It was, however, one of the narrowest victories in the history of presidential elections. A vigorous effort on behalf of Nixon by President Eisenhower in the closing days of the campaign, combined with continuing doubts about Kennedy's

THE PRESIDENTIAL DEBATE.   Senator Kennedy and Vice President Nixon meet in one of the "great debates" of the 1960 campaign. Nixon, confident of his skills as a debater and his experience as a public speaker, accepted the prospect of the debates eagerly. But it was Kennedy, whose poise and relaxed delivery made him an ideal television performer, who benefited more from the encounters. In the debate pictured here, Nixon wears a dark business suit. In the first debate several weeks before, he had worn a light gray suit that had faded into the background, contributing to a general impression of pallidness that apparently harmed him greatly with the voters. Polls taken after the first debate disclosed that those who had watched it on television judged Kennedy the winner, while those who had listened to it on the radio believed Nixon had prevailed. (*NBC*)

youth (he turned forty-three years old in 1960) and religion, almost enabled the Republicans to close what had at one time been a substantial Democratic lead. But in the end Kennedy held on to win a tiny plurality of the popular vote—49.7 percent to Nixon's 49.5 percent—and only a slightly more comfortable electoral majority—303 to 219. If a few thousand voters in Illinois and Texas had voted differently, Nixon would have won the election.

Kennedy and the Presidency

The narrowness of Kennedy's victory placed a serious constraint upon his ability to accomplish his goals. His brief administration, therefore, was less an occasion for dynamic reform than a lesson to the young President in the limits of his office. Kennedy had campaigned promising a program of domestic legislation more ambitious than any since the New Deal, a program he described as the "New Frontier." He was able to steer little of it to completion during his presidency.

Kennedy's most serious problem from the beginning was the Congress. Although Democrats remained in control of both houses, they owed little to the new President, whose "coattails" in 1960 had been exceedingly short. Nor did the presence of Democratic majorities ensure a sympathetic reception for reform proposals; those majorities rested in large part on conservative southerners far more likely to vote with the Republicans than with Kennedy. Moreover, many of those same southerners maintained control, by virtue of their seniority, of the most important congressional committees. One after another of Kennedy's legislative proposals, therefore, found themselves hopelessly stalled long before they reached the floor of the House or Senate.

Kennedy attempted to increase his leverage in Congress by working for changes in legislative procedures. With the support of Speaker of the House Sam Rayburn, he managed to persuade the House to expand the membership of the crucial Rules Committee so as to limit the power of its conservative and autocratic chairman, Howard Smith of Virginia. But the protracted and bitter battle that accompanied the change cost Kennedy much of his already limited political capital in Congress. His legislative proposals continued to languish.

As a result, he had to look elsewhere for opportunities to display forceful, positive leadership. One such area was the economy, which from the beginning of his administration had been his primary concern. Economic growth was sluggish in 1961 when Kennedy entered the White House. Unemployment was hovering at about 6 percent of the work force, far too high by Democratic standards. In addition to such legislative initiatives as requesting tax credits for businesses investing in capital growth, Kennedy attempted to use his executive powers unilaterally to improve the economy. With congressional approval, he initiated a series of tariff negotiations with foreign governments—the "Kennedy Round"—to reduce barriers to international trade, in an effort to stimulate American exports. He began to consider the use of Keynesian fiscal and monetary tools in more direct and positive ways than those used by any previous administration. He even put his personal prestige on the line in a battle to curb inflation. In 1962, several steel companies, led by United States Steel, announced that they were raising their prices by six dollars a ton, a move certain to trigger similar action by the rest of the steel industry. Kennedy was furious at what he considered an irresponsibly inflationary action, particularly since he had helped pressure the Steelworkers Union to accept a restrained wage hike only months before. Angrily denouncing the steel companies both publicly and privately, the President exerted enormous pressure upon United States Steel in particular to rescind its decision —threatening the company with lawsuits and cancellations of government contracts. He even called the president of U.S. Steel, Roger Blough, to the White House for an impassioned tongue-lashing. Finally, the steel companies relented and abandoned the price rise. But the President had won only a fleeting victory. His relationship with the business community was a strained one from that moment on, and a few months later the steel companies quietly raised prices again. The President did not protest.

Where Kennedy found the greatest opportunities to display his vision of presidential leadership was in two areas: foreign policy and style. In his capacity as a world leader, he discovered—like other Presidents both before and after him— that he could act without the constraints that hampered his domestic initiatives. And in adopting a new presidential style, he was able to employ his own most effective political skills. More than any other President of the century (excepting perhaps the two Roosevelts), Kennedy made his own personality an integral part of his presidency and a central focus of national attention. His inspired oratory (most clearly illustrated by his famous inaugural address), his consistent wit, his skill at using the medium of television and at winning the loyalty of the press corps, even his ability to bring public attention to bear on his beautiful wife and his large and energetic family—all combined to win him a measure of public adoration far beyond what his concrete accomplishments could have done. By elevating himself in the national consciousness, he elevated the office of the presidency as well.

Dallas, 1963

Nothing more clearly illustrates how important Kennedy and the presidency had become to the American people than the tragedy of November 22, 1963, and the popular reaction to it. Already, the President was beginning to campaign for reelection the following year; and in November, he traveled to Texas with his wife and Vice President Lyndon Johnson for a series of political appearances. While the presidential motorcade rode slowly through the streets of Dallas, shots suddenly rang out. Two bullets struck the President—one in the throat, the other in the head. He was sped to a nearby hospital, where minutes later he was pronounced dead.

The circumstances of the assassination seemed clearer at the time than they did from the vantage point of later years. Lee Harvey Oswald, who appeared to be a confused and embittered Marxist, was arrested for the crime later that day, on the basis of strong circumstantial evidence. (Among other things, Oswald had shot and killed a police officer who had tried to apprehend him.) Two days later, as

Oswald was being moved from one jail to another, Jack Ruby, a Dallas nightclub owner, stepped from a crowd of reporters and fired a pistol into Oswald's abdomen, an event that was broadcast graphically around the world on television. Oswald died only hours later. The popular assumption at the time was that Oswald had acted alone, expressing through the murder his personal frustration and anger, and that Ruby had acted out of grief and out of a desire to make himself a popular hero. These assumptions received what seemed to be conclusive confirmation by a federal commission chaired by Chief Justice Earl Warren that was appointed to review the events surrounding the assassination. In later years, however, more and more questions and doubts arose about the circumstances of the shooting; and an increasing number of Americans became convinced that the Warren Commission report had not revealed the full story. It seemed unlikely, however, that the mystery would ever be fully resolved.

The death of President Kennedy was one of those traumatic episodes in national history that have left a permanent mark on all who experienced them. The entire nation seemed to suspend its normal activities for four days to watch the televised activities surrounding the presidential funeral. Images of Kennedy's widow, his small children, his funeral procession, his dramatic grave site at Arlington Cemetery with its symbolic eternal flame—all became deeply embedded in the public mind. For months thereafter, the American people displayed an almost obsessive interest in the martyred President and his family. For years, they continued to venerate him in a way reserved in the past for only a very few public figures. When in later times Americans would look back at the optimistic days of the 1950s and early 1960s and wonder how everything had seemed to unravel, many would think of November 22, 1963, as the beginning of the end.

Lyndon B. Johnson

At the time, however, the American public seemed to take comfort in the personality and performance of Kennedy's successor in the White House, Lyndon B. Johnson. A native of Texas, Johnson had entered public life in the 1930s, first as an administrator of the New Deal's National Youth Administration, then as a young Congressman with personal ties to Franklin Roosevelt. After twelve years in the House, he won election in 1948 to the United States Senate. And there, by carefully cultivating the favor of party leaders, he rose steadily in influence to become the Senate Majority Leader. He brought to that post, as he would bring to the presidency, a remarkable level of energy and a legendary ability to persuade and cajole his colleagues into following his lead. He had failed in 1960 to win the Democratic nomination for President; but he had surprised many who knew him by agreeing to accept the second position on the ticket with Kennedy. The events in Dallas thrust him into the White House.

Johnson's personality could hardly have been more different from Kennedy's. Tall, gawky, inelegant in his public speech, he was the antithesis of the modern media politician. Where Kennedy had been smooth and urbane, Johnson was coarse, even crude. Where Kennedy had been personally reticent and almost

NOVEMBER 22, 1963.   Lyndon Johnson had expected to be entertaining
President Kennedy at the LBJ Ranch near Austin, Texas, on the night of
November 22, 1963. Instead, he was standing in the crowded cabin of *Air
Force One* taking the oath of office as President. A stunned Jacqueline
Kennedy, still wearing a pink suit stained with her husband's blood, and a
somber Lady Bird Johnson stand at Johnson's side. Moments later, *Air
Force One* would begin a flight back to Washington, bearing the new
President and the body of the old. (*Wide World Photos*)

unfailingly polite, Johnson was effusive, garrulous, and at times viciously cruel. But
like Kennedy, Johnson was a man who believed in the active use of power. And
he proved, in the end, far more effective than his predecessor in translating his
goals into reality.

Johnson's ability to manage the Congress provided perhaps the most vivid
contrast with Kennedy. Between 1963 and 1966, he compiled the most impressive
legislative record of any President since Franklin Roosevelt. He was aided by the
tidal wave of emotion that followed the death of President Kennedy, which helped
win passage of many New Frontier proposals as a memorial to the slain leader.
But Johnson also constructed a remarkable reform program of his own, one that
he ultimately labeled the "Great Society." And he won approval of much of it
through the same sort of skillful lobbying that had made him an effective Majority
Leader.

Johnson envisioned himself, as well, as a great "coalition builder," drawing into the Democratic fold as many different constituencies as possible. Even more than Kennedy, he tried to avoid the politics of conflict—that is, of winning the support of one group by attacking another. Johnson wanted the support of everyone, and for a time he very nearly got it. His first year in office was, by necessity, dominated by the campaign for reelection. And from the beginning, there seemed to be very little doubt that he would win. As a Democrat in an era of wide support for liberal reform, as the successor of a beloved and martyred President, and as a personification of the same energetic activism that had helped make Kennedy so popular, he was an almost unbeatable candidate. He was further aided by the Republican party, which in 1964 fell under the sway of its right wing and nominated the conservative Senator Barry Goldwater of Arizona. Liberal Republicans abandoned Goldwater and openly supported Johnson. The Democratic party remained united behind the President, despite personal ill feeling between Johnson and Robert Kennedy, the late President's younger brother, who had hoped to be chosen as the party's candidate for Vice President. Johnson had selected Senator Hubert Humphrey of Minnesota instead.

In the fall campaign, Johnson avoided specific, detailed promises, concentrating instead on attracting support from as wide a range of voters as possible and letting Goldwater's stubborn conservatism drive even more Americans into the Democratic fold. The strategy worked. Johnson received more votes, over 42 million, and a larger plurality, over 61 percent, than any candidate in history. Goldwater managed to carry only his home state of Arizona and five states in the deep South. Record Democratic majorities in both houses of Congress, many of whose members had been swept into office only because of the margin of Johnson's victory, ensured that the President would be able to fulfill many of his goals. On election night, Johnson told the nation that he regarded his victory as a "mandate for unity." For a time, that unity seemed to survive; and Johnson seemed well on his way to achieving his own most cherished aim: becoming the most successful reform President of the century.

EXPANDING THE LIBERAL STATE

The domestic programs of Kennedy and Johnson shared two fundamental goals: maintaining the strength of the American economy and expanding the responsibilities of the federal government for the general social welfare. In the first, the two Presidents were simply continuing a commitment that had been central to virtually every administration since early in the century. In the second, however, they were responding to a marked change in public assumptions. In particular, they were responding to what some described as the "discovery of poverty" in the late 1950s and early 1960s, the rather sudden realization by Americans who had been glorying in prosperity that there were substantial portions of the population who remained destitute. Books, newspaper and magazine stories, and at least one memorable television documentary—CBS's *Hunger in America*—all drew attention to the problem. To a nation attempting to present itself as a model to the world, the image of poverty and starvation within its own borders was a severe embarrassment. As a result, first Kennedy and then, to an even greater extent, Johnson set about to construct a series of social programs to assist the needy.

Alleviating poverty, however, was only one of the new commitments of the Democratic administrations. There was, at the same time, a growing concern in the nation about what many Americans termed the "quality of life." In spite of, or perhaps because of, the nation's remarkable economic growth, there were abundant signs of serious maladjustments and decay. Major cities were deteriorating, as wealthy citizens fled to the suburbs, taking jobs, retail businesses, and tax revenues with them. Transportation systems were in chaos, as old facilities struggled to service many more people than they had been designed to handle. Schools faced a series of crises, as rising costs and growing populations placed added strains on their capacities. Books such as Rachel Carson's *Silent Spring* (1962), a study of the effects of insecticides on the environment, began to draw attention to the wider problem of pollution and ecological disorders. Books such as Ralph Nader's *Unsafe at Any Speed* (1966), which exposed the built-in hazards of many American cars, caused wide concern about the vulnerability of consumers to corporations. In one area of American life after another, serious problems were becoming evident that stood in sharp contrast to the nation's image of itself as the wealthiest and most democratic country in the world.

Yet for all such problems, many Americans firmly believed, solutions were readily available. As Presidents Kennedy and Johnson affirmed, all that was required was the will to confront them. Kennedy spoke vaguely of asking Americans to "sacrifice" for their country, but it was clear that what he was asking was less a material sacrifice than a commitment of energy to the solution of problems. Johnson spoke even more expansively of the ability of the nation's economy to support fundamental social reform. Such reform, he implied, would cause no serious distress to anyone. Thus it was that in the first half of the 1960s, the United States undertook a new commitment to social welfare that was in many ways far more ambitious than any before it.

The Assault on Poverty

For the first time since the 1930s, the federal government in the 1960s took steps not only to strengthen and expand existing social welfare programs but to create a host of important new ones. The effort began in the Kennedy administration, although at first without great result. Kennedy did manage to win approval of important changes in existing welfare programs. A revision of the minimum wage law provided considerably fewer new benefits than the President had wished, but it did extend coverage to an additional 3.6 million workers and raise the minimum hourly wage, in stages, from $1.00 to $1.25. Another measure increased social security benefits. He also established several new programs for the unemployed: manpower training to "retool" workers whose skills had become obsolete and Area Redevelopment for chronically depressed regions. Kennedy's most ambitious proposals, however, remained unfulfilled until after his death.

The most important of these, perhaps, was Medicare: a program to provide federal aid to the elderly for medical expenses. Its enactment in 1965 came at the end of a bitter, twenty-year debate between those who believed in the concept of national health assistance and those who denounced it as "socialized medicine." But the program as it went into effect removed many objections. Doctors serving Medicare patients continued to practice privately and to charge their normal fees; Medicare simply shifted responsibility for paying a large proportion of those fees from the patient to the government. With that barrier now hurdled, advocates of national health insurance pushed for even more extensive coverage; and in 1966, President Johnson finally steered to passage the Medicaid program, which extended federal medical assistance to welfare recipients too young to qualify for Medicare. Criticism of both programs continued from all sides. National health insurance advocates continued to insist that coverage be extended to all Americans, a demand that as late as 1981 had made little headway. Others spoke harshly of the bureaucratic problems Medicare and Medicaid created, and of the corruption these programs seemed to encourage. Still more complained bitterly of the tremendous costs the reforms were imposing on the government and the taxpayer; beginning in 1969, as a result, the government began attempting to limit eligibility for assistance in order to reduce expenses. Nevertheless, the two programs made professional medical care available for the first time to millions of Americans who otherwise would have been unable to afford it.

Medicare and Medicaid were the first steps in a far more comprehensive assault upon poverty—one that Kennedy had been contemplating in the last months of his life, and one that Johnson brought to fruition on his own. Determined to eradicate the "pockets of poverty" that were receiving wide public attention, Johnson announced to Congress only weeks after taking office the declaration of an "unconditional war on poverty." The Economic Opportunity Act he then steered to passage provided for, among other things, the establishment of an Office of Economic Opportunity—the centerpiece in Johnson's vision of the Great Society. From the OEO stemmed a vast array of educational programs: vocational training, remedial education, college work study grants, and others. The office funneled government money as well into programs to provide employment for unemployed youths—through the Job Corps, the Neighborhood Youth Corps, and other agencies. And it established VISTA (Volunteers in Service to America), a program reminiscent of the paternal reform efforts of the progressive era. VISTA volunteers moved out across the country into troubled communities to provide educational and social services. Other OEO programs financed housing assistance (as did the Housing Act of 1965, which first established the idea of federal rent subsidies), health care, neighborhood improvements, and many more antipoverty efforts.

The war on poverty was designed to encourage communities themselves to take the initiative in planning reforms, and almost half its funds were disbursed to various Community Action programs. But the reality was often far from the ideal. The nearly $3 billion that the OEO spent during its first two years of existence did much to assist those who managed to qualify for funds. It helped significantly to reduce poverty in certain areas. It fell far short, however, of its goal of eliminating poverty altogether. The job-training programs that formed so important a part of the war on poverty produced generally disappointing results, particularly among the urban black unemployed; blacks continued, once trained, to be barred from many jobs because of racial discrimination, or the jobs simply did not exist in their communities. Community Action programs often fell victim either to local mismanagement or to cumbersome federal supervision, and in either case frequently resulted in a substantial waste of funds. Above all, however, the war on poverty never really approached the dimensions necessary to achieve its goals. From the beginning, funds were inadequate. And as the years passed and a costly war in Southeast Asia became the nation's first priority, even those limited funds began to dwindle. Nearly 17 percent of the American people continued to live in poverty by the late 1960s despite the efforts of the OEO—an improvement over the more than 20 percent who had qualified as poor in 1959, but still a substantial proportion of the population.

Cities and Schools

Closely tied to the antipoverty program were federal efforts to promote the revitalization of decaying cities and to strengthen the nation's schools. Again, many such programs had received support from the Kennedy administration but won passage under Johnson. President Kennedy himself had managed to steer through Congress the Housing Act of 1961, which offered $4.9 billion in federal grants to cities for the preservation of open spaces, the development of mass-transit systems, and the subsidization of middle-income housing. Johnson went even further. He established the Department of Housing and Urban Development, as if to symbolize the government's commitment to the cities. (Its first secretary, Robert Weaver, became the first black ever to serve in the cabinet.) And he inaugurated the Model Cities program, which offered federal subsidies for urban redevelopment.

Kennedy had fought long and in vain to win congressional passage of a program to provide federal aid to public education. Like the idea of federal health insurance, the concept of aid to education aroused deep suspicion in many Americans, who saw it as the first wedge in a federal effort to take control of the schools from localities. Conservatives argued forcefully that once the government began paying for education, it would begin telling the schools how and what they must teach. Opposition arose from another quarter as well: Catholics insisted that aid to education must extend to parochial as well as public schools, something that President Kennedy had refused to consider and that many Americans believed was unconstitutional. Johnson managed to circumvent both objections with the Elementary and Secondary Education Act of 1965 and a series of subsequent measures. Such bills extended aid to both private and parochial schools—aid that was based on the economic conditions of their students, not the needs of the schools themselves. The formula met criteria earlier established by the Supreme Court, and it satisfied some, although not all, conservatives. Total federal expenditures for education and technical training rose from $5 billion to $12 billion between 1964 and 1967.

The Reform Impulse

The great surge of reform of the Kennedy–Johnson years reflected not only a new awareness of the nation's social problems but the boundless confidence of a society that believed its resources and abilities were limitless. By the time Johnson left office, legislation had been either enacted or initiated to deal with almost every imaginable social problem: poverty, health, education, cities, transportation, the environment, the consumer, agriculture, science, the arts. Some of these programs (curbs on air and water pollution, for example) were finally passed or were extended in later years; others, such as the war on poverty, were gradually dismantled or abandoned. But there could be little dispute that the 1960s marked a major expansion of the activities and responsibilities of the federal government—an expansion that many Americans questioned, but from which there seemed no turning back.

The reforms also meant, of course, a radical increase in federal spending. For a time, rising tax revenues from the growing economy nearly compensated for the new expenditures. In 1964, Lyndon Johnson managed to win passage of the $11.5 billion tax cut that Kennedy had first proposed in 1962. Although the cut increased an already sizable federal deficit, it produced substantial economic growth over the next several years that made up for much of the revenue initially lost. But as the Great Society programs began to multiply, and particularly as they began to compete with the escalating costs of America's military ventures, the federal budget rapidly began to outpace increases in revenues. In 1961, the federal government had spent $94.4 billion. By 1970, that sum had more than doubled, to $196.6 billion. And except for 1969, when there was a modest surplus, the budget showed a deficit throughout the decade. In 1968, the deficit rose to $25.1 billion—the highest in history. By 1973, the budget had risen again, to over $246 billion; by 1980, it was in excess of $600 billion. The national debt, in the meantime, had risen from $286.3 billion in 1960 to $458 billion in 1973. In 1981, it was approaching $1 trillion. By the early 1970s, an inflationary spiral had begun that would by the end of the decade produce the highest annual rates of inflation since World War I.

It would be misleading to blame the growth of federal deficits solely on the new social commitments the government had undertaken. During most of the late 1960s and early 1970s, the rise in federal spending was far more a result of military spending. Nor would it be accurate to tie the rise in inflation solely to deficit spending or increasing indebtedness. An enormous range of other factors, both domestic and international, played a role of at least equal importance in producing the wage–price spiral. But it is clear that the possibility that the American economy might have difficulty sustaining an unlimited commitment to social welfare was one that few liberals in the 1960s were willing to consider seriously. In later years, many of the same voices that had demanded new and costly reforms were decrying the "fiscal irresponsibility" of the federal government.

THE BATTLE FOR RACIAL EQUALITY

By far the most important commitment to reform in the 1960s was the effort to ensure justice and equality for American blacks. It was also the most difficult commitment, the one that produced the severest strains on American society. Yet despite the initial reluctance of many whites, including even many liberals, to confront the problem, it was an issue that could no longer be ignored. Black Americans were themselves ensuring that the nation would have to deal with the problem of race.

The Expanding Protests

The Montgomery bus boycott of 1956 was the opening salvo in a massive, rapidly spreading campaign of black resistance to segregation, just as the Little Rock confrontation of 1957 marked the beginning of a protracted legal battle over school integration. In the 1960s, both black efforts and white resistance intensified, and the government found itself forced to act.

John Kennedy had long been sympathetic to the cause of racial justice, but he was hardly a committed crusader. His intervention during the 1960 campaign to help win the release of Martin Luther King, Jr., from a Georgia prison won him a large plurality of the black vote. Once in office, however, he was reluctant to jeopardize his legislative program by openly committing himself to racial reform, fearing that he would alienate key Democratic Senators. Resisting the arguments of those who urged new civil-rights legislation, the Kennedy administration worked instead to expand the enforcement of existing laws and to support litigation to overturn existing segregation statutes. Both efforts produced only limited results. Existing civil-rights laws—and most notably the Civil Rights Act of 1957, which became the principal instrument of the Kennedy effort—were far too weak to produce significant results. And the judicial system proved a slow and awkward route to important reform. Still, the administration hoped to contain the issue of race and resisted pressure to do more.

But that pressure was rapidly growing too powerful to ignore. In February 1960, black college students in Greensboro, North Carolina, staged a sit-in at a segregated Woolworth's lunch counter—an event that received wide national attention. In the following months, such demonstrations spread throughout the South, forcing an increasing number of merchants to integrate their facilities. Of almost equal significance, the sit-in movement aroused the support of a substantial number of northern whites, particularly on college campuses; and in 1961, students of both races began what they called "freedom rides." Traveling by bus throughout the South, they went from city to city attempting to force the desegregation of bus stations. They were met in some cities with such savage violence on the part of whites that the President finally felt obliged to respond. He dispatched federal marshals to help keep the peace, and he ordered the integration of all bus and train stations.

Continuing judicial efforts to enforce the integration of public education produced an even greater test of the President's resolve. In October 1962, a federal court ordered the University of Mississippi to enroll its first black student, James Meredith; and Governor Ross Barnett, a rabid segregationist, refused to enforce the order. When angry whites in Oxford, Mississippi, began rioting to protest the court decree, Kennedy sent federal troops to the city to restore order and protect Meredith's right to attend the university. Events in Alabama the following year proved even more influential. In April 1963, Martin Luther King, Jr., launched a series of extensive, nonviolent demonstrations in Birmingham, Alabama, a city unsurpassed in the strength of its commitment to segregation. Local officials responded brutally. Police Commissioner Eugene "Bull" Connor personally supervised measures to prevent King's peaceful marches, using attack dogs, tear gas, electric cattle prods, and fire hoses—at times even against small children. Hundreds of demonstrators were arrested, as much of the nation watched televised reports of the conflicts in horror. Two months later, Governor George Wallace stood in the doorway of a building at the University of Alabama to prevent the court-ordered enrollment of several black students. Only the arrival of federal marshals forced him to give way. The same night, NAACP official Medgar Evers was murdered in Mississippi.

A National Commitment

The events in Alabama and Mississippi were both a personal shock and a political warning to the President. He could not, he realized, any longer avoid the issue of race. In a historic television address the night of the University of Alabama confrontation, Kennedy spoke eloquently of the "moral issue" facing the nation. "If an American," he asked, "because his skin is dark, . . . cannot enjoy the full and free life which all of us want, then who among us would be content to have the color of his skin changed and stand in his place? Who among us would then be content with the counsels of patience and delay?" Days later, he introduced a series of new legislative proposals prohibiting segregation in "public accommodations" (stores, restaurants, theaters, hotels, and so on), barring discrimination in employment, and increasing the power of the government to file suit on behalf of school integration.

Congressional opposition to the new proposals was strong, and it was clear from the start that only a long and arduous battle would win passage of the legislation. But once again, it was black Americans themselves who made clear that there would be no retreat from the effort. In August 1963, more than 200,000 demonstrators marched down the Mall in Washington, D.C., and gathered before the Lincoln Memorial for the greatest civil-rights demonstration in the nation's history. President Kennedy, who had at first opposed the idea of the march, in the end gave it his open support. And the peaceful gathering, therefore, seemed at the time to denote less the existence of a bitter racial struggle than the birth of a new national commitment to civil rights. Martin Luther King, Jr., in one of the greatest speeches of his career, indeed one of the most memorable of any public figure of the century, aroused the crowd with a litany of images prefaced again and again by the phrase "I have a dream." He closed with words from an old Negro spiritual: "Free at last, free at last. Thank God Almighty, we are free at last." The crowd joined in the singing of what had become the anthem of the civil-rights movement: the hymn "We Shall Overcome."

Johnson and Civil Rights

The assassination of President Kennedy gave new impetus to the battle for civil-rights legislation. The ambitious measure that Kennedy had proposed in June 1963 had passed through the House of Representatives with relative ease; but it seemed hopelessly stalled in the Senate, where a determined filibuster by southern conservatives continued to prevent a vote. Early in 1964, after Johnson had applied both public and private pressure, supporters of the measure finally mustered the two-thirds majority necessary to close debate; and the Senate passed the most comprehensive civil-rights bill in the history of the nation.

At the very moment of passage of the Civil Rights Act of 1964, however, new efforts were under way in the South to win even greater gains for blacks. And

THE MARCH ON WASHINGTON. Martin Luther King, Jr., Roy Wilkins, A. Philip Randolph, Walter Reuther, and others lead more than 200,000 demonstrators down the Mall to begin the march on Washington of August 28, 1963. King's famous "I Have a Dream" speech, which he delivered from the steps of the Lincoln Memorial, marked the high point of the nonviolent civil-rights movement of the early 1960s. (*UPI*)

during the "freedom summer" of that year, thousands of civil-rights workers, black and white, northern and southern, spread out through the South, establishing "freedom schools," staging demonstrations, and demanding not only an end to segregation but the inclusion of blacks in the political process. Like earlier civil-rights activists, they met a hostile and, in some cases at least, a murderous response. Three of the first freedom workers to arrive in the South disappeared; several weeks later, the FBI found their bodies buried under an earthen dam. The movement, however, continued undeterred.

Among other things, activists succeeded in organizing the Mississippi Freedom Democratic party—a predominantly black alternative to the all-white regular party organization. A delegation from the MFDP presented itself at the Democratic Convention in August, demanding that the credentials committee seat it in place of the segregated regular delegation. For the President, who was carefully orchestrating the convention, the issue presented a difficult dilemma. He could not easily ignore the legitimate complaints of the Freedom Democrats about the regular delegation; neither, however, did he want to alienate white Mississippians by unseating their delegates. An awkward compromise, by which several Freedom Democrats were allowed seats alongside the regulars, satisfied no one. Most of the white Mississippi delegates walked out of the convention; and the black delegates resented what they considered token concessions.

Black demands continued to escalate during 1965, and government efforts to satisfy them continued to intensify. In Selma, Alabama, in March, Martin Luther King, Jr., helped organize a major demonstration by blacks demanding the right to register to vote. Confronted with official resistance, the demonstrators attempted a peaceful protest march; but Selma sheriff Jim Clark led local police in a brutal attack upon the demonstrators that horrified the nation. Two northern whites participating in the Selma march were murdered in the course of the effort there—one, a minister, beaten to death in the streets of the town; the other, a Detroit housewife, shot as she drove along a highway at night. The national outrage that followed the events in Alabama helped Lyndon Johnson win passage of the Civil Rights Act of 1965, which guaranteed federal protection to blacks attempting to exercise their right to vote. The traditional criteria for limiting the franchise to whites—literacy tests, knowledge of the Constitution, "good character," and others—were now illegal. (Another, similar device—the poll tax—had been abolished by constitutional amendment in 1964.)

But the civil-rights acts, the Supreme Court decisions, the new social welfare programs designed to help poor blacks, and other government efforts—all were insufficient. As important as such gains were, they failed to satisfy the rapidly rising expectations of American blacks, whose vision of equality included not only an end to segregation but access to economic prosperity. What had once seemed to many liberals a simple moral commitment was becoming a far more complex and demanding issue. Gradually, the generally peaceful, largely optimistic civil-rights movement of the early 1960s was evolving into what would become a major racial crisis.

LIBERAL ACTIVISM AND THE WORLD

In international affairs as much as in domestic reform, the optimistic liberalism of the Kennedy and Johnson administrations dictated a more positive, more active approach to dealing with the nation's problems than in the past. Just as social difficulties at home required a search for new solutions, so the threat of communism overseas seemed to call for new methods and strategies. And just as the new activism in domestic reform ultimately produced frustration and disorder, so did the new activism overseas gradually pull the nation toward disaster.

Diversifying Foreign Policy

John Kennedy's stirring inaugural address was a clear indication of how central to his and to the nation's thinking was opposition to communism. "In the long history of the world," he proclaimed, "only a few generations have been granted the role of defending freedom in its hour of maximum danger. I do not shrink from this responsibility; I welcome it." Yet the speech, which significantly made no mention whatsoever of domestic affairs, was also an indication of Kennedy's belief that the United States had not done enough to counter Soviet expansion. The defense policies of the new administration, therefore, emphasized not only strengthening existing implements of warfare but developing new ones.

Kennedy had charged repeatedly during his campaign that the United States was suffering from a "missile gap," that the Soviet Union had moved ahead of America in the number of missiles and warheads it could deploy. Even before the election, Kennedy received information indicating that whatever missile gap there was favored the United States. Nevertheless, once in office, he insisted on substantial increases in the nation's nuclear armaments. The Soviet Union, which had several years earlier decided to slow the growth of its atomic arsenal, responded with a new missile-building program of its own; and the arms race entered a new phase.

At the same time, however, Kennedy was not satisfied with the nation's ability to meet communist threats in "emerging areas" of the Third World—the areas in which, Kennedy believed, the real struggle against communism would be waged in the future. A nuclear deterrent might prevent a Soviet invasion of western Europe; but in the Middle East, in Africa, in Latin America, in Asia, where insurgent forces had learned to employ methods of jungle and guerrilla warfare, different methods would be necessary. Kennedy gave enthusiastic support to the development of new counterinsurgency forces—a million soldiers trained specifically to fight modern, limited wars. He even chose their uniforms, which included the distinctive green beret from which the Special Forces derived their nickname.

Along with military diversification, Kennedy favored the development of methods for expanding American influence through peaceful means. To repair the badly deteriorating relationship with Latin America, he proposed an Alliance for Progress: a series of projects undertaken cooperatively by the United States and Latin American governments for peaceful development and stabilization of the nations of that region. Its purpose was both to spur social and economic development and to inhibit the rise of Castro-like movements in other Central or South American countries. Poor coordination and inadequate funding sharply limited the impact of the program, but relations between the United States and some Latin American countries did improve. Kennedy also inaugurated the Agency for International Development (AID) to coordinate foreign aid. And he established what became one of his most popular innovations: the Peace Corps, which trained and sent abroad young volunteers to work for two years in developing areas.

Fiasco in Cuba

Kennedy's efforts to improve relations with developing countries were not aided by a hopelessly bungled act of aggression against the Castro government in Cuba. Convinced that "communist domination in this hemisphere can never be negotiated" and that Castro represented a threat to the stability of other Latin American nations, Kennedy agreed in the first weeks of his presidency to continue a project the Eisenhower administration had begun. For months, the CIA had been helping secretly to train a small army of anti-Castro Cuban exiles in Central America. On April 17, 1961, with the approval of the President, 2,000 of the armed exiles landed at the Bay of Pigs in Cuba, expecting first American air support and then a spontaneous uprising by the Cuban people on their behalf. They received neither. At the last minute, Kennedy withdrew the air support, fearful of involving the United States too directly in the invasion. And the expected uprising did not occur. Instead, well-armed Castro forces easily crushed the invaders; and within two days the entire mission had collapsed.

A somber President Kennedy took full responsibility for the fiasco. Governments around the world—not only communist but neutral and pro-Western as well—joined in condemning the United States. But despite the humiliation, Kennedy refused to abandon the principle of overthrowing Castro by force. "We do not intend to abandon Cuba to the Communists," he said only three days after the Bay of Pigs. On the contrary, the failure only redoubled his determination to display American power in the world.

Confrontations with the Soviet Union

In the grim aftermath of the Bay of Pigs, Kennedy traveled to Vienna in June 1961 for his first meeting with Soviet Premier Nikita Khrushchev. Their frosty exchange of views did little to reduce tensions between the two nations. Nor did Khrushchev's continuing irritation over the existence of a noncommunist West Berlin in the heart of East Germany. Particularly embarrassing to the communists was the mass exodus of residents of East Germany to the West through the easily traversed border in the center of Berlin. Before dawn on August 13, 1961, the Soviet Union stopped the exodus by directing East Germany to construct a wall between East and West Berlin. Guards fired upon those who continued to try to escape.

KENNEDY IN BERLIN. One of the greatest triumphs of John Kennedy's brief presidency was his 1962 visit to West Berlin, not long after the East Germans constructed a wall dividing the communist and noncommunist sectors of the city. Addressing a vast and wildly enthusiastic throng, Kennedy declared that, like all free men, *"Ich bin ein Berliner"* ("I am a Berliner"). Kennedy's visit confirmed the status of West Berlin as a symbol of resistance to communism. (*John F. Kennedy Library*)

The rising tensions culminated the following October in the most dangerous and dramatic crisis of the Cold War. During the summer of 1962, American intelligence agencies had become aware of the arrival of Soviet technicians and equipment in Cuba and of military construction in progress. At first, the administration assumed that the new weapons system was purely defensive. On October 14, however, aerial reconaissance photos produced clear evidence that in fact the Soviets were constructing missile sites on the island. The reasons for the Russian effort were not difficult to discern. The existence of offensive nuclear missiles in Cuba would go far toward compensating for the American lead in deployable atomic weapons, giving the Soviet Union the same easy access to enemy territory that the United States had long possessed by virtue of its missile sites in Europe and the Middle East. The weapons would, moreover, serve as an effective deterrent against any future American invasion of Cuba—a possibility that seemed very real both to Castro and to the Soviet leadership.

To Kennedy, however, the missile sites represented an unconscionable act of aggression by the Soviets toward the United States. Almost immediately, he decided that the weapons could not be allowed to remain. On October 22, after nearly a week of tense deliberations by a special task force in the White House, the President announced on television that he was establishing a naval and air blockade around Cuba, a "quarantine" against all offensive weapons. Soviet ships bound for the island slowed course or stopped before reaching the point of confrontation. But work on the missile sites continued at full speed. Preparations were under way for an American air attack upon the missile sites when, late in the evening of October 26, Kennedy received a message from Khrushchev implying that the Soviet Union would remove the missile bases in exchange for an American pledge not to invade Cuba. Ignoring other, tougher Soviet messages, the President agreed; privately, moreover, he gave assurances that the United States would remove its bases from Turkey (a decision he had already reached months before but had not yet implemented). On October 27, the agreement became public. The crisis was over.

The Cuban missile crisis brought the world closer to nuclear war than at any time since World War II. It exposed in dangerous fashion the perils that both

THE MISSILE CRISIS.   The tension of the Cuban missile crisis shows in the President's face as he meets with Secretary of Defense Robert McNamara to discuss America's response to the challenge. Some members of the special committee that met throughout the crisis urged an immediate air strike against the missile sites; in the end, however, the President decided upon a more restrained approach: a naval blockade. One option that apparently received little consideration was a public demand for removal of the missiles coupled with an appeal to the United Nations. UN Ambassador Adlai Stevenson met with open scorn from other members of the committee when he proposed that approach. (*John F. Kennedy Library*)

the Soviet Union and the United States were creating by allowing their own rivalry to extend into Third World countries. But it also, ironically, helped produce a significant alleviation of Cold War tensions. Both the United States and the Soviet Union had been forced to confront the momentous consequences of war; and both seemed ready in the following months to move toward a new accommodation. In June 1963, President Kennedy addressed a commencement audience at American University in Washington, D.C., with a message starkly different from those of his earlier speeches. The United States did not, he claimed, seek a "Pax Americana enforced on the world by American weapons of war." And he seemed for the first time to offer hope for a peaceful rapprochement with the Soviet Union. "If we cannot now end our differences," he said, "at least we can help make the world safe for diversity." That same summer, the United States and the Soviet Union concluded years of negotiation by agreeing to a treaty to ban the testing of nuclear weapons in the atmosphere. It was the first step toward mutual arms reduction since the beginning of the Cold War—a small step, but one that seemed to augur a new era of international relations.

Johnson and the World

Lyndon Johnson entered the presidency lacking even John Kennedy's limited experience with international affairs. He had traveled widely while Vice President, but he had been included in few important decisions. Of all areas of public policy, international relations remained the most unfamiliar to him. He was eager, therefore, not only to continue the policies of his predecessor, but to prove quickly that he too was a strong and forceful leader. To his misfortune, however, he quickly became dependent upon those members of the Kennedy administration with the most assertive, even arrogant, view of the proper uses of American power. They would lead the new President into an unparalleled disaster.

Johnson was even less adept than his predecessor—who had displayed little sensitivity on the subject—at distinguishing between nationalist insurgency and communist expansion. His response to an internal rebellion in the Dominican Republic was a clear illustration. A 1961 assassination had toppled the repressive dictatorship of General Rafael Trujillo, and for the next four years various factions in the country had struggled for dominance. In the spring of 1965, a conservative military regime began to collapse in the face of a revolt by a broad range of groups (including some younger military leaders) on behalf of the left-wing nationalist Juan Bosch. For Johnson, the situation seemed an ideal opportunity to display the effectiveness of American force. Arguing (falsely) that Bosch threatened to establish a pro-Castro, communist regime, he dispatched 30,000 American troops to quell the disorder. The troops remained—although later they came under the auspices of the Organization of American States—until the Johnson administration had assurances that the Dominican Republic would establish a pro-American, anticommunist regime. Only after a conservative candidate defeated Bosch in a 1966 election were the forces withdrawn.

From Johnson's first moments in office, however, his foreign policy was almost totally dominated by a bitter civil war in Vietnam and by the expanding involvement of the United States there. That involvement had been growing slowly for more than a decade by the time Johnson assumed the presidency. In many respects, therefore, he was simply the unfortunate legatee of commitments initiated by his predecessors. But the determination of the new President, and of others within his administration, to prove their worthiness in the battle against communism led to the final, decisive steps toward a full-scale and catastrophic commitment.

SUGGESTED READINGS

On the election of 1960, see Theodore H. White, *The Making of the President, 1960* (1961), a now classic study. On Kennedy himself, see Arthur M. Schlesinger, Jr., *A Thousand Days* (1965), and Theodore Sorensen, *Kennedy* (1965), for admiring portraits by administration insiders; Herbert Parmet, *Jack* (1980); Henry Fairlie, *The Kennedy Promise* (1973); Lewis Paper, *The Promise and the Performance* (1975); and Bruce Miroff, *Pragmatic Illusions* (1976). On the Kennedy assassination, see *The Report of the Warren Commission* (1964) for the official investigation; William Manchester, *The Death of a President* (1967), for an emotional portrait of the days following the slaying; and Anthony Summers, *Conspiracy* (1980), for a discussion of the continuing controversies surrounding the event. Studies of Lyndon Johnson include Doris Kearns, *Lyndon Johnson and the American Dream* (1976), and Eric Goldman, *The Tragedy of Lyndon Johnson* (1968). Johnson's memoirs, *Vantage Point* (1971), offer a defense of his record. George Reedy, *The Twilight of the Presidency* (1970), offers valuable reflections by Johnson's press secretary. Jim Heath, *Decade of Disillusionment* (1975), is an overview of the Kennedy–Johnson years.

On the domestic programs of the Kennedy–Johnson era, see Tom Wicker, *JFK and LBJ* (1968), for a study of congressional politics and the presidency; Jim Heath, *John F. Kennedy and the Business Community* (1969); Victor Navasky, *Kennedy Justice* (1971); James Sundquist, *Politics and Policy* (1968); Sar Levitan, *The Great Society's Poor Law* (1969); Sar Levitan and Robert Taggart, *The Promise of Greatness* (1976); and Daniel Knapp and Kenneth Polk, *Scouting the War on Poverty* (1971). For the maturing of the civil-rights movement, see David Lewis, *King* (1970); Carl Brauer, *John F. Kennedy and the Second Reconstruction* (1977); Martin Luther King, Jr., *Why We Can't Wait* (1964); David Garrow, *Protest at Selma* (1978); and William Chafe, *Civilities and Civil Rights* (1980).

On the foreign policy of the Kennedy–Johnson years, see Richard Walton, *Cold War and Counterrevolution* (1972); Louise Fitzsimmons, *The Kennedy Doctrine* (1972); Godfrey Hodgson, *America in Our Time* (1976), which is also valuable for its study of the domestic climate of the era; Roger Hilsman, *To Move a Nation* (1965); Philip Geyelin, *Lyndon B. Johnson and the World* (1966); and Richard Barnet, *Intervention and Revolution* (1968), which examines American policies toward the Third World. On the disastrous 1961 invasion of Cuba, consult Haynes Johnson, *The Bay of Pigs*

(1964), and Peter Wyden, *Bay of Pigs* (1969). Elie Abel, *The Missile Crisis* (1966); Graham Allison, *Essence of Decision* (1971), an innovative examination of decision making; and Robert Kennedy, *Thirteen Days* (1969), a personal memoir, examine the Cuban missile crisis. Dan Kurzman, *Santo Domingo* (1966), and Jerome Slater, *Intervention and Negotiation* (1970), discuss the American intervention in the Dominican Republic in 1965.

Twenty-Three

Vietnam, Race, and the Crisis of Liberalism

Few Americans would have predicted at the beginning of 1965 that within three years the nation would be embroiled in a major political, social, and cultural crisis. In international affairs, the United States was moving firmly and confidently to combat the expansion of communism, continuing a policy that most Americans had supported for nearly twenty years. In domestic matters, the nation was acting decisively to confront its most serious social problem: racial inequality. Most liberals, at least, continued to believe that the nation possessed the will and the resources to sustain both those commitments.

But the origins of crisis were already apparent to those who cared to look. In extending the historic containment doctrine to dictate a deepening American involvement in the civil war in Vietnam, the United States was embroiling itself in a conflict it did not understand and could not resolve. It soon became the most frustrating and divisive international experience in the nation's history. And in assaulting the problem of racial injustice, the nation was undertaking a far more difficult and wrenching task than most reformers at first realized. It, too, would soon produce deep frustrations and divisions. By the end of the 1960s, the confident assumptions that had fueled the liberal crusades of the first half of the decade lay in ruins. And American society found itself searching for ways to restore stability and unity to the nation.

VIETNAM: THE MAKING OF THE QUAGMIRE

The American involvement in Vietnam had developed so slowly and imperceptibly that when it began spectacularly to expand, in 1964 and 1965, few could remember how it had originated. The first steps toward intervention, certainly,

449

had appeared at the time to be little more than minor events on the periphery of the larger Cold War. From 1946 until 1954, the United States had played an indirect role in Vietnam, supplying French forces in their futile effort to regain control over their former colony. When the French resistance collapsed in 1954 and the Geneva Conference temporarily partitioned the nation, America became more directly involved: first helping to establish Ngo Dinh Diem as the head of a pro-Western government in South Vietnam; then supporting Diem's decision to block the planned 1956 elections, which were to have united the nation under a single government. Both Diem and the Americans had realized that Ho Chi Minh, the nationalist-communist leader of North Vietnam, would win any such election. From that moment on, the United States found itself in the position of defender of the Diem regime; and as such it faced steadily increasing demands as that regime began to lose its grip, shaken by internal opposition and a growing threat from the north.

Guns and Advisers

Ngo Dinh Diem had been an unfortunate choice as the basis of American hopes for a noncommunist Vietnam. Autocratic, aristocratic, and corrupt, he staunchly resisted any economic reforms that would weaken the position of the Vietnamese upper class and the power of his own family. A belligerent Roman Catholic in a nation whose citizens were overwhelmingly Buddhist, he invited dissent through his efforts to limit the influence of Vietnam's traditional religion. By 1958, he was embroiled in a bitter civil war in the south. Two years later, that war intensified, as communist guerrillas (or Viet Cong) organized the National Front for the Liberation of South Vietnam (NLF). The NLF had close ties to the government of Ho Chi Minh and, as the war expanded in the following years, received increasing assistance from the north.

Faced with a steadily deteriorating political and military position, Diem appealed to the United States for assistance. The Eisenhower administration increased the flow of weapons and ammunition to South Vietnam during its last years in office and introduced the first few American military advisers to the area —about 650 in all. But it was the Kennedy administration, with its fervent belief in the importance of fighting communism in emerging areas, that expanded that assistance into a major commitment. Despite misgivings about the reliability of Diem, Kennedy substantially increased the flow of munitions into South Vietnam. More important, he raised the number of American military personnel to 15,500.

But the real depths of the American commitment to the war became clear in 1963, when the Diem regime stood on the brink of collapse. The military struggle against the Viet Cong was going badly. And Diem's brutal tactics in dispersing Buddhist demonstrators in Saigon had produced a religious crisis as well. Several Buddhist monks burned themselves to death in the streets of the capital, arousing further popular resistance to the government and horrifying the American public, which witnessed the immolations on television. Early in November, after receiving tacit assurances of support from the United States, South Vietnamese military

AMERICAN ADVISERS IN VIETNAM.   The introduction of American
military "advisers" to train South Vietnamese troops was the first step toward
the nation's long and disastrous involvement in the war in Vietnam. In this
photograph, American officers instruct Vietnamese soldiers on how to
counter guerrilla warfare. Behind them is one of the American helicopters
that were to become the primary means of transport in the conduct of the
war. (*U.S. Army photo*)

leaders seized control of the government from Diem, executing the deposed
president, his brother, and other associates. The Americans had not sanctioned
the killings, but they had been instrumental in instigating the coup. Faced with
what he considered a choice between allowing South Vietnam to fall or expanding
the American involvement, John Kennedy had chosen the latter. Before he could
indicate what further steps he was prepared to take, he himself fell victim to an
assassin on November 22.

From Aid to Intervention

Lyndon Johnson, therefore, inherited what was already a substantial American
commitment to the survival of an anticommunist South Vietnam. During his first
two years in office, he expanded that commitment into a full-scale American war.
Why he did so has long been a subject of debate.

Many factors played a role in Johnson's fateful decision. But the most obvious
explanation is that the new President faced many pressures to expand the Ameri-

can involvement and only a very few to limit it. As the untested successor to a revered and martyred President, he felt obliged to prove his worthiness for the office by continuing the policies of his predecessor. Aid to South Vietnam had been one of the most prominent of those policies. Johnson also felt it necessary to retain in his administration many of the important figures of the Kennedy years. In doing so, he surrounded himself with a group of foreign policy advisers— Secretary of State Dean Rusk, Secretary of Defense Robert McNamara, National Security Adviser McGeorge Bundy—who strongly believed not only that the United States had an important obligation to resist communism in Vietnam, but that it possessed the ability and resources to make that resistance successful. As a result, Johnson seldom had access to information making clear how difficult the new commitment might become. A compliant Congress raised little protest to, and indeed at one point openly endorsed, Johnson's use of executive powers to lead the nation into war. And for several years at least, public opinion remained firmly behind him—in part because Barry Goldwater's bellicose remarks about the war during the 1964 campaign made Johnson seem by comparison to be a moderate on the issue. Above all, intervention in South Vietnam was fully consistent with nearly twenty years of American foreign policy. An anticommunist ally was appealing to the United States for assistance; all the assumptions of the containment doctrine seemed to require the nation to oblige. Johnson seemed unconcerned that the government of South Vietnam existed only because the United States had put it there, and that the regime had never succeeded in acquiring the loyalty of its people. Vietnam, he believed, provided a test of American willingness to fight communist aggression, a test he was determined not to fail.

During his first months in office, Johnson expanded the American involvement in Vietnam only slightly, introducing an additional 5,000 military advisers there and preparing to send 5,000 more. Then, early in August 1964, the President announced that American destroyers on patrol in international waters in the Gulf of Tonkin had been attacked by North Vietnamese torpedo boats. Later information raised serious doubts as to whether the attack had actually occurred or, if it had, whether it had been, as the President insisted, "unprovoked." At the time, however, virtually no one questioned Johnson's portrayal of the incident as a serious act of aggression or his insistence that the United States must respond. By a vote of 416 to 0 in the House and 88 to 2 in the Senate (with only Wayne Morse of Oregon and Ernest Gruening of Alaska dissenting), Congress hurriedly passed the Gulf of Tonkin Resolution, which authorized the President to "take all necessary measures" to protect American forces and "prevent further aggression" in Southeast Asia. The resolution became, in Johnson's view at least, an open-ended legal authorization for escalation of the conflict.

The Gulf of Tonkin Resolution solved several problems for the administration. It provided congressional authorization for its policies in Vietnam, and it helped mobilize public support for an expanded commitment. But it created other difficulties. Publicly committed now to the defense of what the United States liked to term an independent, democratic government in the south, the administration had to confront the failure of any faction to establish a stable regime there to

LBJ CAMPAIGNING, 1964. The war in Vietnam seemed little more than a faint cloud on the horizon during Lyndon Johnson's triumphant 1964 campaign. The President sharply criticized the Republican candidate, Senator Barry Goldwater of Arizona, for proposing to send "American boys" to Vietnam; but Johnson himself was already expanding the American commitment, and within months of the election he would himself dispatch United States ground troops to Southeast Asia. (*UPI*)

replace Diem. With the South Vietnamese leadership in disarray, more and more of the burden of opposition to the Viet Cong fell upon the United States. In February 1965, seven Americans died when communist forces attacked a military base at Pleiku. Johnson retaliated by ordering the first United States bombings of the north, attempting to destroy the depots and transportation lines that were responsible for the flow of North Vietnamese soldiers and supplies into South Vietnam. The bombing continued until 1972, even though there was little evidence that it was effective in limiting North Vietnamese assistance to the NLF.

A month later, in March 1965, two battalions of American Marines landed at Da Nang in South Vietnam. Although Johnson continued to insist that he was not leading the United States into a "ground war" in Southeast Asia, there were now more than 100,000 American troops in Vietnam. The following July, finally, the President publicly admitted that the character of the war had changed. American soldiers would now, he admitted, begin playing an active role in the conduct of the war. By the end of the year, there were more than 180,000 American combat troops in Vietnam; in 1966, that number doubled; and by the end of 1967, there were nearly 500,000 American soldiers fighting on the ground, while the air war had intensified until the tonnage of bombs dropped ultimately exceeded that in Europe during World War II. Meanwhile, American casualties were mounting. In 1961, 14 Americans had died in Vietnam; in 1963, the toll was 489. By the spring of 1966, more than 4,000 Americans had been killed; and they were continuing to die at a faster rate than soldiers in the ineffective South Vietnamese army. Yet the gains resulting from the carnage had been negligible. The United States had finally succeeded in 1965 in creating a reasonably stable government in the south under General Nguyen Van Thieu. But the new regime was a corrupt and brutal dictatorship, unable to maintain control over a vast proportion of its own countryside. The Viet Cong, not the Thieu regime, controlled the majority of South Vietnam's villages and hamlets.

The Quagmire

For more than seven years, therefore, American combat forces remained bogged down in a war that the United States was never able either to win or fully to understand. Combating a foe whose strength lay not in weaponry but in a pervasive infiltration of the population, the United States responded with the kind of heavy-handed technological warfare designed for conventional battles against conventional armies. American forces succeeded in winning most of the major battles in which they became engaged, routing the Viet Cong and their North Vietnamese allies from such strongholds as Dak To, Con Thien, and later, Khe Sanh. There were astounding (if not always reliable) casualty figures showing that far more communists than Americans were dying in combat—statistics that the United States military referred to as a "favorable kill ratio." There was a continuing stream of optimistic reports, from American military commanders, civilian officials, and others, that the war was progressing—including the famous words of Secretary of Defense McNamara that he could "see the light at the end of the tunnel." But if the war was not actually being lost, it certainly was not being won. It was, moreover, becoming clear to some observers that it was a war that perhaps could not be won.

At the heart of the problem was the fact that the United States was not fighting an army as much as a popular movement. The Viet Cong derived its strength in part from the aid it received from North Vietnam and, indirectly, from the Soviet Union and China. Far more important, however, was its success in mobilizing members of the native population—men, women, and even children—who were indistinguishable from their neighbors and who fought not only openly in major battles, but covertly through sabotage, ambush, and terror. American troops might drive Viet Cong forces from a particular village or city; but as soon as the Americans left, the NLF forces would return. The frustrations of this kind of warfare mounted steadily, until the United States found itself involved in a series of desperate strategies.

Central to the American war effort was the much-heralded "pacification" program, designed in part by General William Westmoreland, whose purpose was

SURVEYING THE QUAGMIRE.   American soldiers search the South
Vietnamese landscape for evidence of enemy troops. The ruggedness of the terrain,
the skill of the Viet Cong at avoiding detection, and the ability of communist
guerrillas to blend in with the native population all contributed to making the
American military effort frustrating and fruitless. (*Philip Jones Griffiths/Magnum*)

to rout the Viet Cong from particular regions and then "pacify" those regions by
winning the "hearts and minds" of the people. Routing the Viet Cong was often
possible, but the subsequent pacification was not. American forces were incapable
of establishing the same kind of rapport with members of an ancient, provincial
culture that the highly nationalistic Viet Cong forces were able to achieve.
Gradually, therefore, the pacification program gave way to the more desperate
"relocation" strategy. Instead of attempting to win the loyalty of the peasants in
areas in which the Viet Cong was operating, American troops would uproot the
villagers from their homes, send them fleeing to refugee camps or into the cities
(producing by 1967 more than 3 million refugees), and then destroy the vacated
villages and surrounding countryside. Saturation bombing, bulldozing of settlements, chemical defoliation of fields and jungles—all were designed to eliminate
possible Viet Cong sanctuaries. But the Viet Cong responded simply by moving
to new sanctuaries elsewhere. The futility of the United States effort was sug-

gested by the statement of an American officer after flattening one such hamlet that it had been "necessary to destroy the town in order to save it."

As the war dragged on and victory remained elusive, some American officers and officials began to argue that the United States should expand its efforts in Indochina. Some argued for heavier bombing and increased troop strength; others insisted that the United States attack communist enclaves in surrounding countries; a few began to urge the use of nuclear weapons. The Johnson administration, however, resisted. Unwilling to abandon its commitment to South Vietnam for fear of destroying American "credibility" in the world, the government was also unwilling to expand the war too far, for fear of provoking direct intervention by the Chinese, the Soviets, or both. Caught in a trap of his own making, the President began to encounter additional obstacles and frustrations at home.

The War at Home

Few Americans, and even fewer influential ones, had protested the American involvement in Vietnam as late as the end of 1965. But as the war dragged on and its futility began to become apparent, political support for it soon began to erode. At first, the attack emerged from the perimeters of government: from intellectuals, from students, and from the press. By the end of 1967, the debate over the war had moved fully into the mainstream of national politics.

DEFOLIATION. The frustration of attempting to find and defeat the elusive Viet Cong forces led American military leaders to adopt extraordinary tactics in South Vietnam, among them the "defoliation" of the jungles to destroy possible communist sanctuaries. These photographs of a mangrove forest before being sprayed with American herbicides (1965) and after (1970) indicate the extent of the devastation wrought on South Vietnam. (*Wide World Photos*)

Many of the earliest objections to the war emerged on college and university campuses. Political scientists, historians, Asian experts, and others began in 1965 to raise serious questions about both the wisdom and the morality of the Vietnam adventure, arguing that it reflected, among other things, a fundamental American misunderstanding of politics and society in Southeast Asia. A series of "teach-ins" on university campuses, beginning at The University of Michigan in 1965, sparked a national debate over the war, long before such debate developed inside the government. College students, in the meantime, were becoming increasingly numerous and outspoken in their denunciations of the war. Some had become radicalized by their participation in the civil-rights movement of the early 1960s and moved naturally into opposition to the war, denouncing it as a reflection of the corruption of American society. Other, more moderate students responded to narrower arguments, opposing the war because they considered it unwise and unwinnable. Whatever their motives, by the end of 1967 American students opposed to the war had grown so numerous and so vocal as to form a major political force. Enormous peace marches in New York, Washington, D.C., and other cities drew increasing public attention to the antiwar movement. Campus demonstrations occurred almost daily. A growing number of journalists, particularly reporters who had spent time in Vietnam, helped sustain the movement with their frank revelations about the brutality and futility of the war.

The chorus of popular protest soon began to stimulate opposition to the war from within the government itself. Senator J. William Fulbright of Arkansas, chairman of the powerful Senate Foreign Relations Committee, became one of the earliest influential public figures to turn against the war. Beginning in January 1966, he began to stage highly publicized and occasionally televised congressional hearings to air criticisms of the war, summoning as witnesses such distinguished public figures as George F. Kennan and General James Gavin. Other prominent members of Congress joined Fulbright in opposing Johnson's policies—including, in 1967, Robert F. Kennedy, brother of the slain President, now a Senator from New York. Even within the administration, the consensus seemed to be crumbling. Secretary of State Rusk remained a true believer until the end; but McGeorge Bundy and Robert McNamara, both of whom had used their political and intellectual talents brilliantly (if dubiously) to extend the American involvement in Vietnam, quietly left the government in 1967 and 1968. Bundy's successor, Walt W. Rostow, was if anything even more committed to the war than his predecessor and one-time mentor. But the new Secretary of Defense, Clark Clifford, became a powerful voice within the administration on behalf of a cautious scaling down of the commitment.

Other factors weakened the position of supporters of the war as well. America's most important allies—Great Britain, France, West Germany, and Japan—all began to criticize the Vietnam involvement. Of more immediate concern, the American economy was beginning to suffer. Johnson's commitment to fighting the war while continuing his Great Society reforms—his promise of "guns and butter"—proved impossible to maintain; and social programs that many Americans believed were now more important than ever were losing funding. The inflation rate, which had remained at 2 percent through most of the early 1960s, rose to 3 percent in 1967, 4 percent in 1968, and 6 percent in 1969. In August 1967, President Johnson asked Congress for a tax increase—a 10 percent sur-charge that was widely labeled a "war tax"—which he knew was necessary if the nation was to avoid even more ruinous inflation. In return, congressional conserva-tives demanded and received a $6 billion reduction in the funding for Great Society programs. The war in Vietnam, in other words, was now not only a source of concern for its own sake but also a direct threat to liberal efforts to redress social injustices at home.

THE RACIAL CRISIS

Concern about those injustices mounted rapidly in the mid-1960s, when the already tense racial climate began to turn bitter and violent. As the scope of black demands widened and as the focus of racial unrest shifted to northern cities, the peaceful, interracial civil-rights movement of Martin Luther King, Jr., began to face competition from more militant and radical organizations. Like the war in Vietnam, therefore, the issue of race was becoming an increasingly divisive force in American life. It had been easy for most white liberals to support the first phase of the black struggle: the peaceful, morally compelling battle against overt, legal discrimination. The second phase, however, proved far more difficult and demand-ing. Some early supporters of the civil-rights movement shifted further to the left, accepting the arguments of militant black leaders. Others moved to the right, gradually losing faith altogether in the possibilities of racial progress. But perhaps the greatest number remained in the center, confused, assailed, and, it sometimes seemed, increasingly irrelevant.

The Changing Context

It was inevitable, perhaps, that the focus of the racial struggle would shift away from the issue of segregation to the far broader demands of poor urban blacks. For decades, the nation's black population had been undergoing a major demo-graphic shift; and by the 1960s, the problem of race was no longer a primarily southern or rural one, as it had been earlier in the century. In 1910, only about 25 percent of all blacks had lived in cities and only 10 percent outside the South. By 1966, 69 percent were living in metropolitan areas and 45 percent were outside the South. In several of the largest cities, the proportion of blacks at least doubled between 1950 and 1968. Blacks constituted 30 percent or more of the population of seven of those cities and nearly 70 percent of the population of Washington, D.C. Conditions in the black ghettoes of most cities were abysmal; and while the economic condition of much of American society was improving, in many poor urban communities—which were experiencing both a rapidly growing population and the flight of white businesses—things were getting worse. More than half of all American nonwhites lived in poverty in the early 1960s. Black unemployment was twice that of whites. Black ghetto residents were far more likely than whites to be victimized by crime, to be enticed into drug addiction, and to be subjected to substandard housing at exploitive prices. They were far less likely than whites to receive an adequate education or to have access to skilled employment.

As the battle against legal segregation progressed in the early 1960s with the passage of the landmark Civil Rights Acts of 1964 and 1965, even such relatively moderate black leaders as Martin Luther King, Jr., began to turn their attention to the deeper problems of racial injustice. By the mid-1960s, the legal battle against school desegregation had moved beyond the initial assault on de jure segregation (segregation by law) to an attack on de facto segregation (segregation by practice, as through residential patterns), thus carrying the fight into northern cities. The nation was taking its first steps toward the busing of students from one school district to another to achieve integration, an issue that would prove as deeply divisive as any social question of its time. Many black leaders (and their white supporters) were demanding, similarly, that the battle against job discrimination move beyond the prohibition of overtly racist practices. Employers should not only abandon negative measures to deny jobs to blacks; they should adopt positive measures to recruit minorities, thus compensating for past injustices. Regulations adopted by the federal government in 1968, and strengthened in later rulings, required all institutions doing business with or receiving funds from the federal government (including schools and universities) to conform to so-called Affirmative Action guidelines. Thus yet another issue had arisen that would soon anger and alienate many whites.

The most important problem, however, remained a far more basic one: urban poverty. Beginning in 1964, moreover, it thrust itself into public prominence when residents of black ghettoes in northern cities participated in a series of riots that shocked and terrified much of the nation's white population. There were a few scattered disturbances in the summer of 1964, most notably in New York City's Harlem. But the first major race riot occurred the following summer in the Watts section of Los Angeles. In the midst of a more or less routine traffic arrest, a white police officer struck a protesting black bystander with his club; and the apparently minor incident unleashed a storm of pent-up anger and bitterness that resulted in a full week of mounting violence. As many as 10,000 rioters were estimated to have participated, attacking white motorists, burning buildings, looting stores, and sniping at policemen. As in most race riots, it was the blacks themselves who suffered most; of the thirty-four people who died during the Watts uprising, which was eventually quelled by the National Guard, most were black. In the summer of 1966, there were forty-three additional outbreaks, the most serious of them in Chicago and Cleveland. And in the summer of 1967, there were eight major riots, including the most serious of them all—a racial clash in Detroit in which forty-three people (thirty-three of them black) died.

Televised reports of the violence horrified the nation. After the Detroit uprising, President Johnson expressed the ambivalence of many white liberals about the riots, calling sternly on the one hand for a restoration of law and order, and appealing simultaneously for an attack upon the social problems that were causing despair and violence. A special Commission on Civil Disorders echoed the latter impulse. Its celebrated report, issued in the spring of 1968, recommended massive spending to eliminate the abysmal conditions of the ghettoes. "Only a commitment to national action on an unprecedented scale," the commission concluded, "can shape a future compatible with the historic ideals of American society." To much of the nation, however, the lesson of the riots was that racial change was moving too quickly and that stern, coercive measures were necessary to stop violence and lawlessness.

Black Power

Disillusioned with the ideal of peaceful change in cooperation with whites, an increasing number of blacks were turning to a new approach to the racial issue: the philosophy of "black power." Black power could mean many different things. In its most moderate form, it was simply a belief in the importance of black self-reliance. Blacks could not rely on the beneficence of whites in their battle for equality; they must mobilize themselves and exert independent economic and political power. In its more extreme guises, black power could mean complete separatism and even violent revolution. In all its forms, however, black power

WATTS, 1965. A seemingly trivial incident in this black neighborhood of Los Angeles sparked the most serious race riot in more than twenty years. Arson, looting, and sniper fire contributed to the mayhem. (*UPI*)

suggested a move away from interracial cooperation and toward an increase in black racial awareness.

The most important and lasting impact of the black-power ideology was a social and psychological one: the instilling of racial pride in black Americans who had long been under pressure from their nation's dominant culture to think of themselves as somehow inferior to whites. The popular phrase "Black is beautiful" best expressed the new impulse of the 1960s. Increasing numbers of blacks began to explore the heritage of their racial culture, to take an interest in their African ancestry, to emphasize the achievements of blacks in American history, to develop their own literary and artistic patterns. Black writers such as James Baldwin celebrated the achievements of black society in their works while expressing increasing hostility toward the white world. Earlier black writers—among them Richard Wright, author of *Native Son* (1940), and Ralph Ellison, author of *Invisible Man* (1952)—experienced triumphant revivals. Schools and universities adopted black-studies programs.

Black power had political manifestations as well, most notably in creating a deep schism within the civil-rights movement. Stokely Carmichael, leader of the Student Nonviolent Coordinating Committee (SNCC) and originator of the phrase "black power," began to lead his organization away from the moderate premises of older civil-rights organizations. Rejecting the Urban League, the NAACP, and even Martin Luther King, Jr.'s, Southern Christian Leadership Conference— from which SNCC had originally emerged—Carmichael began to call instead for more radical and even violent action against the "racism" of white society. The Congress of Racial Equality, long the most interracial of civil-rights organizations, was by the mid-1960s almost entirely black, with whites officially barred from positions of leadership within the organization. Even Martin Luther King, Jr., who was himself the target of criticism from black-power advocates, began to limit the role of white leaders within his own organization, in a reluctant effort to maintain his influence among the more militant members of his race. By 1968, he too was emphasizing the issue of urban poverty and northern racism and was calling for more militant (although still nonviolent) action. He had also become committed, like many other black leaders, to the antiwar movement, speaking out against American involvement in Vietnam as early as 1965.

More disturbing to white Americans than the schism within the civil-rights movement was the emergence of new groups entirely outside it. Particularly alarming were such overtly revolutionary organizations as the Black Panthers. Based in Oakland, California, and led by Bobby Seale, "Minister of Defense" Huey Newton, and "Minister of Information" Eldridge Cleaver, the Panthers openly armed themselves for what they claimed would be a fight for black nationalism. Actual incidents of Panther violence were relatively few; far more frequent were violent attacks on them by law-enforcement agencies, most notably the FBI, which called them the greatest threat to the nation's internal security.

Even more extreme in its objectives, if not in its tactics, was the Nation of Islam of Elijah Muhammed, better known among whites as the Black Muslims. A tightly disciplined movement among northern urban blacks, it rejected white society as inherently evil, referred to whites as "devils," and appealed to blacks to embrace

PANTHERS IN NEW YORK.   Black Panthers demonstrate in New York City in 1968 on behalf of their "Minister of Defense" Huey P. Newton, who had been charged with the murder of a police officer in Oakland, California. By the end of 1969, the FBI and local police forces had succeeded in driving many Panther leaders into hiding or exile. Several were killed, among them two members of the organization shot during a notorious raid upon their headquarters by Chicago police in December. (*UPI*)

the Islamic faith and work for complete racial separation. The most celebrated of the Black Muslims was Malcolm Little, who adopted the name Malcolm X ("X" to denote his lost African surname). His celebrated *Autobiography* (1965) became one of the most influential documents of the 1960s, not only expressing the ideology of black nationalism but exposing the demeaning influence of white society on residents of the ghetto. Malcolm X himself died shortly before publication of his book when black gunmen, presumably under orders from rivals within the Nation of Islam, burst into a meeting he was addressing and assassinated him.

THE TRAUMAS OF 1968

By the end of 1967, the twin crises of the war in Vietnam and the deteriorating racial situation at home, crises that fed upon and exaggerated each other, had helped to create deep social tensions in America. In the course of 1968, those tensions seemed suddenly to burst to the surface and threaten national chaos. Not since World War II had the United States experienced so profound a sense of crisis. Perhaps never before in its history had the nation suffered as many traumatic shocks in such short order. The result, however, was not primarily what many protesting Americans had hoped: a revolutionary change in the nation's domestic and foreign policies. It was, rather, the mobilization of a powerful conservative reaction.

The Tet Offensive

Domestic opposition to the war in Vietnam had been powerful and strident before 1968, but it had remained a distinctly minority sentiment. Fewer than 25 percent of the American people, according to public-opinion polls, opposed the President's policies at the end of 1967. The so-called Tet offensive of early 1968 dramatically changed both the nature of the war itself and the nature of the antiwar movement.

On January 31, 1968, the first day of the Vietnamese New Year (Tet), Viet Cong forces launched an enormous, concerted attack upon American strongholds throughout South Vietnam. The attack displayed a strength that American commanders had long insisted the Viet Cong did not possess. Some major cities, most notably Hue, fell to the communists. Others suffered major disruptions. But what made the Tet offensive genuinely shocking to the American people, who saw vivid reports of it on television, was what happened in Saigon. If any place in South Vietnam had seemed secure from enemy attack, it was the capital city. Now, suddenly, Viet Cong forces were in the heart of Saigon, setting off bombs, shooting down South Vietnamese officials and troops, and holding down fortified areas. Particularly alarming were pictures of Viet Cong forces inside the compound of the American embassy, with United States diplomats trapped in their offices, peering out of windows holding pistols. Enormous numbers of Americans now concluded that the war clearly was not being won.

Even more chilling was the evidence the Tet offensive gave of the brutality of the fighting in Vietnam, of the savagery it seemed to have aroused in those who became involved in it. In the midst of the Tet offensive, television cameras recorded the sight of a captured Viet Cong guerrilla being led up to a South Vietnamese officer in the streets of Saigon. Without a word, the officer pulled out his pistol and shot the young guerrilla through the head, leaving him lying dead with his blood pouring onto the street. No single event did more to undermine support in the United States for the war.

In the weeks that followed, many of the pillars of American public opinion finally began to move into opposition to the war. Leading newspapers began taking editorial stands in favor of deescalation of the conflict. *Time* and *Newsweek* began running searing exposés and urging American withdrawal. Network commentators began voicing open doubts about the wisdom of American policies. (There were reports that when CBS's Walter Cronkite hosted a half-hour special on CBS in which he called the war a hopeless stalemate and urged American withdrawal, the President himself finally realized that he had lost the support of the nation.) The effect of these and other criticisms was devastating. Within weeks of the Tet

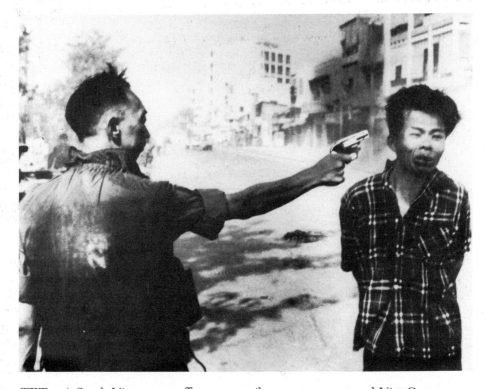

TET. A South Vietnamese officer summarily executes a captured Viet Cong guerrilla in the middle of a Saigon street during the 1968 Tet offensive. Films on American television of the appalling scene did more to turn public sentiment against the war than any other single event. The officer in this picture fled to the United States after the fall of South Vietnam and opened a restaurant in suburban Washington, D.C. When a local newspaper linked him to the 1968 shooting, his business quickly dwindled. (*Eddie Adams/Wide World Photos*)

offensive, public opposition to the war had almost doubled. And Johnson's personal popularity had slid to 35 percent, the lowest of any President since the darkest days of the Truman administration.

The Political Challenge

As early as the summer of 1967, dissident Democrats had been attempting to mobilize support behind an antiwar candidate who would challenge Lyndon Johnson in the 1968 primaries. For many months, they tried to enlist Senator Robert Kennedy, the most widely known critic of the war. But mindful of the difficulties in challenging an incumbent President, Kennedy declined. In his stead, the dissidents recruited Senator Eugene McCarthy of Minnesota, a subdued, cerebral candidate who avoided heated rhetoric in favor of carefully reasoned argument and who attracted a particularly devoted following among college students. A brilliantly orchestrated campaign by young volunteers in the New Hampshire primary produced a startling triumph for McCarthy in March; he came within 1 percentage point of defeating the President.

A few days later, Robert Kennedy finally entered the campaign, deeply embittering many of those who had dedicated themselves to the cause of McCarthy, but bringing his own substantial strength among blacks, poor people, and workers to the antiwar cause. Polls showed the President trailing badly in the next scheduled primary, in Wisconsin. Public animosity toward Johnson was such that he did not dare venture from the White House to campaign. On March 31, Johnson went on television to announce a limited halt in the bombing of North Vietnam —his first major concession to the antiwar forces—and, far more surprising, his withdrawal from the presidential contest. The man who had dreamed of becoming the greatest domestic President of the century was to leave office repudiated by the nation because of his commitment to a disastrous war.

For a moment, it seemed as though the antiwar forces had won—that nothing could stop them from seizing the Democratic presidential nomination and even the presidency itself. Robert Kennedy quickly established himself as the champion of the Democratic primaries, winning one election after another. In the meantime, however, Vice President Hubert Humphrey, with the support of President Johnson, entered the contest and began to attract the support of party leaders and of the many delegations that were selected not by popular primaries but by state party organizations. He soon appeared to be the front runner in the race.

The King Assassination

In the midst of this increasingly bitter political battle, in which the war had been the dominant issue, the attention of the nation suddenly turned again to the matter of race in response to a shocking tragedy. On April 4 Martin Luther King, Jr., who had traveled to Memphis, Tennessee, to lend his support to a strike by black sanitation workers in the city, was shot and killed while standing on the balcony of his motel. The assassin, James Earl Ray, who was captured days later in London, had no apparent motive. Speculation was rampant that he had been hired by others to do the killing, but if so he never revealed the identity of his employers.

The tragic death of King, who had remained the most widely admired black leader among both blacks and whites, deeply affected Americans of all races, producing an outpouring of grief matched in recent memory only by the reaction to the death of John Kennedy. Among blacks, however, it also produced widespread anger. In the days after the assassination, major riots broke out in more than sixty American cities. Forty-three people died; more than 3,000 suffered injuries; as many as 27,000 people were arrested. No one of these riots was as intense as some earlier uprisings, but together the disorders were the greatest manifestation of racial unrest in the nation's history.

MARTIN LUTHER KING, JR.   King, shown here during a press conference in 1963, was the heart of the civil-rights movement for more than a decade. His death in Memphis in 1968 seemed to symbolize what many had already begun to assert: that the peaceful, nonviolent movement of the early 1960s was losing power to a new, more radical approach. (*Magnum*)

The Kennedy Assassination and Chicago

Robert Kennedy, who spoke movingly on the night of the King assassination of the need to abandon violence, continued his campaign for the presidential nomination. Late in the night of June 6, he appeared in the ballroom of a Los Angeles hotel to acknowledge the cheers of his supporters for his victory in that day's California primary. Waiting for him in a nearby corridor, in the meantime, was Sirhan Sirhan, a young Palestinian who had become enraged, apparently, by pro-Israeli remarks Kennedy had made several days earlier in a televised debate with Eugene McCarthy. As Kennedy was leaving the ballroom after his victory statement, Sirhan emerged from a crowd and shot him in the head. Early the next

ROBERT KENNEDY CAMPAIGNING, 1968. In a year of supercharged political emotions, the 1968 presidential candidacy of Senator Robert F. Kennedy evoked remarkably passionate responses. Here he stands among a group of students in Oregon who, like crowds in virtually every part of the country, reach out enthusiastically to touch him. Despite the outpouring of support, Kennedy lost the Oregon primary to Senator Eugene McCarthy, his competitor for the loyalty of the youthful antiwar vote. (*UPI*)

morning, Kennedy died. In reality, he had been the victim of a single, crazed individual. But to much of the nation, stunned and bewildered by yet another public tragedy, Kennedy seemed to have been a victim of national social chaos.

The presidential campaign continued desultorily during the last weeks before the convention. Hubert Humphrey, who had seemed likely to win the nomination even before Robert Kennedy's death, now faced only minor opposition. The McCarthy crusade continued, but it never approached the strength necessary to offer a serious challenge to Humphrey. Support emerged briefly for other antiwar candidates: George McGovern, a Senator from South Dakota; Edward Kennedy, younger brother of Robert and a Senator from Massachusetts. But despite the embittered claims of many Democrats that Humphrey would simply continue the bankrupt policies of the Johnson administration, there seemed no possibility of stopping him. The approaching Democratic Convention, therefore, began to take on the appearance of an exercise in futility; and antiwar activists, despairing of winning any victories within the convention, began to plan major demonstrations outside it.

When the Democrats finally gathered in Chicago in August, even the most optimistic observers were predicting a turbulent convention. Inside the hall, carefully sealed off from all demonstrators by Mayor Richard Daley, delegates engaged in a long, bitter debate over an antiwar plank that both Kennedy and McCarthy supporters wanted to insert in the platform. Miles away, in a downtown park, thousands of students and other antiwar protesters had set up camps and were staging demonstrations. On the third night of the convention, as the delegates were beginning their balloting on the now virtually inevitable nomination of Hubert Humphrey, demonstrators and police clashed in a bloody riot in the streets of Chicago. Miraculously, no one was killed; but hundreds of protesters were injured as police attempted to disperse them with tear gas and billy clubs. Aware that the violence was being televised to the nation, the demonstrators taunted the authorities with the chant, "The whole world is watching!" And Hubert Humphrey, who had spent years dreaming of becoming his party's candidate for President, received a nomination that night that appeared at the time to be almost worthless.

The Conservative Response

The turbulent events of 1968 persuaded many observers that American society was on the verge of a fundamental social upheaval. Newspapers, magazines, the press—all helped create the impression of a nation in the throes of revolutionary change. In fact, however, the prevailing response of the American people to the turmoil was a conservative one. The disorder, the violence, the inflamed demands of radicals and dissidents, the mounting challenges to traditional values and institutions—all were provoking a strong counterreaction among what was, it gradually became clear, a majority of the population. They too were confused and frightened by the events of 1968; but they turned their anger against the protesters and radicals, who were, they believed, disrupting an essentially sound and stable society.

Much of the national media failed to notice until very late the power of what was becoming known as the "silent majority." After the Chicago convention, for example, journalists who had expressed great bitterness toward Mayor Daley and the Chicago police for their heavy-handed tactics against the antiwar demonstrators waited expectantly for evidence of public approval. To their surprise, they received instead a barrage of letters and telegrams expressing support for the police, hostility toward the demonstrators, and anger at the press for its "bias." Similarly, public-opinion polls showing that a growing number of Americans were now opposed to the war in Vietnam also made clear that the nature of that opposition was far different from what antiwar activists liked to believe. Few Americans shared the view of the left that the war was a crime, a moral outrage.

THE SIEGE OF CHICAGO. Helmeted Chicago police charge antiwar
demonstrators in Grant Park during the 1968 Democratic Convention. Despite the
efforts of Mayor Richard J. Daley to limit television coverage of the confrontations,
the networks carried extensive pictures of the violence. Aware of the cameras, many
of the demonstrators defiantly chanted, "The whole world is watching!" (*UPI*)

The majority considered it, rather, a mistake; and they opposed it not because they
rejected the principles motivating American intervention but because the United
States had failed to win. Even at the height of the antiwar movement, fewer than
20 percent of the American people supported an immediate, unilateral withdrawal
from Vietnam. In short, while 1968 had seemed on the surface to be a year of
revolution, in reality, it was a year of conservative reaction to disorder.

The most visible sign of the conservative "backlash" was the surprising success
of the campaign of George Wallace for the presidency. Wallace had established
himself in 1963 as one of the leading spokesmen for the defense of segregation
when, as Governor of Alabama, he had attempted to block the admission of black
students to the University of Alabama. In 1968, he became a third-party candidate
for President, basing his campaign on a host of conservative grievances. Although
he tempered some of his earlier positions on the race issue, he continued to appeal

to those who resented the intrusion of the federal government into local affairs, denouncing the forced busing of students, the proliferation of government regulations and social programs, and the permissiveness of authorities toward race riots and antiwar demonstrations. He chose as his running mate retired Air Force General Curtis LeMay, a bellicose advocate of expanding the war in Vietnam. There was never any serious chance that Wallace would win the election; but his remarkable standing in the polls over many months—rising at times to over 20 percent of those interviewed—was a clear indication that he had struck a responsive chord.

A far more skillful effort to mobilize the "silent majority" in favor of order and stability was under way within the Republican party. Richard Nixon, whose political career had seemed at an end after his losses in the presidential race of 1960 and in a California gubernatorial campaign two years later, reemerged as the preeminent spokesman for "Middle America." Although he avoided the crudeness and stridency of the Wallace campaign, he skillfully exploited many of the same concerns that were sustaining the Alabama Governor. Nixon was far more perceptive than other leaders of public opinion in realizing that many Americans

WALLACE. Analysts were hard put to explain the remarkable popularity of Governor George C. Wallace, who ran an effective third-party campaign for the presidency in 1968. Some believed his appeal rested almost entirely on white resentment of the civil-rights movement; but it was clear that he was tapping as well a wide range of frustrations growing out of the social and political instability of the 1960s. Whatever the reasons, Wallace provided powerful evidence that the American right was still very much alive. (*UPI*)

were now tired of hearing about their obligations to the poor, tired of hearing about the sacrifices necessary to achieve racial justice, tired of reforms that seemed designed to help criminals. By offering a vision of stability, law and order, government retrenchment, and "peace with honor" in Vietnam, he easily captured the nomination of his party for the presidency. And after the spectacle of the Democratic Convention, he and his running mate, Governor Spiro Agnew of Maryland, enjoyed a commanding lead in the polls as the the November election approached.

That lead diminished greatly in the last weeks before the voting. Old doubts about Nixon's character, doubts based in part on the often vicious anticommunism of his earlier career, continued to haunt the Republican candidate. A skillful last-minute surge by Hubert Humphrey, who somehow managed to restore at least a tenuous unity to the Democratic party, narrowed the gap further. And the continuing appeal of George Wallace appeared to be hurting the Republicans more than the Democrats. In the end, however, Nixon eked out a victory almost as narrow as his defeat in 1960. He received 43.4 percent of the popular vote to Humphrey's 42.7 percent (a margin of only about 500,000 votes), and 301 electoral votes to Humphrey's 219. George Wallace, who like most third-party candidates faded in the last weeks of the campaign, still managed to poll 13.5 percent of the popular vote and to carry five southern states with a total of 46 electoral ballots. Nixon had hardly won a decisive mandate. But the election had made one thing clear. The majority of the American people were more interested in the restoration of stability than in fundamental social change.

SUGGESTED READINGS

The one indispensable source on the Vietnam War is the Defense Department studies published as *The Pentagon Papers,* of which several editions are available. One of the most complete is the four-volume Senator Gravel edition (1975). Other books on Vietnam, in addition to those cited after Chapter 21, include David Halberstam, *The Best and the Brightest* (1972), a brilliant study of the decision makers who engineered the commitment; Guenter Lewy, *America in Vietnam* (1978), a controversial defense of the commitment; John Galloway, *The Gulf of Tonkin Resolution* (1970); and Alexander Kendrick, *The Wound Within* (1974). Michael Herr, *Dispatches* (1977), is a collection of essays by a war correspondent expressing the agony of the military experience. Lawrence Baskir and William Strauss, *Chance and Circumstance* (1978), examines the draft during the Vietnam War. Gloria Emerson, *Winners and Losers* (1976), assesses the wide-reaching impact of the war. Thomas Powers, *The War at Home* (1973), and Irwin Unger, *The Movement* (1974), discuss the domestic opposition.

On the rise of black power, see Stokely Carmichael and Charles Hamilton, *Black Power* (1967), the book that gave the phenomenon its name; *The Autobiography of Malcolm X* (1966), which was ghostwritten by Alex Haley; Benjamin Muse, *The American Negro Revolution* (1969); and Archie Epps, *Malcolm X and the American*

Negro Revolution (1969). On the urban riots, consult Robert Fogelson, *Violence as Protest* (1971); Joe R. Feagin and Harlan Hahn, *Ghetto Revolts* (1973); and the *Report of the National Advisory Commission on Civil Disorders* (1968).

The traumas of 1968 are brilliantly examined in Lewis Chester, Godfrey Hodgson, and Lewis Page, *American Melodrama* (1969), as well as in Godfrey Hodgson's important general study of modern America, *America in Our Time* (1976). Arthur M. Schlesinger, Jr., *Robert Kennedy and His Times* (1978), is a thorough and sympathetic biography. Norman Mailer, *Miami and the Siege of Chicago* (1968), is a personalized examination of the political conventions. Ben Stavis, *We Were the Campaign* (1969), is a study of the McCarthy crusade. Marshall Frady, *Wallace*, rev. ed. (1976), is a portrait of the conservative challenger. Theodore White, *The Making of the President, 1968* (1969), is a sober view of the Nixon election.

Twenty-Four

The Turbulent Society

The 1960s produced not only political turmoil in the United States, but cultural changes so profound that those who described them as a "revolution" exaggerated only slightly. The political crises and the cultural transformations were not unrelated. Indeed, in some respects they were almost indistinguishable from one another, for few eras in American history have seen the nation's culture so pervasively politicized.

The most visible cultural events of the era were, like the most visible political events, the assaults upon traditional values and institutions by dissidents and radicals. As in politics, genuine revolutionaries never represented the cultural outlook of more than a tiny minority of the population. Nevertheless, their influence was profound. The radical ideas they supported served as the outer edge of a major cultural shift that affected virtually every area of society. Not all Americans were happy about the changing values of the 1960s, but few could ignore or escape them.

THE NEW LEFT AND THE COUNTERCULTURE

More decisively, perhaps, than in any previous era, American youth dominated the culture of the late 1960s and early 1970s. Their influence could be felt in countless ways—not least in the strenuous and occasionally ludicrous efforts of some older Americans to "relate" to the youth culture by borrowing its language, dress, and life styles. The vanguard of cultural change, however, was a pair of overwhelmingly youthful movements that inspired only limited sympathy from or participation by adults: the New Left and the "counterculture." Although the two movements represented very different impulses, they were in practice closely linked. And each had profound effects upon the larger society.

The New Left

Among the many products of the civil-rights movement and the war in Vietnam was a radicalization of many American students, who in the course of the 1960s formed what became known as the New Left. Its origins were many and diverse. Young radicals of the 1960s rediscovered the social and political critiques of America produced by members of the so-called Old Left of the 1920s and 1930s. And they responded to the writings of several dissident critics of the 1950s and of their own time: Paul Goodman, who in *Growing Up Absurd* (1960) examined the process by which American youth were thrust into a hollow, meaningless existence; Norman O. Brown, who attacked the repressive nature of social and sexual conventions; C. Wright Mills, who in *The Power Elite* (1956) exposed a dangerous concentration of power in American society in the hands of a few corporate and military leaders; and perhaps above all, Herbert Marcuse, who in *One-Dimensional Man* (1964) and other works combined Marxist ideas with psychological theory to produce a gloomy critique of the depersonalized and repressive nature of modern society.

The real origin of the New Left, however, was less in theory than in experience. Above all, it was in the civil-rights movement, in which many idealistic young Americans had become involved in the early 1960s. Exposed as a result to evidence of social injustice, enraged by the violence and racism they encountered at the hands of segregationists and others, some civil-rights activists were by the mid-1960s beginning to consider far more radical political commitments than they once had embraced. As early as 1962, a group of students gathered in Michigan to discuss the nation's political future. In the process, they formed an organization, Students for a Democratic Society (SDS), and issued a creed, the Port Huron Statement, which signaled much of what was to come. "Many of us began maturing in complacency," the statement (most of it the work of student activist Tom Hayden) declared. "As we grew, however, our comfort was penetrated by events too troubling to dismiss." In the following years, as the racial crisis grew more intense and as the war in Vietnam expanded, members of SDS became even more troubled, expanding the scope of their demands and the range of their activities until they had become the cutting edge of student radicalism.

For a time, that radicalism centered upon issues related to the modern university, with which most members of the New Left were associated. A 1964 dispute at the University of California at Berkeley over the rights of students to distribute political leaflets on campus was the first outburst of nearly a decade of campus turmoil. The tumultuous Berkeley Free Speech Movement soon moved beyond the immediate issue of pamphlet distribution and produced far more fundamental protests against the depersonalized nature of the modern "multiversity" and against the role of educational institutions in sustaining corrupt or immoral public policies. The antiwar movement greatly inflamed and expanded the challenge to the universities; and beginning in 1968, campus demonstrations, riots, and building seizures became almost commonplace. At Columbia University in New York, students seized the offices of the president and other members of the administration, occupying them for days until local police forcibly ejected them. At Harvard University a year later, the seizure of administrative offices resulted in an even more violent confrontation with police. Over the next several years, hardly any major university was immune to some level of disruption from radicals and activists among its own student body. Occasionally, there were more serious episodes. Small groups of particularly fervent radicals—most notably the "Weatherman," an offshoot of SDS—were responsible for instances of arson and bombing that destroyed some campus buildings and claimed several lives.

The New Left never succeeded in attracting the support of more than a few students to its most radical tactics and demands. It succeeded brilliantly, however, in elevating the antiwar movement to a major national crusade. Among other

BERKELEY, 1964.   Mario Savio, a graduate student in philosophy, addresses protesters during a rally of the Free Speech Movement at the University of California at Berkeley in 1964. Although the specific issue was an administration effort to ban political activities on campus, the real grievances ran much deeper—to the depersonalizing character of the modern "multiversity." The Berkeley protest, skillfully led by Savio, inaugurated nearly a decade of campus protests nationwide. (*UPI*)

things, student activists were instrumental in organizing some of the largest political demonstrations in American history to protest the war in Vietnam. The march on the Pentagon of October 1967, where demonstrators were met by a solid line of armed troops; the "Spring Mobilization" of April 1968, which attracted hundreds of thousands of demonstrators in cities around the country; the Vietnam "Moratorium" of the fall of 1969, during which millions of opponents of the war gathered in major rallies across the nation; and countless other demonstrations, large and small—all helped thrust the issue of the war into the center of America's politics.

Closely related to opposition to the war—and another issue that helped to fuel the New Left—was opposition to military conscription. The government had relied upon the draft to staff its peacetime army since the early 1950s, generally

THE MARCH ON THE PENTAGON, 1967.   By the fall of 1967, student protests against the war had grown so large and so frequent that they had become a significant political factor. Antiwar demonstrations were also becoming increasingly angry and confrontational. Protesters here face military police during the 1967 march on the Pentagon. (*UPI*)

without controversy. But when in the 1960s draftees began to be called upon to fight in a stalemated, unpopular war, dissent grew quickly. The gradual abolition of many traditional deferments—for students, teachers, husbands, fathers, and others—swelled the ranks of those faced with conscription (and thus likely to oppose it). And the high-handed and often illegal manner in which the draft was being administered by General Lewis Hershey spawned even greater bitterness. The shadow of the draft—the possibility of actually being compelled to join a despised military and fight in a hated war—loomed large over an entire generation of American youth. Draft card burnings became common features of antiwar rallies on college campuses. Many draft-age Americans simply refused induction, accepting what were occasionally long terms in jail as a result. Thousands of others fled to Canada, Sweden, and elsewhere (where they were joined by many deserters from the armed forces) to escape conscription, even though they realized it might be years before they could return home without facing prosecution. Not until 1977, when President Jimmy Carter issued a general pardon to draft resisters and a far more limited pardon to deserters did the Vietnam exiles begin to return to the country in substantial numbers. Many, however, chose to remain permanently abroad—a legacy of how deeply the war in Vietnam had embittered the nation's youth.

The Counterculture

Closely allied to the emergence of the New Left was the growth of a new youth culture openly scornful of the values and conventions of middle-class society. The most visible characteristic of the counterculture, as it became known, and the one that seemed to have the widest influence, was a change in life style. As if to display their contempt for conventional standards, young Americans flaunted long hair, shabby or flamboyant clothing, and a rebellious disdain for traditional speech and decorum. Central to the counterculture were drugs: marijuana smoking—which from 1966 began to become as common a youthful diversion as beer drinking had once been—and the use of other, more potent hallucinogens, such as LSD. Drug addiction was not a new phenomenon; it had long been a problem in poor urban areas. But during the 1960s, the increasing fascination with drugs drew a small but significant number of middle-class youths into dependence on heroin and other addictive substances. There was as well among members of the counterculture a new and more permissive view of sex. Not only did many young people abandon the traditional view that sexual relationships should be restricted to marriage (a view that had, in any case, always been honored largely in the breach); they began to argue that sex need not be related to any sustained emotional involvement. It could be experienced as an immediate physical pleasure for its own sake.

It was these open challenges to traditional life styles that parents and others found most disturbing about the counterculture; and there was a temptation among many in the older generation to dismiss such youths simply as iconoclasts and hedonists. That was no doubt true of many. But the counterculture also encompassed a clear philosophy, one that offered a far more fundamental challenge to the American mainstream than the changes in appearance and social behavior. It was, in effect, the culmination of nearly three generations of lament about the depersonalization of modern society and the alienation of the individual from the environment. More immediately, it was a direct descendant of the ideas of the 1950s' "beats"; and it was no accident that the works of Allen Ginsberg and Jack Kerouac became important forces within the counterculture in the 1960s. Like the New Left, with which it was often closely allied, the counterculture challenged the very structure of modern American society, attacking its banality, its hollowness, its artificiality, its isolation from nature.

The most committed adherents of the counterculture—the so-called hippies, who came to dominate the Haight-Ashbury neighborhood of San Francisco and whose influence spread to many other areas, and the "drop-outs," who retreated to rural communes in Colorado, New Hampshire, and elsewhere—rejected modern society altogether and attempted to find refuge in a simpler, more natural existence. But even those whose commitment to the counterculture was less dramatic shared a pervasive commitment to the idea of personal fulfillment. Such popular phrases as "Do your own thing" and "If it feels good, do it," which became banalized through repetition over time, nevertheless seemed to capture much of the spirit of the counterculture. In a corrupt and alienating society, the new creed seemed to suggest, the first responsibility of the individual is the cultivation of the self, the unleashing of one's own full potential for pleasure and fulfillment.

Thus although the counterculture often seemed simply an adjunct of the New Left, it embodied in fact a different impulse. While political radicalism envisioned a society based on collective, usually Marxist values, the counterculture emphasized individualism and even a rejection of the idea of social progress. Theodore Roszak, whose book *The Making of a Counter Culture* (1969) became a central document of the era, captured much of the spirit of the movement in his frank admission that "the primary project of our counter culture is to proclaim a new heaven and a new earth so vast, so marvelous that the inordinate claims of technical expertise must of necessity draw to a subordinate and marginal status in the lives of men." Charles Reich, in *The Greening of America* (1970), was even more explicit, arguing that the individual should strive for a new form of consciousness—"Consciousness III," as he called it—in which the self would be the only reality.

To Roszak, Reich, and other defenders of the counterculture, the new values promised to create a gentler, more humane society than the industrial, bureaucratic behemoth that America had become. Support for this optimistic view could be found, it seemed, in the new emphasis in the youth culture upon love, peace, and tolerance. In the summer of 1969, for example, 400,000 young music fans gathered near Woodstock, New York, for a festival of major rock groups. They displayed there a spirit of peaceful cooperation that enabled them to survive without serious incident several major rainstorms, a serious shortage of supplies, and a breakdown of transportation. Many believed the experience augured the birth of a new society—the "Woodstock nation." Others, however, were more dubious. Pointing to such episodes as the Rolling Stones concert at Altamont, California, in 1969, in which one spectator was murdered within a few feet of the stage, or the brutal slayings in southern California the same year by members of a "family" of drop-outs led by Charles Manson, critics of the counterculture saw in the youth movement more sadness than hope. Joan Didion, in *Slouching Towards Bethlehem* (1968), presented a particularly bleak picture of life among the hippies of Haight-Ashbury—a community she described as pervaded by crime, drug addiction, and worse, a sense of aimlessness and hopelessness.

Changes in the Mainstream

Although only a relatively few Americans, even only a relatively few young people, embraced fully either the New Left or the counterculture, virtually everyone felt the effects of both in important ways. The fashions, habits, and values of radical

WOODSTOCK. The "Woodstock nation" disperses. The rain-soaked rock festival in Woodstock, New York, in the summer of 1969, spawned a communal social experience that seemed to symbolize the new values of American youth in the late 1960s. Here, the enormous crowd begins to break camp and depart as the festival draws to a close. (*UPI*)

youth intruded upon the mainstream culture to an increasing degree; and some of the changes that resulted were both permanent and fundamental.

In the most obvious sense, the counterculture influenced the society at large by providing a set of social norms that an increasing number of young people chose to imitate. Long hair and freakish clothing became the badge not only of hippies and radicals but of an entire generation. The use of marijuana, the freer attitudes toward sex, the iconoclastic (and often obscene) language: all spread far beyond the realm of the true devotees of the counterculture. And perhaps the most pervasive element of the new youth society was one that even the least radical members of the generation embraced: rock music.

Rock-'n'-roll had first achieved wide popularity in the 1950s, on the strength of such early performers as Buddy Holly and, above all, Elvis Presley. Early in the 1960s, its influence began to spread, a result in large part of the phenomenal popularity of the Beatles, whose music was first heard in the United States in 1964. For a time, most rock musicians—like most popular musicians before them— concentrated largely on uncontroversial romantic themes. But rock's driving rhythms, its undisguised sensuality, its often harsh and angry tone—all made it an appropriate vehicle for expressing the themes of social and political unrest of the late 1960s. By the end of the decade, therefore, rock had transformed itself and had begun to reflect many of the new iconoclastic values of its time. Once again, the Beatles helped lead the way by abandoning their once-simple and seemingly innocent style for a new, experimental, even mystical approach that reflected the growing popular fascination with drugs and Eastern religions. Other groups such as the Rolling Stones turned even more openly to themes of anger, frustration, and rebelliousness. Many popular musicians used their music to express explicit political radicalism as well.

Even those Americans who had no interest in rock music or other aspects of the counterculture could not avoid evidence of how rapidly the norms of their society were changing. Those who attended movies saw a gradual disappearance of the banal, conventional messages that had dominated films since the 1920s. Instead, they saw explorations of political issues, of new sexual mores, of violence, of social conflict. Theatergoers accustomed to optimistic musical comedies and conventional middle-class dramas encountered far more provocative and even disturbing productions: *Hair* (1968), the celebrated rock musical that idealized the counterculture; *Cabaret* (1966), which depicted the decaying society of prewar Nazi Germany; *Company* (1970), a musical that expressed the hollowness of conventional middle-class life. And the most influential entertainment medium of all, television, began similarly to turn away from its evocation of the stable, middle-class, suburban family. Beginning in the early 1970s, it started to offer programming imbued with social conflict—as exemplified by the enormously popular *All in the Family*, whose hero, Archie Bunker, was a lower-middle-class bigot. There remained in popular culture, of course, much that was comforting, conventional, and banal. But the intrusion of new, more abrasive themes was becoming too pervasive to be ignored.

THE COUNTERCULTURE ON BROADWAY. The Broadway musical hit *Hair* was an open celebration of the counterculture. It stunned conventional theatergoers when it opened in New York in 1968, but it soon established itself as one of the most successful shows in Broadway history. It was one of a number of productions in the late 1960s that were bringing rock music and radical values into the mainstream of popular culture. (*Martha Swope*)

RACE, ETHNICITY, AND THE CULTURE OF LIBERATION

The 1960s not only helped inaugurate a search for personal fulfillment among a substantial segment of America's youth. The decade also saw the emergence of powerful "liberation" movements among a number of racial, ethnic, and other minority groups. The emergence of black self-awareness and black political power was, of course, the most obvious manifestation of the new spirit. But at times it seemed as though virtually every group of the American population was engaged in a search for liberation.

Native Americans

Few minorities had deeper or more justifiable grievances against the prevailing culture than American Indians—or Native Americans, as they began to call themselves in the 1960s. Ever since the 1890s, Indians had lived in unalleviated poverty as wards of the federal government, which subjected them to a series of fluctuating and often brutal policies. Early in the century, the government had attempted to force the assimilation of Indians into white society, assaulting the integrity of tribal cultures while failing to provide Native Americans with sufficient resources to make an effective transition into the modern economy. After 1934, federal officials allowed tribal councils a theoretical autonomy; but real power remained in the hands of whites, who maintained ultimate control of the federal subsidies necessary for most tribes to survive. In 1953, even these limited concessions were withdrawn, as the Eisenhower administration, distressed by the high cost of the tribal autonomy program, returned to the policy of forced assimilation.

By the 1960s, not only had the Indian population grown much faster than that of the rest of the nation (nearly doubling between 1950 and 1970 to a total of about 800,000), but Indians had established themselves as the least prosperous, least healthy, and least stable group in the society. Annual family income for Indians was $1,000 less than that for blacks. The Native American unemployment rate was ten times the national rate; joblessness was particularly high on the reservations, where nearly half the Indians lived and where few industries or other sources of employment existed. Life expectancy was more than twenty years lower than the national average. Suicides among Indian youths were a hundred times more frequent than among white youths. And while black Americans attracted the attention (for good or for ill) of many whites, Indians remained all but totally ignored.

Although the Kennedy administration attempted to restore government support for tribal autonomy—a policy maintained by succeeding administrations as well—Indian grievances were, like the grievances of other minorities, soon receiving open expression. In 1961, more than 400 members of 67 tribes gathered in Chicago to discuss ways of bringing all Indians together in an effort to redress common wrongs. The manifesto they issued, the Declaration of Indian Purpose, reflected the same impulse toward cultural liberation that other segments of the population would soon adopt. It stressed the "right to choose our own way of life" and the "responsibility of preserving our precious heritage." In succeeding years, younger and more militant Native Americans formed their own organizations—modeled on the new black-power groups—of which the most prominent was the American Indian Movement (AIM), established in 1968 and drawing its greatest support from those Indians who lived in urban areas. The new activism succeeded in winning some attention from the government to the plight of the tribes. Congress included Indians in the benefits of the Economic Opportunity Act; and Lyndon Johnson promised in 1968 a "new goal" for Indian programs that "stresses

PROTEST AT WOUNDED KNEE. White Americans were shocked in 1973 by pictures such as this one of the Indian occupation of the town of Wounded Knee, South Dakota. This member of the Sioux tribe stands guard in a newly constructed bunker, a row of loaded rifles close at hand and an American flag contemptuously displayed upside down. The new militancy attracted the first serious national attention to the cause of the Indians in many decades, although it did not immediately win them many clear benefits. (*UPI*)

self-determination" and "erases old attitudes of paternalism." The results, however, were negligible.

Leaders of AIM and other insurgent groups soon turned instead to direct action. In 1968, Indian fishermen, seeking to exercise old treaty rights on the Columbia River and in Puget Sound, clashed with officials of the state of Washington. The following year, members of several tribes occupied the abandoned federal prison on Alcatraz Island in San Francisco Bay, claiming the site "by right of discovery." In response to the growing pressure, the new Nixon administration appointed a Mohawk-Sioux to the position of Commissioner of Indian Affairs in 1969; and in 1970, the President promised both increased tribal self-determination and an increase in federal aid. The promises were not fulfilled.

Native American frustration finally produced the most forceful protests in decades in the winter of 1972–1973. In November 1972, nearly one thousand protesters forcibly occupied the building of the Bureau of Indian Affairs in Washington. When they departed six days later, they left behind damage estimated as high as $2 million and a major destruction of files and records. But the most celebrated protest occurred later that winter at Wounded Knee, South Dakota, the site of the 1890 massacre of Sioux Indians by federal troops. In the early 1970s, Wounded Knee was part of a vast Sioux reservation, two-thirds of which was in the control of white ranchers. Conditions for the Indian residents were desperate. Unemployment, illiteracy, alcoholism, and disease were rampant. Poverty was almost universal. Such conditions alone might have been sufficient to spark resistance. Passions among younger and more militant tribal members were aroused further after the 1972 murder of a Sioux by a group of whites, who were not, many Indians believed, adequately punished. In February 1973, members of AIM seized and occupied for two months the town of Wounded Knee, demanding radical changes in the administration of the reservation and insisting that the government honor its long-forgotten treaty obligations. A brief clash between the occupiers and federal forces left one Indian dead and another wounded. Shortly thereafter the siege came to an end.

Far more effective than these militant protests were the increasing victories that various tribes were achieving in the 1970s in a wave of lawsuits in the federal courts. Citing violations by the federal government of ancient treaty obligations, Native Americans began winning judicial approval of their demands for restitution. Beginning with a case in Alaska in 1969, the legal actions spread quickly across the country, establishing the basis for a major change in the economic status of many tribes. Whether these judicial victories would be enough to overcome the effects of decades of poverty, however, remained unclear.

Hispanic Americans

Far more numerous and far more visible than the Indian minority were Hispanic Americans, the fastest-growing minority group in the nation. In 1960, Hispanics had numbered only slightly over 3 million; in 1970, they had increased to more than 9 million; by 1980, most estimates placed their numbers at nearly 20 million, making them the second largest minority (after blacks) in the country. They were also among the poorest.

Hispanics were not, of course, a single, undifferentiated group. There were large numbers of people of Puerto Rican background, concentrated in New York City. A substantial Cuban population was settled in Florida, largely the result of a wave of middle-class refugees who had fled the Castro regime in the early 1960s. (A second flood, of poorer immigrants, arrived in 1980, when Castro temporarily lifted exit restrictions.) The most numerous group—Mexican-Americans—lived in California, Texas, and other states of the Southwest. An uncounted number of them, as many as 7 million according to some estimates, were illegal immigrants (*mojados,* or "wetbacks"). Others were temporary migrant workers *(braceros).*

Many, however, were descendants of families who had been living in Mexican territory when it was incorporated into the United States in the nineteenth century.

Like blacks and Indians, Hispanic Americans responded to the highly charged climate of the 1960s by developing their own sense of ethnic identification and by organizing for political and economic power. Their successes were impressive. Affluent Hispanics became an important force in Miami, where they operated major businesses and filled influential positions in the professions; in Los Angeles, where they organized as an influential political group; and in the Southwest, where they elected Mexican-Americans to seats in Congress and to several governorships. Middle-class Hispanics had never encountered the same rigid forms of discrimination that had afflicted blacks; for example, they had not been forced to attend segregated schools. When opportunities became available, therefore, some Hispanics were able to profit from them more easily than were the members of other minorities.

For the majority of Hispanics, however, the path to economic and political power was more arduous. In New York, Puerto Rican immigrants were crammed into the city's worst slums, including the notorious South Bronx, which became in the 1970s a national symbol of urban decay. In other cities, Hispanics suffered economic deprivation and overt discrimination; in many areas, they became involved in bitter and violent rivalries with blacks. For these poor urban Hispanics, progress seemed as elusive in 1980 as it had ten years earlier.

One Hispanic group, at least, brought the power of organization and political action strongly to bear against problems of poverty and oppression. In California, an Arizona-born Mexican-American farm worker, César Chávez, succeeded where generations of migrants before him had tried and failed: he created an effective union of itinerant farm workers. His United Farm Workers (UFW), a largely Hispanic organization, launched a prolonged and often bitter strike in 1965 against growers to demand, first, recognition of their union and, second, increased wages and benefits. When employers resisted, Chávez enlisted the cooperation of college students, churches, and civil-rights groups (including CORE and SNCC) and organized a nationwide boycott first of table grapes and then of lettuce. In 1968, Chávez campaigned openly for Robert Kennedy, bringing his farm workers into the coalition of the dispossessed that the Senator was attempting to establish and, more important, winning national recognition of the UFW's cause. Two years later, Chávez won a substantial victory when the growers of half of California's table grapes signed contracts with his union. In the ensuing years, his union suffered less from the opposition of growers than from competition with the powerful Teamsters Union, which attempted to entice farm workers into its own vast labor network. Legislation approved by the California legislature and signed by Governor Jerry Brown in 1977 gave the UFW some new legal protection, but its future remained uncertain.

Hispanic Americans also became the focus of another dispute that was to prove increasingly divisive in the 1970s: the issue of bilingualism. It was a question that aroused the opposition not only of many whites but of some Hispanics as well.

CÉSAR CHÁVEZ. Chávez, organizer of the United Farm Workers union in California, rose to become the first widely known leader of Mexican-Americans in the late 1960s. His association with Robert Kennedy during the 1968 campaign made him a liberal hero; and his calls for national boycotts of the products of nonunion growers attracted national support. In 1972, Senator Edward M. Kennedy began a speech to the Democratic National Convention by addressing the delegates as "fellow lettuce boycotters." (*Paul Fusco from Magnum*)

Supporters of bilingualism in education argued that Spanish-speaking Americans were entitled to schooling in their own language, that only thus could they achieve an equal footing with English-speaking students. Opponents cited not only the cost and difficulty of bilingualism but the dangers it posed to the ability of Spanish-speaking students to become assimilated into the mainstream of American culture. Even many Hispanics feared that bilingualism would isolate their communities further from the rest of America and increase resentments toward the minority. The issue was, in part, a dispute over the direction in which Spanish-speaking Americans should move in contemporary society: toward assimilation or toward a strengthening of their own ethnic ties. By the early 1980s, however, it had also become part of the larger dispute over the ability and willingness of the United States to sustain major social programs.

THE WOMEN'S MOVEMENT

American women in the 1960s were hardly a minority. They constituted 51 percent of the population. In the course of the decade, however, a growing number of women began to identify with members of other oppressed groups and to demand a liberation of their own. Sexual discrimination was so deeply imbedded in the fabric of society that when women first began to denounce it, many Americans responded with bafflement and anger. By the 1970s, however, public awareness of the issue had increased dramatically; and the role of women in American life had changed more radically than that of any other group in the nation.

The Rise of the New Feminism

Betty Friedan's book *The Feminine Mystique* (1963), denouncing the "comfortable concentration camp" of the suburban home, was the first salvo in what would soon become a major assault on traditional views of women. Three years later, Friedan joined with other feminists to create the National Organization for Women (NOW), which was to become the nation's largest and most influential feminist organization. "The time has come," the founders of NOW maintained, "to confront with concrete action the conditions which now prevent women from enjoying the equality of opportunity and freedom of choice which is their right as individual Americans and as human beings." Like other movements for liberation, feminism drew much of its inspiration from the black struggle for freedom. "There is no civil rights movement to speak for women," the NOW organizers claimed, "as there has been for Negroes and other victims of discrimination."

The complaints of the feminists were many. They were, they argued, barred from educational institutions, from professions, from politics, and from countless other areas of American life because of ancient male prejudices about the proper role of women. They faced innumerable forms of legal and economic discrimination, including the widespread practice of paying women less than men even when they were doing equal work. Underlying all these problems were male assumptions that women were somehow intellectually and emotionally unfit for male occupations, that their biologically determined role was to serve as wives and mothers. The portrayal of women as mindless "sex objects," feminists charged, was visible in almost every area of American culture—from television commercials that exploited female sexuality to the uninhibited leering and sexual harassment to which women were constantly subjected in the workplace, in schools, and on the streets. "I have been denied a society in which women are encouraged, or even allowed to think of themselves as first-class citizens and responsible human beings," feminist Gloria Steinem charged in 1970. "Women suffer this second-class treatment from the moment they are born. They are expected to be, rather than achieve, to function biologically rather than learn."

The Search for Redress

By the late 1960s, such sentiments had attracted a large following among middle-class women, and the feminist movement had gained substantial strength. Already, women had won important new legal protections and substantial economic and political advances. In 1964, for example, Congress incorporated into the Civil Rights Act an amendment—Title VII—that extended to women the protection of the law in the struggle against discrimination. It had been introduced as a joke by southern Democrats attempting to discredit the entire civil-rights package; but it survived the legislative debate and became the basis for a major federal assault upon sexual discrimination in later years. In 1971, the government extended its Affirmative Action guidelines to include women—linking sexism with racism as an officially acknowledged social problem.

Women were making rapid progress, in the meantime, in their efforts to move into the economic and political mainstream. The nation's major educational institutions began in the late 1960s to open their doors to women for the first time. Princeton and Yale, two of the most prestigious all-male colleges, accepted women undergraduates in 1969. Within a few years, all but a few major academic institutions had done the same. Many women's colleges, in the meantime, began accepting male students. Women were becoming an important force in business and in the professions. The number of women entering law school tripled in the five-year period beginning in 1969. The percentage of Ph.D. recipients who were women doubled in the same period. Nearly half of all married women held jobs by the mid-1970s, and almost nine-tenths of all women with college degrees worked. Two-career families, in which both the husband and the wife maintained active professional lives, were becoming a widely accepted norm. So were such symbolic changes as the refusal of many women to adopt their husbands' names when they married, and the use of the term "Ms." in place of "Mrs." or "Miss" —the latter change intended to denote the irrelevance of a woman's marital status in the professional world.

Women were also advancing in some of the most visible areas of American life. In politics, they were by the early 1970s beginning to compete effectively with men for both elected and appointive positions. In 1981, two women served in the United States Senate—both elected in their own right rather than, like all women Senators before them, to succeed their husbands. A substantial number of women served in the United States House of Representatives throughout the 1970s, and two won election to state governorships. The number of female appointments in the executive branch rose steadily; two women held cabinet positions in the Carter administration.

In professional athletics, in the meantime, women were beginning to compete with men both for attention and for an equal share of prize money. Billie Jean King spearheaded the most effective female challenge to male domination of sports. Under her leadership, professional women tennis players established their own, successful tours and demanded equal financial incentives when they played in the same tournaments as men. King helped legitimize women's sports further in 1973 when she accepted a challenge from retired men's champion Bobby Riggs for a public match, which Riggs claimed would prove that women could not compete athletically with men. King won decisively. By the late 1970s, the federal government was pressuring colleges and universities to provide women with athletic programs equal to those available to men.

There were changes as well in psychological theories about women. Until the 1960s, the reigning Freudian orthodoxy had been that biological differences determined the psychological differences between men and women. Men, the dictum implied, were by nature dominant and aggressive; women were naturally passive and submissive. The publication in 1966 of *Human Sexual Response* by William Masters and Virginia Johnson was the first of many scientific challenges to such assumptions. Masters and Johnson implied that women were not by nature submissive creatures, that they participated actively and equally in sexual relationships. By implication, therefore, they could participate actively and equally in society.

Continuing Controversies

By the beginning of the 1980s, the new women's movement was only fifteen years old. Already, however, it had effected more change than over a hundred years of feminist agitation had done before it. It had also raised issues and demands that continued to provoke debate; and it had shed light on problems that remained unresolved.

Of all the feminist crusades of the 1960s and 1970s, none united more women from more different backgrounds than the campaign for passage of the Equal Rights Amendment (ERA) to the Constitution. Congress approved the amendment in 1972 and sent it to the states; and for a while it seemed that eventual ratification was only a matter of time. By the end of the 1970s, however, the momentum behind the amendment seemed to have died. Approval of the ERA remained several states short of the three-quarters necessary for enactment; and some state legislatures that had earlier voted in favor were trying to rescind their approval. In 1979 Congress granted a three-year extension of the time permitted for ratification. Far more indicative of public sentiment on the issue, however, was the rising chorus of objections to the amendment from those who feared that it would create a major disruption of traditional social patterns. In 1980, the Republican party—after forty years of support for the idea of the ERA—wrote into its platform a new plank opposing the amendment. The Equal Rights Amendment had been the central demand of American feminism since it was first proposed in 1923. In 1981, it appeared to be a hope still far from realization.

Another vital element of the women's movement since the 1920s had been the effort to win for women greater control of their own physical and sexual lives. In its least controversial form, this impulse helped produce an increasing awareness in the 1960s and 1970s of the problems of rape, sexual abuse, and wife beating. Far more divisive, however, was the desire of many women to control their reproductive functions in new ways. There continued to be some controversy over the dissemination of contraceptives and birth-control information; but that issue, at least, seemed to have lost much of the explosive character it had possessed in the 1920s, when Margaret Sanger had become a figure of public scorn for her efforts on its behalf. A related issue, however, stimulated as much popular passion as any question of its time: abortion. Until the 1960s, abortion had been illegal in all but a few states, although it was often performed quietly (and at times dangerously) out of the sight of the law. But the growing strength of the women's movement increased pressure on behalf of the legalization of abortion. Several states had abandoned restrictions on abortion by the end of the 1960s. And in 1973, the Supreme Court invalidated all laws prohibiting abortion during the "first trimester," the first three months of pregnancy. The issue, it seemed, had been settled.

In the following years, however, opposition to abortion revived, growing by the early 1980s into one of the nation's most powerful political forces. The right-to-life movement, as it called itself, managed first to persuade Congress to ban all federal funding for abortions through Medicaid; many state legislatures imposed similar bans. At the same time, pressure was growing for a "human life" amendment to the Constitution, prohibiting abortion even for those women who could afford to pay for it. The moral and religious fervor that the abortion issue had aroused, among American Catholics and fundamentalist Protestants in particular, seemed certain to keep it a focus of controversy for many years.

Yet the greatest dilemma of the women's movement remained one that received only limited discussion. Feminism had by the 1980s become a powerful force on behalf of those educated, affluent women who had chosen to move into careers. It had, however, done far less for poorer, less privileged women, who continued to play only a small role in the larger movement. Women whose economic circumstances were difficult—blacks, Hispanics, working-class women, and others—could evince little enthusiasm for such lofty goals as the Equal Rights Amendment. Many of the feminist programs that proved so valuable to middle-class women reached the lower classes hardly at all. Yet it was lower-class women who suffered most harshly from the failure to control reproduction, from rape, from sexual and physical abuse, and from ancient stereotypes of female roles. Many feminist leaders were aware of and disturbed by the inability of their movement to bridge effectively the barriers of class. Few, however, were certain of how to deal with the problem successfully.

The women's movement was at once the most potent symbol and the most glaring exception to the general impulse toward political and cultural "liberation" of the late 1960s. Feminism expressed both a desire to win social justice through collective political action—a desire that characterized the New Left—and a concern for individual fulfillment and personal freedom—a concern that typified much of the counterculture. But it differed from both in one fundamental respect: its success. The women's movement may not have fulfilled all its goals by the early 1980s. But it had achieved fundamental and permanent changes in the position of women in American life; and it had itself become a lasting political and social force. Most of the other liberation movements of the 1960s, however, suffered a

DEFENDING ABORTION.   Of all the painful controversies aroused by the women's movement, none proved more socially divisive than that over abortion. Feminists insisted that women were entitled to full control over their own bodies and that only easy access to abortion ensured that control. Opponents claimed that abortion was nothing less than the murder of unborn children. By the early 1980s, the "right-to-life" movement had become a powerful political force. Pro-abortion efforts, exemplified by this march in New York City, became less frequent after the 1973 Supreme Court decision legalizing abortion. (*Charles Gatewood*)

far different fate. Either because of decay from within or, more often, because of increasing opposition from without, the crusades for social justice, cultural liberation, and economic reform seemed to fade almost as rapidly as they had emerged.

SUGGESTED READINGS

For an overview of social and cultural aspects of the 1960s, see William O'Neill, *Coming Apart* (1971); Godfrey Hodgson, *America in Our Time* (1976); and Morris Dickstein, *Gates of Eden* (1977). Todd Gitlin, *The Whole World Is Watching* (1981); Irwin Unger, *The Movement* (1974); Lawrence Lader, *Power on the Left* (1979);

Kirkpatrick Sale, *SDS* (1973); and Peter Clecak, *Radical Paradoxes* (1973), examine the New Left. Kenneth Keniston, *Young Radicals* (1968), and Lewis Feuer, *The Conflict of Generations* (1969), are also useful. Sources for examining the counterculture include Paul Goodman, *Growing Up Absurd* (1960), one of the early statements of its philosophy; Theodore Roszak, *The Making of a Counter Culture* (1969), a ringing defense; Charles Reich, *The Greening of America* (1970), an influential contemporary work; and Ronald Berman, *America in the Sixties* (1968), a hostile view. Joan Didion, *Slouching Towards Bethlehem* (1967) and *The White Album* (1979), offer provocative reflections on the mood of the counterculture. Other important works on the political and cultural climate of the era include John Diggins, *The American Left in the Twentieth Century* (1973), and Richard Flacks, *Youth and Social Change* (1971).

On the issue of American Indians, see Wilcomb Washburn, *Red Man's Land/White Man's Land* (1971); Vine Deloria, Jr., *Behind the Trail of Broken Treaties* (1974) and *Custer Died for Your Sins* (1969); D'Arcy McNickle, *Native American Tribalism* (1973); and Stan Steiner, *The New Indians* (1968). A survey of the history of Hispanic Americans is Rodolfo Acuña, *Occupied America,* 2nd ed. (1981). See also Julian Samora, *Los Mojados* (1971); Oscar Lewis, *La Vida* (1969); and Matt Meier and Feliciano Rivera, *The Chicanos* (1972).

Literature on the contemporary women's movement includes William Chafe, *The American Woman* (1972), which traces feminism back to the 1920s; Sheila Rothman, *Woman's Proper Place* (1978), which examines women's roles since the turn of the century; Jo Freeman, *The Politics of Women's Liberation* (1975); and Gayle Yates, *What Women Want* (1975). The book that helped launch the movement is Betty Friedan, *The Feminine Mystique* (1963).

Twenty-Five

The Search for Stability

The election of Richard Nixon in 1968 was the result of more than the unpopularity of Lyndon Johnson's policies and the deep divisions within the Democratic party. It was the result, too, of a changing national mood. A growing number of Americans—a clear majority, it seemed, on the basis of the election returns—were tired of the social turmoil of the 1960s and resentful of the attention directed toward minorities and the poor. The sober, middle-class values of thrift, hard work, and self-reliance were, they believed, under assault. Federal social programs were funneling billions of dollars into the inner cities to help the poor and unemployed, increasing the tax burden on the middle class. Government regulations and court rulings were launching open attacks upon traditional community values and institutions. Hippies and radicals were dominating public discourse with their bitter critiques of everything middle-class Americans held dear. It was time, such men and women believed, for a restoration of stability.

In Richard Nixon they found a man who seemed perfectly to match their mood. Himself a product of a hard-working middle-class family, he had risen to prominence on the basis of his own, unrelenting efforts. His public demeanor displayed nothing of the flashiness of the Kennedys or the stridency of the Democratic left. He projected, instead, an image of stern dedication to traditional values. He avoided the dogmatic attacks on well-established reforms that had helped destroy the Goldwater campaign four years earlier, but he made it clear that he favored new limits on the scope of federal power. He was careful not to endorse an indefinite prolongation of the war in Vietnam, but he indicated too that he would not countenance a humiliating surrender. The extraordinary narrowness of his margin of victory indicated that many Americans continued to consider him sanctimonious, "tricky," and generally unappealing. To much of the nation, however, he was the embodiment of the search for a new, more placid social order.

NIXON, KISSINGER, AND THE WAR

Central to that search, Nixon believed, was resolution of the stalemate in Vietnam. Yet the new President felt no freer than his predecessor to abandon the American commitment in Indochina. On the one hand, he realized that the endless war was undermining both the nation's domestic stability and its position in the world. On the other hand, he feared that a precipitous retreat would destroy American honor and "credibility."

During the 1968 campaign, Nixon had claimed to have formulated a plan to bring "peace with honor" to Vietnam. He had refused to disclose its details. Once

THE NEW NIXON.   Richard Nixon strikes a familiar—and in later years much ridiculed—pose as he campaigns in Santa Barbara, California, during his successful 1968 campaign for the presidency. He provided a symbol of stability and moderation in a year of crisis; and in the course of his campaign, he carefully avoided controversy, preferring instead to benefit passively from the disarray within the Democratic party. (*UPI*)

in office, however, he soon made clear that the plan consisted of little more than a vague set of general principles, not of any concrete measures to extricate the United States from the quagmire. American involvement in Indochina continued for four more years, during which the war expanded both in its geographic scope and in its bloodiness. And when a settlement finally emerged early in 1973, it produced neither peace nor honor. It succeeded only in removing the United States from the wreckage.

The New Policymakers

Nixon had long been far more interested in foreign than domestic affairs. He considered himself an expert on international relations, having read and traveled widely during his years as a private citizen. And like other Presidents, he enjoyed the freedom from legislative and political obstacles that the conduct of foreign policy, unlike domestic policy, provided. Yet despite Nixon's own passionate interest in diplomacy, he brought with him into government a public figure who ultimately seemed to overshadow the President himself in the conduct of international affairs: Henry Kissinger.

Kissinger was a respected and prolific professor of international politics at Harvard when Nixon tapped him to serve as his special assistant for national security affairs. Both Secretary of State William Rogers, who had served as Eisenhower's Attorney General, and Secretary of Defense Melvin Laird, who had been an influential member of Congress, were far more experienced in public life. But Kissinger quickly outshone them both. Nixon's passion for concentrating decision making in the White House was in large measure responsible; but Kissinger's own remarkable adeptness both in fighting for bureaucratic influence and in currying favor with the press was at least equally important. Together, Nixon and Kissinger set out to find an acceptable solution to the stalemate in Vietnam.

Vietnamization

The new Vietnam policy moved along several fronts. Nixon repeatedly insisted that he would not consider a policy of surrender, that only by achieving a "peace to be proud of" could America maintain its international credibility. At the same time, he sought to limit domestic opposition to the war. In the course of 1969, therefore, he initiated several new policies designed to weaken the antiwar movement without ending the fighting. Aware that the military draft was one of the most visible targets of dissent, the administration devised a new "lottery" system, through which only a limited group of nineteen-year-olds—those with low lottery numbers—would be eligible for the draft. The new system would continue to supply the military with its manpower needs while removing millions of potential critics from the danger of conscription. Later, the President urged the creation of an all-volunteer army that would permit the abolition of the draft altogether. By 1973, the Selective Service System was on its way to at least temporary extinction.

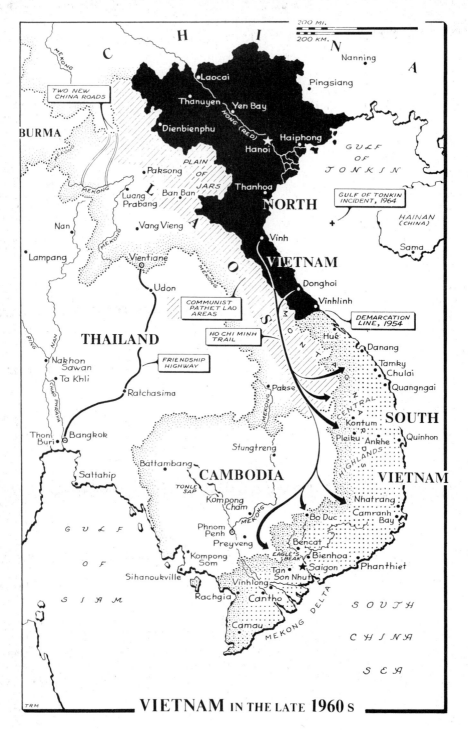

VIETNAM IN THE LATE **1960**S

Far more important in stifling dissent, however, was the new policy of "Vietnamization" of the war—that is, the training and equipping of the South Vietnamese military to assume the burden of combat in place of American forces. In the fall of 1969, Nixon announced the withdrawal of 60,000 American ground troops from Vietnam, the first reduction in United States troop strength since the beginning of the war. The withdrawals continued steadily for more than three years, so that by the fall of 1972 relatively few American soldiers remained in Indochina. From a peak of more than 540,000 in 1969, the number had dwindled to about 60,000.

Yet the Vietnamization process was not only painfully slow, it also did little to reduce the level of fighting in Vietnam. One reason was the persistent inability of American and Vietnamese negotiators to make any discernible progress at the interminable peace talks that had begun in Paris in 1968. The United States continued to insist upon the withdrawal of all communist forces from South Vietnam and the preservation of the Thieu regime as prerequisites to any settlement. The North Vietnamese and the Viet Cong refused to abandon their commitment to reunification of their nation. There was, it seemed, no common ground.

Escalation

To Nixon and Kissinger, therefore, the most effective strategy for settling the conflict seemed to be the strengthening of the South Vietnamese military position through an expansion of the war. That required, they believed, new military efforts to destroy the "staging areas" in Cambodia from which the North Vietnamese had been launching many of their attacks. Very early in his presidency, Nixon ordered the air force to begin a series of secret bombings of Cambodian territory to destroy the enemy sanctuaries. He withheld information about the raids from Congress and the public. In the spring of 1970, with what some have claimed was American encouragement and support, conservative military leaders overthrew the neutral government of Prince Norodom Sihanouk, Cambodia's leader for two decades, and established a new, pro-American regime under General Lon Nol. Lon Nol quickly gave his approval to American incursions into his territory; and on April 30, Nixon went on television to announce that he was ordering United States troops across the border into Cambodia to "clean out" the bases that the enemy had been using for its "increased military aggression."

So successful had Nixon been in seeming to deescalate the war that the once-powerful peace movement had by mid-1970 begun to lose much of its strength. The Cambodian invasion, however, restored it to life, giving it a more determined spirit than ever before. The first days of May saw the most widespread and vocal antiwar demonstrations ever. Hundreds of thousands of protesters gathered in Washington to denounce the President's policies. Millions, perhaps, participated in countless smaller demonstrations on campuses nationwide. Antiwar frenzy was reaching so high a level that to many activists it became possible briefly to believe that a genuine revolution was imminent.

VICTIMS OF NAPALM.   Terrified South Vietnamese children flee
from the village of Trang Ban, southwest of Saigon, after South
Vietnamese government planes had mistakenly dropped napalm bombs
there on June 8, 1972. Despite the Vietnamization program, the war
continued unabated during the first four years of the Nixon
administration. (*UPI*)

The mood of crisis intensified on May 4, when the nation heard the appalling
news that four students had been killed and nine others injured when members
of the National Guard had opened fire on an antiwar rally at Kent State University
in Ohio. A decade of investigations failed to provide any clear explanation for the
tragedy, although it seems clear that Governor James Rhodes and the command-

ers of the Guard had needlessly (and some charged deliberately) inflamed the situation on campus with their heavy-handed tactics. At the time, the incident seemed to many young Americans to confirm their worst suspicions of their government and their society. Ten days later, police killed two black students at Jackson State University in Mississippi during a demonstration there.

The intensity of the public outcry against the use of troops in Cambodia clearly startled the President, and he quickly announced that the American forces would be through with their work there within weeks and would not return. But the clamor against the war continued. Congress angrily repealed the Gulf of Tonkin Resolution in December, stripping the President of what had long served as the legal basis for the war. Nixon ignored the action, claiming that he had the authority to continue military efforts in Vietnam to "protect" American troops already there.

Then, in June 1971, first the *New York Times* and later other newspapers began publishing excerpts from a secret study of the war prepared by the Defense Department during the Johnson administration. The so-called Pentagon Papers,

FOUR DEAD IN OHIO, 1970. Kent State University students react with shock and anguish to the killing of four demonstrators by the Ohio National Guard on May 4, 1970. The burning of a decrepit National Guard armory on campus had provided the Governor with a pretext for sending in the guard, even though officials of the university itself had urged him to close down the campus instead. Two days of escalating tensions between angry students and exhausted guardsmen finally culminated in the shootings. (*UPI*)

leaked to the press by former Defense official Daniel Ellsberg, provided shocking confirmation of what many had long believed: that the government had been consistently dishonest, both in reporting the military progress of the war and in explaining its own motives for American involvement. Publicly, American Presidents had been arguing for years that the United States was fighting to permit South Vietnam "to enjoy a better, freer way of life." Privately, according to the Pentagon Papers, such concerns constituted only about "ten percent" of the real motive. "Seventy percent" was the desire "to avoid a humiliating defeat to our reputation as a guarantor." The administration went to court to suppress the documents, but to no avail. The Supreme Court ruled that the press had the right to publish them.

Particularly troubling, both to the public and to the government itself, were signs of decay within the American military. Morale and discipline among United States troops in Vietnam, who had been fighting a savage and inconclusive war for more than five years, was rapidly deteriorating. The trial and conviction in 1971 of Lieutenant William Calley, who was charged with overseeing a massacre of more than a hundred unarmed South Vietnamese civilians, attracted wide public attention to the dehumanizing impact of the war upon those who fought it. Less publicized were other, more widespread problems among American troops in Vietnam: desertion, drug addiction, refusal to obey orders, even the occasional killing of unpopular officers by enlisted men. Among the disenchanted—deserters, draft resisters, and others—were not simply the radical college students so unpopular with most Americans but many otherwise conventional sons of middle- and lower-class families.

The continuing carnage, the increasing savagery, and the social distress at home were drawing an ever-larger proportion of the population into opposition to the war. By 1971, nearly two-thirds of those interviewed in public-opinion polls were urging American withdrawal from Vietnam. From Richard Nixon, however, there came no sign of retreat. On the contrary, the events of the spring of 1970 left him more convinced than ever of the importance of resisting what he called the "bums" who opposed his military policies. With the approval of the White House, both the FBI and the CIA intensified their surveillance and infiltration of antiwar and radical groups, often resorting to blatant illegalities in the process. Administration officials sought to discredit prominent critics of the war by leaking damaging personal information about them. At one point, government agents broke into the office of a psychiatrist in an unsuccessful effort to steal files on Daniel Ellsberg. During the congressional campaign of 1970, Vice President Spiro Agnew, using the acid rhetoric that had already made him the hero of many conservatives, stepped up his attack upon the "effete" and "impudent" critics of the administration. The President himself once climbed on top of an automobile to taunt a crowd of angry demonstrators.

In Indochina, meanwhile, the fighting raged on. In February 1971, Nixon ordered the air force to assist the South Vietnamese army in an invasion of Laos —a test, as he saw it, of his Vietnamization program. Within weeks, the badly mauled South Vietnamese scrambled back across the border in defeat. American bombing in Vietnam and Cambodia continued to increase, despite its demonstrated ineffectiveness, so that by the end of 1971 the Nixon administration had dropped more explosives on the region than the Johnson administration had done in five years. When in March 1972 the North Vietnamese mounted their biggest offensive since 1968, Nixon responded by escalating the bombing once again, ordering attacks on targets near Hanoi, the capital of North Vietnam, and Haiphong. He called as well for the mining of seven North Vietnamese harbors (including Haiphong) to stop the flow of supplies from China and the Soviet Union.

"Peace with Honor"

The approach of the 1972 presidential election, in which the war promised to be the leading issue, finally did what years of military frustration and escalating public protests had failed to do; it convinced the administration that it must alter its terms for the withdrawal of American forces. In April 1972, the President dropped his longtime insistence on a removal of North Vietnamese troops from the south before any American withdrawal. In July, word leaked out that Henry Kissinger had been meeting privately in Paris with the North Vietnamese Foreign Secretary, Le Duc Tho, and rumors abounded that a cease-fire was near. On October 26, only days before the presidential election, Kissinger announced that "Peace is at hand."

Several weeks later, however, negotiations broke down once again. Although both the American and North Vietnamese governments were ready to accept the Kissinger–Tho plan for a cease-fire, the Thieu regime balked, still insisting that the full withdrawal of North Vietnamese forces from the south be a prerequisite to any agreement. Kissinger tried to win additional concessions from the communists to meet Thieu's objections, but on December 16—despite the American insistence that the agreement was "99 percent complete"—talks broke off.

The next day, December 17, without any prior announcement from the White House, American planes began to bomb North Vietnamese cities in the heaviest and most destructive raids of the entire war. In the past, the United States had made at least token efforts to spare civilian targets from aerial attacks. But the saturation bombing of Hanoi, Haiphong, and other cities allowed of no such distinctions. The Pentagon announced that it was attempting to destroy docks, airfields, railyards, power plants, and the like; but such targets were, of course, located in the middle of heavily populated areas. For twelve days, American B-52s rained terror on the North Vietnamese people. (Fifteen of the giant bombers were shot down, fourteen more than had been lost in the entire course of the war to that point.) Then, on December 30, Nixon terminated the "Christmas bombing" as quickly as he had begun it. The United States and the North Vietnamese returned to the conference table. And on January 27, 1973, representatives of the four interested parties (the governments of the United States, North Vietnam, and South Vietnam, together with the "Provisional Republican Government" of the South—the Viet Cong) signed an "agreement on ending the war and restoring peace in Vietnam." Nixon and Kissinger were fond of claiming that the Christmas bombing had forced the North Vietnamese to relent. In fact, a far more important factor was the increasing American pressure on Thieu to accept the cease-fire and Nixon's promise to him that the United States would respond "with full force" to any violation of the agreement.

The terms of the Paris Accords were little different from those that Kissinger and Tho had accepted in principle the previous fall. The two most prominent components were the establishment of an immediate cease-fire and the return by the North Vietnamese of several hundred American prisoners of war, whose fate had become an emotional issue of great importance within the United States. After that, the agreement descended quickly into murky and plainly unworkable political arrangements. The Thieu regime would survive for the moment—perhaps the only major concession Kissinger was able to wrest from Tho. But there would be no withdrawal of North Vietnamese forces from the south and no abandonment of the communist commitment to a reunified Vietnam. What Nixon boastfully described as a "peace with honor" was really little more than a formula for allowing the United States to extricate itself from the quagmire before the South Vietnamese regime collapsed, a recipe for providing what some officials caustically described as a "decent interval." No knowledgeable military observer believed that the South Vietnamese military could hold off the communists without continuing American support.

The American forces were hardly out of Indochina and the prisoners of war barely reunited with their families before the Paris Accords collapsed. During the first year after the cease-fire, the contending Vietnamese armies suffered greater battle losses than the Americans had endured during ten years of fighting. In Laos, fighting came to an end only after communist forces had established control of more than half the country. In Cambodia, the war raged on, and American planes continued to bomb communist installations in that country until Congress compelled the President to desist in August 1973. In March 1975, finally, the North Vietnamese launched a full-scale offensive against the now hopelessly weakened forces of the south. Thieu appealed to Washington for assistance; Nixon appealed to Congress for additional funding; and Congress, unwilling to pour additional money into what seemed almost certainly a hopeless cause, refused. Late in April 1975, communist forces marched into Saigon, shortly after officials of the Thieu regime and the American embassy had fled the country in humiliating disarray. At about the same time, the Lon Nol regime in Cambodia fell to the Khmer Rouge, the Cambodian equivalent of the Viet Cong.

Still, the war in Indochina did not end. Although Vietnam was soon reunited and freed at last from more than thirty years of civil war, conflict continued in the surrounding nations. In Cambodia, the new communist government of Pol Pot (who renamed the country Kampuchea) launched a reign of terror upon its people perhaps unparalleled in modern history, forcing virtually the entire popula-

THE FALL OF SAIGON.   One of the most humiliating spectacles in recent American history was the chaotic evacuation of Saigon in the spring of 1975. With Viet Cong troops only miles away, desperate South Vietnamese officials and others fought with American soldiers and diplomats for space on the few airplanes and helicopters available for the evacuation. (*UPI*)

tion to uproot itself and causing the death—by murder, exhaustion, or starvation —of more than a third of the country's residents. Conditions grew even worse in 1978 when the new communist government of Vietnam invaded Cambodia (with the support of the Soviet Union) and drove Pol Pot and the Khmer Rouge from power. Not only did the Cambodians suffer from the war itself; but the conflict created a severe famine that threatened virtually to exterminate the population. Massive, if belated, relief efforts from the United States and many other countries alleviated some of the suffering by the end of 1979; but the future of Cambodia remained bleak and uncertain.

Vietnam, in the meantime, faced an invasion of its territory by the forces of communist China, which supported Pol Pot and feared the extension of Russian influence in the region. The two sides established an uneasy truce after several weeks of fighting; but there remained no stable peace between the ancient adversaries. American officials had claimed for years that the collapse of South Vietnam would lead quickly to coordinated communist domination of all of Southeast Asia. In fact, the new regimes were soon fighting each other as bitterly as they had once fought against the West.

Such were the dismal results of more than a decade of direct American military involvement in Vietnam. They had come at a staggering cost. The greatest burden, of course, had been borne by the people of Indochina. More than 1.2 million Vietnamese soldiers had died in combat, along with countless civilians throughout the region. A beautiful land had been ravaged and mutilated; an ancient culture had been all but destroyed. The agrarian economy of much of Indochina lay in ruins, and the social fabric of the region would, it seemed clear, take many years to recover.

But the United States had paid a heavy price as well. The war had cost the nation almost $150 billion in direct costs and incalculably more indirectly. It had resulted in the deaths of over 55,000 young men and the injury of 300,000 more, many of whom were permanently maimed or crippled. American domestic life had been racked by dissent for more than five years. Pressing social problems had gone unaddressed. Members of an entire generation had been scarred by the experience, many of them cruelly disillusioned, some of them deeply and permanently embittered toward their government and their political system. And the nation at large had suffered a heavy blow to its confidence and self-esteem. Only a decade before, Americans had believed that they could create a great society at home and maintain peace and freedom in the world. Now they harbored serious doubts about their ability to do either.

NIXON, KISSINGER, AND THE WORLD

The continuing war in Vietnam provided a dismal backdrop to what Nixon considered his larger mission in world affairs: the construction of a new international order. The President had become convinced that old assumptions of a "bipolar" world—in which the United States and the Soviet Union were the only truly great powers—were now obsolete. The rise of China, Japan, and western Europe, the increasing nationalism of the Third World, the growing disunity within the communist alliance—all augured a new, "multipolar" international structure. To deal with this changing world, Nixon drew on the theories of Henry Kissinger, a longtime student of the nineteenth-century European balance of power. The United States must, Nixon and Kissinger believed, work for a new equilibrium. "It will be a safer world and a better world," the President proclaimed in 1971, "if we have a strong, healthy United States, Europe, Soviet Union, China, Japan—each balancing the other, not playing one against the other, an even balance." The result was a series of new initiatives: the opening of relations with communist China, the establishment of détente with the Soviet Union, and a new posture toward the Third World.

The China Initiative

For more than twenty years, ever since the fall of Chiang Kai-shek in 1949, the United States had treated China, the largest nation on earth, as if it did not exist. There were no official contacts between the two countries. Only a tiny handful of Americans had visited the mainland. News of developments within China was available only in brief and unreliable fragments. One of the world's greatest powers, a nation now in possession of nuclear weapons, was living in almost total isolation from the West, while the United States continued to recognize the decaying exile regime on Taiwan as the legitimate government of China.

Nixon and Kissinger, however, believed that there were now good reasons for forging a new relationship with the Chinese communists. A rapprochement would not only be a belated recognition of reality. It might, in addition, aid the efforts to win a settlement of the war in Vietnam; and it would strengthen China's position as a counterbalance to the Soviet Union, thus inducing the Russians to adopt a more conciliatory attitude toward the United States. The Chinese, for their part, were at least equally eager for a new relationship with the United States. Their own dispute with the Soviet Union—a reflection of the historic antagonism between the two countries, which their mutual commitment to communism had only briefly suppressed—had grown far more bitter than any rivalry with the West. By 1970, Soviet and Chinese forces were massed along both sides of the border, poised, it seemed, for a disastrous war between the two communist powers. The Peking government was eager, therefore, both to forestall the possibility of a Soviet–American alliance against China and to end China's own isolation from the international arena.

Early in 1971, Nixon hinted at a change in American policy when, in a public statement, he made official use for the first time of the legitimate name of the Chinese government: the People's Republic of China. In July, he sent Henry Kissinger on a secret mission to Peking. And when Kissinger returned, the President made the startling announcement that he would visit China himself within the next few months. That fall, the United States dropped its long opposition to the admission of communist China to the United Nations; in October, as a result, the UN admitted the communist delegation and expelled the representatives of the Taiwan regime. Finally, in February 1972, Nixon arrived in China for a week-long visit. American television broadcast vivid pictures of presidential tours of famous Chinese landmarks, which had been invisible to much of the West for more than two decades, of meetings with Chou En-lai and Mao Tse-tung, and of gracious and friendly exchanges of toasts during elaborate state dinners. In a single stroke, Nixon managed to erase much of the deep animosity toward China that the American people had developed over the course of a generation.

The diplomatic results of the summit meeting were similarly important. The United States and China agreed to scientific, cultural, journalistic, and other exchanges and to a series of steps toward the resumption of trade. More significant, Nixon agreed to accept the principle of eventual reunification of Taiwan

NIXON IN CHINA. Nixon reviews a Chinese honor guard upon his arrival in Peking in February 1972. Accompanying him is the Chinese Premier, Chou En-lai. The President's trip provided Americans with their first glimpses of life in China since the 1940s. It also helped dispel a generation of hostility toward the communist government of the mainland. (*UPI*)

with the mainland; and he offered vague assurances that American troops would ultimately withdraw from Taiwan and leave the two Chinese regimes to settle the future of the island between themselves. The United States and China did not agree upon establishing formal diplomatic relations. Nixon was not yet prepared openly to repudiate the Chiang regime, which the United States had supported for so long. But a year after the Nixon visit, the two countries set up "liaison offices" in Washington and Peking that served as embassies in all but name.

Détente

The initiatives in China helped pave the way as well for a new relationship with the Soviet Union, which was as eager to prevent a Chinese–American alliance as Peking was determined to prevent a Soviet–American one. The Russians also hoped to win technological assistance from the United States and to develop trade ties that might enable them to purchase badly needed grain from American farmers. The Soviet leadership had finally decided, moreover, that it had achieved something approaching nuclear parity with the United States; party chief Leonid Brezhnev and others were interested, therefore, in moving to decelerate the costly arms race. The Nixon administration shared the hopes for progress toward arms limitation, and it was hopeful as well that it could win Soviet assistance in settling the war in Vietnam and stabilizing the explosive situation in the Middle East.

The road to what soon became known as "détente" had actually begun in 1968, the last year of the Johnson administration, when the United States and the Soviet Union signed a treaty agreeing to discourage the further proliferation of nuclear weapons in the world. More important, however, was the beginning of talks between American and Russian diplomats in Helsinki in 1969 on a strategic arms limitation treaty (SALT). The negotiations continued for two and a half years, and the result was the conclusion in 1972 of the first phase of a new arms control accord: the so-called SALT I. In May of that year, the President traveled to Moscow for a cordial meeting with the Soviet leadership and a glittering ceremony to sign the agreement. The Moscow summit produced as well a series of accords establishing new trade and other exchanges between the two nations—including the soon to be infamous Soviet–American wheat deal, by which the United States sold nearly one-quarter of the total American grain supply to the Russians at a cost far below the world market price. The federal government made up the price difference through subsidies to American farmers.

Nixon returned from Moscow in triumph, boasting of dramatic progress toward bringing the arms race to an end. In fact, SALT I did not end the arms race or even slow it to any great extent. It simply moved it in a different direction. The two nations agreed to limit themselves to their existing number of intercontinental ballistic missiles (ICBMs), thus institutionalizing Soviet superiority in total missile strength. But the United States continued to possess a substantial lead in the total number of its warheads, largely because it had almost twice as many submarines equipped with nuclear missiles as the Soviets. Each country would, in addition, sharply limit its construction of antiballistic missile systems (ABMs). The treaty thus limited the quantity of certain weapons on both sides. It said nothing, however, about limiting quality or about forestalling the creation of entirely new weapons systems. In the following years, the contest for increased sophistication in weapons systems continued unabated. Both nations, moreover, spent vast sums developing new forms of armaments not restricted by the treaty: the Soviet backfire bomber and the American cruise missile, among others.

SALT I had always been intended as the first step in a far more comprehensive arms control agreement. In June 1973, during a visit by Brezhnev to Washington, the Soviet and American governments pledged renewed efforts to speed the completion of the next phase of the negotiations. Nixon and Brezhnev agreed in principle to abstain from nuclear war, to work for a permanent freeze on offensive nuclear weapons, and to extend Soviet–American cooperation in other areas as well. Basking in the glow of détente, Nixon toasted his Russian guest at a state dinner in the White House. "The question is," he said, "shall the world's two strongest nations constantly confront one another in areas which might lead to war, or shall we work together for peace?"

There could be little doubt that the establishment of détente had produced important benefits for the United States. For one thing, it freed the Nixon administration to pursue its escalation of the war in Vietnam with greatly reduced risk of Soviet or Chinese intervention. Johnson had always refused to allow the mining of North Vietnamese harbors, for example, for fear of provoking the Russians, whose ships made frequent calls there. Now Nixon placed the mines and received no more than a mild rebuke from Moscow in return. There was, in addition, much to be said for reducing tensions between the great nuclear powers for its own sake. Above all, Nixon was taking an important step in replacing the old moralistic, ideological basis of American foreign policy with a more practical and realistic foundation. Yet serious problems remained. The United States and the Soviet Union were powerful and expansive nations, with interests throughout the world that were clearly incompatible at many points. The spirit of détente obscured many of these differences for the moment, but it did not remove them.

The Problems of Multipolarity

The policies of rapprochement with communist China and détente with the Soviet Union reflected several basic assumptions of the Nixon–Kissinger foreign policy. The communist world was no longer a monolithic bloc, the administration now believed, and it required a far more flexible and varied diplomatic approach than it had in the 1950s. The Soviet threat to western Europe, American officials were convinced, was much abated, removing the most serious source of tension from the Cold War. Above all, the new policies reflected a belief that world stability depended primarily on the relationships among the great powers, that the pervasive concern of previous administrations with "emerging areas" had diverted American policy from pursuit of its most important goals. There was ample support for the first two assumptions but less basis for the third. By the last years of the Nixon administration, it had become clear that it was the Third World that remained the most volatile and dangerous source of world instability; that tensions in developing countries had the capacity not only to produce local turmoil but to erode the new relationships among the superpowers.

Central to the Nixon–Kissinger policy toward the Third World was the effort to maintain a stable status quo without involving the United States too deeply in local disputes. The so-called Nixon Doctrine, which the President announced in

1969 and 1970, displayed both the extent and the limits of the administration's concerns in the developing regions. The United States would, the President declared, "participate in the defense and development of allies and friends," but it would leave the "basic responsibility" for the future of those "friends" to the nations themselves. In practice, the Nixon Doctrine meant a declining American interest in contributing to Third World development; a growing contempt for the United Nations, where underdeveloped nations were gaining influence through their sheer numbers; and increasing support to authoritarian regimes attempting to withstand radical challenges from within. In 1970, for example, the CIA poured substantial funds into Chile to help support the established government against a communist challenge. When the Marxist candidate for President, Salvador Allende, came to power through an honest, open election, the United States began funneling more money to opposition forces in Chile to help "destabilize" the new government. In 1973, a military junta seized power from Allende, who was subsequently murdered under mysterious circumstances. There was good reason to believe that the CIA had played a direct role in the coup; undoubtedly, American policies had contributed to creating the circumstances under which the coup became possible. The new regime of General Augusto Pinochet was as brutally repressive as any in the Western Hemisphere. It received warm approval and increased military and economic assistance from the United States.

Far more troubling than Latin America, however, was the Middle East. Long an area of interest to the United States because of its strategic position between the Soviet Union and the Mediterranean, the region was now also of vital economic importance to the West, which beginning in the 1960s had become highly dependent upon the purchase of oil from the Arab states. For the United States, this energy dependence presented special problems. As the most important ally and defender of Israel, America was standing squarely in opposition to the Islamic states, which were unanimous in their condemnation of Zionism.

Hostility toward Israel had grown particularly intense after the humiliating Arab defeat in the Six-Day War of 1967, in which Israeli forces had routed the armies of Egypt, Jordan, and Syria and had seized territory from all three nations. In the following years, Israel remained adamant in its refusal to relinquish the newly occupied territories. The situation grew even more volatile as a result of the desperate plight of hundreds of thousands of Palestinian Arab refugees, some of whom had been virtually homeless since 1948 and whose numbers had drastically increased after the 1967 war. Many of them lived in Jordan, whose ruler, King Hussein, was eager to maintain stable relations with the United States. Disturbed by the activities of the new Palestine Liberation Organization (PLO) and other radical or terrorist groups, Hussein used his own armies to attack the Palestinians after a series of uprisings in 1970, almost precipitating another general war in the region.

In the meantime, the United States was working quietly to repair its relations with the Islamic states and create the framework for a general settlement of the Middle Eastern dilemma, a task the Nixon administration hoped would be eased as a result of its policies of détente with the Soviet Union. Such efforts suffered a serious setback in October 1973 when, on the Jewish high holy day of Yom Kippur, Egyptian and Syrian forces suddenly attacked Israel. The ensuing conflict was far different from the 1967 war, during which Israel had quickly and decisively overwhelmed its opponents. For ten days, the Israelis struggled to recover from the surprise attack; finally, they launched an effective counteroffensive against Egyptian forces in the Sinai. Only then did the United States and the Soviet Union intervene to bring an end to the fighting in the region. Under heavy American pressure, the government of Israel agreed not to press its advantage and accepted a cease-fire.

The imposed settlement of the Yom Kippur War reflected a significant change in the American position in the Middle East. It displayed, first, a new sensitivity to Soviet interests in the region. So worried had the Nixon administration become about Russian intervention in the conflict that at one point the President had ordered American nuclear forces onto a full, worldwide alert. Later, making use of their newly cordial relationship, the two superpowers tacitly agreed to restrain their allies and work for an armistice. The war gave clear evidence, however, of an even more important new reality: the growing dependence of the United States and its allies on Arab oil. Permitting Israel to continue its drive into Egypt would not only have invited Soviet retaliation; it would have jeopardized the ability of the United States to purchase needed petroleum from the Arab states. A brief but painful embargo by the Islamic governments on the sale of oil to America in 1973 provided an ominous warning. The lesson of the Yom Kippur War, therefore, was that the United States could no longer ignore the interests of the Arab nations in its efforts on behalf of Israel.

A larger lesson of 1973 was even more disturbing. The Yom Kippur War and the oil embargo had given clear evidence of the new limits facing the United States in its effort to construct a stable world order. The nations of the Third World could no longer be depended upon to act as passive, cooperative "client states." The easy access to raw materials upon which the American economy had come to depend was becoming a thing of the past. The United States could not even rely any longer upon the automatic support of its NATO allies. None of the principal nations of western Europe had joined the United States in providing military support for Israel in the 1973 war, and most had complained bitterly when American policies had resulted in their own temporary loss of access to vital Middle Eastern oil.

Nixon and Kissinger had been correct in predicting that the bipolar world of the 1950s was giving way to a multipolar world in the 1970s. They had not, however, realized just how many "poles" there would be in the new international order. A dawning recognition in the increasingly nationalistic countries of the Third World of the importance of their natural resources was helping to disperse international power far beyond the four or five major centers of influence that Nixon and Kissinger had been attempting to cultivate. This new reality was ensuring that the great powers would have growing difficulty in the future in shaping the world to their liking.

KISSINGER AND MEIR.   Relations were cordial between Henry
Kissinger and Israeli Prime Minister Golda Meir by the time this
photograph was taken in May 1974. Only months earlier, however,
members of the Israeli government had reacted with great bitterness to
American pressures to halt their advance against the Egyptian army. The
Nixon–Kissinger policies during the Yom Kippur War made it clear that
Israel could no longer expect unlimited and unquestioned assistance from
the United States. (*Wide World Photos*)

THE NEW FEDERALISM

For a time in the 1960s, it had seemed to many Americans that the forces of chaos
and radicalism were taking control of the nation. Seldom had society been so
fraught with conflict; seldom had middle-class Americans found themselves under
such unrelenting assault. The growing fear of disorder had aroused a growing
antagonism toward student radicals, black militants, hippies, and other dissidents.
It had also produced deep resentment of the federal government, which some
Americans believed had become the exclusive preserve of those minorities and
social activists and whose policies, many claimed, were becoming increasingly
disruptive and intrusive. The domestic policy of the Nixon administration, therefore, was an attempt to restore balance: between the needs of the poor and the

desires of the middle class, between the power of the federal government and the interests of local communities. The President himself described the effort as the "New Federalism"—a series of programs to "reverse the flow of power and resources from the states and communities to Washington and start power and resources flowing back . . . to the people."

In some respects, Nixon was extraordinarily successful. By tapping the resentments of the "silent majority," he helped produce a new climate in American political life—one far less receptive to the demands of the poor and minorities, one far more concerned with protecting the values and the economic position of the middle class. But the new climate did not always produce new policies. The federal government remained, despite Nixon's efforts, an expanding force in American life. And it continued to arouse the hostility of large segments of the population. Nixon succeeded brilliantly for a time in expressing those grievances and using them to his own political advantage. He did less, however, to eliminate their causes.

The New Balance

Almost immediately upon taking office, Nixon began to give voice to Middle American resentment of the federal government and to the conservative fear of social decay. Skillfully and effectively, he established himself, in the public mind at least, as the defender of traditional values and local customs. Through his "southern strategy," he began to limit federal efforts to impose integration upon reluctant communities. He tried, unsuccessfully, to persuade Congress to pass legislation prohibiting school desegregation through the use of forced busing. And he forbade the Department of Health, Education, and Welfare to cut off federal funds from school districts that had failed to comply with court orders to integrate (precipitating the resignation of Secretary Robert Finch and other HEW officials).

At the same time, he worked to reduce or dismantle many of the social programs of the Great Society and the New Frontier. He cut off hundreds of federal grants for urban renewal, social welfare, job training, and educational assistance. He attempted to reduce funding for dozens of other social programs, only to be blocked by the Democratic Congress; on occasion, he attempted to defy congressional opposition by simply impounding funds for programs he considered unnecessary. In 1973, he abolished the Office of Economic Opportunity, the centerpiece of the antipoverty program of the Johnson years. And at the same time, he was working to decentralize control of other social programs—both by transferring authority to state and local governments and by establishing a program of "revenue sharing," through which the federal government would return some of its tax revenues to localities.

One of the administration's boldest efforts was an attempt to overhaul the nation's enormous welfare system. The cumbersome, expensive, and inefficient welfare bureaucracy was the most glaring symbol of what Nixon and his supporters considered the excessive intrusiveness of the federal government. The primary vehicle for federal relief—Aid to Families with Dependent Children—was not only costly; it required a large, awkward infrastructure of caseworkers, administrators, and others, and it extended the authority of the federal government directly into the daily lives of families and communities. As an alternative, Nixon proposed what he called the Family Assistance Plan. Designed in large part by the President's urban adviser, Daniel Patrick Moynihan, the FAP established what was in effect a guaranteed annual income for all Americans: $1,600 in federal grants, which could be supplemented by outside earnings up to $4,000. Even many liberals applauded the proposal as an important step toward expanding federal responsibility for the poor. To Nixon, however, the appeal of the plan was its simplicity. It would reduce the supervisory functions of the federal government and transfer to welfare recipients themselves daily responsibility for their own lives. Although the FAP won approval in the House in 1970, concerted attacks by welfare recipients (who considered the benefits inadequate) and members of the welfare bureaucracy (whose own influence stood to be sharply diminished by the bill) helped kill it in the Senate. It was never revived.

Nixon appealed to conservative and provincial sentiments in other ways as well. He issued strident denunciations of protesters and radicals, ordered the Justice Department to arrest demonstrators and dissidents, and unleashed Vice President Spiro Agnew to attack not only youthful critics of the administration but the liberal news media and the "biased" television networks. He rejected as "morally bankrupt" the recommendations of a special commission on pornography, which saw no reason for the government to suppress the distribution of obscene materials. He expressed sympathy for those who opposed abortion. He refused to consider extending amnesty to draft resisters. He issued strong denunciations of those who encouraged the use of drugs. He was, in short, establishing a new stance for the federal government: one that balanced its commitments to helping the poor and minorities against a larger concern for preserving traditional values and protecting the status of the middle class. As campus protests and race riots began to subside after the traumas of 1968 and 1970, his policies seemed to be succeeding.

In fact, however, it was in large part an illusory success; for despite Nixon's efforts, government responsibility for social welfare and federal intrusion into local communities increased dramatically during his administration. The steady growth in the size of the urban "underclass"—impoverished inner-city residents totally and permanently dependent upon welfare—by itself mandated a major expansion in federal assistance. So did the inexorable momentum of a government bureaucracy whose major thrust for decades had been the extension of its own authority. A steady stream of new regulations—on school desegregation, on Affirmative Action, on agricultural practices, and on many other issues—flowed from Washington despite the President's commitment to decentralized power. Nixon succeeded in changing many public assumptions about the proper role of the federal government. It remained for others, however, to attempt to translate the new assumptions into reality.

The Nixon Court

One of the loudest cheers during Richard Nixon's acceptance speech at the 1968 Republican Convention greeted his pledge to change the composition of the Supreme Court. The reaction was unsurprising. Of all the liberal institutions that had aroused the enmity of the "silent majority" in the 1950s and 1960s, none had evoked more anger and bitterness than the Warren Court. Not only had its rulings on racial matters disrupted traditional social patterns in both the North and the South, but its staunch defense of civil liberties had, in the eyes of many Americans, contributed directly to the increase in crime, disorder, and moral decay. One after another landmark decision seemed to tread upon the sensibilities of provincial and conservative Americans. In *Engel* v. *Vitale* (1962), the Court had ruled that prayers in public schools were unconstitutional, sparking outrage among religious fundamentalists and others, who would spend more than a decade fighting the edict. In *Roth* v. *United States* (1957), the Court had sharply limited the authority of local governments to curb pornography. In *Gideon* v. *Wainwright* (1963), the Court had ruled that every felony defendant was entitled to a lawyer regardless of his or her ability to pay; in *Escobedo* v. *Illinois* (1964), the Court had declared that a defendant must be allowed access to a lawyer before questioning by police; above all, in *Miranda* v. *Arizona* (1966), the Court had confirmed the obligation of authorities to inform a criminal suspect of his or her rights. In these and other cases, the Court had greatly strengthened the civil rights of criminal defendants and had, in the eyes of many Americans, greatly weakened the power of law-enforcement officials to do their jobs.

Other examples of "judicial activism" had antagonized both local and national political leaders. In *Baker* v. *Carr* (1962), the Warren Court, in its most influential decision since *Brown* v. *Board of Education,* had ordered state legislatures to apportion representation so that the votes of all citizens would carry equal weight. In dozens of states, systems of legislative districting that had given disproportionate representation to rural areas were thus rendered invalid. The reapportionment that resulted greatly increased the political voice of blacks, Hispanics, and other poor urban residents. By 1968, in short, the Warren Court had become the target of Americans of all kinds who felt that the balance of power in the United States had shifted too far toward the poor and dispossessed at the expense of the middle class.

Richard Nixon shared such sentiments, and he was determined to use his judicial appointments to give the Court a more conservative cast. His first opportunity came almost as soon as he entered office. Chief Justice Earl Warren, who had tried to resign during the last months of the Johnson administration only to be stymied by the refusal of Congress to approve the appointment of liberal Associate Justice Abe Fortas as his successor, announced his resignation early in 1969. Nixon replaced him with a federal appeals court judge of known conservative leanings, Warren Burger.

The President had less success in filling the next Court opening to become available. In May 1969, Abe Fortas resigned his seat after the disclosure of a series

EARL WARREN. Warren's years as Chief Justice saw the Supreme Court take a series of decisive steps in the direction of expanding civil liberties and promoting racial equality. Revered by liberals, Warren became a symbol to conservatives of the increasing intrusiveness of the federal government into the lives of individuals and communities. Right-wing groups erected billboards throughout the South and other areas with the stark message: "Impeach Earl Warren." (*UPI*)

of alleged financial improprieties in which he was involved. To replace him, Nixon named Clement F. Haynsworth, a federal circuit court judge from South Carolina. Although Haynsworth received the endorsement of the American Bar Association and had the respect of much of the judicial community, he came under fire from Senate liberals, black organizations, and labor unions for his conservative record on civil rights. The damaging discovery that he had sat on cases involving corporations in which he himself had a financial interest created even more opposition; and the Senate finally rejected him.

Nixon's next choice was a particularly unfortunate one, motivated some believed by the President's desire to punish the liberals who had scuttled the Haynsworth nomination. G. Harrold Carswell, a judge of the Florida federal appeals court, was almost entirely lacking in distinction. Critics quickly pointed out that an inordinate number of his cases had been reversed by a higher court.

Others uncovered evidence of racist statements that Carswell had made in the past. Most damaging of all, however, was the widely held belief that the new appointee was simply unfit for the Supreme Court—a mediocre man being elevated to a position for which he was unqualified. Nixon supporter Roman Hruska, a conservative Senator from Nebraska, did not help matters by arguing publicly that even if Carswell was mediocre, he should be approved to give mediocre people "a little representation" too. "We can't have all Brandeises and Frankfurters and Cardozos," Hruska explained. The Senate rejected the Carswell nomination.

An enraged President Nixon, ignoring the real reasons for these unprecedented congressional defeats, announced that the votes had been a result of prejudice against the South. But he was careful thereafter to choose men of standing within the legal community to fill vacancies on the Supreme Court. Harry Blackmun, a moderate jurist from Minnesota; Lewis F. Powell, Jr., a respected judge from Virginia; and William Rehnquist, a member of the Nixon Justice Department— all met with little opposition from the Senate. And the Warren Court gradually gave way to what many observers came to describe as the "Nixon Court."

The new Court, however, fell short of what the President and many conservatives had hoped. Far from retreating from its commitment to social reform, the Court in many areas actually extended its reach. In *Swann* v. *Charlotte-Mecklenburg Board of Education* (1971), it ruled in favor of the use of forced busing to achieve racial balance in schools. Not even the intense and occasionally violent opposition of local communities as diverse as Boston and Louisville, Kentucky, was able to weaken the judicial commitment to integration. In *Furman* v. *Georgia* (1972), the Court overturned existing capital punishment statutes and established strict new guidelines for such laws in the future. In *Roe* v. *Wade* (1972), it struck down laws forbidding women to have abortions.

In other decisions, however, the Court did signal a marked withdrawal from its crusading commitment to civil liberties and reform. It attempted instead to create a moderate balance. Although the justices approved busing as a tool for achieving integration, they rejected, in *Milliken* v. *Bradley* (1974), a plan to transfer students across district lines (in this case, between Detroit and its suburbs) to achieve racial balance. While the Court upheld the principle of Affirmative Action in its celebrated 1978 decision *Bakke* v. *Board of Regents of California,* it established restrictive new guidelines for such programs in the future. In other rulings, it confirmed the right of the press to publish free from government restraints (as in the 1971 Pentagon Papers decision), but limited the right of reporters to withhold information about their sources from the courts. The justices were slower to retreat from the unpopular Warren Court rulings expanding the protections available to criminal defendants, but they showed signs of retrenchment there as well. In *Stone* v. *Powell* (1976), for example, the Court agreed to certain limits upon the right of a defendant to appeal a state conviction to the federal judiciary. And Chief Justice Burger, at least, became increasingly outspoken in support of far more conservative changes. "Our search for justice," he said in a speech in February 1981, "must not be twisted into an endless quest for technical errors, unrelated to guilt or innocence."

Nixon had failed to produce a genuinely conservative Supreme Court. But his appointments had ensured that it would be a far more moderate, far less active Court than it had been in the past. By the early 1980s, with five of the nine justices over the age of seventy and with another, even more conservative Republican in the White House, the prospects for a rapid return to liberal judicial activism seemed remote.

The Election of 1972

However unsuccessful the Nixon administration may have been in achieving some of its specific goals, it had by 1972 scored a series of triumphs in enlisting the loyalties of the electorate. The "real majority"—what a 1970 book of that name by Richard Scammon and Ben Wattenberg called the "unyoung, unblack, and unpoor"—responded enthusiastically to the President's attacks upon liberal court decisions; his denunciation of radicals, hippies, and the liberal press; his opposition to busing, abortion, and pornography; his support for traditional moral and religious values; and his appeal for new efforts to combat crime. They approved his call for retrenchment in social welfare programs, and they applauded his restraint —or, as Daniel Moynihan described it, "benign neglect"—in advancing the cause of civil rights. Although the unpopularity of the war in Vietnam continued to plague him as the reelection campaign approached, Nixon's dramatic initiatives in the Soviet Union and China increased public confidence in his ability to end the fighting.

Nixon entered the presidential race in 1972, therefore, with a substantial reserve of strength. The events of that year improved his position immeasurably. His energetic reelection committee collected enormous sums of money to support the campaign. The President himself made full use of the powers of incumbency, refraining from campaigning in the primaries (in which he faced, in any case, only token opposition) and concentrating on highly publicized international decisions and state visits. And agencies of the federal government dispensed funds and favors to communities around the country in a concerted effort to strengthen Nixon's political standing in questionable areas.

Nixon was most fortunate in 1972, however, in his opposition. The return of George Wallace to the presidential fray caused some early concern, for Nixon's own reelection strategy rested on the same appeals to the troubled middle class that Wallace was so skillfully expressing. But although Wallace showed remarkable strength in the early Democratic primaries, the possibility of another third-party campaign in the fall vanished in May, when a crazed assailant shot the Alabama Governor during a rally at a Maryland shopping center. Paralyzed from the waist down, Wallace was unable to continue campaigning.

The Democrats, in the meantime, were making the greatest contribution to the Nixon cause by nominating for President a representative of their most liberal faction: Senator George S. McGovern of South Dakota. An outspoken critic of the war, a forceful advocate of liberal positions on virtually every social and economic issue, McGovern seemed to embody those aspects of the turbulent

1960s that middle-class Americans were most eager to reject. McGovern profited greatly from party reforms (which he himself had helped to draft) that gave increased influence to women, blacks, and young people in the selection of the Democratic ticket. But those same reforms helped make the Democratic Convention of 1972 an unappealing spectacle to much of the public. The party's left wing, flushed with triumph, ran roughshod over Democratic conservatives—among other things, ousting Chicago Mayor Richard Daley's delegation from the convention. To many voters watching on television, the proceedings supported an already growing impression that McGovern was the candidate of hippies, aggressive women, and blacks. The candidate then disillusioned even some of his own supporters by his confused response to revelations that his running mate, Senator Thomas Eagleton of Missouri, had undergone treatment for an emotional disturbance. McGovern first announced that he supported Eagleton "1,000 percent," then suddenly dropped him from the ticket. The remainder of the Democratic presidential campaign was an exercise in futility.

For Nixon, by contrast, the fall campaign was an uninterrupted triumphal procession. After a Republican Convention utterly devoid of controversy, the President made a few, carefully planned appearances in strategic areas of the country. Most of his time, however, he devoted to highly publicized work on behalf of "world peace." And in October, although by then it was clearly unnecessary politically, he sealed the victory with a skillfully orchestrated demonstration that a settlement of the war in Vietnam was near. On election day, as a result, Nixon won reelection by one of the largest margins in history: 60.8 percent of the popular vote compared with 37.5 percent for the forlorn McGovern, an electoral margin of 520 to 17. The Democratic candidate had carried only Massachusetts and the District of Columbia. The new commitments that Nixon had so effectively expressed—to restraint in social reform, to decentralization of political power, to the defense of traditional values, and to a new balance in international relations—had clearly won the approval of the American people. But other problems, some beyond the President's control and some of his own making, were already lurking in the wings.

SUGGESTED READINGS

A fascinating examination of Richard Nixon, written early in his presidency, is Garry Wills, *Nixon Agonistes* (1970). Jonathan Schell, *The Time of Illusion* (1975), is the best overview of the Nixon administration. See also William Safire, *Before the Fall* (1975), for an insider's view; and Nixon's own account, *RN: The Memoirs of Richard Nixon* (1978). On the Nixon–Kissinger policies in Southeast Asia, see Kissinger's memoirs, *White House Years* (1979), for a defense. More hostile are Gareth Porter, *A Peace Denied* (1975), and William Shawcross, *Nixon, Kissinger, and the Destruction of Cambodia* (1978), a devastating attack. General studies of the Nixon–Kissinger foreign policy, in addition to Kissinger's memoirs, include Roger Morris, *Uncertain*

Greatness (1977), and Seyom Brown, *The Crises of Power* (1979). On Kissinger himself, see David Landau, *Kissinger: The Uses of Power* (1972), and Marvin Kalb and Bernard Kalb, *Kissinger* (1974). Other useful works include Tad Szulc, *The Illusion of Peace* (1978), and Roger Hilsman, *The Crouching Future* (1975). On arms control and détente, see Harland Moulton, *From Superiority to Parity* (1973). John Stockwell, *In Search of Enemies* (1977), and Thomas Powers, *The Man Who Kept the Secrets* (1979), examine the CIA. Michel Oksenberg and Robert Oxnam (eds.), *Dragon and Eagle* (1978), discuss the changing Sino-American relationship. William Quandt, *Decade of Decision* (1977), and Robert Stookey, *America and the Arab States* (1975), discuss the United States and the Middle East.

On Nixon's domestic policies, in addition to the general studies mentioned above, see Daniel P. Moynihan, *The Politics of a Guaranteed Income* (1973), and Vincent Burke and Vee Burke, *Nixon's Good Deed* (1974), on welfare reform; and R. L. Miller, *The New Economics of Richard Nixon* (1972), and R. P. Nathan et al., *Monitoring Revenue Sharing* (1975), for economic policy and the New Federalism. Bob Woodward and Scott Armstrong, *The Brethren* (1980), is a gossipy but revealing picture of the Nixon Court. Theodore H. White, *The Making of the President, 1972* (1973), is an admiring account of Nixon's triumphant reelection.

Twenty-Six

The Crisis of Authority

The stunning reelection victory of Richard Nixon obscured for the moment a troubling reality of American political life in the 1970s: the growing public cynicism about authority in general and about the federal government in particular. The war in Vietnam, the social conflicts of the 1960s, the continuing failure of major institutions to perform as the public had come to expect—all had combined to make Americans suspicious of their leaders and mistrustful of their government. Even in triumph, therefore, Nixon was heir to a legacy of eroding public respect for authority.

Yet it was the events of Nixon's own presidency that saw the most rapid erosion of that respect. Already by the time of the 1972 election, the once-vigorous economy had begun a long descent into crisis. The failure in the following years to reverse its course raised serious questions about the ability of elected officials to govern. Of more immediate importance, within months of the President's landslide victory, his administration was embroiled in a series of scandals that not only resulted in Nixon's untimely departure from office, but further increased public cynicism about the nation's leadership.

THE TROUBLED ECONOMY

Although it was the political scandals that most visibly clouded the Nixon presidency, an even more serious national crisis was emerging in the early 1970s: the decline of the American economy. Rising inflation, eroding productivity, and a weakening position in international trade all contributed to a serious deterioration in the nation's once robust economic health. Americans had grown accustomed to boundless prosperity and uninterrupted growth, and they looked to their government to restore both when things began to turn sour. The inability of the government to do so greatly intensified public unhappiness about the quality of leadership.

Sources of Decline

For more than twenty years the American economy had been the envy of the world. The United States had been responsible for as much as a third of the world's industrial production and had dominated international trade. The American dollar had been the strongest currency in the world, the standard by which other nations measured their own monetary health. The American standard of living, already high at the end of World War II, had improved dramatically in the years since. Personal incomes had doubled and spending both on major investments and on consumer goods had soared. Most Americans had begun to assume that this remarkable prosperity was the normal condition of their society. In fact, however, it had rested in large part on several artificial conditions that were by the late 1960s rapidly disappearing.

The most disturbing economic problem, one that was symptomatic of all the others, was inflation, which had been creeping upward for several years when Richard Nixon took office and which shortly thereafter began to soar. Its most visible cause was the performance of the federal government in the mid-1960s. At the same time that President Johnson had persuaded Congress to accept a tax cut in 1964, he was rapidly increasing spending both for domestic social programs and for the war in Vietnam. The result was a major expansion of the money supply, resting largely on government deficits, that pushed prices rapidly upward.

But there were other, more fundamental causes of the inflation and of the economic problems that lay behind it. Much of America's economic strength in the 1950s and 1960s had rested on the nation's unquestioned supremacy in international trade. American industrial goods were in high demand around the world; and the United States had easy access to raw materials, unconstrained by competition from other, weaker industrial nations. By the late 1960s, however, the world economic picture had changed. No longer were American factories unchallenged in pursuit of world markets. They faced stiff competition from West Germany, Japan, and other emerging economic powers. No more did the United States have exclusive access to cheap raw materials around the globe; not only were other industrial nations now competing for increasingly scarce raw materials, but Third World suppliers of those materials were beginning to realize their value and demand higher prices for them. Critics charged that the United States had grown complacent, that its industries had failed to modernize their plants and procedures to compete with the Germans and the Japanese, that its labor costs had become so high as to damage the competitive position of American goods. Such complaints were in many cases undoubtedly justified. But others argued that such internal problems were really secondary to a much more fundamental economic change. In a world with a rapidly growing population and in which popular expectations of dignity and comfort were rising everywhere, the United States was now only one of many competitors for the scarce resources of the globe.

The Energy Dilemma

Central to the problem, it gradually became clear, was access to sources of energy. More than any nation on earth, the United States had based its economy on the easy availability of cheap and plentiful fuels. No society was more dependent on the automobile; none was more profligate in its use of oil and gas in its homes, schools, and factories. As the economy expanded in the 1960s, an already high demand for energy soared much higher. And with domestic petroleum reserves beginning to dwindle, the nation increased its dependence on imports from the Middle East and Africa. The result, ultimately, was a wrenching economic crisis.

For many years, the Organization of Petroleum Exporting Countries (OPEC) had operated as an informal bargaining unit for the sale of oil by Third World nations. Not until the early 1970s, however, did it begin to display its strength. Aware of the growing dependence of Western economies upon the resources of its member nations, OPEC was no longer willing to follow the direction of American and European oil companies. Instead, it began to use its oil both as an economic tool and as a political weapon. In 1973, in the midst of the Yom Kippur War, Arab members of OPEC announced that they would no longer ship petroleum to nations supporting Israel—that is, to the United States and its allies in western Europe. At about the same time, the OPEC nations agreed to raise their prices 400 percent. These twin shocks produced momentary chaos in the West. The United States suffered its first fuel shortage since World War II, and the disruptive effects were a painful reminder to the American people of their dependence on plentiful energy. Motorists faced long lines at gas stations; schools and offices closed down to save on heating oil; factories cut production and laid off workers for lack of sufficient fuel. A few months later, the crisis eased. But the price of energy continued to skyrocket in the following years, both because of OPEC's new militant policies and because of the weakening competitive position of the dollar in world markets. No single factor did more to produce the soaring inflation of the 1970s.

The Nixon Response

Richard Nixon, therefore, inherited an economy in which growth was already sluggish, in which inflation was already troubling, and in which even greater new problems lurked. Within weeks of taking office, he announced a "game plan" for dealing with these various woes. He would, he promised, spend less and tax more. But such policies were easier announced than implemented, evoking as they did both congressional and popular protest. As a result, Nixon turned increasingly to an economic tool more readily available to him: control of the currency. Placing conservative economists at the head of the Federal Reserve Board, he ensured sharply higher interest rates and a contraction of the money supply. But the "tight money" policy did little to curb inflation. The cost of living rose nearly 15 percent

ENERGY CRISIS. Gasoline shortages in 1973 and again in 1979 introduced Americans to the reality of the worldwide energy crisis. Long lines at gas stations tried the patience of the public, producing complaints, arguments, and occasionally, violence. (*UPI*)

during Nixon's first two and a half years in office. In 1971, moreover, the United States recorded its first balance-of-trade deficit (an excess of imports over exports) in nearly eighty years. With inflation unabated and economic growth in decline, the United States was encountering a new and puzzling dilemma: "stagflation," a combination of rising prices and general economic stagnation.

By the summer of 1971, therefore, the President was under strong public pressure to act decisively to reverse the economic tide. First, he released the dollar from the fluctuating gold standard that had controlled its worth since the end of World War II, allowing its value to fall in world markets. The devaluation helped stimulate exports, but it also made it more expensive for America to purchase vital raw materials abroad. At the same time, the President announced an even bolder and more startling new policy. For years, he had denounced the idea of using government controls to curb inflation. His experience as an employee of the Office of Price Administration during World War II had left him with a deep distaste for wage and price regulation; and as late as June 1970, he had insisted: "I will not take this nation down the road of wage and price controls." On August 15, 1971, however, he reversed himself. Under the provisions of the Economic Stabilization Act of 1970, the President imposed a ninety-day freeze on all wages and prices at their existing levels. Then, in November, he launched Phase II of his economic plan: mandatory guidelines for wage and price increases, to be administered by a federal agency. Inflation subsided temporarily, but the recession continued. The unemployment rate for 1971 was 6 percent, compared with 4 percent two years earlier.

Fearful that the recession would be more damaging than inflation in an election year, the administration reversed itself once again late in 1971: interest rates dropped sharply; government spending increased—producing the largest budget deficit since World War II. The new tactics served their purpose. By election day, personal incomes were up and unemployment was down. But there were disastrous side effects. Even though wage and price controls managed to hold down inflation in some areas, consumers were soon paying drastically higher prices for food and other basic goods. At this critical moment, with both domestic and world inflation on the verge of skyrocketing, Nixon abandoned the strict Phase II controls and replaced them with a set of flexible, largely voluntary, and almost entirely ineffective guidelines—Phase III of the administration's economic program.

With the end of wage and price controls, inflation quickly resumed its upward course. The rate for 1973 rose to 9 percent; in 1974, after the Arab oil embargo and the OPEC price increases, it soared to 12 percent, the highest rate since shortly after the end of World War II. The value of the dollar continued to slide, and the nation's international trade continued to decline. Nixon now turned his attention to solving the new "energy crisis," which had become America's most

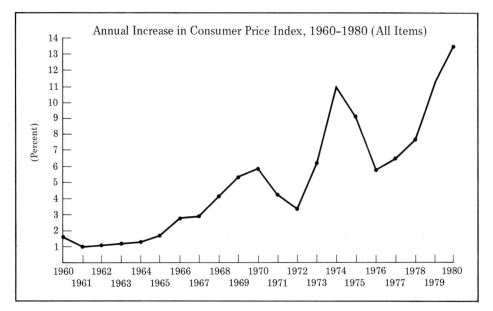

Annual Increase in Consumer Price Index, 1960–1980 (All Items)

pressing preoccupation. But the administration seemed to have no clearer idea of how to deal with that problem than it had of how to deal with the general inflation. The President spoke vaguely of conservation, of increasing production, of restoring "energy independence." But there were few concrete proposals for accomplishing them. And Nixon, in the meantime, was becoming so embroiled in his own political problems that he would have had great difficulty winning approval of a major new program in any case.

The stumbling and erratic economic programs of the Nixon administration were indicative of a broader national confusion about the future prospects for American prosperity. With little understanding of the international forces creating the economic problems, both the government and the people focused on immediate issues and short-range solutions. The Nixon pattern—of lurching from a tight money policy to curb inflation at one moment to a spending policy to cure recession at the next—repeated itself during the two administrations that followed. Such policies had little effect, ultimately, either on inflation or on the general economic stagnation.

WATERGATE AND THE PRESIDENCY

Although economic problems greatly concerned the American people in the early 1970s, a stunning political development almost entirely preoccupied the nation beginning early in 1973: the fall of Richard Nixon. The President's political demise was a result in part of his own personality. Defensive, secretive, resentful of his critics, he brought to his office an element of mean-spiritedness that helped undermine even his most important accomplishments. But the larger explanation lay in Nixon's view of American society and the world, and of his own role in both. Far more than most of his compatriots, the President was convinced that the United States faced grave dangers from the radicals and dissidents who were challenging his policies. Obsessed with what he considered his mission to create a new "structure of peace" in the world, he came increasingly to consider any challenge to his policies a threat to "national security." By identifying his own political fortunes with those of the nation, in other words, Nixon was creating a climate in which he and those who served him could justify virtually any means to stifle dissent and undermine opposition.

The White House Autocracy

Nixon's outlook was in part a culmination of decades of changes in the nature of the presidency. Public expectations of the President had increased dramatically in the years since World War II; yet the constraints on the authority of the office had grown as well. Congress had become more difficult to control; the bureaucracy had become cumbersome and unmanageable; the press, particularly in light of the war in Vietnam, had become suspicious and increasingly hostile. In response, a succession of Presidents had sought out new methods for the exercise of power, often stretching the law, occasionally breaking it.

Nixon not only continued, but greatly accelerated these trends. Facing a Democratic Congress hostile to his goals, he attempted to find ways to circumvent the legislature whenever possible. Saddled with a federal bureaucracy unresponsive to his wishes, he constructed a hierarchy of command in which virtually all executive power became concentrated in the White House. A few cabinet members retained direct access to the President, among them Attorney General John Mitchell, a longtime personal friend, and Henry Kissinger, who became Secretary of State in 1973 but had already established himself as the dominant figure in American foreign policy. For the most part, however, Nixon isolated himself almost completely, relying on a few trusted advisers through whom he exercised his power. At the head of what critics sometimes called the "palace guard" stood two particularly influential aides: H. R. Haldeman, the President's chief of staff, and John Ehrlichman, his chief domestic adviser. Operating within this rigid, autocratic structure, the President became a solitary, brooding figure, whose contempt for his opponents and impatience with obstacles to his policies festered and grew. Insulated from criticism, surrounded by flatterers, he became increasingly blatant in his defiance of the normal constraints on his office. Unknown to all but a few intimates, he also became mired in a pattern of illegalities and abuses of power that late in 1972 began to burst to the surface.

The Spreading Scandals

Early in the morning of June 17, 1972, police arrested five men who had broken into the offices of the Democratic National Committee, which were located in the Watergate Office Building in Washington, D.C. Two others were seized a short time later and charged with supervising the break-in. And when reporters for the *Washington Post* began researching the backgrounds of the culprits, they discovered a series of startling facts. Among those involved in the burglary were former employees of the Committee for the Re-Election of the President (CRP). One of them had worked in the White House itself. They had, moreover, been paid for the break-in from a secret fund of the reelection committee, a fund controlled by members of the White House staff. The further the reporters looked, the more evidence they found that the burglary had been part of a larger pattern of illegalities, planned and financed by the President's closest associates.

Public interest in the disclosures grew only slowly in the last months of 1972. Few Americans, apparently, chose to question the President's assurances that neither he nor his staff had any connection with what he called "this very bizarre incident." Early in 1973, however, the Watergate burglars went on trial; and under relentless prodding from federal judge John J. Sirica, one of the defendants, James W. McCord, agreed to cooperate both with the grand jury and with a special Senate investigating committee recently established under Senator Sam J. Ervin of North Carolina. McCord's testimony opened a floodgate of confessions, and for months a parade of White House and campaign officials exposed one illegality after another. Foremost among them was a member of the inner circle of the White House, Counsel to the President John Dean, who leveled allegations against Nixon himself.

WOODWARD AND BERNSTEIN. Carl Bernstein (left) and Bob Woodward (right) were obscure metropolitan reporters for the *Washington Post* in 1972, assigned to cover routine crimes. As such, they were the first to begin investigating the burglary of the Democratic National Committee headquarters and the first to begin linking the burglars with the White House and the Nixon reelection committee. Their disclosures in the fall and winter of 1972 and 1973 kept the Watergate case alive until judicial and congressional investigations thrust it into the national spotlight. Woodward and Bernstein came under intense attack from the White House, but virtually all of their findings found confirmation in later testimony and in the White House tapes. (*Mark Godfrey/Magnum*)

There were, in effect, two separate scandals emerging from the investigations. One was a general pattern of abuse of power involving both the White House and the Nixon campaign committee. Every week, it seemed, there was a new, even more damaging revelation. White House "plumbers," under the direction of John Ehrlichman, had established illegal wiretaps, intercepted mail, and engaged in burglaries (including the attempt to steal files from Daniel Ellsberg's psychiatrist) in an effort to prevent leaks of sensitive or politically embarrassing information. Members of the reelection committee had solicited illegal contributions, "laundered" the money through accounts in Mexico, and used the funds to support a variety of "dirty tricks" against Democratic presidential candidates and other maneuvers to sabotage the campaigns of Nixon's opponents. And associates of the President had created devious opportunities for Nixon to increase his personal wealth, including several real-estate transactions and income-tax dodges of dubious legality.

The Watergate burglary was, therefore, only a small part of a larger pattern. But it was the break-in itself that became the major focus of public attention for nearly two years. There was never any conclusive evidence that the President had planned or approved the burglary in advance. John Dean and others testified that it had been the responsibility of then Attorney General Mitchell, who had hoped to plant electronic bugs in and steal copies of files from the Democratic offices. (Mitchell had subsequently resigned from the Justice Department to head the President's reelection committee; then, after the scandals began to break, he resigned from CRP as well, citing "personal problems.") But if there was no proof that Nixon had planned the break-in, there was mounting suspicion that he had been involved in what became known as the "cover-up"—illegal efforts to obstruct investigations of and to withhold information about the episode. Testimony before the Ervin Committee provided evidence of the complicity not only of Dean and Mitchell, but of Haldeman, Ehrlichman, and other key White House figures. As interest in the case grew to something approaching a national obsession, only one question remained: in the words of Senator Howard Baker of Tennessee, a member of the Ervin Committee, "What did the President know and when did he know it?"

Nixon, in the meantime, steadfastly denied knowing anything. One by one, he accepted the departure of those members of his administration implicated in the scandals: first a string of lower-level aides; then, with great reluctance, Haldeman and Ehrlichman, who resigned on the same day that Nixon dismissed John Dean. But the President himself remained adamant, declaring at one news conference: "I am not a crook."

There the matter might have rested had it not been for the disclosure during the Senate hearings of a White House taping system that had recorded virtually every conversation in the President's office during the period in question. All the various groups investigating the scandals sought access to the tapes; Nixon, pleading "executive privilege," refused to release them. A special prosecutor appointed by the President to handle the Watergate cases, Harvard law professor Archibald Cox, took Nixon to court in October 1973 in an effort to force him to relinquish the recordings. Nixon, now clearly growing desperate, fired Cox and suffered the humiliation of watching both Attorney General Elliot Richardson (who had succeeded Mitchell) and his deputy resign in protest. This "Saturday night massacre" made the President's predicament infinitely worse. Not only did public pressure force him to appoint a new special prosecutor, Texas attorney Leon Jaworski, who proved just as determined as Cox to subpoena the tapes; but the episode precipitated an investigation by the House of Representatives into the possibility of impeachment.

The Fall of Richard Nixon

Nixon's situation deteriorated further in the following months. Late in 1973, Vice President Spiro Agnew became embroiled in a scandal of his own when evidence surfaced that he had accepted bribes and kickbacks while serving as Governor of Maryland. In return for a Justice Department agreement not to press the case, Agnew pleaded *nolo contendere* (no contest) to a lesser charge, of income-tax evasion, and resigned from the government. With the controversial Agnew no

THE WATERGATE HEARINGS.   White House counsel John Dean, shown here taking the oath before the Ervin Committee, was the most important witness in the investigation. His testimony linked the Watergate cover-up directly to the President. Although Nixon's defenders attempted to discredit Dean's testimony by pointing to his own complicity in the scandals, the White House tapes later proved that Dean had been punctiliously and (from the President's point of view) devastatingly accurate. (*UPI*)

longer in line to succeed to the presidency, the prospect of removing Nixon from the White House suddenly became far less worrisome to Democrats. The new Vice President was House Minority Leader Gerald Ford, an amiable and popular Michigan Congressman whom Democrats considered more acceptable. The impeachment investigation quickly gathered pace. In April 1974, in an effort to head off further subpoenas of the tapes, the President released transcripts of a number of relevant conversations, claiming that they proved his innocence. Investigators and much of the public felt otherwise. Even these edited tapes seemed to suggest not only appalling ill will on Nixon's part but also his complicity in the cover-up.

In July, finally, the crisis came to a boil. First the Supreme Court ruled unanimously, in *United States* v. *Richard M. Nixon,* that the President must relinquish the tapes to Special Prosecutor Jaworski. Days later, the House Judiciary Committee voted to recommend three articles of impeachment, charging that Nixon had, first, obstructed justice in the Watergate cover-up; second, misused federal agencies to violate the rights of citizens; and third, defied the authority of Congress by refusing to deliver tapes and other materials subpoenaed by the committee. Even without additional evidence, Nixon might well have been impeached by the full House and convicted by the Senate. Early in August, however, he provided at last the "smoking gun," the concrete proof of his guilt that his defenders had long contended was missing from the case against him. Among the tapes that the Supreme Court compelled Nixon to relinquish were several that offered incontrovertible evidence of his involvement in the Watergate cover-up. Only days after the burglary, the recordings disclosed, the President had ordered the FBI to stop investigating the break-in. Impeachment and conviction now loomed inevitable.

For several days, Nixon brooded in the White House, on the verge, some claimed, of a mental breakdown. Many of the normal operations of the government ground to a virtual halt as the nation waited tensely for a resolution of the greatest constitutional crisis since Reconstruction. Finally, on August 8, 1974, Nixon addressed the nation and announced his resignation—the first President in American history ever to do so. At noon the next day, while Nixon and his family were flying west to their home in California, Gerald Ford took the oath of office as President.

THE TRANSFER OF POWER. Only moments before this picture was taken, Richard Nixon had delivered an emotional, tearful farewell to the White House staff as he prepared to fly home to California after resigning his office. Here, Gerald Ford—who would later that day take the oath of office as President—walks Nixon to a waiting helicopter on the White House lawn. Between the two Presidents are their wives, Betty Ford and Pat Nixon. (*UPI*)

Americans expressed both relief and exhilaration that, as the new President put it, "Our long national nightmare is over." They were relieved to be rid of Richard Nixon, who had lost virtually all of the wide popularity that had won him his landslide reelection victory only two years before. And they were exhilarated that, as some boasted, "the system had worked." A President had been held accountable to the law; and the transfer of power had been smooth and orderly. But the wave of good feeling could not obscure the deeper and more lasting damage of the Watergate crisis. In a society in which distrust of leaders and of institutions of authority was already widespread, the fall of Richard Nixon seemed to confirm the most cynical assumptions about the character of American public life. The depths of that cynicism were evident in the widespread belief, which public-opinion polls documented, that what Nixon had done, bad as it was, was little worse than what other Presidents had done undetected before him.

THE FORD PRESIDENCY

Gerald Ford inherited the presidency under unenviable circumstances. He faced both the public cynicism that had emerged from the Watergate scandals and the popular fears that were developing as a result of economic decay. His task, therefore, was to restore confidence in the presidency and to revive a stable prosperity in the nation at large. He enjoyed modest success in the first of these efforts but very little in the second.

Few Americans considered Ford a brilliant or an overwhelmingly skillful leader. (Jokes about presidential clumsiness and ineptitude abounded—some of them a result of Ford's apparent propensity for bumping his head on helicopter doors and falling on ski slopes, others because of his frequent verbal slips and political miscalculations.) But the public admired his candor and his obvious integrity. Polls showed that nearly three-quarters of the nation approved his performance during his first months in office.

At first, Ford worked largely through the White House staff and cabinet he had inherited from Richard Nixon. Slowly, however, he began to fill his administration with officials of his own choosing; and in the process he showed signs of trying to reclaim the middle ground in American politics by pulling together the two wings of the Republican party. To fill the vacant post of Vice President, he appointed former New York Governor Nelson Rockefeller, who had for years been the most conspicuous Republican liberal. In his cabinet, he sought to give representation to a far wider spectrum of the population than his predecessor; among his nominees were a university president, a college professor, a woman, and a black.

The President's effort to establish himself as a symbol of candor and integrity suffered a severe setback only a month after he took office when he suddenly granted Richard Nixon "a full, free, and absolute pardon . . . for all offenses against the United States" during his presidency. Ford explained that he was attempting to spare the nation the ordeal of years of litigation and to spare Nixon himself any further suffering. It was, he insisted, an act of "compassion," an effort "to firmly shut and seal this book." To much of the public, however, it was evidence of bad judgment at best and a secret deal with the former President at worst. Resentment of Nixon remained particularly high because the former President still refused to admit his guilt; many Americans believed that until he did, he should continue to suffer the consequences of his actions. Ford defended the pardon decision vigorously, even appearing before a congressional committee to explain it. But his action caused a decline in his popularity from which he never fully recovered.

Seeking International Stability

With the resignation of Nixon, the attention of the nation quickly returned to the more lasting problems confronting the United States, among them America's changing role in the world. At first, it seemed that the foreign policy of the Ford years would differ little from that of the Nixon administration. The new President retained Henry Kissinger as Secretary of State and continued the general policies of seeking rapprochement with China, détente with the Soviet Union, and stability in the Middle East. For a time, there were signs of progress in all these areas.

In particular, there appeared to be major progress in the effort to produce another arms control agreement with the Soviet Union. Ford met with Leonid Brezhnev late in 1974 at Vladivostok in Siberia and signed a new accord that was to serve as the basis for SALT II. The following summer, a European security conference in Helsinki, Finland, produced an agreement that seemed to advance détente even further. The Soviet Union and Western nations agreed, at last, to ratify the borders that had divided Europe since the end of World War II; and, particularly important in American eyes, the Russians accepted the so-called Basket Three clause, which pledged increased respect for human rights.

In the Middle East, in the meantime, the tireless efforts of Henry Kissinger were producing some important results. After months of shuttling back and forth between Cairo and Tel Aviv, Kissinger announced a major new accord by which Israel agreed to return large portions of the occupied Sinai to Egypt, and the two nations pledged not to resolve future differences by force. In China, finally, the death of Mao Tse-tung in 1976 brought to power a new, more moderate government, eager to expand its ties with the United States.

But these successes were, in the end, only minor triumphs within a larger setting of frustration. For the Ford years witnessed a series of major setbacks in America's efforts to create a stable "structure of peace." The new relationship with the Soviet Union was already showing signs of wear by 1975. Critics argued that the Vladivostok accords had set such high ceilings on the construction of armaments that they were virtually meaningless. Members of Congress were raising an increasing outcry over Soviet internal policies of repression toward dissidents and Jews. And there was growing concern as well about alleged Soviet interference in revolutions in Africa and Latin America. Ford and Kissinger continued to defend the idea of détente, but support for the policy was rapidly eroding.

Equally disturbing was what many Americans viewed as a pattern of defeats and embarrassments in all areas of the world. Vietnam and Cambodia fell to the

SUMMIT AT VLADIVOSTOK. Four of the architects of détente meet at Vladivostok in November 1974: from left to right, President Ford, Soviet party leader Leonid Brezhnev, Henry Kissinger, and Soviet Foreign Minister Andrei Gromyko. They agreed at Vladivostok on the general terms of SALT II—the arms control agreement that would become one of the first casualties when the spirit of détente collapsed five years later. (*UPI*)

communists in 1975, underscoring the futility of years of American effort. Arab nations that had once treated the United States with deference were now gleefully raising oil prices and threatening to reduce production. And Third World nations were becoming increasingly vocal in attacking the United States; the United Nations seemed at times to have become little more than a shooting gallery for those who wished to denounce American policies. Humiliation piled upon humiliation, until the government felt obliged to respond.

When members of the Cambodian Khmer Rouge (the communist organization now governing the nation) captured an unarmed American merchant ship, the *Mayaguez,* in the spring of 1975, the administration's patience seemed finally to snap. Ford sent in the Marines to rescue the crew, even though the captors had by then already agreed to release them. This display of American force appealed to the nation's wounded sense of pride; but the result was the unnecessary deaths of several dozen American soldiers. At about the same time, the new American ambassador to the United Nations, Daniel Patrick Moynihan, launched his own campaign to restore American pride. His shrill counterattack against Third World delegates and his strident denunciations of the United Nations itself won him great popularity (and, in 1976, a United States Senate seat from New York); but his confrontational tactics, critics charged, eroded further the nation's already troubled relationship with emerging areas and damaged the already declining viability of the United Nations.

Energy and Inflation

The Ford administration enjoyed little more success than its predecessor in devising a workable approach to the nation's economic problems. Rejecting the idea of wage and price controls, the President called instead for voluntary efforts to curb inflation. He appeared at one press conference wearing a large button with the word "WIN" emblazoned across it—a symbol, he said, of his new campaign to "Whip Inflation Now." The WIN campaign had no discernible effect upon the economy and invited wide public ridicule. Of somewhat greater impact but equally questionable purpose was Ford's pursuit of the now familiar path of tightening the money supply to curb inflation, and then struggling to deal with the recession that resulted. By supporting high interest rates, opposing increased federal spending (largely by use of presidential vetoes), and resisting pressures for a tax reduction, Ford helped produce in 1974 and 1975 the severest recession since the 1930s. Production declined more than 10 percent in the first months of 1975, and unemployment rose to nearly 9 percent of the labor force. There was a temporary abatement of inflation, which dropped briefly below 5 percent in 1976; but by then, the administration was already beginning to reverse its course and support new measures to stimulate the economy.

Complicating these problems was the expanding energy crisis. Despite the rising cost of imported oil, American dependence on OPEC supplies continued to grow. And the nation's use of energy remained the highest in the world. The United States was responsible for nearly a third of the world's energy consumption every year, and it was by 1976 importing almost a third of its energy supply from the OPEC countries. The Ford administration imposed a few new regulations to force energy conservation, but to little effect. More important to the President's strategy was the proposed deregulation of the petroleum industry, which would have allowed the oil companies to charge more for their energy so as to encourage increased production. The Democratic Congress resisted such proposals.

The Election of 1976

As the 1976 presidential election approached, Ford continued to enjoy a wide personal popularity, but his policies were coming under attack from both the right and the left. Conservative critics charged that the President was showing insufficient strength in dealing with America's declining position in the world. Liberals charged that he was attempting to fight inflation at the expense of the poor. In the Republican primary campaign, Ford faced a powerful challenge from former

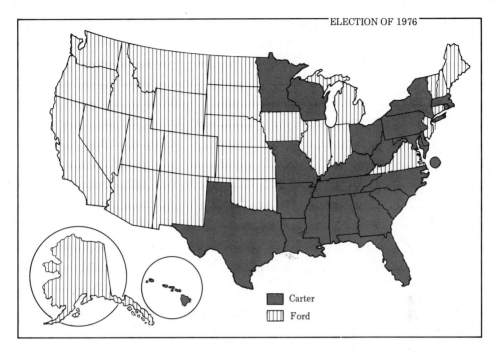

ELECTION OF 1976

Carter
Ford

California Governor Ronald Reagan, leader of the party's conservative wing. He only barely survived the assault, in part because he had agreed to abandon Nelson Rockefeller and choose another candidate, Senator Robert Dole of Kansas, for Vice President.

The Democrats, in the meantime, were experiencing problems of their own. The fiasco of 1972 had left the party numb and confused, and there was little agreement in 1976 about who could best appeal to the troubled electorate. From this disarray emerged a new candidate almost entirely unknown to the nation at large: Jimmy Carter, a former Governor of Georgia, who organized a brilliant primary campaign and appealed to the general unhappiness with government by promising to combat the "bloated bureaucracy." Capitalizing on the momentum of his early primary victories, Carter secured the Democratic nomination before most Americans had developed any very distinct impression of him. His campaign continued after the convention to emphasize "themes"—integrity, compassion, morality, and skepticism of government—rather than issues. And while the tentativeness of Carter's support became clear when his early, mammoth lead dwindled to almost nothing by election day, unhappiness with the economy and a general disenchantment with Ford enabled the Democrat to hold on for a narrow victory. Despite an unusually low voter turnout, which most observers believed was helpful to the Republicans, Carter emerged with 50 percent of the popular vote to Ford's 47.9 percent and 297 electoral votes to Ford's 240. Most Americans welcomed the prospect of a new political regime after eight years of Republican government characterized by frustration and crisis. But there were as yet few indications that Carter had any better ideas of how to deal with the mounting problems than the man he had defeated.

SUGGESTED READINGS

The changing economic climate is examined in Richard Barnet, *The Lean Years* (1980), a controversial study of scarcity, and in Joan Edelman Spero, *The Politics of International Economic Relations* (1977). J. C. Hurewitz (ed.), *Oil, the Arab-Israeli Dispute, and the Industrial World* (1976), examines the energy crisis. The Watergate affair has already spawned a vast literature. In addition to the general studies of the Nixon administration cited after Chapter 25 (of which the best is Jonathan Schell, *The Time of Illusion*), see Theodore H. White, *Breach of Faith* (1975), and Anthony Lukas, *Nightmare* (1976). Bob Woodward and Carl Bernstein, *All the President's Men* (1974), is a personal account by the reporters who first broke the Watergate story. *The Final Days* (1976), by the same authors, chronicles Nixon's last days in the White House. John Dean, *Blind Ambition* (1976), is the best of the many Watergate memoirs by members of the Nixon administration. Richard Cohen and Jules Witcover, *A Heartbeat Away* (1974), chronicles the fall of Spiro T. Agnew. A broad study of the expanding powers of the presidency, culminating in a review of Watergate, is Arthur M. Schlesinger, Jr., *The Imperial Presidency* (1973). The Ford administration has not spawned a large literature, but see Gerald Ter Horst, *Gerald Ford* (1975); Richard Reeves, *A Ford Not a Lincoln* (1976); and Ford's own memoirs, *A Time to Heal* (1979).

Twenty-Seven

America Seeks a New Beginning

America in the late 1970s was a nation in search of its future. But as to what that future could or should be there was little agreement. A decade before, the country had been engaged in a debate over how best to distribute the fruits of its abundant economy. Now it was facing serious questions about how to keep that economy from collapsing. In the 1960s, Americans had argued over how best to use their awesome international power. Now the nation wondered how much of that power still existed. The United States was, in short, mired in a bewildering search for answers to what was coming to be known as the "question of limits." Harsh new realities, both at home and in the world, were requiring major adjustments in virtually every area of American life. But as the decade ended, it remained unclear what those adjustments would be.

THE TRIALS OF JIMMY CARTER

It was Jimmy Carter's misfortune to assume the presidency at a moment when the nation faced problems of staggering complexity and difficulty. No leader could have avoided antagonizing much of the public under such inhospitable circumstances. But Carter made his predicament infinitely worse by a style of leadership that almost invited hostility and derision. And he left office in 1981 as one of the least popular Presidents of the century.

The Outsider in Washington

Carter had campaigned for the presidency as an "outsider," a representative of ordinary Americans who was, like them, deeply suspicious of the entrenched bureaucracies and complacent officials who had dominated American government for decades. He carried much of that suspiciousness with him to Washington. Surrounding himself in the White House with a group of close-knit associates from Georgia, he seemed deliberately to spurn assistance from more experienced political figures. His first weeks in office abounded with stories of insulting behavior by the White House staff toward leaders of Congress. Cordiality was soon restored to most administration actions, but the President continued throughout his term in office to be plagued by his own inexperience and that of members of his staff. When his popularity began to slide, as it soon did, those who repudiated him numbered among their greatest complaints that he displayed little competence as a leader.

In fact, Carter was among the most intelligent and quick-witted men ever to serve in the White House. His greatest problem was less one of ability than of vision. He seemed to have none. Supporters in 1976 had dismissed the "fuzziness" of Carter's campaign as an effective electoral strategy. In the following years, however, they began to question whether it had not also been a reflection of Carter's real view of public policy. Never in the course of his presidency did he succeed in conveying to the public any coherent sense of purpose or overall direction. While he took firm and often courageous stands on individual issues, he failed to demonstrate any recognition of how such issues were linked together. His was, as a disenchanted member of his own White House staff later described it, a peculiarly "passionless presidency."

In the absence of any coherent guiding principles (beyond a strong and openly expressed Christian piety), Carter seemed at times to be governing almost exclusively through the use of symbols. On inauguration day, he spurned the traditional limousine and walked with his family down Pennsylvania Avenue from the Capitol to the White House. In the following months, he missed no opportunity to demonstrate his "closeness" to the people. To explain a new policy, he arranged a televised "fireside chat"; dressed informally in a cardigan sweater, the President spoke to the nation while seated in a wing chair beside a blazing fire (which burned out in the course of the broadcast). On several occasions, he visited "average" communities for "town meetings" with common citizens. And from time to time he participated in radio programs during which members of the public could telephone the White House and speak directly with the President. For a while, such tactics attracted wide popular approval. Gradually, however, much of the public began to look skeptically upon the symbols, wondering if they were not serving as a substitute for policy.

Doubts about Carter's leadership grew particularly strong in response to a widespread perception that he was subordinating public policy to immediate political interests. His was the first administration to make extensive, almost daily use of public-opinion polls in the formulation of decisions. And the result, it often

THE CARTER SMILE. Jimmy Carter's toothy smile became a trademark of his successful 1976 campaign for the presidency. So too did his conspicuous informality. Once in office, he attempted to maintain a "folksy" image by such symbolic gestures as carrying his own luggage on and off airplanes, refusing to use limousines, and forbidding the playing of "Hail to the Chief" within the White House. (*Dennis Brack/Black Star*)

seemed, was a disturbing lack of consistency in direction, a tendency, as some critics put it, for Carter to "lurch from crisis to crisis." This perceived lack of purpose helped as well to make the President the target of criticism from almost every quarter. No political faction could be certain that Carter was its ally. Liberals, who had believed him in 1976 to be an authentic "populist," soon began to complain that he was more conservative than his Republican predecessors. Conservatives, who had taken heart at Carter's antigovernment campaign rhetoric, expressed scorn for his failure adequately to "tame" the federal bureaucracy. Even when Carter adopted a policy to the liking of a particular group, there was always an uneasy sense that the policy might soon be abandoned if political pressures dictated a different approach. Ultimately the President, who had won election by a narrow margin to begin with, lost almost all leverage in his dealings with Congress. So low was his popularity with the public through most of his term that few legislators feared the political costs of opposing him.

In spite of these problems, Carter did achieve a measure of success in his effort to reform and reorganize the federal government. As Governor of Georgia, he had taken great pride in his creation of a more rationally organized bureaucracy. He attempted to do the same in Washington. He instituted a series of important reforms in the civil service, in an effort to make permanent government employees more responsive to the needs of the public and to give administrators more control over their staffs. He reshuffled many of the offices and agencies that had been springing up, often chaotically, for nearly two decades; and he created two new executive departments: the Department of Energy and the Department of Education. He also sponsored a reform of the Social Security System that provided it with at least a temporary reprieve from bankruptcy.

In other areas, Carter made genuine efforts to pursue reform, only to fall victim to congressional opposition. He proposed a major restructuring of the federal welfare system during his first year in office, only to see it die quietly in Congress. He introduced measures to reform the tax system, one of his most conspicuous campaign promises, but proved powerless to keep them from being gutted by special interest groups fighting to preserve or expand their favored status. The President's lack of political clout was, of course, one reason for these failures. So was his tendency to cave in to political pressures without serious resistance. But there is room for doubt as to whether any leader, working in the confused political climate in which Carter was operating, could have moved more rapidly.

Energy and the Economy

Like his two immediate predecessors, Carter was from the beginning of his administration required to devote the bulk of his domestic effort to the problems of the economy, which were becoming increasingly linked to the problems of energy. And like Nixon and Ford before him, Carter followed the familiar pattern of fighting inflation through tight money and fighting recession through economic stimulants. In his case, however, the order was reversed. Entering office in the midst of a severe recession, Carter moved first to reduce unemployment through an increase in public spending for public works and public services and a substantial cut in federal taxes. Unemployment soon began to decline—from nearly 8 percent late in 1976 to only slightly above 5 percent by the end of 1978. But inflation, predictably, soared. The Ford administration had left behind an inflation rate of slightly under 5 percent. In 1977, it rose to 7 percent, and in 1978 to nearly 10 percent. During Carter's last two years in office, things grew even worse, with inflation averaging well over 10 percent ("double-digit inflation," it began to be called) and at one point in 1980 reaching as high as 18 percent.

Carter responded in now traditional fashion. Appointing first G. William Miller and then Paul Volcker, conservative economists both, to head the Federal Reserve Board, he ensured a policy of high interest rates and reduced currency supplies. By 1980, interest rates had risen to the highest levels in American history, for a time exceeding 20 percent. He began to cut back on government spending, vetoing some of the same public works and welfare proposals he had supported during his first year in office. He reduced and delayed the tax reductions he had earlier proposed. And although he introduced nothing as laughable as Gerald Ford's WIN program, he too created a voluntary and generally ineffective system of wage–price "restraint," to be administered through the Council on Wage and Price Stability. Its director, Alfred Kahn, became an energetic and articulate spokesman for fiscal caution, helping to elevate public awareness of the inflation problem. But neither Kahn's efforts nor any other aspects of the administration's policy succeeded in stopping the inflationary spiral. By 1980, the President was making frantic efforts to balance the federal budget. Some economists claimed that a balanced budget was a prerequisite to price stability, others that it would only marginally reduce inflation. But the argument was never resolved because the President never managed to eliminate the deficits. The tight money policy, in the meantime, was by 1980 pushing the economy into another severe recession.

Inextricably tied to the problem of inflation was the problem of energy, which grew steadily more troublesome in the course of the Carter years. One of the President's first acts was to present to the public what he called a "comprehensive energy program," whose success, he insisted, was vital to the nation's future. Solving the energy problem, he claimed (in words borrowed from William James), was "the moral equivalent of war." The specific features of the Carter plan were less dramatic than the rhetoric. Central to the program was a major commitment to energy conservation, which most Democrats applauded. But the policy of encouraging conservation through a system of tax levies, tax incentives, and rebates antagonized countless interest groups. When Congress finally passed the President's energy bill in August 1978, little was left of the original proposals.

A particularly fierce battle had raged over the issue of deregulating the price of natural gas and domestic oil reserves. Carter urged dropping regulations so as to increase prices, which would, he claimed, both encourage conservation and increase production. But he insisted upon coupling deregulation with a "windfall profits tax" on the oil and gas companies that many conservatives opposed. Liberals, in the meantime, wanted no price increases at all, fearful of the effect on the poor. They urged retention of controls. The final bill called for a gradual phasing out of many regulations, to be accompanied by a windfall profits tax far weaker than the President had requested.

In the summer of 1979, the energy battle moved into a new and more desperate phase. Increasing instability in the Middle East produced a second major fuel shortage, forcing American motorists to wait in long gasoline lines once again and creating problems for businesses, industries, and homeowners. In the midst of the crisis, OPEC announced another major price increase, clouding the economic picture still further. Faced with increasing pressure to act (and with public-opinion polls showing his approval rating at a dismal 26 percent, lower than Richard Nixon in his worst moments), Carter went to the presidential retreat Camp David in the Maryland mountains and invited a string of visitors to advise him—not only on a new energy program but on the revitalization of his administration.

Ten days later, he emerged to deliver a remarkable television address. Speaking with what was, for him, unusual fervor, the President complained of a "crisis of the American spirit" and a "national malaise" that had reduced the nation to confusion and despair. As a solution, he proposed a major new commitment to a "positive" energy program. His new proposals included the expansion and strengthening of some of his earlier ones: greater tax incentives for conservation and production, punitive taxes on "gas-guzzling" automobiles, increased use of coal, and research into solar and wind power. The heart of the program, however, was a major federal commitment to the development of new "synthetic fuels." Carter requested Congress to establish a federal corporation with a budget of nearly $90 billion to supervise the creation of the new industry. A scaled-down version of the President's proposals passed the Congress in 1980, but widespread doubts remained about the nation's energy future.

Human Rights and National Interests

Among Jimmy Carter's most fervent campaign promises was a pledge to build a new basis for American foreign policy, one in which the defense of "human rights" would replace the pursuit of "selfish interests" as the cornerstone of America's role in the world. Rhetorically, at least, Carter maintained that commitment during his first months in office, speaking out sharply and often about violations of human rights in many countries (including, most prominently, the Soviet Union) and establishing an Office of Human Rights in the State Department.

Beyond the general commitment to establishing a new "tone" for American foreign policy, the Carter administration focused on several areas of particular concern—the same areas, essentially, that had been the focus of the Kissinger era. (As efforts on behalf of these specific goals began to conflict at numerous points with the emphasis on human rights, the President quietly retreated from his concern with the rights issue.) Carter's first major diplomatic accomplishment was the completion of negotiations on a pair of treaties that would turn over control of the Panama Canal to the government of Panama. In exchange for Panamanian

A MEETING OF OPEC. Members of the Organization of Petroleum Exporting Countries gather in 1976 for one of their frequent meetings to determine a joint strategy on prices and production. The concerted strategy of OPEC succeeded in driving the world price of oil upward with startling rapidity after 1974. Rising fuel costs became one of the major causes of world inflation. (*UPI*)

agreements to maintain the neutrality of the canal, the United States would gradually withdraw most of its troops and supervisory personnel from the Canal Zone, which it had controlled since Theodore Roosevelt's bold maneuvers at the beginning of the century. Domestic opposition to the treaties was intense, inflamed by conservative critics who viewed the new arrangements as part of a general retreat from international power. Such arguments were not without foundation. Carter and his predecessors had supported relinquishing the canal because they recognized that in Panama, as elsewhere, the United States could no longer expect passive acceptance of its wishes. In the face of growing Third World nationalism, the sensible policy, the supporters of the treaties argued, was to remove the most conspicuous irritants. Control of the canal by the United States had become the source of deep resentment in Central America and was one such irritant. Relinquishing the canal was thus the best way to improve relations with the region and avoid the possibility of years of violence. After an acrimonious debate, the Senate ratified the treaties by a vote of 68 to 32, marshaling only one vote more than the necessary two-thirds.

Far less controversial, within the United States at least, was Carter's dramatic success in arranging a peace treaty between Egypt and Israel—the crowning diplomatic accomplishment of his presidency. Inheriting from Henry Kissinger a negotiating process that seemed hopelessly stalled, Carter tried at first to arouse support for a "comprehensive" settlement of the Middle Eastern crisis through an international conference in Geneva. The response from the nations involved was not heartening. It fell to Egyptian President Anwar Sadat and Israeli Prime Minister Menachem Begin, therefore, to initiate the first great breakthrough. In November 1977, accepting a formal invitation from Begin, Sadat flew to the Israeli capital of Tel Aviv for a dramatic state visit, declaring in the course of it that Egypt was now willing to accept the state of Israel as a legitimate political entity. With that, the greatest single obstacle to peace between the two nations —the obstacle that had frustrated nearly thirty years of diplomatic efforts—was removed.

There remained, however, the tortuous task of translating these good feelings into a concrete treaty of peace. When talks between Israeli and Egyptian negotiators stalled, Carter invited Sadat and Begin to a summit conference at Camp David in September 1978, holding them there for two weeks while he, Secretary of State Cyrus Vance, and others mediated the disputes between them. On September 17, Carter escorted the two leaders into the White House to announce agreement on a "framework" for an Egyptian–Israeli peace treaty. Final agreement, the two sides promised, would be completed within three months.

In the months that followed, the euphoria of the Camp David summit faded as new obstacles to the treaty seemed to emerge almost daily, a result in large part of the insistence of the Begin government that Israel continue to establish new settlements in the disputed territory of the West Bank of the Jordan River (which Israel had seized during the 1967 war and which some Palestinian Arabs hoped might become a new homeland for them). Only after Carter himself had intervened again, persuading Sadat to agree to a postponement of resolution of the sensitive Palestinian refugee issue, did the negotiations finally bear fruit. On March 26, 1979, Begin and Sadat returned together to the White House to sign a formal peace treaty between their two nations. Jimmy Carter, whose personal diplomacy had been largely responsible for the moment, looked on proudly.

The Middle East agreement was a tremendous personal triumph for the President. It was also, however, a symbol of America's new problems in the world; and it became, ultimately, the source of still further difficulties. Like his predecessors, Carter was acutely aware of how desperately dependent the United States had become on the resources of the Middle East. Another Arab–Israeli war, accompanied by another oil embargo, could well destroy the American economy. Carter's efforts to produce a settlement were an expression, in some respects, of American strength. But they were also a sign of American weakness, for peace in the Middle East was as important to the United States as it was to the nations of the region. Nor was the treaty a final solution to the problems of the area. Other Arab nations reacted with hostility—not only toward Egypt and Israel but toward the United States as well. And when negotiations to settle the Palestinian question foundered in ensuing months on the rock of Israeli intransigence, tensions in the region escalated further.

THE PEACEMAKERS. The crowning diplomatic accomplishment of Jimmy Carter's presidency was the signing of the Egyptian–Israeli peace treaty on March 26, 1979. Here, Carter stands on the White House lawn shortly before the signing ceremony, flanked by Egyptian President Anwar Sadat and Israeli Prime Minister Menachem Begin. (*UPI*)

Great Power Diplomacy

In the meantime, Carter attempted to continue progress toward improving relations with China and the Soviet Union and toward completing a new arms control agreement. Although he did not share Kissinger's belief in the importance of creating a new great power balance, he did share the concerns of his predecessors for reducing international tensions and dealing more realistically with old adversaries.

The new relationship with China progressed rapidly during 1978, as Chinese leader Teng Hsio-ping began concerted efforts to change the rigid policies of the late Mao Tse-tung and turn his nation toward the outside world. In particular, Teng wanted at least indirect support from the West for China's increasingly tense "cold war" with the Soviet Union. Carter responded eagerly to Teng's overtures; and on December 15, 1978, Washington and Peking issued a joint communiqué announcing the restoration of formal diplomatic relations between the two nations on January 1, 1979. Carter faced strong domestic conservative opposition to the agreement, largely because it required the United States to break relations and abandon its alliance with the Nationalist regime on Taiwan. Once again, critics charged, the United States was displaying weakness and unreliability in its foreign policy. But Carter responded to such criticisms much as he had responded to attacks on the canal treaties, claiming that the new policy represented an intelligent recognition of international realities. In March 1979, America and China exchanged ambassadors, within weeks of Teng Hsio-ping having made a highly publicized visit to the United States.

Only a few months later, Carter traveled to Vienna to meet with a visibly ailing Leonid Brezhnev to complete the final steps in the drafting of the new SALT II arms control agreement. Lower-level negotiators had been working for months to resolve remaining differences; and in Vienna, the Soviet and American leaders took the final step—settling the last details, signing the documents, and clasping each other in a warm embrace. The treaty set new limits on the number of long-range missiles, bombers, and nuclear warheads on each side—limits that some critics denounced as far too high to constitute meaningful disarmament, but that supporters claimed marked an important first step in limiting the construction of new weapons. Future negotiations, the two sides agreed, would work toward actually reducing the existing arsenals. Like SALT I, the new treaty represented no major breakthrough and would, if ratified, limit the future arms race only slightly, if at all. Nevertheless, it attracted the support of most Democratic liberals and most supporters of détente.

Almost immediately, however, SALT II met with fierce conservative opposition. A powerful group of Senate Republicans denounced the treaty as excessively favorable to the Soviet Union, citing in particular provisions that restricted development of the American cruise missile while leaving the Soviets free to proceed with their new backfire bomber. Conservative critics took little comfort from Brezhnev's pledge to limit the rate of production of the new aircraft. Others denounced concessions permitting increases in certain Soviet missile systems that would, some charged, increase an already large Russian advantage in that area. Central to the arguments of the opposition, however, was a larger issue: a fundamental distrust of the Soviet Union that nearly a decade of détente had failed to destroy. Pointing to Soviet activities in Third World countries in Africa, to increasing Russian influence among the radical governments of the Middle East, and to allegations of Soviet support of international terrorism, conservatives argued that ratification of SALT II would represent an unjustifiable endorsement of aggression and subversion. By the fall of 1979, with the Senate scheduled to begin debate over the treaty shortly, the outlook for ratification was already grim. Events in the ensuing months would provide the final blow—both to the treaty and to the larger framework of détente.

CONFUSION AND CONSERVATISM

The years of crisis and turmoil in the 1960s took their toll on the nation's liberal assumptions. America in the 1970s was a society turning increasingly conservative —partly in response to the perceived failures of liberal reform, partly as a defensive reaction against disorder and uncertainty. Yet the new conservatism, unlike earlier versions, was not an expression of confidence in old truths. It was, rather, a reflection of bewilderment—of a search for stable values that would provide a rudder for an aimless society.

The New Demography

The changing tone of American society was in part a result of the changing profile of the American population. After decades of steady growth, the nation's birth rate was in the 1970s beginning to decline, leading some to predict a leveling off of the population by the end of the century. A more immediate result was a significant increase in the proportion of elderly citizens. More than 10 percent of the population in 1980 was over sixty-five years old, as compared with 8 percent a decade before. The median age was steadily rising. In the 1960s, a fascination with youth had dominated American culture. In the 1970s, society was slowly beginning to turn a greater share of its attention to older citizens. To a great extent, it had no choice. The cost, both to private institutions and to the government, of pensions for the elderly had become a staggering burden. The Social Security System, in particular, was by the late 1970s faced with imminent bankruptcy, averted temporarily only by a major increase in the payroll tax that supported the system.

Even more striking was the change in the geographic distribution of the American population. The most dramatic demographic phenomenon of the 1970s was the rise of the "Sunbelt" or "southern rim"—the Southeast, the Southwest, and above all California, which became the nation's most populous state in 1964 and continued to grow in the years that followed. By the end of the 1970s, the population of the Sunbelt had risen to exceed that of the industrial regions of the North and East, which were experiencing not only a relative but in many cases an absolute decline in their numbers. In addition to shifting the nation's economic focus from one region to another, the rise of the Sunbelt was, for the moment at least, producing a change in the political climate. The states of the Sunbelt had traditionally been far more conservative than those of many other regions of the country: the South in part because of the race issue, the West because of the survival of the frontier ethic. But the changes in both areas during the 1960s and 1970s seemed if anything to strengthen that conservatism. The boom mentality of the region conflicted sharply with the concerns of the Northeast, which remained far more committed to social programs and far more interested in controls on heedless economic growth than the Sunbelt.

The nation's major cities in the 1970s continued to confront the specter of social and financial decay. There were signs, it was true, that many members of the middle class were growing disillusioned with the suburbs—which were developing urban problems of their own—and were moving back into urban centers. But the most pressing reality of most major cities remained the burden of caring for the urban poor. New York, the nation's largest city, barely averted bankruptcy in 1975. It was a victim in part of financial mismanagement; but even more, it suffered from a shrinking tax base and the increased costs of the social services it was obliged to provide for its poor. Cleveland, Ohio, became the first major metropolis in the nation to go into receivership, several years later. The crusading liberal leaders of the 1960s—men such as New York Mayor John Lindsay—had no place in the cities of the 1970s. Successful urban politicians were now far more likely to be men such as Edward Koch, a later mayor of New York, who subordinated concern for the poor to a commitment to fiscal stability.

While city governments struggled with the added strains on their budgets, urban dwellers struggled with a gradual decay of services and a rise in social disorder. Urban public schools suffered an increase in violence, drug addiction, and truancy among their students. High-school graduates in some major cities were found to be virtually illiterate. City streets became zones of increasing danger. The rate of violent crime nearly quadrupled between 1960 and 1980. Instead of the centers of commerce and industry they had once been, many cities were becoming little more than repositories for the nation's poor—and thus increasingly prey to violence and decay.

The most important feature of the American population in the 1970s, however, was its sheer size. The United States suffered far less from overpopulation than much of the rest of the world; but it was, nevertheless, becoming an increasingly crowded society. The American population of over 220 million in 1980 was twice as large as the population of sixty years before. There had been many factors contributing to the nation's problems; but the simple reality of more Americans competing for jobs, housing, education, wealth, food, and other finite resources —competing not only with one another but with the rest of the world—may have been the most important cause of frustration and disorder.

The New Religion and the New Right

Throughout human history, a constant feature of rapidly changing societies has been the search for stability, the quest for a haven from uncertainty and confusion. Intellectuals such as Ralph Waldo Emerson might welcome periods of revolution as exciting opportunities for progress and rebirth. But the more common reaction in most societies is a desire to escape from disorder. So it was in the United States as its people faced the new realities of a troubled world. Americans flocked in growing numbers to movements and creeds that seemed to offer refuge from the perils of modern life.

Above all, it seemed, they flocked to religion. Many social critics had in the 1960s predicted the virtual extinction of religious influence in American life. *Time* magazine had reflected such assumptions in 1966 with a celebrated cover emblazoned with the question "Is God Dead?" Nevertheless, America in the 1970s entered the throes of a major religious revival, the most powerful since the Second Great Awakening of the early nineteenth century.

Some of the new religious enthusiasm found expression in the rise of various cults and pseudofaiths: the Church of Scientology; the Unification Church of the Reverend Sun Myung Moon; even the tragic People's Temple, whose members committed mass suicide in their jungle retreat in Guyana in 1978. But the most important impulse of the revival of religion was the rise of evangelical Christianity. It was not a sudden phenomenon. It had, in fact, been in progress at least since the 1950s, when the Reverend Billy Graham had begun to attract a huge national following for his energetic revivalism. For many years, however, the new religion had gone unnoted by much of the press and the media, which had dismissed it as a limited, provincial phenomenon. By the 1970s, they could no longer do so. More than 70 million Americans now described themselves as "born-again" Christians—men and women who had established a "direct personal relationship with Jesus." Christian evangelicals owned their own newspapers, magazines, radio stations, and television networks. They operated their own schools and universities. They occupied positions of eminence in the worlds of entertainment and professional sports. And one of their number occupied the White House itself— Jimmy Carter, who during the 1976 campaign, had talked proudly of his own "conversion experience" and who continued openly to proclaim his "born-again" Christian faith during his years in office.

For Jimmy Carter, evangelical Christianity had served as a prod to social commitment and public service; it had formed the basis for his commitment to racial and economic justice and to world peace. To many others, the message of the new religion was very different—but no less political. Christian revivalism had by the 1970s become closely tied to a deep political and social conservatism. Such organizations as the Reverend Jerry Falwell's "Moral Majority" expressed the dominant political sentiments of the evangelicals. They opposed federal interference in local affairs, denounced abortion, defended unrestricted free enterprise, and supported a strong American posture in the world. Some even reopened issues that had long seemed closed. For example, many "born-again" Christians questioned the scientific doctrine of evolution and urged the teaching in schools of the biblical story of creation instead. Others drew criticism from defenders of civil liberties by demanding stricter censorship of television, movies, and printed materials.

Defenders of the new religion praised it for providing a "moral compass" for many troubled Americans; and they cited its success in redeeming young people, in particular, from crime, drug addiction, and despair. Critics charged that evangelical Christianity too often produced among its members a dogmatic self-righteousness and a dangerous moral absolutism. The religious revival, they warned, threatened to create a climate of oppressive political and social intolerance.

Closely tied to the new religion was a new political right, many of whose members were themselves evangelical Christians. The New Right drew heavily on the conservative dogmas of earlier eras; but in addition to doctrinal enthusiasm, it displayed a remarkable organizing zeal. While earlier right-wing political groups, such as the John Birch Society, had stumbled along in administrative chaos, the new organizations marshaled their influence with awesome skill and effectiveness. Mass mailing campaigns of staggering size raised great sums of money to support conservative efforts. The National Conservative Political Action Committee, for example, spent millions of dollars in support of its chosen political candidates in

1980 and claimed credit for the defeat of many liberal Senators and Congressmen. Leaders of the New Right issued stern warnings to those it had helped to elect: public officials must hew to strict standards of conservative political orthodoxy or risk retribution.

The Changing Left

The New Left of the 1960s did not disappear after the end of the war in Vietnam, but it faded rapidly as an important influence in American political life. Students who had fought in its battles grew up, left school, and entered conventional careers. Radical leaders, disillusioned by the unresponsiveness of American society to their demands, resignedly gave up the struggle and chose instead to work "within the system." Although Marxist critiques continued to flourish in academic

"NO NUKES."   Demonstrators lie down in front of the Pacific Gas and Electric building in San Francisco to protest the company's use of nuclear power to generate electricity. The antinuclear movement became the most widespread popular protest since the end of the war in Vietnam, and it illustrated the changing nature of dissident politics in the 1970s. (*UPI*)

circles, to much of the public they now appeared dated and irrelevant. Yet a left of sorts did survive through the 1970s, giving evidence in the process of how greatly the nation's political climate had changed. Instead of promoting radical change, activists fought instead for preservation and restraint.

Nothing better symbolized the concerns of the changing left than its commitment to protection of the environment. Where 1960s activists had rallied to protest racism, poverty, and war, their 1970s counterparts fought to save the wilderness, protect endangered species, and limit reckless economic development. Above all, they struggled against the expanding use of nuclear power plants to meet the nation's energy needs. Well-organized and often militant antinuclear groups emerged in almost every region of the country to oppose new plant construction and to warn of the dangers of existing facilities. A frightening accident in 1979 at a nuclear power plant on Three Mile Island in Pennsylvania helped to intensify their efforts. In 1980, more than 40 percent of the citizens of Maine voted to support a referendum calling for an immediate shutdown of that state's "Yankee" nuclear power plant. The militant Clamshell Alliance continued to obstruct and bedevil efforts to build a similar plant in Seabrook, New Hampshire, and antinuclear groups in other areas of the country used both public demonstrations and court challenges to advance their cause.

The concern for the environment, the fear of nuclear power—both were reflections of a far more fundamental assumption of the post-Vietnam left. In a sharp break from the nation's long commitment to growth and progress, the new dissidents argued that only by limiting growth and curbing traditional forms of progress could society hope to survive. Industrial society had, they claimed, created a desperate threat to the planet's ecological balance. Continued growth would place intolerable strains on the world's finite resources. Some of these critics of the "idea of progress" expressed a gloomy resignation, urging a lowering of social expectations and foreseeing an inevitable deterioration in the quality of life. It was not surprising, perhaps, that they evoked increasing hostility from conservative Americans seeking to restore the nation's fading glory. Other advocates of restraint believed that change did not require decline: human beings could live more comfortably and more happily if they simply learned to respect the limits imposed upon them by their environment.

Turning Inward

For many Americans, however, the answer to the dilemmas of living in uncertain times lay not in religion or politics but in the cultivation of the self. No aspect of the era aroused more comment than this tendency of individuals to "turn inward," that is, to replace social concerns with personal ones. Journalist Tom Wolfe christened the 1970s "The 'Me' Decade" in a famous 1976 magazine article; historian Christopher Lasch wrote of *The Culture of Narcissism* in a successful 1978 book. Many people disputed their judgments of the phenomenon, but few questioned its existence.

Among affluent Americans, at least, there began to emerge a pervasive concern with personal "life styles." Newspapers introduced special sections devoted to such newly popular pursuits as gourmet cooking, physical fitness, and home decorating. Magazines specialized in helping Americans achieve personal fulfillment through a satisfying life style; among the new periodicals was one with the frank and revealing title *Self*. Along with the interest in life style came a growing concern for self-expression—for "getting in touch with one's feelings." Such pseudoscientific theories as est, Esalen, and Lifespring encouraged their followers to drop traditional social inhibitions against displaying anger, hatred, or jealousy. The key to emotional stability, they claimed, was the open expression of personal emotions. Nor did economic life remain immune from the new spirit. Books such as Robert Ringer's *Looking Out for Number One* (1978) became national best sellers by urging individuals to behave selfishly in the marketplace.

The commitment to self-cultivation and individual fulfillment was not new in American life, of course. It had roots in the "self-made man" ethos of the turn of the century, in the creed of "Lost Generation" intellectuals of the 1920s, in the philosophy of the "beats" of the 1950s, and in the counterculture of the 1960s. But by the 1970s, the impulse seemed to be taking a new and, in the eyes of some observers, alarming form: emphasizing less the idea of personal liberation than the drive for a bland, elitist conformity; placing less value on creative accomplishment than on material comfort. Defenders of the phenomenon described it as the expression of healthy self-respect. Critics denounced it as a defensive reaction to the ominous and bewildering course of contemporary society. It was, they claimed, a retreat from social commitment born of a thinly concealed sense of hopelessness.

"DOONESBURY" ON THE "ME DECADE."   Garry Trudeau launched his celebrated comic strip, "Doonesbury," in the *Yale Daily News* when he was a college student in the late 1960s. In the years that followed, the strip served as one of the most popular and perceptive voices of the generation that came of age during the racial crisis and the war in Vietnam. Here, Trudeau lampoons the middle-class obsession with life styles in the late 1970s. (*Universal Press Syndicate*)

THE YEAR OF THE HOSTAGES

The accumulated frustrations of more than a decade seemed to culminate in the events of the last months of 1979 and the full year that followed. Not since 1968 had the United States experienced such a sense of cascading crisis. If the events of 1979 and 1980 were not as wrenching and disruptive as those of twelve years before, they were at least equally debilitating to the nation's pride and self-confidence. Both at home and abroad, it seemed, America was facing evidence of accelerating decline.

Crisis in Iran

For more than thirty years, the United States had provided political support and, more recently, massive military assistance to the government of the Shah of Iran, depending on that nation as a bulwark against Soviet expansion in the Middle East. By 1979, however, the Shah was in deep trouble with his own people, reaping the harvest of years of unpopular policies. Iranians resented the repressive, authoritarian tactics through which the Shah had maintained his autocratic rule. The SAVAK, the monarch's secret police, which had long made use of torture and arbitrary imprisonment to stifle dissent, aroused particular hatred. At the same time, the Shah was earning the animosity of the Islamic clergy through his rapid efforts to modernize and Westernize his fundamentalist society. The combination of resentments produced a powerful revolutionary movement; and in January 1979, finally, the Shah fled the country for an uncertain exile.

The United States, which had supported the Shah unswervingly until very near the end, was caught unawares by his fall from power. The Carter administration was even less aware, apparently, of the deep resentments that the Iranian people continued to harbor toward America, which had become a hated symbol of Western intrusion into their society. The President made cautious efforts in the first months after the Shah's abdication to establish cordial relations with the succession of increasingly militant regimes that followed. By late 1979, however, such efforts were beginning to appear futile. Not only did revolutionary chaos in the nation make any normal relationships impossible, but what power there was in Iran resided with a zealous religious leader, the Ayatollah Ruhollah Khomeini, whose hatred of the West in general and the United States in particular was deep, abiding, and intense.

The Shah spent most of his first months of exile living in Mexico, having been quietly informed that the American government would not welcome his presence in the United States. Late in October, however, the President succumbed to the urgings of Henry Kissinger, David Rockefeller, and other friends of the Shah and admitted the monarch to New York, where he entered a hospital for treatment of cancer. Days later, on November 4, 1979, an armed mob invaded the American embassy in Teheran, seized the diplomats and military personnel inside, and held them as hostages—demanding the return of the Shah to Iran in exchange for their freedom. Although the militants released a few of the hostages within days, fifty-three Americans remained prisoners in the embassy.

American citizens had been held hostage by foreign governments in the past. In 1968, eighty-two members of the crew of the *Pueblo,* a navy intelligence-gathering ship, were captured and held prisoner by the government of North Korea. It took eleven months for the Johnson administration to win their release, during which time the American public all but forgot about the problem. But the reaction of the nation to the events in Teheran was radically different. Coming after years of what Americans considered international humiliations and defeats, the hostage seizure released a surprising well of anger and emotion. President Carter, facing a difficult reelection battle, did his best to sustain the sense of crisis. But even without his efforts, it was clear, the American people would have reacted strongly. Television newscasts relayed daily pictures of angry anti-American mobs outside the American embassy, the faces of many demonstrators contorted with hatred as they chanted such slogans as "Death to America" and "Death to Carter." Contemptuous statements by the militants guarding the hostages that "The U.S. can do nothing" further inflamed American passions. The nation responded not only with anger but with remarkable displays of emotional patriotism. The surprising victory of the United States Olympic hockey team, which defeated a highly favored Soviet squad and won the gold medal at the 1980 winter Olympics in upstate New York, produced a national celebration of remarkable fervor. It was, clearly, an expression of far more than simple enthusiasm about hockey.

Russia and Afghanistan

Only weeks after the hostage seizure, the nation suffered another dispiriting shock when it learned that Soviet troops had invaded Afghanistan, the mountainous nation lying between Russia and Iran. The Soviet Union had, in fact, been a power in Afghanistan for years, and the dominant force since April 1978, when a coup had established a Marxist government there with close ties to the Kremlin. The invasion, many Soviet experts argued, was Moscow's response to the failure of the new Afghan government to restore stability to the nation; the Soviets were particularly concerned about the activities of Islamic insurgents, whose presence raised the possibility of a fundamentalist revolution in Afghanistan (and perhaps even in Islamic areas of the Soviet Union itself) similar to the one in progress in Iran. But while some observers claimed that the Soviet invasion was simply a Russian attempt to secure the status quo, others—most notably the President—viewed the situation differently. The invasion of Afghanistan, Carter claimed, was a Russian "stepping stone to their possible control over much of the world's oil supplies." It was also the "gravest threat to world peace since World War II." Dire warnings began issuing from the White House about the possibility of a Soviet attack on Iran or other Middle Eastern nations.

TEHERAN, 1979. Iranian militants stand atop the wall surrounding the United States embassy and burn an American flag for the benefit of thousands of demonstrators on the street below. Inside the embassy, American diplomats and soldiers are held hostage in an effort to compel the United States to return the deposed Shah to Iran. Fifty-two of the hostages remained in captivity for fourteen months, until January 20, 1981. (*UPI*)

Whatever the reasons for the Soviet invasion, the situation in Afghanistan became the final blow to the already badly weakened structure of détente. Carter angrily imposed a series of economic sanctions on the Russians, called for an American boycott of the 1980 summer Olympic Games in Moscow, and announced the withdrawal of SALT II from Senate consideration. He also announced a new American policy—what some called the "Carter Doctrine"—by which the United States pledged to oppose, by force if necessary, any further aggression in the Persian Gulf. Critics reacted contemptuously, asserting that the United States lacked the military capacity to defend the Persian Gulf from a Soviet invasion, even if such an invasion were in the offing. But the President persevered, resolved it seemed, to reassert American determination after so many humiliating international setbacks.

The Campaign of 1980

By the time of the crises in Iran and Afghanistan, Jimmy Carter was in desperate political trouble. His standing in popularity polls was lower than that of any President in history. His economic policies were in shambles. Senator Edward Kennedy, one of the most magnetic figures in the Democratic party, was preparing to challenge him in the primaries. Nothing, it seemed, could save the President. But the seizure of the hostages and the stern American response to the Soviet invasion did wonders for Carter's candidacy. His standing in the polls improved dramatically, and his moribund campaign suddenly revived and produced for the President a series of impressive victories in the early primaries.

Carter's troubles were, however, far from over. As month followed month without any discernible progress in efforts to secure the release of the hostages in Iran, public clamor began to build. In April, after the collapse of one round of negotiations, the President ordered a rescue attempt by American commandos. It ended in abject failure when several military helicopters failed in the desert. Eight commandos died when two aircraft collided during the hasty retreat. Secretary of State Cyrus Vance, who had opposed both the rescue mission and much of the new belligerence in the nation's foreign policy, resigned in protest—the first Secretary of State to do so since William Jennings Bryan in 1916. And the President began to suffer a series of damaging defeats in the primaries. Carter, however, continued to benefit greatly from the many personal controversies surrounding Edward Kennedy (most notably a 1969 automobile accident at Chappaquiddick Island in Massachusetts that had left a young woman dead), and he managed in the end to stave off the challenge and win his party's nomination. But it was an unhappy convention that listened to the President's listless call to arms; and Carter's campaign aroused little enthusiasm from the public at large as he prepared to face a powerful challenge.

The Republican party had, in the meantime, rallied enthusiastically behind a man whom, not many years before, most Americans had considered a frightening reactionary. Ronald Reagan, a former film actor of minor talent, a former California Governor with a generally successful record, and a poised and articulate campaigner, seemed in 1980 to be a man in tune with his times. Like Carter before him, he was a strident critic of the excesses of the federal government. More important, he championed a restoration of American "strength" and "pride" in the world. Although he refrained from discussing the issue of the hostages, Reagan clearly benefited from the continuing popular frustration at Carter's inability to resolve the crisis. In a larger sense, he benefited as well from the accumulated frustrations of more than ten years of domestic and international disappointments.

Election day was the anniversary of the seizure of the hostages in Iran, a fact that was not lost on much of the press and the public. It was also the day on which the conservative forces that had been gathering strength in American life for more than a decade finally seized control of the nation's political life. By a startlingly wide margin, Ronald Reagan swept to victory in the presidential election. His popular margin was decisive: 51 percent of the ballots cast, to 41 percent for

KENNEDY'S MOMENT. Senator Edward M. Kennedy waves to delegates at the 1980 Democratic National Convention in New York's Madison Square Garden, shortly before delivering a speech that electrified the party. Jimmy Carter's flat acceptance speech two nights later was a painful contrast; and while the President left the convention with the nomination, Kennedy left, many believed, with the Democratic party's heart. (*UPI*)

Jimmy Carter, and 7 percent for John Anderson—a moderate Republican Congressman who had mounted an independent campaign. Reagan's electoral margin was overwhelming. He swept not only the western half of the nation, which had been Republican territory for years, but virtually all of the traditional bastions of

Democratic strength: the South, the industrial states of the Midwest and North-east, even such traditionally liberal strongholds as Massachusetts and New York. Carter carried only five states and the District of Columbia, for a total of 49 votes to Reagan's 489. Even more startling was the tidal wave of Republican victories in the congressional races. The party won control of the Senate for the first time since the 1950s; and although the Democrats retained a diminished majority in the House, the lower chamber too seemed firmly in the hands of conservatives.

"A New Beginning"

On January 20, 1981, amid a display of wealth and opulence not seen in Washington in decades, Ronald Reagan took the oath of office as President of the United States. (At sixty-nine years of age, he was the oldest man ever to do so.) Pledging "a new beginning" both at home and abroad, he quickly launched an assault on the deficit-ridden federal budget, proposing extensive cuts in spending in all areas of government—except the military, which he intended to strengthen substantially. In the meantime, Secretary of State Alexander Haig, a former general who had served as White House chief of staff during the last days of the Nixon presidency, began issuing stern warnings to the Soviet Union about American resolve, and announced the formal abandonment of Carter's human-rights policy. The new regime, it was clear, was determined to act forcefully to "restore America to greatness." It was equally clear that the President had the support of much of the American public in his effort.

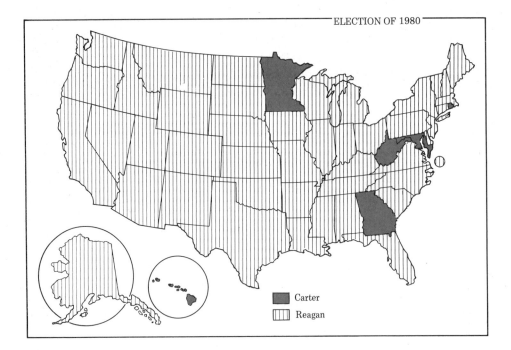

ELECTION OF 1980

Carter
Reagan

THE REAGAN CABINET. President Ronald Reagan holds his first formal cabinet meeting at the White House, January 21, 1981. Seated from left to right are Secretary of Education Terrel Bell, Secretary of Health and Human Services Richard Schweiker, Interior Secretary James Watt (one of the most controversial of the new appointments), Secretary of State Alexander Haig, Reagan, and Secretary of Defense Caspar Weinberger. When President Reagan was wounded during an assassination attempt on March 30, 1981, Haig, Weinberger, and others gathered quickly to ensure official continuity during the tense moments after the shooting. (*UPI*)

Reagan's already high personal popularity soared even higher after an unsuccessful attempt on his life on March 30, 1981. The young assailant, apparently obsessed by a scene from a popular film released several years earlier and infatuated by the actress who had appeared in it, fired several shots as the President walked to his car outside a Washington hotel. Reagan was hit once in the chest; but after emergency surgery, he recovered quickly. A Secret Service agent, a Washington policeman, and White House Press Secretary James Brady were also wounded—Brady most seriously of all.

One result of the assassination attempt was that the President gained additional leverage in his fight for passage of the two major components of his economic program: budget reductions and a tax cut. In one of the most impressive displays of political power of any administration since Lyndon Johnson's, the White House pressured Congress to accept the two proposals virtually without alteration. Both Houses approved the President's proposed budget cuts in June; and early in August, Congress passed the administration's bill calling for a three-year tax cut. Critics argued that the budget cuts—most of them in domestic programs—would not only hurt the nation's poor, but would fail to produce a balanced budget. The enormous increases in defense spending that the President continued to request would, they charged, more than offset the savings. And the tax cut, opponents of the administration charged, would fuel inflation even further. But the Democratic Party, unaccustomed to its role as a minority opposition, had few alternatives to offer.

THE HOSTAGES COME HOME.   Buses carrying the freed American hostages pass through delirious crowds on their way to the United States Military Academy at West Point, New York—the first stop after their arrival in the United States. The release of the hostages from Iran, which coincided almost precisely with the inauguration of Ronald Reagan, sparked a display of patriotism and national celebration that lasted nearly two weeks. The emotional outpouring reflected not only genuine relief at the end of the hostage ordeal, but the accumulating frustrations of the American people in the early 1980s. (*UPI*)

The Reagan administration was, in the meantime, moving in other areas to fulfill the President's conservative campaign pledges. From one department of the government after another came announcements of reversals of longstanding liberal policies. The Justice Department would be less aggressive in pressing for school desegregation; the Departments of Education and of Health and Human Services would reduce pressure for affirmative action on behalf of women and minorities; the Interior Department (under the controversial leadership of Secretary James Watt, an avowed opponent of environmentalists) would begin opening public lands to private development; regulatory commissions would be less aggressive in disciplining corporations. The President signaled a new, more hostile government attitude toward labor in August 1980 when he fired some 12,000 air traffic controllers when they staged an ill-considered and, Reagan charged, illegal strike. Reagan also fulfilled another campaign pledge. When Associate Justice

Potter Stewart announced that he was resigning from the Supreme Court, Reagan nominated as his successor a moderate Arizona judge, Sandra Day O'Connor, the first woman ever named to serve on the highest bench.

Reagan faced no major test of his new, "tough" international stance in the first months of his administration, but he gave ample indication of a new bellicosity in American diplomacy. The President promised to provide military aid (and even to send military "advisers") to the Central American nation of El Salvador, sparking protests from many who claimed that the nation was heading toward another Vietnam. American naval forces staged provocative training exercises in Mediterranean waters claimed by Libya; and in the course of the exercises, United States planes shot down two Libyan jets that had, the government charged, fired first at the Americans. Secretary of State Alexander Haig made frequent public statements denouncing the Soviet Union for its support of "world terrorism" and promising a firmer American stance in its relations with its adversary. And the administration abandoned completely Jimmy Carter's concern with international human rights.The United States even announced a new, more lenient policy toward the government of South Africa, long an international pariah because of its brutal policy of "apartheid"—forced separation of the races. The only criterion of importance in determining the American attitude toward another nation, it seemed, was that nation's policy toward the Soviet Union. Foes of the Russians were, almost by definition, friends of the United States.

By the fall of 1981, there were signs that Reagan's remarkably successful "honeymoon" with Congress and the public might be beginning to fray. New economic projections suggested that even with the proposed budget cuts, substantial deficits would continue into the foreseeable future. High interest rates, sagging stock prices, mounting inflation, and continuing economic stagnation all threatened to erode the President's political standing. But for the moment at least, there seemed still to be a broad consensus of support for the Republican policies of economic conservatism and military strength.

Celebration

Almost at the very moment of Reagan's inauguration, the fifty-two hostages remaining in Iran (one had been released several months before, after he fell ill) were boarding an airplane en route to freedom after their 444-day ordeal. Jimmy Carter, in the last hours of his presidency, had concluded months of negotiations by agreeing to release several billion dollars in Iranian assets that he had frozen in American banks shortly after the seizure of the embassy. The government of Iran, desperate for funds to support a losing war effort against neighboring Iraq, had ordered that the hostages be freed in return. The next few days produced a virtual orgy of national emotion, as Americans welcomed the hostages home with mingled relief, joy, and anger. Not since the end of World War II had there been such demonstrations of patriotism and celebration. But while the joy in 1945 had marked a great American triumph, the euphoria in 1981 marked something quite different. A nation beset with difficulties at home and declining influence abroad was grasping for reassurance that the "American Century," which Henry Luce had proclaimed only forty years before, had not yet come to an end.

SUGGESTED READINGS

Several useful studies of the Carter presidency have already appeared. The most important is the series of articles, "The Passionless Presidency," by James Fallows, a former Carter speech writer, in the *Atlantic Monthly* (1979). Fallows has also published an excellent analysis of the controversial state of the American military, *National Defense* (1981). Jimmy Carter's campaign autobiography, *Why Not the Best* (1975), is unusually revealing for its genre. Bruce Mazlish and Edwin Diamond, *Jimmy Carter* (1980), uses psychoanalytic methods to examine the Carter personality. Jules Witcover, *Marathon* (1977), and James Wooten, *Dasher* (1978), examine the remarkable Carter campaign of 1976. Clark Mollenhoff, *The President Who Failed* (1980), is a hostile account. Roy Blount, Jr., *Crackers* (1980), offers humorous reflections by a southerner about Carter and his region. Jack Bass and Walter DeVries, *The Transformation of Southern Politics* (1976), is a more serious examination of the changing South.

New demographic patterns are examined in Kirkpatrick Sale, *Power Shift* (1975). Douglas Glasgow, *The Black Underclass* (1980), studies the plight of ghetto residents. On the new evangelicism, see John Woodridge, *The Evangelicals* (1975), and Marshall Frady, *Billy Graham* (1979). Peter Steinfels, *The Neo-conservatives* (1979), examines an increasingly important element of the New Right. Christopher Lasch, *The Culture of Narcissism* (1978), is a gloomy view of America in the 1970s. William Boyarsky, *The Rise of Ronald Reagan* (1968), is an early view of the fortieth President; while Hedrick Smith et al., *Reagan: The Man, the President* (1980), is a more recent study. George Gilder, *Wealth and Poverty* (1981), is a clear statement of the conservative economic philosophy of the Reagan administration.

Index

S

About the Authors

Frank Freidel is Bullitt Professor of History at the University of Washington and Charles Warren Professor of History, Emeritus, at Harvard. He is working on a one-volume biography of Franklin D. Roosevelt and a multivolume biography of which four volumes have been published. His other books include *Our Country's Presidents, F. D. R. and the South*, and *American History: A Survey*, with co-authors Richard N. Current, T. Harry Williams, and Alan Brinkley. Past president of the Organization of American Historians, the New England Historical Society, and the New England History Teachers Association, Professor Freidel is coeditor of the 1974 edition of the *Harvard Guide to American History*.

Alan Brinkley is Assistant Professor of History at the Massachusetts Institute of Technology and has served as Visiting Lecturer on History at Harvard. He received his Ph.D. at Harvard and is a former recipient of an American Council of Learned Societies Fellowship. He is the author of *Voices of Protest: Huey Long, Father Coughlin, and the Great Depression* and coauthor of *American History: A Survey*.

A Note on the Type

This book was set via computer-driven cathode ray tube in Avanta, a film version of Electra, a type face designed by W. A. Dwiggins. The Electra face is a simple and readable type suitable for printing books by present-day processes. It is not based on any historical model, and hence does not echo any particular time or fashion.

Composed by Haddon Craftsmen, Inc. Scranton, Pennsylvania. Printed and bound by R.R. Donnelley & Sons, Co., Harrisonburg, Virginia.